Research Methods in Social Relations

Research Methods in Social Relations

Eighth Edition

Geoffrey Maruyama and Carey S. Ryan

WILEY Blackwell

This edition first published 2014
© 2014 John Wiley & Sons, Ltd.

Edition history: Thomson Learning, Inc. (7e, 2002)

Registered Office
John Wiley & Sons Ltd, The Atrium, Southern Gate, Chichester, West Sussex, PO19 8SQ, UK

Editorial Offices
350 Main Street, Malden, MA 02148–5020, USA
9600 Garsington Road, Oxford, OX4 2DQ, UK

The Atrium, Southern Gate, Chichester, West Sussex, PO19 8SQ, UK

For details of our global editorial offices, for customer services, and for information about how to apply for permission to reuse the copyright material in this book please see our website at www.wiley.com/wiley-blackwell.

Library of Congress Cataloging-in-Publication data applied for

Hardback ISBN: 978-1-118-76497-8

A catalogue record for this book is available from the British Library.

Cover image: © Kevin Lau Photography / Getty Images.

Set in 10.5/12.5 pt DanteMTStd-Regular by Toppan Best-set Premedia Limited
Printed and bound in Malaysia by Vivar Printing Sdn Bhd

1   2014

Contents

Preface to the Eighth Edition

What's on your mind? Sorting out a relationship, thinking about what your partner really meant by their last sentence to you, determining which way to drive home today, thinking about when you will be hungry and what you might eat – the possibilities are endless. Of importance for this book, things that you are thinking about and the ways you think about them involve use of a "research" process. So, even if you have never had a research methods course, you have experience with research methods – not necessarily well-designed methods, but methods nonetheless. This happens as we translate our thoughts into questions. In our day-to-day lives, we formulate all kinds of questions, some widely shared, others totally idiosyncratic to us individually: Why do some people speak with accents? Why doesn't everyone use a seat belt when they drive a car or a helmet when they ride a bike? Why do junior high students behave so strangely? Why would anyone dress like that? What kinds of people write research methods books? Although some questions are simply idle musings, most frame our thinking about some issue, and get us thinking about how we might answer them. In effect, they define our individual "research" processes. An exciting aspect of the focus of this methods book on *social relations* is that through that focus readers should be reflecting explicitly on how they study themselves and others, and what they think and do in their everyday lives. Hopefully, readers will realize that social and behavioral sciences have a lot to say about human behavior as well as good tools to continue to add to that knowledge. Importantly, if the things that social scientists studied were not related to everyday life, what good would our science be? In the language of research methods, we would be engaging in research that has no external validity.

In going about answering questions, we all are scientists – not in a career or disciplinary sense, but by engaging in ongoing everyday human processes of observation, action, and inference to make sense of our world and develop expectations for future interactions. Heider (1958) called this process *naïve psychology*, describing ways in which humans engage in processes like those of scientists, but without using scientists' formal methods, rigor, or tools – such as setting up experimental designs, including control groups, generating alternative hypotheses, separating causation from covariation, or engaging in systematic observation using a specific protocol. Thus, this "science" is naïve, for it is imprecise and often inaccurate. (We will discuss issues of naïve psychology in greater detail in Chapter 1.) Most importantly for this book, however, even readers most naïve about social science methods come to the book with beliefs about causality based on their own personal processes of observation and inference, in effect already familiar with some building blocks of science.

Our goal is to translate readers' "naïve" or partly formed ideas about scientific methods into more rigorous and complete ones tied to valid and reliable approaches/ methods. We are humbled by the privilege we have been given by the Society for the Psychological Study of Social Issues (SPSSI) to create the eighth edition of *Research Methods in Social Relations* (RMSR), and hope that our work continues the successes of prior editions. We have great respect for the strong core and tradition in the approaches of the previous seven editions of RMSR, and are grateful to those colleagues who authored them for giving us a great framework and content on which to build. In many instances, we needed to add little to what has previously been said. In other instances, however, because methods and even orientations to research are continually changing, we added new material to address the range of complementary approaches that are prevalent today. But we also are committed to sustaining the historical focus on quantitative and experimental methods, for those remain as important today as ever. If you are not so sure, think as examples about widespread use of clinical trials in biomedical research, of product testing in marketing and other consumer psychology areas, and of use of "effective practices" in education. We have a strong interest in keeping the book aligned with its roots in social relations as we discuss different methods, for such issues are not only central to SPSSI, they still sit front and center in the conflicts that threaten today's world. They are prominent within as well as across countries. Social relations also historically have considered and addressed issues of disparity, disadvantage, discrimination, and privilege, themes that are particularly relevant in our diverse and often stratified world.

Since the seventh edition was written, universities increasingly have been rediscovering their roles and responsibilities in addressing key issues and challenges of today's world. So to us it is important to illustrate the ways that researchers have used various methods to answer questions about social policy and practices, and how methods can engage communities and community partners as co-investigators in the research process. We have added a chapter on working with policy makers and practitioners, included more information about cultural issues, and expanded coverage of methods used for engaged research. Engaged research traditions, often using action research approaches, have long been part of what SPSSI has done and studied, so we are thrilled to see universities move toward what SPSSI has long championed.

We believe that this book is relevant for audiences from an array of fields. Certainly, it is targeted toward the social and behavioral sciences, fields including psychology, neuroscience, sociology, anthropology, economics, and political science. But it also targets researchers in professional schools and other translational programs that draw methods and approaches from basic disciplines in the social and behavioral sciences. Those include business, education, public affairs, law, agriculture and natural resources, and public health and other academic health center units, including medicine, nursing, dentistry, pharmacy, and veterinary medicine. Simply, in today's very interdisciplinary academic world, research methods transcend disciplines, and researchers from a full array of disciplines search for the methods that most effectively help them to address the problems and issues that they study.

Structure of Eighth Edition

The approaches of the previous seven editions of RMSR provide us with a great core and tradition. We have attempted to sustain the strong focus on quantitative and experimental methods, but also to address the range of complementary approaches that are prevalent today. We have kept the book aligned with its roots in social relations as we discuss different methods, for example, illustrating the ways that researchers have used various methods to answer questions about social policy and practices. We have tried to illustrate the role of multiple methods and research programs in providing information that helps researchers and policy makers to arrive at general conclusions.

This edition represents a major restructuring and rewriting of the book, with several new and expanded chapters and consolidation of existing chapters. No major methodological content area has been dropped, although the focus shifts some to reflect newer approaches. We have reordered the chapters, for the most part, to reflect the sequence in which the researcher needs to think about the research process as it unfolds. The first section tries to get readers to think about the research process, how it differs from their everyday lives, the importance of ethics, and the different types of settings in which they might work. The book begins by discussing how theories, ways of thinking, and settings provide the underpinnings of research in the social sciences. It covers in more detail how researchers improve on the processes we all use in our everyday lives to make sense of our world and how it operates, then discusses the nature of theories and how they are evaluated. Then Chapter 3 covers ethics of research, and Chapter 4 discusses relationships of researchers with practitioners, policy makers, and participants in the research process. The first section concludes with chapters on laboratory research and on research in field and community settings.

The second section covers issues of measurement and sampling, and then describes a broad array of approaches to doing research. It begins with three chapters covering issues relevant to all types of research, namely, reliability, validity, and sampling. Then the next seven chapters cover the full range of research types and settings: experimental research, quasi-experimental research, non-experimental research, qualitative research, survey research, evaluation research, and mixed methods research.

The third and final section (Analysis and Writing), which could be placed earlier, covers ways to review literatures and write research reports. It has two chapters, one that covers ways of reviewing existing information on the topic of the research, including quantitative as well as qualitative reviews of research, and a second chapter that covers the process of writing the research report. The final two chapters primarily provide context for the methods that we have described, helping readers to consolidate theory with methods in the processes of conducting and describing research. Obviously, critical reviews of the literature need to be done early in the research process, but at the same time they require background in methods. They were left until the end in part because most researchers come to the task of learning methods already possessing knowledge about substantive literature, namely, theory and empirical research, and the areas in which they will be doing research.

We have omitted chapters that cover basic statistical methods and data coding, for there is much to cover within research methods domains. We believe that statistical issues are better covered in statistics books, that many students have taken statistics coursework prior to or concurrent with their methods course, and that details concerning statistical analyses are readily available on the web. However, we introduce some concepts (e.g., effect sizes and statistical power, confirmatory factor analysis) when they are directly relevant to methodological considerations. And we describe the kinds of descriptive and inferential statistical methods that typically are used along with different methods, so readers can think about the statistical techniques that they will need to use if they choose particular methods. We have expanded coverage of quantitative non-experimental research methods, of doing research in community-based settings, of qualitative methods, and of mixed methods approaches.

We hope readers find the eighth edition useful, and welcome comments about the book.

Acknowledgments

In writing this book, we acknowledge our indebtedness to the many SPSSI members who contributed to the previous seven editions of *Research Methods in Social Relations*. They provided us with a framework that has been highly successful and that has shaped careers of generations of researchers, including the two of us. We own editions 3 through 7 of the book, which should tell readers how influential it has been in our careers. We hope that our efforts will continue that tradition.

In particular, we are grateful to Rick Hoyle, lead author of the seventh edition, for sharing manuscript copies of the seventh edition, providing us with a starting point for our work. We are grateful for the support and suggestions of the SPSSI publications committee and particularly its co-chairs, Chris Crandall and Nilanjana (Buju) Dasgupta; SPSSI, which arranged the move of RMSR from its prior publisher Cengage to Wiley Blackwell; and to our partners at Wiley Blackwell, Olivia Evans, Karen Shield, and particularly Jennifer Bray, our development editor. We have received valuable feedback from two anonymous reviewers as well as many colleagues, in particular Drs. Suzanne Russ (Dickinson State University), Panayiota Kendeau (University of Minnesota), and Norman Miller (University of Southern California). Dr. Kendeau was kind enough to use a manuscript version of the text in a graduate methods course at Minnesota to gather feedback from the students taking the course; to them we also are grateful. Ryan also used the manuscript in her graduate methods course at UNO; we are grateful to those students for their feedback as well. One of Maruyama's graduate students, Martin Van Boekel, both read the book and provided new references and web links for the eighth edition. Finally, Ryan's son, Tim Ryan, created several of the figures for this edition.

We also need to acknowledge the contributions of those who trained us in research methods, our advisors, Dr. Norman Miller and Drs. Charles Judd, Bernadette Park, and Gary McClelland. Finally, we appreciate the support and encouragement of our families, who tolerated us working on the book at strange times and places – like when we were on family vacations.

About the Companion Website

This book is accompanied by a companion website:

www.wiley.com/go/maruyama

The website includes these materials for instructors:

- Sample syllabi
- Suggestions for using discussion questions and exercises
- Test Banks for every chapter
- Power Point lecture slides for every chapter

Part I

Underpinnings of Social Relations Research

Chapter 1

Ways of Thinking and Knowing

Recognizing Importance of Research Methods and Relevance of Research

As was noted in the preface, research methods are of general interest in part because they have developed and employ approaches that in many ways parallel what we all regularly do in everyday life. Even if we know nothing about science or research, we routinely engage in processes of formulating ideas or notions about why things happen or how things work (hypotheses) and seeing whether they happen as we expect them to (testing their plausibility). Such processes give us an intuitive

Research Methods in Social Relations, Eighth Edition. Geoffrey Maruyama and Carey S. Ryan.
© 2014 John Wiley & Sons, Inc. Published 2014 by John Wiley & Sons, Inc.
Companion Website: www.wiley.com/go/maruyama

understanding of research and research methods, and what they potentially can do. Throughout our lives we seek to explain and understand what goes on in the world around us and, in some instances, even control it. We observe what happens, sometimes even creating what happens, and use information from what we observe to draw conclusions.

Think, for example, what people do frequently in their own lives. If you smoke you may decide that you need to stop smoking, and develop ideas and a plan about how you can stop. Similarly, if you would like to lose weight, spend more time studying, or become a more successful athlete, you might develop ideas and plans about how to reach your goal. Assuming you follow your plan, you will see over time whether that plan is successful. How successful you believe you are depends on what you had decided would constitute success – your expectations affect how you identify a goal that would signify success. If the goal is set high, chances of success likely will be lower. You may start with an ambitious goal and later modify it. If the plan is something you decided, you control, and that affects only you, nothing prevents you from modifying your definition of success as time passes. Regardless of how much you change your goal, at some point you likely would reflect on your goal and decide whether you are attaining it. If not, you could try an alternative approach to increase your success. You also could decide that it no longer is important or that it is simply not attainable, and in either case stop trying to attain it.

Similarly, researchers seek to understand and explain phenomena like how and why people do what they do, and, in some instances, to control or change behaviors. Most social and behavioral scientists believe that there are general laws that can explain and predict behaviors, that those laws can be discerned through or derived from collection and analysis of data, and that empirical research can identify those laws and how they operate. Even though researchers today are less likely to express the processes they identify in terms of formal hypotheses, corollaries, derivations, etc. (for an example, see Festinger's (1954) landmark paper on social comparison processes), they nevertheless follow a scientific process of hypothesis generation and testing. In that process, researchers do the same things that we do as individuals except, as will be explained in detail later in this chapter, they are required to worry more about the accuracy of the inferences they draw. And they typically are not allowed to change their hypotheses, target outcomes, or their approach in the middle of an ongoing research study, although they could decide that the research study isn't working and stop it. Further, researchers typically consider a larger set of outcomes than those individuals personally choose to define their success. For example, researchers who study smoking cessation or weight reduction programs need to know how well the programs work (how much do you still smoke, how much do you now weigh?), but also whether they work better than alternative programs, why they work, and whether or not they work only for some people or under specific conditions. They also worry about how sustainable changes are over time. And, tied to the search for general laws, researchers worry about things like generalizability of findings, that is, whether particular findings represent widely applicable outcomes or are specific to the setting and/or the sample.

As you go through this book, we hope that you occasionally step back and appreciate the range of approaches and methods researchers use as they go about gathering information. Some choose laboratory experimentation, others field-based research that may or may not be experimental, still others surveys, and others observational methods or interviews. Some have samples in the thousands, others just one subject. Most researchers specialize, choosing particular techniques and approaches that they find most appealing and with which they are most comfortable. At the same time, however, they recognize and appreciate the richness of information yielded by diverse approaches to particular problems and respect others who are skilled at using different approaches. Knowledge about social phenomena is increased when different approaches are used to provide different perspectives on what is happening. For example, convergence of alternative perspectives and approaches on a single conclusion increases confidence about that conclusion and understanding of the particular phenomena that underlie it, while divergence of conclusions across perspectives and approaches identifies limits or qualifications of phenomena.

As we discuss different approaches to research throughout this book, it is important to recognize that much of research attempts to draw inferences about phenomena – be they sub-microscopic or societal. Regardless of the approach taken, an important goal is to understand social and other phenomena, and to identify variables that can create and/or explain changes in other variables. Understanding has been central to scientific methods throughout history. Even when research was primarily descriptive (in what has been called the **pre-positivist** era; see, e.g., Lincoln & Guba, 1985), the goal still was to observe and understand. Attempts to increase understanding underlie the array of methods that are described in this book. When researchers developed what is sometimes called a **positivist approach** to science and research, they moved from description to active attempts to change outcomes. As science became more active, research findings were used to generate approaches for doing things like creating change, improving lives, and increasing safety and security. After World War II, research changed to view multiple theories being possible in a single setting, and viewed theories as provisional until more refined theories challenged or replaced them. Sometimes this perspective is called **post-positivism**, but the basic "scientific" approach and search for generalizable laws still predominated. (To recognize this shift, we will use the term *positivist/post-positivist* to describe these approaches, which still are dominant.) But the search for generalizable **causal laws** that explain and predict events and that develop interventions to create change and modify outcomes (e.g., social engineering) is not universally held as desirable. Other researchers, called by some **post-positivists** (see, e.g., Lincoln & Guba, 1985) but also called **constructivists or interpretivists** (e.g., Mackenzie & Knipe, 2006), argue that seeking general causal laws is misleading and ultimately will be unsuccessful, for a focus on prediction and control narrows science and decreases its capacity to describe and explain behavior. To lessen confusion, we will refer to that set of approaches as *constructivists*. Among their arguments against positivism are that positivists are:

- *deterministic*, ignoring free will and not recognizing that realities are multiple and constructed;
- *reductionist*, because not all behaviors follow a single set of laws and because positivists attempt to assign causal direction to a complex state in which mutual simultaneous "shaping" is occurring;

- *egocentric*, for researchers often impose their personal reality on situations and participants;
- *dehumanizing* for subjects; and
- *obtrusive and imprecise*, inadequately accounting for the impacts of researchers on their subjects and settings.

Constructivists argue for approaches that are inferential but that develop understandings that include probabilistic and speculative judgments and that are built upon perspectives of the research participants, and they focus work at the local level (e.g., Lincoln & Guba, 1985). Building upon perspectives of the participants rather than coming to the setting with a priori ideas about how things operate explains the terms constructivist and interpretivist. Researchers develop theory or patterns of meaning from participants as they collect data (e.g., Mackenzie & Knipe, 2006).

The approach we are taking to this book is largely what we above have called positivist/post-positivist, for the methods that traditionally have provided content for *Research Methods in Social Relations* (RMSR) are those developed from traditional scientific and related approaches. At the same time, however, RMSR across its various editions has consistently addressed issues that have been viewed as shortcomings of such research:

- sharing responsibility and control of research processes through action research;
- recognizing researcher values;
- respecting research participants; and
- examining the importance of situational factors, of the diverse perspectives that exist in any setting, of the applicability of research findings in real-world settings, and of the obtrusive impacts of researchers on their participants.

Some of the newer sections of this edition of RMSR blend methods used by constructivist researchers with more traditional positivist/post-positivist methods. But our approach is pragmatic, articulating the perspectives underlying different techniques and avoiding identifying approaches as used only by particular types of researchers, for that might limit the methods researchers believe they are supposed to be using. We attempt to present strengths of the different methods and how they are used without taking a position about which approaches might be "best." We don't believe that researchers should be defined as of a single orientation and type, for, as noted above, regardless of approach, all research methods seek to improve understandings and capacity to draw inferences. And **mixed methods** (a new chapter in this edition) provide researchers with richer data that help them to draw more accurate inferences. The methods throughout this book provide various complementary ways of developing understandings and of improving capacity to draw inferences. (At the same time, however, we recognize that our approach may at some points inadvertently adopt positivist/post-positivist orientations, for that is how we were trained.)

In this opening chapter, we describe how social and behavioral sciences[1] are similar to and different from two other ways of knowing with which readers already are

---

[1] Throughout the book we use social science to include behavioral sciences as well as social sciences. Only in this paragraph do we use both descriptors.

familiar: the physical sciences and casual observation. The social and behavioral sciences (e.g., anthropology, psychology, sociology, economics) are similar to the physical sciences (e.g., physics, chemistry) in the logic of inquiry but different in the degree to which the objects (or participants) under observation play an active role in the inquiry. Life sciences (e.g., biology) fall in between, in some instances being more like the physical sciences, in others more like the social sciences dealing with participants. Participants force researchers to consider questions about social and ethical values. The social and behavioral sciences are similar to casual observation in the quest to understand how people behave and relate to each other, but they are different in their rigor and in the systematic methods used for inquiry.

We address two major themes in the remainder of this chapter. The first concerns the place of values in social science research. Social scientists can borrow the logic of the physical sciences but must make use of different methods because the "things" we study are not inert objects but sentient beings engaged in complex social behavior. When we study social behavior involving individuals or groups of people, we encounter their reactions to us as observers/researchers. They, as we, are formulating hypotheses about the setting and what is happening, and their hypotheses may affect ours. In addition, in formulating our hypotheses, we are expressing our values and perspectives, which raise value-laden questions about research. The physical sciences also are not value free, as Einstein pointed out when he discovered the formula for nuclear energy, but the place and prominence of values are more immediately apparent in the social sciences. Also, in research with human subjects, reactions of the observed to the observer or participant to researcher must be taken into account.

The second major theme in this chapter compares the social sciences and casual observation as ways of knowing about and explaining social behavior. As addressed in the beginning of this chapter, examining social behavior scientifically sometimes appears to be "common sense" because most people try to make sense of social behavior daily using processes of casual observation and action. This chapter explains in detail how the social sciences differ from casual observation (sometimes called **naïve psychology**) in their deliberate search for sources of bias or invalidity.

Perspective

Gazing down at people from a tall building or a window of a low-flying airplane gives us a different view of humanity from the embedded perspective with which we are accustomed. A crowded park or congested freeway feels different when we look at the crowds from afar. Somehow the distance gives us a sense of objectivity: We can observe without feeling the congestion ourselves. And it gives us a bigger perspective than we typically have within settings, where we can see only part of what is happening. At the same time, much would be missed if we always observed from afar. We would miss the feelings, the excitement, and the crush and enthusiasm of the crowd if we never entered into it ourselves, and we would not be aware of the many differences among individuals within the social setting. Social scientists observe people and settings from various distances because differing vantage points provide different information – about how people feel, act, and interact, and about contextual variables. Confining ourselves as social scientists to a single method or procedure limits what we can know. No one procedure or method can provide a complete description. Some research methods allow the observer to be a participant in the group that is being observed. Other methods enable the observer to remain hidden or anonymous and to see from a distance. In this book, we describe these different methods in detail.

The Place of Values in Social Science Research

Values might seem to be an odd topic to feature so immediately in a methods text because research strives to be **objective**, namely, "not biased by someone's point of view." As noted in the prior discussion of positivistic and constructivistic approaches, however, the idea that research is value free or totally objective is a questionable and controversial one. That is not to say that research is designed to promote particular views or that many researchers have hidden intentions underlying their research. We believe that most researchers attempt to discover relationships as objectively as possible. At the same time, few researchers go into their research indifferent about possible findings, and many are likely to have strong expectations about which possible outcome is most plausible (and most desirable). Researchers have perspectives and **values**, which represent a point of view, a judgment that "this is good and that is bad," which someone else might dispute. Most importantly for this discussion, their values affect how they see things and what they expect. And they affect what researchers choose to study. Arguments about values often cannot be settled by scientific evidence because disputing parties are likely to interpret evidence as consistent with their perspective or discount evidence contrary to their perspective.

The inextricable connection between values and social science research requires researchers to be aware of the implications their research can have for human welfare. Even though they cannot separate themselves from value questions, they need to be aware of the values that are influencing the approach and the implications of those values for the welfare of various individuals and groups. This tension between objectivity and values is apparent in the case study of a controversial social science study presented in Table 1.1. Using procedures described in Chapter 17 of this book, Rind, Tromovitch, and Bauserman (1998) concluded that victims of childhood sexual abuse do not suffer long-term harm, a conclusion that stands in stark contrast to values held strongly by many members of the public and many victimized by childhood sexual abuse. As detailed in Table 1.1, the published research report received considerable negative attention in the popular press and ultimately was unanimously condemned by both houses of Congress. Other examples of negative attention, including ones in the digital age, can be found in Sleek (2013).

Rind et al.'s (1998) study first illustrates that social science research on an issue of great public interest can attract substantial public attention. It also illustrates the challenges of conducting research that addresses important social issues. On the one hand, it is important to know what the impacts are of social phenomena like childhood sexual abuse. On the other hand, if the results turn out to be inconsistent with widely held public opinion, skepticism about the findings should be considered and perhaps even anticipated. And in this case, individuals who perceived themselves as being victimized by abuse potentially could feel that their credibility and even identity had

---

Table 1.1   Case Study of When Science Clashes with Values: The Rind et al. (1998) Meta-Analysis

In 1998, *Psychological Bulletin*, the premier review journal in the field of psychology, published a meta-analysis of the long-term psychological outcomes of having been sexually abused as a child (Rind, Tromovitch, & Bauserman, 1998). A meta-analysis is a quantitative synthesis or literature review that summarizes a group of studies all bearing on the same topic (see Chapter 17). In their meta-analysis, Rind et al. summarized 59 studies examining the association between psychopathology and childhood sexual abuse history in college students. Somewhat counterintuitively, they discovered that having been abused as a child was only weakly associated with later maladjustment. Moreover, the association between abuse and later psychopathology was even smaller when the abuse was deemed consensual by the victim. Perhaps their most controversial finding was that non-negligible proportions of the samples (11% of women and 37% of men) reported retroactively that their immediate response to the abuse had been positive.

Rind and his colleagues were very careful in their report to state, repeatedly, that the lack of demonstrated long-term negative outcomes for childhood sexual abuse *did not mean* that sexual abuse was acceptable or not immoral. Despite their careful caveats, their paper provoked an intensely negative reaction from the public, who interpreted the findings to mean that the authors were endorsing pedophilia and other forms of childhood sexual abuse. Criticisms of the research findings circulating on the web eventually found their way to Dr. Laura Schlessinger, a media personality whose talk show attracts millions of listeners. After Schlessinger criticized the Rind et al. paper as "junk science" on her show for two consecutive days and generated countless irate phone calls and letters, Congress became involved. Several members of Congress held a press conference demanding that the American Psychological Association (APA; the organization that publishes *Psychological Bulletin*) denounce the Rind meta-analysis and calling for a congressional resolution condemning the study.

Two months of intense public pressure ensued, and ultimately the president of APA wrote a letter to the U.S. House representative who was leading the condemnation campaign. This letter stated that (1) findings reported by Rind et al. were inconsistent with the APA's stated and deeply held positions; (2) the editors should have evaluated the Rind et al. research report based on its potential for affecting public policy and would take such implications into account when reviewing future research reports; and (3) the APA would seek an independent review of the article by a panel of outside experts.

Even these concessions were not enough for Congress, and in July, the House of Representatives voted 355 to 0 (with 13 abstentions) to condemn the Rind et al. meta-analysis. This resolution was passed unanimously two weeks later by the Senate.

---

been undermined by the findings, which would produce anger about the research. Further, contrary to a view of research that separates researchers from their findings, social processes used in everyday life (the **covariation principle**) would associate researchers with their findings, so they may find that despite their intentions to be "dispassionate" researchers conducting the research, they become identified with the findings and the targets of anger.

When viewed from a research methods perspective, issues that would arise in reviewing the article are what Campbell and Stanley (1963) called **threats to validity** – things like: were variables operationalized inappropriately, were data coded incorrectly, were analyses misinterpreted, were incorrect inferences drawn, and so forth. (These issues will of course be covered later in this text.) Researchers surprised by the findings would examine them in detail to see whether they stand up to scrutiny, and they would replicate and extend them using an array of different methods. In thinking about various methodological approaches, in this particular instance, the findings likely were contrary to findings that would have been produced by case study methodologies, which almost certainly would identify individuals who would be able to explain in great detail the harmful effects of the abuse they had experienced. The research can be seen as illustrating that science uses its methods in self-correcting ways, with other researchers reanalyzing, replicating using different as well as similar approaches, and eventually supporting, qualifying, or countering the findings.

Of equal importance is the point that the major professional organization of a discipline was influenced by public reaction and public beliefs and values in its determination of whether a research report should be published. That approach leads to suppression of free scientific inquiry and even censorship of unpopular research. It would be tragic for science if values were to become a justification for preventing important research questions from being asked or for results to be suppressed simply because they convey findings that some people find personally repugnant. As a sidebar, researchers can be at the mercy of the popular press in its depiction of findings. It is distressing that the public media distorted the findings, feeding the public reaction to the research. Finally, returning to the topic – values – the example illustrates the ways that values affect the questions we ask and how we react to what we find.

In sharp contrast to the Rind et al. (1998) research on the effects of childhood sexual abuse, the values in some areas of research are uncontroversial. For instance, a large body of research exists in the field of cognitive psychology on the concept of "natural categories." It shows that people use preferred or basic levels of categorization in perceiving objects and in how they approach and structure their worlds. For example, people first categorize an object they sit in as a "chair," rather than using a more specific ("desk chair") or global ("furniture") category (Rosch, 1988). Natural categories are regarded as providing helpful ways of navigating the overwhelming mass of stimuli that confronts individuals in everyday life.

Research on racial categories, however, has produced observations that evoke values. Although there is little controversy if people use categories to make inferences about pieces of furniture, there is a negative reaction when racial categories (stereotypes) are used to make inferences about individual members of those categories. Indeed, the impact of values is evident even in the title of a research report on racial categories, which begins with the clause: "Just Say No (to Stereotyping)…" (Kawakami, Dovidio, Moll, Hermsen, & Russin, 2000). In short, stereotyping is viewed as acceptable and even helpful when the stereotypes are categories referring to physical objects; when *people* are stereotyped, however, it is viewed as unacceptable. What makes racial category research more controversial than research on furniture categories is the interpretation of the data. The observations or "facts" in both cases are quite straightforward; it is the interpretation that introduces social and political beliefs and values.

The act of framing a question about social behavior also encompasses values, beliefs, and perspectives. For instance, many studies ask, "What are the effects of maternal employment on child development?" but few ask about the effects of paternal employment. Is this asymmetry neutral or does it reflect cultural beliefs and values? Consider another example: In the past there were many studies designed to investigate the "causes" of homosexuality, but few investigating the "causes" of heterosexuality. (*Causes* is in quotation marks because this research typically is correlational, and can only identify relationships rather than causes.) The act of asking a question and framing it, with both an implied answer and an implicit set of values about social behavior, is rarely neutral.

Thus, values can directly influence the type of social science research that is and is not done. Sometimes this influence is positive, as when scientists use their tools to address important issues facing society, for example, struggling intensely to discover a vaccine for HIV/AIDS; ways to prevent birth defects, reduce crime, prevent wars, and lessen intergroup conflicts; or interventions to increase the academic success of at-risk youth. Unfortunately, sometimes values can have a chilling effect on science. Morton Hunt (1999) observed that in the preceding 15 years there was a dramatic increase in the public's efforts to impose limits on the freedom of social scientists to investigate potentially controversial questions. For example, in 1991 an $18 million grant that had already been awarded to researchers to examine sexual behavior in adolescents that placed them at risk for HIV infection was abruptly canceled mere weeks before the project was to begin because of public and congressional pressure on the grounds that it was inappropriate to ask teenagers sensitive questions about sexual practices. Unfortunately, the consequence of this action is that we now know less than we could have known about practices in which teenagers engage that endanger their lives; thus, we are less equipped to intervene and decrease the incidence of a fatal disease.

Contestability in Social and Physical Sciences

Readers who have taken a laboratory course in the life or physical sciences probably remember white laboratory coats and physical equipment that convey the message, "This is serious; this is science." The dissection tools, microscopes, titration jars, eye goggles, and other uncommon instruments make it clear that this is no ordinary way of comprehending the world and that special approaches are required to do the work. This is what people think of when they think of science, and it promises to reveal information far different from that gotten from casual observation, which requires no such tools.

In contrast, the typical first exposure to the social sciences seems much more like casual observation. Usually there are no lab coats or uncommon instruments, and consequently little sense of the mystery and importance that can be engendered by such objects. For example, imagine that someone read that day care centers in the

United States or communal childcare in Israel create self-reliant and sociable children. If that person was not opposed to the idea that mothers of young children can work and their children can thrive, he or she might have believed the results were true; however, if the person believed that mothers of young children should stay home, it would be *relatively* easy to find apparent fault with the research and conclude that the results were erroneous. The results of social science research appear to be more contestable than the results of research in the physical sciences.

We are not suggesting that the physical sciences lack ambiguity. The debate over the existence of cold fusion or dark matter shows that physical scientists are just as capable as social scientists of debating the mere existence of a phenomenon. Even electron microscopes and other sophisticated methods of observation have ambiguity and error. Nevertheless, for the general public, the results of social science research often appear to be more contestable than the results of physical sciences research. It may be because we naturally develop ideas about things like parenting, while dark matter or cold fusion seem far removed from everyday life.

What makes social science research seem more contestable? Few people would say, "Amoebas do not reproduce by dividing in half! They reproduce just like dogs and cats; I don't care what you say with your fancy microscopes!" Such statements simply do not correspond with well-established and observable reality. In contrast, a fair number of people might say, "Children of working mothers do not develop as well as children whose mothers stay home! I don't care what you say with your fancy surveys!" In making such assertions, people dispute / contest findings. Some may think of others they know who "prove" what they say, not realizing that individual cases do not rebut patterns that appear across samples of individuals. Others, however, may have more substantial reasons for disagreeing, pointing to things like wording of items or sampling that could predispose respondents to particular answers.

We do not oppose argumentation and debate; they are essential for a science, physical as well as social, to grow and test itself. The point here, however, is that the public tends to accept observations made by physical scientists but less readily accepts those made by social scientists.

Two features of social science research leave it susceptible to differing interpretations. One is the seemingly ordinary quality of most methods. Instead of using dissection kits or electron microscopes, most social scientists use their unadorned eyes and ears to gather their data. They ask people questions, listen to their answers, and observe their behaviors. In the following chapters we show that the methods used by social scientists differ in significant ways from casual observation; the requirements imposed on measuring techniques are stringent and far from casual. For now, however, we wish to point out that, to the public, the methods commonly used by social scientists may appear to be informal and unimpressive, no different from the methods they use in everyday life, and therefore the conclusions seem contestable.

The second feature that makes the results of social science research seem more contestable is that they often address issues about which there are serious, deeply felt, politically identifiable differences of opinion. It is, therefore, difficult for researchers to persuade someone that they have observed "the facts" when those facts contradict the person's beliefs, values, or political interpretations, and is made even more so in situations where other social scientists report research supporting contradictory views.

For instance, someone who believes mothers should stay home with young children might not be dissuaded by social science research. The prior belief is deeply rooted in the person's beliefs about men and women, about family, about power, and perhaps about religion. The case study of the Rind et al. (1998) meta-analysis is an excellent example of what happens when conclusions from social science research contradict people's very strongly held beliefs (and other social science research).

Exercise: Is research value free?

Because social science research is an investigation of relations between people rather than between objects, it can never (or hardly ever) be value free. We qualify this statement to say "hardly ever" and allow the possibility that some social research might be value free. Think of examples where values have shaped research, and see whether you can think of any example in which the argument could be made that the research is value free. Readers, in reaching their own conclusions, probably will create some very convincing cases that also show how much values come into play in social science research.

We do not want to leave the impression that physical sciences are "really" scientific and social sciences are not. Rather, we want to evoke an appreciation for the features of social science research that make it particularly challenging. Research in the social sciences has many similarities with other forms of research. This book contains language that is technical and teaches methods that are not simple and that are used across life and physical sciences. And if sheer difficulty and complexity were qualifications for being considered "scientific," the social sciences would be high on the scientific ladder, for they try to understand behaviors of complex beings acting in social settings with many changing situational and contextual variables. Nevertheless, because the research is usually embedded in a set of social and political values, results that contradict values elicit emotional as well as cognitive reactions. And, unlike physical sciences, the work is not protected by an aura of respectability, if not reverence, because the research sometimes looks like casual observation.

Casual Observation

As was discussed briefly earlier in this chapter, the study of social behavior is the study of how people behave with and toward others. Defined broadly in this way, we are all social scientists. To see this, imagine a party on a weekend evening. We all have expectations about how people at a party are likely to behave and not likely to behave, as well as when we expect differences across individuals. A party attended by a 20-year-old likely will be different from a party attended by a 50-year-old. Not only do we have expectations about people's behavior at the party, but we also are likely to have explanations for at least some of this behavior. Suppose we saw someone at the party spill a drink on someone else. At least implicitly, we would look around to figure out why the drink was spilled. Was the accident not an accident at all but rather intended? Did it occur because the drinker already had one too many drinks? Was the party too crowded, with the inevitable jostling when too many people are jammed into a small room?

Consider another example: A family is sitting in their apartment when they hear someone shout in a loud voice, "I'm going to kill you!" from the next apartment. Because this is not expected behavior, more or less automatically the family tries to figure out what is going on. That is, they try to find explanations for the behavior they are observing. Is this a serious argument? Is someone in genuine risk of being injured? Or is it merely the kind of joking threat family members are prone to make to one another? Should the family call the police or mind their own business? The family might try to gather more information to arrive at a conclusion, for example, by pressing their ears against the wall to try to hear other parts of the conversation that would clarify the nature of the threatening remark.

As each example illustrates, we are all naïve observers or students of social behavior, regardless of what our actual professions are. That is, we are all engaged daily in the ordinary pursuit of understanding social behavior because we have expectations, hunches, and hypotheses about how people are likely to behave in given situations and why they behave as they do. For instance, we expect certain behaviors at a party and not others. When someone spills a drink, we try to figure out what caused that behavior. The expectations, hunches, or hypotheses of **casual observation** are ultimately utilitarian. If we have ideas about how others are likely to behave in different situations and in response to our own behavior, we can act in ways that elicit desired behaviors from them. Casual observation of social behavior is useful for planning our own behaviors to reach our goals, objectives, or desired outcomes.

This discussion does not imply that our ordinary hunches and hypotheses about others' behaviors are necessarily right. Some expectations about behavior are violated, even routinely. For instance, we might think it inappropriate to have too much to drink at a party. Nevertheless, someone might do just that. Likewise, when driving a car we expect others to look for oncoming cars before making a left turn. Nevertheless, people sometimes turn left in front of approaching traffic.

Not only can our expectations about how others are likely to behave be wrong, our explanations for why they behave as they do can also be wrong. For instance, after seeing someone at a party spill a drink, we might surmise that the accident was caused by clumsiness. This explanation might well be in error; perhaps the spill was intentional and in retaliation against someone who had been insulting. If we hadn't seen or heard about that prior insult, our explanation for the behavior could not be based on it. Similarly, if we hear a threatening shout from a neighboring apartment, we might conclude that it is just a minor argument, and as a result we might not realize a serious crime is about to be committed.

Because our ordinary hunches, hypotheses, and explanations ultimately are constructed to help us achieve our own goals and control our world, and because we must inevitably realize that our hunches are not always correct, part of casual observation involves trying to figure out when our hunches, hypotheses, and explanations are right and when they are wrong. Therefore, two elements characterize our casual observation of social behavior. First, we have hunches and hypotheses about others' behavior. Second, we continue to examine, at least somewhat critically, those hunches and hypotheses. We are motivated both to explain others' behaviors and to figure out whether our explanations are correct. We do both routinely and spontaneously, hardly ever bothering to reflect on the fact that we are in fact studying social behavior.

The same two elements also characterize scientific studies of social behavior, regardless of whether the studies are conducted by researchers from psychology, sociology, political science, public health, education, economics, or business. They all share the goals of constructing theories of human social behavior and critically examining those theories to improve their accuracy.

The goal of this book is to provide an introduction to the methods commonly used by social scientists to study human social behavior and social relations, which encompass a wide range of behaviors and social settings. It covers the methods used to construct scientific theories of social behavior. We first examine how people operate as casual observers of social behavior – routinely using "naïve" methods in constructing and critically evaluating hunches and hypotheses about human social behavior. Then "naïve methods" are compared and contrasted with those that characterize a scientific approach to the same phenomena.

Naïve Hypotheses and Theories of Social Behavior

Most aphorisms or clichés about human social behavior are **naïve hypotheses:**

> Birds of a feather flock together.
> Absence makes the heart grow fonder.
> The early bird gets the worm.

Each of these naïve hypotheses has a characteristic form that is seen most clearly if reduced to its basic meaning:

> Similarity results in increased contact.
> Absence results in increased attraction.
> Immediate action on opportunities results in success.

Each of these naïve hypotheses argues that one phenomenon or behavior – the subject in the sentence – causes or is associated with another phenomenon or behavior – the object. These phenomena, both subject and object, are called constructs. A **construct** is an abstract concept that we would like to measure. Love, intelligence, aggression, self-esteem, and success are all constructs. Although these things are real and affect our lives in many different ways, they do not exist as physical objects. We cannot go down to our local supermarket and pick up a six-pack of love, as much as we might like to. Instead, we can only measure constructs indirectly and imperfectly through an operational definition. The **operational definition** of a construct is the set of procedures we use to measure or manipulate it. For example, one operational definition of intelligence is a person's score on a standardized IQ test. The operational definition of aggression might be the number of electric shocks a participant chooses to deliver to another person. Chapters 2 and 5 address the complex issues of operationally defining a construct and how we determine whether our operational definitions of a construct are correct, or valid.

A social science **hypothesis**, naïve or not, is a falsifiable statement of the association between two or more constructs that have to do with human behavior. These hypothesized associations might or might not be causal. They can state that one construct causes another, or they might simply state that one construct tends to be found with (related to, associated with) another. There are two notions that require elaboration: the notion of constructs and the notion of what is a causal association.

When a hypothesis concerns **causal associations**, some constructs are identified as causes and others as effects. If we believe that the three naïve hypotheses presented earlier are causal, the causal constructs are similarity, absence, and immediate action. The three affected constructs – the effects – are contact, affection, and success. Notice that all these constructs, whether involved in a hypothesized causal association or not, concern general phenomena having to do with social behavior, and they all require further definition or elaboration. What, for instance, is success? Because success is a construct and does not exist physically, it can mean different things to different people. Success for one person might mean having good friends, whereas for someone else it might mean having money or status. And because constructs do not exist physically, they need further definitions tied to actual observable behaviors. To create their definitions, scientists observe and try to identify various ways of defining or measuring success (e.g., someone's stated quality of friendships or someone's average yearly income).

Our naïve hypotheses frequently concern causal associations among constructs. Most of us believe that behaviors have causes and that we can determine at least some of those causes. We also believe that success is not entirely the result of luck or good fortune or random events. Rather, we accept the notion that success is partly affected by activities or constructs like immediate action. Likewise, in arguing that similarity results in contact between people, we implicitly acknowledge that our choice of friends is not random; rather, some phenomena or constructs cause us to like or dislike others. Naïve hypotheses by their very nature imply that human behavior is partially determined or caused. At the same time, we also believe that human behavior occurs as a result of random events, luck, and individual whims. Using the language of Kurt Lewin, behavior is a function of the person *and* the environment.

Hypotheses vary not only in whether they describe a causal association but also in the complexity of the association they describe. Some hypotheses can be linked with other hypotheses to make up a theory. A **theory** is a set of interrelated hypotheses that is used to explain a phenomenon (e.g., attraction, success) and make predictions about associations among constructs relevant to the phenomenon. For instance, the following set of hypotheses forms a small theory. Like many such sets, it takes the form of a syllogism:

Being unemployed frequently leads to personal depression.
Depression is often a cause of divorce.

Therefore, increased unemployment in society is associated with higher divorce rates.

This syllogism consists of three hypotheses, the third being logically inferred from the other two. Some theories of social behavior can be as simple as this, linking a few hypotheses. Others are exceedingly complex, linking many more hypotheses. For instance, some of the founding documents of the United States, such as the Declaration of Independence, set forth relatively complex theories about the conditions under which people will be happy and will prosper.

Hypotheses vary in complexity not only by being linked with others in theories but also by bringing in qualifying conditions or constructs that must be met for the hypotheses to be applicable. For instance, someone might hypothesize that "absence makes the heart grow fonder" holds true only when the absent target is an individual to whom the holder has a romantic attraction. This qualifying condition makes the hypothesis more complex than the original one. Now, instead of maintaining simply that one construct leads to another, the hypothesis states that construct A results in construct B only under condition C.

There is one very common form of qualifying condition that we often add to hypotheses: We frequently specify a group or kind of person for which a hypothesized causal effect should hold. For instance, we might say, "Among individuals actively seeking a job, unemployment increases the probability of personal depression." We have then added a qualifying condition that specifies the group or population for whom the hypothesis is expected to be true. Adding such a condition suggests by implication that the hypothesis might not hold for other groups or populations. Because people having different backgrounds and experiences often behave differently, it is important to increase precision of hypotheses, which also increases the complexity of a hypothesis by adding conditions that specify the population or populations for which the hypothesis should hold.

In addition to varying in whether they describe a causal association and in complexity, hypotheses differ in how confidently they are held or maintained. We might, for instance, firmly believe that being unemployed can cause a person to be depressed. We might feel less strongly, however, about whether personal depression is a cause of divorce. Because theories are made up of sets of hypotheses, often in syllogistic form, and because these hypotheses differ in the confidence with which they are held, the syllogistic conclusion of the theory as a whole ought to be held with no more confidence than the least confident premise. One might even argue that confidence combines multiplicatively, typically yielding lower confidence than the least confident premise. Whether this is in fact how we operate in our casual observation of social behavior, however, is open to question.

So far we have discussed the nature of hypotheses, that is, the form they take and ways in which they vary. Once confidence is considered, we must raise the second question that was posed earlier about our casual observation of social behavior. Why are some hypotheses held with more confidence than others? To answer this question, we must know how people ordinarily gather evidence to test hypotheses.

Sources of Support for Naïve Hypotheses Underlying Casual Observation

At least five sources or types of support are routinely used to develop and modify naïve hypotheses and theories: (1) logical analysis, (2) authority, (3) consensus, (4) observation, and (5) past experience. Each of these sources suffers from at least some weaknesses that make its reliability suspect.

Logical Analysis

We often derive hypotheses and decide whether they are accurate by examining whether they are logically consistent with other hypotheses that we hold. An example of such **logical analysis** is contained in the syllogism presented previously. If we take it to be true that unemployment frequently leads to personal depression, and if we take it to be true that personal depression can often lead to marital discord and divorce, then it necessarily follows that unemployment increases the chance of divorce. This final hypothesis is deduced, or logically inferred, from the combination of the two earlier ones. Schematically, we can represent the syllogism this way:

$$\text{Being unemployed} \rightarrow \text{depression} \rightarrow \text{divorce}$$

As this illustration makes clear, the influence of unemployment on the probability of divorce follows from the intervening or mediating or transmitting role played by depression in the process.

Syllogistic reasoning is frequently used to derive and modify hypotheses based on their consistency with other hypotheses. Generating support for hypotheses by such reasoning, however, is not without its pitfalls. Alan Cromer (1993) argued in his book, *Uncommon Sense: The Heretical Nature of Science*, that the human brain is not wired for the type of logical thought required for science and that instead people hold the mistaken belief that they have intuitive knowledge about the way the world works. The problem is that our "intuition" and logical processes are often incorrect. Cromer gives the well-known physics example: If one were to fire a bullet from a gun straight across a field, while simultaneously dropping a bullet from the same height, which bullet would hit the ground first? Most people would say that the bullet being dropped would hit first, but the answer is that both bullets would hit the ground at the same time. Downward velocity is independent of horizontal velocity. This is elementary physics, but our intuitive reasoning could lead us to the wrong answer. Cromer argued that in order to think scientifically, we need to think in formal logical terms, and this is not something that comes naturally but rather must be taught.

In the social sciences, especially, what we ordinarily regard as a logical conclusion can be influenced not only by pure logic but also by our wishes or desires (Gilovich, 1991), for we have along with our rational and logical capacities tendencies to view the world in ways that would make good things happen to us, that make us look good, and that make the world conform to what we believe. For example, we might invent seemingly logical justifications for hypotheses that we hold simply because we wish these hypotheses to be true. Although we strive for logical consistency in many of our beliefs, we also have a remarkable ability to ignore inconsistencies in other beliefs. For instance, it was not unusual in the 1950s to encounter White Americans who believed both that "anyone in this country can achieve whatever he or she wants" and that "Blacks should not be allowed to attend the same schools as Whites." Today some people believe that government should get out of people's lives and also that government should be able to tell women what they can and cannot do if they get pregnant or that the government should prevent same-sex couples from marrying. Others strongly believe that freedom of expression is important in a democratic society and yet also believe that people who have certain (e.g., bigoted) views should not be allowed to express them. And some people believe that the government should not be involved in health care – except for Medicare and Medicaid. When we want to ignore contradictions in our thinking, we have a remarkable capacity to do so, particularly when issues are complex.

Authority

We are likely to turn to various authorities or experts to determine what hypotheses make sense in our casual observation of social behavior. To figure out how to cope with a difficult child, a parent might consult an **authority** – a pediatrician, a counselor, or a teacher. To decide how to behave in a foreign country we have not visited before, we might consult someone who knows the country well. To understand why riots occur sometimes in some large cities in the summer, we might consult a sociologist or a specialist in issues of race and social class. As long as we have faith in the expert we consult, we might regard the expert's opinion as sufficient justification for a hypothesis.

Using experts to decide which are good hypotheses and which are not is efficient as long as they are indeed expert in the area under consideration. All too often, however, we presume someone to be an expert when he or she only has the trappings of expertise without the actual knowledge to back it up. We rely on the symbols of authority without making sure that the authority is truly knowledgeable (Cialdini, 2001). Another challenge of expert judgments is that experts often do not agree one with another, so our view might depend on the particular expert we consult.

In addition, we are inclined to let our beliefs and values define whom we identify as an expert, which occurs when we seek so-called experts merely to provide a confirmation for our hypotheses rather than a critical assessment. For instance, some might regard an astrologer as an expert on how to choose a spouse. Someone who defines the astrologer as an expert in this area is already convinced of the wisdom of astrological advice on such matters.

A final challenge that comes with reliance on authorities is that authorities can have their own personal interests at heart. Because authorities presumably like their status and position, they might provide advice that perpetuates or justifies the status quo rather than advocating for change. If we wanted to arrive at a solution for our energy problems, the answers we probably would receive from diverse authorities would be likely to differ simply as a result of the positions these authorities occupy. For instance, if we were to ask the chief executive officer of a major oil company, it is unlikely that this person would argue for immediate replacement of or dramatic curtailment of the use of fossil fuels.

In sum, in our casual observation of social behavior, we seek input from authorities to help us evaluate our hypotheses and theories. Just as relying on logical analysis is not without pitfalls, so, too, relying on the wisdom of authorities can lead to biased conclusions.

Consensus

Instead of appealing to the wisdom of authorities, we might appeal to the wisdom of our peers, seeking **consensus** regarding our hypotheses. In part, we decide what are good or bad beliefs or hypotheses by finding out what our friends think about them and whether they agree with us. How might a mother decide when to wean a child? She might appeal to a physician as an authority. It is equally likely, however, that she will ask her friends when they weaned their infants. If a client of our business makes an unreasonable request, we might ask our coworkers why the client acted that way and how we should respond. If we want to evaluate our opinions regarding why high school graduates are not ready for college or why college costs have gone up so much, we might discuss it with our neighbors. All these examples illustrate processes of validating our hypotheses or theories by consensus with peers.

Seeking peer support for hypotheses is not a great deal different from the use of authorities. In both cases, others help us decide what we should and should not believe. As a result, consensus is subject to the same kinds of biases and distortions as is consultation with authorities. With which of our peers will we discuss our ideas on schools? Most probably the discussion will be with people similar to us who are quite likely to agree with us on such things.

In addition, groups of people can be notoriously poor as independent judges. Groups frequently are pushed toward unanimity so that dissenting voices are not heard or are forced to change their publicly espoused views (Janis, 1997). Also, the group might tell the listener what he or she wants to hear, especially if the listener is highly regarded or a person of authority. As a result, group consensus is often inadequate for validating hypotheses. In our casual observation of social behavior, however, we sometimes rely on it heavily.

Observation

To determine whether our naïve hypotheses are correct, we routinely compare them to our own and others' behaviors through **observation**. When our hypotheses are not consistent with what we observe, we might modify or abandon them. Suppose we believe that women are able to "read" nonverbal messages more clearly than men (Hall, Carter, & Horgan, 2000). That is, we think that women are more sensitive in understanding nonverbal signals that are sent to them, intentionally or not. To determine whether this hypothesis is accurate, we might watch members of both sexes in a number of different settings. If we are serious enough about examining our hypothesis, we might even do an informal experiment. For instance, we might try to communicate nonverbally with some female and some male acquaintances and then see who figures out our signals more clearly.

Consider another example. Suppose we believe that prejudice toward other ethnic groups is caused by a lack of personal acquaintance with members of those groups. To learn whether this hypothesis is accurate, we might conduct some informal interviews with various acquaintances, asking about their friendships with members of various ethnic groups. We might then see whether our estimates of each person's degree of prejudice toward each group seem to be (negatively) related to the number of friendships he or she has.

Observational procedures are as full of pitfalls as are other procedures used to support our naïve hypotheses. There are four major problems in using observation to validate hypotheses. We can use the example in the preceding paragraph to illustrate them. First, as we argued in defining hypotheses and theories, the constructs mentioned in a hypothesis (e.g., prejudice or personal acquaintance) can mean different things to different people. One person's impression of an individual's prejudice might not be the same as someone else's because different observers might look for different things. Similarly, what one person means by personal friendships with members of different ethnic groups might be different from what another person means. Hence, we might inadvertently decide to observe behaviors that do not represent or capture the constructs about which our hypothesis is concerned. In the same way, when interviewing individuals about friendships, we might find out how much they desire friendships instead of measuring their actual friendships.

Second, inferring that one construct causes another can be very difficult. Suppose, for example, that we hypothesized and found that people who are married are happier. Such a finding does not necessarily mean that differences in marital status cause differences in happiness. It is also plausible that the causal effects go in the opposite direction: that those individuals who are happier people are more likely to be married because their happiness makes them more attractive. Using observation to support hypotheses can be misleading because causal direction can be very difficult to establish – thus the common statement, "correlation does not imply causation."

Third, we might make our observations on a very select group of people, a group of people, perhaps, for which the hypothesis might be especially true but one that is not representative of the world at large. For instance, although it might be true that prejudice and contact with members of ethnic groups are associated in our select sample of friends, the two variables might not be associated in general or in other samples. Biased sampling could result in us having more or less confidence in our hypothesis than we should.

Fourth, we probably are biased in deciding which observations are relevant. Trope and Ferguson (2000), for instance, have written that when testing hypotheses about individuals, people look for instances that confirm those hypotheses and tend to ignore instances not consistent with them. Thus, the very process of collecting observational data can be biased. Just as we might choose authorities who tend to confirm our hypotheses, so, too, we might judge observations as relevant or not depending in part on whether they support our hypotheses. This phenomenon has been described as "we see what we are prepared to see."

Past Experience

We frequently and regularly generate support for our hypotheses as casual observers of social behavior by reflecting on or remembering past experiences. We think back to instances or events that confirm the hypothesis, and attempt to make modifications to take into account disconfirming instances.

Although the use of past experience is sensible and logical, it is susceptible to all the dangers inherent in the use of observation, plus others. Memory is inherently reconstructive. We do not passively store information about past experiences; rather, we store and organize events selectively. Theories and hypotheses are tools that we use in organizing our memories. It has been repeatedly shown that information consistent with a theory or expectation is more easily remembered than information that is irrelevant (Hirt, 1990). Hence, it is perhaps unlikely that hypotheses will be disconfirmed by recollected experiences.

Exercise: Types of support for reasoning

The text just described five sources of support routinely used to develop and modify naïve hypotheses and theories. They each are rooted in casual observation: (1) logical analysis, (2) authority, (3) consensus, (4) observation, and (5) past experience.

1.   Imagine that you have decided to buy a new car (or new bicycle or computer). How do you use each of the five types? Feel free to use media or any other source in discussing the different sources.
2.   If you were to make the same decision scientifically, how might you modify the approaches that you mentioned above?

Toward a Science of Social Behavior

Try as we might to obtain an accurate understanding of social behavior, we encounter innumerable difficulties in constructing and validating hypotheses and theories in everyday life. Acquiring accurate knowledge about how people behave and why people behave as they do is not easy. Yet we persist. So, too, does the scientist of social behavior, regardless of discipline or problem studied. Although the scientist's path toward acquiring knowledge about social behavior is in many ways just as hazardous and difficult as the path of the casual observer, there are differences in how they proceed. In the remainder of this chapter, we identify some of these differences, most of which are differences of degree rather than of kind. That is, scientists differ from the casual observers not so much in *what* they do as in *how* they do it. The scientific study of social behavior and the casual observation of social behavior engage similar processes, and the differences between them can be subtle and, at times, even difficult to identify. Differences are nonetheless present.

The most important difference concerns the extent to which scientific studies are on the alert for biased conclusions. Scientists ideally operate as if their hypotheses and conclusions about human behavior might be in error. They look for biases and pitfalls in the processes used to support and validate hypotheses. Scientists are aware of the research on such biases and submit their conclusions to the scrutiny of other scientists, who attempt to find biases that were overlooked. In contrast, casual observers, although striving to be as accurate as possible in reaching their conclusions, often gather evidence in support of hypotheses without being aware of or worried about the biases inherent in the process. Although scientists are on the lookout for biases, they also are not aware of them all, which makes the difference one of degree rather than of "do and don't." The heart of the difference is this: The scientist systematically studies how to avoid biases in examining hypotheses, and uses an established set of methods for avoiding many such biases.

Unlike the casual observer, scientists engage in empirical research to try to determine whether hypotheses are accurate and how they need to be modified to make them more accurate. **Empirical research** is the collection of information through observation and other methods that is systematic in attempting to avoid biases. Although scientists might also use logical analysis, authorities, consensus, and past experience in evaluating hypotheses, unlike the casual observer, they must and do ultimately engage in empirical research. Scientists ultimately develop confidence in a hypothesis or a theory if it has been able to withstand empirical attempts to falsify it and if it can explain behavior in the "real world" beyond the research setting.

Because of this reliance on empirical research, social scientists tend to be more concerned about the problem of linking up theoretical constructs with observables than are casual observers. And social scientists also are more likely to be looking at relationships between the theoretical constructs rather than primarily between observable behaviors. A good scientific hypothesis contains statements about associations between constructs of interest and also statements about what observable indicators go with each construct. In other words, scientists who rely on empirical research are necessarily greatly concerned with how to measure or operationalize theoretical constructs. An ordinary observer using observation to support hypotheses is perhaps unlikely to spend much time thinking about what observable qualities indicate constructs of interest. Rather, the observer is more likely to think in terms of observable behaviors or signs, for those are the things occurring in everyday life that can be used to guide behavior.

To rely ultimately on empirical research to validate hypotheses means that social scientists assume that all constructs of interest can indeed be measured or observed. This is the assumption of **operationism**. For each construct of interest in the study of social behavior there must be observable features or manifestations that can be measured that represent the construct. This is not to say, of course, that scientists assume anything can be perfectly measured. In fact, they assume quite the contrary – that all constructs are measured with error, for it is very difficult to identify a measure that is exactly the theoretical variable of interest. Nevertheless, the scientific assumption of operationism means that all constructs of interest can be measured, albeit imperfectly.

Earlier we argued that one of the characteristics of a scientific inquiry is that the scientist is constantly wary of biases in attempting to validate hypotheses. Ultimately this means that scientists can never actually accept a hypothesis as correct or accurate, for the observations that support it might have been biased or in error in unknown ways, or it may be that the hypothesis happens to be consistent with a different hypothesis that actually accounts for what has occurred. Strange as it might seem, scientists never can actually prove a hypothesis based on empirical research because that research could conceivably have been biased or the result could have been a chance event. The best scientists can do is to gather a large quantity of empirical evidence consistent with the hypothesis, while acknowledging that the hypothesis remains unproven in a formal sense because the evidence is, to an unknown degree, faulty. Although scientists of social behavior, like casual observers, are invested in their hypotheses and ultimately wish to support them, to function scientifically means that, regardless of the outcomes of empirical research, we can never accept hypotheses as absolutely true, but note that a body of evidence is consistent with a particular hypothesis.

Let us examine more closely the logic underlying that last statement. When researchers design studies, they are implicitly using the logical argument: "If Theory X is true, then Association Y should be observed." However, the converse does not hold: We cannot say, with confidence, that "Association Y was observed; therefore, Theory X is true." The logical snag is, as noted above, that there could be other reasons besides Theory X – say, Theory Z – for producing Association Y. If Association Y were *not* observed, that is clear evidence against Theory X and we can safely reject the theory. (In reality, scientists do not reject their theories so easily but instead would search for other reasons – inadequate measures or methodological flaws – for why Association Y was not observed.) In short, scientists talk of rejecting hypotheses and theories but not of proving them. We say that the results are "consistent with" or "support" a hypothesis but not that the hypothesis has been accepted. At best, hypotheses can withstand attempts to show that they are incorrect. There almost always are other explanations for a set of findings that seem to support a hypothesis, so a truly scientific stance is always a skeptical one.

What makes a scientific hypothesis a good one, then? A hypothesis gains gradual acceptance if it is repeatedly supported, survives numerous attempts to falsify it, and seems to account for observations conducted by different scientists in different settings. And, if there are competing hypotheses, scientists turn to principles like parsimony or simplicity – the less complex the hypothesis needed to account for the findings, the better. Because any particular observation in support of a hypothesis can be biased or in error, science requires **replication**. That is, empirical research must repeatedly reveal the same conclusions when conducted independently by different researchers. Only in this way can the biases of any one investigator or procedure be overcome.

Another aspect of scientific methods is that scientists submit their interpretations of their research to the critical review of fellow scientists. Before most research reports are published, a journal editor solicits the opinion of several reviewers, experts on the topic of the research. They read the research report thoroughly and critically, looking for biases or alternative explanations of the findings that the authors might have missed, considering alternative hypotheses and related theories. They also assess the importance of the research and its contribution to understanding. Reviewers provide detailed feedback aimed at improving the research report or the research study on which it is based. In many cases the report is deemed not suitable for publication; indeed, rejection rates at the most prestigious scientific journals easily exceed 80%. The review process in the social sciences can be long and grueling, but the system is designed to ensure that research is scrutinized closely and is as accurate as possible before being communicated to policy makers, practitioners, and other researchers. A new challenge posed by the availability of the Internet and minimal costs for making "research" publicly available has been a proliferation of self-publishing and of "online-only" journals with varying amounts of critical review and analysis of the papers that are published. Self-publishing without any review has readily identifiable shortcomings. Some journals have similar shortcomings, for they do not seek experts most knowledgeable about each research paper to review it, and may even publish submissions with limited review if the authors are willing to pay to have their work published. Therefore, it is important to pay attention to the benchmarks set by different journals in their review process, and to be wary of research that does not appear in a journal that uses a credible peer review process.

Although the process built on independent replication and peer review is laudable, in fact, scientists are rarely as noble as an idealized picture of objective science paints them to be. Regardless of whether they are in a role of potential author or of reviewer, they have come to their beliefs through hard work, and are personally invested in their views. And, unfortunately, their efforts are at least in part driven by the requirement at many academic institutions that faculty publish with regularity and frequency, which might pressure them to publish their work prematurely or to submit work that they do not consider to be particularly important but seems publishable. They might even on occasion be a little more vain than most, and stick with their ideas in the face of contradictory information. Even though individual scientists might invest a great deal in trying to "prove" a hypothesis or in trying to demonstrate that all competing hypotheses are in error, the scientific process, by demanding rigorous research and independent replication, should eventually prove to be self-correcting. The scientific community and its journals, by requiring that research be critically reviewed before being published, sees to it that hypotheses are usually critically evaluated and that even the published work is only cautiously accepted by the scientific community as a whole.

A science of social behavior consists of the interchange between theories and empirical research. We do research in an attempt to examine the validity of our theories, and we also draw and develop our theories from observation of everyday social behaviors. Hence, systematic observation starts with a problem, a question, or a hypothesis that motivates it. Research and data, in turn, lead to modification of hypotheses and theories. Ideally the path of science, circling between theory development, hypothesis generation, observation, and hypothesis testing and theory refinement, is always guided by a skeptical and self-critical stance.

Summary

The social and behavioral sciences differ from the physical sciences in a number of ways. First, they concern people rather than objects, and, as a result, questions of value arise more frequently. These questions concern both how the results of the research are to be interpreted, what questions are asked in the first place, and what the role of the research participants is in the research. Second, social and behavioral science methods and conclusions often seem to be little more than common sense because – as casual observers – we routinely think about or try to explain people's behaviors.

As casual observers, all of us routinely develop explanations about our own and others' behaviors so that we can plan our lives and pursue our goals. These explanations take the form of hypotheses and theories about the causes of observed behavior. They are similar to aphorisms or clichés that are commonplace in everyday language. Not only do we put together such explanations, but we also attempt to figure out whether they are valid and appropriate. We rely on five kinds of evidence to help us determine the appropriateness of our explanations:

- logical analysis;
- advice of authorities or experts;
- consensus of our peers;
- further observations that we may make; and
- reflections about past events and behaviors.

Each of these sources of evidence necessarily involves some bias in the appraisal of our explanations.

The social sciences differ from casual observation in at least two ways, although the ultimate goal of both is to arrive at valid explanations for people's behavior.

1. Social scientists ultimately rely on systematic formulation of variables and collection and analysis of empirical data in order to have confidence in a hypothesis.
2. Scientists study the biases that are inherent in attempting to determine which explanations are good and which are poor, and they deliberately design their studies to minimize these biases.

As such, the scientific stance is always a skeptical one. A good scientist never accepts a hypothesis as true. The best that can be done is to gather empirical data that are consistent with the hypothesis. Ultimately, however, the scientist realizes that the hypothesis can never be proven. The research process, including peer review and independent replication, helps identify alternative explanations for different findings and advance science by focusing attention on research that adds to knowledge in important ways.

Go online   Visit the book's companion website for this chapter's test bank and other resources at: www.wiley.com/go/maruyama

Key Concepts

Authority
Casual observation
Causal association
Causal laws
Consensus
Construct
Constructivist/interpretivist approach
Covariation principle
Empirical research
Hypothesis
Logical analysis
Mixed methods
Naïve psychology

Objective
Observation
Operational definition
Operationism
Past experience
Pre-positivist approach
Positivist approach
Post-positivist approach
Replication
Theory
Threats to validity
Values

On the Web

http://home.xnet.com/~blatura/skep_1.html Good description of the scientific method from a website devoted to skeptics, with an emphasis on the need to hold paranormal phenomena to rigorous scientific standards.

http://www.project2061.org/tools/sfaaol/sfaatoc.htm This website contains a textbook, published by Science for All Americans Online, on the scientific enterprise. Especially relevant is Chapter 1, "The Nature of Science."

http://www.scientificmethod.com/b_body.html Description of the 11 major stages of the scientific method.

http://www.dharma-haven.org/science/myth-of-scientific-method.htm A site entitled "The Myth of the Magical Scientific Method," written by Terry Halwes. Halwes argues that scientists deviate in important ways from the logical hypothesis-testing view taught by most science textbooks.

http://www.ems.psu.edu/~fraser/BadScience.html An amusing website that provides numerous examples of researchers making bad mistakes in talking about scientific findings.

Further Reading

Brannigan, G. G., & Merrens, M. R. (Eds.). (1993). *The undaunted psychologist: Adventures in research*. New York, NY: McGraw-Hill.

Cohen, J. (1994). The earth is round (*p* < .05). *American Psychologist, 49,* 997–1003.

Cromer, A. H. (1993). *Uncommon sense: The heretical nature of science*. New York, NY: Oxford University Press.

Gilovich, T. (1991). *How we know what isn't so: The fallibility of human reason in everyday life*. New York, NY: Free Press.

Hunt, M. (1999). *The new Know-Nothings: The political foes of the scientific study of human nature*. New Brunswick, NJ: Transaction Publishers.

Pashler, H., & Harris, C. (2012). Is the replicability crisis overblown? Three arguments examined. *Perspectives on Psychological Science, 7*(6), 531–536.

Simmons, J., Nelson, L., & Simonsohn, R. (2011). False-positive psychology: Undisclosed flexibility in data collection and analysis allows presenting anything as significant. *Psychological Science, 22*(11), 1359–1366.

Stanovich, K. E. (2013). *How to think straight about psychology* (10th ed.). Boston, MA: Pearson.

Chapter 2

Doing Social Science Research

We said in the first chapter that social scientists conduct empirical research, or systematic observation, to generate, support, and modify theories and hypotheses about social behavior. In this chapter, we are more precise about the nature of scientific theories and hypotheses. The roots of this chapter lie in positivist/post-positivist perspectives. Constructivists focus less on generalizable theories and scientific methods shared with natural sciences. We also discuss the ways in which a particular piece

Research Methods in Social Relations, Eighth Edition. Geoffrey Maruyama and Carey S. Ryan.
© 2014 John Wiley & Sons, Inc. Published 2014 by John Wiley & Sons, Inc.
Companion Website: www.wiley.com/go/maruyama

of empirical research may be valid or invalid. In other words, we introduce a set of criteria that are used to evaluate the type of scientific research that focuses on theory and hypothesis testing.

The Nature of Social Science Theories and Hypotheses

In Chapter 1, we defined a **theory** as a set of interrelated hypotheses that is used to explain a phenomenon and make predictions about associations among constructs relevant to the phenomenon. Thus, a theory about social behavior has three features:

- It contains constructs of theoretical interest that it attempts to explicate or account for in some way.
- It describes associations among the constructs. These associations are frequently causal, specifying which constructs affect which others and under what conditions. Hypothesized associations are the heart of a theory.
- Finally, a theory incorporates hypothesized links between the theoretical constructs and observable variables that can be used to measure the constructs. These links specify the behaviors or other indicators of the constructs, which are measured and used to conduct empirical research. Nonscientific or naïve theories of social behavior also consist of constructs and causal relations among them. However, because the scientific study of social behavior relies on empirical research to support and modify theories, scientific theories also specify the observable (measurable) indicators that define the constructs of theoretical interest.

Two examples will clarify what constitutes a theory. A theory of political information processing (Lavine, Borgida, & Sullivan, 2000) holds that when people exhibit greater attitude involvement (i.e., they care more about an issue), they are more likely to engage in biased information-gathering strategies, which results in more extreme and unidirectional attitudes. These attitudes, in turn, result in less decision conflict and greater accessibility of the attitudes in memory. Notice in this example the chain of hypothesized causal associations among constructs: Attitude involvement leads to biased information gathering, which leads to extreme attitudes, which leads to greater attitude accessibility. A good theory also specifies how the constructs of interest could be measured, observed, or manipulated. For instance, attitude accessibility might be indicated by faster responses to items on an attitude scale.

Gaertner and Dovidio (2000, 2012) have developed a social categorization-based theory of intergroup bias known as the Common Ingroup Identity Model. According to this theory, members of different groups or social categories (e.g., Blacks and Whites) who view themselves as belonging to the same larger group (e.g., citizens of the United States), that is, as having a common group identity, have more positive attitudes and beliefs about the subgroup to which they do not belong. Encouraging people to think in more inclusive ways, for example, by increasing the salience of their common identity or introducing tasks that require them to cooperate, leads them to think more inclusively (i.e., to view themselves as belonging to the same larger group), which increases positive expectations, perspective-taking, empathy, and trust, and ultimately reduces prejudice and discrimination.

Gaertner and Dovidio (2012), as well as others, have used a variety of indicators of the constructs that are the focus of the theory. For example, in one experiment, Black interviewers asked White students from either the same or a different university to comply with a request (i.e., to be interviewed about their food preferences). The Black interviewers wore clothing that was associated with either the same university that the White students attended (so that they had a common identity) or a different university. In other words, a common ingroup identity was manipulated via the interviewers' clothing. Discrimination was indicated by lower compliance with the interviewers' requests. The results indicated that White student compliance with Black students' requests was much greater when they shared the same (59%) as opposed to a different (36%) identity. Note that there may actually be a great many specific indicators of particular constructs (e.g., common identity and discrimination) although all of them will have basic features in common.

Both of these examples show the basic structure of a theory. A theory is comprised of hypotheses, which in turn are comprised of statements about associations among constructs (e.g., attitude involvement leads to biased information gathering; creating an ingroup identity reduces prejudice) and associations between constructs and observable indicators (e.g., biased information gathering is indicated by selective attention to attitude-consistent information). The observable indicators are known as variables. A **variable** is any attribute that changes values across people or things being studied. Thus, hair color, IQ test scores, height, introversion, gender, and blood pressure are variables. In a given study, however, they would only be considered variables if at least two levels of them were included. For example, gender would not be considered a variable in a study that examined only men or only women.

A theory is thus made up of two types of **hypotheses**: (1) hypothesized associations among constructs and (2) hypothesized associations between constructs and observable indicators or variables or measures. Both types of hypotheses have characteristic forms. The first, concerning associations among constructs, typically takes the form:

Construct A causes construct B for population X under condition Y.

Each of the examples of theories we discussed earlier contains hypotheses that conform to this model, although the word "causes" might be replaced with "leads to," "produces," or "is associated with." Note, however, that in any given hypothesis, much may remain implicit. For instance, the populations or conditions for which the causal association between construct A and construct B holds might not be explicitly mentioned.

A few further examples illustrate hypotheses about associations among constructs:

• Contact between the members of ethnic groups is more likely to reduce prejudice when the group members have equal status in the contact setting.
• Parents more involved in their children's education have children who perform better academically.

- Media portrayals of women that focus on youth, beauty, and sexuality contribute to gender inequality.
- People more concerned about others are more likely to support environmental protection policies.

The second type of hypothesis concerns associations between constructs and observable indicators. Because constructs are conceptual, they likely are difficult to measure directly and perfectly. Instead, researchers identify measurable yet likely imperfect variables that represent the constructs. The extent to which they are imperfect is called unreliability. For example, body mass index uses only height and weight information, ignoring muscle mass, etc., and is not a perfect measure of obesity or fitness. Associations between constructs and variables / measures usually are of this form:

Behavior X or response Y is a valid indicator of construct A.

Examples include the following:

- Higher scores on the Ambivalent Sexism Inventory indicate more sexist beliefs.
- The SAT or ACT is a valid measure of academic preparation.
- Poverty is indicated by school children's eligibility for free or reduced-price lunches.
- Obesity is indicated by a body mass index that is greater than 30.

What Makes a Theory Productive?

Some social science theories seem to attract a great deal of attention and lead to a great deal of research, whereas others seem to attract very little attention and produce very little research. What characteristics distinguish more and less productive or influential social science theories from each other? Table 2.1 lists the characteristics of a productive theory; our discussion here expands and explains these characteristics.

A good theory must first of all be falsifiable. When we say a hypothesis or theory is **falsifiable**, we mean that we could conceive of a pattern of findings that would contradict the theory. In other words, a falsifiable hypothesis is one for which a researcher can set up an empirical test and, if the findings turned out a given way, the researcher would conclude that the hypothesis had been disproven. The falsifiability criterion of a theory is often difficult for students to understand abstractly, so we borrow an analogy from Meehl's (1978) classic article to illustrate it. We could predict that the high temperature tomorrow will fall between $-100°$ and $+200°$ Fahrenheit. This is not a useful hypothesis because it is not falsifiable; barring cataclysm, the hypothesis will be supported. A hypothesis that allows for every possible imaginable outcome actually explains nothing. In contrast, a hypothesis predicting that tomorrow the high temperature will fall between $70°$ and $74°$ Fahrenheit is both eminently falsifiable and – if supported – potentially very useful.

This example makes two points: First, falsifiability is a necessary and minimum requirement for a theory. Second, the more specific a hypothesis is, the more useful

Table 2.1 Characteristics of a Productive Theory
A productive social science theory • is falsifiable; • states hypotheses as specifically as possible; • is as parsimonious as possible; • addresses an important social phenomenon; • is internally consistent; i.e., the hypotheses do not contradict one another; • is coherent and comprehensible; • specifies its relevant constructs and how they are measured; • agrees with what is already known about the topic; • explains data better than existing theories on the same topic; • agrees with existing theories about related topics; • generates new insights about the topic.

the theory becomes. The second characteristic of a productive theory, then, is that it states specific hypotheses. Meehl (1978) argued that science progresses to the extent that theories have been subjected to and passed risky (i.e., difficult) tests and that the more such risky tests a theory has survived, the better corroborated it is. In Meehl's words, "a theory that makes precise predictions and correctly picks out *narrow intervals* or *point intervals* out of the range of experimental possibilities is a pretty strong theory" (p. 818; emphasis in original).

The third in our list of the characteristics of a good or productive theory is parsimony. Given equal explanatory power, theories that are simpler or more **parsimonious**, that is, those that specify fewer theoretical concepts and relationships, are preferred to those that are more complex. Parsimony may seem surprising given the complexity of human behavior. In an effort to account for this complexity, theories may become quite complex, sometimes involving substantial elaboration to integrate exceptions. The point is that for reasons of precision and clarity and to avoid the pursuit of research that is unlikely to be fruitful, information or ideas that are not necessary to account for a phenomenon ought to be excluded, only necessary elements should be retained, and simpler explanations should be chosen over more complex ones.

Ultimately, the criterion by which we evaluate theories is whether they provide compelling explanations and interpretations for the world around us. There are actually two components to this criterion. First, a productive or useful theory is one that addresses some important or significant phenomenon or social behavior that needs explication (e.g., gender inequality). One implication of this characteristic is that a theory's importance may change over time; a theory may be especially important or productive at one particular time and less so at other times. Phenomena that seem to demand attention change with time. For example, during the late 1980s environmental hazards were of major public concern; more recently, global warming has become a major concern and has thus stimulated a great deal of research. So theories are used and are productive in part if they address phenomena that are socially significant at a particular historical moment.

The second component of this criterion is that a useful theory provides a plausible and empirically defensible explanation for the phenomenon. A plausible explanation means that the theory must be internally consistent, coherent, and comprehensible. It must be accessible to those who use it, that is, to those who conduct the research in support of it, and it must not run entirely counter to common sense or ordinary explanations. It should be more parsimonious and/or do a better job of explaining research findings than existing theories on the topic. In addition, to stimulate research and to be empirically defensible, the theory must be relatively specific about its constructs and how they are to be measured. In other words, a productive theory includes hypotheses about the links between variables and constructs.

There are other criteria for defining a useful or productive theory. One is that the theory must be consistent with both existing research findings and existing theories for related phenomena. The need to be consistent with known research findings is obvious; there is little utility in proposing a theory that has already been empirically disproven. The need to be consistent with related theories is less obvious but also important. For instance, a theory about human memory must be relatively consistent with existing empirically supported theories about reading comprehension, judgment, and perception. Memory does not exist independently of these other cognitive phenomena and neither can an adequate theory of memory. Similarly, a theory about the origins and effects of poverty cannot afford to ignore theoretical approaches describing relations among ethnic groups, social stigma, and crime. The phenomena are linked, and so, too, must be the theories.

Finally, a productive theory is one that yields new insights or offers the possibility of unforeseen implications. That is, good theories grow and prosper as individual researchers examine their implications and extend them logically. Useful theories offer the possibility of growth, allowing researchers to think about connections that they would not have thought about otherwise. This aspect of theory development is exemplified by the use of computer simulations (Hastie & Stasser, 2000; Mosler, Schwarz, Ammann, & Gutscher, 2001). When a theory identifies a complex set of interrelated phenomena and is specific about the forms of the associations among them, one can often use a computer to examine the dynamic implications of the theory. Computer simulations of social phenomena often provide new and empirically testable hypotheses that derive from the theory's basic postulates and that may not have been seen otherwise (e.g., Anderson, 2007; Newell & Simon, 1961).

Exercise: Examining "productivity" of theories

Select a theory that you recently have read about or used in your research. Put it to the test, examining how well it meets the standards set forth: falsifiable, specific in its predictions, parsimonious, addresses an important phenomenon, plausibly explains phenomenon, consistent with prior research, yielding new insights. How does the theory you picked do? In what ways is it strong and in what ways is it not so strong?

The Functions of Research in Constructing Theories

A primary purpose of conducting empirical research is to test hypotheses. Although hypotheses are typically derived from theories, they may develop for other reasons as well. For example, hypotheses may be developed as a way to resolve conflicting research results; from case studies, systematic observation, or other types of qualitative research; or serendipitously as a result of research findings that were unexpected but seem potentially interesting to examine further. Hypotheses even develop because our personal experiences seem inconsistent with or are not explained by existing theories and hypotheses. For this and other reasons, diversity in the characteristics of scientists is critical to the advancement of science. Indeed, scientists generally have a great deal of latitude in their choices of questions to examine and in the types of methods they develop and employ to do so. And they differ in what answers they expect their science to provide (e.g., general laws vs. local solutions), creating healthy dialogues about the nature of scientific inquiry and discovery. Even within approaches, scientists often disagree in their interpretations of results, generating further research in an attempt to resolve the disagreement.

In any case, empirical research is conducted to examine hypotheses about the associations among constructs. In doing this sort of research, we usually make assumptions about the second sort of hypotheses, that is, those linking the constructs with variables or measures, the observable indicators of the unobservable constructs. For instance, we might conduct research designed to demonstrate that interracial contact decreases prejudice. In the process, we make assumptions about how both constructs, interracial contact and prejudice, are to be measured.

Although research that examines hypotheses of the first sort, causal associations among constructs, is more frequent, research on hypotheses of the second sort is also a primary activity of social scientists. Research designed to examine whether a given variable accurately or validly measures a given construct is called measurement research. **Measurement research**, sometimes referred to as psychometric or sociometric research, usually is conducted by examining whether two or more ways of measuring the same construct yield similar results. As will become apparent in later portions of this chapter and in Chapter 8, such research is vitally important to the success of research examining hypothesized causal associations among constructs. Only if we can successfully manipulate, observe, or measure the constructs of interest can we empirically examine hypotheses about the causal associations among them.

We have said that a primary purpose of conducting empirical research is to examine hypotheses. At this point we need to be more specific about what this means. There are four different functions or purposes of empirical research that, in total, constitute the process of examining social science hypotheses: (1) discovery, (2) demonstration, (3) refutation, and (4) replication.

Discovery

Researchers frequently gather information to attempt to discover what might be responsible for some phenomenon or behavior. For instance, in studying depressed clients, we might interview and observe the clients' families to see whether there are any patterns of interaction that might be responsible for the depression. In doing such systematic observation, we do not as yet have a well-defined hypothesis about the causes of depression. Rather, we are attempting to **discover** what might be plausible causes of constructs. Research as discovery is used primarily to develop or generate hypotheses. When conducting research for this purpose, the researcher is operating in an **inductive** manner, attempting to move from observation to the development of hypotheses, rather than the other way around, that is, from hypotheses to observation, which is known as **deductive** research.

Even in inductive research, research is rarely solely about discovery. Insofar as researchers have been thinking about and looking at prior research about the issue of interest, there is some ill-defined or implicit theoretical orientation that guides the research, even when the researchers have no explicit hypotheses they are examining. For instance, in the depression example, a researcher who interviews family members implicitly assumes that understanding the causes of depression might lie in the family and their interactions with the client. A researcher who believes that depression is a result of a genetic or neurochemical malfunction would not look for causes in patterns of family interaction and would likely not interview families. In other words, without some kind of underlying or implicit theory, researchers would not know where to begin looking for the causes of a phenomenon or behavior. Thus, the difference between inductive and deductive approaches is perhaps best thought of as a difference in degree. Even constructivists are not likely to conduct research as pure discovery or to proceed purely inductively, for choice of problem or setting involves presumptions about the problem and how to go about understanding it. Even when research is used primarily to generate hypotheses, researchers inevitably make theoretical assumptions in deciding what to observe or where a potential cause might lie.

Demonstration

If researchers have a hypothesis about the associations among constructs of interest, they are quite likely to gather data in an attempt to **demonstrate** or support it. Suppose, for instance, that researchers believe that living in an integrated neighborhood reduces prejudice. They might then try to generate information or make observations to demonstrate the validity of this hypothesis. For instance, they might interview residents of both integrated and segregated neighborhoods about their attitudes toward various ethnic groups. If the interviews showed that those who lived in integrated neighborhoods had more favorable attitudes, the findings from the research would be consistent with the hypothesis. Such consistency of observation with the hypothesis is the limit of what demonstration research can accomplish.

Research findings can only be consistent with or demonstrate a hypothesis. They can never prove the hypothesis. This point was made in the first chapter but bears repeating here. That residents of integrated neighborhoods express less hostility toward other ethnic groups than do residents of segregated neighborhoods does not mean that the hypothesis, which states that integration *causes* a reduction in prejudice, is correct. There are always alternative explanations that may be equally consistent with the research results. For instance, residents of integrated neighborhoods might express less hostility because they were initially less prejudiced before they moved into the neighborhood, and highly prejudiced people may choose not to live in integrated neighborhoods. Hence, although the research findings are consistent with the hypothesis or demonstrate that it might be correct, alternative explanations that may be equally consistent with the research results always remain.

Research designed to demonstrate a hypothesis is deductive rather than inductive. In other words, in demonstration research, the hypothesis generates the research, whereas in discovery, research is used to generate hypotheses. Scientists, when acting deductively, start with a hypothesis, which they then seek to support or demonstrate using information generated by empirical research.

As was true for inductive research, research is never pure deduction or pure demonstration. Although it could turn out that the research results are nearly perfectly consistent with the hypothesis, inevitably some inconsistencies or results emerge that cannot be entirely explained by the hypothesis. The researcher then proceeds inductively, examining the findings and hypothesis to determine how the hypothesis might be modified to account more precisely for the research findings. In this way, research never exclusively serves a discovery or a demonstration function, just as the researcher never reasons exclusively deductively or inductively.

Refutation

Although a hypothesis can never be proven to be true, it is possible to **refute** competing hypotheses. For instance, suppose we conduct research on the "integration reduces prejudice" hypothesis that we have been discussing. Suppose we find that residents of integrated neighborhoods express less hostility than do residents of segregated neighborhoods. We might then want to refute the competing or alternative hypothesis that residents of the two neighborhoods differed in prejudice initially, before they moved into the segregated or integrated neighborhoods. To do so, we would have to conduct further research, interviewing people when they first move into integrated neighborhoods and then following them over time. If we found that initially they expressed hostility equal to that of segregated residents but that over time they developed more positive attitudes, we would have generated evidence to refute the competing hypothesis.

The process of supporting a hypothesis, and ultimately a theory that is made up of numerous hypotheses, is one of demonstration and repeated refutation of alternative hypotheses. Although in a formal sense there are always alternatives that have yet to be refuted, the remaining alternatives become more and more far-fetched, and gradually we develop confidence in a hypothesis through repeated demonstration and repeated refutations of alternatives to it. This brings us to the fourth purpose of research.

Replication

In Chapter 1, we argued that researcher biases inevitably affect how observations are gathered and interpreted. The only way to overcome these biases is to replicate the research. **Replication** means that other researchers in other settings with different samples attempt to reproduce the research. If the results of the replication are consistent with the original research, we have increased confidence in the hypothesis that the original study supported.

These then are the ways that research is used to develop, examine, support, and modify hypotheses. The functions or purposes of empirical research in examining hypotheses are not mutually exclusive. A given study is likely to serve a number of functions simultaneously. Research to demonstrate a hypothesis usually ends up as discovery as well. Likewise, replication inevitably involves discovery and refutation, as the conditions of replications change and hypotheses must be modified to account for those changes.

The purpose of empirical research is to inform hypotheses, to enable us to build better and more accurate hypotheses about how human beings behave. Of course, not all research is equally informative or useful in constructing and modifying hypotheses. It is to this issue that we now turn: What makes empirical research more or less useful in helping us to discover, demonstrate, revise, and ultimately support hypotheses?

Criteria for Evaluating Social Science Research

We discuss here four major criteria for evaluating social science research: construct validity, internal validity, external validity, and conclusion validity. To do so, we rely on one of the example hypotheses presented earlier:

> Parents who are more involved in their children's education have children who perform better academically.

Let us suppose that we want to examine whether this hypothesis is reasonable. To do so, we would want to gather information in such a way that our observations would be most informative about the merits of the hypothesis.

Construct Validity

To conduct research that will help determine whether our hypothesis is good or bad, that is, reasonable or not, and whether it should be modified in some way, we first need to measure successfully the theoretical constructs of interest. In this hypothesis, two constructs are involved: Parent involvement in children's education is the first theoretical variable. Researchers might assess it by asking parents to report how often they go to parent–teacher conferences and how often they talk to their children about what they are learning in school. Construct validity would then refer to the extent to which these parent reports assess parent involvement. Children's grade point averages or achievement test scores might be used to assess the second construct, that is, children's academic performance. And construct validity would refer to the extent to which these specific measures adequately assess children's academic performance.

Note that, in this example, a measure of the causal construct, parent involvement, is the **independent variable**. The measure of the affected construct, academic performance, is the **dependent variable**. And, again, the degree to which the specific variables accurately reflect or measure the constructs of interest is known as the **construct validity** of the research. A study has high construct validity to the extent that all constructs in the hypothesis are successfully measured or captured by the specific variables on which the researcher has gathered data.

Internal Validity

Assume we had met the first criterion for useful research, and we had good measures of both parent involvement in children's education and children's academic performance. Suppose we then gathered information on a number of parents and their children and found that, indeed, more involved parents' children performed better. Certainly this result is consistent with the hypothesis. What we do not know, however, is whether our research supports the notion that parent involvement *causes* better academic performance. The second criterion for useful or informative research, known as **internal validity**, concerns the extent to which conclusions can be drawn about the causal effects of one variable on another, that is, ensuring that only the independent variable can account for differences in the dependent variable. In research with high internal validity, we are better able to argue that associations are causal ones, whereas in studies with low internal validity, causality cannot be inferred as confidently because alternative explanations for the effects cannot be dismissed. In short, internal validity refers to the degree to which the research design allows causal conclusions to be drawn about the effect of the independent variable on the dependent variable.

External Validity

A third criterion for useful research is known as **external validity**, that is, the extent to which the results of the research can be generalized to the populations and settings of interest in the hypothesis. In the example we are considering, suppose the constructs were well measured (high construct validity). Suppose further that we found an association between parent involvement and children's academic performance and could reasonably claim that association to be a causal one (high internal validity). We then would want to know whether that causal association held in only the relatively few parents and children we observed in our research or whether we could generalize the causal associations to other parents and children whom we did not observe. According to the hypothesis, the effect appears among all parents and children. Clearly, it would not be possible to observe them all. But we might select for observation parents and children who are representative of a larger population, for example, parents and their children who are enrolled in elementary schools in the U.S., so that we would have greater confidence in generalizing the results of our research to others. Such a study would have relatively high external validity. A study from which generalization is difficult has relatively low external validity.

Conclusion Validity

Conclusion validity refers to the degree to which our data analyses – whether those analyses are quantitative or qualitative – allow us to draw appropriate conclusions about the presence or absence of relationships between our independent and dependent variables. It differs from internal validity in that we are not concerned about whether the relationship is a causal one; rather, we are concerned about whether the quality of the data and analyses provides a reasonable basis for concluding whether a relationship exists.

Although conclusion validity applies to qualitative analyses as well, it has most commonly referred to the statistical factors that affect the ability to reach a conclusion about the presence or absence of a relationship. Statistically speaking, it is possible to make one of two types of errors. A **Type I error** refers to incorrectly concluding that there is a relationship when in fact there is not; a **Type II error** refers to incorrectly concluding that there is not a relationship when in fact there is. The factors that affect the probability of making such errors concern the **statistical power** of the study, that is, the probability of finding the predicted relationship if the relationship truly exists. We do not consider issues of statistical conclusion validity in this book. Suffice it to say that drawing correct conclusions about the presence or absence of relationships requires (a) strong research designs in which (b) high-quality measures are used to (c) gather enough data (i.e., an adequate sample size) to see the effect (and thus one must consider the size of the effect that would be reasonable to expect) and (d) the use of data analyses that are appropriate to the research question and the nature of the data. This book focuses on two of these elements, namely, measurement and research design.

All four types of validity, summarized in Table 2.2, are important in evaluating research. However, their relative importance usually depends on the purposes the research is designed to serve. For instance, in the early stages of a research program, it might be sufficient to measure constructs that are associated with the behavior of interest, without worrying too much about whether the association is a causal one. In other words, in discovery research, construct validity might be relatively more important than internal validity. Or consider research in which the primary purpose

Table 2.2 Definitions of Research Validities	
Construct validity:	To what extent are the constructs of theoretical interest successfully operationalized in the research?
Internal validity:	To what extent does the research design permit us to reach causal conclusions about the effect of the independent variable on the dependent variable?
External validity:	To what extent can we generalize from the research sample and setting to the populations and settings specified in the research hypothesis?
Conclusion validity:	To what extent do our analyses allow us to reach appropriate conclusions about the presence or absence of a relationship between the independent and dependent variable?

is replication. Such research is especially concerned with external validity because in replication we are concerned with whether a previously obtained result continues to be found in a new setting at a different time. Because the conditions of the original research and the replication are never identical, we are always examining issues of generalizability in replication research.

The remainder of this chapter concerns the factors that determine whether a study has high or low construct, internal, and external validity; however, our discussion here serves only as an introduction to the subject of how valid and informative empirical research is designed and conducted. The major portion of this book is devoted to this topic as well. Hence, the remaining pages in this chapter serve as an introduction to many of the later chapters, in which some of the same issues are considered in greater detail.

Maximizing Construct Validity

Suppose we wanted to measure children's academic performance to test our hypothesis about the effects of parent involvement. There are a number of ways to measure academic performance. We could give the students achievement tests, look at their grades, ask teachers to evaluate their students verbally, and so forth. Each of these measures is called a variable. Earlier we defined a variable as any attribute that varies across the people or things that we are measuring. Another way to look at variables is to consider them simply as rules or ways of classifying people into different categories so that those who are in the same category are more similar in some way of interest than those who are in different categories. For instance, scores on an achievement test constitute a variable that is thought to measure academic performance. If we line up students according to their scores on the achievement test, we believe that students who are closer together in that rank order are more similar in academic performance than students who are farther apart.

Actually, however, variables never measure only the construct of interest. They measure other irrelevant characteristics as well. Think about an achievement test. To some extent it does measure academic performance; however, it also probably measures test-taking anxiety, motivation to do well, familiarity with English, and so forth. These other factors, in addition to pure academic ability, may influence whether students get relatively high or low scores on the test. To some extent, then, variables reflect not only the construct of interest but also **constructs of disinterest** – things we would rather not measure. Finally, variables contain random errors of measurement. For instance, scores on a test may be affected by recording errors or grading errors. Or students may guess the answers to some questions and these guesses will sometimes be correct and sometimes incorrect.

As shown in Figure 2.1, then, observed scores are made up of three components: (1) the construct of interest, (2) other things that we do not want to measure (constructs of disinterest), and (3) random errors. Thus, if we ordered students based on their scores on the test, that order would not be identical to the ordering that would result if somehow we could order them based on their true academic performance. The best we can do is to develop and administer measures in ways that minimize the

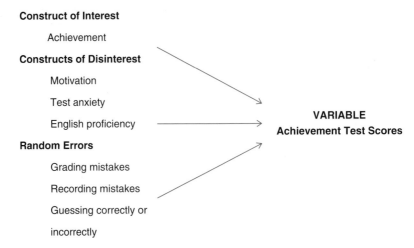

Figure 2.1   Three Components of a Variable.

influences of constructs of disinterest and random errors on the scores that we obtain; to the extent that we are successful, the variable is said to have construct validity.

But how do we know the degree to which a variable has construct validity? We cannot measure true academic performance directly and thus cannot know whether the rank ordering of students on the test is similar to the rank ordering of students on their true academic performance. The only solution is to measure other variables that we think are also measures of academic performance. For instance, school grades measure academic performance – the construct of interest, although they, too, probably measure other things, such as teachers' biases and preferences (e.g., leniency), students' extraversion, and so forth. Nevertheless, we can compare the ordering of students on what we think are our two measures of academic performance, test scores and grades. If the two orderings are similar, and the only thing these two variables measure in common is academic performance, then the similarity of their orderings is evidence for their construct validity.

Let us review the general point. All variables measure not only the construct of interest but other things as well, and we cannot know the true ordering of people on the construct. The best we can do is measure another variable that we think also assesses the construct and then compare orders on the two variables. If the two variables give us similar orderings of people, we have increased confidence that each of them is measuring, among other things, the construct we think they have in common. In short, we need to measure each construct in more than one way. Only if the different measures yield similar results can we have confidence that our variables capture the constructs of interest. Construct validity is thus best evaluated by employing **multiple operational definitions**, or multiple ways of measuring, and then comparing them to see whether they seem to be measuring the same things.

The need for multiple operational definitions and ways to evaluate the quality of variables are discussed in much greater detail in Chapter 8. Here we wish to stress the importance of construct validity. If empirical research is to be useful or informative, it must measure the constructs to which our hypotheses refer. If the observed variables do not have construct validity, there is no way the research can inform our theory. Even worse, poor construct validity may mislead researchers by yielding seemingly positive results that do not actually reflect the constructs of interest. Contributing to this problem is the fact that poor construct validity is harder to detect than problems with other types of validity. For example, there are widely known and accepted procedures for documenting adequate internal validity. If the criteria for establishing internal validity are not met in a given study, it is obvious to other researchers. Establishing construct validity is more challenging, and unless the authors of a research report are careful in describing their measures and validation procedures, it may not be clear whether a given construct was truly assessed.

Exercise: Evaluating construct validity

Construct validity is central to research. It establishes that you are measuring what you think you are measuring. If you are not sure, no one should believe what you find, for you might not be measuring what you think. Find an instrument (personality scale, survey, interview protocol, etc.) that you have used or have read about, and find out how its construct validity has been established. At this point in the book, it would be premature to go further. Anticipating future chapters, we will revisit this example and explore the following questions, so save the instrument that you picked. How was it validated? For what populations has it been validated? Has it been used in ways that go beyond how it was validated? Are there questions about its validity for other populations?

Maximizing Internal Validity

Certain characteristics of the research design affect the internal validity of a study – the extent to which we can infer causal connections from an association between two variables. These characteristics are discussed in more detail in Chapter 10. Our discussion here is intended to provide an intuitive understanding of how to maximize our ability to argue for causal connections.

In the parent involvement example, suppose we were able to assess parent involvement and the academic performance of their children. Suppose further that our research had perfect construct validity: Our measures of both parent involvement and children's academic performance measured those constructs and nothing else. Finally, suppose we found that the children of more involved parents tended to have academic performance scores that were higher than those of children whose parents were less involved. In other words, we found that the two variables, parent involvement and academic performance, were related in the predicted way. Could we argue from this association that we have evidence for a causal effect of parent involvement on children's academic performance? We could not.

Simply showing that people or groups (e.g., parent–child dyads) that have high scores on one variable (i.e., degree of parent involvement) have higher scores on a second (i.e., academic performance) does not necessarily mean that one variable causes the other. Although an empirical association or **correlation** between two variables is necessary, it is not sufficient for reaching causal conclusions. Inappropriately inferring causality from a simple association between two variables is called the **correlational fallacy**. This concept is simple yet utterly important: Correlation does not imply causation.

Consider a couple of classic examples in which two variables are associated, but there is no causal effect of one on the other. Elementary school children who have larger feet tend to be better readers; foot size and reading ability are related. Obviously, however, this relationship does not mean that foot size affects reading ability. Rather, age affects both foot size and reading ability, which is why the two are related. Another example: In some European countries following World War II it was noticed that more babies were born where more storks were roosting. What accounts for this association is population density. Where there are lots of people, there are lots of chimneys, where storks are fond of roosting. Likewise, where there are lots of people, there are lots of babies. Hence, storks and babies are found together. The inability to draw causal conclusions may be obvious in these examples, but when one has strong notions about the specific cause of a given effect, it can be difficult to identify alternative explanations and tempting to draw a causal conclusion.

In sum, whenever two variables are associated with each other, there are four possible explanations for their association: (1) variable X causes variable Y; (2) variable Y causes variable X; (3) variable X causes variable Y and Y causes X, in which case we could talk about reciprocal or bidirectional causation; or (4) some third variable, Z, causes both X and Y. The latter possibility is often called the "hidden third variable" problem, hidden because the researcher might have only measured X and Y and so cannot examine Z, and may not even know what Z is. Figure 2.2 illustrates these possibilities with a research question of social importance: What is the nature of the association between media violence and aggression in children? The research findings are very clear on the existence of an association: As the amount of media violence watched by children increases, so does their aggression.

As Figure 2.2 shows, there are four possible explanations for the association between exposure to media violence and aggression. One possibility is that watching violence on television does cause children to be more aggressive. A second possibility is that aggressive children seek out and watch more violent television programming. In other words, the causal path runs in the opposite direction. To make things even more complicated, it is possible that both of these hypotheses are true and that media violence and aggression cause each other in a complicated pattern over time called **reciprocal causation**. Lastly, it is possible that a third variable causes both aggression and the watching of violent television programming; inadequate parental attention and supervision, for example, is one such plausible third variable. It is the job of researchers to consider and examine all of these possibilities and indeed a great deal of research has examined and continues to examine the association between media

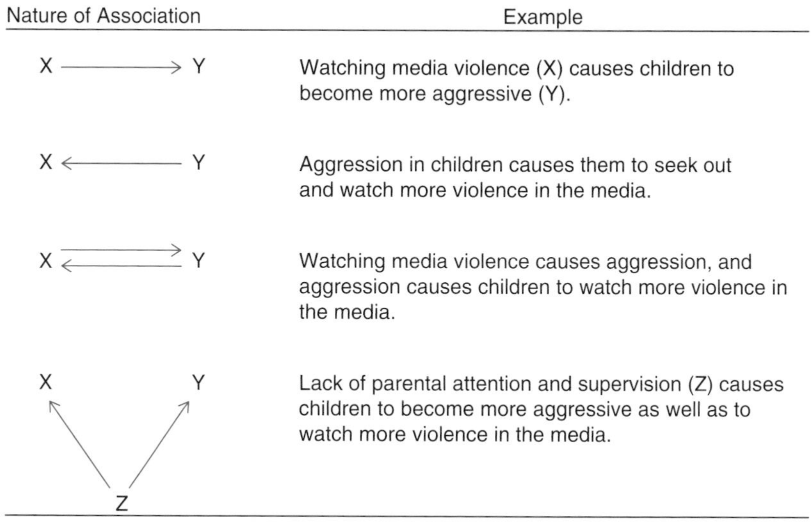

Nature of Association	Example
X ———————→ Y	Watching media violence (X) causes children to become more aggressive (Y).
X ←——————— Y	Aggression in children causes them to seek out and watch more violence in the media.
X ⇄ Y	Watching media violence causes aggression, and aggression causes children to watch more violence in the media.
X Y \ / Z	Lack of parental attention and supervision (Z) causes children to become more aggressive as well as to watch more violence in the media.

Figure 2.2 Possible Causal Pathways to Explain the Association Between Exposure to Media Violence and Aggression.

violence and aggression. We leave it to readers to consider the strength of the research evidence supporting a causal relationship (see, for example, Bushman & Huesmann, 2012; Gentile & Bushman, 2012).

We use this example to highlight two additional points. First, broad conclusions about the effects of one construct on another require a great deal of research conducted by different researchers who have different perspectives, using different research designs and different variables or indicators of the broader constructs. To the extent that the research methodology varies (and thus so too do the strengths and weaknesses of the studies) and yet the research results converge, we are in a much better position to draw broader causal conclusions (as opposed to a causal conclusion about the effect of a specific independent variable on a specific dependent variable in a single study). Second, the ability to draw causal conclusions does not mean that the effect holds for every single individual. In other words, exposure to media violence may indeed cause aggression, but that does not mean that every child who watches violent shows or plays violent video games will necessarily become aggressive – just as not every individual who smokes will necessarily develop lung cancer. Further, most phenomena are multiply determined so that there may be many factors in addition to media violence that cause aggression and many factors in addition to smoking that cause lung cancer.

The issue of establishing causality matters a great deal in science. Scientists are in the business not only of describing and predicting events but also of controlling them. In the social sciences, especially, we wish ultimately to put our findings to the use and benefit of humankind; to design effective interventions for social problems, we must be able to identify the *causes* of those problems and those causes must be manipulable. Returning to the media violence example, if watching media violence causes aggression, decreasing the amount of gratuitous violence in television shows and movies or otherwise limiting exposure to violent media may be an effective way of reducing aggression. However, aggression may also be caused by other factors, for example, inadequate parenting and access to weapons, in which case interventions that target these factors may also be useful. Identifying causes is crucial. So, too, is the evaluation of interventions designed to "treat" the problem – a topic that is discussed in Chapter 15.

We stress this point because this is an area in which the public is sometimes misled by the news media or other information outlets, such as the Internet. Frequently, findings of research studies are presented in a distorted manner because reporters or news anchors draw an inappropriate or unwarranted causal conclusion from a correlational finding. This may occur even when the researchers who conducted the study were very careful to draw appropriate conclusions. For example, a newspaper headline might state "Exercise Makes Pregnancy Easier" and the accompanying article claim that pregnant women who exercise regularly have shorter and less painful deliveries and healthier babies. The causal claim is explicit, but a careful reading reveals that the scientists had only correlational data available; that is, pregnant women were asked how often they exercised, and frequency of exercise was then related to pregnancy outcomes.

We are not trying to argue that exercise is not good for pregnant women. Exercise may indeed cause better deliveries and healthier babies. Our point is merely that one should not draw that conclusion based on the research finding presented in the hypothetical newspaper article. Other explanations exist for the association between exercise and pregnancy outcomes. Women who are concerned with their health in general probably engage in a variety of activities in addition to exercising that are good for their unborn babies. For instance, they might avoid drinking alcohol or smoking during pregnancy; their diets might be healthier; they might take prenatal vitamins; or they might obtain better prenatal care overall. And it could be one or more of these other factors, not exercise, that accounts for the positive outcomes. As detailed in Chapter 10, the only way we can conclude that exercise is a causal factor is to conduct research, especially randomized experiments, that allows us to rule out these alternative explanations.

Misrepresentations of scientific research abound. Because they usually sound plausible, readers may fall into the trap of agreeing with the causal claim. Our hope is that, even if you do not become a practicing social scientist, you will become a discriminating consumer of findings from empirical research on social behavior. We encourage readers to scrutinize newspapers, magazines, and Internet reports with a critical eye, looking for inappropriately drawn causal inferences. Their frequency will be both surprising and disheartening.

To illustrate other threats to internal validity, we return to our example of parent involvement and children's academic performance. Assume that parents were assigned to be either highly involved or not involved in their children's education. Assume further that children in the two groups subsequently differed in their academic performance. We cannot argue for causality in this case because it is possible that the parents and/or children in the two groups differed in other ways that would account for the difference in performance. In particular, the children's academic performance may have differed initially prior to their parents being involved or not. Indeed, participants in the two groups may have differed in many ways that could account for the subsequent difference in children's performance. These types of initial differences between groups of research participants that may affect the dependent variable represent a **selection threat** to internal validity.

How might we get around this selection threat? One way might be to place the parents and their children in the involved and uninvolved groups so that there were no initial differences in academic performance. If we could do so, we could be more confident that differences in performance later on were not due to initial differences in academic performance. As we have suggested, however, the parents and children in the two groups may differ in other ways, for example, motivation, that could influence subsequent academic performance. Indeed, we might observe a difference simply because children in the two groups were changing or learning on their own at different rates. Hence, if we find a difference in academic performance at a later time, we still cannot infer that the difference is caused by the difference in parent involvement. The difficulty of reaching causal conclusions because the individuals in the two groups might be growing or maturing at different rates is known as the **selection by maturation threat** to internal validity.

What is needed is a way to equate the parents and children in the two groups not only now but also in the future. There is really only one way to accomplish the goal of establishing equivalent groups. Suppose for each parent we flipped a coin. Certainly, there is no reason to expect that heads or tails would be related to the child's academic performance now or in the future, nor would we expect the result of the coin toss to be related to hair color, height, or any other person characteristic. By definition, a variable whose values are randomly determined, like the flip of a coin or the throw of a die, is unrelated on average to all other variables now and in the future. Hence, if we decided who was to be in the high involvement group and who is to be in the low involvement group by a flip of a coin, we would expect no differences in academic performance later if parent involvement made no difference.

The lesson is that we can infer causality from the association between two variables only if people have been randomly assigned to the levels of the independent variables. Parent involvement in children's education is the independent variable in our example and it has two levels: highly involved and uninvolved. If it were related to academic performance later and if children were assigned to its levels on a random basis, we would be able to argue that it had a causal effect on academic performance, the dependent variable. Research studies carried out in this manner, with random assignment to the independent variable, are called **randomized experiments**. They are discussed in considerable detail in Chapter 10.

Although randomized experiments are the best choice if causal conclusions are to be drawn from the research, they require researchers to have a great deal of control. Researchers must be able to determine who is in which group, for example. Frequently, such control over the independent variable is impossible. It would be difficult and unethical to ask parents to be uninvolved in their children's education. When such control is not possible, some type of **quasi-experimental research** may be used instead. Quasi-experimental designs are discussed in Chapter 11. Briefly, quasi-experiments are those in which research participants are not randomly assigned to levels of the independent variables. Although they do not permit causal inferences with the same degree of confidence as randomized experiments do, they are essential tools for social scientists. Although some internal validity is sacrificed, quasi-experiments can still yield exceedingly rich and useful information. Randomized experiments are useful and particularly valuable for causation, but they are not the only tools in the researcher's bag.

Maximizing External Validity

In Chapter 9, we consider procedures designed to increase the external validity of research, that is, procedures that increase our ability to generalize the research results to the populations and settings of interest. We introduce these procedures here, again using our example about the effects of parent involvement on children's academic performance.

Suppose we had measured well the two constructs, parent involvement and children's academic performance, and had done what we could to ensure internal validity. How would we ensure that our research results were generalizable to the extent we desired? First, rather than remaining implicit in the hypothesis, the population and setting to which generalization is sought should be made explicit before the research is conducted. We need to define as precisely as possible the group of people and the settings for which we think our hypothesis holds. For instance, we could be a bit more precise by saying that we expect parent involvement to positively affect the academic performance of children enrolled in public schools located in large U.S. cities. If we gathered data from the entire population and found support for our hypothesis, generalization to the desired population would not be a problem.

However, it is neither efficient nor necessary to measure every person in the population or every setting of interest. Rather, we can gather data from a sample of the population. To enhance generalization, we want to select a sample so that it is representative of the population. But how would we do so? The only way we can be confident about generalizing from a sample to a population is to draw a probability sample, for example, a **random sample**. Obtaining a random sample involves doing something like flipping a coin to determine whether each member of the population is to be included in the sample.

Note that random sampling is not the same as random assignment. Using a random process to select a sample from a population is done to enhance our ability to generalize, that is, external validity. Using a random process to assign participants to levels of the independent variable is done to increase internal validity, the ability to reach a causal conclusion about the effect of the independent variable on the dependent variable.

Frequently in the social sciences it is not practical to draw a random sample. We might wish to generalize to parents and children across the country, but it may not be possible to obtain such a sample or to conduct a study that involves people who are spread across such a large geographic area. Generalization must then be done on a theoretical or conceptual basis. We must speculate about how parents and children whom we have not observed might differ from those we have, and then we must decide whether those differences would be expected to influence whether parent involvement affects children's academic performance. Such speculation ultimately gives rise to further research. Indeed, replicating research in other settings and with other samples is an important part of maximizing external validity.

Basic and Applied Research

Throughout this chapter, we have focused on use of research to develop, test, and refine theories. Such research is referred to as **basic research**. But not all research is intended to test theories. Some, for example, is intended to *apply* theories to real-world settings to see whether the theories can help improve outcomes. Other research is intended to answer practical questions about how well different methods or approaches work in particular settings and with specific populations. Some of the latter types of research may not apply any disciplinary knowledge, but examine effectiveness of intuition of practitioners or practices developed atheoretically. Not surprisingly, such research is called **applied research**, or, more recently, **translational research**. If basic and applied research are viewed as ends of a continuum, most research falls somewhere between the end points, for basic research simultaneously can be used to develop practices that work, and applied research can help develop and refine theories. Lewin (1946), for example, argued that practical settings are great places to develop theory, for theories should be relevant to the world and help explain everyday human behavior. In his words, "there is nothing so practical as a good theory." If one agrees with Lewin, then research becomes *both* basic *and* applied, for it develops and applies theories to address practical issues, and we should not view basic and applied research as ends of a continuum but as two dimensions (basic/not and applied/not) of research types.

Summary

There are two major foci of this chapter. The first concerns the purposes of empirical research for the scientific study of social behavior. We argued that research is used fundamentally to examine hypotheses and develop theories. As such, research can be used for discovery, demonstration, refutation, and replication.

Discovery is the inductive process of gathering data to formulate hypotheses. Demonstration is predominantly a deductive process, gathering data that we hope are consistent with a hypothesis. Although such demonstrations can be used to support a hypothesis, the hypothesis can never in fact be proven because there always remain alternative ways to account for a research finding. Research as refutation involves the attempt to refute competing hypotheses, that is, to show that alternative explanations for previous results are not valid. Finally, research as replication involves repeating research with different samples or in different settings to increase confidence in a previous demonstration. In all four cases, discovery, demonstration, refutation, and replication, the ultimate reason for gathering empirical data is to develop, support, evaluate, and refine our hypotheses so that they do a better job of describing and explaining social behavior.

In the second half of the chapter, we defined four criteria that determine the extent to which research is useful in examining hypotheses: construct validity, internal validity, external validity, and conclusion validity. Research has high construct validity if the variables that are in fact measured correspond closely to the constructs that the hypotheses implicate. Research that is internally valid permits us to reach causal conclusions about the association between the independent and dependent variables. Research that is high in external validity enables us to generalize the results from the sample studied to the population and settings of interest. Finally, conclusion validity concerns whether the quality of our data and analyses is adequate for drawing conclusions about the presence or absence of a relationship between our independent and dependent variables. In addition to defining these validities, we discussed the basic conditions for achieving each one. Finally, we introduced the distinction between basic and applied research. This discussion serves to introduce the more complete presentations in subsequent chapters.

Go online   Visit the book's companion website for this chapter's test bank and other resources at: www.wiley.com/go/maruyama

---

Key Concepts

Applied research	Measurement research
Basic research	Multiple operational definitions
Conclusion validity	Parsimony
Construct validity	Quasi-experimental research
Constructs of disinterest	Random sample
Correlation	Randomized experiment
Correlational fallacy	Reciprocal causation
Deductive	Refutation
Demonstration	Replication
Dependent variable	Selection by maturation threat
Discovery	Selection threat
External validity	Statistical power
Falsifiability	Theory
Hypotheses	Translational research
Independent variable	Type I error
Inductive	Type II error
Internal validity	Variable

On the Web

http://www.burns.com/wcbspurcorl.htm Very clearly written discussion of the correlational fallacy, with lots of examples and quotes from relevant readings.

http://faculty.washington.edu/chudler/stat3.html Great web page entitled "How to Lie and Cheat with Statistics." Reviews how graphs and charts can be misleadingly created and reported in the media. Nicely done and interactive.

http://chem.tufts.edu/science/FrankSteiger/theory.htm Good discussion of the distinction between facts and theory, in the context of the evolutionary debate.

Further Reading

Blastland, M., & Dilnot, A. (2010). *The numbers game: The commonsense guide to understanding numbers in the news, in politics, and in life.* New York, NY: Gotham Books.

Cross, C. (1996). *The tainted truth: The manipulation of facts in America.* New York, NY: Simon & Schuster.

Dawes, R. M., Faust, D., & Meehl, P. E. (1989). Clinical versus actuarial judgment. *Science, 243,* 1668–1674.

Huff, D. (1993). *How to lie with statistics.* New York, NY: Norton.

Meehl, P. E. (1978). Theoretical risks and tabular asterisks: Sir Karl, Sir Ronald, and the slow progress of soft psychology. *Journal of Consulting and Clinical Psychology, 46,* 806–834.

Paulos, J. A. (2001). *Innumeracy: Mathematical illiteracy and its consequences.* New York, NY: Hill & Wang.

Stanovich, K. E. (2013). *How to think straight about psychology* (10th ed.). Boston, MA: Pearson.

Chapter 3

Ethical Principles

The Tuskegee Syphilis Study

In 1932, a 40-year longitudinal study was begun by the U.S. Public Health Service (now called the Centers for Disease Control and Prevention) to determine what the natural course of syphilis would be if left untreated. The study involved 399 African American men in Tuskegee, Alabama, who had syphilis and were recruited with promises of "special free treatment" for "bad blood." The researchers never explicitly told the men that they had syphilis. This "special treatment" actually consisted of spinal taps

Research Methods in Social Relations, Eighth Edition. Geoffrey Maruyama and Carey S. Ryan.
© 2014 John Wiley & Sons, Inc. Published 2014 by John Wiley & Sons, Inc.
Companion Website: www.wiley.com/go/maruyama

Figure 3.1   Participants in the Tuskegee Syphilis Study.
Source: Photograph from Records of the Centers for Disease Control and Prevention, maintained by the National Archives; http://research.archives.gov/description/824605.

Figure 3.2   A Physician Draws Blood from a Participant in the Tuskegee Syphilis Study.
Source: Photograph from Records of the Centers for Disease Control and Prevention, maintained by the National Archives; http://research.archives.gov/description/824606.

(performed without anesthesia, by the way) administered to detect the neurological effects of syphilis. Even though it was known as early as the 1940s that penicillin was an effective treatment for syphilis, the infected men were never informed of that fact, nor were they ever treated with penicillin. In 1972, public outcry arising from the first media accounts of the study caused the government to halt the study. By that time, only 74 of the original 399 test participants were alive. Of those who had died, at least

28 – but possibly more than 100 – had died as a direct result of complications of syphilis.

What is right to do to people in the name of science? Is it ethical to withhold treatment from people in order to learn more about a disease and therefore, hopefully, help many more people in the future? Is it ethical to study people without their knowledge? Is it ethical to deceive people about the procedures they are undergoing as part of a study? In the example of the Tuskegee study, the research procedures were clearly unethical. But it would be wrong to conclude that control (i.e., untreated) groups should never be used or that experimenters should never deceive their experimental participants. In this chapter, we describe the history of concerns about ethical issues in social science research with human participants; outline the three broad ethical principles that underlie the formal regulations that have been created to address these issues; describe some specific ethical issues relevant to experimental, quasi-experimental, and non-experimental research; and conclude with a detailed description of the ethical review process.

Why Did Ethical Concerns Arise?

The social sciences differ from some other physical sciences in that our objects of study are people – living, sentient beings who have their own feelings and thoughts. Unlike some physical scientists (e.g., geologists who study rocks, physicists who study molecules), social scientists must take special care to safeguard the rights and dignity of the "objects" they study. Unfortunately, however, scientists have not always taken such care – as the Tuskegee study demonstrates. Indeed, prior to the passing of the National Research Act in 1974, investigators were free to do as they wanted with their human participants; there was no federal or institutional oversight of human research. And many studies that were blatantly unethical or at least questionable were conducted. Now, nearly all research with human participants in the United States is regulated and reviewed by bodies known as **Institutional Review Boards, or IRBs**. Indeed, every study must be approved by an IRB before it can be carried out.

Although the Tuskegee study was instrumental in the development of these regulations, other medical studies also attracted public attention and dismay because participants were physically harmed, seriously deceived, or placed under substantial stress. Some of these have come to light more recently. Skloot (2010), for example, documented the history of Henrietta Lacks and the cells (known as HeLa cells) that were taken from Henrietta without her or her family's knowledge. Henrietta Lacks was a poor Black tobacco farmer who was treated, but died, in the "colored ward" of a hospital in 1951 from an aggressive form of cancer. Her cells were unique, for they could thrive in a lab, an effect not previously achieved for any human cells. Hers were the first human cells grown in culture and continue to be the most widely used cell line in medical research today; they have played a vital role in the development of the polio vaccine, cloning, gene mapping, in vitro fertilization, and cancer treatment.

Companies have made a great deal of money, many scientists have made their careers, and society has greatly benefited from the HeLa cells, all while Henrietta's family remained oblivious, poor, and unable to obtain health insurance. Furthermore, research that was subsequently published (without the family's knowledge) about

HeLa cells included DNA mapping of family members and the details of Henrietta's death. Sadly, Henrietta's daughter first learned the painful details of her mother's death from a book in which medical records were quoted extensively and the autopsy described in graphic detail. As Skloot (2010) and the Tuskegee study suggest, the most egregious ethical violations have involved marginalized populations, for example, people who are poor, members of ethnic minority groups, or mentally disabled, with adverse consequences for families and communities as well as the participants themselves.

Fortunately, the case of Henrietta Lacks finally has a relatively happy ending. On August 7, 2013, it was announced that the National Institutes of Health (NIH) had come to an agreement with the Lacks family to grant them control over how Henrietta Lacks' genome is used. The family will not, however, receive any funds from commercial products that have been produced, finally officially donating her cells. Research reporting the genome and sequencing it are now stored at NIH, and researchers who want to use the data have to apply for access and submit annual reports about their research. Approval for use will be granted by a working group that includes two members of the Lacks family (Zimmer, 2013).

Although they played less of a role in the development of current federal regulations, the social sciences are not without examples of ethically problematic studies. The 1960s Milgram experiments of obedience, in which participants were led to believe they were administering severe (even lethal) electric shocks to an apparently unwilling victim, created considerable controversy among both scholars and the lay public. Although Milgram debriefed his participants and followed up to ensure they had not incurred any lasting harm, some scholars have argued that the stress and unwelcome self-knowledge experienced by the participants (e.g., "I am the sort of individual who would hurt an innocent person") were so severe that the study should never have been done (Baumrind, 1964). Scholars continue to debate the ethics of the Milgram experiments as well as the theoretical significance of the findings (Reicher, Haslam, & Miller, 2014).

Other less prominent social science studies also involved ethically questionable procedures. It was not unusual to deceive participants through **false feedback** about their personality and intelligence. Such studies were generally designed to induce low self-esteem in participants or to investigate the reactions of individuals to threatening feedback. For example, participants might be told that a supposed intelligence test they had taken revealed that they had subnormal intelligence. Alternatively, participants might be told that personality tests revealed that they were latent homosexuals. As we discuss in more detail later, these kinds of studies pose two special risks: first, that participants will be (justifiably) angry when they learn of the deception, and second (and more serious), that participants might not completely believe the debriefing when the deception is revealed, clinging somewhat to the original deception (e.g., "I've always thought I might have homosexual tendencies...").

In other instances, data were collected from individuals who had not given consent for the data collection to take place or indeed were unaware that a study was taking place. In some instances, these studies involved considerable invasion of privacy. For example, in the infamous "tearoom study" (Humphreys, 1970), the experimenter posed as a "lookout" in a men's room, watching for people entering the rest room while homosexual encounters occurred within. The experimenter then followed the homosexual men out of the rest room, surreptitiously recorded the license plate numbers on their cars, and determined their names and addresses through the Department of Motor Vehicles. Weeks later, he called the men and asked to interview them, without disclosing how they were chosen for study.

The Belmont Report

The negative publicity surrounding these and other studies from that time period eventually prompted enough public concern that the federal government decided a formal set of regulations and procedures for evaluating the ethics of both medical and social science studies with human participants was needed. As a direct consequence of the Tuskegee study, the U.S. Department of Health, Education, and Welfare (which has since split into the Department of Health and Human Services and the Department of Education) appointed an investigatory panel in 1972. Their findings led in 1974 to the passage of the National Research Act, which mandated that all federally funded research with human participants must first be approved by an Institutional Review Board and led to the establishment of a special commission given the charge of generating a basic set of ethical guidelines for conducting research.

The final product of this commission was the **Belmont Report**. This report lays out three overarching ethical principles – respect for persons, beneficence (do no harm, practice "good"), and justice – and the implications of these three principles for conducting research with human participants. In this section, we discuss at length each of these ethical principles and how they are translated into research procedures.

Respect for Persons

As described in the Belmont Report, "**Respect for persons** incorporates at least two ethical convictions: first, that individuals should be treated as autonomous agents, and second, that persons with diminished autonomy are entitled to protection." The concept of **autonomy**, obviously an important part of this principle, means simply that human beings have the right to decide to which research experiences, if any, they will be exposed. And in those cases in which research participants have diminished autonomy – for example, because of incapacity, illness, or young age – researchers are particularly obligated to safeguard participants' rights. Respect for persons thus serves as the basis for the most fundamental ethical principle underlying research with human participants, that is, that researchers should obtain **informed consent** from people who are freely and voluntarily choosing to participate in the research.

What does it mean to obtain informed consent? In most research, it means that participants are given forms that describe the purpose of the study, the procedures to occur during the study, risks and benefits of the research, and alternatives to participating. Participants sign the forms, indicating that they have read and understood them and agree to be in the study. Although the process of obtaining informed consent sounds straightforward, in reality it is not as easy as it appears. For many years, consent forms contained a fair amount of obtuse legalese because they were designed to conform to federal regulations. It became apparent that participants were not bothering to read or were unable to comprehend the forms they were signing, which undermines the whole point of obtaining informed consent. This was especially problematic when dealing with less-educated populations – the populations who are most vulnerable and who need the greatest protection of their rights. In recent years, IRBs have been working hard to create templates for consent forms that contain all the necessary information but are written in a user-friendly, easy-to-understand manner. The case study at the end of the chapter includes a sample of such a user-friendly consent form.

There is a certain tension between providing adequate detail about the study versus providing so much detail that biases are introduced into it. If participants are told too much about the study ahead of time, they might be able to guess accurately the study's hypotheses, which may influence their behavior in the study. For example, they may behave in ways they feel are expected by the experimenter, try to please the experimenter, or deliberately act in ways that oppose what they think the experimenter expects. A good consent form describes the procedures that participants will undergo and the risks accompanying those procedures in enough detail that participants can reasonably judge whether they want to participate, but not so much that the hypotheses are revealed.

The opposite of informed consent and, consequently, respect for persons is **coercion**. Forcing somebody to be in a research study is clearly unethical, with the Nazi medical experiments on concentration camp inmates the most egregious example. However, coercion lies on a continuum, with the Nazi medical experiments on one end and truly free and informed choice on the other end; it is the cases that fall in the middle that present special ethical concern.

Such cases are more common than one might think. For example, a study of prisoners presented by prison administrators might be perceived as coercive; that is, the prisoners might feel pressure to "volunteer" for the study to gain good behavior credit or to avoid being perceived as uncooperative. Does this mean that no research on prisoners should be allowed? Not necessarily. The principle of respect for persons would imply that it is not fair to deprive persons, including prisoners, of opportunities to volunteer for research, especially if the research involves some sort of benefit or financial remuneration. But it does mean that, in general, the persons soliciting participants for a research study should not be in positions of authority or power over potential participants, due to the very real potential for dual role conflict or perceived coercion. For example, it is generally not a good idea for professors to ask students in their classes to participate in their own studies because the students may not feel comfortable saying no to those who directly control their grades.

The issue of payment to participants raises other ethical concerns of coercion. What seems like a small amount to some potential participants might seem very large to others, for example, prisoners, children, and people with low incomes. The amount might seem so large that people feel pressured to participate even if they have misgivings about the research procedures. For example, a desperately poor family might agree to participate in medical research because it includes free checkups and other medical care, despite grave concerns and reluctance about the discomforts of the procedures (e.g., blood draws). A delicate balancing act therefore exists between appropriately compensating people for the inconveniences involved in being part of the research versus placing people in situations where they do not feel they can afford to decline. Ironically, then, an IRB can decide that a researcher is proposing to offer too much money to participants and that consent would therefore not be freely given but coerced by the magnitude of the inducements.

A special case of coercion concerns the widespread practice of **subject pools** at research universities. At most colleges, students are asked to participate in social science research as part of their course requirements. The rationale includes the educational value of viewing research from the perspective of a participant and the idea that it contributes to a science from which students benefit. Indeed, if it were not for the many college students who have participated in social science research over the years, there would be much less knowledge to share with them in their college courses. One review of the social psychological literature (Sears, 1986) indicated that college undergraduates were participants in 74% of the research studies reported in the top scientific journals.

Nevertheless, subject pools exist primarily so that researchers have a convenient source of participants. Certainly, some educational benefit may derive from participating in research, but it is unclear whether much more is gained by participating in several as opposed to a single study. In any case, to address the coercion issue, students must be offered an alternative means of obtaining the same course credit (e.g., writing a brief summary of a research article). Although such alternatives may be designed to be perceived as relatively unpleasant so that students "choose" to participate in research, the alternative is at least available for those who have or develop objections to research participation.

Exercise: Subject pools (groups of 4)

Subject pools have been a typical part of introductory psychology courses and an integral part of psychological research. Because psychology is a popular field and large numbers of students from major fields other than psychology take introductory psychology, it is the most representative sample of any psychology course. And a rationale for the students is that experiencing a psychology experiment helps students understand other psychological research. Other social sciences have typically not followed that model, both because they believe that they can provide different experiences for their students and because they have been less likely to conduct the types of research that require human subjects.

Based either on your experiences or on your ideas of what it might be like to participate in a psychology experiment, evaluate the research participant experience from the perspective of the participant. Discuss the experiences within your group, and generate at least five arguments for their value, and five focused on their limitations.

The ethical principle of respect for persons also has important implications for the practice of **deception** in social science research. Deception raises two major ethical concerns. The first is the broader moral question about whether it can be ethically permissible to do something – that is, lie – for the sake of science when it is not acceptable to do so in the course of daily life. The second concern is narrower in scope and involves the fact that participants cannot provide true informed consent to participate in a research study if they are being deceived about important aspects of the procedure. Deception may be the most problematic ethical issue in social science research, and considerable attention has been devoted to untangling the thorny issues involved. However, because it arises primarily in experimental research, we postpone our discussion of these issues to a section later in the chapter devoted specifically to ethical issues in experimental research and move instead to the second broad ethical principle delineated in the Belmont Report, that of beneficence.

Beneficence

The word **beneficence** means being kind or charitable. In a research context, the ethical principle of beneficence means that researchers should maximize the benefits to participants and minimize potential harms. The principle of beneficence has greater ramifications for medical research than for social science research, as the latter is less likely to involve the potential for physical harm to participants. That does not mean, however, that social scientists can ignore the principle of beneficence; as described earlier, participants in social science research may be greatly distressed by the research procedures. Recall that the primary ethical objection to the Milgram studies of obedience to authority was not the considerable deception involved but rather the severe stress and anxiety experienced by participants.

Most readers are familiar with the Hippocratic oath taken by physicians since ancient times: "First, do no harm." This edict embodies the spirit of the beneficence principle. Our quest for knowledge should not come at the price of harm to participants. However, the edict of "do no harm" is easier to follow in a routine clinical practice, in which treatment validity and dangers have been long well-established, than it is in the context of research, which by definition involves procedures and treatments whose benefits and risks are not yet fully understood. The dilemma for researchers is that they may have a promising treatment, but they have no way of knowing for sure that it is effective nor can they guarantee that no harmful unanticipated side effects will occur. They may think there will be few or no adverse effects, but until it is actually tried out on humans, there is no way to know for sure. Animal models and computer simulations can help in gauging the risks and harm likely to occur from a given treatment, but they cannot substitute completely for human trials.

Most experimental treatments and research procedures pose some degree of risk or harm; however, the researchers obviously also believe the research holds the potential to help, if not the research participant directly, large numbers of people in the future. The key to resolving this ethical dilemma – and indeed, all ethical dilemmas in research – is a careful weighing of the risks versus the benefits of the research. If the risk of harm is low, then there is little ethical concern in conducting the study.

However, a treatment or procedure may involve substantial discomfort or risk of serious side effects and still be considered ethical, for example, if the potential benefits of the treatment are large (e.g., alleviating a serious disorder suffered by the patient) and both the researchers and the participant decide that the benefits outweigh the risks. Thus, the ethical task faced by researchers and IRBs is a **risk-benefit analysis**: the careful determination of the magnitude of the potential harm to participants and whether that risk is outweighed by the potential benefits.

Many recent ethical controversies in science have involved research in which the calculation of risks and benefits went awry. For example, gene therapy received a lot of early enthusiasm as a technique holding great promise as a cure for many serious diseases. In 1999, however, an 18-year-old man named Jesse Gelsinger died suddenly after receiving experimental gene therapy. This death was clearly tragic and unexpected and, as a result, IRBs all over the country halted gene therapy clinical trials until researchers could develop a better understanding of what went wrong in this trial and the likelihood of it happening again. (A moving description of the Gelsinger case, written by Jesse's father, is available on the Internet using the address listed at the end of the chapter.)

In other instances, the risks and harm are clearer before the research begins. A good example would be the intense controversy over the use of embryonic stem cells in biological research. Embryonic stem cells are undifferentiated cells that can be cultivated to grow into different types of human tissues (unlike differentiated human cells, which can be used for one function only; e.g., skin cells can only divide into other skin cells). Biomedical researchers believe that embryonic stem cells can be used to grow replacement tissues or organs, as well as for treatments for Alzheimer's disease, cancer, or spinal cord injuries.

The use of embryonic stem cells in research has raised ethical concerns because in most instances the process of extracting the cells destroys the human embryo. Indeed, many people, including archbishops from the Roman Catholic Church, have argued that embryos should be treated as human beings and that the use of cells from embryos can never be ethically justified. Most researchers using stem cells, however, have obtained them from aborted fetuses or leftover frozen embryos from in vitro fertilization procedures. They argue that embryos have only the potential to develop into human beings and that the stem cells used in research would only be derived from embryos that were aborted or never implanted and therefore do not have that potential.

Fortunately, in most social science research, the ethical ramifications of the beneficence principle are rarely this thorny. However, this does not mean social scientists can ignore the risk-benefit calculations, as one can argue that the benefits of social science research are also lower. The knowledge obtained from a social science study rarely has any direct benefit for the participants involved; at best we can usually only argue that the benefit to society in general is intangible and delayed. Yes, we find out more about prejudice, or overconsumption of resources, or any other social problem, and this knowledge could lead to improvements in these problems someday. But social scientists are often hard-pressed to point to actual concrete results of their research, particularly those that would benefit the participants in the research. The ethical question thus becomes whether we have the right to subject our participants to the inconvenience, potential discomfort, and time investment of participating in our research when we can promise them no tangible benefit.

Ethical considerations also demand that researchers monitor the well-being of their participants continuously throughout the experiment and halt the experiment when circumstances demand it. For example, a large-scale study examining the efficacy of a daily aspirin in preventing heart attacks was ended as soon as it became clear that the aspirin was effective. The researchers concluded that it would be unethical to continue administering the placebo to the control group. Studies might also be halted if ill consequences occur to some participants, as was the case in a clinical trial of a blood pressure-reducing medication. Several unexplained deaths occurred in the experimental group, and although the deaths did not appear to be related to the experimental drug, the researchers concluded that they had no choice but to discontinue the experiment.

In social science research, negative consequences are typically not as severe, but researchers nonetheless are obligated to track their data collection efforts and ensure that participants do not experience unanticipated negative reactions or distress. Part of the federal regulations of the IRB process, in fact, requires researchers to report each and every "**adverse event**" that occurs during the course of a study.

In sum, the principle of beneficence is translated practically into the assessment of the risks and benefits involved in participating in the research. Only when the benefits outweigh the risks can the proposed study be deemed ethical. The investigator's responsibility is to minimize the risks to participants, and the IRB's responsibility is to make informed judgments about whether the risks are appropriate in light of the presumed benefits.

Justice

The **justice principle** is relevant to the investigator's choice of participants. Researchers should seek representative samples and avoid choosing certain groups of participants (e.g., the economically disadvantaged, the very sick, or the institutionalized) simply because they are more accessible. In short, the Belmont Report cautioned against adding the "burdens" of participating in research to members of populations already burdened. In particular, it is not fair to utilize a disadvantaged population as research participants for interventions that primarily would benefit more advantaged populations. This concern has been raised about AIDS research in Africa. Africa (especially sub-Saharan Africa) has the highest incidence of AIDS cases of any region, making it an attractive locale for obtaining research participants, but many of the drug treatments under investigation are extremely expensive and would be out of reach for most of the local population. Is it fair to try out a new drug – one that might not work and could have harmful side effects – on people who would not have access to it once it was deemed effective? Again, this ethical issue is not easily resolved. Proponents of the research argue that the clinical trials might be the only way such impoverished populations can gain access to the latest and best medical treatments. Opponents argue that, if so, then researchers are, in effect, coercing individuals into participation, raising yet another set of ethical concerns.

Another example from educational research is the attention given to schools that have patterns of low student achievement. As we are writing this book, a major focus of research is on the achievement gap, the disparity between achievement of White students and students of color, and between lower- and higher-income students. As a result, schools that had previously been ignored are being flooded with requests to conduct research. We have seen instances in which an investigator asks to work with a school's fifth-graders in math, only to be told that another researcher (in one instance from the same university) was already working with the fifth-graders in math, using a very different approach from that proposed. Although the schools often appreciate the help and many are reluctant to turn down research assistance, the disconnected nature of the help and the idiosyncratic nature of the different investigations often result in a failure to produce a coherent approach that can be integrated with the approach already in place at the school. We have seen researchers propose to do research in a school using an intervention they have developed who pick the school because they know someone there or because it is convenient, but who have no idea about what currently is being done or even whether what they want to do is consistent with it. In such instances, even with a well-designed intervention, the research can be counterproductive for students. An important point is that targeting students with needs is no guarantee that the research fulfills a justice criterion, for if the research, however well intentioned, is not compatible with what and how students are currently learning, it is not likely to benefit them.

The justice principle also has implications for how individuals within a given study are treated. The main concern is the ethicality of control groups. Is it fair to give a potentially helpful treatment or intervention to one group of participants but withhold it from another? As we discuss in detail in Chapter 10, the only way to conclude with certainty that a given treatment or manipulation is effective involves, in part, comparing a group that receives it to one that does not. In much research, the control group does not "miss out" on anything significant. But in medical research, in which the treatment might be a cure to a deadly disease, or in social policy research, where the treatment may be an educational intervention that could lead to a lifetime of accomplishment, participants in the control group could miss out, literally, on their lives.

This ethical dilemma is poignantly highlighted in the classic book, *Arrowsmith*, by Sinclair Lewis (1925). Arrowsmith is a young scientist who has invented what he hopes will be a cure for a deadly tropical disease. He is in the process of conducting a randomized trial to assess the drug's effectiveness when an epidemic of the disease strikes. The local citizens plead with Arrowsmith to make his drug available to all. He must deal with the conflict between the emotional impulse to do everything he can to help – people are dying all around him, after all – and the more scientific need to adhere to the randomized trial that will enable him to decide whether the medicine even works in the first place. We will not spoil the book for readers by revealing what he ultimately decides, though we will pique readers' interest further by saying that Arrowsmith's dilemma becomes agonizingly acute when his own wife contracts the disease.

One might argue that researchers should simply ask for volunteers to be placed in the control group, thus obviating the ethical problem of withholding treatment from individuals who believe they are receiving it. However, this is not a satisfactory solution. People who volunteer to be in a control group likely differ in many ways from those who volunteer only for the treatment group. Certainly, individuals who know they are not receiving the treatment will have expectations and perceptions that differ from those of participants who know they are receiving it. These differences would make it impossible to know whether outcome differences between the two groups resulted from differences in the treatment or something else.

The potentially different expectations of control and treatment group members are controlled through the use of **placebos**, which make it impossible for participants to know whether they are getting the treatment or not. In medical experiments, placebos are treatments of the same size and format as the experimental treatment (e.g., pills of similar size, color, and even sometimes yielding similar side effects) but which typically are medically inert. In clinical psychology research, the control group might receive what is called an "attention placebo" therapy, in which clients meet regularly with a therapist for the same amount of time they would in the experimental therapy, but standard therapeutic techniques are not incorporated. In experimental psychology, the control group generally receives materials that are matched in terms of length, intensity, format, etc., except for the critical dimension(s) being manipulated.

The ethical problem is that, to be effective, participants cannot realize they are in the control group even though in some cases they volunteer for the experiment because they hope to receive the experimental treatment. This problem is especially acute in clinical trials of experimental treatments for fatal diseases; people with advanced cancer or HIV/AIDS, for example, are often desperate to be accepted into a clinical trial that might offer some hope, however slim, of curing their disease.

Fortunately, there is a solution to this ethical dilemma. The first step is to make full disclosure to participants during the consent process. Participants must be told that it is necessary both to include control groups in the experiment and to prevent participants and researchers from knowing which experimental condition participants are in. Participants must also be explicitly told what their chances are of being assigned to the control condition. Finally, participants can be assured that if the researchers find at the conclusion of the experiment that the intervention is effective, the researchers will offer the intervention to all control participants at no expense. (Of course, researchers must fulfill that promise.) If participants come into the experiment ahead of time knowing that they might not receive the actual treatment until the conclusion of the study and are still willing to participate, ethical concerns of justice are allayed.

Focus on Ethical Issues in Experimental Research: Deception

Earlier, we noted that deception is perhaps the trickiest ethical issue facing social scientists. Deception tends to be especially prevalent in experimental research, as most experimental manipulations involve some element of deception. There are two major forms of deception in experimental research: deception by omission and active deception. In **deception by omission**, participants are not told any outright untruths; rather, detail is left out about the research purpose or procedures. For example, a study examining whether participants would cheat on a test if given the opportunity might be described to participants as a "study of mental and behavioral processes." Strictly speaking, this is not actively deceptive (cheating is a behavioral process), but it is misleading in that participants are not told that cheating is the behavior of primary interest in the study.

When deception is defined this way, most research contains an element of deception, as few researchers divulge the precise behaviors or hypotheses being studied – for the obvious reason of avoiding demand characteristics or expectancy effects (Chapter 5). In most cases, instances of deception by omission are not cause for ethical alarm, as participants are still given adequate information about the nature of the experiment and what they will experience so that they can give meaningful informed consent. Deception by omission becomes an ethical problem primarily when the detail omitted is something that might have affected people's willingness to participate in the study had they known the true purpose of the study. For example, it is possible that some people would not have volunteered for the cheating study described above had they known that it was about cheating; these participants might become offended and distressed once debriefed about the real purpose of the study. One implication is that deception is primarily problematic when it leads participants to behave in ways that they would regret. For example, Sieber (1992) notes that, although participants were deceived, the Isen and Levin (1972) study examining the effects of cookies on helping behavior does not pose an ethical problem, because the behavior elicited by the manipulation was socially desirable. In dealing with deception, then, the primary challenge for IRBs is to review the consent form and the experimenter's cover story and then judge whether participants might react too negatively to the deception involved in the study.

Active deception is a more serious ethical problem. In these cases, participants are actively misled about aspects of the experiment. Milgram's (1974) studies of obedience are a famous example of this type of deception, as participants were lied to about the identity of the confederate, the purpose of the study, and the supposed shocks they were administering to the confederate. Although active deception of any kind is problematic, the form that is most problematic involves studies that deliver **false feedback** to participants; that is, people are given information about themselves that has no basis in fact but rather was assigned randomly. As described earlier, it is not uncommon in social science research for experimenters to manipulate mood or self-esteem of participants by giving them either positive or negative feedback about their alleged performance on ability or personality tests. Also as noted earlier, this kind of deception creates two problems: potential anger felt by participants when they realize they've been lied to and the possibility of **perseverance effects**, that is, that participants will continue to believe the false feedback even after having been told about the deception. Research shows that such perseverance effects do occur, but they can be ameliorated by a "process debriefing" that addresses not only the fact of the deception but also the existence of perseverance effects themselves (Ross, Lepper, & Hubbard, 1975). Once participants are told that there is this tendency for people to cling to the originally deceptive feedback, they are much less likely to do so.

Another particularly problematic form of deception in experimental research is called **double deception** or **second-order deception** and refers to the once-standard practice of experimenters telling participants that "the experiment is over" but then going on to collect additional data. A famous example of such double deception is the classic Festinger and Carlsmith (1959) study of cognitive dissonance, in which the entire dissonance manipulation and measurement of the dependent variables did not take place until after the participants were told the experiment was over. The problem is that when participants are told a second time that the experiment is now "really" over, they may be angry or unconvinced. Such deception can also seriously undermine the individual's general trust in science. Kelman (1968) argues, and most IRBs concur, that double deception is ethically unacceptable and that no further data collection should take place after telling participants the study has been concluded.

Using Deception in an Ethical Manner

Is deception in social science research necessary? Some ethicists have argued that it is not, that valid data can be obtained through deception-free procedures. Kelman (1968) has argued that deception is wrong on moral grounds and almost never warranted on practical grounds; he advocated instead for relying on role-playing in collecting data. For example, if we wanted to see how threats to self-esteem affect later behavior, rather than administering false feedback, we could ask participants to go through the experimental procedures while pretending they have received negative personal feedback. Kelman offers data to suggest that role-playing participants provide results that are comparable to those yielded by participants who are deceived in the traditional manner. The obvious shortcoming of this recommendation is that one can never be sure that role-playing will yield realistic data, especially when the focus of study is sensitive or socially undesirable behavior. For example, it seems highly unlikely that the same high percentage of participants asked to role-play Milgram's procedure would shock to the limit as was actually observed. Because of this fear, role-playing has not been considered a viable alternative to deception.

What, then, can researchers do to ameliorate the ethical problems raised by deception yet still obtain high-quality data? There are several creative approaches to the problem, most involving participants giving **consent to conceal** (Sieber, 1992). First, researchers can obtain participants' permission to be deceived. In this approach, participants are told during the consent process that there may be misleading aspects of the research procedure that will not be revealed until the end of the study. Alerting participants to the possibility of deception is certainly less deceptive and may prevent them from feeling badly about having been "duped." However, tipping off participants may cause them to behave atypically as they try to determine the nature of the deception during the experiment. An alternative approach is to ask participants to waive the right to be fully informed; that is, they are told that the researchers are unable to give full detail about the study beforehand but that they will be debriefed following the experiment. Unlike the former approach, this approach does not explicitly warn participants that they will be deceived, which may prevent participants from becoming suspicious, but may still cause them to become upset upon learning of the deception.

An additional method of dealing with deception involves the thorough **debriefing** of participants about all aspects of the deception and then giving them the opportunity to withdraw their data from the study (with no penalty or loss of benefits). The ethical reasoning behind this approach is clear: If deception, as we have argued, subverts the informed consent process, then participants have the right to say, after debriefing, that they would not have participated in the study had they known the full details. It is impossible to turn back time and erase the fact that participants completed the study, but a compromise is for participants to refuse to let their data be used. An increasing number of IRBs require that researchers who use deception obtain during the debriefing portion of the research a signed consent form from participants to use their data; the consent form describes the nature of the deception, explains why it was necessary, and explicitly offers participants the option of withdrawing their data.

Focus on Ethical Issues in Quasi-Experimental Research: Confidentiality and Anonymity

As we discuss in Chapter 11, nonrandomized, or quasi-experimental, studies are generally done when random assignment is impossible but researchers would like to draw causal conclusions. Much quasi-experimental research takes place in the field and involves survey administration, program evaluation, and the like. This type of research often involves asking participants to provide information that they would not want to share with others. In a workplace setting, for example, people who are asked to give their impressions of certain managerial practices may feel very strongly that they do not wish their individual responses to be divulged. Thus, maintaining confidentiality and anonymity of the data is especially important.

The key to addressing issues of confidentiality and anonymity is to be aware of the distinction between them and to be sure not to promise anonymity to participants unless anonymity can be assured. **Anonymity** means that absolutely no identifying characteristics are recorded with the data so that it would be impossible for researchers to determine who contributed a given piece of data. **Confidentiality** means that although researchers can determine whose data are whose, within certain legal limits (described later), researchers promise never to share that information.

In many situations, anonymity of data cannot be guaranteed. Often, identifiers are placed on the surveys so that individuals can be contacted later to remind them to complete the survey, for follow-up data collection purposes, or so that their responses can be related to data about participants that come from other sources, or so participants could be measured again in the future and those responses linked to the earlier responses of each individual. Furthermore, even if the researchers originally intended for survey responses to be anonymous, responses to a combination of questions could identify participants (or at least some of them), especially if the sample were small. If, for example, participants are asked to indicate their ethnicity, gender, and the department in which they work, it may be possible to identify some participants because very few may have a particular combination of characteristics. Anonymity can also be unintentionally undermined if raw data (which lack identifiers) are stored with the signed consent forms (which contain participants' names). The simple solution, of course, is to store consent forms separately – under lock and key – from the raw data.

Confidentiality should always be assured to the fullest extent possible, which means that no one besides members of the research team should have any access to the raw data. However, in a few circumstances, researchers are legally obligated to violate confidentiality. Participants who admit to planning suicide or murder or who reveal evidence of child abuse would have to be reported, as most states have "**duty to warn**" laws that require researchers to report them to appropriate authorities. Such circumstances are not as rare as one would think; for example, the Beck Depression Inventory (one of the most commonly used measures of depression) has an item that asks specifically about whether the respondent is considering suicide. Researchers would be legally obligated to refer to authorities all participants who indicate that they are considering committing suicide, even if confidentiality had been promised in the consent form. The solution to this ethical dilemma is to design one's study so that participants remain anonymous; if there is no possible way of identifying participants, there is no longer any obligation to report. If anonymity is not possible, then participants should be warned of the limits to confidentiality in the consent form.

This issue also arises when research participants are children and adolescents, especially when the research involves sensitive or illegal behaviors like sexual behavior or substance use. Obviously, researchers want participants to feel that their responses would be kept private, for otherwise participants may not respond honestly. Nevertheless, if parents were to insist on viewing their child's questionnaire, researchers would be legally and ethically forced to comply unless parents had agreed when consenting to their child's participation that they would not have access to their child's data. Researchers might also design the study so that participants' responses were truly anonymous; then parents could be told honestly that there would be no way to retrieve their child's individual responses.

Focus on Ethical Issues in Non-Experimental Research: Participant Observation

The method of participant observation has enjoyed a resurgence of popularity in social science research, as qualitative methods have become increasingly popular. Qualitative methods generally provide an alternative to the deception problem described earlier, for their epistemological roots lead them to engage participants as partners in the research process and to avoid any deception. Participant observation, described in Chapter 13, however, can be an exception. In participant observation, the researcher joins a naturally occurring social group and observes its proceedings, keeping detailed field notes about what happens. In some instances group members are not aware that the researcher is observing them for scientific purposes, sometimes not even at the conclusion of data collection. Later, a description of the group may be published, with identifying features deleted or changed.

Ethical concerns with surreptitious participant observation studies are rather obvious: A great deal of deception occurs if researchers do not inform participants that research is being conducted or identify themselves as researchers. Further, this type of deception means that informed consent is unlikely to be obtained. Invasion of privacy is another, related ethical concern. Because participants are often unaware of the study, they might say and do things that they would not normally or intentionally disclose to a researcher. (Note that researchers are bound by ethical constraints that other professionals are not bound by. Reporters often infiltrate groups to gather material for articles or broadcasts without divulging what they are doing.)

Confidentiality and anonymity are also of concern in participant observation. Most researchers follow basic ethical guidelines of keeping identifying information strictly confidential and locked in a secure location, as well as changing identifiers in publications. But the possibility remains that people (particularly those familiar with the group) could determine who is being discussed, especially if the group were of a highly specialized nature. For example, in the mid-1950s, there were not many cults predicting the destruction of the world and subsequent salvation by alien beings, so readers of Festinger, Riecken, and Schachter's (1956) classic participant observation work, *When Prophecy Fails*, readily could have determined the identity of the individuals involved.

How might these ethical concerns be resolved? Some researchers avoid the deception problem by informing group members ahead of time about the study and requesting their permission to be observed. This solution clearly satisfies most ethical objections (although confidentiality and identifiability concerns still remain), but it does so at the cost of introducing substantial reactivity into the data collection. How reasonable is it to think that people would behave normally if a researcher were present and taking notes or tape-recording the proceedings? However, as advocates of this solution and years of "reality TV" can attest, people eventually do become largely accustomed to the presence of observers and video cameras, and might very well start to behave naturally even when they know they are being studied.

Is Not Doing a Study Ethical?

The major theme underlying our discussion of research ethics is that determining whether and how a given study should be done ultimately rests on a consideration of the costs and benefits of doing the research. Rosenthal and Rosnow (1984; Rosenthal, 1994) suggest, however, that a thorough ethical review also requires a consideration of the costs and benefits associated with *not* doing the study. In some cases, the long-term social costs of not discovering a cure for a disease or an intervention for an acute social problem, such as poverty or prejudice, might be so high that one could argue that researchers have an ethical obligation to undertake the research, even if the risks and costs associated with such research are high.

Taking such a perspective can help to resolve some of the ethical controversies currently raging in the biomedical sciences, such as the debate over using embryonic stem cells mentioned earlier. The perennial debate over the use of animals in research provides another good opportunity to consider the ethics of not performing research. Some would ban completely the use of animals in biomedical or behavioral research. Their arguments are often emotionally compelling: What right do we have to hurt or kill an innocent puppy? Although a puppy may be the face of opponents of animal research, do people feel the same about mice or pigs? Would saving or improving human lives be worth experimenting using animals to help solve genetic diseases in children or dementia in older adults? Although arguments could focus on the merits of research on different animals, we believe that a primary question should focus not only on the relative costs and benefits of doing the research, but also the costs of not doing the research. Suppose, for example, a treatment is under investigation for cerebral palsy, a disorder that affects about three of every thousand babies born. If this hypothetical treatment were effective, it could restore mental and physical capabilities to children who might otherwise be doomed to a lifetime of mental retardation and wheelchairs. The prospect of a cure that would help thousands of children this year, and the same number the next year, and for each year after that unto perpetuity, from a cost/benefit perspective is likely worth the lives of a hundred laboratory animals, even puppies.

Some bioethicists argue that not only is such research ethical, but also that it would be unethical to refuse to do the study. Indeed, the potential risks of any study can be entirely eliminated simply by not doing the study; however, in making that decision, we should consider not only the risks that have been avoided but also the benefits that would be forgone. In some cases, the potential benefits that would not be fulfilled if the research were not done are tremendous indeed. As Kaplan (1988) once eloquently asked, "Who speaks for the sick, for those in pain, and for the future?"

We are not suggesting that there are no ethical problems in using animals in research and don't expect all readers to agree with our perspective. As researchers we have an obligation to protect all living organisms from unnecessary pain and to use animals only when no feasible alternative exists. Computer simulations are sometimes possible, but they are not always adequate; sooner or later many treatments must be tried on living organisms. Assuming the proposed benefits of the research are great enough, research on animals seems to us ethically justified, even if it means their ultimate death. As Dr. Benjamin Trump of the University of Maryland Medical School once said in an interview, later quoted widely by Ann Landers, "We in the medical profession find it painful to accept a dead child over a dead mouse."

The Ethical Review Process

The ethical review process begins in the planning stages of a study. Researchers should consider ethical issues when planning the design of a study and choosing the procedures and measures to be administered. More formally, the researcher must obtain IRB approval prior to the collection of any data. It is important to note that IRB processes have been developed for research designed and controlled by the researchers, where the entire project can be planned in advance. In contrast, for engaged and many types of qualitative research discussed later in the book, where the work is a partnership with the participants and other community partners and is developed jointly with them, researchers cannot design the entire project in advance, which makes the IRB process especially difficult. Fortunately, many IRBs are developing better ways to accommodate such research. Nevertheless, it is likely to involve many iterations between the researcher and the IRB as approaches are refined and changed, and the IRB is informed about the "changes." Fortunately, such approaches rarely involve any kind of deception, for participants who are partners in designing the research are well aware of what it is attempting to accomplish.

The IRB process is generally lengthy. The first step is to prepare the IRB proposal, which involves completing forms with basic information about the researcher and all other research personnel who will be involved in data collection, indicating the number and type of participants to be enrolled in the study, and providing a full description of the proposed research project. The project description includes several critical sections:

1. A background and introduction section that summarizes relevant past empirical and theoretical work, thereby providing a basis for the research, and indicates why the research is important. This section provides a context for IRB members, most of whom are not from the researcher's discipline.

2. A section listing the specific objectives of the proposed research, which helps IRB members to gauge the adequacy of the proposed methods.

3. A description of the study population, including number, age range, gender, and ethnic/racial background. Researchers must also specify whether any vulnerable populations will be included. Special IRB regulations govern the protection of vulnerable populations, including children, pregnant women, prisoners, and people who have mental or physical disabilities.

4. A description of how participants will be recruited. IRBs play close attention to recruitment, as they want to ensure that no coercion is involved. If the researcher is planning to recruit via advertisements or flyers, the IRB will want to see a copy of the recruitment ad prior to approving the study. If the researcher is gaining access to participants through some other channel (e.g., school system, medical clinic), the IRB will need to be assured that the researcher has the legal right to view names and contact information for potential participants. In many school systems, for example, it is illegal for a principal to provide a list of names and addresses of students to researchers. Further, if one is doing research in a preK-12 school district, one's research must usually go through the school district's IRB and an approval form obtained before the university's IRB will approve the research (sometimes both "wait" for the other). The same can be true in healthcare settings, where clinics or hospitals have IRBs that need to approve the research. Regardless of sequencing, the two IRBs are likely to want to see the other's approval before the research begins.

5. A short section describing the overall study design. The IRB will want to know how many experimental conditions there are, if any, and whether random assignment will occur.

6. A longer section describing the research procedures to be carried out. This section is analogous to the method section in a journal article; it should describe everything that happens to participants. Copies of all research instruments to be administered should be included. In many ways, this section is the most important part of the IRB proposal, for it is difficult to gauge the extent and magnitude of risks without knowing exactly what participants will be doing.

7. A description of all potential risks – physical, psychological, social, legal, and other. This section provides a more explicit description of the risks that are inherent in the procedures described in the preceding section.

8. The researchers must also describe the precautions they will take to protect against or minimize potential risks. When procedures are particularly stressful,

a common safeguard is for researchers to have available counselors to whom they can refer participants. An explicit description of the debriefing procedure, including a script, may also need to be provided depending on the seriousness of the deception.

9. The next step is to provide an explicit risk-benefit analysis, explaining why the risks to participants are reasonable in relation to the anticipated benefits. We would describe what we believe are the risks resulting from any deception (e.g., whether they are minor or not), whether such procedures have been used without problems in previous research, and so forth. In the case of a relatively minor deception, for example, we might point out that psychological research indicates that not only are participants generally not angered by deception in an experiment, but also that they find deception experiments on the whole more interesting and enjoyable to participate in than other types of studies (Christensen, 1988; Epley & Huff, 1998; Smith & Richardson, 1983).

10. A summary of relevant incentives and research-related costs. IRBs want to know what kinds of incentives will be offered so that the possibility of coercion can be assessed. The IRB also wants to make sure that all incentives and research-related costs (including such things as transportation to the study, time required to participate, etc.) are clearly spelled out in the consent form.

11. A listing of any available alternatives to the study. This section is relevant primarily in health fields, in which it is important to provide potential participants with the knowledge of any comparable treatments that might exist besides participating in the study. In research that involves undergraduates, we would describe the alternative method of earning research credit (e.g., the student writing a summary of a research article).

12. A description of how and where research materials will be stored and a discussion of confidentiality. The IRB wants to know what kinds of data are being obtained from participants, where the data will be stored (e.g., under lock and key, in password-protected electronic files, on secure websites), and how participants' confidentiality will be preserved.

13. A copy of the informed consent form that will be used. These forms should be written in everyday, easy-to-understand language. Some studies require multiple consent forms; for example, a longitudinal study with measurements widely separated in time may require a separate consent form for each phase of the study. Studies that address disparate populations might need a different consent form for each class of participant. For example, a qualitative study examining communication between healthcare providers and Latino patients probably would need two sets of consent forms, one for the healthcare providers and one for the patients (not to mention a Spanish translation for the patient version). When participants are minors, obtaining consent is more complicated. Legally, the consent form must be directed to and signed by parent(s); however, the children themselves should also be consulted and fully informed as to the nature of the research, and their wishes regarding participation should be honored whenever possible. Some IRBs require written assent from participants who are considered minors in the state where the research is conducted. Table 3.1 shows an example of a consent form that could be used in a laboratory study that

Table 3.1 Sample Consent Form for a Case Study of Interpersonal Expectancy Effects

Consent to Participate in a Research Study
Personality and Social Interactions

Why am I being invited to take part in this research?

You are being invited to take part in a research study about the personality factors that are related to how people interact with other people. You are being invited to participate in this research study because you are enrolled in Psychology 101. If you take part in this study, you will be 1 of about 240 undergraduates to do so.

Who is doing the study?

The person in charge of this study is Dr. Jane Doe of the Psychology Department at the University of Social Science. There may be other people on the research team assisting at different times during the study.

What is the purpose of the study?

By doing this study, we hope to learn more about the relations between personality and people's social interactions.

Where is the study going to take place and how long will it last?

The research procedures will be conducted in Research Hall at the University of Social Science. The session should last no longer than 50 minutes.

What will I be asked to do?

First, we will ask you to complete a number of questionnaires. These questionnaires are designed to measure aspects of your personality, such as extraversion, friendliness, dominance, and anxiety. We will then ask you to work on a problem-solving task with another undergraduate. This interaction will be videotaped. Following the interaction, we will separate you and your partner and ask you to complete some questionnaires asking for your impression of the interaction and your partner.

What are the possible risks and discomforts?

To the best of our knowledge, the things you will be doing have no more risk of harm than you would experience in everyday life. There is a slight possibility that you may feel self-conscious or uncomfortable about being videotaped. You can discontinue being in the study at any time, and you can have the videotape erased at any time.

Do I have to take part in this study?

If you decide to take part in the study, it should be because you really want to volunteer and participate. You will not lose any benefits or rights you would normally have if you choose not to volunteer. You can stop at any time during the study, and you will still keep the benefits and rights you had before volunteering.

What will it cost me to participate?

There are no costs associated with taking part in this study.

Will I receive any payment or rewards for taking part in the study?

You will receive one hour of experimental credit toward your Psychology 101 grade for participating in this study.

Who will see the information I give?

Your information will be combined with information from other students taking part in the study. When we write up the study to share it with other researchers, we will write about this combined information. You will not be identified in these written materials. We will make every effort to prevent anyone who is not on the research team from knowing that you gave us information or what that information is. For example, your name will be kept separate from the information you give us, and these two things will be stored in different places under lock and key. Only members of our research team will see the videotape we made of your interaction.

(Continued)

Table 3.1   *(Continued)*

Consent to Participate in a Research Study
Personality and Social Interactions

Can my part in the study end early?

If you decide to take part in the study, you still have the right to decide at any time that you no longer want to continue. You will not be treated differently if you stop taking part in the study.

What if I have questions?

Before you decide whether to accept this invitation to take part in the study, please ask any questions that might come to mind. You can contact the investigator at 000-555-1234 if you have any questions following your participation. If you have any questions about your rights as a research volunteer, contact the staff in the Office of Research Integrity at the University of Social Science at 000-555-5678. You may keep a copy of this consent form.

What else do I need to know?

You will be told if any new information is learned that may influence your willingness to continue participating in this study.

_____   _____

Signature of person agreeing to participate in study   Date

_____

Printed name of person

_____

Name of person providing information to participant

involves minor deception. Note the question-and-answer format and straightforward language contained in the form. Note also that the consent form emphasizes that participants can discontinue the study at any time. But also note that the consent form is an example of deception by omission; the experimental manipulation is not mentioned nor is the specific focus of the study identified.

Once completed, the proposal is sent to the IRB for review. Although the makeup of IRBs varies widely across institutions, federal regulations require that IRBs contain at least five members (most contain far more than that), representing both genders, varied professions, and scientists as well as nonscientists. At least one member of the IRB must be a layperson who is not otherwise affiliated with the institution. Upon receiving the proposal, an IRB staff person determines whether the protocol needs to undergo an expedited or full review. An **expedited review** (meaning that it can be done by only one IRB member and thus can be handled more quickly than a full review) is restricted to those studies that involve no more than minimal risk and otherwise fall into one of several specified categories, such as survey research on nonsensitive topics. **Minimal risk** is defined in federal regulations as the "probability and magnitude of harm or discomfort anticipated in the research are not greater in and of themselves from those ordinarily encountered in daily life or during the performance of routine physical or psychological examination or tests."

In a **full review**, all members of the IRB receive the protocol and read it carefully before meeting to discuss it and the other studies on the agenda. IRB members first raise among themselves the concerns they had upon reading the proposal. The researchers may also be invited in to answer specific questions from the IRB members. These questions can address any and all aspects of the research procedures, down to details as minute as the wording of a given item on a questionnaire. An IRB member might ask, for example, whether deception is necessary. Research that involves videotaping of participants may also warrant further discussion, for example, about how confidentiality of the tapes would be ensured. Note that the American Psychological Association no longer considers covert videotaping (i.e., without the participant's knowledge) to be ethical. (Different disciplines are governed by different sets of ethical principles. IRBs, however, are obligated only to follow and enforce federal regulations. Federal regulations are usually in close agreement with disciplinary guidelines, but there can be discrepancies. For example, nothing in the federal regulations prohibits covert videotaping.) Following the discussion, IRB members vote on the protocol, almost always voting to withhold approval until certain changes are made. (Approving a protocol with no changes rarely happens.) Imagine that the IRB asked researchers to provide a "**consent to use data**" form that participants would be asked to sign during the debriefing process for a study that involved deception. Table 3.2 shows what such a form might look like. After the researchers have made the necessary changes and resubmitted the revised protocol, IRB approval is granted, and the IRB provides a version of the consent form that bears an official IRB approval stamp. Only such stamped consent forms can be used in collecting data. IRB approval can be granted for only one year at a time, and approval applies only to the protocol as described in the most recent revision. Any subsequent changes, whether minor or not, that the researchers wish to make to the research procedures must be submitted to the IRB for approval before implementing them. The IRB must always have full documentation of the entire research procedures at all times. At the end of the year, researchers must submit a continuation review form, in which they describe how many participants have been enrolled in the study, where the data and consent forms are being stored, and whether any adverse reactions have occurred during data collection. (Such adverse reactions must also be reported immediately after their occurrence.)

We have gone to such detail for two purposes. The first is to clarify some of the important terms we have discussed, such as informed consent and deception. The second purpose is to convey how seriously researchers and institutions take the issue of protection of human participants. Literally thousands of hours are devoted every year to the oversight of research involving human participants. The time and paperwork demands seem grueling at times, but the ultimate payoff – the protection of human participants – is worth the cost.

Closing Thoughts

This chapter began with the question, "What is right to do to people in the name of science?" Our discussion of ethical principles in the social sciences has hopefully clarified the important issues that must be taken into account when answering that

Table 3.2   Consent to Use Data Form for Case Study of Interpersonal Expectancy Effects

Personality and Social Interactions
Consent to Use Data

I understand that I was not originally told of some aspects of the experimental procedure. Specifically, I was led to believe that my interaction partner had scored either very high or very low on a test of problem-solving ability. I have been told that this information was randomly determined and that the experimenter actually has no knowledge of my partner's problem-solving ability. I understand that the purpose of this deception was to see how my expectations regarding my partner's ability affected our subsequent interaction. The purpose of this deception has been thoroughly explained to me, and I understand that it was necessary for the validity of the experiment.

However, because I was misled about this aspect of the experiment, I understand that I now have the right to have my data withheld from the experiment if I so wish. If I decide to withhold my data, I understand that my questionnaires will be destroyed immediately and the videotape of my interaction will be immediately erased. I understand that I will still receive full credit for my participation and that no penalties will be applied if I decide to withhold my data.

_____ I hereby give permission for the experimenters to use my data in their study.

_____ I do not give permission for the experimenters to use my data in their study; instead, I wish for my data and videotape to be destroyed immediately.

I have read and understood the above.

_____   _____

Participant's signature   Date

_____

Experimenter's signature

question. Although specific guidelines are hard to outline without knowing the precise procedures involved in a study, in general, participants' rights are protected as long as researchers adhere to the three principles of respect, beneficence, and justice, and as long as the benefits of the research outweigh the costs. It can be easy or tempting to get so swept up in the excitement of doing research and analyzing data that we almost forget the source of our data: other human beings just like us, human beings who have feelings and can be hurt.

Summary

Protecting human research participants' rights, safety, and dignity is essential. Prior to the 1970s, no regulations governed research with human participants, and studies were sometimes conducted that involved clearly unethical practices. Following the adverse publicity surrounding one such unethical study, the Tuskegee Syphilis Study, the U.S.

government established Institutional Review Boards, whose sole function is to approve the procedures involved in human research studies. The ethical principles underlying the federal regulations were first described in the Belmont Report and consist of respect for persons, beneficence, and justice. Respect for persons means that anybody who participates in a study should be a true volunteer and fully informed about the nature of the research. The principle of beneficence means we should do no harm to our participants; it requires a careful risk-benefit analysis of the proposed research. Justice means that we should not take advantage of overburdened populations in recruiting participants and that participants are fully informed about the odds of being placed in a control group and thus not receiving treatment.

Deception is of particular ethical concern in experimental research. Deception is sometimes necessary, but is ethically problematic because by definition participants are unable to provide full informed consent. One solution is to obtain participants' consent to use their data after a thorough debriefing and disclosure of the deception. In survey research, issues of confidentiality and anonymity are central. Every effort must be made to keep participants' data confidential, and anonymity must not be promised unless it can be ensured. In participant observation research, both deception and confidentiality are of special concern.

Obtaining IRB approval for a study is a time-consuming process that involves a thorough description of the methodology of the proposed study. The IRB members perform a detailed risk-benefit analysis, in which they determine whether the risks involved in the procedures are greater or lesser than the benefits to be gained from doing the study. Finally, one needs to consider not only the risks and costs involved in conducting the study but also the potential social costs if the study is not done.

Go online   Visit the book's companion website for this chapter's test bank and other resources at: www.wiley.com/go/maruyama

---

Key Concepts

Active deception	Deception by omission
Adverse event	Double deception
Anonymity	Duty to warn
Autonomy	Expedited review
Belmont Report	False feedback
Beneficence	Full review
Coercion	Informed consent
Confidentiality	Institutional Review Boards (IRBs)
Consent to conceal	Justice principle
Consent to use data	Minimal risk
Debriefing	Perseverance effects
Deception	Placebo

Respect for persons
Risk-benefit analysis
Second-order deception

Subject pool
Tuskegee Syphilis Study

On the Web

http://www.hhs.gov/ohrp/archive/irb/irb_guidebook.htm The IRB Guidebook
– very detailed and informative, but easy to read – issued by the Office for Human
Research Protections under the U.S. Department of Health and Human Services.

http://www.circare.org/submit/jintent.pdf "Jesse's Intent" (Gelsinger, 2001) is a
moving description of the case of Jesse Gelsinger, the young man who died suddenly
after participating in a gene therapy study, written by his father.

http://www.apa.org/ethics/ The ethics section of the American Psychological
Association website. It contains a draft of the latest version of the Ethical Principles
for Psychologists.

http://www.nlm.nih.gov/archive//20061214/pubs/cbm/hum_exp.html A bibliography compiled by the National Library of Medicine listing books and journal
articles on ethical issues in research involving human participants. The bibliography
covers 1989–1998 and includes 4,650 citations.

http://www.cnn.com/HEALTH/bioethics/archive.index.html A biweekly online
column written by Dr. Jeffrey P. Kahn, entitled "Ethics Matters," sponsored jointly by
the University of Minnesota Center for Bioethics and CNN Interactive.

http://www.nih.gov/sigs/bioethics/outsidenih.html A web bibliography compiled by the National Institutes of Health (NIH) providing links to other bioethics
Internet resources.

Further Reading

Fried, A. L. (2012). Ethics in psychological
research: Guidelines and regulations. In
H. Cooper, P. M. Camic, D. L. Long,
A. T. Panter, D. Rindskopf, & K. Sher
(Eds.), *APA handbook of research methods
in psychology, Vol. 1: Foundations, planning,
measures, and psychometrics* (pp. 55–73).
Washington, DC: American Psychological
Association.

Kimmel, A. J. (1988). *Ethics and values in
applied social research*. Thousand Oaks, CA:
Sage.

Knapp, S. J., Gottlieb, M. C., Handelsman,
M., & VandeCreek, L. D. (Eds.). (2012).
*APA handbook of ethics in psychology, Vol. 2:
Practice, teaching, and research*. Washington,
DC: American Psychological Association.

Mays, V. M. (2012). The legacy of the U.S.
Public Health Service Study of untreated
syphilis in African American men at Tuskegee on the Affordable Care Act and health
care reform fifteen years after President
Clinton's apology. *Ethics and Behavior, 22,*
411–418.

Mertens, D. M. (2012). Ethics in qualitative research in education and the social sciences. In S. D. Lapan, M. T. Quartaroli, & F. J. Riemer (Eds.), *Qualitative research: An introduction to methods and designs* (pp. 19–39). San Francisco, CA: Jossey-Bass.

Mertens, D. M., & Ginsberg, P. E. (Eds.). (2009). *The handbook of social research ethics*. Thousand Oaks, CA: Sage.

U.S. National Commission for the Protection of Human Subjects of Biomedical and Behavioral Research. (1979). *The Belmont Report*. Bethesda, MD: Author. [Reprinted on numerous websites.]

Wassenaar, D. R., & Mamotte, N. (2012). Ethical issues and ethics reviews in social science research. In M. M. Leach, M. J. Stevens, G. Lindsay, A. Ferrero, & Y. Korkut (Eds.), *The Oxford handbook of international psychological ethics* (pp. 268–282). New York, NY: Oxford University Press.

Chapter 4

Roles and Relations among Researchers, Practitioners, and Participants in Engaged Research

Research Methods in Social Relations, Eighth Edition. Geoffrey Maruyama and Carey S. Ryan.
© 2014 John Wiley & Sons, Inc. Published 2014 by John Wiley & Sons, Inc.
Companion Website: www.wiley.com/go/maruyama

In 1948, Lewin argued that training of social scientists should include developing their ability to work with non-academics on important issues: "The training of large numbers of social scientists who can handle scientific problems but are also equipped for the delicate task of building productive, hard-hitting teams with practitioners is a prerequisite for progress in social science" (Lewin, 1948, p. 211). Despite that plea, few social scientists today are formally trained as part of their graduate education to work in and with communities, and the array of important social challenges and problems is as great as ever. We provide in this chapter an introduction to both the logic and the issues that are part of developing partnerships with practitioners and policy makers that can work directly to address important issues.

The chapter focuses in particular on **engaged research**, that is, research conducted in partnership with practitioners, policy makers, and other community partners. It can be called engaged research, partnership research, collaborative research, action research, or participatory action research. Although engaged research has been around for a long time, recently there has been resurgence of interest in it and of its use. For example, a researcher interested in intergroup relations might develop a partnership with organizations that have been trying to reduce intergroup conflict to collaboratively design an intervention (research study) that the community organizations can help implement. Or a public health researcher might develop a partnership with a community health clinic to improve its procedures for addressing needs of immigrant populations. Or a psychologist might conduct collaborative research with a social service profession on its screening and selection techniques and how they limit diversity of the work force.

The points in this chapter are applicable to any field-based research, but are focused on engaged research in particular. Engaged research is structured somewhat differently; it requires discussion of different orientations to such work, an understanding of the historical and logical grounding for the work, and an articulation of the principles for guiding the work. We don't believe there is a toolbox for such work, for it varies widely across many dimensions, including the nature of the issues, the types of partners and their strengths, the scope of the work, and the length of the projects. But the work is characterized by engagement of practitioners and participants with researchers in designing, carrying out, analyzing, and interpreting the project's findings. Providing feedback about the findings to the practitioners and participants is an integral part of the work. Given its description, it should be clear that not all applied or field-based research could be called engaged research. Even work that is not engaged, however, should attend to the principles of engaged research, for those principles enhance mutual respect among researchers, practitioners, and participants.

Some of the motivations for conducting engaged research come from outside universities, as our publics ask why they should support research and what it has contributed to their lives. More importantly, however, such research hopefully represents universities turning more outward and defining their place and role in society in terms of engaged research as well as educating students. This is not to say that basic research has not contributed to societal improvements or that basic research is not important. Rather, we consider engaged research an important component of research, for it addresses practical concerns and enriches theory while identifying points of intersection between research, policy, and practice.

As an example, the Minneapolis Public Schools are in the process of changing how they assign grades to their high school students. They want to align the grades with state standards, and establish a set of performance goals for students that can be reliably and accurately assessed by teachers. Concurrently, a group of faculty at the University of Minnesota is interested in improving the way that readiness for college is measured because of its use in college admissions and course placement decisions; this group views better measures of content mastery from high school courses as integral to improved measurement of college readiness. Given their common interests, the two groups have begun working together and have submitted a grant proposal to support shared work. Each group can accomplish its goals more effectively by collaborating with the other, as well as with the Minnesota State Department of Education (a third partner), which developed the state standards. Together these groups can change state policies as well as practices concerning the ways that grading and knowledge acquisition are measured, and can provide dissemination of information and training through regional centers across the state that would drive adoption of similar approaches if the project were found to be effective.

The example illustrates how it is possible to find "sweet spots" where the interests of researchers, practitioners, and policy makers converge. In such circumstances, the interests of different stakeholders can all be moved forward through collaboration. Even more importantly, the joint actions of researchers, practitioners, and policy makers in planning and executing a collaborative project can produce a partnership that accomplishes its goals more efficiently and effectively than the partners could do on their own. Imagine in contrast if only the researchers wanted to change how teachers grade. Their efforts would not align with those of the schools or teachers, so even if they were willing to participate, the teachers "helping" the researchers would be taking on work not related to their jobs. At times when their work demands are particularly heavy, the teachers' attention to the research project would likely diminish.

In this chapter, we discuss types of research and the array of roles in which researchers might find themselves. Some clearly are engaged research, other approaches not. Both types are needed; this chapter is not intended to suggest otherwise. The focus is largely on **collaborative research** and the different types of partnerships that might develop as well as approaches for developing relationships. As is true for every method described throughout the book, not all researchers want or need to do collaborative research. In talking about engaged research and action research in particular, Chein, Cook, and Harding (1948) stated, "[it] is a field which developed to satisfy the needs of the socio-political individual who recognizes that, in science, he can find the most reliable guide to effective action, and the needs of the scientist who wants his labors to be of maximal social utility as well as of theoretical significance" (pp. 43–44). Not all social scientists have or should be expected to have such needs, and not all researchers who do such research are attracted to it from their socio-political needs. More broadly, engaged research appeals to researchers who want their work to have practical impact; they are likely to engage in such research at some times during their careers. Collaboration provides a way to develop research projects that contribute to knowledge. A unique element of collaborative research is its likelihood of producing results with immediate practical as well as conceptual value.

Exercise: Addressing social challenges

We all have lives outside of what we study in psychology. Think about your community, and the main challenges it faces. They may be about the environment, the schools, safety, civility, or even competing values. Pick one that you know something about and think about who is involved in it, how they perceive the challenge, and how they might solve it. If you were brought in as a researcher, imagine how you would include the different stakeholders (e.g., the people and the agencies involved). What knowledge do the different stakeholders bring, and how can they contribute to your research? Without looking ahead in this book, how do you imagine you might design a research study that gets at the issue?

We are asking you to do this before we discuss the range of methods/tools that you would have to help you. To the extent possible, we want you to have context when you think about different methods. When we talk about processes for building trust, you can think about the different stakeholders and how they feel about each other in your setting. When we describe methods and designs, we hope that they might extend how you think about the types of research that might be done.

If you have a good example, please share it with the class.

Roles of Researchers in Work with Practitioners, Policy Makers, and Participants in Social Research

Researcher roles can range widely within collaborative research. In some cases, practitioners or communities identify a specific need that they have for a researcher who is knowledgeable and who can guide or assist them. In such situations, the researcher is unquestionably the expert, and may be able to dictate what needs to be done and how to do it. The expert status of the researcher and role (e.g., paid consultant) limits the extent to which the researcher needs to negotiate with the practitioners or policy makers about the work to be done. The researcher may dictate what is to be done, and often has final say regardless of input from or concerns of others. At the other end of a continuum of roles are some types of **action research**, particularly variants often called **participatory action research (PAR)** or **critical PAR**, where the researcher is more of a partner, a facilitator, or even an observer rather than a guide or director, and the role may not be either to design the research or to collect the data. In such instances, researchers would cede control to the partners. Community partners design the research with advice from the researchers, *community researchers* collect the data, and then the partners and researchers interpret the data. In educational settings, for example, researchers may try to build research capacity of teachers and support them as they develop as researchers of their teaching practices. An attractive element of this approach is that it creates research capability within the community where the research is being done.

Arguments for involving community researchers are that they:

- have credibility within the community because they are part of it;
- interact more comfortably with residents and may be more effective in getting participants to be serious about the research; and
- are likely to be more accurate in determining what respondents are trying to say and in probing when respondents' statements are incomplete or not clear because they understand the culture of the community.

Limitations of involving community researchers as opposed to academic research-ers include:

- their range of research skills (collect, code, analyze, and interpret data) is typically narrower;
- they are thus likely to require greater training;
- they are less likely to be familiar with and interested in the theories being tested and to have taken research methods courses; and
- they may turn over more rapidly unless they are hired for full-time work.

Although community researchers are more likely to be engaged in PAR or similar approaches, it is certainly possible to involve them in many different types of research. As much as anything, it requires thinking during the planning stage of securing resources to cover both the training of community researchers and paying them for their work time. And there is a tradeoff, for supporting community researchers means fewer resources for other research expenses, for example, the support and training of graduate students or university researchers.

Between the expert researcher controlling the setting and the participatory researcher advising participants as researchers is a range of engaged research methods. They include research partnerships in which the project is a collaboration between researchers and practitioners, but the particular investigation is largely defined by the researcher. In quite different types of partnerships, projects are largely identified and defined by the community and practitioners, but guided by the researchers' expertise about research methods and design. In still others, the work can truly be called a co-creation of researchers and practitioners because they share the design, execution, and interpretation of the work. Each of those methods may contain elements of action research (e.g., Lewin, 1946).

Given the nature of community-based research, researchers have articulated par-ticular approaches that are effective for community engagement. Of particular note are action research approaches (Lewin, 1946). Our perspective on collaboration is grounded in the work of Lewin and his colleagues (e.g., Lewin, 1946), and reflected in action research and Lewin's statement that "nothing is so practical as a good theory." This orientation to research suggests that problems grow from the ways people live their lives in communities, and that communities are ideal places for testing theories. It further argues that scientists should be engaged in research that addresses important practical issues and problems, that there is natural convergence of interests of scientists, policy makers, and practitioners around such issues, and that the combination of researchers with their theories and practitioners with their knowledge of local conditions and limitations is key in driving effective research in non-laboratory settings. In attempting to emphasize the importance of research in solving practical problems and contributing directly to life quality, Lewin (1948) stated that "Research that produces nothing but books will not suffice" (p. 203). The particular roles may vary from situation to situation depending on the skills and interests of the engaged partners as well as the setting. (Readers familiar with Lewin's field theory will recall his focus on both individuals and environmental factors.) This perspective is one that positivists, post-positivists, and constructivists share – researchers working with practitioners can create knowledge that is both practical and conceptually important.

One might wonder why theories and conceptual importance matter in research that focuses on practical issues and problems. In other words, if the research addresses the specific question of interest, does it matter whether it also addresses a conceptual or theoretical issue? From a "traditional" scientific perspective, the answer is typically yes, for it is the conceptual basis or theory that allows researchers to explain and understand the phenomenon and to therefore address similar types of issues in other contexts. If we know why and how something works, under what conditions it works, and for whom it works best, we can use that information to understand related phenomena and to devise ways of addressing similar issues in other contexts. If, in contrast, we believe the constructivist view that the search for general laws will be unproductive and limits understanding of local conditions, the theories that are of interest are local and emerge from or are refined by the research.

Brief descriptions of different action research approaches follow. For readers seeking greater detail and sources for action research, Maruyama and Van Boekel (2014) provide an extensively annotated bibliography of action research approaches.

Action Research Approaches

What we are calling action research comes directly from Kurt Lewin's work (e.g., Lewin, 1946); it also has been called **action science** (e.g., Argyris, Putnam, & Smith, 1985). As articulated by Lewin, it employs fairly traditional approaches to collaborative research, engaging practitioners as partners to identify problems and explain local conditions, and to help with translational aspects of the work. Lewin spoke about university "experts in theory" working with community "experts in practice," and about work growing out of community problems and issues. His approach, unlike some others, views attempts to create and test theory as a central feature of action research. For Lewin, the work is driven by researchers drawing on their conceptual and methodological expertise to work collaboratively with community partners. In contrast to much current action research, Lewin assumed that much of this work would be experimental. Also unlike much work that is "one shot," a single study done in one setting, Lewin's work assumes an ongoing relationship with the partners. It sets up cycles of problem definition, approach selection, action, observation/data collection, data analysis and interpretation, and then problem redefinition. Argyris et al. (1985) take a position between that of Lewin and the methods described next.

They argue that action research/science should integrate theory and practice by informing action and testing theory. Action research sometimes fulfills a hypothetical-deductive function to explain and predict patterns and regularities of behavior, but it also needs to consider the counterview that interpretive understanding of meanings cannot be reduced to regularities because that would ignore the ways in which people create meanings in their everyday lives.

Participatory Action Research

Other models, clustered under participatory action research (PAR) or critical PAR, share the cyclic approach and the centrality of collaboration, but view research as self-examination of practices and as an unfolding process. Such research heavily involves community members throughout the process, namely, in defining the research questions that examine the ways in which they behave, in collecting the data, and in making meaning of what is happening. There also often is a commitment to social change in PAR research. As is true of all the major types of action research, there is much variability in what is called PAR (e.g., Baum, MacDougall, & Smith, 2006; see Fals Borda, 2001, for a view of its history and development). In many instances, rather than directly conducting the research, researchers are training practitioners to become researchers of their own practices (e.g., McTaggart, 1991). In PAR, all relevant parties collaboratively examine current action and problems with a goal of transforming practice in applied settings. It puts the university researcher in a role of collaborator or advisor to the researchers, who are the practitioners or even the participants. In some projects, community members are trained to be researchers, because it is believed that they understand the local conditions better and have access to information that outsiders would not have in evaluating practices. As noted above, because community researchers are known and trusted within the community, they are more likely to elicit honest responses and interpret the responses as they are intended to be interpreted by the participants. A challenge working in diverse communities is that communities are not singular in their perspectives, so any filtering of responses is susceptible to misinterpretation, irrespective of who is asking questions or interpreting responses. A second challenge, mentioned above, is that many researcher positions are short-term or part-time, which may make it difficult to find and keep skilled community people to work on action research projects.

Community-Based Participatory Research

Yet another variant of action research is one that has been particularly popular in health fields, namely, **community-based participatory research** (CBPR; e.g., Minkler & Wallerstein, 2008). CBPR is explicit in the importance of engaging all the stakeholders throughout the process, and in disseminating the research to all the stakeholders. CBPR is recognized by the National Institutes of Health Office of Behavioral and Social Sciences Research (2011) as "an effective method for transferring evidence-based research from clinical settings to communities that can most benefit thereby improving health. CBPR's community-partnered research processes offer the potential to generate better-informed hypotheses, develop more effective interventions, and enhance the translation of the research results into practice. Thus, CBPR is an essential tool for action-oriented and community-driven public health research" (p. 1). Community partners participate in the full process of developing the research, from conceiving and designing the study to formulating its hypotheses, to conducting the study and data collection, to data analyses and interpretation, to drawing conclusions from the data and presenting the findings to the local community as well as the research community. From some perspectives, CBPR provides a middle ground between PAR and action research, although in practice it seems in various forms to be like each of them. One area where there is variability across CBPR studies is whether or not research participants are represented on the research team.

In general, from our perspective, it is good to employ a full array of approaches in conducting engaged research, for the different approaches can answer different questions and/or bring different perspectives to bear on community issues. Virtually all focus in their own way on using partnerships to build community capacity to do and understand research, which is beneficial both to future research and to the community. They all also focus on gaining perspectives of community partners to inform the research so it is attentive to local conditions that could affect the implementation of the study and its findings. Most importantly, the different approaches complement other approaches as well as one another and, when used optimally, allow researchers to take on a range of roles and address a full complement of possible issues. And they provide complementary information that when pooled across methods can provide a richer view of the issues and the communities in which the research is being conducted.

Exercise: Traditional scientific and post-positivist approaches

Chapter 4 is a good place to think about the different epistemologies that underlie research. For the sake of this exercise, we exaggerate differences between the divergent perspectives, recognizing that many researchers work between these end points. Those working from traditional scientific approaches tend to begin from theory as they think about application, and view collaborative research as an opportunity to test theories while conducting research with both conceptual and practical implications. They find theories that can be applied to practical problems. Post-positivists/constructivists tend to begin from community knowledge, arguing that researchers don't have the understanding of local conditions, and that many theories will come from the participants. Some view researchers as advisors who support the community members as they conduct the research on their practices and become researchers of those practices.

Identify a practical problem or issue. Describe how you would address it from a traditional perspective, and, alternatively, how you would address it from a constructivist perspective. Finally, see if you can find a pragmatic approach that blends the two different approaches. If you are successful, you may well have created a mixed methods study (Chapter 16).

Importance of Work that Engages Practitioners and Is Relevant to Policy

[M]ost universities continue to do their least impressive work on the very subjects where society's need for greater knowledge and better education is most acute. (Bok, 1990)

Derek Bok captures a challenge to researchers, namely, that an important role of research is to address and help ameliorate society's problems and challenges. This position was also articulated by Lewin as well as the authors of earlier editions of this book. Yet it is difficult to point to problems and challenges that have been solved by social science research. From one perspective, Bok's statement should not be surprising, for the topics and issues about which society's needs are greatest are complex, multifaceted, value-laden, and thus not easily addressed, or they would be solved readily once identified. But from another perspective, what Bok pointed out is that insufficient attention has been devoted to addressing issues of greatest importance for society. Much of the research done by social and behavioral scientists ignores or at best speaks indirectly to the most challenging and impactful issues of the day. In part, the focus may reflect the fact that for the last half century applied research often has been viewed as less important than basic experimental research focusing on theory development. For example, federal research funding has supported basic research more than applied research. The Institute of Education Sciences at one point suggested that it might support only experimental research, which would in our view greatly limit the knowledge creation process as well as external validity of research.

As will be described in a following section, the status of applied research may be changing, for external pressures and accountability needs are helping to focus research on important societal issues. In many instances, such issues simply cannot be addressed using an experimental design. And, as also will be discussed later in this chapter, applied work has taken on a somewhat different identity as translational research. But such research still is messy, less controllable, less predictable, and often frustrating. Researchers directing their energies toward challenging issues frequently experience lack of control and incomplete understanding of the research settings and their dynamics, for they are outsiders to those settings. As noted above, they need partners familiar with the settings and their characteristics and idiosyncrasies. They also have to recognize that the participants in the research process are unlike typical college student participants in that they are looking for particular outcomes for themselves and their communities, and are perfectly willing to challenge researchers.

The intent of this chapter is not to be dismissive of research that does not address society's needs. Basic research that increases understanding of social processes will always hold a prominent place among research methods (e.g., Festinger's theory of social comparison processes analyzed how people use their perceptions of others to judge their own behaviors), and much of that research may have translational uses. Researchers who are both more enthusiastic about and better at working in laboratories with highly controlled settings and very specific phenomena should focus their energies there. In contrast, however, this chapter focuses on work done with partners in field settings, and is directed toward researchers who want to do work that has more immediate practical impact on people's lives. There are a lot of different settings where research involves practitioners, including for example studies in education with educators, parents and families, and with students; in health care with service providers and patients; in public policy with government officials and service providers; and in other fields including marketing and business, law, social welfare, and public affairs. Such work is not for researchers whose desire is experimental elegance and control, for researchers doing engaged research need to share control, work in settings where many other things are occurring concurrently with any research, and work with partners who usually are simultaneously working toward other goals in addition to those of the research. Often so many things are changing that it is difficult to attribute a particular finding uniquely to a specific intervention or approach. Nevertheless, as we explain next, we believe that as part of research methods training, prospective twenty-first-century researchers need to develop appreciation for and understandings of issues of partnership and approaches for conducting engaged research.

Historical Roots of Engaged Research

Engaged research dates back at least to the development of public research universities in the United States. The **Morrill Land Grant Act of 1862** created public research universities whose purpose was to address the needs of their communities. Historically, the **land grant mission** formalized a unique role for land grant universities as a partner with the state in generating, applying, and teaching about new knowledge and discoveries. The act promoted integration of knowledge generation, teaching, and application. While once relegated primarily to the "agricultural" and "mechanical" arts and sciences, the role is now understood as more broadly applicable to the generation of new knowledge and discoveries in the arts, sciences, and humanities that profoundly shape and influence the U.S. future on every level. Desired outcomes from this role include human progress, improved achievement and creativity, global competitiveness, environmental protection, and a higher quality of life. The move that some might view as an expansion of the land grant mission seems to us simply an updating of a broad and enduring mission of public service and partnership in addressing social needs and supporting economic development. Many non-land grant institutions would agree, arguing that they also share that mission. Affirmation of the importance of post-secondary education and research in urban and metropolitan areas in the U.S. comes in part from more recent creation of higher education institutions dedicated to urban areas and issues (e.g., University of Illinois, Chicago). And, as universities beyond the U.S. have flourished in our current information age, the multiple missions of universities have been translated and applied to universities around the world.

Ernest Boyer has argued that work like that described in this chapter is integral to the future of research universities. In *Scholarship Reconsidered* (1990), he posed questions about how knowledge can responsibly be applied to consequential problems, and whether social problems can themselves provide an agenda for scholarly work. His questions are key, for they firmly anchor engaged work to the core missions of land grant and other research universities. Linkages come through the four different scholarships identified by Boyer – *discovery, integration, engagement,* and *teaching.* And they touch the three key missions of land grant and other research universities: research, teaching, and outreach/public service. Engaged research of universities includes basic research conducted in field settings, applied research translating theory to practice, and problem-driven research applying academic tools and approaches to better understand complex social issues. And the research informs training experiences for graduate and professional students, research and service learning experiences for undergraduates, and work of outreach professionals in numerous areas like health care, nutrition, youth and family development, education, community and economic development, and gardening/farming.

In addition to moving beyond the traditional land grant disciplines to include social sciences and all other disciplines, today's engaged work differs in that it is being done during an **urban age**. Society in the U.S. and the world has become metropolitan/ urban, with a substantial majority of the population now living in urban areas. Challenges of an urban age (disparities in educational outcomes, crime rates, employment, health care, crowding, etc.) have become prominent and are closely tied to economic success. A major change produced by the urban age is in the nature of the communities in which the work is done. In smaller rural communities of the past, disadvantaged populations were relatively small and interspersed among more affluent others, and communities were socioeconomically diverse. In contrast, in larger metropolitan areas today, along with larger populations there is substantial stratification, and many urban communities or parts of communities are largely comprised of economically and socially disadvantaged populations whose challenges go largely unnoticed by others sharing the metropolitan area but not the specific community. The concentration of poverty and disadvantage changes somewhat the nature of the work, for many of today's neighborhoods and communities struggle to meet the needs of their population. They confront researchers with entire communities facing multiple challenges, markedly changing the scope of challenges. Universities in such circumstances are not just "value adders" but core providers of knowledge and also services through their research and outreach. Along with the larger and complex challenges come great opportunities for researchers interested in conducting research that has societal benefits.

Despite substantial research activity, research programs have not been able to ameliorate or produce substantial sustained impact on the growing array of issues facing today's society. Limits of impacts underscore the complexity of the challenges faced as well as the need for new approaches that change the scale, coherence, and even fundamental assumptions guiding how the challenges are addressed. Our experiences suggest to us that universities are key partners but that they are unable to create changes of sufficient magnitude without engaging partners and building community capacity. A major role of universities is to convene stakeholders and work to create broad partnerships that go deep into communities while engaging major governmental and non-governmental organizations (see, for example, Kania & Kramer, 2011). Work needs to be sustained rather than episodic, and institutional rather than investigator driven. Such changes are beginning to occur, and we believe that future generations of social and behavioral science researchers will need to have skills and understandings that enable them to conduct translational research in partnership with practitioners and policy makers as well as with other researchers. We explain next why it is important today and then focus on issues to consider when doing such work.

Importance of Collaborative Engaged Research

Collaborative research is important both to post-secondary institutions and to the research community. For post-secondary institutions, Harkavy and Puckett (1994) suggest that there are many arguments supporting university research engagement, including self-interest (e.g., personal safety), costs of being withdrawn from the community, advancement of knowledge, teaching, and human welfare, as well as promoting civic consciousness and engagement. Support for urban engaged research has come from major associations of United States university presidents, for example, through the Association of Public and Land Grant Universities (APLU) and its Coalition of Urban Serving Universities (USU). Many university presidents have spoken individually in support of engaged research. For example, former Syracuse University President (and social psychologist) Nancy Cantor (2007) pointed to the importance of reasserting the public benefits of higher education, of reconnecting with the American people, and of leaving the "ivory tower" to engage in public scholarship with community partners.

Collaborative engaged research is important in advancing research knowledge for a number of reasons:

- Such research goes beyond the college student subject population that has been so prominently a part of social science research, and also may get beyond the criticism that too much of social science is based on samples that are WEIRD (White, Educated from nations that are Industrialized, Rich, and Democratic; see, e.g., Henrich, Heine, & Norenzayan, 2010) through inclusion of immigrant and economically struggling samples. Through collaboration, researchers have better access to diverse research participants who are more representative of broader society.
- It is responsive to today's most important issues, counteracting the criticism that social science has been unable or unwilling to contribute in any important ways to the betterment of society, in contrast with fields like medicine or public health.
- The work develops collaboration as a **mutually beneficial** arrangement, a **quid pro quo** that meets the needs of all the partners. In the illustration described at the beginning of the chapter, the school district gets help in developing its new assessment system, in particular seeing how consistently and reliably teachers can assess mastery of core content from courses plus having information on validity of the ratings. The state department gets a chance to see how readily and effectively the array of standards can be aligned with curriculum and assessment practices as well as some ideas and practices it can disseminate to other school districts about aligning assessments with standards. And post-secondary education benefits insofar as high school assessments and standards are better aligned with post-secondary curriculum and preparation, and they get information that potentially helps them make better decisions about college admissions and course placement.

As the example illustrates, in many instances it makes good sense for research to be done collaboratively.

• As articulated by Lewin in the quote at the beginning of this chapter, a benefit of research in "real-world settings" is that it grounds theory in what is happening in the world outside academia. Such grounding is particularly important for work on social relations, for such processes can look very different in natural settings, and ignorance about the setting may undermine even a well-conceived study. A final reason for collaborative research is that it is time for universities to acknowledge that research is no longer the exclusive domain of post-secondary education. Universities no longer are exclusive access points for scholarly information, for the Internet has made journal articles accessible from anywhere in the world. And today many highly skilled, credentialed, and qualified researchers are working outside academia in and with community partners and government agencies, not to mention the many "think tanks" that compete for research funding. Many of these researchers have substantial experience developing skills working with practitioners in applied settings that few of their university colleagues are able to match. They can provide a bridge between university researchers and practitioners. And, if universities choose not to engage communities, other researchers can bypass universities in addressing the needs of communities.

Prior Social Relations Research Affecting Policy and Practice

In a number of instances, social scientists' summaries of empirical studies and their implications have shaped policy decisions and thereby affected practice. The earliest and perhaps best known is the 1952 **Social Science Statement** that was cited in the 1954 *Brown v. Board of Education* U.S. Supreme Court school desegregation case. In that case, social science evidence provided to the Court documented the harms of segregation (see, e.g., Clark, Chein, & Cook, 2004), leading to a court decision that included the powerful phrase that draws from the social science evidence: "generates a feeling of inferiority as to their status in the community that may affect their hearts and minds in a way unlikely ever to be undone." The social science brief has been touted as the first time social science evidence was included in arguments in support of a U.S. Supreme Court ruling. Since that time social science evidence has been summarized and synthesized to address a number of Supreme Court cases, including as examples racial profiling and use of race in college admissions decisions (both for the Michigan *Grutter* and *Gratz* cases and the 2013 Texas *Fisher* case). As long as justices do not hold the position that current Justice Clarence Thomas has been said to hold, namely, that all social scientists need to agree in order for research findings to be acceptable and persuasive, social science research should continue to influence policies.

Similarly, in many instances, social science evidence has changed practices, for example, increasing the use of cooperative student groups in schools to improve both student achievement and intergroup relations, or developing long-term diverse work teams with equal status and common goals as a way to reduce intergroup conflicts and increase performance. Such research is done in field settings, typically in collaboration with practitioners, and is exactly the kind of work that this chapter describes.

Social science research has changed how job interviews are conducted and the type of information that is considered acceptable and unacceptable to request during interviews, the skills that are sought in leaders, how police use background information in identifying offenders, and how political campaigns and advertising are done.

Applied versus Translational Research

Earlier, we suggested that applied research has received increased status through the use of different language to describe the work and its potential impacts. In particular, describing work as **translational** has provided greater credibility. In health fields, phrases like "bench to bedside" have captured the importance of work that applies discoveries of basic laboratory research (referred to as bench science) immediately to improve patient well-being, living conditions, and general health. Such work has been reinforced by a focus on the relevance and impact of universities. Within the United States, for example, calls have gone out to make research universities more attentive to and directly engaged with the country's changing demographics and needs. In fall 2003, the National Institutes of Health (NIH) Roadmap (Zerhouni, 2003) called for a model that extended beyond the "ivory tower," using a translational approach that applies basic research to provide real solutions for social problems facing today's communities. Using the word translational rather than applied or practical provides a more positive perspective on engaged, relevant work within the academy, with status in many universities comparable to basic research. In addition, the National Science Foundation (NSF) now asks directly about translational issues, explicitly requiring investigators to articulate broader impacts of their research. At times when all governmental expenditures are being closely scrutinized, being able to show that the work is supported by the community and to articulate the practical as well as conceptual benefits of research matters.

Practical Suggestions for Developing Relations with Policy Makers, Practitioners, and Communities

At this point, we focus on issues researchers need to consider in particular as they think about engaged research, but also for any work outside a laboratory, for some concerns of field and engaged research are quite different from those facing laboratory researchers. Schon (1995) described such work as "the swamp," where problems are messy and confusing and sometimes seem intractable, in contrast to the hard high ground of manageable problems more typical of laboratory research. With less control, translational researchers depend on partners to help guide the work and inform them about what is happening.

One of the challenges of collaborations and engaged research is identifying areas where interests converge and collaboration is potentially productive for all partners. Although in some instances research may largely occur through researchers asking practitioners to help them, such instances may not yield the quality of findings or partnerships that are desired. Rather, effective partnership research needs to draw on the knowledge and skills of all the partners, which occurs when all are invested in the work and see the work as meaningful, as their work, and as meeting their needs. If they see research as someone else's project, the commitment and attention they devote to it will be less. Simply, for collaborative partnership research, engaging partners is an important challenge. To do such research effectively and respectfully, needs, goals, and aspirations of the different partners have to be negotiated.

The remainder of this section draws on experiences of the authors doing engaged research. Our experiences include work by the first author to develop university partnerships with an urban community across an array of projects involving three different research areas (education, community development, and health) and four working groups (e.g., Maruyama, Jones, & Finnegan, 2009),[1] and from work by the second author in program evaluation (e.g., Dempsey, Riley, Ryan, & Kelly-Vance, in press; Esquivel, Ryan, & Bonner, 2008; McCall, Ryan, & Plemons, 2003). We discuss a range of issues in partnership development: developing relationships, linking the research with other ongoing research and partnership efforts, organizing meetings, developing commitment to the work, power dynamics, communication, developing timelines and a work plan, and finding support for the research. The work that is drawn upon focused on projects where there was strong agreement about importance of the work. We avoided projects that would be politically sensitive, controversial, or potentially divisive, like research identifying differences across communities in things like pregnancy rates, sexual behaviors, achievement levels, or drug use. If research on such issues is proposed, researchers need to recognize that some partners will opt out of participation. Community agencies are often concerned that research findings will reflect negatively on their work or that they will be seen as supporting research that makes their communities look bad. They simply can't afford alienating their supporters and constituents, for their livelihood depends on those relationships. In contrast, our work focused on improving achievement levels, job readiness, and health of residents from all backgrounds.

Developing Relationships

Building partnerships between university and community partners requires **developing trust** to bridge the gaps across differences in size, scale, needs, and available resources. Based on our experiences, trust can be built through developing a common understanding of community needs, and recognizing what different partners have already done and are doing to address them and where convergence of interests and opportunities lies. Trust can also be built upon professional and personal relationships between partners, based upon common interests in identifying and implementing approaches to improve conditions and outcomes for residents, organizations, and institutions. A list of effective approaches appears below. They are intended to be illustrative, but a common element is that relationship building takes time; developing working relationships is central to partnership efforts and will not happen overnight.

[1] The work was supported by a three-year grant from the U.S. Department of Education's Fund for the Improvement of Postsecondary Education (FIPSE).

- Convene partners for meals, which contributes to developing a sense of community and trust. Although partnerships cannot ultimately just be "about the food," sharing of food and fellowship include symbolic meanings that are important. Most people eat lunch, so holding meetings with food over lunch is effective in attracting partners. But don't expect food alone to create commitment to your work.
- Take time in meetings and discussions to share perspectives, establish common interests and goals, and acknowledge contributions of various partners to the work – while recognizing and publicly acknowledging that meetings need to move to action.
- Make informal time outside of meetings to meet partners one-on-one or in smaller groups. Such meetings provide opportunities to go into greater depth about specific personal and organizational interests and goals, and to discuss strategies for how to move forward, develop program planning, and establish approaches for addressing effort and engagement issues. Such meetings are often simpler to organize, more convenient for partners, and better for finding out about particular needs and interests of each partner, because they allow for greater candor, provide opportunities to learn more about historical relationships among different partners, and provide time to develop relationships beyond what generally can happen in larger group settings.
- Attend meetings of partners and others in the community; be visible and involved in work that extends beyond specific research projects and interests. Attend events or work with community partners when no benefit (and particularly no university benefit) is apparent. Researchers can meet others, and others from the community can see that researchers are there, which can improve how the researchers are perceived and thus community partners' willingness to work with them.

One final point about relationships is that university partners need to differentiate two distinct situations. The first are instances when the researchers aren't sure about the exact project they want to do or the direction the work needs to go and/or where the main goal is partnership building and developing relationships to establish a research program. The second are those instances in which, because of circumstances like previous agreements or funder limitations, there already are commitments to a particular approach or restrictions to particular activities. The latter cases simply should not be presented as if the direction and work still are being decided, but should be described clearly. Based on our experiences, university partners need to avoid giving community partners the impression that options beyond those already defined can be considered, for later inflexibility to pursue some suggested options may result in bad feelings due either to a sense that input was disregarded or that time was wasted making a project look like it was a full partnership when it was not.

Being Aware of and Acknowledging Other Ongoing Research and Partnership Efforts

It is likely that large universities will have other projects and initiatives addressing issues related to research being initiated, but that might not be specific to a particular community setting or partner. Integrating emerging work with existing work is not just sensible, it is critically important for establishing credibility in the community – if university work seems unconnected and people from various parts of the university are unaware of what their colleagues are doing, partners will be skeptical about participating, and for good reason. It is difficult to coordinate research, particularly at large universities, for people from all across the university seek community partners and projects, and do so for different reasons and with different purposes. In many instances, contacts are made and projects initiated by individuals within units without the administrative leaders in those units knowing about them (e.g., church-initiated projects, or ones initiated by community partners contacting a faculty "expert" whom they think might be able to help them). Because there are so many reasons for developing partnerships (e.g., to consult as an expert, to test or apply a particular theory, to meet NIH guidelines for representative subject populations), much work probably doesn't align well for collaboration even if that were desired. Nevertheless, it is important to build bridges to existing work and at least become aware of it.

Organizing Meetings

Again, our experiences may be idiosyncratic to our particular projects (although they have been largely consistent across projects). Nevertheless, listed below are approaches/experiences that were helpful in developing and sustaining partnerships:

- Have a clear agenda and share it widely before the meeting.
- Engage in specific discussions within the broad topic of interest to the group in order to narrow down interests and create a focus for the research.
- Find out about existing community efforts that are similar in any way to the research being developed/proposed, and try to coordinate with or complement those efforts.
- Determine common goals among the broader set of specific and shared organizational interests (recognizing that in some instances there may be fundamental differences in values and approaches that make identification of common goals very difficult).
- Develop agreement about objectives, outcomes, shared efforts, and individual (organizational) contributions from each partner/organization.
- Address evaluation issues, establishing process and outcome criteria early on, so measurement and documentation can take place throughout the entire project.
- Develop and maintain communication and opportunities for follow-up and review throughout the time of project activity.
- Promptly address any issues and misunderstandings that may occur, particularly with respect to maintaining clear and effective communication.
- Ensure that there are at least some outcomes that will be attained as the project is nearing completion and that can be shared as success stories.
- Share information about outcomes with all project partners and broadly throughout the community.

- Expect projects to be dynamic and fluid, which requires maintaining flexibility and tolerance for changing conditions that can alter activities of community partners or those participating in research or other partnership activities.
- Expect conflict and differences that may extend to basic values, for in diverse groups all individuals are not likely to view things in common ways.
- Work hard to maintain an atmosphere of equality and inclusiveness, for it is easy to underestimate the power others may perceive researchers to possess and how intimidating researchers can seem.
- Follow through on commitments, for researchers definitely will be judged by their actions more than their words.

Building Commitment to the Work

Developing projects that are viewed not as university work but as partnership work can prove challenging. In instances where grants provide resources to support research projects (what Kania and Kramer (2011) call backbone or infrastructure), partners may be happy to have the researchers do much of the work. A challenge of that circumstance is that when the grant ends, no capacity exists for continuing the work. Researchers in partnership work need to resist accepting control of and responsibility for the projects so that partnerships remain more egalitarian and projects are shaped collectively. The processes that unfold are unlikely to be linear, and are not for people who like predictability. Groups start working in a particular direction, then pause and reconsider, sometimes even pulling back and rethinking their direction. Eventually, they move forward again, although often in a somewhat different direction. Until each group reaches a point where sufficient trust is established, it is difficult to move very far in any direction. Neither university nor community partners are likely to engage fully until they trust that their participation will help them fulfill their reasons for being part of the partnership. Until there is agreement about direction and purpose, adding partners may slow down the work insofar as revisiting of processes and decisions is needed. Once there is agreement, bringing on additional partners is much simpler, for different partners then are able to articulate the project in consistent ways. Developing and sharing written summaries of the decisions made and their justifications is important for increasing shared understandings of what agreements have been made and why decisions were made the way they were. But that task typically falls to the researchers, which makes it more difficult to cede direction and control to the partnerships that researchers are trying to develop.

Dynamics of Power in Relationships with Communities

University researchers face challenges tied to their institutions' power, reputations, size, and status. Universities are massive in comparison to most non-government partners in community partnerships. Some community partners may expect that because university budgets are large, university people have access to substantial resources. On the university side, researchers typically believe they have expertise, but often don't feel particularly powerful or that they have access to the sorts of resources that others might expect. And students who work as research assistants or as part of a service learning class certainly don't feel a sense of power from being "from the university." University people, however, need to be aware that how they are perceived is a balance between the positions they hold and the institutions they implicitly represent. Some university employees (e.g., faculty) may be perceived enviously by partners who are paid hourly and may have to attend meetings without being compensated. But even students can be perceived enviously, for they are privileged to attend college – and particularly if it is a highly selective one to which many other students sought admission but were not accepted or if it is expensive to attend. Perceived differences in power and resources can create complex power dynamics between communities and universities throughout the engagement process – even ignoring dynamics tied to preexisting relationships within communities, within universities, and between communities and universities.

We consider it important to take time to explicitly discuss the perceptions that exist among community and university partners. Major challenges are to build relationships based on accurate perceptions of what different partners have to offer in the particular setting and circumstances, and to ensure that each partner contributes something to the partnership. If community partners believe that the university has funding available, they might think that as long as they follow the lead of the university they will eventually secure some of the funding. This type of thinking can create or perpetuate an unequal power dynamic between partners, and limit their candor. In contrast, when partners have an accurate understanding of the resources that are available, they are able to think more concretely about what they need to advocate for and promote as well as what they can contribute and what they need to pursue to attain their goals. Throughout the partnership, community and university partners need to continue to discuss expectations and work to continue to develop and strengthen honest, open relationships.

Communication

Once specific projects begin, partners with lesser interest in the specific work tend to reduce their involvement in the partnerships. Keeping partners – both university and community – engaged can be difficult. One area that should not be overlooked is **communication**. Good communication helps keep the work visible, which increases momentum and keeps project efforts moving forward. We recommend developing key messages in advance of the work that can be shared with the community, and shaping reports of successes and accomplishments in ways that reinforce those messages and help increase awareness of what the researchers and the university are doing and why. Most community residents and potential community partners don't have a lot of direct contact with universities; in such circumstances, messaging needs to be consistent, fairly simple, and focused on accomplishments and who community partners are.

Establishing Timelines for Work and a Work Plan

As partnerships develop, flexibility and openness to diverse perspectives are essential, for this gives partners a sense of inclusion rather than exclusivity. At the same time, however, participants can focus better if they see the specific things they have to do and dates by which they have to do them. They need to know what they are expected to do and when the work needs to be completed. Also, having a timeline and work plan with assignments allows group members to see the resources that have been contributed by different partners. Once decisions are made to move forward, it is beneficial to establish specific **timelines** and agenda **priorities** so that partners can see how they are moving forward to the implementation stage of the work. Establishing timelines sometimes exposes differences between the pace of movement in universities, which is often slow and on different timelines (e.g., semesters), and the pace in community organizations. (The standing joke of the first author's community partners was to ask whether we would be working on "university time" or "real time.") Work with partners at the beginning to define clear and reasonable timelines that adapt to community timelines and schedules as much as possible, and try to stick to them.

Finding Support for the Research

A major challenge for partnership work occurs if the researchers do not come with funding already secured. (When there is funding, if the proposal did not involve the partners, a major challenge is to engage community partners to do work designed by the researchers.) In such a case, it is important to attract funding that will support the work, which is difficult until one knows exactly what resources are needed. If the work is to support efforts of some partners as well as researchers, the proposal can't be submitted until a budget can be put together that reflects efforts of all the partners, and a proposal that includes at a minimum input from the partners. Even if a proposal is submitted quickly, the delay in receiving funds can be a year (e.g., the U.S. Department of Education Institute on Education Sciences September deadline has July 1 as the earliest starting date). Lags in finding out whether the work will be funded and go forward create challenges, for in putting together a proposal the partners are engaged and planning the work. Given community timelines for doing work, partner expectations are likely that work will start shortly after the proposal is submitted. If it is not funded, enthusiasm for a second cycle may be substantially less. Even if the project is funded, by the time funding comes much of the enthusiasm is likely to have waned and needs to be reignited, assuming that the partners have not already moved on.

Such challenges suggest that initial research projects with a partnership-building goal should be relatively focused, "doable" projects, ones that already have enough support to conduct (e.g., seed money) or ones where the researcher partners initially seek infrastructure support – which is difficult to get, because external funders don't like to support infrastructure, for that is an ongoing (think never-ending) expense. And, assuming that initial funding is secured, the other side of the challenge is finding support to sustain the partnership projects. A potential limiting factor in attaining success is the extent to which both community and university partners are able and willing to sustain existing efforts so that projects can reach successful outcomes and continue over time. An ideal situation is one where existing community partner agencies can take over effective research projects and sustain their interventions or programs through ongoing funding streams.

In concluding this section, we provide a list of specific points from our experiences that build understanding and help improve the quality of engaged research in field or community settings. The list represents reflections about our roles as researchers. They may be somewhat idiosyncratic to our work and communities, but provide ideas about partnerships that should prove helpful to researchers who are developing partnerships, for they largely draw attention to practical issues that can undermine partnerships if not anticipated. The settings where these occurred were ones where university researchers attempted to develop partnerships that addressed common interests, and not ones where the research design was finalized before seeking partners. It is adapted from a final report on urban partnerships from a federally funded project, and expands on and refines an earlier list from Maruyama, Jones, and Finnegan (2009). Readers who have done community-based research are encouraged to suggest additions or changes to the list to the authors; we will add them to the website.

1. Receiving a grant to conduct research in a community setting is not sufficient to ensure community interest and participation. Community members want to see tangible impacts of the research in their community. That would include beneficial outcomes like jobs and job skills, improved community programs, better outcomes in areas like education or health, and long-term engagement.
2. Tied to point 1 is that in challenged communities, researchers need to consider issues of inequality when thinking about expectations for participation. For example, there may be much less true volunteer labor available, for residents may have to work multiple jobs to get by. And their employers may not be willing to pay them while they attend meetings.
3. Trust is key to success, and needs to be earned.
4. It is very important to think about and track indirect impacts of projects, for many interesting and potentially important community outcomes may not be measured by the dependent measures of initial interest to the researchers.
5. Flexibility in approaching the research is essential, for changes may be necessary and obstacles surmounted.
6. Expect challenges if you try to engage practitioners and policy makers simultaneously, for their focus can be very different.
7. If there are clear directions that one wants to pursue, be honest about them, and don't present the situation as if different possibilities are being considered.
8. Preexisting relations – be they good or poor, will strongly shape the work. These may be individual or institutional reputations or histories.
9. Expect participation not only from allies but also from cynics and critics.
10. Virtually all parties, university and community, come to the table with their own goals and agendas, and they will promote those. You as a researcher need to figure out what those are.
11. Researchers from large universities have to deal with perceptions about them as powerful and controlling.
12. Expect to learn a lot about yourself through partnerships (e.g., your culture, perspectives, perceptions and expectations, blind spots).

13.   Expectations of university and community partners need to be managed. Setting modest and achievable goals is a way to build realistic expectations and seed sustainable partnerships.

14.   Expend effort in advance to define what success will be, so you know it when you experience it and can celebrate it.

15.   People come with different views about what research is. Plan to spend time explaining what your research is and what the immediate and desired impacts are of your research. For example, some opposed to university work in a community referred to the Tuskegee Syphilis Study, suggesting that it represented the kinds of research we would be doing.

16.   One of the unique opportunities for university researchers is that they have both credibility and an absence of self-interest in convening community and civic partners to develop new, unique partnerships that can create improved outcomes and community change.

17.   Researchers need to be clear about the resources that they have available and how those resources will be used.

18.   Think about your expectations for the location where you are working, and revisit those expectations as the project unfolds.

19.   Before starting the research, researchers should take time to meet with key community organizations to explain their interests and goals.

20.   Researchers need to be ready to provide support and technical assistance to make efforts successful.

21.   Researchers need to determine the capacity of initial partners (university as well as community) to set and achieve goals and outcomes as partnerships are formed and develop.

22.   Universities have not been particularly successful in creating mechanisms that effectively support faculty members interested in engaged partnership research.

23.   Communication about what is happening and how it is working is critical to partnership success.

24.   Work, particularly in challenged communities where there are many unaddressed needs, may be complicated by large numbers of small non-profits trying to help address those unmet needs, for your research may overlap with what they are trying to do.

25.   Many times researchers won't be leading the partnership process – but if we want to be engaged in meaningful ways, we should be sure we are part of the process throughout so we understand what is going on.

26.   Whenever reasonable, set clear expectations for partners and get partnership agreements in writing.

Exercise: Pros and cons of engaged research

As you finish the chapter, make a list of the features of engaged research that you view as attractive, and then make a list of features that are less desirable. Get together with your small group and share the different set of strengths and shortcomings of engaged research. How many of you want to do engaged research?

Summary

In summary, social science research can say much about policies and practices. In some instances, influence has occurred without conducting a lot of engaged partnership research, but rather by applying theories and findings from cumulative research to analyze everyday problems. The arguments central to this chapter are that such work has been important, but that it can and should be extended by complementing it with engaged research conducted in partnership with practitioners and policy makers. Such research maximizes external validity of the research and provides immediate application of the findings in community settings. It provides visible evidence that research done by universities is of practical value and worth supporting. And it also may contribute to the development or refinement of basic knowledge and theories. In the near future, as public funding decreases, research needs to make the case that it provides a "return on investment" that warrants funds that could also be used for social programs, public safety, infrastructure maintenance, or other important needs.

Illustrative Examples

The two following examples illustrate just how challenging and frustrating it can be to work in changing environments. We present them as examples of the amount of time it can take to get research going and the different types of barriers or impediments that can hinder work. Not all research goes as smoothly as published articles may suggest, and persistence is important. Incidentally, variants of each of the two projects are still ongoing.

1. Schoolyard Gardens

The first author has worked for several years with local elementary schools building partnerships and developing research that focuses on the construction and use of schoolyard gardens to engage students in hands-on and discovery learning to increase their understanding of science. We started with three sites where science achievement was very low – with single-digit "passing" rates on fifth-grade science tests. Immediately after the first year, one school was moved to a different site because it was outgrowing the current one – not good for us, for we had put in about 200 linear feet of garden, brought in dirt and compost, and planted a full garden. We simply had to abandon that site (and much of the produce it yielded) and move to the new site, where we repeated the process.

Things were going well and developing through the second year at all three sites, with gardening curriculum and nice gardens, but at the end of that year each of our partner schools had to be reorganized because it failed to meet No Child Left Behind (NCLB) achievement levels. NCLB required that, as part of restructuring, principals had to be changed, and the principals not only were all supporters of the program, but also were the gatekeepers, controlling access, and our primary partners in the work. The new principals brought into the schools were charged with addressing the math and reading issues that landed the schools in reorganization, with subjects like science and gardening being lower priority.

Furthermore, because we had no prior relationships with the new principals, we were just one of many programs ongoing within their schools, and they had no context for understanding or valuing our work. We lost two of the sites. At one, the new principal was too busy and not interested. At a second, the local community organization was allowed to use the school gardens as a membership Community Supported Agriculture (CSA), where members paid an annual fee and got weekly bags of produce that the gardens yielded. The CSA effectively cut the students off from the gardens. We continued with the third school, which was successful, and started at a fourth site that earlier had been disinterested in participation, but was now ready and had space for a large garden. We worked with a local non-profit, which made the work there sustainable. And we put garden beds in yet another school site just before our funding ended. That work is still getting under way, led by a science education professor who has taken over the work at the three sites.

This illustration provides a good example of why many faculty do not get more involved in this type of research. The people we choose as partners – even if the right people for the project and who are interested – often leave, with a result that the partnership disintegrates. It can be the same on the opposite side – a university researcher may retire or move, causing a project to fall apart. In many ways, the issues are the same as or parallel to those that can occur for evaluation research (Chapter 15), where project outcomes can be decided by seemingly irrelevant factors like changes in administration of a partner organization or loss of a key partner. As was noted earlier, rewards and structure of universities often do not lend themselves to development of community partnerships, for they don't yield the faculty productivity indicators that other activities do.

2. After-School Programs

The first author also started working to develop after-school programs on youth entrepreneurship designed to build business and interpersonal skills of high school students and also help students see linkages between school and jobs. There were again three partners, in this case, non-profit organizations. One partner was gone within a year, a victim of the economic downturn that left the organization unable to raise sufficient resources to continue operations. A second managed to keep afloat, but had to lay off the youth program worker who was the primary contact, which effectively ended the partnership. The third organization continued, but initially decided not to be a partner, and ran a program on its own. After a summer they came back to work as a partner, and have continued partnership projects with various university partners, including with us. In this project our timing was unfortunate, for many small organizations were unable to withstand the economic shocks produced by the 2008–2009 recession. But it also illustrates the importance of trust; even the partner who stayed afloat and eventually worked with us was initially reluctant to do so.

> **Go online**   Visit the book's companion website for this chapter's test bank and other resources at: www.wiley.com/go/maruyama

Key Concepts

Action research

Action science

Collaborative research

Communication

Community-based participatory research

Critical PAR

Developing trust

Engaged research

Land grant mission

Morrill Land Grant Act of 1862

Mutually beneficial research (Quid pro quo)

Participatory action research (PAR)

Priorities and timelines

Social Science Statement

Translational research

Urban age

On the Web

http://www.ourdocuments.gov/doc.php?doc=87&page=transcript Link to the *Brown v. Board of Education* decision narrative.

Further Reading

Cox, D. N. (2006). The how and why of the scholarship of engagement. In S. L. Percy, N. L. Zimpher, & M. J. Brukardt (Eds.), *Creating a new kind of university* (pp. 122–135). Bolton, MA: Anker Publishing.

Harkavy, I. (1997). The demands of the times and the American Research university. *Journal of Planning Literature, 11(3),* 333–336.

Percy, S. L., Zimpher, N. L., & Brukardt, M. J. (Eds.). (2006). *Creating a new kind of university*. Bolton, MA: Anker Publishing.

Weiwel, W., & Perry, D. (2008). *Global universities and urban development: Case studies and analysis*. Armonk, NY: M. E. Sharpe.

Chapter 5

Research in Laboratory Settings

Research Methods in Social Relations, Eighth Edition. Geoffrey Maruyama and Carey S. Ryan.
© 2014 John Wiley & Sons, Inc. Published 2014 by John Wiley & Sons, Inc.
Companion Website: www.wiley.com/go/maruyama

The laboratory is a unique setting for research in many ways. Perhaps the best way to understand its special features is to think of it not as a single type of environment for research but as a medium in which research settings can be constructed. The laboratory's uniqueness lies in its flexibility. It can take on whatever physical, social, or other characteristics that are needed for the particular research study. Further, the laboratory allows researchers to take all participants through the same planned and consistent sequence of events in the same physical setting.

The three primary reasons for using the laboratory are to:

- attain control
- implement an experimental manipulation
- construct a setting for the experiment

The laboratory's isolation from external influences makes it possible to **control** or minimize the effects of extraneous factors on whatever the research is designed to investigate. Participants are obviously less likely to be distracted by passersby or other activities. In addition, however, some factors that vary and that may influence human behavior, for example, participants' social status as well as more mundane factors, such as the weather, become less relevant as participants are socially and physically isolated from the larger world; other factors (e.g., posters on the wall, illumination) can be held relatively constant. The laboratory thus helps control variability in the dependent variable that may be caused by extraneous factors.

Control over extraneous variables increases **statistical power**, that is, the likelihood of detecting an effect if that effect truly exists, and the precision of the conclusions that can be drawn from the research. In most field or survey research studies, many factors that may affect the dependent variable are free to vary. Because those factors vary much less in laboratories, smaller effects are easier to detect in laboratory studies than in field studies – including effects that may be theoretically important but too small to be of practical significance outside the laboratory.

Independent variables are also more easily manipulated in laboratory settings. As described in Chapter 10, the manipulation of independent variables is a critical feature of experimental design. Of course, non-experimental research is conducted in the laboratory (e.g., because certain types of observation are most easily conducted there), and experimental research is conducted outside the laboratory. But it is easier to implement experimental manipulations in the laboratory. Manipulation is really just another side of control. Instead of contriving a single controlled setting, task, and the like, two (or more) treatments are constructed that differ in only the intended ways, and participants are randomly assigned to experience one or the other treatment.

Various features of the setting that can influence research participants' behavior or otherwise facilitate research can also be arranged in the laboratory. For example, researchers might wish to explore physiological reactions to some experimental stimulus. The physiological equipment requires a computer, psychophysiological recorders and accompanying finger/muscle leads, and, in some cases, a specially constructed room that is electrically isolated. This kind of research can be conducted only in a laboratory setting.

The flexibility of the laboratory is used to attain control, implement a manipulation, and construct an appropriate setting in different ways for different research topics and goals. Thus, practical advice concerning specific laboratory-based studies depends on the particular procedures used to study a particular phenomenon. The factors that are important to consider for a group interaction study, for example, differ from those that should be considered for a study of the effects of pornography on sexual aggression. Researchers must generally refer to published reports of relevant studies to identify specific methods that can be adopted or adapted for a given study. We therefore describe here only general principles.

When Should the Laboratory Be Used?

The particular strengths and weaknesses of the laboratory make it more appropriate for some types of research topics and goals and less appropriate for others. Several conceptual contrasts define types of research that vary in their suitability for the laboratory. Although these contrasts are expressed as dichotomies, they actually are continuous dimensions; specific studies may fall anywhere along these dimensions.

Universalistic versus Particularistic Research Goals

The goal of some research is to investigate hypothesized associations, such as "use of pornography causes sex crimes." Such propositions, intended to have broad limits of generalizability, contrast with more local or focused questions, such as "Will flexible work schedules increase job satisfaction among the employees of Acme Inc.?" In other words, some research goals are relatively universalistic, whereas others are more particularistic.

Universalistic research is intended to investigate theoretically predicted associations between abstract constructs (e.g., pornography and sex crimes). Tests of such hypotheses are important because they shed light on the validity of the theory from which the hypotheses were derived. The primary question is whether the hypothesized association can be demonstrated at all. For this purpose, the details of the setting, population, and other particulars of the demonstration are often considered less crucial. However, the empirical universality of many associations has only recently begun to be examined as a result of advances in technology, which facilitate cross-cultural research. Some of this work has called into question the extent to which many associations, previously thought to be universal, actually are (Henrich, Heine, & Norenzayan, 2010). We therefore caution researchers not to assume too much about the extent to which any association applies to all humans or across all sorts of what appear to be theoretically irrelevant conditions. In any case, universalistic research focuses on detecting associations between general, abstract constructs; the particular operationalizations of the constructs are considered less important and are thus chosen for practical reasons. Similarly, the participant sample may be any group from the relevant population (e.g., all humans). Of course, if an association can be replicated – observed in many studies that use diverse operationalizations of the theoretical constructs and diverse participant populations – our confidence in the existence of that association is increased.

In contrast, the specification of a particular concrete setting, population, and time period to which the results are intended to apply is an intrinsic part of **particularistic research**. For example, we might not be interested in whether flexible work schedules produce good results in other places where they have been tried but only in whether they benefit a specific organization (with its particular workplace methods, corporate culture, and employees). Rather than general statements, a specific target of generalization for the research results is intended. Therefore, there is little or no interest in replicating the results across multiple settings, operationalizations, or populations.

Particularistic research goals often involve questions of how much, how often, how strong, or how many – quantitative questions of how large an effect is. Such questions cannot be answered in the abstract but require substantial involvement with the details of the target setting and population. For instance, estimating how large the effects of pornography are requires knowledge about the types of people who are susceptible to the effects and their relative prevalence in the population; the size of effects associated with different types of pornographic material and the amount each type is used in the population; the ways in which the conditions of use influence the size of the effects; the conditions under which use takes place in the population; and many other similar questions.

Laboratory settings are well matched to universalistic research goals. If a theory specifies that under conditions X, Y, and Z, outcome C should be observed, it might be possible to set up the required conditions in the laboratory. Whether the conditions occur *anywhere* in the "real world" outside the laboratory is not significant for the purpose of testing the validity of the theoretical prediction. The laboratory is less often suitable for pursuing particularistic research goals. It is difficult to answer questions about the impact of a program, or the effect of a variable, in a specific setting with specific people unless the research is actually conducted under those same conditions, implying the use of a field, survey, or observational study.

Basic versus Applied Research

A distinction that partly overlaps with the preceding one is that between basic and applied (or translational) research. This distinction is frequently misunderstood. It is not the case that research conducted in the laboratory is always basic, whereas non-laboratory (field or survey) research is always applied. Also, it is not the case that one type of research is superior to the other. In fact, it is often difficult to separate the two; many researchers seek both to develop and refine new knowledge – **basic research** – and to use that knowledge for the improvement of the human condition

– **applied research**. These goals are inextricably linked because, as Lewin (1951) noted, attempts to apply theoretically based knowledge to solve real social problems will almost always reveal new knowledge – even if it is only the knowledge that the theory is incomplete or inadequate. Lewin's famous dictum underscores this linkage: "There is nothing so practical as a good theory."

Basic and applied research can perhaps best be distinguished by the ways research findings are used. The same theory might serve as the basis for research on the social and personality processes underlying coping and reactions to stress in general (Endler, Macrodimitris, & Kocovski, 2000) or to examine the effects of an intervention to improve coping among stroke patients (Frank, Johnston, Morrison, Pollard, & MacWalter, 2000). Although the two studies have the same conceptual or theoretical basis, the former would be considered basic research, whereas the latter would be considered more applied. As another example, consider the finding in cognitive psychology that repeated testing (vs. repeated studying) after learning improves delayed recall. This finding could be used to develop further basic theories of memory storage and retrieval (basic research) or to design instructional programs for students (Karpicke & Roediger, 2008).

Although most basic research is universalistic and most applied research is particularistic, this is not always the case. For example, a study to develop a theory of coping processes in a specific population, such as persons infected with HIV, might be considered basic and particularistic. Similarly, research dedicated toward developing teaching techniques that are intended to be effective across a wide range of curricula and students might be considered universalistic and applied. Perhaps the best way of understanding the difference between the two dimensions is to consider the research *goals* versus the *end use* of the results. The universalistic–particularistic distinction involves the researcher's underlying goals in conducting the study; the basic–applied distinction involves the use that is made of the study's results.

Examining What Does Happen versus What Would Happen

Some research is aimed at investigating what happens in a particular situation. For example, what is the structure of a naturally occurring "get-acquainted" conversation? How much, and when, do people self-disclose? To answer such questions, we must find or construct the situation of interest. Pairs of college students who are strangers can have a "getting acquainted" conversation in the laboratory (Gable & Shean, 2000); however, other situations (e.g., an organizational setting or a family) would be more difficult to investigate in the laboratory. The key concern is whether the theoretically significant elements of the situation can be constructed in the laboratory.

In contrast, sometimes the goal is to see what would happen under specific circumstances. This type of research includes most theory-testing research, in which the hypothesis specifies a set of circumstances and the goal is to create those circumstances and see whether the predicted result occurs. Consider research designed to identify the conditions under which intergroup contact is more likely to reduce prejudice (Pettigrew & Tropp, 2006). It might sometimes be necessary to create the setting and other conditions in the laboratory because the intergroup contact and the specific conditions of interest would be unlikely to occur otherwise.

Other examples of what-if questions include research in which the goal is to strip away elements of natural settings to determine the minimal conditions that are necessary for a behavior to occur. For example, some research has examined intergroup behavior using the "minimal group paradigm" (Tajfel, 1982; Turner, 1987). It is easy enough to find real-life instances of negative intergroup interactions but difficult to explain them theoretically because multiple contributing factors, both present and historical, coexist. To remove the effects of historical antagonisms between groups, cultural stereotypes, conflicts over economic rewards, and the like, individuals can be brought into the laboratory and divided into two groups on some trivial – even explicitly random – basis. Even in these situations, in which social categorization is the only element, people discriminate in favor of the "group" to which they belong; develop stereotypes of the other "group"; and believe that the other "group" is homogeneous ("They're all alike."). The powerful effects of merely categorizing people into ingroups and outgroups would not have been possible to discover without the ability to experimentally separate social categorization from the other historical and cultural factors with which it is usually associated.

As these examples illustrate, research aimed at determining what would happen under specific circumstances – whether or not those circumstances actually exist anywhere in concrete form – is important for theory testing and for exploring the limits of a phenomenon of interest. Such research, in contrast to research aimed at determining what actually happens in a real situation, is particularly well suited to the laboratory setting, where the circumstances required by the research goals can be constructed.

Manipulable versus Nonmanipulable Independent Variables

Of course, certain types of independent variables cannot practically or ethically be set up and manipulated in the laboratory. We cannot use the laboratory to study, for example, the psychological effects of learning that one has a terminal disease; the researcher would have to seek out a cancer treatment center or other natural setting in which this event occurs. Nor can the laboratory be used to examine the consequences of experiencing a natural disaster. In short, some research questions are difficult or impossible to investigate in the laboratory.

Short versus Long Time Frames

A related point is that laboratory research rarely extends beyond a relatively short time period. The majority of laboratory studies are completed within an hour or two. A few might last weeks, as in one 12-week study of a prejudice reduction intervention (Devine, Forscher, Austin, & Cox, 2012). But many important phenomena in the social sciences develop only over weeks, months, or years, and the practical limitations of the laboratory require that they be studied in more natural and less controlled settings. For example, research on the determinants and consequences of peer victimization (e.g., Perren, Ettekal, & Ladd, 2013) or the relationship between parent involvement and children's academic achievement (Cheung & Pomerantz, 2012) would be difficult to conduct in the laboratory.

Participants' Awareness of the Research

Keeping people unaware of the fact that they are participating in research is difficult if not impossible in a laboratory study. As we explain later in this chapter, this fact can undermine the validity of the research, as participants might formulate hypotheses about the purpose of the study, which may influence their behavior in ways that would not occur in more natural settings.

One way to minimize the effects of participant awareness is to conceal the focus of the research. For example, laboratory studies of helping behavior might involve staged "emergencies," which occur while participants are performing another task that is the ostensible focus of the research (e.g., completing questionnaires). Participants would then be unaware that their reactions to the emergency are of primary interest – as far as they are concerned, the emergency simply happened.

A related method is to use dependent measures that are less obvious than directly asking participants what they think or how they feel. Participants who are unaware of the particular behavior of interest are more likely to act naturally with respect to that behavior. For example, participants might realize that a study of the getting acquainted process concerns how much they like their partners and their ratings on a self-report measure of liking might therefore be higher than they would normally be as a result of social desirability concerns. However, liking might also be measured by recording how close to their partners participants choose to sit. Participants would probably be unaware that researchers were recording sitting behavior and this measure may thus more accurately reflect participants' true feelings. Chapter 8 describes the issues involved in designing and interpreting such nonreactive measures.

Finally, we should note that participants' awareness that they are in a study can also be a problem in non-laboratory research. Except for innocuous observations of publicly accessible behavior, ethical considerations usually require that participants in field research be informed that they are being studied. Thus, although the laboratory setting makes the individual's role as a research participant highly salient, awareness of such a role and the validity problems it presents are not limited to laboratory research.

Summary

Despite its popular association with such high-prestige scientific fields as physics and chemistry, the laboratory is by no means a perfect setting for social science research. Like every research setting, the laboratory has strengths and weaknesses that make it more appropriate for some types of research than for others. The laboratory can be particularly useful for testing theoretical hypotheses of universalistic scope, to answer questions about what *would* happen rather than what *does* happen in some setting, and to investigate the relatively short-term effects of manipulable independent variables. It is less suitable for answering questions about what does happen in particular settings, for describing particular populations in particular places, or for examining long-term effects of fixed and nonmanipulable variables. Researchers who view the laboratory as an inappropriate setting for any social science research commit as serious an error as do those who adopt it unquestioningly for every research problem. The suitability of the laboratory depends on the particular research goals. Advances in our understanding of social phenomena ultimately require research in both the laboratory and the "real world."

Types of Laboratory Study

Laboratory studies can be divided into categories, which differ in the nature of the independent variable and often in the participants' task as well. Wilson, Aronson, and Carlsmith (2010) distinguished between impact and judgment experiments, and we add a third category, observational studies.

Impact Studies

An **impact study** is one in which the manipulation is intended to directly affect participants' behavior. Participants experience some event or series of events (the experimental manipulation) to which they must react. Classic examples include Milgram's (1974) study of obedience and Darley and Latané's (1968) "bystander intervention" study of helping behavior in which participants were confronted with a (staged) emergency while they were performing mundane experimental tasks. The researchers examined how and whether participants would seek help. Impact studies in general require careful staging so that participants perceive the events as real.

More recently, researchers have asked participants to play video games in which participants experience different types of events. For example, Anderson and Dill (2000) asked undergraduates to play either a violent or nonviolent video game. (Pilot testing indicated that the games were similar in enjoyment, difficulty, frustration, action speed, and cardiovascular activation while playing.) After playing the games, participants completed a measure of aggressive thinking and then played another game in which they could punish their opponents by administering an aversive blast of white noise. Results showed that participants who had played the violent video game thought and behaved more aggressively than did participants who played the nonviolent game.

Similarly, Correll and colleagues (2007) asked police officers and community members to play a video game in which they were confronted with armed and unarmed Black and White men; participants were instructed to "shoot" as quickly as possible only those targets who were armed. Although both police officers and community members exhibited racial bias, only community members exhibited a greater willingness to shoot Black targets than White targets.

Judgment Studies

In **judgment studies**, events do not happen to participants; rather, researchers create stimulus materials that vary in some way (the independent variable) and ask participants directly to respond to them. Participants might read, listen to, or watch stimuli and then make various types of judgments. In one study, for example, Scambler, Harris, and Milich (1998) asked children to watch one of three versions of a video portraying three children (actually actors following a script), one of whom was teased by the others after revealing that he had repeated third grade. In one version of the video the child responded in a hostile manner; in the second, the child ignored the teasing and changed the subject; and in the third, the child responded with a humorous comeback. After watching the video, participants rated their impressions of the children in the video and the effectiveness of the child's response to the teasing.

Observational Studies

A third category of laboratory research includes **observational studies**, that is, studies that use the laboratory mainly for convenience in arranging controlled observation. The key element of such studies is intensive observation; although different experimental conditions might be used, there is not a strong emphasis on impactful manipulations nor are participants directly asked to provide judgments of stimuli. Rather, the focus is on detailed observation of interaction or behavior as it unfolds over time. In some developmental psychology studies (e.g., Farver & Howes, 1993), for example, researchers have drawn conclusions about children's social and cognitive structures and ability based on how the children played with each other and their parents.

Researchers have also conducted observational studies in an effort to understand group processes, often making detailed records of the interactions among group members. Sommer, Horowitz, and Bourgeois (2001) videotaped jury-eligible men and women participating in mock juries deliberating a negligence lawsuit. Coders rated the videotapes for references to evidence that favored the plaintiff and references to evidence that favored the defendant, and examined impacts of the presence of a person who advocated disregarding the jury instructions in favor of doing what was "fair." Analyses indicated that jurors selectively discussed evidence that justified their decisions and when a person raised justice concerns the juries were less likely to comply with instructions.

Summary

As the diversity of the examples suggest, there is little practical advice that can be applied to all types of laboratory studies. For example, in an impact study, the staging and pretesting of an "unexpected" event might consume most of the researcher's efforts, whereas in a judgment study, the careful, controlled construction of multiple stimuli might be the focus. Anyone planning to conduct or evaluate laboratory research should carefully consider the key issues for the particular study of interest – depending on its type, its topic, the variables being manipulated, the special nature of the population, and so on.

Artifact and Artificiality

Research has revealed several types of artifacts that can contaminate the results of laboratory studies if appropriate precautions are not taken. Moreover, laboratory studies sometimes impress readers or observers as trivial or unnatural in various ways.

The presumed "artificiality" of laboratory research has become a kind of catchword for critics who advocate increased use of more naturalistic types of research. We examine the merits of these concerns and criticisms to see what lessons can be learned about threats to the validity of laboratory research.

The Laboratory and Types of Validity

As noted in Chapter 2, all research studies – not just laboratory studies – must be evaluated in terms of their internal, construct, and external validity. Special considerations that arise concerning laboratory settings affect each of these types of validity.

Internal Validity.   The laboratory setting in itself carries no positive or negative implications for internal validity. However, as noted, the laboratory facilitates random assignment and the control of extraneous factors as well as the manipulation of independent variables, all of which maximize the internal validity of research. In fact, a well-designed experiment allows few if any plausible threats to internal validity, as detailed in Chapter 10.

Construct Validity.   In the laboratory, we face questions about the extent to which independent and dependent variables truly match their intended theoretical constructs. For the independent variable, at times there are no problems in capturing the intended causal construct in a laboratory manipulation. Consider a study on the effects of persuasive messages delivered by print versus television. A laboratory manipulation in which some participants read messages and others see messages on videotape certainly seems to correspond in all relevant ways to the intended theoretical construct. Yet, at times the issue is more difficult. We might wish to investigate the effects of authority relationships on social interaction, for example, by bringing pairs of college students into the laboratory and assigning one to a "supervisor" role and the other to a "subordinate" role. But questions arise about how well this manipulation captures the theoretical construct of "authority" as it exists in organizations or other settings. The manipulation lacks such features as a history over time, actual control by the "supervisor" over significant outcomes for the "subordinate," differential access to organizational resources, and so on. For such reasons, we might wonder about the construct validity of some laboratory manipulations.

For the dependent variable, laboratory studies often rely on pencil-and-paper measures, which can be criticized from the viewpoint of construct validity. (Of course, much survey and field research is subject to the same criticism.) However, as discussed in Chapters 7 and 8, questionnaire measures can be constructed with good reliability and validity. In addition, laboratory research often uses other types of dependent variables, including response latencies, physiological activity, and observations of real behavior. In fact, the ability to arrange settings, tasks, and instruments (e.g., cameras or physiological monitoring equipment) to record behaviors of theoretical interest, instead of having to depend on participants' self-reports, is a significant advantage of the laboratory over most field settings.

How do we assess construct validity? As we describe in Chapters 2 and 8, any operationalization can be demonstrated to match its intended theoretical construct by showing that its associations with other variables follow theoretical predictions, both in the sense of convergent and discriminant validity. This strategy is as applicable in the laboratory as anywhere else. A good example of demonstrated convergent validity is found in Isen's (e.g., 1984) research on the effects of moods on memory and judgment. Across a number of studies, she induced positive moods in research participants by giving them gifts, offering them cookies and soda as they entered the laboratory, having them read a series of positive statements about themselves, and showing them comedy films. The research showed that all these manipulations had similar effects, laying to rest most concerns about the construct validity of each.

Note that the construct validity of a manipulation or dependent measure is not determined by its **mundane realism**, that is, the degree to which surface features of the manipulation or measure resemble objects or events outside the laboratory. Strictly speaking, the extent to which an operational definition resembles some other instance of a construct is irrelevant. Rather, construct validity is indicated by **experimental realism**, that is, the extent to which the manipulations or measures are truly perceived in the intended ways by research participants. Mundane realism is not a precondition for experimental realism.

For example, the construct validity of the manipulation of authority in Milgram's (1974) experiments on obedience depends on the extent to which research participants perceived the experimenter's authority as real (experimental realism). Its construct validity should be judged by the correspondence of its effects to theoretically expected patterns, not by its superficial resemblance to particular "real-life" instances of authority (mundane realism). The degree to which the number of shocks participants delivered to a confederate has construct validity as a measure of aggression cannot be assessed by considering how often people in real life give shocks to others when they are angry, but rather by comparing the results obtained with this measure, over a series of studies, with those that would be theoretically expected for a valid measure of aggression (Berkowitz & Donnerstein, 1982).

In sum, the construct validity of a laboratory operational definition cannot be assessed simply by examining the superficial aspects of the operational definition, for example, by asking whether it resembles anything that participants encounter in real life. Experimental realism is not the same as mundane realism. Nor can construct validity generally be assessed on the basis of the outcome of a single study. Instead, evidence of construct validity emerges as the results of multiple studies using the operational definition are found to concur with theoretical expectations: The empirical associations found using the operational definition match the theoretically predicted associations that the construct is expected to have.

In our view, the construct validity of laboratory manipulations and measures is the most important and most difficult issue to address in laboratory research. Questions about construct validity ordinarily cannot be answered definitively in the short run, in contrast to internal validity, which can in many cases be confidently attributed to a particular study. Construct validity can also be problematic more often in the laboratory than in field settings because operational definitions used in the laboratory typically are devised from simplifications or abstractions about a general situation of interest. With the researcher's creative act of abstraction and construction comes the obligation to assess the correspondence between the operation and the construct of interest.

External Validity.   As defined previously, external validity refers to the range of settings, populations, and the like to which the research results can be generalized or applied. As with construct validity, external validity is an empirical question. Unlike construct validity, which is important in all research, the importance of external validity depends greatly on the specific research goals. Two cases can be distinguished using labels previously introduced: particularistic versus universalistic research.

The goal of particularistic research is generalization from the laboratory or other research setting to a specific target setting and population. Research results are therefore of little use if they do not apply to the target setting. Thus, care is usually taken to make the research setting (and population and operational definitions of dependent and independent variables) as similar as possible to the target. Of course, absolute similarity cannot generally be attained, and an appeal to theory must be made to establish which variables are important and which ones are not. For example, the color of the walls in the research setting probably does not need to match the color of the walls in the setting of interest, unless theory or prior evidence demonstrates that wall color affects the phenomenon of interest. For particularistic research, external validity is a key goal, and researchers generally attempt to increase it by making consequential features of the research setting, population, and manipulations as similar as possible to those about which inferences are to be drawn.

In universalistic research, there is no specific target setting, population, and so on, to which researchers wish to generalize. Instead, the goal of the research is to test theoretically derived hypotheses. The issue of external validity therefore takes a different form. For example, a researcher might note that in a specific laboratory study a certain manipulation of frustration increases a certain measure of aggression by 9% in a given population. The researcher would be unjustified in extending this finding in quantitative detail to any larger population, for instance, by claiming that "frustration on the job increases the likelihood that parents will physically abuse their children by 9%." The nonrepresentative sampling of research participants (e.g., undergraduate volunteers) and other arbitrary aspects of the experimental manipulation and setting rule out this form of generalization. But such generalization is not the point of universalistic research. The research is intended to support or falsify theoretical predictions about the conditions under which frustration increases aggression.

In universalistic research, the external validity question takes this form: To what range of settings and populations does the theory apply? External validity is a property of the theory, not the research findings. From this perspective, consider the conclusions that could be drawn if a particular theoretical association were demonstrated in a laboratory study but was absent in a field setting: (1) The operational definitions of the theoretical constructs used in the laboratory research had poor construct validity. (2) The operational definitions in the field setting had poor construct validity. (3) The theory is inadequate, failing to specify one or more conditions that limit the range of situations in which the key association applies. The external validity of a theory in this sense is most clearly demonstrated by **replication**, that is, by reproducing the

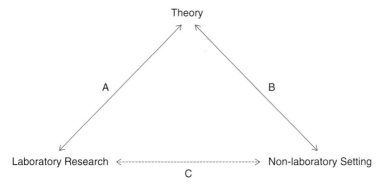

Figure 5.1 Schematic Illustrating the Association of Laboratory Research with Theory and Setting Outside the Laboratory.

finding across various settings, populations, and operational definitions of the theoretical constructs.

In short, once construct validity has been established, external validity questions for universalistic research are not questions about the research results per se but about the adequacy and completeness of the theory. In the case of universalistic research, generalization from the laboratory to other settings and populations is indirect. The research is used to test and support a theory; the theory is used to generate predictions for other settings and populations of interest. This principle is schematically illustrated in Figure 5.1. The links, A and B, correspond respectively to the construct validity of the research operations and to the predictive power and completeness of the theory. Link C, the extent of direct correspondence or similarity between the laboratory operational definitions and elements of the target situation, is of little or no importance in the logic of universalistic research; however, as noted earlier, C is the key link in particularistic research and is appropriate to emphasize in evaluating the external validity of research that investigates phenomena as they occur in specific settings or populations.

"Artificiality" of the Laboratory

Some criticize laboratory research for being artificial, pointing to differences between events and tasks in the laboratory and those in the "real world." Laboratory research is artificial; it is used precisely because it permits the creation or construction of settings, tasks, and manipulations that are suited to achieving the research goals. As the earlier discussion indicates, however, resemblance to events in everyday life is not a criterion for the evaluation of universalistic research.

The most problematic form of validity for laboratory research that is intended to test a theory is construct validity, which is established by careful comparisons between research results and theoretical expectations, not by examining the superficial attributes of the research operations. The critic is inappropriately applying to universalistic research a standard that is suited for evaluating particularistic research. However, artificiality can contribute to one particular kind of threat to construct validity, demand characteristics. This concern is discussed later in the chapter.

The message to critics, then, is to look beneath the surface. A seemingly artificial manipulation might turn out to be a valid operational definition of the intended theoretical construct – or it might not. The question is an empirical one, not to be settled by pointing at superficial attributes of the research but by evaluation of the results of research, using the operational definition in question.

Overcoming Threats to Validity of Laboratory Research

Laboratory research is subject to many of the same threats to validity as other types of research. The main strength of the laboratory is its conduciveness to randomized experiments, which rule out the most significant threats to internal validity. The most significant weaknesses of laboratory research involve construct validity, which can be threatened by several factors, including experimenter expectancies and demand characteristics.

Experimenter Expectancy.   Imagine that an experimenter asks research participants in a laboratory study to judge photos of people's faces for a study of perception. The experimenter shows them a series of photos, one at a time, and asks them to judge how much each face reflects "success" or "failure." The students do not know, but the experimenter was previously told that people generally judge these particular photos as highly successful (or in another condition, that they are generally judged failures). The remarkable findings of experiments like these, pioneered by Rosenthal and his collaborators (Rosenthal, 1976; Rosenthal & Rosnow, 1969; Rosnow & Rosenthal, 1997), demonstrate that **experimenter expectancies** can influence research participants' actual responses. When the experimenter was told that the photos were generally judged as successful, research participants rated the photos as more successful than when the experimenter was told that the photos were generally judged as failures – even though the label of success or failure was randomly assigned.

These hypothesis-confirming results do not occur because experimenters (or participants) consciously attempt to bias the results (Rosenthal, 1969). Instead, the influence stems from subtle, nonverbal cues that are not under the experimenter's conscious control but that can nevertheless influence participants' behavior. For example, studies have shown that differential vocal emphasis can elicit expectancy-consistent ratings from participants (Adair & Epstein, 1968; Duncan & Rosenthal, 1968).

Laboratory research is particularly susceptible to experimenter bias for two reasons. First, researchers are ordinarily in direct communication with participants, which is less often the case in survey or field research. Second, in the isolated and controlled environment of the laboratory, participants might be particularly attentive to subtle aspects of the researcher's behavior or the setting, trying to discover the purpose of the study. When the influence is such that participants give "correct" responses, that is, responses that would be evaluated positively by others, the responses are said to be influenced by **social desirability**. Such biases constitute a threat to construct validity, for the experimental manipulation might represent not only a manipulation of the

Table 5.1	Strategies for Coping with Experimenter Expectancy Effects

Strategies that Prevent Expectancy Effects
- Keep experimenters unaware of participants' conditions.
- Eliminate experimenter–participant interaction, e.g., conduct study on the Internet or have participant respond to instructions delivered by computer or audiotape.

Strategies that Minimize Expectancy Effects
- Minimize experimenter–participant interaction, e.g., deliver crucial instructions, manipulations, or measures on paper or computer.
- Use multiple experimenters within sessions, one to deliver the manipulation who is not unaware of the participants' experimental condition(s) and one to administer the dependent variable who is kept unaware of participants' experimental condition(s).
- Keep experimenters unaware of participants' conditions as long as possible.
- Keep experimenters unaware of experimental hypotheses.
- Use multiple experimenters across sessions.
- Train experimenters carefully and emphasize importance of adhering to standardization.

Strategies that Permit the Detection and Assessment of Expectancy Effects
- Observe experimenters' behavior, either online or through videotaping.
- Adopt an expectancy control group design.

intended construct but also a confounding variable. We could never be certain whether the manipulation or the researcher's expectations produced the results.

Table 5.1 lists a number of strategies that can be used to prevent or minimize expectancy effects. First are strategies that would prevent such effects. The most effective one is to keep experimenters unaware of the experimental condition that participants are in. Consider a study designed to test the hypothesis that people in a good mood judge others more positively than do people in a neutral or bad mood. If experimenters are aware that participants are in the good-mood condition, they might unintentionally give nonverbal signals that lead participants to make positive judgments. If experimenters do not know which condition participants are in, there is no way that their cues can bias the results. Experimenters can know the hypothesis that is being tested, but without knowing what condition participants are in, the experimenter cannot have firm expectations for participants and thus cannot bias the results.

Eliminating *all* experimenter–participant contact is the other surefire strategy for preventing experimenter expectancy effects. If the experimenter is not present, expectancy effects cannot occur. Internet studies, for example, eliminate experimenter expectancy altogether. Experimenter contact can also be avoided through the practice of having participants show up at the laboratory to find signs instructing them to start a tape recorder or computer program that delivers further instructions, or having all instructions in writing. Such procedures have obvious disadvantages. There is no way to answer any questions participants might have. There also is no quality control over responding, including no way to ensure that the intended participant is the person who actually provides the responses. Lastly, written or computer-administered instructions often are less motivating and have less impact on participants, thus reducing experimental realism and response quality. For these reasons, automated data gathering is not used often and is probably appropriate only for short, simple studies.

Table 5.1 also lists strategies that can minimize, but not prevent, experimenter expectancy effects. Limiting experimenter–participant contact reduces the opportunities for experimenters' nonverbal cues to influence participants' behavior. Having crucial instructions or manipulations handed to participants on a sheet of paper or delivered by computer also enhances the standardization of procedures, as it can be guaranteed that instructions or manipulations are identical across participants.

Although keeping experimenters unaware of treatment condition is the best strategy for avoiding expectancy effects, it is not always possible. Some manipulations must be delivered orally and others cannot be enacted without the experimenter's awareness. There are nonetheless creative ways of minimizing expectancy effects, including the use of two experimenters, one to deliver the manipulation and the other, who remains unaware of what manipulation was given, to collect the dependent variable. Harris, Milich, Corbitt, Hoover, and Brady (1992), for example, delivered both experimental manipulations and dependent measures orally because their participants were children whose reading and writing skills were uncertain. To minimize the potential for expectancy effects, one experimenter briefly delivered the experimental manipulations and another, unaware of condition and the goals of the study, gathered responses to the dependent measures.

An alternative strategy, when the use of multiple experimenters is not feasible, is to keep the experimenter unaware of the experimental condition of the participant as long as possible. In the mood and judgment study example discussed earlier, the experimenter could remain unaware while obtaining informed consent and delivering the cover story. When the manipulation is to be delivered, the experimenter would open an envelope revealing the participant's experimental condition and then insert the proper stimulus videotape to show. This solution works best for studies in which there is little need for experimenter–participant interaction during and after the manipulation.

Another strategy is to keep experimenters unaware of the research hypotheses. The experimenter could be aware that a person is in the good-mood condition but would not have been told that a good mood is hypothesized to lead to more positive interpersonal judgments. However, experimenters might form their own expectations. Even expectations that do not correspond to the research hypotheses can be problematic. Having multiple experimenters running fewer sessions each makes it less likely that experimenters will generate experimental hypotheses and less likely that they will pick up on the subtle operant conditioning strategies that lead participants to provide the expected results. It also increases the generalizability of the research findings. But it also introduces another source of variability that might reduce the magnitude of the treatment effect.

A final strategy for minimizing expectancy effects is to train experimenters carefully, emphasizing the need for standardization in all aspects of the experimental procedure. Training and standardization generally increase control and reduce error in laboratory research, but might only reduce, rather than prevent, expectancy effects.

It is simply impossible for experimenters to continuously monitor and control the subtle nonverbal behaviors through which expectations might be communicated.

Two additional strategies do not prevent expectancy effects, but allow researchers to determine whether they are occurring and, if so, their magnitude. The first involves monitoring experimenters' behavior, either during the experimental sessions or afterwards by watching videotapes of the sessions. Naïve observers could rate the experimenter's behavior on relevant dimensions, and analyses could be done to see whether experimenter behavior varied systematically across conditions. For example, do experimenters look happier and smile more when they interact with participants in the good-mood condition compared to participants in the bad-mood condition? This strategy might reduce expectancy effects as well, because experimenters may adhere more closely to standardization if they know their behavior is being scrutinized. When observations are made as the study is being run, experimenters who appear to be biased can be retrained or replaced. When observations are made after the fact, it is too late to salvage the study, but at least the researcher has gained important knowledge about the source of participants' behavior.

The second strategy for detecting and assessing the magnitude of expectancy effects is to use an **expectancy control group design**, also known as a balanced placebo design. In this design, experimenters' expectancies are manipulated as an independent variable along with the major independent variable in a factorial design. (Factorial designs are described in Chapter 10.) A classic example (Burnham, 1966, cited in Rosnow & Rosenthal, 1997, pp. 60–61) underscores the potential for expectancy effects to occur. Twenty-three experimenters each ran a rat through a maze. Half of the rats had a brain lesion; the other half did not. In addition, about half of the experimenters were told that their rat's status (i.e., whether it had a brain lesion) was opposite of what it actually was. The dependent measure was performance on the maze task. Analyses revealed that rats with brain lesions ran the maze more slowly than did rats without lesions, which tells us that it is better to have an intact brain. The surprising result was the effect of experimenter expectancy: Rats whose experimenters *thought* they had lesions ran the maze more slowly than did rats whose experimenters thought they did not. Moreover, this effect was slightly larger than the effect due to actual brain lesions. In other words, what the experimenter believed to be the case affected rats' maze performance more than what actually was the case. This basic result is consistent with other research in which this design has been used; that is, the effect of experimenter expectancy can be significant and comparable in magnitude to the effect of the theoretical variable.

Unlike other strategies, the expectancy control group design allows a precise estimate of the magnitude of an expectancy effect and a comparison to the effect of the independent variable. The design is not without limitations, however. First, it can be used only when it is possible to mislead experimenters about the experimental condition of the participants. Second, the design reveals only whether expectancy effects occurred; it does not prevent them from happening. Third, the design requires researchers to gather twice as much data for the sole purpose of detecting an effect that they do not want. Consequently, the expectancy control group design is underutilized and tends to be restricted to those research areas in which expectancies are of substantive interest, such as the large literature on behavioral effects of alcohol, in which both experimenter and participant expectancies about the participant's consumption of alcohol are often manipulated (George, Gilmore, & Stappenbeck, 2012).

Demand Characteristics.   Imagine students walking into a laboratory to participate in a study. In a setting with few if any familiar elements, and confronted with a novel set of tasks, they might be particularly attentive to elements of the environment as they try to make sense of the situation. They may even be motivated to figure out what behaviors would make them appear psychologically "normal" or more likely to be evaluated positively by the researcher. This is the key idea behind the notion of **demand characteristics**: that participants pick up subtle cues in the researcher's behavior, the task, or the setting, which then influence their behavior. Demand characteristics undermine the validity of research because participants are not responding as they naturally would to the experimental manipulations or stimuli.

Orne's (1969) classic work demonstrated how even innocuous studies can be affected by demand characteristics. His interest in demand characteristics grew out of an experience he had in his research on hypnosis. Orne (1962) wanted to create a task that would be so tedious and dull that a nonhypnotized person would refuse to do it. So he brought participants into the laboratory and presented each of them with a huge stack of paper that had hundreds of thousands of simple arithmetic problems (adding two-digit numbers). Orne told participants to work on the problems until he told them to stop. *Five and a half hours later* Orne himself gave up and told participants to stop. When Orne made the task even more pointless by instructing participants to tear each sheet of paper into no fewer than 32 pieces after they had finished it, participants kept working for hours until Orne finally told them to stop. What could account for participants' ceaseless toil? Orne (1962) concluded that participants were reacting to the demand characteristics of the situation. Because the researcher obviously was not interested in mathematical ability (the problems were too easy, not to mention that the pages were being torn up before the researcher could see them), participants concluded the study had to be about something else. And the "something else" they came up with was task persistence. No one wanted to score low on a measure of task persistence, so they all kept working until they were told to stop.

There are two morals to this story:

- Research participants actively search for meaning when they participate in an experiment (think how much easier it is to study rocks!). If the researcher does not provide them with the meaning of the experiment, or if the researcher's explanation contradicts what they actually experience, participants will generate their own meaning.
- The meaning participants generate is not random. Rather, participants react to the demand characteristics of the situation in similar ways. The vast majority of Orne's (1962) participants concluded that the boring task was a test of task persistence. And therein lies the insidious danger of demand characteristics: Because they lead participants to behave in systematic ways, they undermine the construct validity of the experiment.

Demand characteristics can never be eliminated. Unless participants go through the study completely unaware, incurious, and unquestioning, they will react to *something* in the experimental setting and that something will influence their behavior. Thus, the strategy for experimenters is not to eliminate demand characteristics but to carefully control them. The first step is to identify the demand characteristics that are salient in a given study. This can be accomplished through **pilot testing**, in which individuals from the same population as the eventual participants are led through the procedures and periodically queried as to what they think the hypothesis of the study is and which features of the setting led them to that hypothesis. Researchers should not use their own reactions to the laboratory setting as a substitute for more time-consuming pilot testing, as they are too familiar with the experiment and its goals and thus are unable to view the procedures and setting as naïve participants would.

Second, researchers need to attend carefully to the details of the laboratory setting and procedures. Disguising the independent variable is often the key, for example, by exposing each participant to only one level of the independent variable rather than several or by making the independent variable appear to be an event unrelated to the experiment. Examples of some methods researchers have used to reduce the effects of demand characteristics are given in the next section. But demand characteristics remain a concern in any research in which participants are aware of their participation, even in non-laboratory research settings. It would be rare for people to complete a survey questionnaire or to perform tasks in the presence of a researcher without asking themselves the question, "What are they trying to find out here?" and the almost inevitable sequel, "What should I say?" or "How should I act?"

Elements of a Laboratory Study

Practical advice on a number of aspects of laboratory research has been developed and refined by experienced researchers over the years. Here we present some basic suggestions and guidelines.

Setting

The physical context of the research setting, though easy to overlook, can play an important role in influencing participants' reactions and behavior. However, the central element of the setting is participants' overall interpretation of "what is going on" in the research. Ordinarily, researchers do not allow participants to construct an interpretation freely but give them one, commonly called a **cover story**. This term suggests that the interpretation provided is often misleading or deceptive, and sometimes it is. More often, though, researchers give participants a truthful but nonspecific account of the research purposes.

For example, in a study focusing on the helping behavior of participants in response to a staged emergency, the cover story would be quite simple but deceptive: Participants would simply be told that their task is to complete a questionnaire about life in college. While they are doing so, smoke might begin to filter into the room. In an investigation of the effects of stereotypes on judgments of individuals, participants might be told that the researcher is interested in how people form impressions of others and that they will be given information about individuals and then asked to answer some questions about them. This example of a cover story is truthful but overly general; the researcher accurately conveys the general focus of the study but does not mention that the key manipulation, which is embedded in the information given to participants, is the individual's ethnicity. Finally, studies of persuasive communications often use deceptive cover stories to prevent participants from focusing on how they "should" react to the stimulus materials. They might be told, for instance, that they are going to watch a videotape of a speaker delivering a message and are to judge it for technical quality or for the speaker's skill and eloquence in conveying the message.

In all cases, the primary purpose of a cover story is to give research participants the sense that they know what is going on, an overall framework in which to interpret the events and tasks called for by the research. A cover story is successful to the extent that participants are satisfied that they understand the research purpose (so they have no need to speculate about what the researcher really wants) and they remain interested and motivated. For both ethical and practical reasons, it is best to avoid deception when possible. But in some instances, it is difficult to imagine how the research could be conducted without some measure of deception.

The details of the physical setting can bolster the cover story. For example, in an investigation of the effects of anticipated group discussion on people's opinions or attitudes, the cover story would focus on the upcoming discussion. If the researcher simply told participants there would be a group discussion after they complete a questionnaire, participants might believe it. But if participants are taken through a room containing a table surrounded by several chairs, hear sounds that suggest the presence of other participants in adjoining cubicles, and see other people's books and coats in the research waiting room, belief in the cover story becomes much more likely. Similarly, research on the effects of fear might involve telling participants they will receive electric shocks. The chances of arousing fear would be increased by allowing participants to notice an impressive electrical apparatus or by having the researcher dressed in a white laboratory coat.

In summary, the setting for a laboratory study ideally provides a framework (1) that enables participants to interpret the events they will be going through and that prevents them from generating their own interpretations and thus the effects of demand characteristics on their behavior, and (2) that keeps participants interested and motivated. Physical details, task instructions, and above all a sensible, coherent cover story are essential for these purposes.

Independent Variable

Laboratory research most often is experimental in design; the independent variable is manipulated and participants are randomly assigned to conditions. Of course, non-experimental laboratory studies are sometimes performed, as in observations of how different types of people (e.g., people high and low on power motivation) respond to a laboratory-constructed situation (e.g., a group discussion). In such cases the independent variable is a property of the participants rather than a manipulation. In this section we focus on the special considerations involved in creating a laboratory manipulation of an independent variable.

The first requisite for a manipulation is construct validity or experimental realism (Wilson et al., 2010). How that is attained differs for impact and judgment studies. In an impact study, the believability of the manipulation is crucial; a carefully constructed cover story, corroborating physical details, and skillful acting by the experimenter might all be necessary. If the research goal is to make participants angry to investigate the effects of anger on interpersonal evaluations, it might be decided that a negative comment by a **confederate**, an accomplice of the experimenter posing as a participant, is the best way to accomplish it. A cover story must be constructed to make the delivery of the comment believable – perhaps that the research topic concerns peer evaluations and that participants will write a paragraph that will be evaluated by a fellow student. The stage has now been set for the manipulation, a direct negative evaluation of the participant's writing. Obviously, the details could vary greatly, depending on the specific nature of the manipulation, and the researcher can be quite creative.

In other cases, a manipulation is embedded in the experimental stimuli rather than in an event that participants experience. For example, Norton, Sommers, Apfelbaum, Pura, and Ariely (2006) conducted a set of studies that examined the effects of a colorblind ideology on Whites' strategies for appearing unprejudiced. In one study, each White participant was assigned to interact with a Black or White partner who was actually a confederate. (Analyses indicated that the confederates performed the task similarly.) Participants and their partners were given photographs that varied on several dimensions, including whether the person in the photo was Black or White. Participants' goal was to determine which photo their partners were looking at by asking as few yes/no questions as possible. Analyses revealed that participants were less likely to ask about the race of the person when their partners were Black even though not asking impaired their performance. Further, participants who avoided the topic of race made less eye contact with and appeared less friendly toward their Black partners.

In judgment studies, manipulations are often similarly embedded in stimulus materials that participants study and evaluate, and making the materials believable is critical. For instance, if the research concerns the effects of job applicants' gender on evaluations of their suitability for a job, materials (perhaps in the format of résumés) would be prepared that differed only in that one respect: the applicant's gender. As in the study above, the rest of the material on the résumé serves mainly as a context for the gender manipulation; its effects on judgments are somewhat beside the point, for it does not vary from one experimental condition to another. Using several different résumés allows one to establish that the effects of the gender manipulation are relatively constant regardless of the other information.

In the case of judgment studies, it might not be important for participants to think that the résumés were provided by real job applicants, although some researchers might prefer to use a deceptive cover story including this statement. As long as the materials are plausible, participants generally are able to make judgments and evaluations as if they describe real people, events or situations, much in the same way that the psychological impact of a well-written novel does not depend on readers' belief that it describes actually existing persons and events.

Across all types of manipulations, unintentional confounding must be avoided. A **confound** occurs when the levels of the independent variable vary directly with some other, nonessential factor(s). For example, if two experimenters are available, one might be tempted to divide the participants between them by condition, but it would be extremely unwise to do so. The manipulation that is intended to constitute the sole difference between conditions would be confounded with other differences between the experimenters, for example, their treatment of research participants. Of course, this confound is quite obvious and would not be seen in any experienced social scientist's work. Other equally problematic, but less obvious, confounds are more often encountered. Consider, for example, manipulating a job applicant's gender by means of a photograph. A photograph of a woman or man could be attached to otherwise identical résumés to create stimulus materials for two different conditions. However, target gender would be confounded with any number of unique attributes of the photos, such as the physical attractiveness of the targets, whether they are smiling, and their backgrounds. The solution to problems like these is to use more than one representative of each desired level of the manipulation (e.g., five photographs of women and five of men). Irrelevant characteristics of the photographs would then vary within as well as between conditions, lessening the problem of confounding and allowing the researcher to separate out the variability due to differences across photos.

A question that can arise in any type of experimental design is whether to expose each participant to more than one condition. As noted in Chapter 10, the advantages are that fewer participants are needed and statistical power and precision are greater. The disadvantage is that participants who see more than one condition are more likely to determine the purpose of the experiment, which may affect their responses. In some cases, it makes no sense for participants to experience more than one condition. We would not want to stage a serious "accident" to measure participants' helping behavior and then turn around and stage a less serious one for the same participants. Nor could we show the same participant an identical résumé with a different photograph. The decision to expose participants to multiple conditions has to be made with careful thought about the specifics of each research project.

Finally, participants in any experiment must understand what they are to do and pay attention to the stimulus materials, the manipulation, and their task. The instructions that participants receive at the outset are the key means for reaching these goals. A researcher who states instructions too briefly or not clearly enough risks gathering meaningless data from participants who do not understand or do not care. Repetition of key elements of the instructions, examples, probes to make sure that the participants understand, and pilot testing the entire experimental procedure, from cover story through instructions to manipulation, are all strategies that can be used to improve the quality of data that are ultimately obtained. Participants in the pilot test can be questioned about their reactions, their understanding of the task, their belief in the cover story, and so on. Actual data gathering should not begin until pilot testing indicates that the procedure works as intended.

We have focused in this section on independent variables that are experimentally manipulated and to which participants are randomly assigned. If participants are randomly assigned to conditions, we should end up with roughly equal numbers of participants in each of the conditions, or cells of the design. However, there can be differences in cell sizes, especially if the number of conditions is high and the sample size relatively low. Such disparities are more problematic when another independent variable or blocking factor is used. A variation of random assignment, randomly assigning participants in blocks, can be used to assure equal cell sizes for any factor or combination of factors. The general strategy involves identifying the total number of conditions to which participants will be assigned (e.g., four) and then randomly assigning that number of participants (i.e., the first four participants) to all (four) conditions and then beginning again with the next (four) participants. So, for example, in the case of four conditions, the second four participants would be randomly assigned such that one participant would be in each of the four conditions. Of course, once all but one of the participants in a block are assigned, the last participant would be automatically assigned to whatever condition remained. This procedure ensures equal numbers of participants across conditions, assuming that the total sample size is an even multiple of the number of conditions. When another independent variable to which participants are not randomly assigned is involved (e.g., gender), the procedure can be adapted to assure equal cell sizes – simply randomize by blocks separately for each level of that variable (e.g., randomize by blocks separately for men and women). Such procedures ensure that one does not by chance end up with, for example, few or even no participants in a particular condition.

Another practical issue involving random assignment emerges when participants take part in a laboratory experiment in groups. For instance, if the conditions are defined simply by variations in stimulus materials, the researcher might recruit as many participants as there are chairs in the room in which the study is to take place. In such situations, it is desirable for all experimental conditions to be represented in each group. Otherwise, any special properties of that group's experience (e.g., the fact that many members of the group were annoyed by an inattentive participant who did not listen to the instructions and had to have them repeated) would be confounded with condition. Of course, at times this representation is impossible because the procedure obviously differs between experimental conditions (e.g., participants in two conditions are shown different films as a means of inducing happy and sad moods or the task involves sorting cards). But in most judgment studies it is easy to randomly distribute different versions of the materials within each group of participants who participate together, thereby ensuring that any effects of experimenter, time of day, or other session-specific differences are randomly distributed across all conditions. Further, other strategies may be used when differences in procedure would be obvious to participants, for example, presenting films on individual computer monitors with headphones, using cubicles so that participants cannot see what other research participants are doing, or conducting the study in very small groups and statistically evaluating potential group effects.

Manipulation Checks

As part of the pretesting procedure, and in many cases during the actual study, researchers ask questions – termed **manipulation checks** – to assess whether the manipulations had the intended effects on participants. For example, if the manipulation is intended to induce anxiety, participants could be asked to complete a mood checklist, including such terms as "anxious," "fearful," and "afraid." Manipulation checks are desirable for two reasons:

- They help establish the construct validity of the manipulation. If the manipulation has the theoretically predicted pattern of effects on manipulation checks, a stronger case can be made that it truly operationally defined the intended construct.
- They are helpful in understanding what happened when a study does not produce the predicted results. Manipulation checks help researchers determine whether (1) the manipulation did not work or (2) the manipulation worked but failed to produce the predicted effects on the dependent variable. The first possibility suggests the desirability of repeating the experiment with a stronger or better manipulation, whereas the second possibility means that the results did not support the hypothesis, which may occur for a variety of (sometimes related) reasons, for example, a lack of statistical power, poor dependent measures, a manipulation that was too weak to affect the dependent measure, chance, or that the research hypothesis was wrong and no such effect truly exists. Manipulation checks help researchers evaluate the situation and decide how to proceed.

Some researchers advocate using manipulation checks as a rationale for omitting participants from the sample prior to analysis. The logic is that if a mood manipulation, for example, is supposed to put participants in a happy mood, we really do not want to include them in that condition unless they are truly happy. If by some chance a participant is assigned to the happy condition but, just prior to arriving at the laboratory, had terminated a five-year-long relationship and hence is feeling miserable despite the funny movie, the manipulation check will reveal that the person is not feeling happy. Is it then a fair test of the hypothesis to keep that participant in the happy condition? Some researchers argue that a true test of the hypothesis is whether happy moods affect the dependent variable of interest, and the movie manipulation is simply the vehicle by which happy moods are achieved. As such, they argue further, science is better served if that person were dropped from the study. Other researchers argue that manipulation checks are not an adequate basis for dropping participants, for it may invalidate random assignment.

Our position is that because it is often tempting to drop participants who give us "inconvenient" data, manipulation checks should be used only rarely, if at all, to justify omission of participants. And in such rare cases, the analyses should be done twice, once using all participants and once omitting any participants with offending manipulation check data. Ideally, identical patterns of statistically significant results will be obtained, and the researchers need only indicate so in their written report. Should there be discrepancies across the two sets of analyses, with the most common case being nonsignificant findings when all participants are included and significant findings after omitting participants, researchers should report the outcomes of both analyses. The chore of deciding which set of analyses to believe then falls on readers whose decisions will likely depend on concerns about internal validity; dropping participants undermines the purpose of random assignment to conditions and thus internal validity.

A related issue concerns the use of manipulation checks for **internal analyses**. In internal analyses, manipulation check responses are not used as a basis for dropping participants. Instead, the manipulation check becomes an independent variable that is related to the dependent variable instead of using participants' randomly assigned conditions. Using the mood manipulation example again, participants would be randomly assigned to watch the happy or sad movie. A manipulation check would be administered, and instead of using the two-level treatment variable in analyses, participants' ratings on the manipulation check mood scale (e.g., 1 to 7) would be used. The logic is that it makes more sense to use individuals' "true" mood states, as reflected by their self-reports in the manipulation check, to predict their subsequent impressions.

A major drawback to such internal analyses, however, is that doing them transforms the study from a true experiment into a correlational study, with all the interpretational ambiguities that a correlational study involves. When hypotheses are tested with respect to participants' randomly assigned treatment conditions, researchers can conclude that a significant effect of the independent variable *caused* differences in judgment. But when internal analyses are performed, even if the correlation is consistent with the hypothesis, the researchers can conclude only that the independent and dependent variables are related. The cost in terms of increased threats to internal validity often outweigh the benefits of conducting internal analyses or omitting participants whose manipulation check responses indicate that the experimental treatment did not have the intended effect. Manipulation checks are thus most useful during the pilot-testing stages of research or to provide evidence that the manipulations were effective.

Finally, we need to acknowledge that manipulation checks may arouse participants' suspicion by alerting them to the independent variable. For example, in research on interpersonal expectancy effects, participants might be told something that is not true about their interaction partners, for example, that the partner scored either extraverted or introverted. The purpose of such research is to see how the perceiver's expectancies about the target affect the interaction and, in particular, whether the expectancies elicit self-fulfilling prophecies. For such a study to work, participants must pay attention to the expectancy manipulation and believe their partners to be either extraverted or introverted. However, a manipulation check that is administered prior to interaction with the target ("On a 7-point scale, how extraverted do you think the target will be?") could cause participants to wonder why the researchers are concerned about their partners' extraversion. Participants who previously would have accepted the expectancy manipulation at face value without thinking twice might now suspect that the manipulation was not true. Researchers might therefore wish either to avoid using manipulation checks when the independent variable is deceptive or use them only during pilot testing.

Exercise: Manipulation checks and multiple dependent variables

We put these two types of measures together for an exercise because they can create the same complex situation. First, if we include more than a single dependent variable, what additional complications does it produce? Ideally, additional measures allow us to get at different aspects of the phenomenon that we are trying to study. But what if one dependent measure is significant and another is not? What should we conclude? Discuss what you might do in interpreting your findings. What factors might you consider? An extension of this situation is one where you add a manipulation check to see if your treatment worked as you had hoped. But what if the dependent variable is significant and the manipulation check is not? It suggests that the manipulation was not successful, for the groups did not differ as expected. Discuss what you might do here and what factors you might consider in deciding how to interpret your findings.

Dependent Variable

The construct validity of the dependent variable should be developed and assessed with the same care as the manipulations. All too often, however, a carefully executed experiment is weakened by a dependent variable that is a one- or two-item measure having questionable reliability and validity. In Chapters 7 and 8 we discuss some basic aspects of measurement that apply to laboratory dependent variables as well as surveys.

As we have noted, multiple measures are better than a single measure, and the greater the diversity among the measures (as long as they tap the same theoretical construct) the better, because error and invalidity in one measure will be unlikely to be shared with a different measure. Common patterns of findings on different measures strengthen confidence in the study's construct validity: the inference that the results are produced by the intended theoretical construct rather than by extraneous factors.

There can, however, be too much of a good thing: Just as we would recommend that researchers not stake an entire study on a single dependent variable, we also would recommend that researchers not make the opposite error of including too many dependent variables. It is tempting to add dependent variables, on the logic that it only takes a minute or two to have participants complete another measure, and if a certain measure does not work out, another measure might. The problem is that having lots of dependent variables increases the possibility of some results being significant by chance alone, a problem that is termed **capitalizing on chance**, and there is no way of knowing which results are genuine and which are statistical flukes (i.e., not likely to replicate). Having a large number of dependent variables also increases the possibility of inexplicable patterns of findings – what does it mean if we obtained the predicted results for dependent variables A, B, and C but not for D, E, and F? Does it mean our theory is not correct? Not necessarily, but it is not as reassuring as if we had collected only A, B, and C and gotten significant results for all three. In sum, it is generally best to use two or three highly reliable and well-validated dependent measures.

Most laboratory studies use self-report measures; the great majority of judgment studies fall into this category. Many considerations are important when self-report measures are used, including the thoughtful wording of questions and careful conceptualization of what is to be asked. For instance, participants can be asked to report on their judgments, experiences, past behaviors, beliefs, memories, or attitudes (e.g., "What were you thinking about when you were rating the textbook?") but cannot be expected to make reliable inferences about their behaviors (Ericsson & Simon, 1984; Nisbett & Wilson, 1977). Therefore, questions such as "Why did you behave as you did?" which call for inferences should be avoided, unless the research concerns people's theories about the causes of their behaviors. These types of measurement issues are described in more detail in Chapter 7.

At times, laboratory dependent measures go somewhat beyond self-report, as usually defined, to elicit people's willingness to make commitments concerning future behavior. For instance, if a particular attitude change technique is hypothesized to increase people's motivation to help the poor, the dependent measure might be based on a sign-up sheet in which participants actually commit themselves to some number of hours of community service over the next month (ranging from 0 hours to 40 hours, say). Such measures are sometimes termed **behavioroid**, as they seem to fall somewhere in between a pencil-and-paper report of how much participants care about the poor and an actual behavioral measure based on observations of participants' volunteer behavior over an extended period of time. They do not have the concreteness and realism of behavioral observations (for participants make a commitment that they might not keep), but they are vastly easier to measure. This type of procedure sometimes involves deception: Participants sign up for some activity, believing that they are making a true commitment, which is essential for this type of measurement, but the experimenter has no intention of holding participants to it and terminates the research after the measure is completed. Of course, in some instances it would be ethically superior if researchers avoided deception and took participants' commitment seriously, for example, by referring them to a community agency that actually needs volunteers.

Non-self-report measures can be broadly categorized as observational or behavioral, but many distinct types of observation are used in laboratory research. Usually, research participants are given an opportunity to perform some behavior, and observers or recording devices record what they do. Research on small group interaction or nonverbal behavior would typically use such methods. Observations of this sort are not much different in the laboratory than in the field, except that the laboratory setting can make it easier to arrange for the appropriate type of observation, with one-way mirrors, carefully placed video cameras, and the like. The issues involved in the use of observation are described in Chapter 13.

Other measures used in some laboratory studies are observational in that they do not depend on participants' reports about their internal states but make use of tasks that participants are instructed to perform. They might be called **performance measures**. One example is research on goal setting and performance in which people are induced to set different types of goals and then to perform some task as well as they can for a given period of time (Locke & Latham, 2006). Patterns of performance demonstrate which types of goal setting are most effective. Implicit measures are another example. In social cognition research, for example, the way information is organized in memory can be inferred from the type of information that participants recall and the order in which they recall it, and attitudes can be inferred from response latencies, that is, how quickly participants make judgments (Gawronski & Payne, 2010). As these examples suggest, performance measures can be less susceptible than other types of measures to demand characteristics or other social desirability effects.

With any type of dependent measure, however, it might be necessary to disguise either its existence (e.g., a hidden camera) or its purpose (e.g., a questionnaire presented as being from an unrelated experiment). Disguise can prevent demand characteristics or guesses about the purpose of the research. For example, consider an experiment on attitude change. Reading a persuasive message on some topic followed by a questionnaire about attitudes relevant to that topic would be reactive, leading participants to wonder whether the "right" response is to agree with the message they read to show consistency, firmness by not changing their original views, and so on. Any naturalness in answering the question would be lost. Instead, researchers can embed questions on the key topic in a longer questionnaire covering diverse topics and label it "Social and Political Attitudes" or something equally broad. Alternatively, researchers can represent the purpose of the question as something other than what it actually is. For instance, the cover story in some studies on attitude change is that the research concerns the audio or video quality of the presentation (the persuasive message). Researchers can then say to participants that people's attitudes about the content of the message might influence their ratings and that to control for this possibility the researchers would like to know what participants' opinions are. Of course, deceptions such as these should be used only when necessary and participants should be fully debriefed regarding the deception, as described in Chapter 3.

As this section suggests, the dependent measures used in laboratory research are diverse. But in all cases, the underlying goal is to use measures that are high in reliability and validity, which can be accomplished by employing multiple measures, giving clear instructions and eliminating distractions, and eliminating – or at least minimizing – demand characteristics.

Debriefing

Debriefing ordinarily involves a two-way exchange of information in an interview with participants after the study is concluded, a process that is important for several reasons:

- If the experiment involved any deception or other stressful procedures, the researcher can ensure that all participants leave in a psychologically positive state.

- Debriefing can help make participation in research an educational experience; learning how and why research is conducted is often the most valuable payoff participants receive in return for their help.
- Researchers can learn from their participants whether the procedures, instructions, and tasks were clear; whether the manipulations were perceived as intended; and whether participants formulated hypotheses about the purpose of the experiment and tried to behave accordingly.

It is generally most natural to begin the debriefing by inviting participants to ask any questions they might have. Then participants can be asked to comment on matters that are important from the researcher's viewpoint, for example, the comprehensibility of the instructions. Finally, the researcher gives a detailed description of the methods and purpose of the study so that participants understand why the experiment was conducted in the way it was. Often, participants do not have the background knowledge to understand the details of the research hypotheses, but it is almost always possible – and desirable – to convey the key ideas in terms that are meaningful to most people.

For research that involves deception, special procedures are important, both for the researcher's and the participant's sake. The researcher generally wants to find out whether participants were suspicious about the particular deception that was used or other aspects of the study. A **funnel questioning** technique generally works best. That is, the researcher initially asks general questions, such as "What do you think the study was about?" and "Did you think there may have been more to the experiment than meets the eye?" The questions then become increasingly narrow, ending with questions focused on the specific deception, such as "Did you suspect that the questionnaire we said was unrelated was actually a key part of this research?" The disadvantages of beginning with a specific question or, even worse, simply telling participants that they have been deceived are that (1) participants might feel naïve or foolish to be told so directly that they were deceived and thus (2) to protect their self-image, they might say, "Of course, I knew it all along." This response prevents one from identifying participants who really had reasonably accurate suspicions.

Sensitive researchers make a special point of explaining why deception was used and convey to participants that it was not undertaken lightly, that is, that it was used only because no other methods would serve the purposes of the research. These statements should be true. For ethical reasons, deception should not be used lightly.

A debriefing generally ends with the researcher urging the participant not to discuss the study with other people before it is completed. Participants have to be persuaded not to reveal the "clever" and potentially interesting details of the setting and deception to others who might become participants in the future. Even if no deception is involved, participants who enter the study forewarned about its overall purposes may behave differently than naïve participants whose knowledge is limited to the cover story. A valid question, of course, is how much we can trust our participants when they agree not to divulge the details of our studies. Fortunately, there is reassuring although "old" data on this question. In a clever experiment, Aronson (1966) enlisted three undergraduate confederates to approach individuals who were known to have participated in a previous experiment. Despite repeated pleas from the confederates to divulge the true purpose of the study, the participants steadfastly refused to say or merely repeated the cover story originally given to them.

In summary, debriefing is important for the researcher's purposes of identifying participants who were inattentive or held accurate suspicions and learning whether the procedures were clearly understood and accurately followed or were confusing. But protection of the participants' interests is even more crucial. Ideally, debriefing accomplishes the purposes of uncovering and dealing with any negative reactions to the study, gently disabusing participants who were taken in by deceptive research procedures, and making sure that participants emerge from the study wiser – but no sadder – than when they entered it.

Summary

Laboratory settings allow researchers to control extraneous factors, implement an experimental manipulation, and construct a setting for the experiment. Laboratories are appropriate research settings when independent variables are practically and ethically manipulable, the time period is short, and the ability to draw inferences about causality is central to the research goals. Research with particularistic goals involving generalization of findings to specific target populations or investigations of the effects of nonmanipulable variables over long time periods are generally best conducted in other settings.

Laboratory studies fall roughly into several categories: impact studies, in which something actually happens to the participants and their reactions are of interest; judgment studies, in which people's perceptions, judgments, or evaluations of stimulus materials are the focus of the research; and observational studies, in which the laboratory setting is used to facilitate detailed observation, with or without manipulation of independent variables.

With all types of laboratory studies, as with all research in general, the construction of the setting, manipulation of independent variables, measurement of dependent variables, and debriefing are specifically aimed at increasing the validity of research conclusions. Internal validity is the chief strength of laboratory-based research, for the setting facilitates randomized experimental designs. Construct validity can be strong, although the setting carries specific risks of artifacts, that is, experimenter expectancy effects and other demand characteristics. External validity in laboratory research often refers to generalization of the theory (as opposed to the specific findings themselves) to other populations and settings. External validity in the sense of the generalizability of findings directly to specific target populations is often low in laboratory research.

Finally, although practical advice about laboratory-based research depends on the particular procedures used to study a given phenomenon, some general advice was provided for each element of a laboratory study. These elements included the setting, independent variables, manipulation checks, dependent variables, and the debriefing. Researchers should refer to published research reports to identify specific methodologies that can be adopted or adapted for a particular study.

> Go online   Visit the book's companion website for this chapter's test bank and other resources at: www.wiley.com/go/maruyama

Key Concepts

Applied research
Basic research
Behavioroid measure
Capitalizing on chance
Confederate
Confound
Control
Cover story
Demand characteristics
Expectancy control group design
Experimental realism
Experimenter expectancies
Funnel questioning

Impact studies
Internal analysis
Judgment studies
Manipulation check
Mundane realism
Observational studies
Particularistic research
Performance measure
Pilot testing
Replication
Social desirability
Statistical power
Universalistic research

On the Web

http://psychclassics.yorku.ca/topic.htm#experimental Website entitled *"Classics in the History of Psychology"* created by C. D. Green, containing links to a number of classic papers about experimental psychology and the psychological laboratory.

We also suggest that, using a search engine such as Google or Yahoo!, readers input the phrase "psychology laboratory," which will return hundreds of links, some providing access to pages featuring descriptions (even photographs) of laboratories in which work such as that described in this chapter is done.

Further Reading

Brannigan, G. G., & Merrens, M. R. (Eds.). (1993). *The undaunted psychologist: Adventures in research.* New York, NY: McGraw-Hill.

Rosnow, R. L., & Rosenthal, R. (1997). *People studying people: Artifacts and ethics in behavioral research.* New York, NY: W. H. Freeman.

Stanovich, K. E. (2013). *How to think straight about psychology* (10th ed.). Boston, MA: Pearson.

Strohmetz, D. B. (2006). Rebuilding the ship at sea: Coping with artifacts in behavioral research. In D. A. Hantula (Ed.), *Advances in social and organizational psychology: A tribute to Ralph Rosnow* (pp.

93–112). Mahwah, NJ: Lawrence Erlbaum Associates.

Wilson, T. D., Aronson, E., & Carlsmith, K. (2010). The art of laboratory experimentation. In S. T. Fiske, D. T. Gilbert, & G. Lindzey (Eds.), *Handbook of social psychology* (Vol. 1, 5th ed., pp. 51–81). Hoboken, NJ: John Wiley & Sons.

Chapter 6

Research in Field and Community-Based Settings

Many of the important conceptual advances in the social sciences and in psychology in particular have been based on experimental research done in laboratories. Going forward, laboratory experimentation will remain a prominent part of research in psychology as well as a method that all social scientists need to understand because of its emphasis on controlling extraneous factors and testing or excluding competing explanations for effects. Such principles are relevant outside the laboratory, whether we are thinking about experimental, quasi-experimental, or non-experimental research, even in settings where control is not possible. Nevertheless, there is much more to social science research than the laboratory. A number of landmark research studies have been conducted in natural settings. Their enduring impact at least in part can be

Research Methods in Social Relations, Eighth Edition. Geoffrey Maruyama and Carey S. Ryan.
© 2014 John Wiley & Sons, Inc. Published 2014 by John Wiley & Sons, Inc.
Companion Website: www.wiley.com/go/maruyama

attributed to their **external validity**, for their results were immediately applicable for understanding everyday human behavior as well as enriching theory. Early examples include much of Lewin's World War II attitude change research on Americans' eating habits, Sherif and colleagues' (Sherif, Harvey, White, Hood, & Sherif, 1961) Robber's Cave study of group conflict, and Festinger, Schachter, and Back's (1950) housing study. More recent field research is illustrated by the large bodies of experimental and quasi-experimental research on cooperative learning in classrooms (see, e.g., Johnson & Johnson, 2005), and on environmental psychology addressing issues like recycling or energy conservation (e.g., Oskamp, 2007).

Furthermore, there is a view going back to the first edition of this text that research should contribute to the solution of practical problems as they emerge in society. In the words of Jahoda, Deutsch, and Cook (1951, p. v), "Experience has demonstrated that research conducted without concern for immediate application is neither easily nor promptly put to use. Research concerned with immediate application requires throughout the research process a collaborative effort between social scientists and those who are to act upon their findings." Such research is not likely to be laboratory experimentation, for such work is fraught with challenges tied to external validity and typically does not engage practitioners as partners.

This chapter provides the counterpoint for Chapter 5, discussing advantages of research conducted outside the laboratory. Such work covers a broad array of approaches, ranging from quantitative studies including experiments as well as studies where no variable is manipulated and controls are limited, to qualitative studies that focus in detail on a small, nonrandom sample. The advantage of immediate **relevance of the findings** to the natural setting in which the study is conducted (an aspect of external validity) has already been discussed. Most notably, in Chapter 5 we suggested that **particularistic research** is likely to be done in field settings, for it is focused on immediate applicability for a specific setting. It might lead readers to think that perhaps we could just turn Chapter 5 on its head, and say that the strengths of 5 (internal validity, control of extraneous factors) are the weaknesses of this chapter, and vice versa. Although that idea is at least partly true, some highly controlled experiments are conducted outside the laboratory. If in those studies the control part is prominent, some external validity is likely sacrificed in order to maintain control and fidelity of treatments within the non-laboratory setting. The point of course is that we speak generally about strengths and benefits, recognizing that for any particular study strengths and weaknesses are determined by the setting, design, and controls put in place. But regardless of the control that researchers attempt to impose on their field settings, a mantra of such research is "Life happens." It succinctly recognizes that no matter what one might plan, circumstances intrude. A study of traffic patterns is disrupted by a fire that totally stops traffic or by an unexpected bridge closure; a school study is thrown off by a flu epidemic or weather that closes the school; a health study is upset by changes in health policies and reimbursements; a worker productivity study is halted as workers go out on strike or as the government shuts down; a key community partner and the site of a study closes, and so forth.

Once one moves outside the laboratory, a number of factors become important. One was discussed in Chapter 4, namely, the importance of partners familiar with the setting who understand local conditions and how those might affect a research study.

A second is the **level at which data are analyzed**. For example, in U.S. public schools, students study within classrooms within schools and within school districts. Depending on the level at which a treatment is delivered, data may be analyzed with class or school as the "observation," for that may be the level at which independence of observations occurs. Studies of teachers with interventions delivered at the level of the class would likely examine data at classroom levels, those of principals at school levels. Similarly, in business settings the level may be the work team/group or office/factory/plant, or even the business. In health settings, level may be a clinic or department or even practitioner, depending on the level at which an intervention is administered. In some instances, data are analyzed using **multilevel approaches** so that effects at different levels can be examined simultaneously – separately (e.g., student effects from teacher effects) and in combination. A third factor, also discussed previously, is **randomization**, whether or not subjects are assigned randomly to conditions.

In the remainder of this chapter, we discuss the issues that should be considered when conducting research outside laboratory settings. We next discuss in more depth issues of level of analysis and randomization. Then we provide illustrations of different types of non-laboratory research, including a study illustrating the importance of non-laboratory experimentation in determining effectiveness of interventions, a non-experimental study helping develop and refine theory, and an action research study engaging community members as partners. Next we discuss what is lost if we were to no longer do applied research beyond laboratories on important social issues, the importance of understanding the setting when developing relationships with non-university partners, and the importance of cultural issues. Finally, we close with a short discussion of how **extraneous factors** might be controlled in non-laboratory settings.

Levels of Analysis

Imagine as an example a study in which 1,000 people are interviewed about their political attitudes and behaviors. For this study, the question of defining the unit of analysis is apparently easily answered. Individuals naturally constitute the independent observations, and each individual presumably has a value on each of the variables. There is, however, no requirement that individuals must always be the **unit of analysis**. In fact, there are many studies in which the unit of analysis is at some other level; for instance, in cross-cultural or cross-national research, the unit of analysis is quite likely to be a nation (e.g., Glick et al., 2000). Likewise, smaller groupings of individuals can be the unit of analysis. For instance, in studies of marital relationships, partner pairs or dyads might be the unit of analysis. And group might be the unit of analysis in studies of social interactions among members of differently structured groups (e.g., Bales & Cohen, 1979). In all of these examples, the units of analysis have been defined as aggregates or groupings of individuals. The unit of analysis might also be defined in any particular study *within* individuals. For instance, a psychophysicist might be interested in examining how different temperatures are perceived when different parts of the body are exposed to them. In such a study, all of the data might be collected from a single individual and the unit of analysis becomes body part. Similarly, in **time-series designs**, such as experience sampling studies (Chapter 11), a single individual might be repeatedly observed over time and then the unit of analysis defined as each individual observation.

All of these examples illustrate the fact that there is no single appropriate unit of analysis that should be used in any and all studies. Viewed differently, it is not the case that observations must always correspond to individuals. Rather, the choice of the unit of analysis depends on the research questions that are being addressed and the level at which the researcher wishes to generalize. If generalization to individuals is sought, the individual is most appropriately the unit of analysis. If we are interested in group processes, generalization across groups might be desired and groups are the appropriate unit of analysis. Units of analysis may be classes, schools, teams, groups, offices, businesses, organizations, cities, states, or even countries.

Errors of generalization often occur when the unit of analysis is not at the same level as the unit to which we seek to generalize. For instance, assume that a set of data about voting trends and income is gathered from different U.S. counties. Here county is the unit of analysis. Assume further that wealthier counties tend to be on average more Republican and less Democratic. If we attempt to generalize these results, which apply to counties, to the individual level, we might well commit what is called the **ecological fallacy**. It is inappropriate to assume, on the basis of these group-level data, that the individuals within the counties necessarily behave in a way analogous to the way their counties on aggregate behave. Wealthier individuals might indeed be inclined to cast Republican ballots, and less affluent individuals might well be inclined to cast Democratic ballots. But the individual and the ecological (group) associations are not necessarily the same. Typically, associations found when the unit of analysis is a group of individuals are stronger than the same associations would be if the individual were the unit of analysis. So, for instance, in this example, the association between counties' wealth and voting trends is likely to be considerably stronger than that between individuals' wealth and their voting records.

Sometimes it makes sense to employ multiple levels of analysis within the same study. This was the case in the Glick et al. (2000) study cited earlier. Glick and his colleagues were interested in cross-cultural differences in hostile and benevolent sexism. They had over 15,000 individuals from 19 countries complete the Ambivalent Sexism Inventory. Some of their research questions were aimed at the individual unit of analysis; for example, they tested differences between men and women within each country, for a total of 19 analyses. Other research questions used country as the unit of analysis; for example, Glick et al. computed the average hostile and benevolent sexism scores for each country and then correlated those scores with two United Nations' indices of gender equality for each country.

In sum, the decision regarding the appropriate unit of analysis is a joint function of the nature of the data (we cannot use individual as the unit if all we have are group-level data) and the research question being asked. The critical determinant is that observations at the chosen unit of analysis should be **statistically independent**; in other words, the data from one case should not influence or have been influenced by the data from another case. Take, for example, a study looking at marital conflict negotiation in which nonverbal expressions of anger were coded from 50 heterosexual couples as they discussed a current problem in their relationship. We could not use individual as the unit of analysis (i.e., setting up a data set with 100 participants and their corresponding anger scores) because the anger expressed by the husband in a discussion surely affects the anger expressed by the wife. The proper unit of analysis in this hypothetical example is therefore the dyad (couple). Independence of units of analysis is a critical assumption for most of the statistical analyses used in the social sciences, and violating this assumption can lead to badly biased results. (See Judd, McClelland, & Ryan, 2009, for illustrations of what can happen when nonindependence is ignored.)

The issue of the appropriate unit of analysis is even more complex than we have portrayed it, for it raises statistical issues that are beyond the scope of this book. For example, when data are collected at more than one level, current multivariate analytic techniques (e.g., hierarchical linear modeling, multilevel modeling) allow simultaneous examination of variance accounted for by variables at different levels. So analyses of student achievement levels might include student-level variables as well as class- or teacher-level variables in accounting for achievement outcomes. The important points for our purposes are that generalization should always be at the same level as the unit of analysis and units should always be statistically independent. Hence, to define what constitutes the observations for the analyses, we need to think about whether we wish to generalize to individuals, groups, nations, or some other meaningful entity.

Randomization: Pro and Con

Balance between principles and practicalities is perhaps nowhere more apparent than in the decision regarding whether determination of a program's effectiveness should employ a randomized experimental design. From the perspective of solid scientific practice, the randomized experiment, when feasible, is highly desirable. For instance, the effectiveness of jigsaw classroom cooperative learning to be described later in this chapter initially was assessed in nonrandomized studies. Although the results appeared to favor the program, there were too many plausible alternative explanations to confidently assert that the program was effective. Only when the program held up under the scrutiny of a randomized experiment was it reasonable to assert its effectiveness.

Although the randomized experiment is the only method that allows researchers to make assertions about program impacts with confidence, there are strong differences in opinion about the importance and value of experimentation across different types of field research. One type in particular that has a long history of controversy about research approaches is called **program evaluation**. Program evaluation is discussed in more detail in Chapter 15. In this section, we present different perspectives on the use of random assignment of participants to conditions for program evaluation. Despite the allure of randomized experiments, practical considerations specific to the evaluation context often argue against their use. Researchers opposed to limiting evaluations to experimental approaches have made the following arguments against randomized experiments as a strategy for program evaluation:

1. They are not feasible because one cannot ensure that participants in social programs adhere only to the requirements of the condition to which they were

assigned, it is impossible to ensure that the program is implemented properly, and good outcome measures do not exist for many social programs (e.g., those that focus on improving quality of life).

2. They have a narrow scope and are limited because they "fail to include qualitative information... [and] are unable to recognize subtle human reactions to a social program" (Boruch, 1975, p. 122).
3. They are useless in providing information on how to make a program better.
4. They are unethical because they either deprive the control group of a desirable treatment or subject the treatment group to a questionable treatment.

An evaluator supportive of use of experimental approaches, Robert Boruch, responded to each of the above criticisms in a 1975 paper as follows.

1. Randomized social experiments are feasible because more than 200 evaluations of social programs successfully used random assignment. This does not mean that it is easy to implement true experiments, but it is proof that they are feasible. Boruch's (1975) list of over 200 evaluations using an experimental design shows a wide range of programs that include job training, education, mental health, social welfare, medical care, economic incentives, criminal justice, the mass media, and many others. Random assignment is possible in more places than the critics believe.

The critics might still have a point, however, if we ask whether there are some special conditions that make random assignment particularly difficult and other conditions that make it easy. Boruch (1975) noted:

> The examples... serve as a basis for examining conditions under which controlled tests appear to be most readily mounted. For example, many such tests compare the effects of various material products, such as two different income subsidy plans, rather than the effects of social programs which are based heavily on personal skills or program staff, such as two rehabilitation programs for the mentally ill.

It is conceivable that experimental tests of the latter sort are more difficult to conduct because we do not know enough about designing tests that are especially sensitive to staff skills or that do not threaten the status of program staff. Program administrators often resist random assignment and true experimental designs because they do not want an evaluation that looks foolproof – and they could be right. It is one thing to design experiments for treatments that have no immediate practical consequences. However, when the research might lead to programs being changed or closed, we want to be particularly certain about program effectiveness before we use research findings to recommend program changes. For example, we might not know enough about designing treatments and measuring the effects of particular social programs to conduct a truly fair test of an idea. It would be unfortunate if a good idea or program were to be jeopardized by having a rigorous evaluation conducted on an inadequate implementation of the idea.

2. Randomized experiments need not preclude gathering qualitative data, and gathering quantitative data need not preclude discovering "subtle human reactions to a social program." Data in true experiments can be either quantitative or qualitative; what matters is that they be systematic: "systematic and reliable information is essential for dispelling erroneous ideas generated by casual observation, dramatic anecdote, and unchecked impressions. That systematic information may be quantitative, or qualitative, or both" (Boruch, 1975, p. 122).

Another part of the second criticism is that experiments are narrow and limited in scope because they are "one-shot affairs." Boruch (1975) replies that "nothing in experimental design methodology demands one-shot tests, and, for a variety of reasons, sequential assessment should ordinarily be the rule rather than the exception" (p. 125). Both the critics and the defenders of experiments are correct. Experiments and evaluations often are one-shot tests and do not follow the program or the participants over many months or years, but they need not be so limited. The 30-year follow-up evaluation of the Cambridge–Somerville experiment described later in this book is a notable exception. In general, most non-laboratory research, experimental or not, could be criticized for lacking continuity, for few research programs engage in cycles of design/planning, implementation, data analysis and interpretation, conceptual refinement and reconceptualization, and design/planning and reimplementation. And, practically, most summative or outcome evaluations are not longitudinal studies because the answer to the question "Does it work?" cannot wait for years.

3. The third criticism, that experimental evaluations are not useful because they provide little guidance on how to make the program better, also has a grain of truth. If we discover that job-training programs do not succeed in getting higher wages for the trainees, we do not know what will succeed. All we know is that this attempt failed. Experiments do not necessarily provide ideas for innovations, but they can provide clear answers about whether a particular innovation worked. Whenever it is possible to compare two innovations and appropriate outcome measures are available, an experimental test will show which one is better. If we accept experiments for what they are – tests of effects – they do enable us to make decisions about whether a program is good and which of several alternative programs is the best.

Another part of the third criticism is that "rigorous evaluations of social programs, including experiments, can destroy any incentive to be creative in program development" (Boruch, 1975, p. 128). Boruch answers that experimental design and evaluation cannot guarantee creativity but that there is also no reason they must stifle it. The experimental approach is very compatible with creativity – people who are willing to experiment are innovative and creative. And those who experiment generally want to know the results of their experiments.

Barriers to innovation can arise when the results of the innovation threaten the innovator's career; in this sense, experimental evaluations can stifle creativity. For this reason, Campbell (1969) has said the ideal strategy is to compare two innovations, with the program administrators' jobs guaranteed no matter what the evaluation reveals, so that administrators and evaluators can be impartial judges of the value of social programs. "This is a useful strategy to the extent that multiple comparisons inhibit premature emotional endorsement of what might be thought of as the solution to a complex social problem, and that they reduce the staff anxieties usually associated with a test of only one solution" (Boruch, 1975, p. 129).

4. The fourth criticism of randomized experiments in evaluation research concerns the ethics of experimentation, and it takes several forms. On the one hand, critics say that the untreated or control group is unfairly deprived of a potentially good program. On the other hand, critics also say the treated or experimental group ("guinea pigs") is unfairly subjected to questionable treatments that might not help and might even harm them. Whether the treatment be helpful or harmful, experimentation is called unfair. Boruch (1975) has a simple answer: "Failure to experiment... [can be] unethical" (p. 135) because we will never know if a treatment is effective if we do not put it to a rigorous test.

In those cases in which we know that a program will not be harmful but want to decide whether it is helpful or simply ineffective, we ideally want to permit as many people as possible to participate. The limit on how many people can participate is usually determined not by any principle of experimental design but by budgets. If this is the case and if more people volunteer or express an interest in a program than can be served, randomization is a fair way of deciding who can participate in the program and who will be in the control group (Brickman, Folger, Goode, & Schul, 1981; Wortman & Rabinovitz, 1979). Some people participate in lotteries, hoping for pleasure and profit. They might also be willing to participate in lotteries for access to social programs for which there are more volunteers or applicants than there are places available. Social psychologists who examined the perceived fairness of lotteries found that people regard random assignment as fair when all the people in the participant pool are equally deserving (Brickman & Stearns, 1978). If prior screening of people's merits or needs still leaves a pool of people larger than the number who can receive a special program (e.g., scholarships), a lottery seems fair, and a lottery is random assignment.

Seligman's research on energy conservation is a good example of how it is possible to conduct randomized experiments in the real world. Seligman and his colleagues wanted to see whether homeowners would reduce their energy consumption if they were given feedback about how much energy they were consuming (e.g., Becker & Seligman, 1978; Becker, Seligman, & Darley, 1979; Seligman & Hutton, 1981). They randomly assigned homeowners to two groups; one received conservation feedback and the other did not. They first recruited a large number of potential participants, more than they could accommodate. The homeowners who were willing to participate were told that if they were selected for the experiment, they would have a small device installed in one wall of their home. They also were told that the experimenter might not have enough devices for everyone who was interested, in which case the devices would be allotted randomly. After the random assignment was made and the participants were informed of their luck, all remained willing to participate. Those who did not receive the feedback meters remained in the experiment as a control group. They were willing to answer questionnaires and have their energy consumption monitored because they shared an initial commitment to the goal of energy conservation. This feature, of course, makes the entire sample a special one, not a randomly selected sample. It limits the external validity of the experiment. Nonetheless, it gives the evaluation high internal validity, and it demonstrates the willingness of people in the real world to participate in randomized experiments.

Illustrations of Non-Laboratory Research

Experimental Research: The Jigsaw Classroom

In instances where drawing causal inferences is desired, an ideal applied research study would be a truly randomized intervention in a real-world setting. Such a study would have high internal and external validity. Classrooms are attractive settings for such studies. Because teachers often experiment with innovative educational methods, a research intervention is not out of the ordinary experience of teachers or students. Students are accustomed to taking tests or filling out questionnaires, so using a test or questionnaire as a dependent variable is consistent with what occurs in classrooms. If teachers, parents, students, and school administrators want to choose whether to participate in an innovation, the selection of treatment and control groups might be voluntary rather than random, and the research would be quasi-experimental. In some instances, however, they might consent to random assignment, permitting the researchers to conduct a true randomized experiment in a real-world setting.

Students and teachers in Austin, Texas, took part in a series of randomized and nonrandomized experiments designed to change intergroup relations and student achievement levels in United States classrooms. Eliot Aronson and his colleagues (1978) worked with teachers to develop classroom conditions that were cooperative rather than competitive and that would facilitate peer teaching. They wanted to create a climate in which Black, Latino, and White children would all participate and benefit.

The cooperative classroom activities were modeled on the activity of piecing together a puzzle. Children worked in small groups of five or six and were given assignments for which each child had one piece of the solution. The students were to piece together the whole solution by learning from and teaching each other. For instance, in one assignment the students were expected to learn about the life of Joseph Pulitzer. His life story was divided into six periods, each described in a paragraph written by the researchers. They cut and distributed the separate paragraphs to fifth-grade students, who had been put into *interdependent learning group*s of six children each. Each child in the group had a different paragraph describing one of the six periods in Pulitzer's life, and they were not allowed to pass their paragraphs around or read one another's. Instead, they were to teach and learn from one another. This meant the other five needed to pay close attention to the one who was speaking because that person had valuable information and was an important resource. Each child was essential for the others' solutions; no one could be dismissed as unimportant or unintelligent. And no one could benefit from studying all alone, trying to be the "best," independent of the others in the group.

The students who were in these interdependent jigsaw groups liked each other and liked school better than did children who were in traditional classrooms. They also came to like themselves better – they developed higher self-esteem. These positive effects were evident across ethnic groups. For example, in some of the predominantly White classrooms there were Latino children who had previously remained silent in class. When they had been called on to speak in the traditionally competitive classrooms, they had sometimes been embarrassed, so they and their teachers learned it was safest for them to be silent. With the jigsaw problem, these children had information essential for the solution, and what they said became valuable to others. The transition was not easy for them or their classmates, but their role in the class did change and so did their performance. The grades of ethnic minority children went up almost a whole letter, as did their self-esteem and that of all the students who participated. Most of the teachers also liked what they saw happening in the interdependent groups, and many continued to use the technique after the intervention ended.

The first of these jigsaw classroom interventions was a quasi-experiment. Ten teachers who had participated in a weeklong workshop with the researchers volunteered to use the jigsaw method in their classrooms. The school administrators then identified three other teachers who were known as very competent and committed to their own methods of teaching to serve as a comparison group. The teachers were, therefore, self-selected rather than randomly assigned into the treatment and "control" conditions.

At the end of six weeks, the researchers found that students in the jigsaw classrooms had higher self-esteem, liked school more, were more convinced they could learn from one another, and had higher grades than did students in the regular classes (Blaney, Stephan, Rosenfield, Aronson, & Sikes, 1977). The only problem with these glowing results was that no one could be sure it was the jigsaw method itself that was responsible because the teachers in the jigsaw classrooms were self-selected rather than randomly assigned. Perhaps those teachers who volunteered to use the new method were doing all sorts of other things differently. Could it have been their personal enthusiasm, their expectations that the "experiment" would succeed, their commitment to do something (anything) for which they had volunteered?

To rule out these alternative explanations, the researchers next obtained permission to assign classrooms randomly to the jigsaw method or to a control group that would conduct business as usual (Lucker, Rosenfield, Sikes, & Aronson, 1977). In the randomized experiment among 11 fifth- and sixth-grade classes, 6 classes used the jigsaw method and 5 classes were taught by equally competent teachers using their traditional methods. At the end of just two weeks, students in the jigsaw classrooms showed gains in their test scores compared with students in the traditional classrooms; this was particularly true for ethnic minority students.

Non-Experimental Research: Engaging and Persisting in Volunteerism

Snyder and Omoto (2008) have developed a model explaining how and why people choose to volunteer. The social phenomenon that they are trying to explain is one that could possibly be developed through analogue studies that emulate ongoing social processes, but it seems to us much more reasonable to do what they chose to do, namely, initially to develop and test their theory in natural settings with people who choose to volunteer. Their model begins with *antecedents*, namely, personality, motivational, and circumstantial characteristics of individuals that help determine who actually volunteers. Then it moves to *experiences*, the psychological and behavioral aspects of the relationships that develop among volunteers, between volunteers and staff members in agencies and organizations, and between volunteers and recipients of their direct services. The model posits that the behavioral patterns and relationship dynamics are important determinants of continued volunteering as well as of benefits to recipients of the volunteer efforts. The model ends with *consequences*, which include impacts of volunteer service on changes in attitudes, knowledge, and behavior. Snyder and Omoto examine the different components at levels of individuals, social groups, agencies, and societies.

As Omoto and Snyder (1995) began to examine volunteerism, they developed and cross-validated an instrument that measured motivations for volunteerism. Then they used it for a long-term field study looking at persistence of volunteering. They used research methods that allowed them to examine the plausibility of their conceptual model, using multiple measures of each conceptual variable to improve the reliability and validity of their constructs, and then examined how well the data fit a model dictated by the theory using a **structural equation modeling** approach. That methodology combines correlation and regression approaches interrelating variables with factor analysis approaches that relate measures to underlying variables. The former approaches describe the nature of relationships among variables, and the latter address issues of reliability and construct validity. Although their findings were mixed, the findings led to continued research examining the plausibility of their model in explaining when and why people choose to volunteer, and how long they persist.

Non-Experimental Research: Impacts of Post-Secondary Education on Inmate Recidivism Rates, an Action Research Study

Michelle Fine, Maria Torre, and a large group of co-investigators (2001) examined the effectiveness of college education programs for female inmates in a maximum security prison in New York State, using an action research approach. The research was stimulated in part by prior decisions by the federal government in 1994 to deny Pell Grants to incarcerated prisoners. Prior to that decision, over 350 college programs were operating, mostly supported by Pell Grant funding. Shortly after the federal support was eliminated, states followed suit and withdrew state-level educational support as well, effectively eliminating most college education programs in prisons.

It is no surprise that free college education for criminals would be controversial, for many people would be thinking, "I'm paying for my children's education, but these convicted felons living in state facilities don't have to pay for their education because they all qualify for Pell Grants." Yet many people also realize that the costs of incarcerating prisoners, which are paid by taxpayers, are much higher than the costs of education. Any interventions that reduce recidivism and its associated costs are important – and not readily found. This study illustrates the kinds of political challenges that can face researchers. If college education provides inmates with alternatives to lives of crime once they are released from prison and reduces recidivism rates, then there are societal-level benefits to providing education. If people focus on those, then they might be persuaded by data from research like that of Fine and colleagues. But if people focus on the fact that criminals are getting a free education that non-criminal taxpayers are not getting, namely, on individual-level costs and benefits, then the data on program outcomes may matter little.

Fine, Torre, and colleagues evaluated a program started by a consortium of private colleges in New York, in cooperation with the prison superintendent, interested community members, and a group of inmates. The consortium was initiated in response to inquiries by prisoners, who argued that the education programs that they had previously produced positive benefits that were being lost, and that female prisoners were losing any sense of hope about their futures. The prison population was uneducated, with only a little over half of the inmates having a high school diploma or GED (General Educational Development) diploma. A substantial majority were women of color, with over 80% African American or Latina. The researchers used an action research approach, developing the research design collaboratively with the inmate committee, and engaging them as co-researchers throughout the research process. Researchers employed a combination of qualitative and quantitative analyses to document the processes that occurred and to draw out the richness of the responses of the inmates. Analyses of recidivism rates employed a comparison group of inmates with similar backgrounds but who had not participated in the education program.

The research findings are ones that should make the government review its decision about college programs in prisons. Participating inmates' reincarceration rate was less than 8%, compared with a rate of about 30% for other inmates from the same facility. Lower rates of reincarceration meant lower prison costs, reducing costs substantially. An important side benefit of the educational intervention was that the prison became a safer place, with fewer behavioral incidents and fewer management problems. The differences in reincarceration rates were attributed to the participating women developing skills, knowledge, and social networks that kept them from reverting to criminal activity. Of course, because the research did not include random assignment and evaluates only one education program, we cannot be sure that the effects would occur for all inmates or for all education programs. For example, the program engaged inmates as co-investigators, which probably is atypical of research in prisons. So a competing explanation would be that the findings might be in part a "**Hawthorne effect**," named after a business plant where a number of different interventions were introduced to see which increased productivity. The major finding was that it was not the specific intervention, but the attention given to the workers that increased their productivity. Similarly, the respect and roles given to the women inmates could have made them feel special and valued, which may have shaped their senses of self-worth independently of the actual educational program and put them on a path to success. Nevertheless, the set of measures and rich data provide strong findings, warranting at the very least additional studies examining effectiveness of educational programs in different settings and with different prisoners.

Can We Afford Not to Do Applied Research?

An important subset of non-laboratory research, tied to the name "Social Relations" of this text, is research that examines relations among people and relations of people with their environments. This work is important because it gives us insights into the human condition and why we behave in the ways that we do. Such research examines in natural settings things like friendships, particularly across groups (e.g., the jigsaw studies just described), how attitudes and beliefs about different things affect our behaviors (e.g., how to increase volunteerism), situational motivators of aggressive and other antisocial behaviors, and how decisions humans make affect other humans. The study on ways of engaging female prisoners to reduce future criminal behavior is an excellent illustration of such research. The research examines effectiveness of governmental policies, documenting benefits of programs closed for political and not empirical reasons. In contrast to the decision, we would like to believe that social science research can help design policies from its empirically supported theories, help evaluate their effectiveness, and help refine them. In the remainder of this section, we examine another study with implications for governmental policies, namely, research on impacts on humans of nuclear power.

Illustration: Living Downwind of Nuclear Reactors

Rosalie Bertell, a mathematician and medical researcher, examined environmental influences on the survival of low-birth-weight infants in Wisconsin between the years 1963 and 1975 (Bertell, Jacobson, & Stogre, 1984). Bertell and her colleagues chose Wisconsin because the state has routinely tested milk for radioactive materials, and these tests provide a measure of radioactive contamination of pasturelands. The researchers chose six regions based on their proximity to nuclear power plants. Three regions – Eau Claire, La Crosse, and Green Bay – are close to and downwind of nuclear power plants. The other three – Rice Lake, Wausau, and Madison – are distant from or upwind of nuclear power plants.

Bertell et al. studied the effects on low-birth-weight infants (weighing less than 5½ pounds, or 2,500 grams) because these infants are very fragile and sensitive to environmental influences that might threaten human health or life. They are more vulnerable to respiratory infections that other infants survive. Radioactive gases and particles, which are released into the atmosphere by nuclear power plants, suppress infants' immune systems and make them more vulnerable to respiratory diseases than they already are. When these infants contract respiratory infections, they are more likely to die, and their death records usually state the cause of death as "pneumonia."

To assess the health effects of nuclear power plants, one must take into consideration not only proximity but also prevailing wind patterns. For instance, the three downwind regions were affected by the start-up of seven nuclear power plants, four in Wisconsin and three in Minnesota. The prevailing winds are from the west or northwest, so the residents of Eau Claire are downwind of the Minnesota nuclear plants.

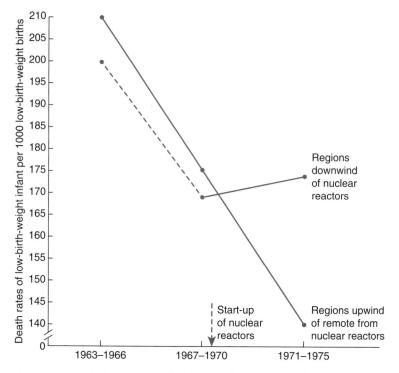

Figure 6.1   Relations of Living Downwind of Nuclear Plants and Infant Deaths across Three Time Periods.

The power plants whose effects Bertell and her colleagues examined were started up between 1969 and 1974. Therefore, the researchers compared the death rates of low-birth-weight infants for three time periods: 1963 to 1966, 1967 to 1970, and 1971 to 1975. They used the first two time periods to see whether there was an overall upward, downward, or level trend in the infants' death rates. They then compared the death rates during the third time period with those during the previous two to see whether there was a change after the start-up of the nuclear power plants.

During the period from 1971 to 1975, which was after the start-up of the nuclear power plants, the death rates in two of the remote or upwind regions were below the state level. The death rates in the regions downwind and close to the nuclear power plants were all above the state level. After the start-up of the nuclear reactors (1971–1975), death rates in all three downwind regions were higher than in the upwind regions. Figure 6.1 summarizes the effects by showing the average death rates for infants in the downwind and the upwind or remote regions.

Before the introduction of the reactors, the death rates declined between the first and second time periods in both sets of regions. This decline probably resulted from advances in health care and medical technology. The decline in death rates continued in the upwind or remote regions from the second to the third time period. In the downwind regions, however, the death rates rose again after 1970. This rise in deaths corresponds with the start-up of the seven nuclear reactors between 1969 and 1974.

Before concluding that the increased death rates of these infants were caused by the nuclear power plants, Bertell and her colleagues examined some potentially **confounding variables** to see whether there were plausible alternative explanations. The researchers were rightly concerned about the internal validity of their research, for the results could alarm people in Wisconsin and elsewhere and so needed to be carefully scrutinized before being made public. They considered several sets of potentially confounding variables. We consider two here: (1) the existence of other environmental pollutants that could adversely affect the health of infants and adults, such as waste products from chemical plants and fossil fuel plants, and (2) the availability of quality medical facilities, particularly infant intensive care units, which are known to affect the survival rates of low-birth-weight infants.

The researchers found no association between the existence or operation of chemical and fossil fuel plants and the infant death rates. For instance, in Eau Claire, a downwind area where infant death rates increased, there are only 2 fossil fuel generators, whereas in Madison, where the infant mortality rates decreased, there are 11 fossil fuel generators. So fossil fuel plants cannot be implicated in the infants' deaths. The same pattern appears for chemical plants. In Eau Claire there are only 2 chemical companies and in Madison there are 28, but the death rates are higher in Eau Claire and lower in Madison.

The researchers also considered the second alternative explanation – that the availability of medical facilities, particularly infant intensive care units, was the major determining factor in the infants' deaths. The evidence on the existence of perinatal care units shows that all three downwind regions, with the increased death rates, were served by perinatal care units, so the deaths could not be attributed to lack of medical care. In fact, within one of the downwind areas, La Crosse, the highest rates of low-birth-weight deaths were in those parts of the county with the best access to specialized medical care. In contrast, of the three upwind regions, two had no perinatal or infant intensive care units, so their better survival figures could not be attributed to better medical care.

As a final check on their findings and interpretations, the researchers examined the association between reports of radioactive gases released and low-birth-weight infant death rates. They encountered several difficulties with this analysis. The first was that not all gaseous releases are reported by the operators of nuclear power plants. The Nuclear Regulatory Commission does not require operators to report the gases released during start-up and testing phases (Bertell et al., 1984). A second difficulty is that there are seasonal shifts in prevailing winds. Eau Claire, for instance, is downwind of one nuclear reactor about 50% of the year and downwind of another reactor 25% of the year, so the gaseous releases that affected Eau Claire came from different reactors at different times of the year. The researchers, therefore, had to proceed with the knowledge that not all gaseous releases were reported, and they had to combine seasonal wind factors with the timing of reported gaseous releases. They did find an association between gaseous releases and infant death rates and concluded,

Despite the many unknown factors, such as exact dates of "batch" releases of radioactive gases, wind direction at release times and probable doses to the downwind population, there is a discernible trend with greater excess in low birth weight infant deaths coinciding with years of larger radioactive gaseous releases, and fewer excess low birth weight infant deaths occurring during years with smaller radioactive gaseous releases. (p. 19)

Even though their research cannot establish causality because it is not experimental, it creates a plausible case for cause and effect. If this research had not been done, no one would know about the connection between infant deaths and the location of nuclear power plants. These deaths would still be attributed to other causes. It took empirical research to demonstrate that living downwind of nuclear power plants seems very likely to cause a rise in the death rates of infants. This research did not set off great alarms, perhaps because it was not widely publicized, the persons most directly affected were not informed, the causal relationship could be disputed, or the appropriateness of the particular dependent measure could be questioned.

In any case, this scenario raises several questions. Does the fact that fragile low-birth-weight infants die when they are born downwind of nuclear reactors mean that hardy adults are also affected? Does the hospital record, which says the cause of death is "pneumonia," accurately identify the cause? Could it reasonably be said that the child died from "radioactive gaseous releases" or from "living downwind of a nuclear reactor"?

We come back to a question raised in Chapter 1 and that has been implied elsewhere in this book. Is it possible to conduct social science research – research that examines human relations and human welfare – without considering questions of social values? Does applied, and perhaps also basic, research not force us to consider whose purposes are served by an intervention or an evaluation or even a research question? And must we at least sometimes choose sides?

Exercise: Sharing results from controversial research

As has just been described, Bertell and colleagues (1984) found evidence that nuclear plants were adversely affecting the health of individuals living downwind of nuclear power plants. If you were the researcher, what would you do with your findings and why? Discuss what you think might happen after you share your results. Given what happened in the case of the Rind, Tromovitch, and Bauserman (1998) abuse research (Chapter 1), researchers should expect criticism and be prepared to respond to it, regardless of whether their approach is to be resistant to the criticism or accepting of it.

Conducting Research in Community Settings

This section builds from the section of Chapter 4 that focuses on roles of researchers in partnership research. Field and community-based research is conducted in communities with residents, organizations, and cultures. By **culture** we mean the process of meaning-making and interpretation that exists in a setting and is shared by people in that setting (see, e.g., Smith, 2012). Cultures exist at many levels. Sometimes the terms "subcultural group" and "subculture" are used to describe subgroups or specific settings where norms for behavior are different. It may be, for example, that a field study is done in a coffee shop within a university, in which case the workers and patrons are likely university people, and the setting likely will be familiar to the researcher. Even then, however, the coffee shop has its "regulars" and its patterns of behaviors, which may differ greatly from other places on campus and reflect its own culture.

Most field research is done beyond universities, in places like community clinics, social service agencies, retail stores, businesses, schools, factories, community centers, bus stops or stations, or airports. In these settings, there are the people who work there, the leaders or others who set cultural parameters (and who may be partners in the research), and the constituents who frequent the location. Working outside a university results in researchers navigating settings about which they may know little, which takes us back to the Lewinian idea about experts in theory – researchers – working with experts in practice – those who understand the cultures in which we are working. Without understanding, even a well-designed research study may fail because it ineffectively considers or adapts to local conditions.

Because of challenges of conducting research outside laboratories and universities, researchers gravitate to sites that seem to provide relatively easy access to participants and where there is acceptance of and interest in research. Pragmatism in choosing locations for conducting field research is often sensible, for some settings simply may not readily lend themselves to research. At the same time, if the field settings chosen are always ones similar to universities, generalizability of findings will be limited. Regardless of ease of access, it is important to remember that the setting chosen has its culture and that people in that setting value the patterns of behavior that the setting has developed. A school, for example, has its schedule, its rules and norms (e.g., methods and patterns of discipline), its habits, and its structure. The students are used to particular ways of doing things, and research in which they are participants should be compatible with those ways. Effective research in that setting would fit the research to existing patterns of the school so the research seems like a part of the school rather than something alien imposed upon it. Interventions designed to change behaviors need carefully to consider the specific things that need to change in order for the interventions to be effective, for they do not want to change a lot of extraneous elements of the setting that might produce reactive responses from students or teachers. Said differently, if too much changes or if changes independent of the intervention occur, the research might produce unwanted effects unrelated to the specific intervention but possibly attributed by the researcher to the research.

Given the challenges, it is important to remember the strengths of research in field and community settings.

- First, the results have external validity for that setting. If the setting is changed too much by the research, external validity is lessened.
- Second, participants are providing data in a setting with which they are familiar, and around others whom they already know and trust. They may not need to make a special trip to participate in research, for the research often comes to them.

In such settings, there should be fewer demand characteristics operating, and people should behave more naturally.
- Third, there are fewer translational issues to consider, most notably wondering whether the effects of the research might also appear in natural settings.

Taken together, these reasons argue that research in field settings generally has greater immediate applicability, and is more likely to provide solutions to practical problems as they emerge in society.

To summarize, the point of this section is that to realize advantages that come from working in field and community settings, research in those settings needs to be designed with an understanding of the setting so the research is not unduly influenced by extraneous features of the setting. In the absence of compelling reasons to design a study that imposes its particular culture, it is valuable to design research studies so they blend with the existing setting as much as possible. Then the research maximizes the advantages of working in natural settings.

Cultural Issues

In the preceding section culture, the habits, patterns, expectations for, and classifications of behaviors that are held by different people in different settings, was discussed as an important aspect of any setting. Cultural psychology, for example, is a relatively recent area of study within psychology; researchers have found that our understanding of basic cognitive, motivational, and behavioral phenomena is limited without considering, and increased by examining, cultural differences in phenomena and the various factors that give rise to differences (a detailed analysis of culture can be found in Wyer, Chiu, & Hong, 2009). Wyer et al. (2009) define culture as *"networks of knowledge,* consisting of learned routines of thinking, feeling, and interacting with other people, as well as a corpus of substantive assertions and ideas about aspects of the world"* (p. 4). They further note that culture is unique in that it is: shared, visible through symbols, artifacts, etc., providing common ground for communication, transmitted from old to new members, and dynamic, undergoing changes. An interesting feature of cultures is that by looking at other cultures, we better understand our own culture, for we learn about things we take for granted. Applied to research settings, individuals who don't share all of the beliefs or values of the researcher help researchers understand their assumptions and beliefs, which can markedly improve the quality of the research.

While all settings can be viewed as having cultures, within communities many of the key aspects of culture typically are shared. In contrast, substantial differences across cultures exist as we move across countries. Smith (2012) describes what **cross-national replications** of landmark U.S. studies have found, noting large differences in rates of conformity and obedience as well as differences in preferred leadership types and in how deviates in groups are treated and whether or not they are excluded. Earlier in this chapter, we described the Glick et al. (2000) study that included analyses done at a country level, which also illustrated how cultures can differ. But even for research within a researcher's country, there are important reasons to consider culture, for differences in key values and beliefs (e.g., religion, race/ethnicity, political ideology) are common. In such cases, many assumptions and beliefs about how people behave are not shared. Such cultural differences can greatly affect research, for many of the assumptions of the researcher about how things happen are not shared with the participant sample. If, for example, a researcher were to assume that participants in research would interpret instructions or background materials in a specific way, and if no one from a particular cultural background were to do that, the intervention would not have the expected effects. Consider, for example, the case of parent involvement in children's education (Ryan, Casas, Kelly-Vance, Ryalls, & Nero, 2010). U.S. schools assume that parents will be the family members who are involved in children's education rather than, for example, older siblings, aunts and uncles, or other extended family or community members. As a result, researchers might assess only parent involvement and not even ask about others who may be involved. It may be that in some families others are better able to help the children because of work schedules, expertise, or language issues. If we only ask about parents' involvement, we may miss a great deal and reach erroneous conclusions about the extent to which parents value their children's education. Ryan et al. discuss this issue in the context of assessing Latino parent involvement, but the more general issue of defining involvement in education in terms of parent involvement applies to families from other backgrounds as well, for example, immigrant families where the parents' English is poor and where an older sibling educated in the U.S. becomes the person involved with schools.

In the United States, we often focus on culture at a group level, specifically at the level of an ethnic, racial, gender, social class, or immigrant subgroup. Such research is reasonable, for in fact those variables may account for major differences. When researchers are concerned about such differences, they include those variables explicitly in the design, either as **individual difference variables** in their analyses or as selection variables, namely, including only people from a specific background as research participants. A notable feature of background or demographic variables is that they can never be randomly assigned, so research including them cannot be viewed as pure experimental research. Experiments can examine the different ways in which, for example, men and women respond to a stimulus, but differences cannot automatically be attributed to gender differences. Rather, researchers have to go through the process of eliminating alternative explanations that researchers using quasi-experimental approaches use.

A prominent example of research on group differences is research on what is called the "achievement gap," which refers to racial, ethnic, or class differences in student academic outcomes. Those outcomes include achievement levels as well as attainment levels. Group differences are large, accounting for major differences in high school dropout and graduation rates, college admissions at selective colleges, and college graduation rates. Focusing on culture at such a level allows us to examine the roots of such differences as well as the processes that seem to sustain them. And, as was noted above about background variables, true experimentation is not possible, for one cannot be randomly assigned to gender, race, national origin, or family social class. Further, external validity of findings when studying issues like the achievement gap is integral, for the challenge is not to change student achievement levels in artificial settings like a laboratory, but to change them in actual educational settings and in ways that can be taken to scale so they affect large numbers of students. Finally, tying back to the social relations part of the title of this book, one determinant of the achievement gap may be unrelated to academic skills, but due to motivations of students to do well, attitudes about the importance of school, or classroom practices that differ from and perhaps even conflict with students' cultural values and practices. Ignoring social factors and their roots prevents researchers from looking broadly at causes of achievement and attainment.

The major point of this section is consistent with and overlaps with the preceding one. It is that in field or community settings, researchers need to attend to the social context and dynamics of the setting, and that cultures existing in any setting can strongly shape effectiveness of research conducted in them. Once again, the perspective is that articulated by Lewin, namely, that researchers need partners familiar with the settings in which they are working who can help design and conduct the research in ways that allow the intent of the research to emerge.

Control of Extraneous Factors, Statistical and Otherwise

In concluding this chapter, we address issues alluded to throughout the chapter, namely, that when working in non-laboratory settings researchers need to explicitly attend to alternative explanations for their findings and, to the extent possible, eliminate those alternatives. Sometimes alternatives can be eliminated through the design, rendering alternative explanations implausible. For example, if a school study examines a condition where students learn their science through hands-on experimentation in a setting where they are moving around rather than sitting in desks, an alternative explanation of increased learning would be that students are physically active, which keeps them engaged and reduces the nervous energy that makes them fidgety and inattentive. To eliminate this explanation, a comparison condition would need to be created in which students are equally active but don't engage in hands-on experimentation.

In other instances, the design simply cannot pit competing explanations one against the other. It may be that in a school, comparable alternative conditions cannot be designed, for they would not fit a school day schedule or would be too disruptive to the school environment. Or they might not fit the philosophy of the school. In still other instances, competing explanations do not emerge until the data are being collected and participants raise issues or researchers realize that some respondents are articulating perspectives that were not sufficiently considered in advance of the study. In such instances, the options are more limited.

One option is to employ **statistical controls** using covariates to explore alternative explanations. For example, if an alternative explanation is that particular findings are caused by increased activity levels and there is a measure of each participant's activity level, that measure could be "controlled for" by looking at a residual relationship between the treatment and outcome variable after eliminating activity level as an explanation for the findings. For analysis of variance designs, such analyses are called **analysis of covariance**, and for correlational data, **partial correlation**. These analyses remove variance related to the controlled variable, leaving a residual relationship that is statistically independent of that variable. (Note, however, that statistical control is not a substitute for random assignment to conditions; rather, it is one strategy that can be used to examine the plausibility of alternative explanations when random assignment is not possible.) Of course, if in the study just described the intervention was designed to increase activity level, the covariate could be viewed as a measure of the effectiveness of the intervention. Taking it out would weaken or even eliminate the effects of the intervention. The point is one that has been made regularly in the methods literature – before using covariates, be sure that you understand what the covariates really measure, and be sure that they are not measures of treatment or outcome variables of interest (e.g., Gordon, 1968). For example, residual relationships can be absent for very different reasons, including if the controlled variable were a mediator or a common cause, or if there was conceptual overlap between the control variable and the other variables.

To summarize, the point of this section is to remind readers that during the design and analysis stages of their research in field and community settings, they have the ability to consider and address competing explanations for findings. To the extent that they can anticipate alternative explanations, they can determine ways of at least exploring the viability of different perspectives and, ideally, of eliminating some.

Summary

This chapter complements Chapter 5 and its focus on research done in laboratory settings, covering research done outside the laboratory. Non-laboratory or field research has strengths in its external validity and applicability to real-world settings and phenomena. But the price that typically is paid is loss of control, likely diminishing internal validity and control of extraneous variables. This chapter ties back to Chapter 4, for much of this work is done in collaboration with practitioners, and is best if it engages them as partners to help researchers understand the effects of local conditions on the research. The chapter discusses use of statistical controls that are often necessary to tease out possible confounds, challenges tied to levels of analysis of data and design, and how issues of randomization are viewed. For randomization, we present arguments for and against using it, leaving it to readers to decide what is best in particular circumstances. We illustrate non-laboratory research describing one experimental and quasi-experimental study from a school setting, one non-experimental quantitative study conducted in a community setting, and a qualitative quasi-experimental study conducted in a women's prison. We argue that non-laboratory research is highly important, and that without it we would be without significant knowledge that affects our daily lives. We closed the chapter by revisiting the importance of engaging community partners, discussing the significance of culture in shaping responses of participants, extending the culture point to a discussion of international research and the variability that has been found across nations, and finally addressing the importance of attempting to control extraneous factors in non-laboratory research.

Go online   Visit the book's companion website for this chapter's test bank and other resources at: www.wiley.com/go/maruyama

Key Concepts

Analysis of covariance	Multilevel approaches
Confounding variables	Partial correlation
Cross-national replication	Particularistic research
Culture	Program evaluation
Ecological fallacy	Randomization
Errors of generalization	Relevance of the findings
External validity	Statistical controls
Extraneous factors	Statistically independent
Hawthorne effect	Structural equation modeling
Individual difference variables	Time-series analysis
Level of analysis	Unit of analysis

On the Web

http://www.aral.com.au/ A valuable resource for all topics related to action research.

http://ccdl.libraries.claremont.edu/cdm/ref/collection/lap/id/17/ This is a link to a video on measurement issues in field-based research. (Please note, this video takes a while to load before you can watch it.)

Further Reading

Dipboye, R. L., & Flanagan, M. F. (1979). Research settings in industrial and organizational psychology: Are findings in the field more generalizable than in the laboratory? *American Psychologist, 34(2)*, 141–150.

Paluck, E. L., & Cialdini, R. B. (2014). Field research methods. In H. T. Reis & C. M. Judd (Eds.), *Handbook of research methods in social and personality psychology* (2nd ed., pp. 81–97). New York, NY: Cambridge University Press.

Reis, H. T., & Gosling, S. D. (2010). Social psychological methods outside the laboratory. In S. T. Fiske, D. T. Gilbert, & G. Lindzey (Eds.), *Handbook of social psychology* (pp. 82–114). Hoboken, NJ: John Wiley & Sons.

Part II

Research Approaches in Social Relations Research

Chapter 7

Measurement and Reliability

Research Methods in Social Relations, Eighth Edition. Geoffrey Maruyama and Carey S. Ryan.
© 2014 John Wiley & Sons, Inc. Published 2014 by John Wiley & Sons, Inc.
Companion Website: www.wiley.com/go/maruyama

A major challenge that researchers often face is developing or identifying measures or scales that assess abstract ideas, such as social power and prejudice. Ultimately, researchers who attempt to assess abstract concepts can never be absolutely sure they are successful. But various methods can be used to maximize the likelihood that research measures capture the abstract concepts of interest and help researchers evaluate the extent to which they are successful.

We discuss measurement methods in this chapter, beginning by describing the basic conceptual task of assessing broad, abstract concepts or constructs and then discussing how social scientists go about developing specific questions and items to assess them. We conclude the chapter by outlining procedures for creating multiple-item scales and assessing their reliability.

From Abstract Concepts to Concrete Representations

The general process of measuring *abstract concepts* involves developing concrete representations or *variables*, which can be measured more directly. The specific procedures for measuring concrete representations or variables are known as *operational definitions*.

Constructs

Constructs are the abstractions that social scientists discuss in their theories. They are the rich theoretical concepts that make the science interesting and include terms as wide-ranging as social status, power, intelligence, popularity, and gender roles. Because these concepts are intangible, researchers must find concrete representations that approximate what they mean when they use these terms.

Any one construct can be measured in many different ways because there are a variety of concrete representations of any abstract idea. Each one will be an approximate representation of the construct, which also means that the different representations should be related one to another. In some cases, the different approximations represent different settings in which the construct is manifested or different facets of a construct. For instance, social power could be represented by the amount of influence a person has at work, at home, in the neighborhood, or in the mass media, and self-concept could be examined with respect to individuals' sense of their physical skills, their social skills, or their academic skills. Each of these more concrete representations gives some indication of a person's power or self-concept; no one alone contains the whole truth. And although each one is a different variable, they are all related to their underlying construct. Taken together they provide a better approximation of what is meant by the conceptual variable they measure.

Variables

Variables are representations of constructs. They cannot be synonymous with a construct because any construct can be assessed using many different variables. Therefore, variables are partial, fallible representations of constructs; researchers work with them because they are measurable. Variables must have at least two values, or they would be constants and not variables. They suggest ways in which we can decide whether someone has more or less of a construct (e.g., social power, femininity, or masculinity) or is better categorized as one type (e.g., female) of a construct (e.g., gender) than another (e.g., male). For instance, if we select "influence at work" as the variable to represent social power, we can devise ways to determine whether one person has more or less of the variable than does another person. Being more concrete than the construct, the variable suggests some steps that can be taken to measure it. These steps are called operational definitions.

Operational Definitions

An **operational definition** specifies how to measure a variable so that scores on that variable indicate how much of a construct people have; it is the steps or procedures researchers follow to obtain measurements. For example, a researcher might refer to an organizational chart to count how many subordinates an individual has. The variable might have only two possible scores such as "present" and "absent" or "high" and "low," or it might have many possible scores, as with intelligence or achievement tests.

Operational Definitions Are Necessary but Rarely Sufficient

Operational definitions are necessary but rarely sufficient to capture the rich and complex ideas contained in a construct. The beauty of an operational definition is that it specifies precisely how to measure a variable so that anyone could repeat the steps and obtain the same measurements. Its very specificity and concreteness, however, limit the breadth and depth of what is measured.

A thermometer reading of someone's temperature, for example, is an acceptable operational definition because it is a clear procedure that can be easily repeated. But what does a thermometer reading measure? We usually accept it as a measure of whether a person has a fever (a temperature that is too high), but that is debatable. Thermometer readings vary throughout the day as well as across individuals, and one must decide which temperature indicates a fever. The connection between temperature and fever is not entirely clear. The thermometer reading, therefore, is an imperfect measure of whether someone has a fever. It is also a less-than-adequate measure of health because the connection between temperature and physical health is even more uncertain than the connection between temperature and fever. To adequately assess physical health, one must take many readings and ask many questions, as a physician does during a general medical checkup. Any single measurement, such as a red blood cell count, is an operational definition of a component of physical health, such as degree of anemia. And each operational definition is acceptable as a scientific measure of physical health because it is publicly accessible. People can learn to measure blood pressure or count red blood cells, and they can agree in their measurements – not necessarily exactly, but to a reasonable extent. Scientific measurement is accomplished with operational definitions that can be used and repeated by others, which makes operational definitions objective.

The emphasis on objectivity in operational definitions does not mean that all measurement or all observations must be quantified. Good observations and measurement can also consist of words rather than numbers. It also does not mean that the result from an objective measure, for example, a number like 100 on a thermometer or achievement test, *is* that person's temperature or level of achievement. If the same person were retested with another instrument or at another moment, the number might be different. Each measurement only approximates a person's true standing (or score) on the construct; each measurement also contains error. Objectivity also does not guarantee truth or accuracy. Rather, it permits social scientists to communicate with each other and with the public. It also permits anyone to challenge and check research because the operational definitions are instructions for replicating the observations or measurements and for articulating the logic linking the measures to the conceptual variable that underlies them.

Definitional Operationism

As we have noted, any single operational definition is always limited to some degree. It is therefore important to avoid **definitional operationism**, that is, the assumption that operational definitions are synonymous with the constructs they represent or, in other words, that an operational definition *is* the construct (e.g., scores on an intelligence test are intelligence). Such an assumption ignores the facts that every measure (a) taps irrelevant features not related to the underlying construct (e.g., characteristics of the person administering the study or observing the behaviors, a lack of familiarity with wording), (b) includes measurement error, and (c) fails to tap all the relevant features of the theoretical construct. We therefore advocate the use of *multiple* operational definitions. Each one provides a check on the other, and each has a different set of errors or biases.

Measurement Presupposes a Clearly Defined Construct

The construct is the starting point for all measurement. In a way, the basic problem with definitional operationism is that it reverses the order by *defining* the construct in terms of an operational definition. The approach we advocate is first to define constructs in terms of other, theoretically related constructs. This definition constitutes the construct's **nomological net**: the theoretical network of associations derived from theory and stated at an abstract level (e.g., Cronbach & Meehl, 1955). The construct's nomological net then becomes the starting point for decisions about operational definitions.

For example, a theory might define social power as the ability to influence other people's actions. One might then investigate whether individuals can give commands that others must follow, whether they generally win others over to their viewpoints in arguments or discussions, and so on. However, it probably would not be reasonable to consider an individual's income as a measure of social power. Although income might be associated with power or even be a reasonable measure of power in some circumstances, it is not closely associated with social power *in terms of the theory* we are using. In sum, measurement always presupposes a clearly specified construct, and the construct's specification should guide the choice of operational definitions.

Commonsense knowledge and personal observations about constructs also have a place in choosing operational definitions and measurement strategies. For example, it is intuitively clear that income is one component of social status. But how can we decide what form the association between income and status takes? Both intuition and common sense tell us that income and social status are associated in a curvilinear rather than linear fashion (see Figure 7.1). As we move higher and higher along the income scale, a particular difference (e.g., $1,000) in income means less and less (Carter, 1971), for it becomes a smaller and smaller proportion of one's total income. We cannot prove that the association is curvilinear because we have no direct measure of social status. But we will probably make fewer errors and reach more insightful conclusions if we assume the relationship is curvilinear.

In contrast, the association between social status and (years of) education is probably neither linear nor curvilinear, given what we know about the meaning of education. Graduations from high school and college make a bigger difference, for example, in employment decisions, than does completion of any previous year of schooling. Education as a measure of social status has plateaus, and graduation is one of them. We can therefore best approximate the association between education and status by assigning status increments to each plateau rather than to each year of schooling (see Figure 7.2). Each graduation signals an increase in status and preparation.

Fitting quantitative variables to abstract constructs is a major challenge in social science research. Although we would like nice, uniform linear relations among measures, the world is much more complex than that. Our measures do not always bend where they should and it is unclear which portions of a construct we have measured and which portions we have not. When we use the numbers we obtain to describe people's standing on the construct, part of our description must be based on what we

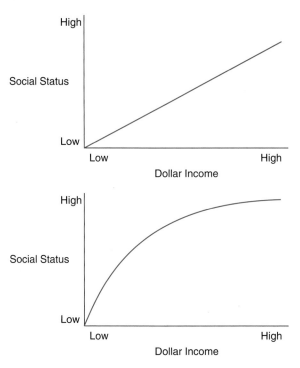

Figure 7.1 Depiction of Linear (Top) and Curvilinear (Bottom) Association Between Income and Status.

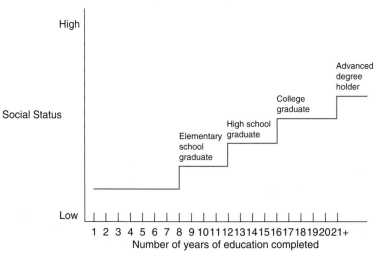

Figure 7.2 Association Between Number of Years of Education and Social Status.

already know – our intuition and commonsense knowledge about the nature of the constructs.

Developing Questionnaire Items

We now turn to the issue of developing specific questions and items to assess the constructs in which we are interested. Our focus here is on direct questioning, although social scientists use many other measurement methods as well. We say more about other methods in Chapter 8. Regardless of the specific method used, the key concern is the degree to which responses are high in construct validity. Ultimately, such details as question wording, content, and the sequence in which questions are asked affect the construct validity of participants' responses.

In direct questioning, the content and wording of the questions or items must clearly convey to respondents what information is desired. Consider, for example, the statement "I am the first in my family to attend college." This item was developed and intended to identify students who were what is commonly called "first-generation" college students, the first from their family ever to attend college. But when college students were asked to indicate whether this statement was true of them along with a question about their parents' education, it became clear that some first-born children considered themselves the first in their families to go to college because they were oldest and went to college before any of their siblings, regardless of the educational attainment of their parents. In other words, its validity as a measure (or operational definition) of first-generation college students was seriously undermined.

We can broadly categorize the constructs of interest to social scientists with respect to whether they concern what research participants know (facts); what they think, expect, feel, or prefer (beliefs and attitudes); or what they have done (behaviors). A questionnaire generally includes questions referring to more than one of these categories, and at times a single question has aspects of more than one category; however, we use these distinctions to discuss the issues involved in developing questions.

Exercise: Developing questionnaire items

Identify a construct that you might want to measure in your own research. Assume that you plan to use questionnaire items to assess it. That is, your operational definition will consist of responses to a set of 2–3 questionnaire items. Write 2–3 questions that you might use. Keep these questions in mind as you read the remainder of this chapter. In what ways might the questions you generated be problematic? How might you improve the questions you wrote? What other factors might you want to consider if you were to use these questions in your research? How could you evaluate whether your questions yield scores that are reliable?

Questions Aimed at Facts

Often the simplest way of ascertaining facts is to approach people who know them and ask. We expect people to know a variety of facts about themselves and their situations, and a significant portion of many questionnaires is devoted to obtaining factual information, such as the respondent's age, education, religion, income, marital status, and occupation. Questions about events, circumstances, or conditions known to the respondent, such as details of recent illness or medical treatment, also are common.

The possibility for error in reporting facts must always be considered. Errors can arise from memory problems, from response biases, or from different interpretations of questions. In one study of potential bias in reporting charitable contributions, Bekkers and Weipking (2011) found substantial inaccuracy – similar to findings reported 60 years earlier (Parry & Crossley, 1950) with respect to misreporting of charitable contributions (40% inaccurate), voter registration and voting (25% errors), and even age (17% misstatements). In reporting their ages, people tend to round off (to 30, 40, 50, etc.) rather than reporting exactly, and it is not unusual for people to misstate their ages. This problem can usually be avoided by asking for year of birth rather than current age.

Memory failures are more likely for events that are farther in the past or that are more trivial and routine. The structure of the questionnaire can ease respondents' task; for example, fertility, occupational, or medical history data are often collected in a chronological format. Remembering temporally related events can aid recall of more of the desired details. Reassessments can also increase the probability of recall. **Memory telescoping**, that is, the tendency to recall events as being more recent than they actually were, can also be problematic (Thompson, Skowronski, & Lee, 1988). For example, an episode of illness that was actually 16 months ago might be reported in response to a question about illnesses in the past 12 months, perhaps leading the researcher to overestimate illness frequency.

Specificity and precision are important in factual questions to avoid interpretation of questions in terms of respondents' own frame of reference. For example, the term "income" is vague – it could mean respondents' job earnings, total income (including unearned income like interest, dividends, or capital gains, or other payments in addition to earnings), or total family or household income; it could mean before-tax or after-tax income; and so on. The question would have to be worded carefully and differently depending upon the information sought.

Specific facts from the recent past that are nontrivial and therefore memorable are generally reported relatively well – if they are nonthreatening to respondents. This is particularly true if question wording, questionnaire forms, and administration procedures are properly designed. But even such major events as hospitalizations can be substantially underreported just a year later; memory cannot be completely trusted (Cannell, Fisher, & Bakker, 1965).

Questions Aimed at Beliefs or Attitudes

Questions that require more subjective judgments, such as those about beliefs or attitudes, are probably the most difficult to write, for a number of reasons:

- Respondents might not have attitudes because they never thought about the issue until the interviewer asked about it. Researchers cannot count on respondents saying they don't know; many people simply respond with an opinion that is reached on the spot and therefore not well considered. Some research indicates, however, that people who have formed attitudes toward an object can be distinguished from those who have not by the shorter time they take to answer an attitude question (Fazio, Powell, & Herr, 1983). Assessing the amount of time between question and response might help overcome the problem of respondents expressing opinions they don't hold with any certainty. Fazio and Williams (1986) used this technique in face-to-face interviews and found that the more quickly respondents reported their attitudes toward presidential candidates the better those attitudes predicted their actual votes several months later.
- Attitudes often are complex and multidimensional – an issue we discuss later in this chapter and in Chapter 8. For example, a person might not have a single overall attitude toward abortion, but might favor it in some circumstances and reject it in others, or favor it on medical grounds but disapprove of it on moral grounds.
- Attitudes have a dimension of intensity. People who have the same attitude can differ widely in the intensity of the attitude. It might thus be important to measure attitude intensity. For example, the costs of a position could be pointed out and respondents asked whether they would still support it. To determine those who most intensely favor stronger environmental protection policies, for example, respondents might be asked whether they would be willing to pay $10, $100, or $1,000 more in taxes to attain them.

As these factors suggest, expressed attitudes depend a great deal on question wording, question sequence, and interviewer effects. For example, the public expresses much greater support for "assistance for the poor" than for "welfare," although welfare refers to assistance for the poor. And in one U.S. survey (Schuldt, Konrath, & Schwarz, 2011), the difference in beliefs about whether "global warming" versus "climate change" was real depended on whether respondents were members of the Republican or Democratic political party. Republicans were more likely to believe that "climate change" (vs. "global warming") was real, whereas there was no difference among Democrats. Thus, although the two terms refer to the same phenomenon, the difference between the two parties was much greater (42.9%) when the term "global warming" was used than when the term "climate change" (26.2%) was used.

Question specificity is as important for questions about attitudes as it is for questions about facts or behaviors. General and specific questions often do not elicit the same responses, as when a person expresses a negative attitude toward an ethnic group but a positive attitude toward individual members of that group. Usually, specific questions yield more valid responses. For example, asking people whether they favor more educational television programs would not reveal whether they would watch them; they might simply think that they are generally good for other people. However, answers to seemingly specific questions sometimes reflect general attitudes, making the answers subject to misinterpretation by the researcher. For example, people might be asked, "Are qualified Black teachers as likely to be hired in the schools in this city as qualified White teachers?" Unless respondents have specific knowledge about practices in the school system, it is likely they would answer on the basis of a general opinion about whether Blacks are treated fairly. The answer would not be based on the specific issue, although it might seem to be. This question also might produce the same (No) responses from two groups that are very different, one consisting of individuals who believe that they would be less likely to be hired because of discrimination, and a second of those who believe they would be more likely because of preferential hiring. Questions need to be framed at an appropriate level of specificity, avoiding questions that are so general as to be meaningless, questions that are too specific to be answered meaningfully, and questions that inadvertently combine disparate respondents with differing motivations for selecting a particular response.

Questions Aimed at Friendship Patterns and Attitudes toward Specific Others

Positive and negative attitudes about or actual interactions among people who all are members of a group or social network are sometimes assessed using **sociometric questions**. In sociometric questionnaire studies, all members of the group are asked to indicate which other members they would like to have as a partner in some interaction (e.g., "eat lunch with," "work with") and which group members they would not like to have as a partner. Sometimes they are asked to rate all members of their social network on desirability, while in other instances respondents might be allowed to name as many others as they wish in a particular category or might be restricted to naming a limited number, for example, three others.

Sociometric data can provide information about individuals' position in the group, the social subgroups or "cliques" within the group, the relations among subgroups, the group's cohesiveness, the leadership structure, and other matters. Sociometric measures have been used in studies of various social phenomena, including leadership, peer relations in racially mixed schools, bullying and relational aggression, effects of experimental treatments on group structure, and so on. For example, Maruyama and colleagues (Maruyama, Miller, & Holtz, 1986) examined the relations of sociometric ratings of school peers (work with, have on sports team, sit next to) with school achievement, examining whether or not popularity seemed to "cause" achievement in desegregated schools.

Later in this chapter and in Chapter 8, we outline principles for developing various types of multiple-item scales to assess attitudes. Those scales could assess friendships, but can cover a range of issues and topics. Attitudes are generally best measured using multiple questions and constructing scales. As we discuss later, a properly constructed scale almost always has better reliability and validity than does a single item.

Questions Aimed at Behavior

Questions asking about behaviors should be specific. For example, it is better to ask, "For whom did you vote in the last mayoral election? What made you vote for this person? Did you know the religion of any of the candidates? Were you influenced for or against any candidate by knowledge of that person's religion?" rather than "Do you usually consider a candidate's religion in deciding for whom to vote?" The first question anchors respondents to concrete instances, which facilitates recall.

As with questions about facts, response accuracy is generally lower when respondents are asked to recall behaviors that occurred farther back in time. Because of the problems of memory, studies of behavior often use techniques, such as diaries, in which respondents log their behavior as it occurs rather than relying on recall after the event (e.g., Swim, Hyers, Cohen, & Ferguson, 2001).

Question Content: General Issues

Some considerations apply to nearly all questions regardless of type. One concerns the number of questions to devote to a topic. Unnecessary questions and unnecessary details should be avoided. For example, it might be sufficient to ask about the number of children under age 16 rather than the age of each child in a family. However, enough questions should be included to permit full understanding of the responses, particularly for those topics that are the focus of the research. Usually, this principle implies using multiple-item scales to measure key attitudes so that reliability and validity are maximized, but it has other implications as well. For example, asking about respondents' attitudes toward a particular ethnic group should be done in the context of parallel questions about other groups. Otherwise, we would not know whether responses suggesting a negative attitude were specific to the group or reflected a negative view of all ethnic outgroups or even of all people in general.

Sometimes the overall research purpose involves the replication of a question or an entire study. In these cases, questions should be worded exactly as they were in the original study (not surprisingly, called **exact replication**). As we have seen, even seemingly minor wording changes – such as the use of the term "forbid" instead of "not allow" – can result in large differences in responses. A similar situation arises when information derived from the questionnaire is to be compared to other sources of information (e.g., U.S. Census data, personnel records, or directory listings); the question and the response categories should follow those used in the other source. An exception might occur if the second group of respondents was culturally different from the first. In that case, it might be more important to gather responses on the same conceptual variables (**conceptual replication**) rather than ask the exact same questions.

Even when replication is not a primary purpose, the ability to compare results from a study with those of earlier research often greatly increases the meaningfulness of the results by placing them in context. It is therefore common for researchers to use questions that are identical to those used in previous research. This also allows them to avoid spending time and effort developing a new measure of a construct that other researchers have measured in the past. In addition to published research papers, statistical archives, such as those that the U.S. Census Bureau makes available on the Internet, and compilations of questions and scales, such as Tests in Print (Buros Center for Testing) and the American Psychological Association's PsycTESTS database, are useful sources of existing measures.

If new measures are developed or the wording in existing measures needs to be adapted or updated, identifying the specific terms to use can be difficult. As noted, the use of terms such as "earnings" versus "income" can completely change the meaning of a question. Terms should be exact, reflecting just what the question content is intended to mean. However, terms must also be simple – comprehensible even to the least-educated respondents. Keep in mind also that respondents may be familiar with the terms when they hear them, but not when they see them in writing; the reverse can also be true. Many commonly used terms are frequently misunderstood, including personal characteristics such as "nationality," "marital status," or "unemployed" and attitude objects such as "guaranteed wage" or "mass media." If there is concern, questions should be pretested to see whether they are understood. Terms that are misunderstood should be avoided and simpler equivalents substituted, or terms should be clarified in detail. For example, instead of asking, "What is your marital status?" which might elicit reports of marital problems, plans for the future, opinions about marriage, or feelings about personal fitness for marriage, it is best to ask, "Are you currently married, widowed, divorced, or separated or have you never been married?"

Ambiguous or vague words are frequent sources of trouble. Even familiar, simple words can give rise to ambiguity: In "What kind of headache remedy do you usually use?" the word "kind" might be understood by some respondents to refer to a "brand" and by others to mean "pills versus powder." Quantifying words (e.g., "frequently," "often," "sometimes," "almost never," "usually") are intrinsically vague and should be avoided in favor of numerical ranges when possible. In "Do you attend religious services regularly?" one respondent might take "regularly" to mean weekly, whereas for another it might mean once a month.

Biased words in questions can produce biased responses. Terms that produce powerful emotional responses, such as "freedom," "equality," "justice," "loss," "bureaucrat," or "big business," should generally be avoided. Two people holding opposite viewpoints might word questions about wage and price controls in two different ways: "Do you think that government bureaucrats should be involved in regulating workers' wages and the prices charged by businesses?" versus "Do you think that big business and powerful union leaders should be able to set prices and wages at whatever levels they choose, or should the government step in to protect consumers from increases in the cost of living?" The second version is likely to elicit more pro-control responses. These examples of biased questions, although extreme, are not fanciful; newsletters sent by congressional representatives to their constituents often contain "surveys" that use equally biased questions. One suspects that the purpose of such questions is as much to persuade voters of the wisdom of the representative's position as to determine the voters' true opinions, a strategy that can backfire if respondents feel as if they are being manipulated (Schuman & Presser, 1996).

Finally, the sensitivity or level of threat posed by the question content needs to be carefully considered. If responses are likely to be viewed as private or personal by respondents, special precautions in wording and presentation can maximize the chance of obtaining valid answers instead of misinformation or refusals to answer. Techniques for measuring opinions on sensitive topics are discussed later in this chapter.

Question Structure

Questions should be short and simple. Complex and lengthy sentences are likely to be misunderstood by respondents. However, the need to use simple words may result in lengthy sentences, and compromises must sometimes be struck. The key idea in the question should come last to avoid a premature formulation of an answer. Qualifications and conditional clauses should come first. For example, researchers ask, "If your party nominated a woman for president, would you vote for her if she were qualified for the job?" instead of, "Would you vote for a woman for president if ..." Even the standard wording might be improved by moving the phrase about qualification for the job to the beginning.

Questions should also simplify respondents' task as much as possible. For example, instead of asking what percentage of income is spent on rent, it is preferable to ask about both monthly income and monthly rent payments. Instead of asking about the average length of recent vacation trips, ask for the length of the three most recent trips. The researcher can calculate the desired percentage or average from respondents' answers.

Expressing All Alternatives

Questions should make all response alternatives clear. Even when an implied alternative is clear, stating it explicitly can make it more salient and hence place possible responses on a more equal footing. Omitting some alternatives or not treating them equally in the question actually constitutes a form of bias. The question "In the mayoral election, do you plan to vote for Mayor Jones or the challenger?" is blatantly biased; the names of both candidates should be given, and perhaps the fact that one is the incumbent should be omitted ("... do you plan to vote for Jones or Brown?").

Similarly, one fairly common practice is to describe a policy by introducing it with "Some people say we should..." to lead in to a question about "Do you agree or disagree?" or "What do you think?" The result can be a biased question unless the opposing position is treated equally, as in, "Some people say that women should have more leadership roles in business, industry, and government. Others say that women do not need to be in more leadership roles. What do you think?" An alternative strategy is to use a forced-choice format. For example, instead of "Some people say that individuals are more to blame than social conditions for crime and lawlessness in this country" followed by an agree or disagree response scale, we might ask, "Which in your opinion is more to blame for crime and lawlessness in this country – individuals or social conditions?" (Schuman & Presser, 1996). Forced-choice wording sometimes elicits more valid responses than agree or disagree wording, perhaps because the latter is more susceptible to response biases, such as a general tendency to agree with statements regardless of their content (Petty, Rennier, & Cacioppo, 1987).

Avoiding Unwarranted Assumptions

The question "What is your occupation?" assumes that all respondents have an occupation. "For whom did you vote in the last presidential election?" assumes that all respondents voted. Such questions annoy respondents and are likely to produce invalid data. The general solution to this problem is to ask a preliminary question about whether the respondent is working, did vote, or whatever is appropriate, and then ask the question of interest for only those respondents who fall into the relevant category. Other respondents can be instructed to skip the irrelevant question.

Another way unwarranted assumptions can be introduced into questionnaires is by **double-barreled questions**, which inappropriately combine two separate ideas and require a single response. Asking about the attitude of respondents' "parents" is inappropriate, for the father's and mother's attitudes might differ. Other examples are "Do you think that the government's policy on inflation is effective and fair?" and "Do you think that taxes on corporations should be increased and taxes on individuals lowered?" The last example might be appropriate if a specific policy proposal combining those two elements is being considered; a question about the respondents' attitude on the proposed policy would necessarily be double-barreled in form.

Open-Ended versus Closed-Ended Questions

Questions and response options can be broadly categorized as either open-ended (or free-response) or closed-ended (or fixed-alternative). Open-ended questions allow respondents to answer in a relatively unconstrained way, either writing or typing a response or telling it to the interviewer, who is instructed to record the response verbatim. Later, the researcher instructs judges or raters to code the responses in terms of categories or themes. In contrast, closed-ended questions are those that provide two or more response alternatives and respondents are instructed to select the choice closest to their own position.

Open-ended and closed-ended questions have complementary strengths and weaknesses. Open-ended questions allow respondents to convey the fine shades of their attitudes to their own satisfaction instead of forcing them to choose one of several statements each of which might seem unsatisfactory. Responses can thus be more representative of the true range and complexity of participants' opinions. Open-ended questions can be used when the researcher does not know the full range of attitude positions in the population under study; construction of closed-ended questions requires such knowledge in advance. Open-ended questions may therefore be especially useful in research with populations for whom existing measures have never been used (e.g., in cross-cultural research) and it is thus unclear whether existing measures are valid. If open-ended questions are to be used, researchers should be clear about the kind of information they want, as participants are likely to ignore open-ended questions that are vague or otherwise difficult to answer. One helpful strategy, in addition to pretesting, is to provide specific instructions, such as "Please write 3–5 sentences to describe your impressions so that 5–10 years from now you could read your response and know what your impressions were at this time."

Open-ended questions also have disadvantages, however. The most important are the cost and difficulty of coding responses. Open-ended responses are frequently contradictory, incomprehensible, or irrelevant, and a significant portion usually defy all efforts at meaningful categorization. They are functions of respondents' attitude positions but also of their intensity, knowledge about the issue, involvement, education, general verbal fluency, communicative style, and other factors (e.g., the quality of instructions that were provided). To code such responses meaningfully requires a great deal of work and is sometimes simply impossible. In contrast, closed-ended questions are easily scored to produce meaningful results for analysis.

Another advantage of closed-ended questions is that the provision of response categories can help clarify the intent of the question or facilitate recall. For instance, respondents might be unable to recall the name of their preferred political candidate before a primary election but might be able to pick the name out of a list of candidates. Or people might not be able to remember all the state parks they have visited in the past year without the aid of a list of names and locations. Often, open-ended questions concern respondents' reasons or explanations for a response. The follow-up might be worded, "Would you tell me more about your thinking on that?" Full information often requires more than one question. For example, the question "Why do you feel the way you do about abortion?" might elicit answers involving personal or educational experiences, beliefs about legal restrictions, political attitudes, moral or religious values, or beliefs about when human life begins. (This variety of possible responses illustrates the difficulties of coding open-ended responses in ways that permit comparisons across respondents.) The goals of the research might be best served by using a series of questions to ask each respondent about each of these different aspects of the issue.

Researchers often seek to obtain the benefits of both open-ended and closed-ended questions. One approach is to present an open-ended question first followed by closed-ended questions. Another is to present a set of fixed-response alternatives and also an open-ended "other" category, allowing people who are not comfortable with any of the given alternatives to provide their own; however, this type of question rarely obtains enough "other" responses to warrant analysis. Most respondents choose one of the offered response categories rather than create their own. This type of question is nevertheless useful in determining whether important response alternatives were not included among the fixed set: A relatively large number of "other" responses indicates that the set of responses is incomplete and should be revised.

Perhaps the best way to combine the advantages of open- and closed-ended questions is during the early stages of questionnaire development. Initially, open-ended questions are asked of a small pretest sample of the population that is to be studied. Closed-ended questions can be constructed that represent the most common response categories found in the pretest sample. This approach saves work (for only the open-ended responses from the pretest, not from the whole study sample, need to be coded), while ensuring that the closed-ended question that is finally used adequately represents the diversity of opinions on the issue. Closed-ended questions constructed in this way generally have equal or superior validity to the open-ended questions from which they were constructed (Schuman & Presser, 1996). Most researchers today use mainly closed-ended questions in attitude measurement but with a few open-ended questions to obtain reasons for or illustrations of attitudes on key issues. Open-ended responses can help in the formulation of new hypotheses and often are quoted to lend interest and concreteness to research reports.

Response Options for Closed-Ended Questions

If closed-ended questions are used, additional decisions have to be made. The question might call for a response scale along a single dimension, for example, "How frequently do you attend religious services: never, a few times a year, about once a month, about two to three times a month, about once a week, or more often than once a week?" For attitude items, a common response scale involves the dimension of agreement versus disagreement, using qualified categories like "strongly agree," "agree," "disagree," and "strongly disagree." These are usually among the easiest types of questions for respondents to answer because the response dimension is so clearly identified. In this case, an issue is whether each response alternative has a label, or only the end points are labeled (strongly agree; strongly disagree). To the extent that labeling every response alternative clarifies the task, doing so will reduce measurement error. At the same time, however, labeling each point results in a categorical scale, whereas labeling only the end points produces a scale often treated as interval.

Closed-ended questions can also involve response options that do not fall along a single dimension, for example, "If the election were being held today, which presidential candidate would you vote for: Barack Obama or Mitt Romney?" or "Would you say the group most responsible for causing inflation is business, labor unions, government, or some other group?" As the last example illustrates, a residual "other" category can be included in a set of responses. One danger with lists of unordered response categories is that they might fail to include the preferred choice of some respondents, a possibility that can be reduced by pretesting or by including an "other, please specify" option. Another problem is that respondents must consider each response option individually, which makes the question difficult to answer. A final problem is that the categories might not be mutually exclusive, forcing respondents to choose between equally true alternatives, for example, "How did you first hear about the proposed freeway: from a friend or relative, at a meeting of an organization to which I belong, at work, from my spouse, over television or radio, or from a newspaper?" (Dillman, 1978). What if some respondents heard about it from a friend at work? Poorly constructed response options are among the most common problems in questionnaires.

Response options must strike the appropriate balance between vagueness and overprecision. Most respondents would find it hard to answer a question such as, "How many meals did you eat at restaurants last month: _____ meals," for too much precision is implied by the request for a specific number. On the other hand, "very many, quite a lot, not too many, just a few, none" would be vague. Ranges of numbers are usually the best solution in such cases. An example is "none, 1–2 meals, 3–5 meals, 6–10 meals, 11–20 meals, more than 20 meals." Income is generally measured using numerical categories because respondents often are more comfortable placing their income in a category like $15,000–$19,999 than giving an exact figure. As with any set of response categories, the ranges should be mutually exclusive and exhaustive. Income categories, for instance, should not be given as $15,000–$20,000, $20,000–$30,000, and so on. This point might seem minor (not many respondents will have an income of exactly $20,000), but the manner in which such details are treated creates an overall impression of sloppiness or care in question construction and might there-fore influence respondents' motivation to take the task seriously.

Filters and the Assessment of No Opinion

People have an unfortunate tendency to answer questions even if they have no knowl-edge of, or opinion on, the issue. Unless the purpose of the research includes the measurement of off-the-cuff, uninformed reactions, the assessment of "no opinion" or "don't know" responses should be allowed, for example, by listing "don't know" as one response alternative.

Sometimes the "don't know" response is explicitly mentioned in the question, as in, "Do you favor or oppose... or haven't you thought much about it?" A variant of this approach is to include a neutral point in the response scale, for example, "strongly agree," "agree," "no opinion," "disagree," or "strongly disagree." Of course, more "don't know" responses are obtained when the possibility is explicitly mentioned than when it is not, and one has to decide whether people who "neither agree nor disagree" are the same as those who have "no opinion." Sometimes the opinion question is preceded by a filter question: "The governor has recently taken a position on the issue of layoffs for state employees. Have you heard or read enough about this to have an opinion on the matter?" Respondents who answer affirmatively might even be asked to describe the governor's position to verify their understanding. Respondents who claim not to have an opinion would not be asked to respond to a subsequent opinion question.

Research indicates that a substantial number of people, perhaps as many as 25% of the population, give a "don't know" response when a filter question invites it but give a substantive opinion to an unfiltered question. Such respondents are called float-ers (Schuman & Presser, 1996). Using unfiltered questions and therefore including the floaters' responses can seriously affect conclusions drawn from attitude surveys. An overall recommendation is to use filters to screen out uninformed respondents if the measurement of only informed opinion on the issue is the goal, but to use standard (unfiltered) questions to assess basic values, ideologies, or general attitudes.

Question Sequence

The sequence of questions in a questionnaire or interview is also important. An appropriate sequence can ease respondents' task, which is particularly important at the very beginning to capture respondents' interest and motivate completion. The sequence of questions can also either create or avoid biases that influence responses to later questions. Context effects, effects of preceding questions on responses to later questions, pose the same sorts of issues as effects of question wording, although they seem to be less powerful. The following guidelines help minimize bias and make questionnaire completion easier.

Respondents often doubt whether they can provide meaningful information. They are not experts on the topic or (perhaps) even highly educated. They may worry about embarrassing themselves by not knowing the answers. Every questionnaire should therefore begin with a few easy and unchallenging questions (probably closed-ended questions offering only two or three response categories). At the same time, initial questions should be interesting, and clearly important and relevant to the stated study purpose (Dillman, 1978). One common practice, beginning the questionnaire with easy-to-answer background items like age, marital status, or education, is thus unwise.

The main questions come next; they might be concerned with respondents' beliefs, behaviors, attitudes, or whatever concerns the purpose of the study. Questions about respondents' social and demographic background should be put at the end when respondents are ordinarily more willing to give such personal information. And if they are not willing, at least replies to the belief and attitude questions will not be affected by the suspicion or resentment that personal questions might arouse.

In addition, topically related questions should be kept together. Respondents can become confused and annoyed if questions skip around from topic to topic. Moreover, each topic should be linked in respondents' minds to the overall purpose of the study. Questions with no evident connection to the topic arouse suspicion and resentment, for example, if a questionnaire about "how people feel about the Social Security system" suddenly turned to questions on drug use. Respondents often resist even demographic questions if their relevance is not understood, which is another reason for putting such items at the end of the questionnaire; the implicit or explicit message is then that they will be used to compare the beliefs or opinions of people with different characteristics. Thus, respondents can see their relevance.

Clear and meaningful transitions between topics that clarify the relevance of the new topic to the study purpose are essential. At a minimum, transitional statements signal that one topic has been completed and a new one is coming up. These statements might be as simple as "The next few questions are about your experiences with the members of other ethnic groups." Transitions can also explain – although not with great technical detail – the rationale for the succeeding questions in terms of the study purpose or their association with the preceding topic. An example is, "An important part of understanding people's attitudes toward Social Security has to do with their feelings about retirement from work. So, next we would like to ask some questions about your plans and thoughts about retirement," or to introduce the personal background items at the end of the questionnaire, "Finally, we would like to ask some questions about yourself, to help us interpret the results." Well-written transitions smooth the flow of a questionnaire or interview, ease respondents' task, and motivate them to continue by showing the inquiry to be meaningful and relevant.

Sequence within a Topic Area

Within specific topic areas, two general guidelines relate to question sequence:

*   Present general questions first, followed by increasingly specific and detailed questions; this is known as the **funnel principle**. More general questions (e.g., satisfaction or dissatisfaction with one's work in general) are more easily justified in terms of their relevance to the study purpose. They then serve as a natural lead-in to more specific questions. The general-to-specific sequence also produces less bias than the reverse. For example, specific questions about satisfaction with wages that

precede a general question about job satisfaction would lead respondents to over-weight wages in their overall judgments.

* Look for possible associations among questions that might produce bias if they are presented close together. For example, we would not want to ask questions about strikes and labor troubles before a question about attitudes toward unions.

Question sequence effects can be quite large (Schuman & Presser, 1996). They are more likely to occur with general or summary questions than with others (Tourangeau & Rasinski, 1988); however, order effects influence attitude and even factual responses. In one survey, respondents reported that they had been the victims of more crimes if a series of crime-related attitude items preceded the factual questions, perhaps because the attitude questions aided recall (Schuman & Presser, 1996). Our ability to predict what questions are susceptible to order effects is not complete, but common sense must be applied in questionnaire construction to avoid obvious problems. Questions that are administered by computer can be presented in a different random order for each respondent. To the extent that a greater number of orders is possible, it is unlikely that a particular order would have any practical consequence.

One implication of order effects involves the assessment of changes over time. Although researchers have long known that even seemingly minor wording changes can greatly influence responses, confounding intended replications, it now appears that the context of a question, and particularly the few preceding questions, can have similar effects. As such, the most persuasive replications carry over a whole sequence of questions, rather than a single question.

Researchers have used split-ballot experiments within surveys to determine the effects of differences in question wording and sequence. A **split-ballot experiment** uses two (or more) versions of a questionnaire, with different wordings or sequences, for different, randomly assigned subsets of respondents. Random assignment means that respondents receiving the different forms can be assumed to be equivalent so that any differences in responses can be attributed to the wording or sequence. Split-ballot experiments are useful for any study in which the researcher wishes to rule out question wording effects as a major influence on results. For example, we could use two different wordings of a crucial question in a split-ballot experiment. If the results are similar, wording effects probably did not play a major role in the results.

Item Wording for Sensitive Questions

When question content might prove embarrassing or threatening to respondents or is viewed as private or personal, direct questioning can elicit deceptive responses or refusals to answer. Questions about illegal behaviors, sexual practices, and attitudes toward outgroups pose obvious problems. Even questions about income and political affiliation are sometimes viewed as threatening. Various techniques have been developed in an effort to obtain truthful answers to sensitive questions. The basic issue, however, is whether respondents believe that researchers are taking appropriate steps to ensure that the information they provide is not disclosed in such a way that their identity can be ascertained. It is also important that sensitive topics be fully introduced by transition statements in the questionnaire and that their relevance to the study topic is made clear. Respondents are more willing to respond if they understand the need for the information than if the questions seem gratuitous or unnecessary.

Certain precautions in wording are typical for topics of only marginal sensitivity. For example, question wording can "explain away" the behavior and make respondents more comfortable in giving that reply. Examples are "Did you vote in the presidential election last November, or didn't you find the time to vote?" and "Do you favor or oppose the program of . . . or haven't you happened to hear much about this?" Not having voted or not knowing enough to have an opinion are implicitly excused in the wording to encourage respondents to answer truthfully.

Other practices also seem to encourage valid responses to threatening behavioral items. Wording variations have little effect on yes or no responses to simple "Have you done it?" questions about socially undesirable behaviors, but have major effects on quantitative responses to questions about how much or how often (Bradburn & Sudman, 1979). The most valid results seem to come from long (vs. short) questions and open-ended (vs. closed-ended) formats. Another practice may also help: the use of respondents' own preferred words for the behavior, determined from a prior question, rather than a standard term. A recommended strategy is to embed a threatening behavioral question in a connected sequence of questions (Dillman, 1978). Respondents might be asked about how frequently they think other people engage in the behavior, how much they approve or disapprove of it, and whether anyone they know personally has done it, before asking whether they have done it.

An additional issue concerns how to assess ethnic identity. Society is becoming increasingly diverse and the numbers of multiethnic or multiracial people are increasing as well. Further, some respondents object to terms such as "African American," whereas others object to alternatives like "Black." The term "Native American," if used without further clarification, is selected by many White people as well as by American Indians (whom it is intended to denote). The best solutions are to instruct respondents to "check all that apply," to use alternative labels for each response category, and to provide an "other" category and ask respondents to write or type their ethnicity. So, for example, possible responses might include: Asian/Asian American/ Pacific Islander; Black/African American; Hispanic/Latino/a/Chicano/a; Northern American Indian/Native American/Alaskan Native; White/Caucasian; Other, please specify: _____. Different categories and terms are likely to be necessary, depending on the geographic areas from which respondents are expected to come. Depending on the research goals, for work in the U.S., one could use the U.S. Census categories, which were agreed upon after extensive work and consultation.

Creating Multiple-Item Scales

Some scaling methods use single-item global ratings – by the respondent or by observers – to assign scores to people or other objects; these scores are intended to reflect the underlying construct. For example, individuals might rate their liberalism or conservatism in response to: "Do you consider yourself to be very liberal, liberal, middle of the road, conservative, or very conservative?" The response places the individual in a particular position on the scale. Or judges might rate news stories as "favorable," "neutral," or "unfavorable" with respect to a controversial issue. The judges evaluate the story based on standardized rules that they have been trained to use, assigning scores that locate the stories along a single scale from favorable to unfavorable.

In the remainder of this chapter, however, we focus on creating multiple-item measures. Even though both single-item and multiple-item measures, or scales, serve the basic function of providing a usable measure of a theoretical construct, multiple-item scaling procedures are generally preferred. Creating a single score to summarize several observed variables in a meaningful way can simplify the analysis. For example, it would be simpler to test hypotheses about congressional representatives based on one total support for gun control score than on a large number of individual votes or on a single important vote.

The most important advantage of a multiple-item scale is that it almost always has better reliability and validity than do the individual items or variables that make it up. As our discussion thus far suggests, responses to individual items are influenced by many factors in addition to respondents' standing on the construct that the items are intended to measure. This variability can be called **item-specific error**. Such influences might include response errors, different interpretations of or familiarity with item content, fatigue, distractions, and so forth. But across a large number of items, such varying influences would be expected roughly to average out, leaving the scale formed from all the items as a purer measure of the underlying construct. This is basic reliability theory, where true score variance is expected to combine additively, while random errors, because they are random, do not increase as items are combined. It also is a specific application of the logic of multiple operations initially described in Chapter 2. Note, however, that nonrandom variability (e.g., common method variance) does not combine randomly, lessening the value of combining items.

Issues Concerning Item Construction in Multiple-Item Scales

Several issues – in addition to those we have already discussed – are important in constructing items for multiple-item scales:

- The items must be empirically related to the construct that is to be measured; otherwise, they can contribute nothing (except error) to the measurement. Items that have more in common correlate more highly with each other, leading to the greater reliability of scores. At the same time, if all the items selected were identical, they would not be tapping the full domain of the construct, but only a subset of that domain. Therefore, one should not just look for items with high correlations, for they may be too redundant and not allow a researcher to assess the full domain as defined by the construct.
- The items must differentiate among people who are at different points along the dimension being measured. Items need to discriminate not only between extreme positions but also among individuals near the midpoint of the scale, so items that tap different points along the scale should be included. Items that assess the most extreme positions are often not worth including. For example, an item that elicits 97% agreement and only 3% disagreement would do little to discriminate among people along the attitude dimension (especially considering that some of the 3% probably represent random errors).

- Items should be worded so that the construct is represented by "yes" or "agree" responses about half the time and by "no" or "disagree" the rest of the time. This strategy avoids confounding the measure of the construct itself with an **acquiescence response style**, that is, the tendency to agree with statements regardless of their content. Although this bias is not as prevalent as once thought, it typically requires little extra effort to create balanced scales with roughly equal proportions of "agree" and "disagree" items.

Levels of Measurement

Not all variables have numerical scales in which higher numbers indicate more of the construct. Indeed, four **levels of measurement** are commonly distinguished: nominal, ordinal, interval, and ratio.

Nominal

Nominal scales contain qualitatively different categories to which we attach names rather than numerical meaning. The simplest are dichotomies, having only two values, such as male and female or homeowners and renters. The categories are *qualitatively* rather than quantitatively different. If we were to use numbers like 1 and 2 to stand for male and female, respectively, the numbers would have no arithmetic value. The number 2 would not mean that cases placed in that category have more of the quality than cases placed in the category numbered 1.

The list of alternatives need not exhaust all possible categories, but it should include those categories relevant to the theory and the population tested and should allow for the classification of every case. For instance, if we designed a study to test the effects of living in one's own home, in someone else's, or in an institution, these three categories plus an unspecified "other" category would be sufficient for the purposes of that study. The inclusion of "other" ensures that every case can be classified.

Ordinal

An **ordinal scale** contains categories that can be ordered by rank on a continuum. The categories indicate more or less of the quantity being measured. For example, we might ask respondents to indicate their annual incomes by checking a category, such as "$20,000–$29,999" or "$30,000–$39,999." We could then assign numbers (e.g., 1–9) such that higher values indicate higher incomes. Ordinal scales do not provide any information about the interval, or degree of difference, between the values. The interval between 1 and 2 could be larger or smaller than the interval between 2 and 3.

Interval

When numbers attached to a variable imply not only that 3 is more than 2 and 2 is more than 1 but also that the intervals between values on the scale represent equal quantities of the variable being measured, they constitute an **interval scale**. The Fahrenheit scale is an example of an interval scale; the temperature difference between 33° and 34° is the same as the temperature difference between 36° and 37°. Numbers on an interval scale can be meaningfully added or subtracted because the properties of the scale are such that $20 - 10 = 40 - 30$. But numbers on an interval scale cannot be multiplied or divided because the scale does not have a true 0, indicating the absence of the variable. We can multiply and divide the values only if we have a *ratio scale*.

Most constructs in the social sciences are measured using ordinal scales. For example, even though annual income is an equal interval variable, if we were to use it as a measure of social status, we could not assume that it represented equal intervals of social status. (This was illustrated in Figure 7.1.) The status difference between $20,000 and $40,000 is much larger than the status difference between $1,220,000 and $1,240,000. Annual income would therefore be considered an ordinal scale measure of social status.

Ratio

Ratio scales have a true 0 and the scale values thus represent multipliable quantities expressed in a unit scale, for example, length in feet or meters, weight in pounds, and so forth. Physical scales measuring length and weight are ratio scales: A 4-foot length of board is twice as long as a 2-foot piece; 10 pounds of feathers weigh twice as much as 5 pounds. For these physical scales, 0 is real and meaningful. Although we cannot point to anything that has 0 inches or 0 pounds, we know what those mean on rulers or scales, and 0 is not arbitrarily located at just any point on the scale; 0 represents the absence of the attribute. So for temperature, the Kelvin scale is a ratio scale, for its temperature of 0 is absolute zero.

Some variables used to measure constructs in the social sciences appear to be ratio measures because they have 0 as the lowest score, but they may be ratio variables only for certain purposes. Money (monetary wealth) as a measure of social status, for instance, appears to be a ratio scale because the variable has an absolute true 0. A person can be penniless. This does not mean, however, that the penniless person has 0 social status. A monk who takes a vow of poverty, for instance, has no money but has social status among people who respect religious orders.

The level of measurement is important to understand because of its implications for analyzing and interpreting data. For example, it would not make sense to ask research participants to indicate whether they consider themselves male or female and then to report the average or mean gender. However, the implications of levels of measurement for statistical analysis are not always as obvious and have, in fact, been the subject of some debate. Some authorities claim that the typical data in social science research (e.g., ratings of agreement vs. disagreement on a 1–7 scale) can only be considered ordinal rather than interval-level data. Some have further argued that ordinal-level data cannot be analyzed using powerful parametric statistics (e.g., multiple regression) because such analyses require interval or ratio-level data.

However, other authorities disagree with these claims (e.g., Dawes & Smith, 1985; Norman, 2010). Their basic argument is that the level of measurement of a particular set of data is an empirical question, to be settled – like other issues of scale validity – by examining the associations of the scores to other measurements. If the associations are essentially linear associations – they are the same at all points across the range of values the measures can take – the responses can be treated as interval scaled, and powerful data-analytic methods may be used. In other words, the level of measurement is not an intrinsic property of measures that is guaranteed by the use of a particular scaling method – any of the rating scale or multiple-item scaling techniques discussed in this chapter could, in principle, produce scores that have interval properties. Indeed, studies have shown that responses to single-item scales often approach linear associations with physical measurements (e.g., height) and that multiple-item scales do even better (Dawes, 1977). Finally, parametric statistics have been shown to be robust to the use of ordinal-level data. In short, there is a great deal of empirical and logical justification for the common practice in social science research of analyzing responses to ordinal scales, using powerful (parametric) statistics that assume an interval or ratio level of measurement.

Types of Multiple-Item Scales

Three general procedures for developing multiple-item attitude scales have been widely used. They are differential, cumulative, and summative. In addition, a multidimensional summative approach, the semantic differential, is described. The approaches differ in their assumptions about the association between people's attitudes and their responses to the individual items that make up the scale. Other differences – in the types of item used, the way the individual responses are combined to produce a scale score, and so on – follow from this difference. All the scaling methods assume that attitude questions or statements can be thought of in terms of their position along the attitude dimension that ranges from favorable to unfavorable. The logic for each procedure is presented, followed by a critique addressing strengths and weaknesses.

Differential Scales

Differential scales (Thurstone, 1929) include items that represent known positions on the attitude scale. Respondents are assumed to agree with only those items whose position is close to their own and to disagree with items that represent distant positions. The construction process involves gathering or constructing a large number of statements related to the attitude. Working independently, judges classify the statements into categories on the basis of the statements' favorability toward the attitude object or position on a dimension (e.g., liberalism–conservatism). The first category includes the statements that the judge considers most favorable to the object; the second, the next most favorable statements; and so on. The scale value of each item is then calculated as its average category placement by the judges. Finally, items representing a wide range of scale values are selected to form the scale and presented to respondents, usually in a random order, with instructions to check each statement with which they agree. Respondents' attitudes are calculated as the mean of the scale values of the items with which they agree.

In contrast to other scale types, differential scales require items that elicit agreement from people with positions near the item's scale value but disagreement from others whose attitudes are either more favorable or less favorable. For example, "Affirmative action is a necessary evil" will obtain agreement from people with an attitude position near the midpoint of the scale, but people who either strongly favor or strongly oppose affirmative action will disagree with the item. This is an example of the type of **nonmonotone item** that differential scales use. Cumulative and summated scales, in contrast, require **monotone items**: items that are either clearly favorable or unfavorable to the object. The probability of agreeing with such items should increase (or decrease) consistently as respondents move from one end of the attitude dimension to the other. For example, "Affirmative action programs increase the overall fairness of our society" would presumably elicit consistently more agreement from people who favor affirmative action than from those who oppose it.

The differential scaling method has certain advantages. The responses offer a check on the scale's assumptions. Respondents are supposed to agree with only a narrow range of items around their own position (such as items with scale values of 6.7, 7.1, and 8.0). If a respondent checks a wide range of noncontiguous items (e.g., scale values of 3.3, 7.1, and 9.4), it might mean that the respondent does not have an attitude on the issue or that the attitude is not organized along the dimension assumed by the scale. For respondents who meet the assumptions of the scale, the **latitude of acceptance** (defined as the range of scale values with which the subject agrees) can be calculated from the responses. This measure is related to the degree of the respondent's involvement with the issue or the attitude: People who are more involved in an issue tend to agree with a narrower range of positions.

The differential scaling technique is little used today. The construction procedure is lengthy and cumbersome. Although the use of judges' ratings allows the discarding of items that are ambiguous or meaningless, other scaling techniques achieve similar results with less effort. And there is much evidence that the attitudes of the judges themselves influence their assignment of scale values to the items, which is undesirable in the context of this measurement technique. Finally, and perhaps most important, differential scales have generally lower reliabilities than summated scales with the same number of items.

Cumulative Scales

Cumulative scales also are made up of items with which respondents indicate agreement or disagreement. The special feature of cumulative scales, pioneered by Guttman (1944), is that items are associated in such a way that respondents who hold a particular attitude will agree with all items on one side of that position and disagree with other items. As noted, cumulative scales thus require each item to be monotone: either clearly favorable or unfavorable to the object or issue.

One of the earliest social attitude scales, the Bogardus Social Distance Scale (Bogardus, 1933), was intended to have a cumulative pattern. The scale lists a number of relationships between a respondent and members of a particular social or ethnic group and respondents are asked to indicate which ones they consider acceptable. An example is shown in Table 7.1. Note the monotone items and the expected cumulative

Table 7.1   Bogardus Social Distance Scale

	To Close Kinship by Marriage	To My Club as Personal Chums	To My Street as Neighbors	To Employment in My Occupation	To Citizenship in My Country	As Visitors Only to My Country	Would Exclude from My Country
English	1	2	3	4	5	6	7
Black	1	2	3	4	5	6	7
French	1	2	3	4	5	6	7
Chinese	1	2	3	4	5	6	7
Russian and so on	1	2	3	4	5	6	7

Directions: For each race or nationality listed on the scale, circle each of the classifications to which you would be willing to admit the average member of that race or nationality (not the best members you have known or the worst). Answer in terms of your first feeling reactions.

pattern. That is, respondents who circle number 4 (acceptance of group members into occupations) should also circle number 5 (willing to allow group members as citizens in the country) and should not circle 6 and 7 because they are worded negatively. Similarly, respondents who did not circle 3 would not be expected to circle 2 or 1.

Response patterns that allow the formation of cumulative scales also occur in other domains. One scale, for example, assesses the conditions under which physicians recommend abortions (Koslowski, Pratt, & Wintrob, 1976). The items range from those conditions in which most physicians sampled would recommend abortion, such as the pregnancy constituting a threat to the mother's life, to those in which most would reject abortion, such as the pregnancy disrupting the mother's career or education. For the most part, the physicians' acceptance of abortion under the 11 different circumstances studied followed the cumulative pattern of a cumulative scale. For example, physicians who accept abortion if the pregnancy disrupts the mother's career also accept abortion if the pregnancy threatens the mother's life.

The main advantage of a cumulative scale is that a single number (the person's scale score) carries complete information about the exact pattern of responses to every item – under the crucial assumption that there is no random error in responses. For example, respondents with scores of 5 for a particular group on the social distance scale (Table 7.1) would be known to favor allowing group members into their neighborhoods, country, and occupations but not into their social clubs or close kinship by marriage. Thus, the scale score from a cumulative scale is unusually informative.

The scale also provides a test of the unidimensionality of the attitude. Items that reflect more than one dimension generally do not form a cumulative response pattern; indeed, Guttman (1944) originally proposed his technique as a means of examining unidimensionality rather than constructing scales. This advantage is tempered by the fact that simple random error in responses can distort the perfect cumulative response pattern, making it difficult to determine whether the attitude domain is "really" unidimensional when error is present (as it usually is).

Disadvantages of the cumulative scaling technique concern its limitation to unidimensional domains. Unidimensionality is a pattern of an attitude within a given population of individuals rather than a property of a set of items. A set of items might show a unidimensional pattern for one group of individuals but not for another, or it might be unidimensional at one time but not later. Further, most domains are not unidimensional. Consider attitudes toward government. People might have attitudes toward government regulation of business that are distinct from their attitudes toward taxation, civil rights, and so on. One dimension would not completely index attitudes toward the complex concept of government or provide the sole basis for predicting voting or other behaviors. The best approach in such cases is to accept the fact that the attitude of interest might be multidimensional and to measure it with summated scales, which do not require strict unidimensionality.

Summated Scales

Summated scales of the form developed by Likert (1932) are the most widely used in the social sciences today. Like differential and cumulative scales, a summated scale consists of a set of items to which research participants respond with agreement or disagreement; however, there are a number of differences. Only monotone items are used in summated scales – that is, items that are definitely favorable or unfavorable in direction, not items that reflect a middle or uncertain position on the issue.

Respondents typically indicate their degree of agreement or disagreement with each item by selecting a number (e.g., "strongly disagree" = 1, "disagree" = 2) or selecting a response (e.g., "strongly disagree") that is numerically coded (e.g., 1) by the researcher. Scale scores are derived by reverse scoring negatively worded items and then averaging (or summing, assuming that all respondents responded to all items) across items. As with any scaling method, scale scores are interpreted as representing respondents' standing on the construct being measured. In the case of attitudes, the basis for the interpretation is that the probability of agreeing with favorable items and disagreeing with unfavorable ones increases directly with the degree of favorability of the respondent's attitude. (This is the definition of monotone items.)

The measured response to any single item is considered to reflect in part the construct of interest, and in part measurement error. The summation of responses to many items into a single scale score should result in error variance components combining randomly. This means that errors will not increase as true score variance on the construct increases additively, which strengthens the common construct reflected in the set of items.

The procedure for constructing a summated scale involves several steps:

1. Based on a theoretical conception of the attitude or other construct to be measured, the investigator assembles a large number of items that are relevant to the attitude and that are either clearly favorable or unfavorable (i.e., are monotonic).
2. The items are administered to a group of pilot participants drawn from a population similar to that for which the scale is to be used. Participants indicate their agreement on a multipoint response scale.

3. Scale scores are computed.
4. Responses are analyzed to determine which items contribute most to the (internal consistency) reliability of scores.

The **item analysis** stage is the most important in the development of a scale. Several techniques are available. A simple approach is to calculate the associations between the responses to each item and the total scale scores. Items that are not strongly associated with the scale scores are not as effectively measuring the desired construct/dimension and should be examined carefully to see whether they should be discarded. More sophisticated and complex approaches also are available, such as **factor analysis**, which is used to evaluate the underlying dimensionality or degree of statistical commonality in a set of items – that is, the degree to which responses to them appear to be influenced by the same construct (e.g., Kline, 1994). Exploratory and confirmatory factor analytic techniques, in particular, also allow researchers to evaluate structural validity – an issue we discuss in Chapter 8. It is sufficient for now to note only that the final multiple-item scale can be unidimensional or multidimensional, depending on the informed decisions of the researcher. Even if several dimensions emerge, however, if they are to be combined, they need to be positively associated to some extent, as otherwise the concept of a single overall scale score makes no sense.

The advantages of summated scaling methods are several. First, a summated scale is usually simpler to construct than a differential scale. Second, summated scales can be used in many cases in which differential or cumulative scales cannot (e.g., multidimensional constructs). Third, a summated scale is generally more reliable than a differential scale of the same length. Finally, the range of agreement–disagreement responses permitted with summated items might make respondents more comfortable in indicating their position than the simple agree versus disagree choice forced by differential items.

Summated scales also have shortcomings. Unlike differential scales, they do not yield information about the respondents' latitude of acceptance to measure the degree of issue involvement. Unlike cumulative scale scores, scores from a summated scale do not provide information about the pattern of responses to all the individual items. The same scale score might be based on quite different combinations of responses to individual items; however, it is not clear whether this should be seen as a disadvantage. The individual items in a unidimensional summated scale are considered to be basically interchangeable; their individual identity is not as important as the fact that each reliably reflects the underlying attitude. Some differences in response patterns that lead to a particular scale score can derive from simple random error, which it is desirable to ignore. The fact that the scale contains a number of items means that random variations on individual items tend to cancel each other out when the variations are not associated with the construct being measured.

Further, when a scale is considered to be multidimensional, meaningfully different response patterns yield the same total score. In response, the researcher could use subscale scores as well as the total scale score to test hypotheses involving the construct. The subscale scores would differentiate the specific patterns of responses. Thus, an advantage of the summated scale construction technique is that multiple correlated

Table 7.2 Example of a Semantic Differential Scale

			Me as I am					
Fair	1	2	3	4	5	6	7	Unfair
Clean	1	2	3	4	5	6	7	Dirty
Light	1	2	3	4	5	6	7	Heavy
Large	1	2	3	4	5	6	7	Small
Passive	1	2	3	4	5	6	7	Active
Strong	1	2	3	4	5	6	7	Weak
Slow	1	2	3	4	5	6	7	Fast
Bad	1	2	3	4	5	6	7	Good

Note. Respondents are instructed to circle a number from 1 to 7 on each scale to rate the given concept.

dimensions can be included within a scale when it is empirically and theoretically meaningful to do so. We discuss this issue further in Chapter 8.

Semantic Differential Scales

The **semantic differential** is a specialized scaling method that has been applied to the measurement of social attitudes. It shares the basic characteristics of summated scales but also has some unique features. Respondents are asked, in effect, to make a series of ratings on multiple-point response scales. Total scores are then derived from the individual item responses by statistical techniques that might include factor analysis. In these ways the semantic differential resembles other summated scales.

The semantic differential was developed by Osgood, Suci, and Tannenbaum (1957) as a method for measuring the meaning of an object to an individual. It can also be thought of as a series of attitude scales. The respondent rates a given concept (e.g., "Irish," "Republican," "me as I am") on a series of seven-point **bipolar scales**, of the type shown in Table 7.2. Any concept – a political issue, a person, an institution, a group – can be rated. Factor analyses have demonstrated that these scales generally group together into three underlying attitude dimensions: (1) respondents' evaluations of the object, corresponding to the favorable–unfavorable dimension of traditional attitude scales (fair–unfair, clean–dirty, good–bad, valuable–worthless); (2) respondents' perceptions of the potency or power of the object or concept (large–small, strong–weak); and (3) respondents' perceptions of the activity of the object (active–passive, fast–slow, hot–cold). Responses to the individual bipolar scales can be summed to give scores that indicate individuals' positions on these three underlying dimensions of attitude toward the object being rated. This use of semantic differential ratings thus resembles a summated scale with three subscales.

Among strengths of the approach, Osgood et al. (1957) suggested that the semantic differential allows the measurement and comparison of diverse objects by diverse people because it is not greatly affected by the nature of the object being measured or the type of person using the scale. Some results, including several cross-cultural studies, support this claim, but other evidence indicates that the semantic differential is not completely comparable across concepts. The meanings of scales and their associations with the other scales vary depending on the concept being judged. What is good, for example, depends on the nature of the concept: "Strong" might be good in judging athletes but bad in judging odors. The implication is that the rating scales do not always provide consistent measurements of the underlying dimensions independently of the concepts being judged.

Reliability and Sources of Unreliability

Reliability refers to the extent to which the scores from a measure are free from random error. **Validity** is the extent to which scores reflect only the desired construct without contamination from other systematically varying constructs. A measure can yield perfectly reliable scores that are completely invalid, as in the case of a math test that measures test-taking ability rather than knowledge of math. When a measure yields scores that are both reliable and valid, we can confidently use it in research. Reliability is usually addressed prior to validity and, as we shall see, it is also easier to address.

All scores on a measure contain some components in addition to the desired construct. This idea is expressed in a simple equation:

$$\text{observed score} = \text{true score} + \text{systematic error} + \text{random error}$$

Here the **true score** is a function of the construct we are attempting to measure; **systematic error** reflects influences from other constructs besides the desired one or unique variance of individual items; and **random error** reflects nonsystematic, ever-changing influences on the score.

Consider, for example, observed or obtained scores on a math achievement test. The true score would refer to a test-taker's true math ability. But other constructs, such as motivation, also influence observed scores. Test-takers who don't care whether they do well might doodle in the margins of the test instead of working to solve the problems and end up with scores that are lower than their true ability. And some people are better than others at understanding test instructions and guessing intelligently when they are unsure of the answer, leading to scores that are higher than their true ability. Random error includes such factors as lucky or unlucky guesses; random slips of the pencil in filling in answers; simple mental mistakes in solving the problems; inability to concentrate because of a lack of sleep; feeling sick, and the like. Observed math achievement scores would partly reflect these sources of systematic and random error.

When individuals rate the attributes of others, various sources of error may affect the reliability of their responses. A common form of systematic error is **halo bias**, which refers to the tendency for overall positive or negative evaluations of the object or person being rated to influence ratings on specific dimensions (Cooper, 1981). For example, Thorndike (1920) found that supervisors' ratings of teachers yielded a very strong association between rated intelligence and rated ability to discipline. Because the actual association (based on intelligence test scores) is probably only modest,

Thorndike concluded that the raters were unable to judge each dimension independently. Instead, their global evaluations of the teacher influenced their ratings of both intelligence and ability to discipline, inflating the association. Another type of error, related to halo bias, is the **generosity error**, in which raters overestimate the desirable qualities of people whom they like.

Other types of errors reflect differences among raters in the translation of subjective judgments into overt rating scale responses. These errors stem from differences between raters in **response styles**. Some raters, for example, seem to avoid extreme response categories and assign ratings using only the more moderate categories (a **midpoint response style**), whereas others do the reverse (an **extreme response style**). Similarly, as we indicated earlier, some have an acquiescence response style, whereas others have a **disacquiescence response style**, tending toward the use of negative response categories. These styles influence not only responses to items within the same questionnaire, but also responses to questionnaires administered across time (Weijters, Geuens, & Schillewaert, 2010) and contribute to findings of differences between cultural groups (Johnson, Kulesa, Cho, & Shavitt, 2005). **Contrast error**, a tendency for raters to see others as opposite to them on a trait, arises from using one's own position on a dimension as an anchor for rating others. For example, raters who are very orderly tend to rate others as relatively disorderly and vice versa.

Besides systematic errors or biases, random errors can enter into any ratings of oneself and others and reduce their reliability. The most obvious source of random error is simple mistakes caused by things like fatigue, inattention, or improper training.

A number of steps can be taken in the construction and use of rating scales to minimize the impact of rater biases and errors. In addition to training and motivating the raters, using multiple raters (e.g., two or more judges, collateral reports) whose ratings are averaged almost always reduces the impact of random errors (unreliability) because the independent errors tend to balance out in the averaging process. The use of multiple raters also reduces halo bias (Kenny & Berman, 1980). Of course, combining multiple ratings is generally more feasible when the ratings are based on recorded material or observations of a sample of behavior. It is often impossible to have more than one rater on hand to observe live social behavior.

Increasing raters' familiarity with the object or person being rated also reduces halo bias, although it can increase generosity errors. This effect might account for the fact that self-ratings (which are obviously made by a familiar rater) are less subject to the halo bias than are ratings by others (Thornton, 1980). Ratings made concurrently with observation of behaviors are less subject to the halo bias than are ratings made from memory after witnessing the behaviors (Shweder & D'Andrade, 1980). However, one frequently used technique does *not* seem to be effective in reducing halo bias: rating all objects or people on one category before going on to the next category instead of rating each one on all categories in succession (Cooper, 1981).

Many precautions essentially are efforts to give all the raters a common frame of reference so that they use the rating scale in the same way. The use of a common frame of reference is more likely when clear, concrete definitions of the characteristic being measured are provided. Such definitions might include illustrations of behaviors or other responses that exemplify the various rating categories. Raters' tendency to avoid extreme positions could be counteracted by giving less extreme labels to these positions. People would be more likely to choose "There are many things about my job that I do not like" than "There is nothing about my job that I like."

The labeling of response categories should also take account of generosity biases. For example, in rating their instructors, college students rarely use any category worse than "good." Therefore, on a five-category scale, with "average" as the middle category, almost all the responses would fall in the upper two categories. Some universities therefore use asymmetrical or unbalanced wording, with "good" at the center of the scale, to obtain a more symmetrical response distribution: "superior," "very good," "good," "average," and "poor" (Dawes, 1972). This example also points out the common fallacy of interpreting rating scale responses literally. On a scale like this one, 80% to 90% of the responses might be above the "average" category, although it is obviously impossible for 90% of the instructors to be above average in their teaching effectiveness. The information in a rating scale response is not literally contained in the specific category label that the rater chooses (such as "good" or "average") but is implicit in the scale's demonstrated associations with other measures.

Despite our best efforts to minimize systematic and random errors, observed scores cannot be assumed to reflect the desired construct only. The key question becomes how to separate the various contributions to the score so that we can improve the test and do a better job of classifying or ranking people on the construct. Knowing how much systematic and random error influence scores would suggest ways to improve the test or the need to consider alternative measures. And, of course, better measures would enable us to classify or rank people more accurately; that is, observed scores would better reflect true scores because the effects of error would be weaker.

Fortunately, there is a way to achieve these goals. The underlying logic involves assessing the contribution of different components of observed scores by comparing the similarity of observations made under circumstances in which particular components are expected to vary. For example, we could assess the similarity of two sets of scores in which the true score and systematic error components are expected to remain constant, and only random error is expected to vary. Greater similarity between the two sets implies that random error is less influential, whereas greater differences imply that random error is more important.

We can assess the similarity of sets of scores using correlation coefficients. A **correlation coefficient** is a statistical index of the strength of association between two variables; it provides an answer to the question, "To what extent do two variables measure the same thing?" The possible values of a correlation coefficient range from -1.0 to $+1.0$. The absolute value of the coefficient indicates the degree to which the two sets of scores are similar; the sign indicates whether the scores are positively or negatively related. Because scores are intended to assess the same construct, they should be positively related to at least some degree. Thus, **reliability coefficients** range from 0 to $+1.0$, with 0 indicating a complete lack of reliability and 1.0 indicating perfect reliability. Once reliability is known, it can be used to estimate the strength of relationship between two variables in the absence of measurement error (e.g., through correction for attenuation).

Test–Retest Reliability

The source of random error that is the focus of concerns about reliability is expected to vary, rather than remain constant, from one occasion to another. Specific mental mistakes, slips of the pen, and the like would not recur if the test were repeated after some time delay. Therefore, the correlation between scores on the same measure administered on two separate occasions – a **test–retest correlation** – provides an estimate of the measure's reliability. The two occasions should be far enough apart so that respondents cannot remember specific responses from the test to the retest but close enough together so that change in the true score is expected to be minimal. A completely unreliable measure, in which all the variation in scores stems from random errors, would show a complete lack of correlation between test and retest. A perfectly reliable measure, in which no random error whatever affected the score, would produce scores that correlate perfectly over a short period of time.

Internal Consistency Reliability

Test–retest reliability estimates are conceptually easy to understand and are widely used. But they can be difficult to obtain; it is cumbersome to assemble a group of people twice to repeat the measurement, and issues of memory for responses and of change in the true construct being measured can make an appropriate time period difficult to select. An alternative estimate, called **internal consistency reliability**, is not subject to these concerns and, therefore, more widely used.

This estimate rests on the idea that random error varies not only over time but also from one question or test item to another within the same measure. That is, making a mistake, misunderstanding a word in a test question, or other sources of random error would be expected to influence some specific items on the measure but not others. If all the questions or items on the measure are measuring the same construct, lack of correlation among specific items can serve as the basis for an estimate of the influence of random errors. If random error has a strong effect, it would make scores on some individual items high and others low, reducing the item-to-item correlation. On the other hand, a weak effect of random error would mean that each item more strongly measures the same underlying construct, so a high score on one item would go together with a high score on another; the items would be highly correlated.

This basic insight has been used in different ways to develop methods of estimating the reliability of a measure without having to assess people on two separate occasions. For example, the set of items in the measure might be split into two halves, separating the full set of items into odd-numbered and even-numbered sets to ensure that an equivalent number of items from early and late in the measure appear in the two sets. The correlation between the two half-tests provides an estimate of reliability known as **split-half reliability**.

The exact value of a split-half reliability estimate, however, depends on how the items were split (e.g., odd vs. even, first half vs. last), introducing a degree of arbitrariness into reliability estimation. For this reason, the preferred measure of internal consistency reliability is now **coefficient alpha** (Cronbach, 1951). This estimate is derived from the correlations of each item with each other item and so does not rest on an arbitrary division of the items into two halves. In fact, coefficient alpha can be shown to be numerically equal to the average of all possible split-half reliabilities.

Inter-Rater Reliability

In some studies, the operational definition of a construct requires the direct observation of behavior. For instance, the operational definition of toddlers' activity level might be the amount that each toddler moves about a room during a 10-minute period of free play. As a means of quantifying movement, the room could be divided into a grid made up of equal-size cells and observers could count the number of times a toddler crosses from one cell to another. Or the quality of communication between romantic partners could be measured by observing or listening to conversations about what each likes least and most about their partner and rating them on a 5-point scale anchored by "destructive" and "constructive." In either case, a particular observer's rating of behavior is, like an item on a questionnaire, subject to error. For instance, while counting toddlers' movements from cell to cell in the grid, an observer might lose concentration and fail to record all instances of crossing from one cell to the next. Or certain children might move about the room in such a way that it is not always clear whether they moved from one cell to another. Similarly, different observers might take a different view of the quality of a conversation between romantic partners as a result of the current status of communication in their own romantic relationship.

In much the same way that random errors in responses to items on a questionnaire reduce the reliability of scores, inconsistencies between observers who are rating participants as well as random errors in observer ratings reduce the reliability of behavioral ratings. The strategy for addressing this problem is to enlist multiple observers. We can then use the logic of internal consistency reliability to estimate **inter-rater reliability**. If observers rate the behavior on a continuum (e.g., the quality of conversation between romantic partners), then their ratings can be treated like items on a questionnaire and reliability estimated using coefficient alpha. If the task given observers is to rate whether a research participant did or did not enact a behavior, then a statistical measure of agreement, such as **kappa** (Cohen, 1960) or **intraclass correlation**, can be used to estimate inter-rater reliability.

Factors that Affect Reliability

As we have indicated throughout this chapter, responses to individual items are influenced by various sources of random error. Random error causes some observed scores to be higher than the true values and some observed scores to be lower than the true values. One way to lessen effects of error is to aggregate scores across a number of items. Errors are likely to cancel each other out when multiple items are used. For this reason, measures that have a greater number of items are more reliable than shorter ones, other things being equal. Another way to lessen impacts of error is to increase the variability on the construct of interest; a larger range of variation on the measured construct among the individuals being tested also leads to higher reliability. It is easier to make reliable distinctions among individuals when they vary a lot than when they are all very close together on the target characteristic. Minimizing ambiguity in wording and instructions also helps; distractions, misunderstandings, and the like can be minimized by clear instructions and an optimal testing situation, which also decrease people's tendencies to make random errors and simple mistakes. Finally, the number of categories on the response scale can influence reliability. Providing fewer than five categories seems to limit reliability, although providing more than five categories helps little, if at all (e.g., Masters, 1974).

Summary

We began this chapter by saying that operational definitions are essential to scientific measurement. They provide a public process for reproducing and replicating measurements and manipulations so that we can assess their reliability and validity.

Operational definitions are necessary but also inevitably inadequate. They contain errors by including irrelevant components and omitting other relevant portions of the underlying construct that we want to tap. For this reason, no single operational definition completely defines a construct. Each definition is only an approximation. Because no single measure is perfect, we advocate using multiple operational definitions of any construct.

Most measures involve directly questioning individuals about facts, beliefs, attitudes, or behaviors, and careful attention must be paid to item development and questionnaire construction. Research and experience have provided guidelines for decisions on question content, wording, sequence, and the like. And various methods of constructing multiple-item measures have been developed, summated scales being the most widely used. Reliability indices, such as coefficient alpha, help researchers evaluate the extent to which such scales are free from error. All measures contain at least some error; combining responses to multiple items yields more reliable measures than do responses to single items. Measurement error can be minimized in other ways as well, for example, through the use of well-written items or questions and clear instructions and test-taking conditions.

Go online   Visit the book's companion website for this chapter's test bank and other resources at: www.wiley.com/go/maruyama

---

Key Concepts

Acquiescence response style
Bipolar scales
Coefficient alpha

Conceptual replication
Construct
Contrast error

Correlation coefficient
Cumulative scales
Definitional operationism
Differential scale
Disacquiescence response style
Double-barreled questions
Exact replication
Extreme response style
Factor analysis
Funnel principle
Generosity error
Halo bias
Internal consistency reliability
Inter-rater reliability
Interval scale
Intraclass correlation
Item analysis
Item-specific error
Kappa
Latitude of acceptance
Levels of measurement
Memory telescoping

Midpoint response style
Monotone items
Nominal scale
Nomological net
Nonmonotone items
Operational definition
Ordinal scale
Random error
Ratio scale
Reliability
Reliability coefficients
Response styles
Semantic differential scales
Sociometric questions
Split-ballot experiment
Split-half reliability
Summated scales
Systematic error
Test–retest correlation
True score
Validity
Variable

On the Web

http://www.brocku.ca/MeadProject/Mead/pubs2/philpres/Mead_1932_toc .html Writings by George Herbert Mead that provide a sense of how the earliest social scientists thought about measurement.

http://buros.org/ Home page of the Buros Center for Testing. Provides links to thousands of tests of potential interest to social scientists.

http://www.fairtest.org/ Home page of the National Center for Fair and Open Testing, a group committed to responsible use of test results.

http://www.testpublishers.org/ Home page of the Association of Test Publishers, containing useful information and resources about the responsible use of tests.

http://www.apa.org/science/programs/testing/find-tests.aspx FAQ/Finding information about psychological tests from the American Psychological Association (APA).

http://www.apa.org/pubs/databases/psyctests/index.aspx APA PsycTESTS is a database of psychological tests, measures, scales, and other assessments.

Further Reading

John, O. P., & Benet-Martínez, V. (2014). Measurement: Reliability, construct validation, and scale construction. In H. T. Reis & C. M. Judd (Eds.), *Handbook of research methods in social and personality psychology* (2nd ed., pp. 473–503). New York, NY: Cambridge University Press.

Kalton, G., & Schuman, H. (1980). The effect of the question on survey responses: A review. Retrieved March 8, 2014, from http://www.amstat.org/sections/srms/Proceedings/papers/1980_005.pdf

Schwarz, N. (1999). Self-reports: How the questions shape the answers. *American Psychologist, 54,* 93–105.

Schwarz, N., & Oyserman, D. (2011). Asking questions about behavior: Self-reports in evaluation research. In M. M. Mark, S. I. Donaldson, & B. Campbell (Eds.), *Social psychology and evaluation* (pp. 243–264). New York, NY: Guilford Press.

Shrout, P. E., & Lane, S. P. (2012). Reliability. In H. Cooper, P. M. Camic, D. L. Long, A. T. Panter, D. Rinkskopf, & K. J. Sher (Eds.), *APA handbook of research methods in psychology, Vol. 1: Foundations, planning, measures, and psychometrics* (pp. 643–660). Washington, DC: American Psychological Association.

Chapter 8

Evaluating the Construct Validity of Measures

As noted in Chapter 7, measures high in reliability would be high in validity only if they measure what they are supposed to measure. Sometimes highly reliable measures measure the wrong construct, a construct that actually is different from what is intended. A measure intended to tap people's levels of conscientiousness might instead reflect only the extent to which they are biased in the direction of reporting good things about themselves. Or if we gave a standard IQ test in English to a group of

Research Methods in Social Relations, Eighth Edition. Geoffrey Maruyama and Carey S. Ryan.
© 2014 John Wiley & Sons, Inc. Published 2014 by John Wiley & Sons, Inc.
Companion Website: www.wiley.com/go/maruyama

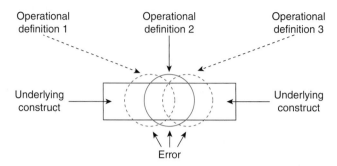

Figure 8.1 Operational Definitions Include Irrelevant Components and Fail to Include All Relevant Portions of the Underlying Construct.

French high school students, their scores might be high in test–retest reliability, but they likely would be invalid indicators of those students' intelligence. For most French students, an English IQ test would be a measure of English-language proficiency rather than a measure of intelligence. That test would be an inappropriate and, therefore, invalid test of intelligence for that group of respondents.

Most measures in the social sciences do not contain such gross errors, but all measures share problems of validity to some extent. Operational definitions inevitably assess constructs that are not supposed to be assessed and do not assess portions of the underlying construct that should be assessed. Because the underlying construct can be tapped only indirectly through operational definitions, we can never be sure what portion of the construct the operational definition taps and what portion is unmeasured. This principle of measurement is illustrated in Figure 8.1. Notice that a substantial majority of each circle representing an operational definition overlaps with the rectangle representing the underlying construct. However, the circles themselves do not overlap completely; a portion of each circle does not overlap with the rectangle at all; and a portion of the rectangle is not covered by any of the circles. Figure 8.1 also indicates that coverage of the underlying construct is greatly improved through the use of multiple operational definitions, which we discuss below.

In this chapter, we consider ways to maximize and evaluate the extent to which our operational definitions overlap with the rectangle (Figure 8.1). We begin by describing the advantages of using multiple measures that rely on different methods for obtaining them and describe methods other than direct questioning of participants, which we discussed in detail in Chapter 7. We then focus on ways to evaluate the degree to which our measures yield scores that assess the constructs they are intended to assess; in other words, we discuss evidence for their **construct validity**.

Using Multiple Methods of Measurement

Findings demonstrated across multiple measures are more compelling when they are acquired in different ways. When data are obtained in multiple ways, researchers can be even more confident that overlap between the measures represents the construct of interest rather than overlapping errors of measurement due to **common method variance**. This is because some variation in scores results simply from the method used to obtain them. In other words, although two paper-and-pencil measures of a construct are better than one, a paper-and-pencil measure coupled with an observational measure would be better still. The use of two or more measures of the same type thus does little to overcome the fallibility of each. The reasoning follows from the basic principle that we discussed in Chapter 7, that is, that all measures are fallible. And to some degree, the fallibility of a measure is tied to the method of measurement. For instance, all paper-and-pencil measures, regardless of the construct they are designed to measure, are subject to similar systematic and random errors. Systematic errors include, for example, halo bias (i.e., the tendency for overall positive or negative evaluations to influence ratings on specific dimensions) and response styles (i.e., differences between raters in the way they use response scales). Random errors include lucky guesses and slips of the pencil. (We discussed these biases and errors in Chapter 7.) Differences between raters in degree of bias and response styles can produce strong mean response differences between them even when inter-rater reliability is high. This is because inter-rater reliability measures relative ratings; as long as raters view the same items highest and the same ones lowest, their ratings will generally highly correlate even though one rater uses only response categories 1, 2, and 3, and another uses only 3, 4, and 5. In short, the sources of error that undermine reliability undermine construct validity as well. And some sources of error result from the method of measurement.

Of course, there are other reasons that social scientists cannot rely completely on direct questioning of research participants. One concerns research participants' capacity for understanding. For example, if participants are children it might not be possible to phrase questions about certain constructs in a way they can understand. A second is when the research involves constructs that reflect socially undesirable qualities. In such instances, we cannot assume that people will accurately describe themselves, particularly when they do not feel as if they are responding anonymously. Social scientists have therefore devoted a great deal of attention to developing multiple methods of measurement in addition to questionnaires and rating scales.

In the next section, we consider measurement methods other than direct questioning – methods that, not surprisingly, are referred to as indirect measurement methods. We discuss the advantages of three classes of indirect measures: collateral reports, observation, and physiological monitoring. We also touch on three additional approaches: the Implicit Association Test (IAT; Greenwald, McGhee, & Schwartz, 1998), which makes use of response latencies to assess the strength of associations; the card sort technique; and autophotographic (sometimes called photovoice) measures. These indirect methods of measurement are indispensable in some research domains and an asset in domains that generally rely on direct questioning because they involve different measurement methods, thereby minimizing common method variance. As will become clear later in this chapter, the use of multiple methods of measurement also facilitates the evaluation of construct validity.

Indirect Methods of Measurement

Collateral Reports

Collateral reports are third-party responses to a questionnaire or interview. By "third party" we mean someone other than the participant provides information about the participant. We refer to such reports as collateral because they are gathered in addition to, rather than instead of, information provided by the participants. Moreover, the information provided by the informant is in response to the same questions posed to the participant. By gathering the same information from multiple sources, it is possible to detect biases that might contaminate self-reports.

Collateral reports are commonplace in research on children. Typically, informants are parents and teachers. For instance, Chassin, Pitts, and DeLucia (1999) studied the influence of alcohol and drug use by adolescents on their adjustment as young adults. During adolescence, measures of key constructs were obtained from participants and informants. It is worth noting that at least some of the constructs involved in these studies concerned illegal behavior of the sort that participants might either under- or over-report. By obtaining collateral reports, which should not be subject to the self-serving biases that influence self-reports of such behaviors, the researchers were able to probe for biases and, in the end, increase confidence in the validity of participants' reports.

McDowell and Parke's (2009) longitudinal study is a particularly remarkable example of the use of collateral reports and multiple measurement methods more generally. Their data included child and parent reports, teacher and peer ratings, and behavioral observations of parent–child interactions. They used collateral reports, assessing the same construct from different participants' perspectives (e.g., teacher and peer ratings of social acceptance). They also used completely different methods of measurement to assess the same construct (e.g., parent reports and observations of parent–child interactions). The assessment of relationships between constructs was based on variables that relied on different measurement methods. For example, behavioral observations of parent–child interactions predicted peer and teacher ratings of social acceptance.

The primary advantage of collateral reports is the potential to assess biases in self-reports. The strategic selection of informants makes it possible to use collateral reports to evaluate the veracity of self-reports as well as to pinpoint sources of potential biases. In this regard, obtaining collateral reports is a good example of the use of multiple operational definitions. Although the items on the survey do not vary, the sources of the information used to respond to them do. This variability in source permits the use of statistical techniques, such as factor analysis (discussed later in this chapter), to tease apart the construct of interest from constructs of disinterest, which should vary from one source to the next. To the extent that the same relationships are demonstrated using measures from participants and measures obtained from third parties, our confidence in the findings is greatly increased.

A drawback of collateral reports, however, is the dilemma that researchers face when multiple third-party reports do not agree with each other or when third-party reports differ from participants' self-reports. For instance, Chassin et al. (1999) found stronger support for their hypothesis using collateral reports as opposed to adolescents' own reports of their drinking behavior and adjustment. Such departures in findings between collateral reports are well documented in research with younger children, in which parents' and teachers' ratings depart not only from students' self-ratings, but also from each other. It is easy to see how this could be true. Parents, teachers, and the children themselves witness the child's behavior from different perspectives, in different contexts, and with reference to different comparison groups. Although this diversity is an asset, it can create a conundrum for researchers. What is the correct inference if the results are consistent with the hypothesis when the children's own ratings are used but inconsistent with it when parents' or teachers' ratings are used? Resolution to this inferential dilemma often requires additional research that focuses on the unique characteristics of the perspectives represented by the different sources.

The use of collateral reports introduces a number of additional complications because of the need to gather data from both participants and informants. First, the use of collateral reports increases the cost of the study, potentially doubling (or even tripling) it without adding to the size of the sample. Of course, if the quality of the information about participants is greatly improved, or if collateral reports are the only way to measure certain constructs given the target population, then the cost is justified. Second, recruitment strategies for informants may need to be different from those used to enlist participants. This is not a concern if, for instance, the informants are parents; the parents of minors typically would need to be contacted for permission to recruit their children anyway. If, however, the informants are peers or coworkers, then it is unlikely that the strategy used to recruit participants will work for informants. Moreover, the kind of recruitment that is required might result in informants who are not comparable from one participant to the next. For instance, if high school students are asked to recruit best friends, there is no guarantee that every participant will interpret "best friend" in the same way, that every participant's best friend will be accessible, or even that each child has a best friend. It can also be difficult to ensure that participants do not work with informants to provide information, thereby defeating the purpose of obtaining information from different perspectives. Thus, despite the appeal of acquiring information about participants from multiple sources, the costs and potential problems mean that researchers rarely obtain collateral reports unless the research question or characteristics of the population they are studying requires them.

Observation

Although collateral reports move outside respondents to gather information not directly influenced by them, they often are combined with responses obtained by questioning the respondent directly. As such, they only partially extricate the process of measurement from the biases and shortcomings inherent in participants' self-reports. **Observation** is an approach to measurement that does not rely at all on participants to report their preferences, opinions, or behaviors. Instead, judges are trained by the researcher to detect and record observable indicators of the construct of interest.

In Chapter 13, we provide detailed coverage of observational techniques. For our purposes here, we give readers a feel for the ways in which observation can be used to measure constructs. As noted above, McDowell and Parke (2009) used both observations of parent–child interactions and parent reports to assess parental influences on children's peer relations. In a study of the effects of family influences on relationship quality, Conger, Cui, Bryant, and Elder (2000) visited families in their homes for a two-hour session. During the session, family members were videotaped while they took part in four structured interactions. Five years later, adolescent family members who were in romantic relationships were videotaped interacting with their partners while engaged in tasks designed to generate discussion or create conflict. Videotaped interactions were rated by multiple judges on characteristics, such as supportiveness and hostility. In another longitudinal study, Caspi et al. (1997) were interested in the degree to which temperament at age 3 predicted personality at age 18 and health-risk behaviors at age 21. Of course, 3-year-olds do not have the facility with language necessary to provide responses to direct questions about their personality. Instead, these researchers used observational methods to classify the children at age 3 as undercontrolled, inhibited, reserved, or well adjusted. As illustrated by these examples, observational methods are useful when participants might not be willing or able to accurately report their standing on a construct.

An obvious advantage to observation is the relative objectivity of ratings. Presumably, judges are unbiased observers trained by researchers to document what they see or hear without interpretation. As such, their ratings of participants should not be contaminated by sources of bias that threaten the validity of participants' self-ratings. Moreover, observers can take note of subtle, nonverbal cues to participants' motives and emotions, constructs that might not be apparent to the participants themselves.

Occasionally, a researcher finds audio- or videotaped recordings relevant to a hypothesis that were gathered for other purposes (e.g., surveillance video in a food market). In such cases, the costs of measurement are greatly reduced and the observation itself is in no way affected by the goals of the research. The latter feature adds an additional layer of objectivity and distance between the hypotheses of the study and the means by which the information used to test the hypotheses was gathered.

Another advantage to observation is that it can often be accomplished while participants are in a natural setting. For instance, the Conger et al. (2000) study involved observing families interacting in their homes. In this study, the families knew they were being observed, and the observations were of interactions manufactured by the research team. A purer form of naturalistic observation is unobtrusive observation, in which research participants are not aware they are being observed. For instance, we might obtain information about the radio station preferences of people in a city by recording the station to which radios are tuned in cars that are being serviced. A limitation on such studies, discussed in Chapter 13, is the invasion of privacy without participants' consent. Such concerns aside, unobtrusive observation in naturalistic settings can generate information that is high in external validity relative to information gathered in artificial or contrived settings in which researchers are present.

Perhaps the greatest disadvantage to observational measurement is that many constructs are not amenable to observation. Most overt behaviors are readily observed, and independent judges often are in near-unanimous agreement in their ratings of whether participants did or did not engage in a behavior. Other constructs are not so readily observed. For instance, emotions are not always manifested outwardly. People do not always communicate their motives, desires, or preferences in their actions. For constructs such as these, observation is not particularly useful.

Another disadvantage concerns the use of observational information to test causal propositions. Typically, observational measurement involves neither manipulation of putative causes nor random assignment of participants to levels of the causal variable. As such, even when certain behaviors regularly co-occur with certain features of the setting, it is not possible to draw firm causal inferences. So, with observational research in natural settings, there is a trade-off between external validity and internal validity. For this reason, observational research often is an adjunct to research in which the researcher exerts more control over the setting and the critical constructs.

Physiological Measures

Whereas observational methods are used to measure overt characteristics, physiological measures target covert characteristics, such as emotions, evaluations, and preferences. **Psychophysiology** is the study of the interplay of physiological systems and people's thoughts, feelings, and behaviors. By "physiological systems" we mean bodily systems, for instance, the endocrine (hormonal), cardiovascular, and immune systems. It is now apparent that these systems influence and are influenced by people's experience of themselves and the world around them (Blascovich, 2014). Moreover, it is possible to identify particular patterns of physiological activation that indicate constructs of interest to social scientists. We illustrate with three examples.

Blascovich, Mendes, Hunter, Lickel, and Kowai-Bell (2001) proposed that individuals interacting with a stigmatized person would feel threatened, although they might not report it when asked directly. They tested this stigma-threat hypothesis by creating laboratory interactions between participants and stigmatized confederates (accomplices of the researchers posing as participants). Threat was operationally defined as a pattern of cardiovascular activity indicative of decreased blood volume and flow. The results were consistent with their hypothesis. Confirming the researchers' suspicion that the threatening nature of the interaction would not be apparent using more traditional measures of threat, they found no support for their hypothesis using paper-and-pencil measures or observational measures provided by confederates.

Another social science study using physiological measures comes from Harmon-Jones and Sigelman (2001) who examined the effects of an insult on anger and aggression. Of relevance to this discussion is their operational definition of anger. Harmon-Jones and Sigelman recorded electroencephalographic (EEG) activity in order to test their hypothesis that anger is indicated by increased left-prefrontal activity in the brain. Results confirmed their expectation: Participants who were insulted evinced greater activity in the left-prefrontal cortex, and their level of activity was associated with their self-reports of anger and their engagement in aggressive behavior.

A third example is the increasing use of cortisol, which is a hormonal indicator of stress and anxiety. Page-Gould, Mendoza-Denton, and Tropp (2008) examined the effects of cross-group friendships among Latinos/as and Whites on anxiety in intergroup situations. They found that greater experience with cross-group friendships resulted in decreased cortisol reactivity among people who were more sensitive to race-based rejection. Other work has further shown that Whites' concerns about appearing prejudiced are associated with higher cortisol levels during and after interracial contacts and with interracial experiences during the course of an academic year (Trawalter, Adam, Chase-Lansdale, & Richeson, 2012) and that the patterns of chronic cortisol levels among ethnic minority group members differ from those of Whites in ways that are consistent with negative health consequences. These findings suggest that the stress resulting from factors associated with ethnic minority status (e.g., experiences with racism and discrimination) may contribute to poorer health among the members of ethnic minority groups (DeSantis et al., 2007).

There are two primary advantages of physiological monitoring relative to other measurement methods. First, despite the fact that participants know they are being assessed, they cannot control the outcome of the assessment. Thus, unlike direct questioning in all its forms and intrusive observational methods, there is little or no concern that participants' biases are reflected in their scores. A second advantage is that measurement is continuous in real time. It permits the introduction of time into hypotheses and research design. Thus, we can go beyond the relatively simple question of *whether* a stimulus has an influence to the more refined question of *when* it exerts an influence relative to the onset of a stimulus or event.

This latter advantage carries with it a disadvantage: Because multiple measures are needed (e.g., some signals are read at 1-second intervals or less), the sheer amount of information produced can be overwhelming. For instance, if a researcher monitors participants during a 15-minute period at 1-second intervals, the result would be 900 pieces of information for each participant. Extracting signals from noise in such large amounts of information requires considerable expertise and sophistication.

Indeed, it is the "noise" factor that often proves the most challenging for researchers interested in measuring social constructs using physiological measures. For, while the cardiovascular system is responding to a stimulus presented by the researcher, it is also responding to other factors, such as room temperature, physical health, novelty of the laboratory setting, events that took place just prior to entering the laboratory, and so forth. For this reason, many research studies in which key constructs are operationally defined using physiological measures include numerous control variables aimed at determining the degree to which the physiological measure is influenced by factors not relevant to the hypothesis.

Three additional concerns limit the use of physiological measures. First, as must be apparent by now, a considerable amount of expertise is required both to understand the functioning of the physiological systems to be monitored and to run monitoring equipment. Second, the necessary equipment is expensive and fragile. As such, equipment is often shared by multiple research groups whose members are well trained in its use and maintenance. Finally, the extreme sensitivity of some physiological monitoring equipment may require that participants be seated and relatively still throughout measurement (salivary cortisol samples, which involve taking mouth swabs, are relatively easy to obtain from participants). Invasive procedures and those that severely restrain participants' behaviors or the social context of the research limit the ability to examine many behaviors of interest to social scientists.

Other Indirect Methods

Social scientists regularly develop new and creative ways to buttress research findings that are suspect because they are based solely on direct questioning. To give readers a flavor of these other approaches, we describe three.

An approach to measurement that focuses on constructs that can only be measured indirectly are **implicit association methods** (Gawronski & De Houwer, 2014; Sekaquaptewa, Vargas, & von Hippel, 2010; Teige-Mocigemba, Klauer, & Sherman, 2010), which use various indirect ways of assessing the strength of associations between attitude objects (e.g., ethnic groups, the self) and specific attributes. A widely used measure is the Implicit Association Test (IAT; Greenwald et al., 1998; Greenwald, Poehlman, Uhlmann, & Banaji, 2009; Nosek, Greenwald, & Banaji, 2005) to measure automatic evaluative judgments. The term "automatic" is used here to refer to thoughts and feelings that are not under the conscious control of the individual. Such *implicit* thoughts and feelings about an object (e.g., another person, a group of people, oneself) can be contrasted with *explicit* thoughts and feelings, of which an individual is aware and able to control. The latter typically are measured using one of the direct questioning methods described in Chapter 7. The logic of the IAT is as follows: Participants are seated at a keyboard facing a computer screen. They are instructed to indicate as quickly as possible by pressing designated computer keys the correspondence between evaluative attributes (e.g., pleasant, ugly) and concepts (e.g., young–old, black–white, self–other). The computer records the amount of time that lapses between the presentation of the stimuli and key press for the different pairings of evaluative attributes and concepts. (The best way to understand how the IAT works is to experience it firsthand. Try one of the demonstration tests at implicit.harvard.edu/implicit/.) Implicit attitude measures are computed using an algorithm that takes into account the differences in speed of responses to the different attribute–concept pairings. Faster responses to pairings of negative attributes and a given concept compared to positive attributes and the same concept indicate a negative implicit evaluation. The implicit association method has been used to study implicit attitudes toward a variety of groups, products, and activities.

Another indirect means of gathering information from people is the card sort. In the **card sort**, research participants are given a stack of cards, each containing a single adjective or descriptive phrase. Participants are asked to sort the cards into piles that in their opinion belong together when describing a person, group of people, or themselves. Linville (1987) used the card sort effectively to measure self-complexity, the number of different ways people view themselves and the degree of overlap among their self-views. She found that self-complexity is not a quality that people can effectively report about themselves in response to direct questions, but it is nonetheless consequential in their emotional reactions to stress. Others have used similar techniques to assess, for example, the complexity of individuals' perceptions of social groups (e.g., Park, Wolsko, & Judd, 2001) and leader self-complexity (Hannah, Balthazard, Waldman, Jennings, & Thatcher, 2013).

A novel approach to gathering information about participants is autophotography (sometimes called photovoice when the participants write summaries for each photo). In **autophotographic research**, participants carry disposable cameras with them for a short period of time and photograph aspects of their experience as directed by the researchers. For instance, Dollinger, Preston, O'Brien, and DiLalla (1996) asked college students over the course of a semester to create a photo-essay by taking 20 photographs that "describe how you see yourself and tell something about who you are" (p. 1270). Trained judges then coded the photographs for various features relevant to the research questions. The findings both corroborated and extended similar research using paper-and-pencil measures. Burke and Dollinger (2005) used similar autophotographic procedures to assess individuality and social connectedness. And, more recently, Langhout (2014) described her use of photovoice methodology with young immigrants and children of immigrants.

Exercise: Developing and evaluating indirect measures

Identify a construct that you might want to measure in your own research. What types of indirect measures (i.e., measures that do not involve direct questioning) might you use? Identify 2–3 possible ways you might assess the construct. Be as specific as possible. What challenges might you encounter? What other factors might you want to consider if you were to attempt to use these types of measures in your research? How could you evaluate their construct validity?

Summary

Although direct questioning continues to be the measurement approach of choice among social scientists, not every construct of interest to social scientists can be measured by direct questioning. Moreover, findings from research studies that rely solely on direct questioning are strengthened when they are replicated using measurement methods that do not rely on participants' self-reports of the key constructs.

We reviewed three categories of measurement that do not rely on participants' self-reports and, as with the various approaches to direct questioning, each has strengths and weaknesses. When the research questions concern populations that cannot be counted on to provide valid self-reports, collateral reports are an effective means of bolstering confidence in the veracity of information about participants. Another approach is to circumvent self-reports altogether and gather information about participants by observing their behavior either in strategically created environments or in natural settings. And, for a select category of hypotheses, physiological monitoring is a compelling means of operationally defining constructs for which self-reports are suspect. Other indirect methods of measurement include implicit association methods, such as the IAT; card sort techniques; and autophotographic or photovoice research. Each of these indirect measurement approaches is a necessary and appealing adjunct to the questionnaires and interviews that dominate research in the social sciences.

Evaluating Construct Validity

Recall that in the discussion of reliability in Chapter 7, measures of any particular variable were made up of true score, unique (systematic error), and random error variance. To evaluate reliability, we compared scores that should measure the same variable, but that could be differentially influenced by random errors. Test–retest and internal consistency reliability estimates use this basic approach in different ways. The basic idea can be extended to the assessment of construct validity. The key concept again involves examining correlations between sets of scores that are expected to have different blends of components. Validity assessment, however, involves looking for variance that is due to what is supposed to be measured, so things like systematic error – the extent to which a measure measures something other than what it intends to measure – should not be part of validity.

For example, if two measures are expected to measure the same characteristic but have different sources of systematic error, the extent to which they correlate is an indication of the extent to which they measure that characteristic or construct. A higher correlation would indicate greater construct validity. If both measures were completely pure and valid measures of the construct, they would correlate perfectly. However, if the measures were useless as assessments of the target construct, showing only systematic biases or errors, the correlation between them would be zero, assuming that the sources of systematic error are different. If the sources of systematic variance are not different, we need other approaches to tease variability related to the construct of interest apart from other systematic variance. Before describing variations on this fundamental idea and the ways it can be used to assess validity, we describe two other approaches to validity assessment, namely, face validity and content validity.

Note that ways of conceptualizing and talking about validity and construct validity have varied a great deal over the years and have been the subject of some debate (Newton & Shaw, 2013). This debate is important both theoretically and practically as psychological tests and measures are often interpreted and used in ways that have significant consequences for individuals' lives – as in the use of IQ tests to help identify students who have special needs. A measure of a construct may yield scores that are more or less valid for different groups of people, situations, and purposes. One aspect of validity is whether individual scores from a measure have the intended meaning for particular samples, for example an English-language achievement measure with second-language learners for whom English is not a native language. In contrast, our focus here begins with whether or not a theoretical variable shows expected patterns of relationships with other variables, distinguishing among the various methods that social scientists use to evaluate construct validity. These methods have typically been given distinct and specific labels, such as content validity, criterion validity, and so forth. But the ultimate goal is to determine the construct validity apparent within our data.

Face Validity

Face validity is evaluated by judges, sometimes experts, who read or look at a measuring technique and decide whether it appears to measure what the researchers intend for it to measure. For instance, professional speech therapists could look at a test designed to measure degrees of speech impairment and decide whether the test seems to measure what the testers claim. Evaluating face validity is highly subjective and is considered the least scientific means of evaluating construct validity. Still, most instruments must pass the face validity test, at least informally, as other researchers are likely to question the validity of a measure that does not appear to measure the intended construct. Further, a measure that does not appear to be meaningful to research participants may limit the extent to which they "buy in" to the research and therefore limit the validity of their responses. Similarly, the public may question the usefulness of research findings if the measures that were used do not appear to be valid. Nevertheless, face validity does not provide sufficient evidence for construct validity. Indeed, indirect, subtle, or implicit measures that lack face validity are often used when it is important to disguise the purpose of the measure from the people whose characteristics are being measured. An example would be a hypothetical measure of prejudice that is based on asking people about their color preferences.

Content Validity

Content validity refers to the extent to which the items in a measure represent the full range of the construct that one is attempting to assess. Maximizing the content validity of a concept involves first defining a universe, that is, a set of all possible behaviors or characteristics that are believed to constitute the conceptual variable, and then developing items that assess the full range of those behaviors or characteristics.

The logic of domain sampling is relevant here. A **domain** is the hypothetical population of all items (say, attitude statements) relevant to the construct we wish to measure. The "true underlying attitude" would be the aggregate of the person's responses to all the items in the domain. Conceptualized in this way, it is natural to think of measurement as an application of sampling. In **domain sampling**, we draw a sample of items from the domain and use the person's responses to those items to estimate the person's standing on the desired construct. Construct validity would be the person's true standing on all of the items in the domain and the difference between the person's true standing and the person's responses to the selected items would be sampling error. The domain sampling model makes clear that the amount of variation in item content is a key determinant of construct validity. The greater the variation in the domain, the greater the number of items needed to assess it. If the domain of items were completely homogeneous in content, people would respond identically to every item so that only one item would be needed to assess it.

This domain sampling strategy has perhaps been most commonly used in educational and industrial psychology contexts where maximizing content validity is considered especially important. Consider, for example, the development of standardized tests to assess achievement. If we were developing a test that purports to measure quantitative knowledge, we would not assess only geometry or algebra. Similarly, an industrial/organizational psychologist might use the full range of knowledge, skills, and abilities identified in a job analysis to develop instruments to select and evaluate employees. Course instructors also use this general approach to maximize the content validity of exams, identifying the full range of skills and knowledge that students are expected to have acquired, and then developing or selecting items to represent that range so that the underlying dimension is effectively sampled.

Of course, it would be quite challenging – if not impossible – to identify the full range of attributes that represent each and every construct in which social science researchers are interested. Consider, for example, the range of attitudes, cognitions, and behaviors that would be needed to represent constructs such as prejudice or extraversion. For research purposes, then (as opposed to diagnostic purposes, that is, making decisions that directly affect individuals' outcomes), investigators rarely go through the painstaking process of establishing the content validity of their measures. Instead, researchers write items that tap the desired construct and define the domain as the hypothetical population of items with characteristics equivalent to those that were written. (But see Graham et al., 2011, for a description of their impressive work developing items for the Moral Foundations Questionnaire.) Nevertheless, as we have indicated, the approach is relevant in many applied contexts. Further, the concept is useful to consider when developing new measures (see, e.g., Graham et al., 2011) and evaluating existing ones; thinking about the full range of attributes believed to represent a construct is an integral part of instrument development, and often is helpful in developing new items and in identifying limitations of existing measures.

Criterion Validity

To be useful, a measure ought to predict or relate to some criteria, that is, other variables or outcomes, such as academic achievement, job promotions, or therapeutic success. To the extent that scores from a measure do so, they are said (or, less accurately, the measure is said) to have high **criterion validity**. Researchers have sometimes distinguished between two types of criterion validity: **concurrent validity** and **predictive validity**. As their names suggest, the former concerns the extent to which scores from a measure predict criteria that were obtained at the same point in time, whereas the latter concerns the extent to which scores from a measure predict criteria that occur in the future. For example, one would generally expect a valid measure of intelligence to correlate with students' educational achievement (criterion validity). This relationship could be assessed in a cross-sectional design such that students complete a measure of intelligence (an "IQ" test) and their scores on this measure are correlated with educational achievement measures, for example, whatever grades students have at the same point in time (concurrent validity) or with the grades they earn in college 10 years later (predictive validity).

Criterion validity is limited in terms of its usefulness for evaluating construct validity. Every criterion is itself an imperfect measure or indicator of a different, albeit conceptually related, construct (John & Benet-Martínez, 2014). In the previous example, for instance, general intelligence is measured by "IQ" test scores, and school achievement by school grades. Grades assess the knowledge acquired in particular subject areas (e.g., math), the ability to follow instructions, appropriate classroom behavior, class participation, and so on, not all of which are necessarily measures of educational achievement as it is generally conceptualized. However, to the extent that the two measures represent different methods of measurement that are subject to different sources of error, a relationship between them increases our confidence in the construct validity of our measure.

Convergent Validity

We now focus more directly on ways of comparing scores from different measures to arrive at a picture of the relative contributions of the desired construct and other, undesired constructs to the observed scores. The tests a measure must pass are twofold: assessments of *convergent* and *discriminant* validity.

Convergent validity refers generally to the extent to which two measures that should be related are in fact empirically related. With respect to measures of a single conceptual variable, it refers to the overlap between alternative measures that have different sources of systematic error. For example, suppose we wish to measure the intelligence of French students. We could use an English-language intelligence test as operational definition 1, a French IQ test as definition 2, and a face-to-face interview conducted by a panel of French educators as definition 3. Table 8.1 shows a hypothetical rank ordering of students' intelligence scores obtained from the three measures.

By counting the number of agreements in the rank ordering between any two tests, we get a rough picture of the correlation between them. The greater the number of agreements, the higher the correlation. Here, the amount of agreement between definitions 2 and 3 is quite high; two students reverse position and seven remain the same. The amount of agreement between definition 1 and the other two is much less; five or six students reverse positions in each case. The amount of agreement between any two measures tells us the extent to which they are measuring the same thing. It

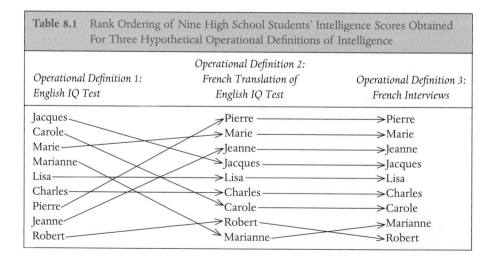

Table 8.1 Rank Ordering of Nine High School Students' Intelligence Scores Obtained For Three Hypothetical Operational Definitions of Intelligence

Operational Definition 1: English IQ Test	*Operational Definition 2: French Translation of English IQ Test*	*Operational Definition 3: French Interviews*
Jacques	Pierre	Pierre
Carole	Marie	Marie
Marie	Jeanne	Jeanne
Marianne	Jacques	Jacques
Lisa	Lisa	Lisa
Charles	Charles	Charles
Pierre	Carole	Carole
Jeanne	Robert	Marianne
Robert	Marianne	Robert

is represented conceptually as the overlapping portions of the circles in Figure 8.1 and is numerically equal to the square of the correlation coefficient.

Measures based on operational definitions 2 and 3 thus show good levels of agreement, indicating the convergent validity of the two measures. That is, both are intended to assess intelligence, and they tend to rank-order respondents in the same way. To what can this correspondence be attributed? Obviously, to the extent that both measures effectively tap intelligence, they will correlate highly. But random and systematic errors should lessen the correlation because the nature of the errors in the three measures would be expected to be different. Systematic errors in the three measures include knowledge of English for definition 1 (the English-language intelligence test) and conversational skills and poise for definition 3 (the interview). Indeed, the English-language assessment does not correlate highly with the other two, showing that it does not have good convergent validity. Most of the variability in responses to this measure appears to be due to knowledge of English rather than intelligence, for if this were not the case, it should correlate with the other two measures of intelligence.

These biasing factors or errors are not part of what we mean by intelligence, for an intelligent French student might be unable to answer any questions on the English test because he or she has never studied English. Similarly, a student might do well on written tests but become anxious during an interview. Knowledge of English and the tendency to become anxious are irrelevant constructs that could enter as biases into these measures of intelligence. But comparing the three measures allows us to assess the amount of overlap between them, learning the extent to which the measures tap what we intend them to tap and to what extent they tap other factors. Convergent validity indicates that the correlated measures are picking up the common intended construct.

Discriminant Validity

A valid measure has to show good convergence with other measures of the same or similar things, as already noted. It should also correlate substantially less with measures that are supposed to tap different constructs, and not at all with things to which it should not be related; this is the definition of **discriminant validity**. Consider a self-report measure of conscientiousness as an example. We might be concerned that the test only taps the tendency to give socially desirable responses. We could assess this suspicion by a convergent validity strategy, looking for correlations between the measure and other measures of conscientiousness that do not rely on self-reports. We also could use a discriminant validity strategy. A measure of socially desirable responding (Paulhus, 1991, 2002) could be administered to people along with the conscientiousness measure. To the extent that the measure is valid, it should not correlate highly with social desirability, for there is no reason to think that conscientiousness and the tendency to give socially desirable responses are associated constructs. In contrast, a high correlation supports the suspicion that social desirability bias is a strong contributor to the conscientiousness scores obtained from our measure.

In short, a measure should correlate substantially with alternative measures of the same construct that vary in potential sources of invalidity. In addition, a measure should correlate much less with other measures that do not tap the target construct but that pick up expected sources of systematic error. These dual types of evidence provide strong empirical support for a measure's validity.

Validity and the Nomological Net

Both convergent and discriminant validity can be put into a common framework by considering the nomological net of the target construct. Recall from Chapter 7 that the nomological net is the theoretically derived set of associations with other constructs that serves to define the target construct. With this definition, the assessment of validity can be summed up in a single sentence: Validity is demonstrated when the associations observed with a measure match the theoretically postulated nomological net of the construct. In some cases, a hypothesized variable is predicted to correlate highly with some variables, moderately with others, and not at all with still other variables. Its construct validity is affirmed to the extent that it shows the predicted pattern of relationships. In effect, the measure correlates with what it is supposed to correlate with and does not correlate with what it is not supposed to correlate with. This statement is more general than the previous illustration under the heading of convergent validity. There we stated that a measure should converge with alternative ways of assessing the same construct. Now we are restating the broader point, namely, that theory might tell us that constructs, although not identical, should be correlated; correlations between measures of such constructs also furnish evidence of a measure's validity. In other words, any demonstration of a relationship between a measure and measures of other theoretically related constructs provides evidence for convergent, and thus construct, validity. Pratto and her colleagues (Pratto, Sidanius, & Levin, 2006; Pratto, Sidanius, Stallworth, & Malle, 1994), for example, developed a measure of social dominance orientation, showing that it did not correlate with interpersonal dominance (discriminant validity), but did correlate with sexism and ethnic prejudice (convergent validity). Figure 8.2 shows the general notion schematically. Note how the pattern of associations among the measures, indicated by circles labeled with lowercase letters, mirrors the theoretical pattern of associations among the constructs.

The Multitrait–Multimethod Matrix

Validity, then, is based on an assessment of how much one measure of a construct agrees with other measures of the same or theoretically similar constructs and disagrees with measures of theoretically dissimilar constructs. A challenge to convergent/ discriminant validity is the extent to which measures are collected using common methods. If a group of variables is collected by a common instrument using a common method, they all will share method variance, and each of the variables may correlate with all the others. To the extent that method variance is strong, there may only be moderate to large correlations within a set of variables that share method

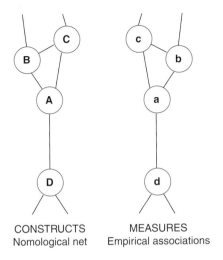

CONSTRUCTS
Nomological net

MEASURES
Empirical associations

Figure 8.2   Schematic Depiction of Desired Correspondence Between the Construct's Nomological Net and the Measure's Empirical Pattern of Associations.

variance, even though their predicted relations range from none to strong. Clearly, method variance creates challenges and needs to be somehow removed.

Campbell and Fiske (1959) directly addressed issues of method variance in their paper on **multitrait–multimethod (MTMM) matrices**. A multitrait–multimethod matrix is a table of correlation coefficients that is made up of multiple constructs measured using multiple methods. The presence of multiple methods allows researchers to extract method variance independently of trait or construct variance, which improves the capacity of researchers to evaluate the convergent and discriminant validity of constructs (Campbell & Fiske, 1959). As an example, suppose we are interested in the theoretical construct called "attitudes toward women" and we design an instrument to measure it. In order to demonstrate the validity of our measure, we would need to show not only that it converges with other measures of the same attitude but also that attitudes toward women are distinct from other attitudes such as political liberalism or attitudes toward men. To demonstrate validity in these ways, we would have to measure those other attitudes, too, and find patterns of correlations that distinguish our measure and other measures of attitudes toward women from measures of political liberalism, attitudes toward men, and the like.

To construct an MTMM matrix, we must have at least two constructs measured with at least two methods, and ideally would have at least three constructs measured using three different methods. A minimal example of a matrix for evaluating the validity of our hypothetical measure of attitudes toward women is shown in Table 8.2.

Interpretation of the matrix is based on the principle that the more features two measurements have in common, the higher their correlation will be. Measurements can share two types of features: traits and methods. **Traits** are the underlying construct the measurement is supposed to tap – attitudes toward women in our example. **Methods** are the mode of measurement. For our example, we select two methods

Table 8.2   Multitrait–Multimethod Matrix of Correlations between Attitudes toward Women and Attitudes toward Men

	Paper-and-Pencil Questionnaire		Observations of Behavior	
	Attitudes toward Women (ATW)	Attitudes toward Men (ATM)	Attitudes toward Women (ATW)	Attitudes toward Men (ATM)
Questionnaire				
ATW	(.90)			
ATM	.30	(.90)		
Behavior				
ATW	.70	.10	(.90)	
ATM	.10	.70	.30	(.90)

Note: The coefficients in parentheses are reliability estimates.

that vary considerably in terms of potential threats to validity: paper-and-pencil questionnaire and observations of behavior. Referring to Table 8.2, you can see that our selection of two traits and two methods yields a matrix of correlations arrayed in four columns and four rows. The first two columns and rows include correlations involving attitudes toward women and attitudes toward men measured using a paper-and-pencil questionnaire. Similarly, the last two columns and rows include the same correlations using behavioral observation. The correlations of the first two rows with the last two rows show relations of the two types of attitudes across the different methods. Only the lower portion of the matrix is printed because a correlation matrix is symmetric about its diagonal (e.g., four measures have only six correlations). The values on the diagonal are reliability coefficients, which could be estimated using either a test–retest or internal consistency strategy, but which generally would use the latter. Ideally, the reliability coefficients are for your sample rather than for a sample or even population that differs from yours.

In a fantasy world, scores would reflect only the intended construct and not be influenced by the method of measurement. In our world, reality world, the method of measurement also affects the score, and some of the variation in observed scores is a product of the method used to obtain them. For instance, look at coefficients in the first two columns of the illustration in Table 8.2. The correlation between attitudes toward women and attitudes toward men is .30 when both are measured using a paper-and-pencil questionnaire; however, the correlation between them is only .10 when they are measured using different methods. In light of this pattern, we conclude that scores on our hypothetical measure of attitudes toward women are, to some degree, influenced by the way they are measured. To the extent that the two correlations we just highlighted were the same, we could conclude that method of measurement is not a threat to the validity of our measure (and that we might have come close to fantasy world).

The MTMM matrix lets a researcher assess the extent to which scores on a measure reflect the trait (i.e., construct) the measure was designed to tap as opposed to the method (i.e., mode of measurement) by which scores were assigned. Because every score is made up of two systematic elements – a trait and a method – the correlation between two sets of scores depends on how much they share both the trait and the method, and on how strong each of the sources of variance is. By comparing coefficients representing different combinations of trait and method in the MTMM matrix, a researcher can learn a great deal about the validity of a measure. Correlations between scores that reflect the same trait and the same method (monotrait–monomethod) are **reliability coefficients**. Although these coefficients are not themselves indicative of validity, as we noted at the beginning of the chapter, they indicate the upper limit to the validity of our measure, for they identify the maximum amount of variance that can be valid. Correlations between scores that reflect the same trait measured by different methods (monotrait–heteromethod) are **convergent validity coefficients**. They ideally will be strong, for they represent the types of relations we have been promoting, a single trait measured in different ways. The reliability coefficients of an instrument should logically be higher than its validity coefficients because the former are based on shared method variance as well as shared trait variance. The MTMM matrix includes two additional types of correlation coefficients that help assess the validity of an instrument. These both correlate different traits. One type, **discriminant validity coefficients**, are correlations between different traits measured by the same method (heterotrait–monomethod). Those correlations provide information about the magnitude of the method variance. The final type is the correlations that measure different traits measured by different methods (heterotrait–heteromethod), sharing neither trait nor method variance. Those correlations, called by our predecessors **nonsense coefficients**, should be the smallest in the matrix.

Ideally, the reliability and convergent validity coefficients should be high, whereas the discriminant validity and nonsense coefficients should be low. Practically, that may not exactly happen if method variance is strong, which may happen with some methods. But regardless of the strength of the method variance, the nonsense coefficients that share neither trait nor method variance should be smaller than other correlations. In general, if the latter two types of coefficients are as high as the convergent validity coefficients, the two traits are not different but the same or highly similar. For instance, our hypothetical measures of attitudes toward women and attitudes toward men should not be too highly correlated if they tap truly separate attitudes. If the correlations between these measures were like those shown in Table 8.2, we would be satisfied that they measured two distinct traits or attitudes. The convergent validity coefficients (.70) are higher than the discriminant validity coefficients (.30) and the nonsense coefficients (.10), indicating that the measures tap two different traits. If, however, the matrix looked like the one in Table 8.3, the measures would be invalidated because some of the correlations were too high and because the convergent validity correlations were disappointingly low.

The correlations in Table 8.3 show that the two attitudes are very similar because they are highly correlated with one another. There are several issues of concern. First, method variance is very strong; the correlations between two different traits measured by the same method (.80) are really high. Method variance that high makes it difficult for trait variance to emerge, as can be seen by the lack of discriminant validity. Second, the nonsense correlations, which should be close to zero, are almost as large as the convergent validity correlations, suggesting that there is little trait variance across

Table 8.3   Multitrait–Multimethod Matrix of Correlations between Attitudes toward Women and Attitudes toward Men Showing Lack of Convergent and Discriminant Validity

	Paper-and-Pencil Questionnaire		Observations of Behavior	
	Attitudes toward Women (ATW)	Attitudes toward Men (ATM)	Attitudes toward Women (ATW)	Attitudes toward Men (ATM)
Questionnaire				
ATW	(.90)			
ATM	.80	(.90)		
Behavior				
ATW	.40	.30	(.90)	
ATM	.30	.40	.80	(.90)

Note: The coefficients in parentheses are reliability estimates.

the measures (note that in the example, it is true for both attitudes, not just attitudes toward women). Third, the construct is not a strong one, for the correlations of the same trait measured by different methods (.40) are low. There may be a few elusive traits that are very difficult to measure and that would be expected to show low convergent validity, but they are not the norm. Changing measurement techniques should not produce low correlations of alternative measures of a single construct. In general, if two measures tap different attitudes, the discriminant validity correlations between them should not be higher than the convergent validity correlations of the same trait measured by different methods (.40).

Particularly if a researcher is trying to develop a measure of a newly conceptualized construct, choosing a MTMM approach is recommended. MTMM provides both convergent and discriminant validity information, and it is particularly important to assess its discriminant validity to demonstrate that it is indeed new and different. Such measures can be invalidated not only because of low correlations but also correlations with other measures that are too high to justify the claim that they measure different constructs. If we observed the pattern of correlations shown in Table 8.3, we would conclude that the two measures tap the same attitude; and rather than talk of attitudes toward women and attitudes toward men, we might combine the measures and reconceptualize the construct as attitudes about gender and gender roles.

In 1959 when Campbell and Fiske developed the MTMM approach, their recommendations for analysis were guided by logic (e.g., any monotrait–heteromethod correlation should be larger than the corresponding heterotrait–monomethod correlations) rather than by specific statistical tools. As statistical methods developed, however, and confirmatory factor analysis approaches became widely available, analyses largely turned to use of confirmatory factor models, which seemed natural since, in a confirmatory factor analysis (described later in this chapter), researchers specify factors a priori, specify and extract both trait and method factors (e.g., Kenny, 1976), and obtain better estimates of the relationships between different traits independent of the methods used to measure them. Unfortunately, some models (e.g., a 3-trait,

3-method MTMM data set) can have problems in estimation, which has led to a series of papers discussing challenges of confirmatory factor analysis for MTMM problems (e.g., Kenny & Kashy, 1992). That discussion is beyond the scope of an introductory methods book such as ours. To obtain closure for this discussion, the ideal approach to use for work on construct validity involves measurement using multiple methods of multiple traits, and in many instances can employ confirmatory factor analysis approaches to analyze MTMM data (e.g., if one method doesn't have common method variance).

To summarize the broader section on construct validity, the validity of a measure, like its reliability, can be assessed by comparing scores obtained under conditions in which different components of the observed score are assumed to vary. The three components of any observed score are the true or desired construct itself, systematic errors, and random errors. Logically, examination of the validity of a measure always involves assessing the match between the empirical associations demonstrated by the measure and the theoretically expected set of associations: the construct's nomological net.

Exploratory and Confirmatory Factor Analyses

None of the methods described so far tells us directly whether a measure made up of multiple items assesses a single or multiple dimensions. Further, as noted in Chapter 7, high internal consistency reliability (i.e., a high value of coefficient alpha) does not mean that a measure made up of multiple items assesses a single dimension. Other methods, **exploratory factor analysis** (EFA) and **confirmatory factor analysis** (CFA), can determine whether a measure assesses a single or multiple dimensions and, if it assesses multiple dimensions, whether those dimensions reflect the underlying construct (or constructs) in expected ways. Both of these approaches, but CFA in particular, require large sample sizes. Some of the material in this section is fairly advanced, so individuals with limited research backgrounds should focus on the logic of the section and not worry if they do not understand all the technical details.

Both types of factor analyses assume that participants' responses to the items in a measure result directly from a smaller number of **latent** (i.e., unobserved or inferred) constructs. And both allow researchers to evaluate the extent to which a measure taps a single or multiple dimensions. In general, EFA, as the name suggests, is used when it is not possible to predict precisely the number and nature of dimensions that a measure assesses, or which items go with which dimension. Because EFA is exploratory, the results of EFAs are often ambiguous and interpretations involve much subjectivity. Sometimes there could be a reasonable solution that has three dimensions, and another that has four. Because EFA does not yield a unique solution, it has no corresponding significance tests to compare different solutions. In contrast, CFA, again as the name suggests, is used when one has an a priori prediction about the number and nature of dimensions (i.e., which items are associated with – "load on" – which factors). It also could be used when the number of competing predictions or hypothesized models is limited. Because there is a single unique solution with CFA, it provides a set of statistics including confidence intervals for relations of items with dimensions and for relations among the dimensions. They allow significance of all parameters estimated in the model to be determined. Although violating the confirmatory nature of the approach, CFA also provides detailed information (e.g., modification indices) that allows one to make changes to the model so that it more precisely describes the data. Although CFA can thus be used in a somewhat exploratory fashion, it is not exploratory insofar as researchers still must specify the model or models to be tested. CFA also potentially allows for covariation among residuals (measurement errors). More importantly, CFA provides a general framework for addressing convergent validity, discriminant validity, and random error and thus can be used to assess construct validity more broadly than can EFA (John & Benet-Martínez, 2014). And it gives a unique solution for each model.

We do not go into detail here about the statistical procedures (see, e.g., Kline, 2011; Maruyama, 1998); instead, we provide an example of a CFA. Graham and his colleagues (2011) created a measure called the Moral Foundations Questionnaire, which is intended to assess five moral concerns. More than 30,000 participants (recruited via the Internet) responded to a set of 30 items about the factors (e.g., emotional suffering) that affect their judgments of morality; these responses were then analyzed, using CFA. The final five-factor model is reproduced in Figure 8.3. Note that each of the five latent factors or dimensions (i.e., harm, fairness, ingroup, authority, and purity) is indicated by an oval and each measured variable (i.e., participants' responses to each item) is indicated by a box. The arrows point from each latent factor to each measured variable to indicate that participants' responses result from their standing on the latent construct. For example, Harm is assessed with six measured variables or

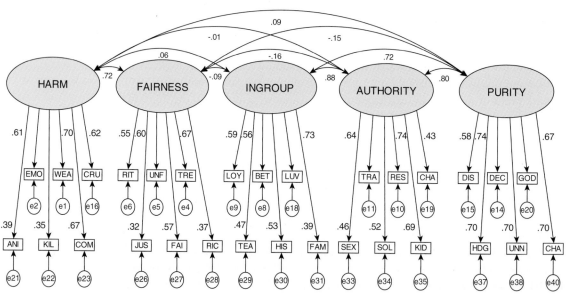

Figure 8.3 Moral Foundations Questionnaire Confirmatory Factor Analysis Model with Five Correlated Factors.
Source: Graham et al. (2011). Reproduced with permission of APA.

items. Measurement error is indicated by a small oval with a lower case "e"; again, the oval reflects the fact that errors are not directly observed but are inferred from the data. Arrows point from each error to each item to indicate that participants' responses to the items result not only from their standing on the latent factor but also from measurement error (all other unmeasured causes of the item). Thus, each of the six items that assesses Harm is also influenced by error. Double-headed arrows (e.g., between latent factors) indicate that the factors are correlated, but that causal relationships are not implied.

Graham et al. (2011) reported various fit indices, which showed that the model in Figure 8.3 described their data well. In CFA (and other structural equation modeling or SEM models), the basic statistic that is reported is a goodness-of-fit chi-square statistic for the model. Unlike most statistical tests, such as analysis of variance and regression, that researchers employ to identify statistically significant relations among variables, this test is one where lack of significance is desirable. It is a test of the difference between the hypothesized model and the observed data. In particular, *nonsignificant* chi-square statistics indicate that discrepancies between the data and the theoretical model are small. If the only challenge of interpreting the overall goodness-of-fit statistic were understanding that it measures the magnitude of the differences between the observed data and hypothesized model, things would not be too bad. In addition, however, the chi-square is directly related to sample size ((N–1) * function). If the sample size were to double, the chi-square statistic for the exact same discrepancies would more than double. So a model that fit with a sample of 100 subjects would not fit as well with a larger sample, and in any large sample the chi-square statistic is likely to be significant. Thus, researchers rely on an array of fit indices to assess the fit of their models. Some indices provide information about "absolute" fit compared to a perfect fit, while others provide information "relative" to the worst possible fit of the particular data set that is being analyzed, and still others balance fit with model parsimony (Maruyama, 1998, provides a detailed discussion of the various types of fit indices). Although explanation of why we prefer the following fit indices goes beyond the scope of an introductory book, we recommend the following fit indices: Non-normed fit index (Tucker Lewis), Incremental fit index, Comparative fit index, root mean squared residual, and root mean square error of approximation (RMSEA). When the various indices reach established guidelines (e.g., .08 in the case of RMSEA; Kline, 2011), the model is considered to be an appropriate fit or description of the data. At the level of the parameter, CFA also provides statistical tests indicating whether each variable or item loads on its hypothesized latent factor; here statistical significance indicates that the variable or item is indeed associated with the latent construct. For example, the parameter estimate linking Harm and EMO, that is, emotional suffering, is .61, which although not reported, is statistically significant.

A major challenge of approaches that examine factor structures is that there can be many models that are consistent with the data. Said differently, for any theoretical model, there are alternative models with the same underlying data structure. So models are never confirmed; the best one can say is that the data are consistent with the theoretical model. At the same time, there often are competing or distinctive conceptual perspectives. CFA allows one to compare these competing views. Graham and colleagues (2011), for example, tested whether their five-factor model with correlated factors described the data better than did various other models. They showed that the model fit the data significantly better than did models that had more factors, models that had fewer factors, and a model that did not allow the factors to correlate. Comparing models like those of Graham et al. could be done using the RMSEA, the expected cross-validation index (ECVI) or the AIC/CAIC fit indices. The analyses thus provided evidence of discriminant validity in that the five factors were distinct (e.g., the five-factor model fit the data better than did alternative models with fewer factors) and convergent evidence in that the five factors were correlated; the model also accounted for the role of measurement error. Discriminant and convergent validity were further demonstrated by showing that the pattern of correlations of the five moral concerns with measures of other theoretically related and unrelated constructs was as expected. For example, other fairness measures, such as (reverse-scored) social dominance orientation (Pratto et al., 1994), correlated more strongly with the moral concern for fairness than with the other four moral concerns (convergent validity). But these correlations were not too high (i.e., .44 to .56), suggesting that moral concern with fairness is conceptually distinct from other fairness constructs (discriminant validity).

Methods for assessing construct validity continue to develop. For example, Asparouhov and Muthén (2009) described exploratory structural equation modeling or ESEM, which combines the benefits of EFA and CFA. Such developments, combined with more widespread availability of technology and the ability to use it, have led to a dramatic increase in the numbers of published CFAs and Structural Equation Models (SEMs, of which CFA is a special case). Researchers continue to examine, for example, the convergent and discriminant validity of the widely used Positive and Negative Affect Schedule (PANAS; Watson, Clark, & Tellegen, 1988). This work has shown, for example, that although positive and negative affect are distinct constructs (vs. opposite ends of the same continuum), the two are correlated rather than completely independent (Crawford & Henry, 2004).

Cultural Issues in Measurement

Additional measurement issues emerge in cross-cultural research. One might wish to determine whether two or more cultural groups differ in their standing on some construct. Or, rather than directly comparing two cultural groups, one might wish to determine whether relationships between constructs obtained in one cultural group are also found in other cultural groups. In other words, one might want to determine the universality of research findings.

Assessing differences between groups and evaluating the universality of research findings, however, requires the establishment of **measurement equivalence**. One cannot assume that a measure shown to be valid in one group necessarily has the same meaning or relevance for people in a different cultural group. This issue is especially problematic when the cultural groups differ in language – although whether measures are equivalent across same-language gender, ethnic, and age groups in the U.S. can also be questioned (e.g., Carlo, Knight, McGinley, Zamboanga, & Jarvis,

2010). Fortunately, the factor analytic procedures we have already described have greatly enhanced researchers' ability to evaluate measurement equivalence – both within and across language groups.

Research involving use of a measure that was developed for a different language group requires that the measure be translated into the language of interest. The procedure most often used is called **back-translation** (Brislin, 1980; John & Benet-Martínez, 2014). In this method, a person who is fluent in the languages of interest translates the original measure, most commonly in English, into the other language. A second bilingual expert then independently translates the new version of the measure back into the original language. The researchers, working with the first translator, compare the original and back-translated versions of the measure to identify discrepancies. Efforts to resolve discrepancies depend on the degree to which they are discrepant. Minor discrepancies might be resolved through discussions with both translators. Major discrepancies might require more substantial revisions and a continuation of the back-translation procedure. Ideally, additional steps would then be taken to evaluate the success of the back-translation procedure in promoting measurement equivalence. Such steps might include administering each version of the measure to participants in the respective language groups followed by a comparison of item and scale statistics and confirmatory factor analyses (John & Benet-Martínez, 2014).

Note that the back-translation procedure does not ensure the construct validity of the measure. Manifestations of the same construct might be very different in different cultural groups; using translated measures ignores potentially unique and culturally distinct meanings and indicators of constructs. Thus, some researchers have advocated an **emic** approach in which a construct is defined within the specific cultural group of interest, and this definition and perhaps other cultural norms (e.g., about the mode of measurement or instructions to participants) form the basis for creating a culturally relevant measure to assess the construct. This approach stands in contrast to the **etic** approach described above, in which the construct is assumed to be interculturally comparable or universal (John & Benet-Martínez, 2014). However, most researchers generally agree that both approaches are needed to fully understand human behavior. Emic approaches enable researchers to understand factors that are unique to specific cultural groups, whereas etic approaches help us understand the extent to which various phenomena are similar across cultures. Thus, a complete understanding of social behavior – both within and across cultures – requires both emic and etic approaches (Cheung, 2012; Cheung, van de Vijver, & Leong, 2011; John & Benet-Martínez, 2014).

Summary

Either to buttress findings from research in which constructs are operationally defined using direct questioning or to study phenomena for which direct questioning is not feasible, a number of measurement strategies are available. As with direct questioning methods, the choice between collateral reports, observation, physiological monitoring, or some other indirect method of measurement requires careful consideration of the population under study and the constructs implicated in the hypotheses to be tested. The strongest hypothesis tests are those in which key constructs are operationally defined using multiple methods that offset the strengths and weaknesses of each.

With multiple measures of multiple constructs, a researcher can construct a matrix of reliability and validity correlations known as the multitrait–multimethod matrix. This provides a thorough assessment of construct validity by allowing the researcher to examine both the convergent and discriminant validity of the methods and the traits being measured, and to tease apart method from trait variance. Factor analysis approaches, confirmatory as well as exploratory, help determine underlying structures of sets of items and provide information helpful in determining the construct validity of a particular measure. They provide tools integral for understanding the underlying structure of the data, for few individuals could look at the 190 correlations in a 20×20 matrix and discern their underlying structure.

The need to consider cultural issues in measurement has also become increasingly more important as the population becomes more diverse and our daily lives become more global. Measures cannot be assumed to be equivalent across diverse populations – particularly across different language groups. Ultimately, both emic and etic approaches will be critical to further development of measures and understanding of diverse groups.

Go online   Visit the book's companion website for this chapter's test bank and other resources at: www.wiley.com/go/maruyama

---

Key Concepts

Autophotographic research
Back-translation
Card sort
Collateral reports
Common method variance
Concurrent validity
Confirmatory factor analysis
Construct validity
Content validity
Convergent validity
Convergent validity coefficients
Criterion validity
Discriminant validity
Discriminant validity coefficients
Domain
Domain sampling

Emic
Etic
Exploratory factor analysis
Face validity
Implicit association methods
Latent
Measurement equivalence
Methods
Multitrait–multimethod (MTMM) matrix
Nonsense coefficients
Observation
Predictive validity
Psychophysiology
Reliability coefficients
Traits

On the Web

http://ericae.net/ft/tamu/Valid.htm Complete text of an essay entitled, "Controversies Regarding the Nature of Score Validity: Still Crazy After All These Years."

http://psychclassics.yorku.ca/Cronbach/construct.htm Cronbach and Meehl's classic 1955 paper, "Construct Validity in Psychological Tests," first published in *Psychological Bulletin, 52*, 281–302. Website entitled "Classics in the History of Psychology" created by C. D. Green.

Further Reading

Gawronski, B., & Payne, K. B. (Eds.). (2010). *Handbook of implicit cognition: Measurement, theory, and applications*. New York, NY: Guilford Press.

Grimm, K. J., & Widaman, K. F. (2012). Construct validity. In H. Cooper, P. M. Camic, D. L. Long, A. T. Panter, D. Rindskopf, & K. J. Sher (Eds.), *APA handbook of research methods in psychology, Vol. 1: Foundations, planning, measures, and psychometrics* (pp. 621–642). Washington, DC: American Psychological Association.

John, O. P., & Benet-Martínez, V. (2014). Measurement: Reliability, construct validation, and scale construction. In H. T. Reis & C. M. Judd (Eds.), *Handbook of research methods in social and personality psychology* (2nd ed., pp. 473–503). New York, NY: Cambridge University Press.

Messick, S. (1980). Test validity and the ethics of assessment. *American Psychologist, 35*, 1012–1027.

Messick, S. (1995). Validity of psychological assessment: Validation of inferences from persons' responses and performances as scientific inquiry into score meaning. *American Psychologist, 50*, 741–749.

Newton, P. E., & Shaw, S. D. (2013). Standards for talking and thinking about validity. *Psychological Methods, 18*, 301–310.

Chapter 9

Sampling Methods

A crucial issue of any research concerns the extent to which conclusions can be generalized beyond the immediate settings and samples that have been studied. In Chapter 2 we labeled this issue external validity. A research study that has high external validity is one from which we can confidently generalize the results to the population and settings that are of theoretical interest.

Research Methods in Social Relations, Eighth Edition. Geoffrey Maruyama and Carey S. Ryan.
© 2014 John Wiley & Sons, Inc. Published 2014 by John Wiley & Sons, Inc.
Companion Website: www.wiley.com/go/maruyama

In this chapter, we describe how the process of selecting a sample from a population can affect the validity of generalizations from the sample to the population. Most of the discussion focuses on sampling people (e.g., to interview or to serve as research participants in some other way). However, we also consider issues involved in sampling units other than people (e.g., newspaper stories) and conclude the chapter by providing an overview of experience sampling.

We begin with two general points. First, the importance of external validity varies for different types of research. In most survey research, external validity is quite important. Consider, for example, a national survey designed to estimate the proportions of voters who favor various presidential candidates. It is not practical to interview all voters, and hence only a relatively small sample of voters is surveyed. Whether the sample is well chosen affects the success of the entire enterprise. In laboratory research, however, internal validity is usually the primary concern; indeed, randomized experiments are often conducted in laboratories, because they facilitate the control of extraneous variables that would otherwise undermine internal validity. But prospective research participants are not always willing to come to a laboratory. Hence, laboratory researchers frequently must make do with whatever participants are available, for example, college students who participate in research as a course requirement. Sampling procedures that allow one to generalize the conclusions directly to a population are usually not possible.

The second point is that even when external validity is a primary concern, the type of generalization that is desired depends on the type of research. The purpose of some research is to draw conclusions about a population, for example, a study of a new teaching method in which the goal is to determine whether the new method, as implemented by a city's teachers, can improve learning among that city's population of third-graders. For this type of **particularistic research goal**, external validity involves the ability to generalize the research results from the studied sample to the target population, and sampling is crucial to enhancing that ability.

Other research is designed to test theoretically hypothesized associations; the specific population or setting of interest is usually not specified. For example, one might conduct an experiment to test a theory about the conditions under which frustration leads to aggression. For such **universalistic research goals**, the consistency of the findings with the theoretically based hypotheses is the primary goal, for inconsistency implies that the theory is inadequate and requires revision. The ability to extend the research findings from the sample to the population is of less concern. Instead, the applicability of the theory outside the research context is the central question.

In short, research can serve a variety of purposes. For some purposes (e.g., testing theoretical hypotheses of a causal nature) internal validity is crucially important. External validity becomes a theoretical question (i.e., how broadly applicable is the theory) rather than a methodological question. For other purposes, the extent to which the results apply directly to a larger population is the key concern, and sampling is critical. The relative priority of research validities depends on what the researcher is trying to accomplish.

We now turn to an introduction to the fundamentals of sampling. We begin by providing some basic definitions and concepts that are used throughout this chapter.

Some Basic Definitions and Concepts

A **population** is the aggregate of *all* of the cases that conform to some designated set of specifications. Thus, the specifications "people" and "residing in the United States" define a population consisting of all the people who reside in the United States. We could similarly define populations consisting of all the households in a particular city district, all students who are enrolled fulltime at a particular university, or all the case records in an agency's files.

One population might be included in another. For example, the population consisting of all the women residing in the United States is included in the population consisting of all the people who live in the United States. The included population is known as a subpopulation, a population stratum, or simply as a **stratum**. A stratum is defined by one or more specifications that divide a population into mutually exclusive segments. For instance, a given population could be subdivided into **strata** consisting of women 21 through 40 years of age, men 21 through 40 years of age, women 41 through 60 years of age, and so on. Similarly, we could specify a stratum of the U.S. population consisting of Latina college graduates between 21 and 40 years of age; or we might have some reason for regarding this group as a population in its own right, that is, without reference to the fact that it is included in a larger population.

A single member of a population is referred to as a **population element**. We often want to know how certain characteristics of the elements are distributed in a population. For example, we might want to know the age distribution of the elements, or we might want to know the proportion of the elements that prefer one political candidate to another. A **census** is a count of all the elements in a population and/or a determination of the distributions of their characteristics, based on information obtained for each of the elements.

It is generally much more economical in time, effort, and money to obtain information for only some of the population elements rather than for all. When we select some of the elements with the intention of finding out something about the population from which they are taken, we refer to that group of elements as a **sample**. We hope, of course, that what we find out about the sample is true of the population as a whole. However, this might or might not be the case; how closely the information we receive corresponds to what we would find by a comparable census of the population depends largely on the way the sample is selected.

For example, we might want to know what proportion of a population prefers one political candidate to another. We could ask 100 people from that population which candidate they prefer. The proportion of the sample preferring Jones might or might not be the same as the corresponding proportion in the population. For that matter, the actual votes in an election might not accurately represent the preferences of the population. Unless there is a 100% turnout, the actual voters constitute only a sample of the population of people eligible to vote. People who prefer Smith might be overconfident about their candidate's chances and neglect to come to the polls; or they might be discouraged from coming to the polls by heavy rain. The election results determine which candidate takes office, but they do not necessarily indicate which candidate is preferred by a majority of the population. Similarly, the early returns in an election can be taken as a sample of the population of returns; and as everyone knows, they can be quite deceptive.

In the case of elections, there probably is not much we can do to guarantee that the samples accurately represent their populations. We usually accept the outcome of an election as a reflection of the popular will. And if we are misled by early returns, our errors are soon corrected. In other situations, however, we can to some extent control the properties of the sample – we can draw the sample in a way that increases the likelihood that the sample results are similar to the true population figures. We can never guarantee that the sample results reflect the population unless we have also conducted a complete comparable census. We can, however, devise sampling plans, which, if properly executed, can guarantee that if we were to repeat a study on a number of different samples selected from the same population, our findings would not differ from the true population figures by more than a specified amount in more than a specified proportion of the samples.

Suppose that we select numerous samples from the same population, asking the individuals who were selected to indicate whether they agree or disagree with a policy statement. For each sample, we compute the percentage who agree, and take that result as an estimate of the proportion of the population who agree. We could devise various **sampling plans** that would ensure that our estimates do not differ from the true population figures by, say, more than 5% on more than, say, 10% of the samples; the estimates will be correct within 5 percentage points (the **margin of error**, that is, the limits of accuracy of the sample estimate) 90% of the time (the probability or **confidence level**, that is, the probability of obtaining an estimate within the margin of error upon repeated sampling). We could similarly devise sampling plans that would produce correct results within 2 percentage points of the true population value 99% of the time or within any other margin of error and any assigned confidence level.

In practice, of course, we do not repeat the same study on an indefinite number of samples drawn from the same population. But our knowledge of what would happen in repeated studies enables us to say that with a given sample, there is, say, a 90% probability that our figures are within 5 percentage points of those that would be shown by a census of the total population using the same measures. (We discuss the underlying principles of these concepts later in this chapter.) Having set the desired levels of accuracy and confidence in the findings, we would select from the available alternatives the sampling plan that could be most economically achieved. Of course, the higher the levels of accuracy and confidence we desire, other conditions being equal, the higher the cost of the study.

A sampling plan that provides this type of assurance is referred to as a **representative sampling plan**. Note that in this usage the word "representative" does not qualify "sample" but "sampling plan" for a representative sampling plan might not result in a representative sample. The sampling plan must be properly carried out and even then, as we have indicated, there is a chance that the sample figure is further from the true population figure than we had planned. A representative sampling plan only ensures that the likelihood that the selected sample is sufficiently representative of the population is high enough to justify the risk of taking it as representative; it decreases the likelihood of misleading sample findings.

Another way to decrease the likelihood of misleading sample findings involves taking steps to guarantee the inclusion in the sample of diverse elements of the population and to make sure (either by controlling the proportions of the various types of elements or by statistical procedures) that those diverse elements are taken account of in the proportions in which they occur in the population. We consider this issue at greater length later in this chapter when we discuss quota sampling and stratified random sampling.

As we have noted, the dependability or accuracy of survey findings is affected not only by:

- the sampling plan and
- the faithfulness with which it is carried out,

but also by

- the measurement procedures used.

For this reason, sample surveys of a large population can produce more dependable results on some matters than can a census. For example, there are not enough highly skilled interviewers to get anything more than superficial information in a national census; a survey on a smaller scale requires fewer interviewers and also permits more intensive training. Similarly, a smaller-scale survey can make it economically feasible to spend more time with each respondent, making it possible to use measures that could not be used for a census of a large population.

The basic distinction in modern sampling theory is between probability and non-probability sampling. In **probability sampling**, one can specify for each element of the population the probability that it will be included in the sample. In the simplest case, each of the elements has the same probability of being included. But it is not necessary that the probability be the same for every element. Rather, for each element there must be some specifiable probability that it will be included. In **non-probability sampling**, there is no way to estimate the probability each element has of being included in the sample and no assurance that every element has *some* chance of being included.

Probability sampling is the only approach that makes representative sampling plans possible. Probability sampling makes it possible to estimate the extent to which the findings from a sample are likely to differ from what would have been found by studying the population. If investigators use probability sampling, they can specify the size of the sample (or the sizes of various components of complex samples) that they will need if they want to have a given degree of certainty that their sample findings do not differ by more than a specified amount from those that a study of the total population would yield.

The major advantages of nonprobability sampling are convenience and economy – advantages that can, for some research purposes, outweigh the benefits of probability sampling. We turn next to a discussion of specific types of nonprobability sampling and probability sampling.

Nonprobability Sampling

Haphazard Samples

Haphazard, **convenience**, or **accidental sampling** involves taking the cases at hand until the sample reaches a designated size. For example, we might take the first hundred people we meet on the street who are willing to be interviewed. Or college professors, wanting to make some generalization about college students, study the students in their classes. Or a television reporter, wanting to know how "the people" feel about a given issue, interviews available shoppers, store clerks, barbers, and others who are presumed to reflect public opinion. There is no known way of evaluating the **biases**, that is, systematic deviations of sample values from true population values, introduced in such samples. If we use haphazard samples, we can only hope that we are not being too misled.

Haphazard samples include those obtained via recently developed crowdsourcing websites, such as Amazon.com's Mechanical Turk (MTurk). MTurk has available more than 100,000 workers from over 100 countries (although most are from the U.S. and India) who complete various types of tasks, including web-based surveys, in exchange for small amounts of money. The use of MTurk is gaining in popularity among researchers because data can be obtained anonymously, quickly, and at a very low cost. It is also possible, although not always easy, to restrict eligible participants to those who have certain demographic or other characteristics. Research so far indicates that the reliability of data obtained from crowdsourcing samples is as good as or better than that of university samples (Behrend, Sharek, Meade, & Wiebe, 2011). Buhmester, Kwang, and Gosling (2011), for example, compared the responses of participants recruited via MTurk to those of college students enrolled in psychology courses – the traditional source of research participants for psychology studies – and found that MTurk participants were somewhat more demographically diverse than both "standard" Internet samples and typical American college samples and that the data were just as reliable. We expect to see an increased use of such crowdsourcing sampling strategies in the years to come, as well as additional research on how they can be best utilized.

Quota Samples

Quota sampling (sometimes misleadingly referred to as "representative" sampling) helps to guarantee the inclusion of diverse elements of the population and to make sure that they are taken account of in the proportions in which they occur in the population. Consider an extreme case: Suppose that we are sampling from a population that includes equal numbers of women and men and that there is a sharp difference between the two in the characteristic we wish to measure. If we did not interview any women, the results of the survey would almost certainly be an extremely misleading picture of the total population. Minority group members are frequently under-represented in haphazard samples. Anticipating possible differences among subgroups, quota samplers seek to guarantee inclusion of enough cases from each stratum.

The basic goal of quota sampling is the selection of a sample that is a replica of the population to which one wants to generalize; hence, the notion that it "represents" that population. If it is known that the population has equal numbers of men and women, the investigators attempt to include equal numbers of men and women. If it is known that 10% of the population lies within a particular age range, the investigators sample so as to ensure that 10% of the sample falls within that age range.

However, quota sampling is otherwise similar to haphazard sampling. The part of the full sample in a particular class is a haphazard sample of the corresponding stratum of the population. The women in the sample are a haphazard sample of the women in the population; the 20- to 40-year-olds in the sample are a haphazard sample of the 20- to 40-year-olds in the population. Even if the sampling procedure yields correct proportions of the compound classes (e.g., White women in the 20 to 40 age range), the sample cases in these classes are still haphazard samples of the corresponding compound strata in the population. The total sample is thus a haphazard sample.

Researchers who use quota sampling procedures tend to fall prey to several types of bias. They might include their own friends, who will tend to be like themselves and thus potentially nonrepresentative of the overall population. They might concentrate on areas in which large numbers of people are available, for example, large cities, college campuses, or airport terminals. Such samples would overrepresent the kinds of people who tend to gravitate to these areas and underrepresent those who do not. Or interviewers doing home visits might avoid rundown buildings in dangerous-looking neighborhoods, building a socioeconomic bias into the sample.

Such factors are not easily corrected using statistical correction procedures. We might know in advance the true relative proportions of the two sexes and the various age groups, which would allow us to correct for disproportions in the sample. But what true proportion of what definable population is most likely to be found at an airport terminal during the course of a survey? Investigators using quota sampling procedures can only try to ensure that important segments of the population are not entirely unrepresented, sample in such a way that potentially relevant variables are not too distorted in their sample, and hope that whatever disproportions remain do not have an undue bearing on the opinions, preferences, or whatever it is that they seek to know.

Purposive Samples

Purposive sampling involves handpicking cases to form samples that researchers deem satisfactory for their needs. A common strategy is to select cases that are judged to be typical of the population, assuming that errors in selection judgments will tend to cancel out; however, experiments on purposive sampling suggest that this assumption is not dependable. In any case, without an external check, there is no way of knowing whether the "typical" cases are indeed typical.

Purposive samples selected because of assumed typicality have been used in attempts to forecast national elections. One such approach involves selecting for each state a number of small election districts whose election returns in previous years have approximated the overall state returns, interviewing all the eligible voters in these districts about their voting intentions, and hoping that the selected districts are still typical of their respective states. However, when there are no marked changes in the political atmosphere, one can probably do as well by basing forecasts on the returns from previous years without doing interviews; when changes are occurring, we need to know how they are affecting the selected districts in comparison with other districts.

Impact evaluations of social programs have often relied on purposive sampling as well, that is, purposive sampling of program sites. Often selection judgments are made so that the sites vary with respect to some characteristic, for example, urban versus rural (Olsen, Orr, Bell, & Stuart, 2013). Although the cost of purposive sampling might be lower, the ability to generalize the findings from these evaluations is undermined. A lack of external validity might not be a problem if the study is designed to determine only whether the program can work. However, if the impact of the program varies across sites or the results are to be used as a basis for broad policy decisions, which is more often the case, this type of sampling can be problematic. Biased estimates of program impacts do not provide a good basis for making policy decisions that affect large numbers of people and might therefore result in higher costs in the long run. (See Olsen et al., 2013, for a more in-depth discussion, including the derivation of a mathematical expression to estimate bias.)

Snowball Samples

When the research question concerns a special population whose members are difficult to locate, researchers might resort to snowball sampling. **Snowball sampling** is a multistage sampling procedure by which a small initial sample "snowballs" into a sample large enough to meet the requirements of research design and data analysis. The snowballing results from members of an initial sample of the target population enlisting other members of the population to participate in the study. If participants enlisted in this way bring additional people into the study, then the sample size grows geometrically, quickly reaching a size much larger than the initial sample.

The starting point for a snowball sample is the initial sample of population members, each of whom is asked to name all the other population members he or she knows. After these individuals complete the survey or interview, they, too, would be asked to list all others of the target population whom they know. The newly named individuals form the next "layer" of the snowball. This procedure continues until either no new prospective participants are listed or the sample of enrolled participants reaches a predetermined size. The investigators either directly contact and attempt to enlist the new individuals who are identified or, if members of the research team cannot directly contact prospective participants, offer an incentive for members of the initial sample to enroll individuals in the study.

As with all nonprobability sampling methods, it is impossible to know how representative the final sample is of the population from which it was drawn. Even if the initial sample is obtained using a probability method, the lists provided by members of the initial sample are haphazard and, therefore, subject to the biases described earlier. It is wise to begin with a stratified random sample (though this would require a list of population members) or, minimally, a quota sample and seek the largest initial sample possible. Even then, inferences must be made with caution given the unknown association between the sample and the population. Nevertheless, the snowball sampling method might make sense when the population of interest is understudied and its members are difficult to find. As is always the case, researchers must consider whether the potential increase in knowledge and basis for further research is worth the effort.

Concluding Thoughts about Nonprobability Sampling

Advances in sampling methods, including nonprobability sampling methods, continue to occur. For example, respondent-driven sampling (RDS) (Heckathorn, 1997) uses a specific variation of snowball sampling and a mathematical model to adjust for sampling bias as a means of obtaining representative samples of difficult-to-reach, but socially interconnected populations (see, e.g., Kogan, Wejnert, Chen, Brody, & Slater, 2011). Similarly, the work of Olsen et al. (2013) suggests that it is possible to estimate and adjust for bias resulting from certain types of purposive sampling.

There are also circumstances in which nonprobability sampling might be more appropriate than probability sampling. Researchers do not necessarily carry out studies of samples only for the purpose of being able to generalize to the populations. If we use samples for other reasons, the ability to evaluate the likelihood of deviations from the population values is irrelevant. For example, if our goal is to obtain ideas, insights, and experienced critical appraisals, we would select a purposive sample. The situation is analogous to expert consultants being called in on a difficult medical case. These consultants – a purposive sample – are not called in to get an average opinion that would correspond to the average opinion of the entire medical profession. They are called in precisely because of their special experience and competence. Or the situation can be viewed as analogous to our more or less haphazard sampling of foods from a famous cuisine. We are sampling not to estimate some population value but to get an idea of the variety of elements available in this population.

Finally, as we noted in the introduction to this chapter, for some social scientists, the need for experimental control overrides sampling considerations. That is, social scientists who use experimental methods in a laboratory setting frequently trade some external validity for increased internal validity. There also are times when concerns about construct validity and external validity conflict. That is, it is necessary on occasion to decide whether we want a better sampling design or more sensitive and generally more informative measurements.

Probability Sampling

Probability samples are those in which every element of the sampled population has a known probability of being included. It is not necessary that all elements have an equal probability, although that is frequently the case. Probability sampling plans decrease the likelihood of obtaining misleading results in the two ways we identified earlier:

- They allow us to specify the chances that the sample findings do not differ by more than a certain amount from the true population values.
- They can guarantee that enough cases are selected from a population stratum to provide an estimate for that stratum of the population.

Probability sampling plans thus provide samples that can support firm conclusions about the characteristics of a population. We discuss four types of probability samples: simple random sampling, stratified random sampling, cluster sampling, and finally, multistage sampling, which involves combining two or more of the first three strategies.

Simple Random Samples

Simple random sampling is the most basic probability sampling design; it is incorporated in all more complex probability sampling designs. A simple random sample is selected using a process that gives every element in the population an equal and independent chance of being included in the sample. Independence means that the inclusion of one element does not depend at all on the inclusion of any others. In combination, these properties mean that every possible combination of elements of a particular number also has an equal probability of being drawn.

Suppose, for example, that we want a simple random sample of 2 cases from a population of 5 cases. Let the 5 cases in the population be *A*, *B*, *C*, *D*, and *E*. There are 10 possible pairs of cases in this population: *AB*, *AC*, *AD*, *AE*, *BC*, *BD*, *BE*, *CD*, *CE*, and *DE*. If one were to write each combination on a card, put the 10 cards in a hat, mix them thoroughly, and have a blindfolded person pick one, each card would have the same chance of being selected. The 2 cases corresponding to the letters on the selected card would constitute the desired simple random sample.

In this illustration, each of the cards (i.e., each combination of 2 cases) has 1 chance in 10 of being selected. Each of the individual cases also has the same chance of being selected – 4 in 10 because each case appears on 4 of the cards. There are, however, many ways of giving each case the same chance of being selected without getting a simple random sample. For example, suppose we were to arbitrarily divide an illustrative population of 10 cases into 5 pairs as follows: *AB*, *CD*, *EF*, *GH*, and *IJ*. If we write the designations for these pairs on 5 cards, blindly pick one of the cards, and take as our sample the 2 cases designated on this card, every case has 1 chance in 5 of being selected; but not every possible combination has the same chance of being selected as every other – in fact, most of the combinations (e.g., *AC*) have no chance at all as they have not been included on the cards.

In principle, we can use this method for selecting random samples from populations of any size, but in practice it would be difficult to list all the combinations of the desired number of cases. The same result is obtained by selecting each case individually, using a list of **random numbers**, which are sets of numbers that were generated in such a way that there is no systematic order. We discuss the generation and use of random numbers in the next section.

Selecting a Random Sample

The first task in selecting a random sample is to list or otherwise specify the population from which elements are drawn to form the sample; this list or other specification of the population is referred to as the **sampling frame**. Establishing an accurate and complete sampling frame is a critical step in any probability sampling plan. It is difficult to meet for many real populations (e.g., all the residents of a particular city), but lists exist for other types of populations (all currently enrolled students in a university or all the physicians licensed to practice medicine in a state). Sometimes a clear and systematic way of enumerating all the population elements already exists and is readily available. For example, if we wish to sample 5-minute time periods from a population of 24 hours, there would be 12 × 24, or 288, time periods in the population.

Obtaining and Using Random Numbers

The second task is to obtain random numbers. **Random number tables** can be found in many statistics textbooks as well as on the Internet (e.g., http://www.nist.gov/pml/wmd/pubs/upload/AppenB-HB133-05-Z.pdf). Typically, tables include a series of numbers, usually four to six digits in length, arrayed in matrix format (i.e., columns and rows). Table 9.1 is a small random number table we created for illustrative purposes, using numbers generated by Research Randomizer (Urbaniak & Plous, 2013). Note that the columns and rows are numbered, a feature that facilitates movement through a large table. The table is used as follows: Suppose our sampling frame included 500 people, and we wanted to select a simple random sample of 20 people. Our first step would be to array names or some identifier of the 500 people in a list and give each a unique number from 1 to 500. Next, we would select an arbitrary

Table 9.1	Example of a Random Number Table				
	1	*2*	*3*	*4*	*5*
1	12580	31823	22653	27734	47**403**
2	29525	48**314**	58762	60704	50241
3	60798	76190	23514	29173	33917
4	71**407**	11789	76**269**	18456	16527
5	99**098**	52177	84710	11274	24956
6	36998	16917	53341	16**151**	02600
7	56802	06**327**	37**068**	69581	70**150**
8	56315	13969	98**018**	16**050**	86985
9	73**094**	57414	37955	87909	60581
10	49390	15483	30627	77**030**	59252

place in the table to begin, for example, by dropping a coin or other small object onto the random number table from such a distance that we could not anticipate where it would land. We would begin with the number closest to the object. For purposes of illustration, let us pretend that this exercise pointed to column 1, row 5. Because our sampling frame includes only 500 people, we need only three of the five digits in each table entry. We could use either the first or the last three; we have chosen to use the last three. Beginning with the number in column 1 and row 5, we systematically move through the table (either across rows or down columns), looking for values from 1 to 500 in the last three digits of each entry. We have highlighted numbers in the table that fall in this range. As you can see, our first number ends in 098; hence, the person assigned 98 in our sampling frame becomes the first member of our sample. Moving down the column, the last three digits of the next number, 998, falls outside our range, so we move to the next number and the next until we encounter another three-digit number within our range. If a number corresponding to an element that is already in the sample comes up a second time, it is simply ignored and the next number is used; this corresponds to **sampling without replacement**. In the end, our sample of 20 comprises the people holding the following positions in the sampling frame: 98, 315, 94, 390, 314, 190, 177, 327, 414, 483, 269, 341, 068, 018, 173, 274, 151, 50, 30, and 403.

Often researchers *generate* random numbers specific to the sampling situation rather than consulting generic random number tables. Software-based **random number generators**, such as those provided in Microsoft Excel, SPSS, or SAS, are, technically speaking, *pseudo*-random number generators. These generators begin with a seed, an arbitrary starting value (e.g., the time of day). The seed value is transformed according to some algebraic rule and then the outcome of that transformation is itself transformed. This process proceeds until the desired number of random numbers is generated (Marsaglia, 1984). Because one can document the process by which such numbers are produced, they are not genuinely random. *Genuine* random numbers do not involve algebraic manipulation, instead relying on some naturally occurring random process as the basis for generating numbers. For instance, the HotBits hardware (http://www.fourmilab.ch/hotbits/) builds lists of genuinely random numbers based on the inherent randomness in the amount of time it takes the Krypton-85 nucleus to decay. The algebraic transformations that underlie pseudo-random number generators have become increasingly sophisticated, however, yielding numbers that approach genuine randomness and suffice quite well for random sampling.

We illustrate the use of a pseudo-random number generator, Research Randomizer (http://www.randomizer.org), using the same example of drawing 20 cases at random from a population of 500. The input screen offers users a number of choices to tailor the generated list to the specific requirements of the sampling situation. We thus asked for one set of 20 numbers falling in the range from 1 to 500 with no repeats. We also asked that the generated numbers be ordered from lowest to highest. A screen shot of the output appears in Figure 9.1. Note that this procedure is much more efficient than the manual search through a random numbers table because only numbers in the desired range are generated; choosing sets of four digits from a printed table yields many numbers that are out of range and unusable.

Whether using a random number table or a random number generator, the definition of simple random sampling is met because each number is chosen randomly and

Research Randomizer Results

1 Set of 20 Unique Numbers Per Set
Range: From 1 to 500 – Sorted from Least to Greatest

Job Status:

Working... Please be patient...

Finished

Set #1:

71, 157, 165, 172, 231, 233, 237, 271, 273, 274, 295, 360, 386, 419, 428, 438, 439, 441, 472, 483

Figure 9.1   Results from Web-Based Pseudo-Random Number Generator, Research Randomizer, When Given the Problem of Generating 20 Unique Random Numbers from the Range 1 to 500. Source: Urbaniak & Plous (2013). Retrieved June 22, 2013, from http://www.randomizer.org/

independently (by the definition of what random numbers are). Each population element thus has an equal and independent chance of being included in the sample.

Principles Underlying the Use of Probability Sampling

We next illustrate the underlying principles of probability sampling. Consider, for this purpose, a hypothetical population of 10 individuals, or cases, as follows:

Case	A	B	C	D	E	F	G	H	I	J
Score	0	1	2	3	4	5	6	7	8	9

The score represents some attribute of the individual, such as his or her performance on a test of mechanical aptitude. The mean score for this population of 10 cases is 4.5. If we did not know this figure, we could estimate it based on the scores of the elements in the sample that is drawn. According to the definition of simple random sampling, the method of selecting the sample must give equal probability to every combination of the desired number of cases; in other words, over the long run, with repeated sampling, every combination should come up the same number of times. We can, therefore, determine what will happen in the long run in our illustrative population by considering all the combinations; that is, we can take every combination of the desired number of cases and compute a mean for each combination. What results is a distribution of sample means – known as a **sampling distribution**. For example, there are 45 possible combinations of 2 cases in our hypothetical population

Table 9.2   Mean Scores of Simple Random Samples of 2, 4, and 6 Cases from
Illustrative Population of 10 Cases with Population Mean Score of 4.5

Sample Means	Sample Size		
	2 Cases	4 Cases	6 Cases
.5	1		
1.0	1		
1.50–1.75	2	2	
2.00–2.67	5	10	2
2.75–3.25	3	25	10
3.33–4.00	8	43	52
4.17–4.83	5	50	82
5.00–5.67	8	43	52
5.75–6.25	3	25	10
6.33–7.00	5	10	2
7.25–7.50	2	2	
8.00	1		
8.50	1		
Total number of samples	45	210	210
Mean of sample means	*4.5*	*4.5*	*4.5*
Percent of sample means between 4.00 and 5.00	11	24	39
Percent of sample means between 2.67 and 6.33	60	89	98

Note. With the small number of different scores in the illustrative population, the number of possible sample means is limited. Thus, for samples of 2 cases, there is no combination that can yield a mean of 2.25; but there are 3 samples of 4 cases (*ABDF, ABCG, ACDE*) with a mean of 2.25. Similarly, a mean of 2.67 is not possible for 1 sample of 6 cases. For convenience of tabulation and to highlight the characteristics of the sampling distribution, the means of the samples have been grouped.

of 10 cases. One, and only one, combination (cases *A* and *B*) yields a sample mean of .5; there are 5 combinations (*A* and *J*, *B* and *I*, *C* and *H*, *D* and *G*, *E* and *I*) that yield sample means of 4.5; and so on. Similarly, there are 210 possible samples of 4 cases. One of these combinations (*A, B, C,* and *D*) yields a sample mean of 1.5; 1 (*A, B, C,* and *E*), a sample mean of 1.75; and so on. Table 9.2 shows the sampling distributions for sample means based on simple random samples of 2, 4, and 6 cases from our illustrative population.

Notice that for samples of a given size the most likely sample mean is the population mean; the next most likely are values close to the population mean; the more a sample mean deviates from the population mean, the less likely it is to occur. (Because of the grouping of means, this pattern is obscured for samples of two cases, for which there are 5 possible samples with a mean of 4.5, four possible samples with a mean of 4.0, and so on.) Also, the larger the sample, the more likely is it that its mean will be close to the population mean. For instance, whereas 39% of the means for samples of 6 fall between 4.00 and 5.00, only 11% of the means for samples of 2 fall within this narrow range centered around the population mean.

These characteristics of probability samples (not only for samples of means but also for samples of proportions and other types of statistics) make it possible to estimate the population characteristic (e.g., the mean) as well as the likelihood that the sample figure differs from the true population figure by a given amount. This knowledge enables us to estimate margins of error and confidence levels to which we referred earlier and to which we return later in this chapter when we discuss sampling error.

One interesting feature of simple random sampling ought to be mentioned, even though it is hard for most people to believe it without mathematical proof. When the population is large compared to the sample size (say, more than 10 times as large), the variabilities of sampling distributions are influenced much more by the *absolute number* of cases in the samples than by the *proportion* of the population that is included; that is, the magnitude of the errors that are likely depends more on the absolute size of the sample than on the proportion of the population it includes. Thus, the estimation of popular preferences in a national pre-election poll, within the limits of a given margin of error, would not require a substantially larger sample than the estimation of the preferences in any one state in which the issue is in doubt. Conversely, it would take just about as large a sample to estimate the preferences in one doubtful state with a given degree of accuracy as it would to estimate the distribution of preferences in the entire nation. This is true despite the fact that a sample of a few thousand cases obviously includes a much larger proportion of the voters in one state than the same-size sample does of the voters in the nation. Thus, estimating the preferences of 100 million U.S. voters within 3 percentage points requires only 1,150 randomly selected voters (Dillman, Smyth, & Christian, 2009). We consider this issue again when we discuss sampling error.

Common Errors in Random Sampling

Two problems commonly occur in the selection of simple random samples. First, sometimes people use **systematic sampling**, which involves choosing elements in such a way that choices are not independent. For instance, if the desired sample size of 160 is approximately 1 in 10 population elements, we might pick a random number between 1 and 10 (say, 6) and sample every tenth element after the random start. Although this method would provide a sample in which every element has an equal chance of being chosen (because of the random choice of starting point), it is not a simple random sample because the selection decisions are not independent. If the sixth element is included, the sixteenth must be and the seventh cannot be. Systematic sampling can create important biases when the list involves any type of regularity or systematic cycle, such as a list of names in alphabetical order. The procedure for drawing a simple random sample involves little additional effort and should thus be used instead of systematic sampling.

Another pitfall involves the treatment of population elements that are ineligible for sampling. For example, we might have a list of graduates of a job training program, from which a sample is to be drawn for a follow-up study of the program's effects. The decision might be made to sample only people who completed the program a year or more ago. Thus, the list would include some eligible elements and some ineligible ones. It might seem appropriate simply to select the next element on the list when the sampling procedure comes up with an ineligible name; however, this method would introduce bias and violate the nature of a probability sample. Names that follow ineligible ones would have double the usual probability of selection (because they might either be drawn in their own right or selected because the previous element was drawn but found ineligible). The correct procedure is to draw a larger sample in the first place – a sample that is large enough to compensate for the loss of ineligible elements. For instance, if a final sample of 160 is desired and it is estimated that 20% of the listed population is ineligible, we would draw an initial sample of size 160 × 1.20, or 192 (perhaps rounding up to 200). After the expected 20% loss, the remaining sample would approximate the desired size and would retain the property of being a statistically correct simple random sample.

In summary, simple random sampling plans are indeed simple – provided that a list of the population elements exists. However, in some research situations other types of samples are used, either for reasons of efficiency (stratified samples) or practicality (cluster samples). These more complex probability sampling techniques are variations of simple random sampling. We turn to these next.

Stratified Random Sampling

In **stratified random sampling**, the population is first divided into two or more strata. The strata can be based on a single criterion (e.g., sex, yielding the two strata of male and female) or on a combination of two or more criteria (e.g., age and sex, yielding strata, such as females under 21, females 21 and over, males under 21, and males 21 and over). In stratified random sampling, a simple random sample is taken from each stratum, and the subsamples are then joined to form the total sample.

To illustrate how stratified random sampling works, we refer to this population of 10 cases.

Case	A	B	C	D	E	F	G	H	I	J
Sex	F	F	F	F	F	M	M	M	M	M
Age	Y	O	Y	O	Y	O	Y	O	Y	O
Score	0	1	2	3	4	5	6	7	8	9

The first five cases are females; the last five, males. The cases designated *Y* are younger, and the *O*s are older. The score represents some attribute of the individual, such as performance on a test of mechanical aptitude.

Consider samples of four with equal proportions of females and males. To satisfy this last condition, many samples of four that were possible under the conditions of simple random sampling are no longer possible – for example, samples consisting of cases *A, B, C, D* or of cases *A, B, C, F* or of cases *D, F, G, I* – because they do not have two males and two females. In fact, there are now exactly 100 possible samples as compared to the 210 possible simple random samples. We have computed the mean score for each of the possible samples and thereby obtained the sampling distribution of the mean. Table 9.3 compares the sampling distribution of the mean for samples

Table 9.3 Mean Scores of Samples of 4 Cases from Illustrative Example of 10 Cases with Population Mean Score of 4.5 (Simple and Stratified Random Samples)

Sample Means	Type of Sample		
	Simple Random Sample	Samples Stratified by Sex	Samples Stratified by Age
1.50–1.75	2		1
2.00–2.50	10		7
2.75–3.25	25	3	8
3.50–4.00	43	25	26
4.25–4.75	50	44	16
5.00–5.50	43	25	26
5.75–6.25	25	3	8
6.50–7.00	10		7
7.25–7.50	2		1
Total number of samples	210	100	100
Mean of sample means	**4.5**	**4.5**	**4.5**
Percent of sample means between 4.00 and 5.00	24	44	16
Percent of sample means between 2.50 and 6.50	89	100	84

Note. The means of the samples have been grouped.

of four obtained on the basis of simple random sampling, stratified sampling with sex as a criterion for stratification, and stratified sampling with age as a criterion.

There is a marked improvement over simple random sampling when the sampling is based on a stratification of our hypothetical population by sex; the number of samples that give means very close to the population mean is much higher and the number of sample means that deviate widely from the population mean is much lower. When the population is stratified by age, however, there is no such improvement in the efficiency of sampling; in fact, the means of individual samples are somewhat less likely to be very close to the population mean.

In general, stratification contributes to the efficiency of sampling if it succeeds in establishing classes that are internally comparatively homogeneous with respect to the characteristics being studied – that is, if the differences between classes are large in comparison with the variation within classes. In our illustrative population, the difference in scores between females and males is relatively large and that between age groups is relatively small; that is why stratification by sex is effective and stratification by age is ineffective in this case. The general principle is that if we have reason to believe that stratifying according to a particular criterion or set of criteria will result in internally homogeneous strata, it is desirable to stratify. If the process of breaking down the population into strata that are likely to differ sharply from one another is costly, we have to balance this cost against the cost of a comparable gain in precision obtained by taking a larger simple random sample. The issues involved in the decision of whether to stratify have, basically, nothing to do with trying to make the sample a replica of the population; they have to do only with the anticipated homogeneity of the defined strata with respect to the characteristics being studied and the comparative costs of different methods of achieving precision. Both simple and stratified random sampling are representative sampling plans.

When using stratification, there is no reason for sampling from the different strata in the same proportion; that is, even with respect to the criteria selected for stratification, it is not necessary for the sample to reflect the composition of the population. For example, in sampling from a population in which the number of males equals the number of females, it is permissible (and might be desirable) to sample five or two or some other number of females to every male. Note that in such a procedure, the cases in the total population do not all have the same chance of being included in the sample. But the probability of inclusion of each case can be specified, thus meeting the basic requirement for probability sampling. When this is done, however, the mean score (or the proportion of elements with a given characteristic or whatever measure is desired) for the sample must be adjusted to estimate the mean score of the total population. In other words, the estimate for each stratum must be weighted so that it contributes to the score for the total sample in proportion to its size in the population.

There are several reasons for sampling the various strata in different proportions. Sometimes it is necessary to increase the proportion sampled from classes having small numbers of cases to ensure that these classes are represented. Consider, for example, a survey of retail sales volume in a given city in a given month. Simple random sampling of the stores might not lead to an accurate estimate of the total volume of sales because a few very large department stores account for an extremely large proportion of the total sales, and there is no guarantee that any of these large stores would turn up in a simple random sample. In this case, we would stratify the population of stores in terms of some measure of their total volume of sales (e.g., the gross value of sales during the preceding year). Perhaps only the three largest department stores would be in our topmost stratum. We would include all three in our sample; in other words, we would take a 100% sample of this stratum. Any other procedure would greatly reduce the accuracy of the estimate – no matter how carefully samples were taken from other strata. Of course, we would then need to adjust or weight the figures from the strata to estimate the total volume of sales in the city.

Another reason for taking a larger proportion of cases from one stratum than from others is that we might want to subdivide the cases within each stratum for further analysis. Let us say that in our survey of retail sales we want to be able to examine separately the volume of sales made by food stores, by clothing stores, and by other types. Even though these classifications are not taken into account in selecting the sample (i.e., the sample is not stratified on this basis), it is clear that we need a reasonable number of cases in each volume-of-sales stratum to make possible an analysis of different types of stores within each stratum. If a given stratum has relatively few cases, so that sampling in the proportion used in other strata would not provide enough cases to serve as an adequate basis for this further analysis, we might take a higher proportion of cases in this stratum.

One of the major reasons for varying the sampling proportions for different strata cannot be fully explained without going into the mathematical theory of sampling, but the principle involved can be understood on a more or less intuitive basis. Consider two strata, one of which is much more homogeneous with respect to the characteristics being studied than the other. For a given degree of precision, fewer cases are needed to determine the state of affairs in the first stratum than in the second. Consider an extreme example: Suppose we knew that every case in a given stratum had the same score; we could represent that stratum on the basis of a sample of one case. Of course, in such an extreme case we would likely not know that the scores were all the same without also knowing what the common score was. But sometimes we can anticipate the relative degrees of homogeneity or heterogeneity of strata before carrying out the survey. For example, if with respect to certain types of opinion questions, men were expected to be more alike than women, we could sample men less thoroughly than women for a given degree of precision. Or consider using states as strata in a stratified sample for predicting a national election. It would be wiser to sample more heavily in more doubtful states rather than to sample each state in proportion to its population of eligible voters. In general, we can expect the greatest precision if strata are sampled proportionately to their relative variabilities with respect to the characteristics under study rather than proportionately to their relative sizes in the population.

In summary, the reason for using a stratified rather than a simple random sampling plan is essentially a practical one: More precise estimates of population values can be obtained with the same sample size under the right conditions, as Table 9.3 illustrated. This result reduces the overall cost of the research. The "right conditions" involve relative homogeneity of the key attributes within each stratum and easy identification of the stratifying variables. The concrete procedure for drawing a stratified random sample involves drawing a simple random sample within each population stratum, treating each as a separate population list. The complexities involved in assigning unequal sampling probabilities for different strata and the like take us beyond the scope of this chapter, although we touched on some of the major considerations.

Cluster Sampling

Except when dealing with small and spatially concentrated populations, there are enormous expenses associated with simple and stratified random sampling – for example, in the preparation of classified lists of population elements and in drawing participants from scattered localities. Other factors can also make it difficult or impossible to satisfy the conditions of random sampling. For example, it might be easier to get permission to administer a questionnaire to three or four classes in a school than to administer the same questionnaire to a much smaller sample selected on a simple or stratified random basis; the latter might disrupt the school routines much more. For such practical reasons, large-scale survey studies seldom use simple or stratified random samples; instead, they use the methods of cluster sampling.

Cluster sampling involves sampling in terms of larger groupings or clusters that are selected by simple or stratified methods; if not all the elements in the clusters are to be included in the sample, elements within the clusters are selected on a simple or stratified random sampling basis. Suppose, for example, that we want to do a survey of seventh-grade public school children in some state. We could proceed as follows: Prepare a list of school districts, classified perhaps by size of community, and select a simple or stratified random sample. For each district in the sample, list the schools and take a simple or stratified random sample of them. If some or all of the selected schools have more seventh-grade classes than can be studied, take a sample of the classes in each of the schools. The survey instruments would then be administered to all the children in these classes or, if desirable and administratively feasible to do so, to a simple random or stratified random sample of the children in those classes. Similarly, a survey of urban households might involve selecting a sample of cities followed by a sample of districts within each city, and finally, a sample of households within each district. Note that the procedure moves through a series of stages, hence the common term **multistage cluster sampling**, from more inclusive to less inclusive sampling units until we finally arrive at the population elements that constitute the desired sample.

In this kind of sampling procedure, it is no longer true that every combination of the desired number of elements in a population (or in a given stratum) is equally likely to be selected. Hence, the effects we noticed in our analysis of simple and stratified random sampling of our hypothetical population of 10 cases (i.e., that the population value was the most likely sample result and that larger deviations from the population value were less likely than smaller ones) cannot develop in quite the same way. Such effects, however, do occur in a more complicated way, provided that each stage of cluster sampling is carried out on a probability sampling basis. We pay a price, however, in terms of sampling efficiency. On a per-case basis, effective cluster sampling is much less efficient in obtaining information than comparably effective stratified random sampling; that is, for a given number of cases, the probable margin of error is much larger in the former case than in the latter. Moreover, the correct statistical handling of the data is apt to be more complicated. These handicaps, however, are more than balanced by the associated economies, which generally permit the sampling of a sufficiently larger number of cases at a smaller cost.

The comparison of cluster sampling with simple random sampling is a bit more complicated. Stratified sampling principles can be used to select the clusters so that what is lost in efficiency because of clustering effects can be regained by stratification. Depending on the specific features of the sampling plan in relation to the object of the survey, cluster sampling might be more or less efficient on a per-case basis than simple random sampling. But again, even if more cases are needed for the same level of accuracy, cluster sampling is usually more cost effective for large-scale surveys.

In summary, cluster sampling, like stratified sampling, is done for practical reasons – but the specific reasons are different. The costs of sampling (e.g., making a list) and of data collection (e.g., sending interviewers to scattered individual locations) can be reduced by sampling cases in clusters. However, sampling efficiency (the number of cases required to produce population estimates of a given quality) is reduced, so more cases are required. Clustering is reasonable whenever the reduction in costs per sampled element outweighs the increased number of elements required.

Sampling Error

As we have indicated throughout this chapter, even if our sampling frame is accurate and complete and our method of random selection is without error, our sample will not exactly match the population from which it is drawn on any given characteristic. This discrepancy is referred to as **sampling error**, the difference in the distribution of characteristics between a sample and the population as a whole. Because we cannot measure the entire population, we can only estimate the extent of sampling error for a given sample. Inasmuch as any value we derive for sampling error is an estimate, we tend to cite such values according to degree of confidence. In the social sciences, the convention is to accept estimates about which there is 95% confidence that the estimate is correct. (Occasionally, the more stringent 99% confidence criterion is used.) Thus, when speaking of sampling error, we tend to make statements such as, "With 95% confidence we can say that there is X% sampling error given the size of our sample."

It probably comes as no surprise that sampling error decreases – that is, characteristics of the sample more closely match characteristics of the population – as the size of a random sample increases. This property of random samples is easy to see in the formulas used to calculate margin of error. For instance, if we want to estimate with 95% confidence the margin of error associated with an estimate of a proportion (e.g., the percentage of registered voters who will vote for a particular candidate in an election), we can use the formula,

$$1.96 \times \sqrt{\frac{P(1-P)}{N}}$$

where N represents sample size and P represents the proportion of the sample that displayed the behavior of interest to us. For illustrative purposes, let us assume that $P = .50$ and $N = 100$. Substituting these values into the equation and solving it yields a value of .098. The corresponding percentage, that is, 9.8%, is the margin of error. Hence, if we are willing to make several key assumptions, we can say with 95% confidence that the true percentage of the population who displayed the behavior of interest falls between 40.2% and 59.8%. With the same degree of confidence, if we boost sample size to 1,000, the range shrinks to between 46.9% and 53.1%. If we need a higher level of confidence, say 99%, we increase the multiplier to 2.58, expanding our range for $N = 1,000$ to between 45.9% and 54.1%. The important point for our purposes is that, because N is in the denominator, increasing N always reduces the estimate of sampling error.

The impact of sample size on sampling error is illustrated in Figure 9.2. On the x axis is sample size and on the y axis is sampling error expressed as a percentage. Consistent with computations described in the previous paragraph, the sampling error when sample size is 100 is about 10%. Note that increasing the sample size an

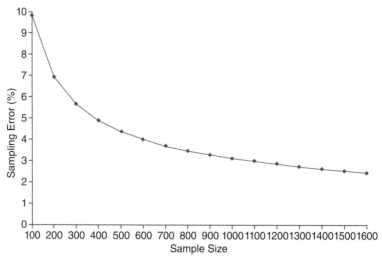

Figure 9.2   Theoretical Percentage Sampling Error (95% Confidence) Associated with Estimates from Random Samples Ranging in Size from 100 to 1,600.

additional 100 dramatically reduces the sampling error to just under 7%. Adding another 100 elements to the sample reduces the sampling error further but to a lesser degree. In fact, after sample size reaches about 600, sampling error is reduced very little by adding additional elements. This explains why the preferences of 100 million U.S. voters can be estimated within 3 percentage points with only 1,150 randomly selected voters (Dillman et al., 2009). Another way of describing this pattern is to consider the proportionate increase in sample size required to achieve a specific reduction in sampling error. Assume that we wanted to cut sampling error in half. To accomplish this for a given sample size, we would need to quadruple the number of elements. Referring back to Figure 9.2, note that the sampling error for $N = 400$ is about half the sampling error for $N = 100$. To realize this same reduction in sampling error for $N = 400$, we would have to increase sample size to 1,600. Clearly, there is a pattern of diminishing return in the association between sample size and sampling error.

We want to emphasize that sampling error and the oft-cited margin of error associated with public opinion polls are *estimates* based on a set of assumptions that rarely are met. Such estimates are idealized values that assume a truly random sample from the population and no extraneous influences associated with other aspects of the polling. Unfortunately, there are several other possible sources of error in polls and surveys, for example, nonresponse, measurement error, interviewer bias, and weighting procedures, whose effects are difficult to quantify. We discuss some of these sources of error in Chapter 14.

Random Digit Dial (RDD) Telephone Sampling

One commonly used probability sampling method is known as **random digit dial (RDD) telephone sampling**. Rather than relying on telephone listings, which are biased as a result of unlisted numbers, people who have recently moved, and the use of cell phones instead of landlines, random digits are used to create a list of telephone numbers to be contacted. First, a list of three-digit area codes and three-digit central exchange numbers is obtained from telephone companies. The phone numbers are then sampled by combining a randomly drawn valid area code–exchange combination (six digits) with a random four digits, giving a potential number within an existing exchange. The number is dialed, and if it is answered, screening questions are asked to determine whether an eligible household has been contacted as opposed to, say, a business, a computer, or another type of nonhousehold number; ineligible numbers are frequent, which means that much time is wasted on screening them out.

An alternative is to randomly sample from telephone directories or electronic white pages, using a method that avoids most of the problems of straight sampling of listed numbers. That is, one can draw randomly a household listing, and then replace the last three digits of the number with three random digits. This method increases the proportion of sampled numbers that will actually be households because of methods that phone companies use to assign phone numbers (i.e., assigning numbers in consecutive blocks of 100 or 1,000). At the same time, unlisted numbers and numbers of new residents not listed in the directory have the same chance of being called as do numbers that are in the directory.

The increasing popularity of cell phones has made the issue of conducting RDD telephone sampling more complex and more expensive. For many people, cell phones have partially or completely replaced landlines. Although it is possible to conduct RDD of cell phone numbers in addition to more conventional list-assisted RDD sampling, the task is more challenging. Brick and colleagues (2007) examined the feasibility of including cell phone numbers in a RDD telephone survey and concluded that RDD sampling of cell phone numbers was indeed feasible; however, they also reported a lower response rate, a higher refusal rate, and a lower refusal conversion rate (i.e., a lower rate of agreeing to participate in a subsequent contact attempt) in their cell phone sample than in their landline sample. Methodological developments are likely in the coming years as the popularity of cell phones is a relatively recent phenomenon, and technology and the telecommunications infrastructure continue to evolve.

Sampling Elements Other Than People

Research sometimes requires representative samples of elements other than people or groups of people. One example would be samples of time periods for an observational study in which the phenomenon of interest is to be observed at discrete times rather than continuously (see Chapter 12). For example, 30 five-minute observation periods might be randomly chosen over the course of a day. Another example is drawing samples of media content for content analysis (see Chapter 13). It might be impractical or unnecessary to code all the content of a particular newspaper for an extended period of time, so only a sample of days or pages might be chosen for examination. In these situations, a clear goal of the research is to generalize to the entire population from observations or analyses of a sample of elements. Probability sampling is therefore the approach that should be chosen. In such cases, a simple random sample is likely to be both theoretically and practically satisfactory because of the ease of listing the elements of the population (e.g., all the five-minute time periods in a day, all the days and page numbers for the newspaper).

A more specific application of the logic of sampling to measurement theory makes use of the concept of sampling items to construct a multiple-item measure of a desired construct (Nunnally & Bernstein, 1994). Suppose that we could define a domain (population) of items that measures the construct of interest, for example, the domain of two-digit addition problems (e.g., $37 + 74$) or the domain of statements describing positive or negative attitudes toward abortion. We could describe the theoretical goal of measurement as assessing the individual's responses to all the items in the domain. But doing so explicitly is impractical (we cannot generate all the attitude statements that would fall into the defined domain) and unnecessary (we probably do not need to administer all 10,000 arithmetic problems to get a good idea of the person's addition ability). Therefore, the domain can be sampled.

The logic of **domain sampling** (see also Chapter 8) is identical to the logic of sampling in general. Individuals' performance on the sample of items contained in a measure is used as a basis for estimating their hypothetical performance on the entire domain. The sample might sometimes be a probability sample; for example, it would be easy for a computer to draw a simple random sample of addition problems from the domain described. More often, the sample is a nonprobability sample because the boundaries of the domain (e.g., domains of attitude statements) are ill-defined. In practice, we simply construct a set of attitude statements and define the domain as being the hypothetical population of similar items. It should be clear, based on the principles of sampling, that a larger sample (i.e., a measure with more items) would permit a closer approximation to the desired construct (the person's responses to the entire population of items) by reducing sampling error. Indeed, as we showed in Chapter 7, measures with more items have higher reliability. However, such measures might not have adequate construct validity, which requires sampling from the entire domain of the construct. In other words, and as we noted in Chapter 7, items that are more similar to each other will have higher reliability, but if they are too redundant they are unlikely to assess the full domain of interest.

Another type of sampling is known as experience sampling, a sampling procedure used in **daily diary studies**, which are intensive studies of people's naturally occurring thoughts, feelings, and behaviors as they unfold over short periods of time, usually from seven days to two weeks. During waking hours, people are thinking, feeling, and behaving continually, making it impossible to record every thought, feeling, or behavior they experience. **Experience sampling methods** make use of sampling procedures typically used to assemble representative samples of people to obtain representative samples of experiences. They have been used to study a variety of phenomena, including intrinsic motivation and subjective experiences of time (Conti, 2001), motives for drinking alcohol (Mohr et al., 2001), self-control (Hofmann, Baumeister, Förster, & Vohs, 2012), self-expansion and flow among couples (Graham, 2008), and impression formation (Denrell, 2005). In some cases, researchers are interested in accurately describing the subjective experiences of participants and thus seek random samples of participants' lives. In other cases, researchers are interested only in particular experiences and purposive sampling is used.

To apply the experience sampling method, the researcher develops a means to signal participants that they are to complete the brief questionnaire they were provided. Participants might be instructed at the outset of the study to complete a questionnaire each day according to a set schedule as in a daily diary study; instructed to complete a questionnaire each time they recognize the occurrence of something about themselves or their environment (**event-contingent sampling**); or be alerted by an electronic device, such as a handheld computer or smartphone, that it is time to complete the questionnaire (random sampling). In the latter case, researchers must also determine (1) during what hours experiences will be sampled; (2) how many times during those hours experiences will be sampled; and (3) other constraints that should be imposed on the sampling (e.g., that signals cannot occur within 30 minutes of each other or that participants can disable or ignore the device during certain activities). When researchers are interested in accurate estimates of the quality or quantity of particular experiences or events, the standard procedure is to sample experience on random occasions throughout the day for a number of days.

Summary

The focus of this chapter is sampling as a vehicle for maximizing the external validity of research. We noted that for a sampling procedure to result in a representative sample, the first thing that must be done is to specify the population to which one wants to generalize. Then one can proceed to use either probability or nonprobability sampling procedures. In the former, every element in the population has a known, nonzero probability of being included in the sample. In the latter, we do not know the probability of inclusion for each element and some of the elements have zero probability of inclusion. Only in probability sampling do we have a firm basis for estimating how far sample results are likely to deviate from the true population figures.

Four types of nonprobability sampling were described: haphazard, quota, purposive, and snowball sampling. The first involves interviewing whomever is convenient, accessible, or otherwise accidentally encountered. Quota samples are also haphazard samples; the only difference is that in quota samples we specify strata from each of which haphazard samples are to be gathered. In purposive samples, we use our best judgment to decide which elements are most representative of the population and include them in the samples. Finally, snowball samples capitalize on the knowledge of and access to members of special populations by a small number of people from the population initially enrolled in the study to build a sample.

Probability sampling was illustrated through a description of the simplest form, simple random sampling. In such a sample, each element has an equal probability of being included in the sample, and the inclusion of each element is an independent decision. This property makes all possible samples of the desired size equally likely to be drawn. Stratified random samples involve selecting random samples from strata or subgroups of the population and combining them to form the total sample. Stratification is more efficient when the differences between strata are large in comparison with the variation within strata. For large-scale research projects, such as national surveys, sampling becomes more complex and demanding. In such cases, cluster samples or random digit dialing methods might be used.

Finally, we briefly described ways in which the logic of sampling can be used in the selection of other types of elements besides people. Time periods, elements of media content, and test items are all subject to sampling when the goal is to generalize results to a population that is the main focus of interest. Even experiences from the stream of people's lives can be sampled in the same way that people are sampled from populations.

Go online   Visit the book's companion website for this chapter's test bank and other resources at: www.wiley.com/go/maruyama

---

Key Concepts

Accidental sampling

Biases

Census

Cluster sampling

Confidence level

Convenience sampling

Daily diary studies

Domain sampling

Event-contingent sampling

Experience sampling method

Haphazard sampling

Margin of error

Multistage cluster sampling

Nonprobability sampling

Particularistic research goals

Population

Population element

Probability sampling

Purposive sampling

Quota sampling

Random digit dial (RDD) telephone sampling

Random number generator

Random number table

Random numbers

Representative sampling plan

Sample

Sampling distribution

Sampling error

Sampling frame

Sampling plan

Sampling without replacement

Simple random sampling

Snowball sampling

Strata

Stratified random sampling

Stratum

Systematic sampling

Universalistic research goals

On the Web

http://www.gallup.com/poll/faqs.aspx?ref=f In the "Frequently Asked Questions" section of the Gallup Organization's website is a detailed description of how samples are drawn by an organization that specializes in the use of samples to describe the U.S. population. Begin at the home page, **http://www.gallup.com/**, to read about results from Gallup's latest polls.

http://www.randomizer.org/ Home page for Research Randomizer, a JavaScript program for random selection and random assignment. Research Randomizer has a user-friendly graphical interface that allows considerable flexibility in specifying the characteristics of the list of random numbers it generates. Like most computer-based random number generators, Research Randomizer is a *pseudo*-random number generator.

http://www.fourmilab.ch/hotbits/ Home page for HotBits, web-based applications for research that requires a true random number generator. A hardware-based generator, HotBits capitalizes on the inherent randomness in the decay of a Krypton-85 nucleus.

http://www.pollingreport.com/ This website features highlights of national polls, including nonpartisan analysis.

http://www.ncpp.org/ The National Council on Public Polls works to "promote better understanding and reporting of public opinion polls." In its web pages are a variety of commentaries on the proper use of polling information (e.g., "20 Questions a Journalist Should Ask About Poll Results").

http://www.experience-sampling.org/ Information and download page for The Experience Sampling Program, software for conducting experience sampling studies using handheld computers such as Palm Pilot.

Further Reading

Henry, G. T. (1998). Practical sampling. In L. Bickman & D. J. Rog (Eds.), *Handbook of applied and social research methods* (pp. 101–126). Thousand Oaks, CA: Sage.

Krosnick, J. A., Lavrakas, P. J., & Kim, N. (2014). Survey research. In H. T. Reis & C. M. Judd (Eds.), *Handbook of research methods in social and personality psychology* (2nd ed., pp. 404–442). New York, NY: Cambridge University Press.

Levy, P. S., & Lemeshow, S. (2008). *Sampling of populations: Methods and applications* (4th ed.). New York, NY: John Wiley & Sons.

Mehl, M. R., & Conner, T. S. (Eds.). (2012). *Handbook of research methods for studying daily life.* New York, NY: Guilford Press.

Reis, H. T., Gable, S. L., & Maniaci, M. R. (2014). Methods for studying everyday experience in its natural context. In H. T. Reis & C. M. Judd (Eds.), *Handbook of research methods in social and personality psychology* (2nd ed., pp. 373–403). New York, NY: Cambridge University Press.

Chapter 10

Randomized Experiments

Research Methods in Social Relations, Eighth Edition. Geoffrey Maruyama and Carey S. Ryan.
© 2014 John Wiley & Sons, Inc. Published 2014 by John Wiley & Sons, Inc.
Companion Website: www.wiley.com/go/maruyama

Research designs differ in many ways. Some are more efficient than others, some make fewer demands on the researcher or on participants, and some take more time to implement. Recall from Chapter 2 that research designs also differ in **internal validity**, that is, the extent to which one can draw causal conclusions about the effect of one variable on another. Indeed one of the most important distinctions among designs is how effectively they rule out threats to internal validity. In this chapter, we consider designs that are highest in internal validity: randomized experiments.

Randomized experiments are highly specialized tools, and like any tool they are excellent for some jobs and poor for others. They are ideally suited for the task of causal analysis, that is, for determining whether differences in one variable *cause* (as opposed to simply relate to) differences in some other variable. Randomized experiments are used a great deal in the social sciences. Yet they also have their weaknesses. In this chapter, we describe their strengths and weaknesses and show how they differ from other research designs. The chief strength of randomized experiments, their internal validity, requires that researchers be able to decide which participants are assigned to which levels of the variable that is believed to be the causal variable. Experiments also require the researcher to minimize the effects of extraneous variables that might otherwise be confounded with the causal variable of interest. Frequently, this control, although maximizing internal validity, compromises construct and external validity.

Indeed, the sort of control that is necessary for a randomized experiment is most easily achieved in laboratory settings, where extraneous variables can be controlled so only the variable of interest changes across conditions. By controlling variables that may vary in natural settings, experiments typically differ from real-life, everyday settings in ways that limit our ability to generalize research conclusions to other settings. In other words, external validity can be compromised. Randomized experiments can also be conducted in real-world settings. However, real-world or field experiments, although often stronger in external validity, tend to be weaker in internal validity because it is usually more difficult to control the effects of extraneous factors. To see this more clearly, let us examine the kind of control a randomized experiment requires.

Controlling and Manipulating Variables

All research requires the manipulation or measurement of variables. As defined earlier, variables represent the constructs that researchers are interested in theoretically. They represent those things that researchers want to study and draw conclusions about. For instance, if we want to understand why people vote as they do, voting preference would be a variable that must be measured. Variables, as the name suggests, must vary; that is, they must have at least two values. Therefore, to understand voting preferences, we must study people whose voting preferences vary; some people prefer one candidate and other people prefer another. If everyone in the study preferred the same candidate, voting preference would no longer be a variable; it would be a constant.

Most research involves at least two variables, one variable usually called the independent variable, and one the dependent variable. The **independent variable** is the variable we believe to have a causal influence on our outcome variables, and is the variable in experimental research that the researcher manipulates. The **dependent variable** is the outcome variable; its values *depend* on the independent variables. In most cases, whether something is considered an independent or dependent variable depends on the research questions being asked. For example, if we wanted to demonstrate that teachers who hold high expectations for their students treat those students with greater nonverbal warmth, teacher expectations would be the independent variable and teacher warmth would be the dependent variable. But if our research looked instead at the influence of teacher nonverbal warmth on students' subsequent achievement, teacher warmth would be the independent variable and student achievement would be the dependent variable.

Clearly there are many variables besides teacher expectations or teacher nonverbal warmth that might also influence children's achievement. Family members' education, income, and expectations for children and children's motivation, health, and attendance would also influence achievement. If we wanted to be able to predict children's achievement, we would try to include as many of these variables as possible in our research. If, on the other hand, we wanted to understand the influence of a single variable, to see whether it has a causal effect on children's achievement, we would try to control all the other variables. Isolating and controlling other possible independent variables is the strategy followed in experimental research.

Experimenters ask questions, such as "What is the effect of others' expectations on children's achievement?" Notice that the question refers to a variable an experimenter can possibly control – expectations. Experimenters study variables that either they or someone else can manipulate, such as the timing, content, or strength of others' expectations. Thus, they can decide to vary whether others have positive or negative expectations about a target; that is, they can control which individuals have positive expectations and which have negative expectations of a particular child or children, for example, by telling some individuals that a child has high ability and telling others that the child has low ability. Variables that can be so controlled are called experimental independent variables or more simply experimental variables. Other sorts of independent variables, such as religion, income, education, gender, ethnicity, and personality traits, are all variables that people bring with them to a study and are virtually impossible to manipulate. These sorts of independent variables are called **individual difference or subject variables**. They are properties that people already possess. In contrast, **experimental variables** can be manipulated. This is a major difference between experimental and non-experimental or quasi-experimental research. Experimenters can control the variables whose effects they wish to study; they can control who is exposed and how they are exposed to those variables.

Why is it necessary to isolate and control extraneous variables and manipulate the independent variable to maximize internal validity? To answer this question, consider a study of the influence of television advertising on voting preferences. Assume we were not interested in the effects of education, religion, and parents' political preferences, or any other independent variables on voters' choices. All we wanted to know was whether seeing a particular television advertisement influenced voting preferences. Now suppose we did *not* manipulate who watched the television advertisement and who did not. Suppose that instead, we simply found some individuals who saw the advertisement and some who did not, and we asked them about their preferred candidate. If we found a difference in candidate preferences between those who saw the advertisement and those who did not, we could never be sure that this difference was due to having watched the advertisement or not. Instead, it might be due to a host of other individual difference variables on which the two groups happen to differ, such as political views or education.

We might try to conduct our research with individuals who all had the same political views and education. That is, we might try to equate the two groups on these individual difference variables or control these variables by holding them constant. In the social sciences, however, controlling for other variables by holding them constant is never sufficient to ensure internal validity. Even if we controlled political views and education, there might be many other individual difference variables that differ between the two groups. And any of these might also influence candidate preference. For instance, the two groups might differ in how late they stayed up at night, in how many children they had, in their age, or in what they preferred to eat for breakfast. Any of these other variables might be responsible for the difference between the two groups in candidate preference.

In other words, any preexisting difference between groups could serve as a **plausible alternative explanation** for our conclusion that exposure to advertisements affects voting behavior. Some rival explanations are more plausible than others (e.g., it would be difficult to think of a reason that breakfast preference would determine voting behavior), but *any* systematic difference between groups other than the experimental variables threatens the study's internal validity. And, because no study measures all extraneous variables, there are many possible rival explanations that cannot be dismissed, as well as alternative explanations for the results that might account for them but that are never even considered. For example, among people there is an unknown, but surely large, number of variables that might be responsible for voting choices (or almost any other dependent variable in which we might be interested). Thus, in social science research one can never maximize internal validity or reach causal conclusions about the effect of an independent variable simply by making sure that research participants do not differ on a limited number of other potentially confounding variables. There are simply too many other variables that need to be controlled.

The solution to this problem is to conduct a **randomized experiment** in which individuals are randomly assigned to levels of the independent variable. In our study of the effects of televised advertisements on voting preferences, we would randomly determine whether each individual did or did not watch advertisements featuring the political candidates. Obviously, to conduct this sort of randomized experiment, we must be the ones to decide who watches the advertisement and who does not. The researcher must be able to manipulate the independent variable.

Random Assignment

Random assignment is the only way to equate two or more groups on all possible individual difference variables at the start of the research. This step is essential for drawing causal inferences about the effects of an experimental independent variable because the experimenter must be reasonably confident that the differences that appear at the end of the experiment between two treatment groups are the result of the treatments and not of some preexisting differences between the groups.

Random assignment (also called **randomization**) is not the same as random sampling, which we covered in detail in Chapter 9. Random sampling is the procedure we might use to select participants for the study. It serves not to equate two or more experimental groups but to make sure that participants are representative of a larger population. As discussed in Chapter 9, random sampling allows us to say that what we have found to be true for a particular sample is likely to be true of people in the larger population from which the sample was drawn. It maximizes the external validity of research.

In contrast, **random assignment** is a procedure we use after we have a sample of participants and before we expose them to a treatment or independent variable. It is a way of assigning participants to the levels of the independent variable so that the groups do not differ when the study begins. Random assignment ensures that all participants have an equal chance of being assigned to the various experimental conditions. Dividing participants on the basis of their arrival to the laboratory or alphabetically would not be truly random as it does not ensure equal probabilities of assignment to condition and could introduce systematic biases in the data. For example, personality differences might be associated with early versus late arrival to the laboratory, and thus we would not want our experimental groups to differ on those traits. Random assignment requires a truly random process, such as the use of a random numbers table, a computerized random number generator, or the flip of a coin in the case of an experiment that has only two conditions. (Use of random numbers tables and random number generators is discussed in Chapter 9.) Random assignment enables us to say that X caused Y with some certainty. That is, random assignment maximizes the internal validity of research.

Exercise: Random assignment and random sampling

Random assignment and random sampling are sometimes difficult to keep distinct, for they both are important for drawing inferences from research. Discuss them in your group, and see what you can create that helps everyone in your group to distinguish between them and keep them straight.

To appreciate what random assignment accomplishes and why, consider a new example – determining whether students learn more about research methods through a traditional lecture format or through an interactive web-based format. Assume that a company was able to bring together a random sample of undergraduate students from across the country to participate in the study. We would therefore not have to worry about the representativeness of the students. Our only concern would be determining whether students learn more from traditional lectures or the web-based format. The best way to design this experiment is to assign students randomly to one of two conditions: group L, which takes the traditional lecture-based course, and group W, which takes the web-based version of the course. We measure how much they learn by giving them all the same examination at the end of the semester. Assume that the web and lecture versions of the course cover exactly the same material and that the final examination is a valid measure of how much people know about research methods.

If our sample were large enough or if we did the study repeatedly, we could be confident, because of random assignment, that the two groups of students – those attending lectures and those doing the web course – were equivalent in all possible ways. To appreciate this statement, suppose we randomly assigned the students by flipping a coin. About half of the students would get "heads" and about half would get "tails." With a large enough sample, would we expect all the students with light hair to be in one group and all the students with darker hair in the other? Of course not, for every student regardless of hair color has the same likelihood of being in group L and of being in group W. Chances are that there would be a mixture of dark- and light-haired students in both groups. Would we expect all the men to get "tails" and all the women to get "heads"? Of course not. On average, the two groups would include both women and men. In fact, as a result of random assignment, on average, the two groups would be equivalent in *all* possible ways. We would not expect them to differ on any individual difference variables. Thus, random assignment and randomized experimental research designs control for all possible individual difference variables that could interfere with our ability to reach causal conclusions about the effect of the independent variable.

Of course, if we had only two students in the study, one female and one male, the student attending the traditional lecture course would differ in gender from the student taking the web course whether we randomly assigned them to conditions or not. But if we were to do this study over and over again (randomly assigning the two students each time), across the studies, gender would not be confounded with the independent variable. Thus, random assignment works *on average*, given a large enough sample or given a sufficient number of times that a study is conducted. In any one study, with a limited sample size, there can be differences between the experimental groups simply by chance. But on average, if we did the study over and over again, all such differences would disappear. As was illustrated with a sample of two participants, random assignment works only on average. Nevertheless, it is the only procedure that can ensure the equivalence of people across experimental conditions and is therefore critical for maximizing internal validity.

Because random assignment works on average, it is important for researchers to be cognizant of the possibility of **failures of randomization**, which are much more likely with small samples. In other words, in any single study, it is possible that particular kinds of participants will not be evenly distributed across experimental conditions (e.g., all the African American participants might end up in one condition, or there might be disproportionately more women in one group than another). Failure of randomization is a problem because it means that despite random assignment, the groups were not equivalent at the beginning of the study and therefore the internal validity of the study is compromised. Thus, it is often wise to measure important individual difference variables or administer pretests for important dependent measures. Analyses comparing experimental groups on these individual difference and pretest variables should ideally reveal no differences between experimental conditions. If the analyses indicate a failure of randomization, the researcher is in a difficult position. It would not be acceptable to shuffle the experimental assignment of participants until the groups "looked" equivalent, as that undermines the whole point of randomization. Replicating the study – perhaps with a larger sample to minimize the likelihood of a failure of randomization – is often the only satisfactory solution.

Independent Variables that Vary Within and Between Participants

In the research examples presented so far, the independent variable has varied between research participants. That is, some individuals were exposed to the political advertisements and some were not; some students went to the lectures and some took the course on the web. There are many independent variables, however, that can be manipulated *within* participants, which usually results in a more efficient research design.

Consider another example: We want to examine whether using the term "climate change" or the term "global warming" in an online advertisement affects people's concern for the environment. We must decide how to manipulate the independent variable. We consider two options. We can assign some individuals to the "climate change" condition and others to the "global warming" condition. If a total of 40 individuals were available, there would be 20 participants in each of the two conditions of the study (i.e., if we were lucky or if we constrained our random assignment procedure so that the two conditions would have equal numbers of participants).

The second option for manipulating the independent variable involves measuring all 40 participants' concern for the environment in both conditions, once after reading the message with "climate change" and once after reading the message with "global warming." In this case, the independent variable varies within participants rather than between them. Rather than some participants being in one condition and some in the other, all participants are in both conditions. This is called a **within-participants** or **repeated measures design**.

We introduce this distinction between independent variables that vary within participants and those that vary between participants because it helps to clarify the list of threats to internal validity that we consider in the next section of the chapter. At this point, it is only necessary to understand the distinction and also what random assignment means in the two cases. When the independent variable varies between participants, participants are randomly assigned to one condition or the other so that participants in the two conditions will not, on average, differ on any variables that are not part of the experimental procedure. When the independent variable varies within participants, random assignment involves randomly determining the order in which each participant is exposed to the levels of the independent variable. Suppose we did not do this. Instead, all 40 participants first rated their concern for the environment after the "global warming" message and then after the "climate change" message. Participants might read the first message more carefully than the second or deduce the purpose of the study after the first message (we discuss this issue further later in this chapter), or become tired after reading the second message, or notice characteristics of the room or the experimenter in between the two ratings. All of these other things might influence participants' ratings. If we then found a difference in environmental concern, we could not be sure whether it was due to our experimental manipulation or to any or all the other differences between the two times at which participants provided their ratings.

It is simple to overcome this problem by randomly assigning half of the participants to read the "global warming" message first and the "climate change" message second and the other half to read the "climate change" message first and the "global warming" message second. In this way, differences in, for example, attention or fatigue would not account for differences in ratings between the two levels of the independent variable. This practice of varying the order of experimental conditions across participants in a repeated measures design is called **counterbalancing**. Counterbalancing is important not only because it helps to assure internal validity but also because it controls for possible contamination or carryover effects between experimental conditions, for example, the possibility that people would become more concerned after reading the second message simply as a result of greater exposure to environmental issues.

To recap, when the independent variable varies between participants, we randomly assign each participant to one condition or the other. When the independent variable varies within participants, each participant is measured under each condition, and we must then randomly assign participants to experience the various conditions in different orders. Later we consider some of the advantages and disadvantages of using designs in which the independent variable varies within rather than between participants.

Threats to Internal Validity

Making causal inferences is what doctors do when they try to diagnose the cause of a patient's pain or what detectives do when they attempt to identify the cause of a crime. The researcher, doctor, and detective must each rule out a list of alternative explanations to arrive at the most probable cause. The alternative explanations are threats to the internal validity of the research proposition. The strength of randomized experiments is that through randomization these threats are, on average, eliminated. If we use a research design other than a randomized experiment, these threats make causal inference very difficult indeed. Six such threats to internal validity are defined in this section. Other threats exist as well; fuller discussions of them can be found in the classic primer on research design by Campbell and Stanley (1963) as well as in work by Shadish, Cook, and Campbell (2002) and Judd and Kenny (1981).

Selection

Selection refers to any preexisting differences between individuals in the different experimental conditions that can influence the dependent variable. As should be clear from our earlier discussion, selection is a threat to validity whenever participants are not randomly assigned to conditions. An extreme example makes it obvious why selection poses such a serious threat to internal validity: Pretend a researcher is interested in testing the hypothesis that bungee jumping has mental health benefits. The researcher explains the study to a group of prospective participants, and all those who want to try bungee jumping are placed in the experimental group, whereas the participants who decide they would rather not bungee jump are placed in the control group. Of course, no experienced researcher would design a study in this manner. Clearly, the two groups differ in many important ways, including risk-taking tendencies and attitudes toward bungee jumping. It would be impossible to determine at the conclusion of the study whether any differences between the two groups were caused by the bungee jumping itself or these preexisting differences.

The threat posed by selection is obvious in cases like these where participants *self-select* into experimental conditions. Less obvious, but just as much of a threat, are cases where participants do not self-select, but rather preexisting groups are used that could differ on any number of characteristics. For example, a researcher might wish to test a new method of increasing sales productivity. The method might be used in one car dealership and monthly sales compared to those of a neighboring dealership using traditional sales techniques. The inferential difficulty is that the sales personnel at the two dealerships might differ in many respects that affect their productivity above and beyond the effects due to the experimental sales techniques. The same threat to validity occurs when selecting participants for various treatment conditions from different businesses, health facilities, or schools.

In short, *unless participants have been randomly assigned to an experimental condition*, selection is always a threat, and in most cases causal inferences about the independent variable cannot be drawn.

Maturation

Maturation involves any naturally occurring process within persons that could cause a change in their behavior. Examples include fatigue, boredom, growth, or intellectual development. A rather obvious example of the threat to internal validity caused by maturation would be a study testing the effects of intensive speech therapy on 2-year-old children over a 6-month period. At the conclusion of the study, the children are pronouncing words significantly more clearly than at the beginning. Of course, children of that age are experiencing rapid improvement in their speech as a natural function of language development, and they might have improved just as much without the speech therapy. Fortunately, such biases can be easily cured by including a control group (i.e., children who do not receive intensive therapy) in the study.

Normal developmental changes should affect participants in both the experimental and control groups to the same degree.

In addition to developmental changes that occur in individuals over extended periods of time, maturation also refers to short-term changes that can occur within an experimental session. Consider a reaction time task in which participants are instructed to attend to a complicated visual pattern and press a button whenever a certain stimulus shape appears. Participants are likely to become fatigued or bored after doing the task for 30 or 40 minutes. Reaction latencies probably will increase and more errors will be committed toward the end of the study, posing an inferential problem if all of the experimental trials are located in the beginning or end of the session. This type of maturational bias, too, has a simple cure: Present stimuli in a counterbalanced order so that all types of stimuli are evenly distributed across the experimental session.

History

History refers to any event that coincides with the independent variable and could affect the dependent variable. It could be a major historical event that occurs in the political, economic, or cultural lives of the people we are studying, or it could be a minor event that occurs during the course of an experimental session – such as a disruption in the procedures because of equipment failure, a fire alarm going off, a participant in a group session behaving inappropriately, or an interruption from any unwanted source. In short, history is anything that happens during the course of the study that is unrelated to the independent variable yet affects the dependent variable. Sometimes the event actually has historical significance, but the threat to validity refers to any event that provides a competing explanation for findings.

Imagine that a researcher is conducting a study of attitudes toward the death penalty. A well-publicized execution that takes place during data collection could affect participants' attitudes in ways unintended by the researcher. History threatens not only internal validity, but also external validity of this study. The threat to internal validity caused by such events can be remedied by including a control group, as participants in both conditions should be aware of and affected by the execution to the same extent, so we can infer that any additional differences between the groups were caused by the independent variable. The threat to external validity, however, is not so easily removed. There is no way of knowing whether participants would have reacted similarly to the dependent measures if they had *not* been exposed to the publicity surrounding the execution.

With respect to unique events that occur during the course of a study, the degree of damage caused depends on how the data are gathered. If participants are run individually, such events would presumably affect only one participant, whose data could be dropped from analyses. At worst, the disruption would merely add a slight amount of noise or random error to the data. Intrasession history becomes more problematic when participants are run in group sessions, as is often done to gather data quickly and easily. Malfunctioning computers or other equipment can disrupt or ruin a significant portion of a study, and the researcher is faced with the unfortunate choice of either dropping the affected data or contending with considerable noise in the data analyses. Moreover, if the data are gathered in such a way that all of the experimental participants are run in one group and the control participants in another, history becomes an insurmountable threat to internal validity. If any differences are obtained between conditions, we do not know whether it is because of the independent variable or because of the unique events that occurred within each group. For that reason, if participants are run in groups out of necessity or convenience, researchers should ensure that the different experimental conditions are represented within each group if at all possible. If that is not possible (e.g., if the manipulation must be administered orally), then multiple groups for each condition – as many as possible – should be run so that potential history effects can be statistically evaluated.

Instrumentation

Instrumentation is any change that occurs over time in measurement procedures or devices. If researchers purposefully change their measuring procedures because they have discovered a "better" way to collect data, or if observers gradually become more experienced or careless, these changes could have effects that might be confused with those of the independent variable. As was the case with maturation, this problem is a particular threat to internal validity if the various experimental conditions are run at different times. Instrumentation is a bias that should not happen. The cure is careful training and monitoring of observers or measurement procedures and ensuring that the order of experimental conditions is counterbalanced or randomized throughout the course of the study. Pilot testing also helps, for weaknesses in the measurement instrument often can be identified by asking participants what they inferred from each question and why they answered the way they did.

Mortality

Mortality refers to any attrition of participants from a study. If some participants do not return for a posttest or if participants in a control group are more difficult to recruit than participants in a treatment group, these differential recruitment and attrition rates could create differences that are confused with effects of the independent variable. Take, for example, a study testing an experimental drug designed to help people quit smoking. The drug reduces the desire for nicotine substantially, but it has the rather distressing side effect of causing unrelenting diarrhea. As a result, 70% of the treatment group drops out of the study. At the conclusion of the study, the remaining 30% in the treatment group are smoking significantly fewer cigarettes than the participants in the control group (none of whom dropped out). Can we conclude that the new drug works? No, because the 30% who stayed in the study are almost certainly no longer equivalent to the control group participants on important variables such as motivation. Presumably, the people who are truly motivated and committed to quitting smoking are the ones who would keep taking the drug despite the troubling side effects. The opposite case is also possible, where participants in the control condition see no benefits and withdraw from a study in proportions much greater than those in the treatment condition.

Mortality is particularly problematic in longitudinal research, in which data are gathered at multiple points in time. Imagine an intervention study designed to improve school success for at-risk adolescents. At the five-year follow-up, 45% of the original sample could not be located. Analyses of the data showed significant gains in achievement test scores; however, the high mortality rate precludes us from drawing the causal inference that the gains were caused by the intervention. The adolescents who could not be located for the follow-up probably include those whose performance was worse; perhaps the reason they could not be located is that they dropped out of school or were even incarcerated.

Mortality always presents a threat to external validity; at the end of a study, we are only able to conclude that our results are representative for the kinds of individuals who are likely to finish the study. The greater the mortality, the less representative our final participant sample becomes. On the other hand, **differential mortality**, that is, mortality rates that differ across experimental groups, creates a threat to internal validity. Because experimental groups are no longer equivalent except for the independent variable, we cannot determine whether it was the independent variable that caused any group differences or the other ways in which the groups differ. Thus, it is always important to look for problems caused by mortality and differential mortality. At the conclusion of data gathering, researchers can count the number of participant dropouts and determine whether the number varies systematically across conditions.

Unlike some of the other threats to internal validity, there is no easy cure for mortality. There are steps researchers can take to reduce mortality in a longitudinal study, such as keeping in close contact with participants by sending them newsletters or birthday cards or obtaining the names and addresses of contact persons who would be expected to know how to find participants over the duration of the study. With adequate preparation and effort, attrition in even a 10-year study can be kept under 20%. Differential mortality is harder to prevent, especially if the experimental treatment involves aspects that make it substantially more or less desirable than the control group's experience, or if the treatment affects mortality (which likely would be a dependent variable in such research). The antismoking drug with the unpleasant side effects would naturally result in more dropouts than the control condition, as would a study in which the experimental participants must agree to experience painful electric shocks. In such cases, the problem of differential mortality can be addressed by carefully designing the experience of the control participants to be equally desirable or aversive. Making both conditions equivalently aversive might increase the total amount of participant mortality (as more people in the control group will likely drop out of the study), but external validity might be a necessary cost to pay for increasing the internal validity of the study.

Selection by Maturation

Selection by maturation occurs when there are differences between individuals in the treatment groups that produce changes in the groups at different rates. Differences in spontaneous changes across the different groups can be confused with effects of the treatment or the independent variable. For example, imagine we were conducting social skills training groups for preadolescents. If analyses showed significant improvements in girls but not in boys, we might be tempted to conclude that our treatment is effective for girls; however, an alternative explanation is that girls simply mature socially earlier than boys and that our treatment had no effect at all.

Random assignment is the best way to address this threat to internal validity. When participants are randomly assigned to treatment groups, any variability in rates of maturation is spread across all groups to an equivalent degree. When random assignment is not feasible, one can attempt to assess the degree of change that would have been expected in the absence of the treatment. For example, one might ask comparison groups of female and male preadolescents (i.e., individuals who seem similar to the research participants, such as female and male preadolescents in a similar school) to complete the same measures as the research participants and at the same points in time. Hopefully, you will not encounter this type of challenging situation in most studies, for the solutions are complicated. One is a cross-sequential design where the treatment is delivered at two different times, with data being collected at three time points. The first data collection would be a pretest for both treatment groups, the second would occur after one group gets the treatment but before the second group gets the treatment, and the third after both groups have had the treatment. Each group would provide both a treatment condition and a control condition, and only if the impact of the treatment were the same for the two groups could this threat be eliminated.

Illustrating Threats to Internal Validity with a Research Example

Some of the threats to internal validity are particularly troublesome when the independent or treatment variable varies between participants (selection and selection by maturation). Others are likely to be more problematic when there is no control group or the treatment variable varies within participants (history, maturation, instrumentation, mortality). To help understand these threats and how they are in fact threats if a randomized experiment is not conducted, consider the following examples of non-experimental research designs.

Imagine that the trustees of an educational foundation want to know whether receiving a liberal arts education actually makes people more liberal. The researcher decides to answer the question by comparing the people she knew in high school who went to college with those who did not. A high school reunion provided the opportunity to make some observations. These observations revealed that the researcher's high school friends who had not gone to college were more politically conservative than the people who had gone to college.

The independent or treatment variable in this example is whether the participants went to college. The researcher wishes to ascertain whether this independent variable has a causal effect on political attitudes, the dependent variable. Because some of her classmates went to college and others did not, and because she was comparing the political leanings of these two groups of classmates, the independent variable varies between classmates. Obviously, classmates were not randomly assigned to the levels of the independent variable: The researcher did not flip a coin for each classmate at high school graduation to determine who went off to college and who did not.

The internal validity of this design is particularly threatened by selection and by selection by maturation.

Selection

We need to consider the possibility that the people who did not go to college and the people who did were different types of people to begin with. They might have had different political attitudes even before their educational paths diverged. Because they were not randomly assigned to the college and no-college groups but rather selected their own paths or had their paths selected for them by admissions committees, parents, school counselors, and other advisors, there is no guarantee that they were similar at the outset. Such selection effects are serious threats to the internal validity of studies in which there is not random assignment. Whenever people select their own treatments or are selected by others for treatments or end up in different treatment groups by some unknown process instead of by random assignment, we have no assurance that the people in different groups were equivalent before exposure to the independent variable. Chances are they were not because the very fact that they selected or were selected for different treatments indicates that they were different types of people, with different preferences, abilities, or other characteristics that made them seem more suitable for one treatment rather than another.

Selection by Maturation

Now suppose the researcher had thought about the selection threat and tried to eliminate it. Perhaps she gathered some information from the past about her classmates in an attempt to show that the political leanings of those who went to college were the same as the leanings of those who did not go to college back when both groups were finishing high school. Suppose she found some records of interviews about the then-current presidential election and became convinced that at that time the two groups of classmates had approximately the same political attitudes. The researcher then argued that selection was no longer a threat and that causal conclusions about the impact of college on political attitudes were more defensible.

The problem is that the researcher also needs to consider the possibility that the two groups of classmates would have grown apart in their political leanings even if one of the groups had not gone to college. Even if the two groups were the same politically during senior year in high school, they probably still were very different groups in other ways; their political attitudes might have been changing at different rates and in different directions even if, for some reason, the college-bound classmates had not in fact enrolled in college.

Realizing the impossibility of eliminating these two internal validity threats, the researcher decides to gather some more data, using a research design that she hopes will not be as subject to the threats of selection and selection by maturation. This time she decides to follow a group of students as they go to college for the first time.

She initially measures their political leanings when they graduated from high school and then again two years later, after their sophomore year in college.

Again, the researcher finds that the political attitudes after two years in college were more liberal than they were two years earlier. On the plus side, this research design has effectively eliminated the threats of selection and selection by maturation because this time the researcher is not comparing two different groups of individuals. Rather, she is looking at the political attitudes of the same students at two different times: before they went to college and after they had been there two years.

Note that the research design is now a repeated measures design in which the independent variable varies within participants. That is, the political attitudes of each individual are measured twice, once before and once during college. Obviously, the researcher has not randomly assigned individuals to different orders. That is, everyone's attitudes were measured the first time without having been to college and the second time after having been there for two years. This is an example of a study in which counterbalancing the order of experimental conditions is impossible. Thus, the design is not a randomized experimental one, and its internal validity is threatened in the following ways.

Maturation

We need to consider the obvious problem that individuals might simply change in their political attitudes as they mature or grow older. Accordingly, the individuals followed for two years might have developed more liberal political attitudes even if they had not gone to college during those two years, simply as a function of growing older.

History

We also need to consider the possibility that different sorts of historical events were taking place at the two times and everyone at the second time might have been more liberal than they were at the first, whether or not they went to college in the interim. It is well known that the American populace as a whole seems to change in its political leanings across time. The decade of the 1960s was characterized by relatively liberal sentiments throughout the country compared to the 1950s. Thus, historical events change everyone's outlook, and such events might have affected the outlook of the students over the two-year period that they were followed.

Instrumentation

We need to consider whether the way in which the dependent variable was measured changed from the first time to the second. Perhaps after the first phase of data collection, the researcher thought of better ways to ask the political attitude questions for the second phase of data collection. If the measurement procedures were not exactly the same at the two times, differences in the measurement instruments could be responsible for the differences in attitudes obtained.

Mortality

In all probability, after a two-year period, the researcher was not able to gather data successfully from all of the individuals who participated in the first phase of the study. Some of them, despite the best efforts of the researcher to track them down, might have moved away, become ill, or for other reasons become unreachable. It is possible that these individuals happen to be those with the most conservative political attitudes. Thus, the relative liberalness of those from whom data were gathered the second time, after two years in college, might be due not to their becoming more liberal but to the fact that the most conservative individuals have not been included in the sample at the end of the study.

Construct Validity of Independent Variables in a Randomized Experiment

A randomized experiment requires the experimenter to be able to control or manipulate the independent variable so that a random assignment rule can be used. To do so, a researcher must first define and create an operational definition of it. As discussed in Chapter 7, an **operational definition** is the procedure used to manipulate or measure the variables of the study. All research contains operational definitions of abstract concepts; they are not unique to laboratory experiments. Sometimes the operational definition of an independent variable is clear and straightforward. For example, if we are interested in the impact of jury size on verdicts, the independent variable is easy to conceptualize and manipulate: We simply compare juries composed of 6 versus 12 jurors. In many cases, however, the operational definition of a given independent variable is not so straightforward. The independent variable might be complex, requiring a complex operational definition; or it might be a general construct that can be operationally defined in any number of ways, and the researcher must choose an operational definition that is valid, practical, and convincing.

Consider, for example, urban stress. Urban stress is a complex, abstract notion that could be measured or manipulated in a number of ways. We could ask people living in large cities to rate how stressed they feel on a 7-point scale, which might be adequate if we were interested in stress as a dependent variable. But we could not readily use that operational definition if we wanted to manipulate stress. Glass and Singer (1972), in their classic work on urban stress, manipulated stress in the laboratory by subjecting participants to noise that was either controllable or uncontrollable. Their reasoning was that uncontrollable noise in the laboratory is a noxious stimulus that could serve as a substitute for urban social stressors. In order for their findings to be compelling, however, they had to convince others that it was reasonable to equate uncontrollable noise with the abstract construct urban stress.

In Chapter 7, we discussed the importance of **construct validity**, that is, making sure that our variables capture the constructs we wish to measure. The same problems of assessing validity pertain to variables that are experimentally manipulated. For instance, instead of measuring anxiety, a researcher might manipulate people's anxiety, creating high anxiety in some persons and low anxiety in others. Or rather than measure existing levels of motivation, an experimenter might manipulate motivation by giving some participants instructions that motivate them to do well on a task and giving others instructions that cause them to care little about their performance.

When researchers create rather than measure levels of an independent variable, we call it a **manipulated variable**. When independent variables are obtained by measurements rather than manipulations, a researcher uses the same logic for assessing reliability and validity that is used for dependent variables. With manipulated independent variables, however, the researcher must test the manipulation by measuring its effects to determine its construct validity. For instance, a researcher might try to create high motivation by telling some participants that their performance on a task is an indicator of their intelligence and create low motivation by telling others that the task is a measure of willingness to practice dull tasks. The researcher needs to know whether these instructions really created different levels of motivation. Perhaps the manipulation resulted in no differences in motivation because participants did not believe the instructions or because participants wanted to do well regardless of the task. Perhaps the researcher created differences – but in anxiety instead of motivation. To demonstrate the validity of the manipulation, the researcher must also *measure* participants' motivation after the instructions – in the same experiment, if possible, or in a separate experiment if including the additional measure in the primary experiment would undermine the effect of the manipulation on the primary measures of interest. If those who received the "intelligence test" instructions rate the task as more important and their desire to do well as higher than do those who get the "willingness to practice dull tasks" instructions, the researcher would have some evidence that the manipulation was successful. However, the instructions might also have created different levels of anxiety along with levels of motivation. We would like to see evidence that only motivation, and not anxiety, was manipulated by the instructions. To do this, a researcher would have to demonstrate both the discriminant and convergent validity of the manipulation.

When researchers demonstrate the validity of their manipulated variables, they generally obtain a measure of the independent variable construct after they have manipulated it. This is called a **manipulation check**, and it can provide evidence of the convergent validity of the manipulation. More than one variable might also be manipulated, as in a factorial design, which we discuss later in this chapter. In such designs, obtaining evidence for the construct validity of a manipulated independent variable requires that (1) the manipulated variable affect its corresponding manipulation check measure (e.g., that our motivation manipulation affects our measure of motivation) and (2) that the effect of that manipulated variable on the manipulation check measure does not depend on, or interact with, the other manipulated variable (e.g., that the effect of our motivation manipulation on our motivation measure is the same whether people are low or high on the other manipulated variable). Researchers rarely take the further step of demonstrating discriminant validity by showing that their manipulation has not created different levels of some other variables, for example, that it has not changed participants' anxiety levels. Occasionally, however, when research includes this additional step, it becomes all the more persuasive. Manipulation checks are discussed in greater detail in Chapter 5.

Constructing good operational definitions requires appropriate and accurate procedures to measure and manipulate variables. The art of finding suitable procedures cannot be taught with a set of rules but is acquired by experience. The real test of external validity for both measured and manipulated variables, however, rests on the confirmation of the findings in other settings. In short, the best test of external validity is a replication of a study – a demonstration that the results can be repeated with different participants, procedures, experimenters, and operational definitions.

Alternative Experimental Designs

We already have briefly discussed two alternative designs for randomized experiments. In one, participants were randomly assigned to the levels of the independent variable and each participant was measured only once. In this case, the independent variable is said to vary between participants. In the other design, the independent variable varies within participants and each participant is measured under every level of the independent variable; the order of exposure to those levels is randomly determined. These two designs, both of which we talk about in more detail in this section, are not the only alternatives. A variety of other randomized experimental designs are also possible and useful. We use the following notation to describe different research designs:

$X =$ a treatment, an independent variable, a cause
$O =$ an observation, a dependent variable, an effect
$R =$ participants who have been randomly assigned to the treatment condition

Design 1: Randomized Two-Group Design

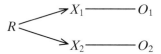

Participants are randomly assigned to the experimental treatment group (X_1) or to a control group (X_2). This is the design discussed earlier in which the independent variable varies between participants and has only two levels: treatment and control. The word "treatment" is simply verbal shorthand to identify the group that experienced the variable of interest; it does not necessarily imply some kind of intervention designed to help people.

This design contains all the bare essentials for a randomized experiment:

* random assignment
* treatment and no-treatment groups
* observations after the treatment

We must have at least two groups to know whether the treatment had an effect, and we must randomly assign individuals to groups so that the groups will be, on average, equivalent before treatment. Then we can attribute any posttreatment differences to the experimental treatment.

We can rule out several rival explanations or threats to internal validity by using this design. We know that any posttreatment differences are not the result of a selection threat (barring any failure of randomization) because participants were randomly assigned rather than self-selected or systematically assigned to the two groups. We know also that the posttreatment differences are not a product of maturation because the two groups should have matured (e.g., aged or fatigued) at the same rate if they were tested at the same intervals after random assignment.

We can rule out other alternative explanations not just by referring to random assignment but also by looking carefully at the experimental procedures to see whether it is plausible that the treatment group might have been exposed to some other events (historical events in the outside world or events within the experimental session) that the no-treatment group did not experience. If not, we can eliminate history as a rival explanation. If the two groups were tested or observed under similar circumstances, we can eliminate instrumentation differences as an explanation. Once we have eliminated these alternative explanations, we can feel quite confident that the experimental treatment caused any observed difference between the two groups (O_1 and O_2).

Design 2: Pretest–Posttest Two-Group Design

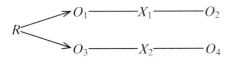

This design has an additional set of tests or observations of the dependent variable, called **pretests**, before the experimental treatment. Pretests have several advantages. They provide a check on the randomization and let the experimenter see whether the groups were equivalent before the treatment. Pretests also provide a more sensitive test of the effects of the treatment by letting participants serve as their own comparison. Instead of comparing only O_2 and O_4, the experimenter can compare the difference between participants' pretest and posttest scores. In other words, O_2 minus O_1 can be compared with O_4 minus O_3. Because participants' pretest scores all differ from one another and their posttest scores reflect some of these preexisting individual differences, the experimenter gains precision by making these sorts of comparisons rather than simply comparing O_2 and O_4. Researchers can compare change scores or include pretest scores as covariates in the analyses.

To understand the benefits of this design, suppose two people were randomly assigned to different groups in an experiment on weight loss; Person A was assigned to the no-treatment control group and Person B to the weight-loss treatment group. If Person A weighed 130 pounds on the pretest and 130 pounds on the posttest, it is clear that being in the control group did not affect Person A's weight. If Person B weighed 160 pounds on the pretest and 150 pounds on the posttest, it is plausible that the treatment caused Person B to lose 10 pounds. However, if the experimenter did not take pretest measures and looked only at the posttest weights, Person B's 150 pounds compared to Person A's 130 would make the treatment look bad. Therefore, having pretest information in this pretest–posttest two-group design gives the experimenter a more precise measure of treatment effects.

The pretest also has some disadvantages, however. It can sensitize participants to the purpose of the experiment and bias their posttest scores. If this occurs for the experimental and control groups alike, their posttest scores should be equally elevated or depressed; pretesting alone would then not be an alternative explanation for a difference between O_2 and O_4. However, the pretest might affect the treatment group differently from the control group; this would appear as a difference on the posttest and would be indistinguishable from a difference produced by the treatment alone. In sum, when pretesting affects both experimental conditions equally, it is a threat to external validity; participants' responses to the second testing are not representative of how people would respond if they had not been given a pretest. When pretesting affects the experimental groups differentially, however, it becomes a threat to internal validity.

Unfortunately, this kind of differential effect of pretesting is common. Take, for example, a persuasion study trying to change people's attitudes toward capital punishment. A pretest asking for participants' attitudes about capital punishment probably will alert participants to the focus of the study and thus make them particularly sensitive to the persuasion manipulation. Alert participants might realize that the experimenter is interested in capital punishment and that the persuasive message is supposed to change their attitudes, perhaps causing participants to change their responses on the posttest in an attempt to please the experimenter. Participants in the control group, however, who do not receive a persuasive message on the topic of capital punishment, do not realize that capital punishment is the focus of the experiment and hence feel no demand to change their attitudes on the posttest.

Design 2 provides no solution to this problem. Experimenters must therefore decide whether this is a plausible occurrence for any particular study. If it is plausible, they should avoid this design in favor of the simpler Design 1 or opt for the more complex Design 3 described next.

Design 3: Solomon Four-Group Design

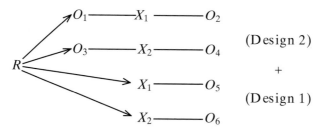

The third design combines Designs 1 and 2. With this design an experimenter can test decisively whether the posttest differences were caused by the treatment, the pretest, or the combination of treatment plus pretest. Design 3 is an expensive design because it requires four groups of participants to test the effects of only two levels of a treatment. The four groups are needed because in addition to the treatment and control groups, there are pretested and non-pretested groups.

This design offers the separate advantages of Design 1 – no interference from pretesting effects – and Design 2 – greater precision from the pretest scores as baselines against which to measure the effects of the treatment. In addition, it enables the experimenter to see whether the combination of pretesting plus treatment produces an effect that is different from what we would expect if we simply added the separate effects of pretesting and treatment. Such combinations, if they are different from the sum of the two individual effects, are called **interaction effects**. They are similar to what occurs when two natural elements combine to produce a new effect, as hydrogen and oxygen together produce a new compound, water. The whole is different from or greater than the simple sum of the parts. For many problems studied by social scientists, interaction effects are important, for variables can affect other variables in complex ways. We need more than two-group designs to study these, and we need more than one independent variable because an interaction results from a combination of two or more causes, or independent variables. Designs with two or more independent variables are called factorial designs.

Design 4: Between-Participants Factorial Design

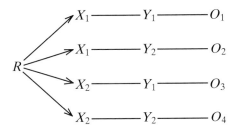

The X is one independent variable; the Y is another. In a **factorial design**, two or more independent variables are presented in combination. The entire design contains every possible combination of the independent variables (also known as factors; hence the name, factorial design). If there are more than two independent variables and if each has more than two values, the design rapidly mushrooms because each additional variable or value greatly increases the number of conditions. We illustrate this fact using tables, which are the form most commonly used to diagram factorial designs.

Table 10.1 illustrates the combination of two factors, or independent variables. In the language of experimental design, we call this a 2×2 (where the "$\times$" is read out loud as "by") factorial design, which means there are two factors and each has two levels. In this particular example, the two factors are feedback (positive/negative) and confederate gender (male/female). If we added a third factor, we would double the number of conditions if the additional factor also had two levels, triple it if the new factor had three levels, and so on. For instance, if we added the relative status of the confederate as another factor to the two factors in Table 10.1 and used three status categories – lower, same, or higher than the participant – we would have a $2 \times 2 \times 3$ (between-participants) factorial design, with 12 conditions, shown in Table 10.2. This 12-cell design is much more complex than the original 2×2. It is triple the size and, therefore, either requires three times as many participants or spreads the same number of participants thinner, with one-third the number in each condition.

Table 10.1	A 2 × 2 Factorial Design	
Factor Y	*Factor X*	
	Confederate Gender	
Feedback	*Male*	*Female*
Negative	Male Negative	Female Negative
Positive	Male Positive	Female Positive

Table 10.2	A 2 × 2 × 3 Factorial Design		
Factor Y	*Factor Z*	*Factor X*	
		Confederate Gender	
Feedback	*Confederate Status*	*Male (M)*	*Female (F)*
Negative (N)	Lower (L)	N, L, M	N, L, F
	Same (S)	N, S, M	N, S, F
	Higher (H)	N, H, M	N, H, F
Positive (P)	Lower (L)	P, L, M	P, L, F
	Same (S)	P, S, M	P, S, F
	Higher (H)	P, H, M	P, H, F

The advantage of a factorial design involving more than a single independent variable is that we can examine interaction effects involving multiple independent variables in addition to the separate or main effects of those variables by themselves. Suppose we were interested in two independent variables, X and Y, and their effects on some dependent variable, O. We could design two different experiments, one in which we randomly assigned participants to levels of X and then examined effects on O, and a second in which we randomly assigned participants to levels of Y and examined effects on O. Alternatively, we could create a factorial design and randomly assign participants to all of the $X-Y$ combinations of levels: X_1-Y_1, X_1-Y_2, X_2-Y_1, and X_2-Y_2. The advantage of this factorial design over the two separate single-factor experiments is that we can ask whether the effect of one of the independent variables is qualified by the other independent variable. If it is, the two independent variables are said to "interact" in producing O. Then, we cannot simply talk about the effect of X on O because the effect of X on O depends on the level of Y. Similarly, we cannot simply talk about the effect of Y on O because that effect depends on the level of X. We must talk about their joint or interactive effects on O.

To describe an interaction effect more concretely, we consider a published example of a 2 × 2 design (Sinclair & Kunda, 2000, Study 2). The study examined how participants responded to receiving either positive or negative feedback from a male or female manager. Participants were told that the study was a collaborative venture on the part of the university with local businesses to train personnel managers. Participants were asked to respond orally to an interpersonal skills test while a manager-in-training (actually a videotaped accomplice of the experimenter posing as a research participant) was allegedly listening from another room. Following the task, participants were shown one of four videotapes showing the alleged manager-in-training giving an evaluation of participants' interpersonal skills. Half of the time the person on the videotape was female and half the time the person was male. Half of the time the feedback given was positive and half the time the feedback was negative. Participants were then asked to rate how skilled the manager was at evaluating them.

This 2 × 2 (Manager Gender × Feedback) factorial design is depicted in Table 10.1. Notice that the gender variable in this study refers not to participants' gender but to the people whom the participants rated. This distinction is important. Participants' age and gender are characteristics they bring with them rather than experimental conditions to which people can be randomly assigned. The portion of a study that examines such individual difference variables is therefore not a true experiment. In contrast, the gender of an actor or stimulus person to whom participants respond is an experimental variable, because participants can be randomly assigned to interact with or observe a male or female actor.

The researchers combined two independent variables – manager gender and the valence of the feedback – because they were particularly interested in the effect of the combination. The dependent variable was participants' ratings of how skilled they thought the confederate manager-in-training was. The experimenters expected that the effects of the confederate's feedback would depend not only on whether the feedback was positive or negative but also on whether the feedback was delivered by a man or a woman.

Table 10.3 displays the results of the experiment. Higher scores mean that participants evaluated the confederate's skill more positively. Let us review the effects that we can examine with a factorial design. All factorial designs provide information about the separate main effects of each independent variable and the interaction effects among the independent variables. The main effect shows whether one independent variable has an effect when we average across the levels of any other variable. Do not be misled by the term "**main effect**"; it does not mean the most important or primary

Table 10.3	Ratings of Male and Female Confederates who Delivered Positive or Negative Feedback		
	Confederate Gender		
Feedback	*Male*	*Female*	
Negative	M = 8.0	M = 6.8	M = 7.4 (Mean for negative)
Positive	M = 8.8	M = 9.2	M = 9.0 (Mean for positive)
	M = 8.4 (Mean for males)	M = 8.0 (Mean for females)	

result but rather the effect of one independent variable averaging across the other. In Table 10.3, the main effects for each variable are shown in the margins. Looking first at the results for the feedback factor, we can see that participants who received positive feedback rated the confederate much more positively (average = 9.0) than did participants who received negative feedback (average = 7.4). And, indeed, statistical analysis confirmed that this difference was statistically significant (i.e., not likely a chance occurrence). Looking at the results for the confederate gender factor, we see that male confederates are rated slightly higher (average = 8.4) than are female confederates (average = 8.0), but the difference is small and not statistically significant.

The primary benefit of the factorial design is that it shows us how independent variables interact in their effects on dependent variables. In other words, we can test interaction effects, that is, whether the effect of one independent variable on the dependent variable depends on, or is moderated by, the other independent variable. An independent variable or factor that alters the effect of another independent variable or factor on the dependent variable is referred to as a **moderator variable**. Deciding which variable moderates the other is drawn from the theory, not just from the statistical outcomes.

The values inside the four cells of Table 10.3 show the interaction effect. Interactions are often depicted in graphical form for ease of interpretation. Figure 10.1 displays the data from Table 10.3 in the form of a figure. The non-parallel lines indicate that there is an interaction that the statistical analysis revealed to be significant. The interaction indicates that the effect of feedback was negligible when the confederate was a man but considerable when the confederate was a woman. In other words, just because the main effect of confederate gender was not significant does not mean it had no effect; instead, participants rated the male confederate as equally skilled whether he had delivered flattering or unflattering feedback, but they rated the female confederate as more skilled when she had just delivered flattering feedback than when she had delivered negative feedback. Thus, one could say that the effect of confederate

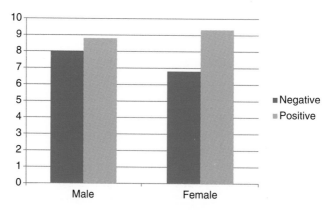

Figure 10.1   Effect of the Interaction of Confederate Gender and Valence of Feedback on Participants' Evaluations of the Confederate's Skill at Providing Feedback.

gender on participants' ratings was moderated by (or depended on) the valence of the feedback.

Notice that testing an interaction is equivalent to asking whether two differences are different from each other. In this case, for example, the interaction indicates that the positive–negative feedback difference in ratings of the male confederate is different from the positive–negative feedback difference in ratings of the female confederate. Notice also that the same interaction can be interpreted in more than one way. In this case, for example, the interaction can also be interpreted as indicating that ratings of the male confederate were higher than those of the female confederate when the feedback was negative, but somewhat lower than those of the female confederate when the feedback was positive. The effect of one factor (e.g., male vs. female confederate) looking at only one level of another factor (e.g., positive feedback only) is known as a **simple effect**. The interaction thus tells us whether two simple effects differ from each other. But an interaction does not usually tell us whether either simple effect is significantly different from zero. In our example, the simple effect of feedback valence (positive vs. negative) for the female confederate must be significantly different from zero because the feedback valence difference for the male confederate is 0.8 and the interaction tells us that the two differ. However, it is not clear whether the simple effect of male versus female confederate was significant when feedback was negative. The significant interaction tells us that the male–female difference of 1.2 in the negative feedback condition differs significantly from the male–female difference of $-.40$ in the positive feedback condition, but we cannot be sure whether 1.2 differs from 0. Researchers therefore often report the results of additional "simple effects" significance tests to aid in the interpretation of interactions. They sometimes also interpret the same interaction in more than one way as the interpretations can yield different insights about the nature of the phenomenon being investigated.

Interaction effects require more complex theoretical explanations than do main effects. Researchers must sufficiently develop their theories to explain why effects of one independent variable are different at different levels of the other independent variable. This complexity, however, is also one of the major strengths of factorial designs: By including more than one independent variable, the researcher is better able to identify and understand multiple and complex causes of a dependent variable. Thus, a major reason to use factorial designs is to test for interaction effects. Another reason is to be able to generalize the effects of one variable across levels of another variable. For instance, if we wanted to study the effects of being able to control noise (variable 1) on people's ability to solve puzzles, we might vary the type of puzzle as a second independent variable. This would enable us to demonstrate that people perform better on not just one but two (or more) types of puzzles (variable 2) when they can control the noise in their environment. We add the second variable not because we expect it to make a difference but to demonstrate that it makes no difference. A third reason to include more than one independent variable in an experiment is to study the separate effects of the variables. We might design a factorial study even if we expect to find only two main effects and no interaction because we can test the two main effects more efficiently and with fewer total participants in a factorial design than we could with two separate studies.

Repeated Measures Designs

Earlier we discussed the fact that experimental or independent variables could be manipulated within as well as between participants. Rather than assign different people to different treatments, the experimenter exposes the same persons to multiple treatments. Each participant is repeatedly treated and tested, and the variations caused by different treatments appear within the same person rather than between different groups of people. Such designs are randomized experimental designs as long as we randomly assign participants to be exposed to the various conditions in different orders.

Not all independent variables can be used in repeated measures designs, just as not all variables can be manipulated experimentally. We earlier made the distinction between manipulated experimental variables and individual difference variables. Manipulated variables are designed by the experimenter and participants can be randomly assigned to manipulated treatments. In contrast, individual difference variables, such as age, height, personality traits, gender, race, and so on, come with participants. Individual difference variables impose restrictions on research design as well as analysis because they cannot be used as within-participants or repeated measures factors.

When factors can be varied within participants, experimenters can use a design that requires fewer participants and provides more sensitive measures of the effects of a variable. For instance, if we wanted to study how quickly men and women can solve puzzles that are labeled "masculine problem" and "feminine problem," we could use either a between-participants or a within-participants design. The participants' gender is an individual difference variable and must be a between-participants factor. The label on the puzzle could be either a between-participants or within-participants factor. If it were between participants and we wished to have 15 observations in each condition, 60 participants would be required, as shown in Table 10.4. The 60 observations would come from 60 different people.

We could, however, make the gender labeling of the task a within-participants factor and have each participant solve both a "masculine" and "feminine" labeled puzzle. In this case, as shown in Table 10.5, we would need only 30 participants, 15 men and 15 women, to get the same number of observations in each condition because each person would solve two puzzles. Note that we now have one repeated measures or within-participants factor and one between-participants factor. Designs

Table 10.4 Illustration of the Number of Participants Needed for a Between-Participants Design		
	Gender Labeling of the Task	
Participant's Gender	*Masculine*	*Feminine*
Male	$n = 15$ men	$n = 15$ men
Female	$n = 15$ women	$n = 15$ women
	Total $N = 60$ participants	

Table 10.5   Illustration of the Number of Participants Needed for a Within-Participants Design

Participant's Gender	Gender Labeling of the Task	
	Masculine	*Feminine*
Male	15 men	(15)
Female	15 women	(15)
	Total $N = 30$ participants	

that include both within-participants (e.g., masculine vs. feminine puzzle) and between-participants factors (e.g., participant gender) are known as mixed models. In this case, however, participant gender is not manipulated and thus gender cannot be said to *cause* differences in the dependent variable.

The other efficient feature of repeated measures designs is the precision gained by using participants as their own comparisons. Like the pretest observations of the pretest–posttest two-group design, the repeated measures give us individual baselines for each participant. The 15 men who solve the "masculine" puzzle in Table 10.4 might vary widely in the time they require. One might solve the puzzle in 10 seconds and another might take 10 minutes. If each person takes one minute longer to solve the "feminine" than the "masculine" puzzle, it would not appear as a noticeable difference between the two puzzle groups if we used a between-participants design, but it might be a noticeable difference in a repeated measures design. In other words, repeated measures are more statistically powerful than are between-participants designs because analyses do not just compare differences between groups, but compare changes of each individual within groups. Recall from our discussion of statistical conclusion validity in Chapter 2 that statistical power refers to the likelihood of seeing an effect if the effect truly exists.

Again, individual difference variables cannot be used with repeated measures; not even all manipulated variables are suitable as within-participants or repeated measures variables. Some manipulated variables would arouse participants' suspicions about the purposes of the experiment. For instance, suppose we tried to use the ethnicity or gender of job applicants as a within-participants variable. If we presented prospective employers with two hypothetical job applications and résumés in which everything was identical except the ethnicity or gender of the applicant, the prospective employers could see immediately that we were testing to see whether they practice race or sex discrimination in hiring. Similarly, asking the same participants to judge the same message twice, once using the term "global warming" and once using "climate change," as in our earlier example, would make the purpose of the experiment quite obvious. Researchers therefore sometimes use "filler tasks," that is, asking participants to complete additional tasks to disguise the true purpose of the experiment.

Other variables are not suitable for repeated measures designs if they produce long-lasting effects that would carry over from one testing to the next. For instance, if we tried to compare the effects of alcohol and hallucinogenic drugs on drivers' reaction times, we would not have them drink alcohol, give them a driver's test, and then give them hallucinogenic drugs immediately after for a second test. In addition to the obvious ethical problems of administering drugs to experimental participants, we also would encounter practical problems. If we use repeated measures designs, we must be sure the effects of the first level of a treatment are gone before we try to administer subsequent levels. For this reason, repeated measures designs are generally not appropriate for examining factors that affect learning. Consider, for example, an experiment to determine which of two teaching strategies is more effective in helping participants learn a task or acquire certain knowledge. Once participants have learned the task or acquired the knowledge, they are unlikely to unlearn it.

Analyzing Data from Experimental Designs

Because data from experimental designs are typically scores that reflect the effects of treatments, the appropriate approaches for analyzing data are those that compare the means of the different treatment conditions. In the simplest instances of two groups, the analysis could be a *t*-test. More generally, however, analyses use a form of analysis of variance (ANOVA). Variations of the approach include those where there are multiple dependent variables, called multivariate analysis of variance (MANOVA), and those where there may be control variables whose effects are eliminated before looking at the mean differences, called analysis of covariance (ANCOVA). Perhaps most common are those ANCOVAs that control for pretest scores when looking at posttest scores. Sometimes researchers use a general linear model approach, which involves using regression approaches to produce the mean comparisons. The methods may look different, but are actually the same, as are *t*-test and ANOVA analyses of the same data. They can also easily accommodate cases in which the number of participants varies across conditions (see, e.g., Judd, McClelland, & Ryan, 2009).

Strengths and Weaknesses of Randomized Experiments

We have emphasized the strengths of randomized experiments. By randomly assigning people to experimental conditions, experimenters can be confident that subsequent differences on the dependent variable are caused, on average, by the treatments rather than preexisting differences among groups of people. Manipulated experimental variables, unlike individual difference variables, enable experimenters to conclude "This caused that." No experimenter can be 100% sure that "this" experimental treatment was the cause of "that" effect, as there is always the possibility of a failure of randomization or undetected artifact, but randomized experiments can rule out many alternative explanations.

Yet randomized experiments are not without their weaknesses. In this section, we describe some of the major drawbacks of randomized experiments. It is important to keep in mind, however, that these drawbacks are not inevitable condemnations of experimental designs. Not all experiments have these limitations and not all non-experimental studies are without them.

Experimental Artifacts

One set of extraneous variables that undermines the validity of research conclusions is artifacts. In research design, the word **artifact** refers to an unintended effect on the dependent variable that is caused by some feature of the experimental setting other than the independent variable. Even with selection, history, maturation, instrumentation, and the other threats to internal validity taken care of, the results of research might not be true effects of the experimental treatment but instead be artifacts, or effects of some extraneous variables. For instance, experimenters can unwittingly influence their participants to behave in ways that confirm the hypothesis, particularly if the participants want to please the experimenter. Findings that result from such attempts are artifactual in the sense that they do not represent participants' true responses to the independent variables of interest. Another example would be when participants respond in socially desirable ways rather than in ways that represent what they really believe and would do. A detailed discussion of such artifacts and their potential threats is given in Chapter 5, where we consider laboratory research in detail. Artifacts can occur regardless of the research design that is used. In laboratory settings, artifacts are just as likely when non-experimental or quasi-experimental designs are used. Artifacts can also occur in the field if, for example, the independent variable is confounded or covaries with some unintended aspect of the field setting.

External Validity

Experimental designs and procedures maximize the internal validity of research – they enable the researcher to rule out most rival explanations or threats to internal validity. There can be a trade-off, however. Experimenters might maximize internal validity at the expense of the external validity or generalizability of the results. Because many randomized experiments are conducted in laboratory settings (although they need not be), we might ask whether the findings extend beyond the laboratory. Can the experimenter talk about these phenomena in the world outside, or do they appear only in highly controlled and sometimes artificial conditions?

A common criticism of laboratory experiments in particular is that they are poor representations of natural processes. Some laboratory experiments, like Glass and Singer's (1972) studies of noise, use remote analogues of real-world variables, like urban stress. Although some readers criticize such analogues as being artificial, we also can argue that the artificial conditions in these experiments are more effective ways to study the problem than are some more realistic conditions. The laboratory noise and laboratory measures of physiological and cognitive effects are all substitutes for the real phenomena; they are analogues and therefore artificial. Being artificial is not necessarily a disadvantage, however. Some laboratory analogues are more effective than their realistic but mundane counterparts and therefore make the research more persuasive, an issue we discuss in Chapter 5. In the final analysis, how realistic or generalizable any treatments and effects are can be discovered only by trying to replicate the findings in another setting.

The Problem of College Sophomores in the Laboratory

A third major criticism of experiments is not about the methods but about the subject populations. It questions the representativeness of typical research participants, who particularly in psychology often are college students participating in research to fulfill course requirements. Are college students representative of the larger population? It depends on how one defines the larger population as well as the particular research question. For many research purposes college sophomores are often considered to be no different from anyone else. For instance, to study a physiological variable such as the eye blink response, we might be able to assume that what is true for 18-year-old college students is also true for 6-year-old elementary school students and 40-year-old employees. And some researchers argue that the particular population being studied is largely irrelevant if the desire is to establish that a causal relationship occurs between two variables. Once the existence of the relationship has been established, then researchers can worry about how generalizable the findings are and what their implications are. However, researchers who study social processes, such as the effects of contact with ethnic outgroup members on prejudice, would certainly be wise to study more heterogeneous people – in the same or different studies. Similarly, to study the effects of an economic variable, such as tax incentives for purchasing energy efficient appliances, it would be wise to include people with a range of incomes and some practical experience with the issue.

Sears (1986) documented social psychologists' overreliance on college students as participants, providing a compelling critique of the practice. More recently, other researchers have questioned our tendency to overgeneralize findings from research that typically relies on research participants in Western, Educated, Industrialized, Rich, and Democratic (WEIRD) societies (Chiao & Cheon, 2010; Henrich, Heine, & Norenzayan, 2010). Many research conclusions that have been considered universal – even those concerning basic perceptual processes, such as visual illusions – appear to depend on one's experiences. In short, the unique characteristics of our research participants can indeed affect our findings.

What can be done about this problem? First, in many instances, researchers could reduce their reliance on college students and include other populations in their studies. The convenience of the college "subject pool" is hard for researchers to resist; many university-based researchers decide that they prefer to increase the volume of their research by using inexpensive and readily available college undergraduates, even at the cost of external validity. Fortunately, the reliance on college undergraduates appears to be declining, partly as a result of technology that makes diverse populations more accessible. For example, the ability to develop cross-cultural research collaborations has improved dramatically and some studies can be conducted successfully via the Internet. Second, regardless of the population that is studied, researchers must be more circumspect in discussing the generalizability of their research findings rather than assuming that findings based on specific groups generalize to very broad populations (e.g., all people). As global awareness has increased and social science research has blossomed across the world, failures to replicate widely accepted Western findings have increased awareness of cultural boundaries on research. Finally, researchers can provide more thoughtful evaluations of the factors that might affect the generalizability of their research findings when they publish their findings. Indeed, more thoughtful evaluations often reveal interesting avenues for further research and interesting boundary conditions on social phenomena. Looking forward, we are hopeful that by improving the rewards (e.g., research funding and opportunities to publish) for replicating research findings among diverse populations, researchers will continue to reduce their reliance on college undergraduates and WEIRD populations more generally.

We are not suggesting that all areas of the social sciences are guilty of the college sophomore bias, for, as we noted above, experimental psychologists have been most guilty of relying on college student populations for their research. Indeed, for many social science questions, participant populations simply must be more heterogeneous than college students; participants must vary in age, income, education, or occupation if these are variables to be examined. For instance, sociological research more often addresses questions about demographic groups – people of different economic, ethnic, educational, and cultural backgrounds – as well as the effects of situations and social structures much more diverse than those typical of college campuses.

Certainly, there is nothing about experimental designs that *requires* studying college undergraduates. Although laboratory experiments are criticized for relying too heavily on college students, the truth is that the choice of design is independent of the choice of sample. The only requirement of a randomized experiment is random assignment; and with manipulable variables, ingenuity, and a little tact, experimenters are able to use random assignment in many places outside the college community. Said differently, the college sophomore problem is not a weakness of experimental designs per se but rather an unfortunate feature of the preponderance of research in the social sciences that features randomization and manipulation of independent variables.

The Failure of Experiments to Provide Useful Descriptive Data

Another drawback of randomized experiments is that they rarely yield descriptive data about frequencies or the likelihood of certain behaviors that we can generalize to larger populations. For instance, if 20% of the people in the treatment group agree with a statement about the usefulness of therapy, it tells us nothing about the percentage of people who agree with this statement in any larger population unless we have recruited the participants for our experiment by selecting a representative sample from the larger population. In theory this can be done; in practice it is exceedingly rare.

An important difference between how probability surveys and experiments are usually conducted is that probability surveys enlist random samples of respondents who are representative of some larger population (see Chapter 9). Therefore, if 80% of the people in a representative sample say they support marriage equality, we can generalize this result to the population from which they were drawn. Because the sample is a random selection of people from a population, the distribution of beliefs and preferences in that sample is approximately the same as the distribution in the population. The survey, therefore, provides descriptive data about the population. In contrast, an experiment usually does not make use of a representative or random sample because the purpose of the experiment is not to provide descriptive data about percentages of people in the population who profess certain beliefs; the purpose of an experiment is to provide information about causes and effects.

Summary

Randomized experiments are the best method for examining causal associations and concluding that "This caused that." The defining characteristic of such designs is that participants are randomly assigned to the levels of the independent variables. Randomized experiments enable researchers to test and rule out the primary threats to internal validity: selection, maturation, history, instrumentation, and mortality. Experiments that comprise more than one independent variable provide tests of both the main effects and the interaction effects of those variables. The high internal validity of randomized experiments is sometimes achieved at the cost of external validity, especially when randomized experiments are conducted in laboratory settings with relatively select samples of participants. However, two things must be kept in mind about this possible limitation. First, the limitation is not a necessary consequence of the use of a randomized design. Randomized experiments can be conducted in field settings using representative samples. Second, even if this is a limitation of some experimental designs, the goal of experimental research is not to maximize external validity; it is to maximize internal validity. We use the diverse designs of social science research to accomplish a set of diverse and partially incompatible goals. We should use randomized experiments for what they are particularly good at – that is, answering questions about causal processes – and we should rely on other sorts of designs to answer other sorts of questions.

Go online   Visit the book's companion website for this chapter's test bank and other resources at: www.wiley.com/go/maruyama

---

Key Concepts

Artifact

Construct validity

Counterbalancing

Dependent variable

Differential mortality

Experimental variables

Factorial design

Failure of randomization

History

Independent variable

Individual difference or subject
    variables

Instrumentation

Interaction effect

Internal validity

Main effect

Manipulated variable

Manipulation check

Maturation

Moderator variable

Mortality

Operational definition

Plausible alternative explanation

Pretests

Random assignment or randomization
Randomized experiment
Repeated measures design
Selection

Selection by maturation
Simple effect
Within-participants design

On the Web

http://www.socialresearchmethods.net/kb/desexper.php A very nicely written and organized website that contains information about various types of experimental and non-experimental designs, internal and external validity, threats to internal validity, and other topics covered in this book.

http://webstat.une.edu.au/main/index.htm A tutorial designed by the School of Psychology at the University of New England that has several relevant units, including a discussion of experimental and non-experimental designs, internal and external validity, and between-participants and within-participants designs.

Further Reading

Campbell, D. T., & Stanley, J. C. (1963). *Experimental and quasi-experimental designs for research*. Chicago, IL: Rand McNally.

Huck, S. W., & Sandler, H. M. (1979). *Rival hypotheses: Alternative interpretations of data based conclusions*. New York, NY: Harper & Row.

Shadish, W. R., Cook, T. D., & Campbell, D. T. (2002). *Experimental and quasi-experimental designs for generalized causal inference*. Boston, MA: Houghton Mifflin.

Smith, E. R. (2014). Research design. In H. T. Reis & C. M. Judd (Eds.), *Handbook of research methods in social and personality psychology* (2nd ed., pp. 27–48). New York, NY: Cambridge University Press.

West, S. G., Cham, H., & Liu, Y. (2014). Causal inference and generalization in field settings: Experimental and quasi-experimental designs. In H. T. Reis & C. M. Judd (Eds.), *Handbook of research methods in social and personality psychology* (2nd ed., pp. 49–80). New York, NY: Cambridge University Press.

Chapter 11

Quasi-Experimental and Other Nonrandomized Designs

As we have explained at several points earlier in this text, science is much more than just randomized experiments. Science is a process of discovery in which researchers use the best tools available to answer their questions. In instances where the independent variables cannot be manipulated or where random assignment would not be ethical, experimental designs are not viable tools. In such circumstances, researchers have available an assortment of research designs that are preferable to randomized experimental designs. This chapter illustrates different types of non-experimental

Research Methods in Social Relations, Eighth Edition. Geoffrey Maruyama and Carey S. Ryan.
© 2014 John Wiley & Sons, Inc. Published 2014 by John Wiley & Sons, Inc.
Companion Website: www.wiley.com/go/maruyama

designs, discusses the meaning of causality in this context, discusses some classic **quasi-experimental designs**, and describes some newer approaches for drawing inferences from these types of designs.

In nonrandomized research designs research participants are not randomly assigned to levels of the independent variable. Instead, the comparisons between treatment and control conditions or between different treatments must always be made with the presumption that the groups are *nonequivalent*. As a result, the internal validity of these designs is threatened by the full range of threats discussed in Chapter 10. Accordingly, causal inferences about the effects of independent variables on dependent variables are difficult to draw.

Despite their shortcoming with respect to causal inferences, for some questions these designs have distinct advantages over randomized experimental designs. The relative sacrifice in internal validity can well be worth the cost, depending on the goals of the researcher and the context in which the research is conducted. For instance, a primary goal of a researcher might simply be to explore the distribution of some variable in some population of interest. Alternatively, it might be to see whether a treatment can be implemented in a particular setting. In the former case, considerations about internal validity are not relevant because the researcher is not interested in determining processes of causation. Rather, the researcher wishes to know how many people believe something or act in a certain way or have a certain characteristic. For such questions, a **survey research** approach is appropriate. Although discussion of many survey designs could be placed in the following chapter about nonexperimental designs, survey methods appear in a separate chapter (Chapter 14) to provide readers with a better sense of their range and usage. In the latter case, which will be described in detail after we provide examples of survey research, the research may look like an experimental design but lack random assignment or a comparison group.

Survey research approaches are used in a wide variety of situations and to fulfill a range of purposes, as can be seen in the following examples of their use:

- Sociologists gather information from a representative sample of the U.S. labor force to study their training and occupational attainments.
- Public opinion polling organizations conduct studies of the popularity of various presidential candidates among potential voters.
- Market research organizations conduct studies of consumers to find out what kinds of soft drinks they prefer.
- Medical researchers survey the nation's population to determine the incidence of disease-related factors.
- Political scientists interview members of the U.S. House of Representatives to monitor their reactions to increasing public attention to the ethics of public figures.
- A national women's magazine asks its readers to answer a questionnaire that solicits information about their occupational aspirations.
- Psychologists survey students to determine levels and types of harassment or bullying experienced by students in schools.
- Political sociologists survey a sample of students in large universities to determine whether they support or oppose a military draft in the United States.

• A national broadcast rating organization uses electronic recording devices to measure the distribution of television watching each week.

In each of these examples, the researchers are not interested in establishing cause-and-effect conclusions, but are concerned about measuring constructs well and gathering information from a representative sample of individuals. The designs discussed in this chapter are perfectly appropriate for addressing such purposes. Other details of survey research are discussed in Chapter 14, and non-experimental research is discussed in Chapter 12.

In other instances, researchers want to do more than simply describe a sample of respondents. As was mentioned above, they might want to see how a treatment works in a particular setting, or discover or document an association between two or more variables in some target population. For example, they might select a single group (with no comparison group) and administer a particular intervention to learn how to implement it effectively, comparing data collected before and after the intervention to see if it appears to have any effects. In such a case, the primary goal is to find an intervention that works in the setting rather than establishing a causal relation between independent and dependent variables. Because the design is not experimental, even if the outcomes are the ones desired, they cannot be sure that the intervention caused the outcome. At the same time, however, because they are not worrying about random assignment, the intervention could be given to everyone seeking it, and no participants would be denied inclusion in a treatment that attracted them to participate.

Finally, consider the methods available for a researcher interested in the effects of independent variables that cannot be effectively manipulated. It would be impossible, or at least unethical, for example, to design a manipulation that would allow researchers to examine people's reactions to a natural disaster. Yet psychologists are certainly interested in the behavioral and mental health implications of how people cope with natural disasters. The solution to this dilemma – that is, being interested in the effects of a variable that cannot be manipulated – is not to abandon empirical research strategies. Rather, a viable solution is to employ the best **nonrandomized research design** available, recognizing its internal validity limitations and attempting to overcome the limitations as much as possible.

Examples of Nonrandomized Designs

Before considering the formalities of alternative designs and their relative strengths and weaknesses, consider two examples of research that have made effective use of nonrandomized designs.

Survey Study

Starting in 1968, the Panel Study of Income Dynamics (PSID), a longitudinal study of a representative sample of American families, has been conducted by researchers at the Institute for Social Research at the University of Michigan (http://psidonline.isr.umich.edu/). Interview data were gathered annually through 1997 and have been gathered biennially since then. By following the children of sample families as they grew and formed families of their own, the sample size has grown substantially from its initial sample of 5,000 families. And by following individuals across time, data now follow individuals across entire work lives, for over 40 years. The interviews elicit information on a host of economic and social variables. A set of core variables is publicly available, including: income sources and amounts; poverty status and whether the family receives any public assistance; family structure and basic demographic variables; employment, housing, and socioeconomic background; and general health status. Other supplemental topics are addressed in different time periods and include measures, such as housing and neighborhood characteristics, education, savings and retirement plans, health expenditures, and childcare issues. Given the large amount and scope of data now available, it is no surprise that PSID was selected as one of the National Science Foundation's "Nifty Fifty," the 50 most interesting research projects, at NSF's 50th anniversary celebration in 2000.

The massive amounts of information accumulated in this panel study can be and have been used to address many important social science questions. Many different researchers have approached these same data from different vantage points and with different theoretical interests and yet have found them a rich source of information. Since the beginning of the study, more than 3,000 peer-reviewed publications have been written to communicate findings from the data set.

Consider the strengths of this study. First, the sample is obviously large and representative. Regardless of one's theoretical interest, it is difficult to imagine a randomized experiment involving a representative sample of 5,000 respondents. Second, considerable amounts of time were spent interviewing each family and refining the questions that were asked. Therefore, hundreds of constructs were measured and issues of reliability and validity of measurement could be addressed relatively easily. Again, it is difficult to imagine a randomized experiment within which such massive amounts of information about family life in America could have been gathered. Third, because the survey was administered in a **panel design**, meaning that the same families were reinterviewed regularly, it is possible to document variations in economic conditions both between families in any given year and longitudinally within the same families over time.

Consider the advantage of being able to make both cross-sectional and within-subject longitudinal comparisons, in more detail. Suppose we were interested in examining the association between employment status and family composition variables. Given the 2008–2009 economic downturn and massive job losses, we might want to study consequences of job loss. We may hypothesize that when the parents in a family are unemployed, stress within the family increases, which in turn might lead to divorce and family breakup. It would be impossible to conduct a randomized experiment to examine this hypothesis. Manipulating employment status is not something that any experimentalist would choose to do. Yet this panel design permits researchers to look at the hypothesized association in a variety of different ways. First, within any given year, family compositions of employed and unemployed respondents can be compared. This **cross-sectional comparison** can be done for each year of the panel study, yielding many replications of any particular finding. Second, the longitudinal design allows the same sort of comparisons to be made *within* individual families when the employment status of the parents changes over the course of the study. Thus, families in which the parents either become newly unemployed or employed during the course of the study can be identified, and then corresponding changes in their family composition and stresses can be examined. If both sorts of comparisons lead to the same conclusion – that is, if employment status of parents is associated with family composition variables both between families and within families over time – we can have increased confidence in the correctness of the hypothesis despite the fact that a randomized experimental test of it is not feasible. If, in contrast, the results were inconsistent, with one supporting the hypothesis and one not, we would need to find more data to test our hypothesis further. If neither approach revealed a relationship, we could feel confident that our hypothesis is wrong. Finally, a researcher could design a quasi-experimental design that matches individuals losing their jobs on a range of background characteristics with similar individuals who did not lose their jobs. Later we describe propensity score matching, an approach for identifying a comparison group that in principle is matched to the "intervention" group in ways that equalize the likelihood that individuals in the two groups would lose their jobs.

Quasi-Experimental Intervention Study

Consider now a nonrandomized design that involved an intervention. Researchers have long been interested in designing public service announcements (PSAs) that would be effective in reducing drug use. This topic would be difficult to address experimentally. Although it would be possible to bring people into the laboratory and randomly assign them to watch either an experimental (antidrug) PSA or a control (neutral topic) PSA, such a limited onetime exposure probably would not have much impact, and, more importantly, it would not be representative of the real world in which the PSAs would ultimately be used. A quasi-experimental field study was deemed a more appropriate approach for answering the question of the effectiveness of antidrug PSAs (Palmgreen, Donohew, Lorch, Hoyle, & Stephenson, 2001). In quasi-experimental designs, one or more independent variables are manipulated but participants are not randomly assigned to levels of the manipulated variables. In this quasi-experimental study, the researchers created PSAs that were designed to be particularly effective for high sensation seekers, who were identified as a population at high risk for drug use. (In Chapter 13, we revisit the Palmgreen et al., 2001, study when we discuss how focus groups were used to create the PSAs.) The PSAs were then shown at different points in time in Fayette County, Kentucky, and Knox County, Tennessee, two counties that were deemed comparable on demographic and cultural variables (but to which participants obviously were not randomly assigned). During a 32-month interval, individual interviews were conducted each month with samples of 100 randomly selected adolescents in grades 7 through 10 from each of the two counties. The main dependent variable was whether respondents had used marijuana during the previous 30 days. The independent variable was whether the antidrug PSAs were running on local television. The PSAs were televised between January and April 1997 in Fayette County and between January and April 1998 in both Fayette County and Knox County. Because drug use was tracked continuously starting 8 months before the first Fayette County PSA campaign, and because adolescents in Knox

County were not exposed to the PSAs at the time of the first campaign in Fayette County, the researchers could determine whether self-reported marijuana use appeared to be affected by the presentation of antidrug PSAs.

This study is an example of an **interrupted time-series design**. "Time series" refers to the strategy of measuring a set of variables on a series of occasions (e.g., monthly) during a specified period of time (32 months in the example). "Interrupted" refers to the strategy of introducing an intervention – the stimulus or event (the PSA campaign) during the period of assessment in order to evaluate its effect on the variables being measured (e.g., 30-day marijuana use). Time-series designs are a type of **longitudinal design**, typically referring to designs where multiple measures are collected on a single group of participants and the analyses examine how responses to the measures change across time, before, at, and after the introduction of the intervention. This implementation of an interrupted time-series design conveys several important advantages. First, it controls for trends in marijuana use prior to the PSA campaigns in both counties by providing a long baseline period before the campaigns were initiated. Second, the fact that three separate campaigns were used (two in Fayette County, one in Knox County) helps to rule out threats due to history effects; it would be highly unlikely that any given external event would coincide exactly with the three PSA campaigns. The fact that Knox County serves as a control for the first campaign in Fayette County further helps to rule out history effects that might be occurring at a national level; in other words, if a federal antidrug campaign coincided with the first PSA campaign in the Palmgreen et al. (2001) study, it should affect marijuana use equally in both Fayette and Knox Counties. The design also controls for maturation effects, again because Knox County acts as a control group. Lastly, the design includes elements of both a between-participants (cross-sectional) design (Fayette vs. Knox County) and a repeated measures (longitudinal) design (the two administrations of the campaign in Fayette County), thus providing the advantages of both types of design.

Figure 11.1 shows the results for the Palmgreen et al. (2001) study. We provide more detail about interrupted time-series designs later in the chapter, but the main results emerge clearly from their pattern. The top half of Figure 11.1 displays the data for the Knox County samples; notice that marijuana use increased steadily from May of 1996 to December of 1997, but when the PSA campaign was introduced in January of 1998, marijuana use declined. In Fayette County (bottom half of the graph), however, the pattern of drug use was quite different. Again, we see a steady increase of marijuana use at the beginning of the study, but the first peak occurs in January of 1997, at the introduction of the first PSA campaign. Marijuana use declined steadily until the fall of 1997, when it started increasing again. But with the introduction of the second PSA campaign in January of 1998, marijuana use again declined.

These results illustrate the value of a carefully designed and well-executed quasi-experiment. Although participants were not randomly assigned to conditions, thus precluding a definitive causal inference, it would be difficult to imagine any alternative explanation that could account for the pattern of marijuana use that was obtained in the two counties. Thus, the researchers could be fairly confident that the PSAs were in fact effective in reducing marijuana use among high-sensation-seeking adolescents.

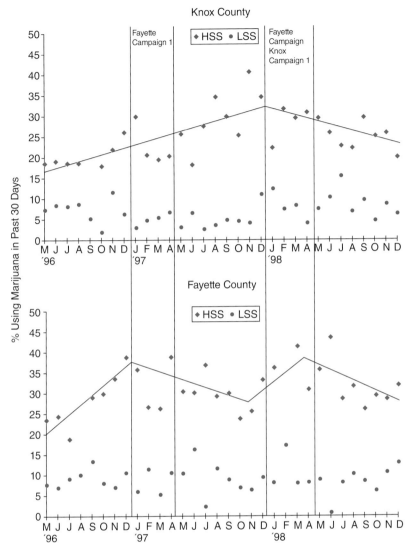

Figure 11.1   Example of Findings from an Interrupted Time-Series Design.
Note: HSS → high sensation seeking; LSS → low sensation seeking
Source: Palmgreen et al. (2001), p. 294. Copyright 2001 by the American Public Health Association.
Reprinted with Permission.

Conditions for Causality

There are three criteria for inferring causality: (1) *X* and *O* covary (relationship is functional), (2) *X* precedes *O* in time (*X* has time precedence), and (3) there are no alternative explanations for group differences in *O* (it is non-spurious). First, two variables covary (i.e., they are associated or related) when certain values of one variable are more likely to be found with particular values of the other variable. For example, if education and income positively covary, then lower levels of income tend to occur with lower levels of educational attainment and higher levels of income tend to occur with higher levels of educational attainment. Variables that negatively covary have high values of one tending to occur with low values of the other, and vice versa. Covarying is a necessary condition for causality, but not sufficient to establish causality, for two variables can covary for other reasons, for example, because they both are caused by a third variable. Thus, the dictum: "Correlation does not imply causality." The opposite, however, is true, for in order for there to be causality, variables must be related (covary), leading to the statement: "Causality does imply correlation." Finding an association between two variables in different populations and different research conditions is necessary for and lends credence to a causal hypothesis involving the two variables, for each instance is a test of the hypothesis that could disconfirm or limit it. But finding relations across multiple settings and samples is not enough; each instance has to be examined for plausible alternative explanations before even tentative causal interpretation is reasonable.

Second, the assumption of **temporal order** may seem challenging, for often two variables that are related are measured at approximately the same time. Each may be measured by responses to items in a questionnaire, or each collected at a single point in time. In such instances it cannot be said that one variable comes before the other in time, at least in terms of when the information was gathered. Rather, the researcher must assume that one variable as measured in the questionnaire represents the accumulation of earlier influences and has influenced other responses on the questionnaire through prior life experiences. Sometimes it can be determined that one preceded the other in time even if the variables were collected at the same time. For example, for most Americans, the end of schooling comes before the beginning of their first full-time employment. If we used survey data to study the occupational attainments of American workers, we could say that for most Americans, educational attainment came before occupational placement. But even if this is in general true, the temporal order does not describe every worker. Some people work for years on a full-time basis at a job they consider to be permanent before they attend or complete their schooling. To the extent that respondents differ in the ordering of education and first job, there is ambiguity in the interpretation of the association between them. Such ambiguity is another reason for researchers to exercise caution in making causal inferences from survey or questionnaire research designs. To provide a more precise test of their hypothesis (but also potentially limiting generalizability of the findings), they may select a sample for which the direction of the relationship is less ambiguous, for example, selecting only workers who went straight through their educational years as full-time students before taking any full-time job. Instead of limiting the sample, however, one might argue that at a particular point in time the jobs people hold reflect their educational preparation for those jobs, so later changes in educational attainments that lead to later job changes would not affect the findings. Regardless of the position one wants to take, it is important to think carefully about the hypotheses that are being formulated and tested, and to consider their applicability for different groups and settings.

If our purposes are limited to assessing the incidence or distribution of characteristics, say, the number or proportion of men and women in a given occupation, an experimental design is not needed, nor is it needed when we wish to assess the degree of covariation among variables. Most non-experimental designs are adequate for such a task. We could readily gather data from which to calculate the degree of association between or among variables. For example, we could determine relations of family background measures (income and parents' educational attainments) with perform-ance in school (grades, grade point average, highest level of education completed) and earnings. In addition, we could order variables so that the variables we hypothesize as causal temporally precede those we identify as effects. However, whenever we wish to go beyond the estimation of associations to the interpretation of them, the limita-tions of non-experimental designs are apparent, for that is when the third condition for causality becomes important.

In the social sciences, it is difficult to attribute causal ordering to relationships unless there is random assignment to conditions, for the complexity of humans and human interactions offers many viable alternative explanations. This is true in contrast to the physical sciences, where in many instances alternative explanations for phenom-ena are limited even when random assignment has not been used. Consider, for example, a study of the effects of different plant foods in the four quadrants of a field. Because the same field is used and all four plant foods are used during the same growing season, we can be fairly confident that all the other things that affect plant growth have been controlled and cannot be responsible for observed differences between quadrants of the field. In this case, even without random assignment, a per-suasive case for internal validity can be made simply because there are no viable alternative explanations for any differences found. In essence, the selection threat to internal validity is eliminated by controlling for all plausible alternative differences, which might be done even without the use of random assignment. In principle, we might contemplate cases in which such control is possible in the social sciences. In practice, however, it is rarely if ever possible to have sufficient confidence in the belief that all competing explanations for group differences on the dependent variable have been eliminated. For example, in the study just described, a skeptic might still point out possible alternatives like differences in underground water supplies in different quadrants or other factors not considered by the researchers. But that criticism could be addressed by another quasi-experimental study replicating the initial study the next year while rotating the quadrants so different quadrants were now in different treat-ment conditions.

Exercise: Causation

Although the approaches described in Chapter 11 are rigorous, they fail to meet necessary and sufficient conditions for establishing causality. We articulate those above as: (1) X and O covary (relationship is functional), (2) X precedes O in time (it has time precedence), and (3) there are no alternative explanations for group differences in O (it is non-spurious). What are the alternative explanations that the approaches in Chapter 11 fail to meet, and what can be done about them? For example, some researchers describe single subject designs as experimental. Analyze them with respect to the conditions for establishing causality, and decide if you think we should have described them as experimental.

Illustrative Nonrandomized Designs

There is a wide variety of nonrandomized research designs (for comprehensive treatments, see Campbell & Stanley, 1963; Shadish, Cook, & Campbell, 2002; Judd & Kenny, 1981). Much of the remainder of this chapter illustrates some of these designs and discusses the major threats to internal validity that are posed by each one. In general the hallmark of nonrandomized designs is the absence of assigning individuals randomly to levels of the independent variable(s).

As in Chapter 10, a fundamental distinction to be made among designs concerns the way in which the independent variable varies. It can vary either between participants or within them, just as it did in randomized experimental designs. Recall that in the former case, different individuals are measured in different treatment conditions (levels of the independent variable). Research participants who are exposed to the treatment are not the same as those who are in the control group. In contrast, when the independent variable varies within participants, each participant is observed under all of its conditions or levels. That is, the same individual is observed both in the treatment and in the control condition. As we will see, there are different threats to internal validity depending on whether the independent variable varies within or between participants in nonrandomized designs. Finally, in some designs, such as the one used in the Palmgreen et al. (2001) study discussed previously, independent variables of interest vary both between and within participants. In that study, exposure to the PSA campaign varied between counties during the first year of the study, but, because adolescents in both counties ultimately were exposed to the campaign during the time series, it varied within each county as well.

As in Chapter 10, we use the following notation to describe different research designs:

X = a treatment, an independent variable, a cause
O = an observation, a dependent variable, an effect

(Note that the R used in Chapter 10 to denote randomization is not needed here.)

Static-Group Comparison Design

Group 1 $X \text{———} O_1$

Group 2 $\text{not-}X \text{———} O_2$

In this design, people are not randomly assigned to group 1 and group 2; instead, these are either naturally occurring groups or groups to which people are assigned for some reason other than a random one (e.g., self-selection).

If we imagine the **static-group comparison design** with a naturally occurring X having several levels (e.g., socioeconomic status – low/medium/high), it becomes the following:

Group 1 X_1————O_1

Group 2 X_2————O_2

Group 3 X_3————O_3

This design has as many groups as there are levels of the independent variable. As such, the independent variable varies between participants. Data analysis for these designs would be variants of analysis of variance (ANOVA). In the first case, one would do either an ANOVA with two groups or a t-test; they provide equivalent tests. In the second case, one would do a one-way ANOVA with three levels of the independent variable. Alternatively, one could conduct all of these analyses in regression, using contrast-coded predictors as described by Judd, McClelland, and Ryan (2009).

Because participants have not been randomly assigned to the groups, **selection** is a serious threat to the internal validity of this research design and limits interpretations of the findings. Suppose X represents education (no college, some college, college graduate) and O represents income. If the groups differ in income, it is tempting to interpret this difference as the effect of education on income. Such an interpretation would be analogous to our interpretation of the effects of X in a randomized experiment. The difficulty with interpreting the results of a static-group comparison is the possibility that there are other differences between the education groups that might also affect income. For example, the education groups probably differ on academic abilities or parental socioeconomic status (SES). Such differences are plausible **alternative explanations** for any differences in income between groups. They and other viable explanations would have to be dismissed empirically before researchers could assert with confidence that education causes income, and the conditions for causality described earlier in this chapter (and elsewhere in this book) would have to be met.

Data from any static-group comparison design can be used to establish that two variables covary (the first of the three criteria for causality). Ambiguity in the interpretation of the nature of the association between variables, however, is a reason for researchers to exercise caution in making causal inferences from this sort of research design. If our purposes are limited to assessing the degree of covariation among variables, a static-group comparison design is adequate for the task. Using this design, we could readily gather data from which to calculate the degree of association between or among variables. For example, we could determine relations of family background measures (income and parents' educational attainments) with performance in school (grades, grade point average, highest level of education completed) and earnings. It is when we wish to go beyond the *estimation* of associations to the *interpretation* of them that the limitations of the static-group comparison design are realized, for that is when the third condition for causality becomes important. And, as has already been argued, that condition is very difficult to meet with this design.

Pretest–Posttest Nonequivalent Control Group Design

The **pretest–posttest nonequivalent control group design** is an extension of the static-group comparison design that includes measures of the dependent variable at multiple points in time. Each group is given both a pretest and a posttest, measuring the dependent variable both before and after exposure to the independent variable:

$$\text{Group 1} \quad O_1 \text{———} X \text{———} O_2$$
$$\text{- -}$$
$$\text{Group 2} \quad O_3 \text{——————} O_4$$

With three or more levels of the independent variable, this design is simply extended to additional groups, as in the static-group comparison design:

$$\text{Group 1} \quad O_1 \text{———} X_1 \text{———} O_2$$
$$\text{- -}$$
$$\text{Group 2} \quad O_3 \text{———} X_2 \text{———} O_4$$
$$\text{- -}$$
$$\text{Group 3} \quad O_5 \text{———} X_3 \text{———} O_6$$

Like the static-group comparison design, in this design the independent variable varies between participants, but a random rule for assigning individuals to its levels has not been used. There are two advantages of this design over the static-group comparison design. First, because the pretest measurement is taken before exposure to the independent variable, and because the posttest measurement is taken afterward, the temporal precedence of the independent variable to the dependent variable can be firmly established. Unlike the static-group comparison design, then, the longitudinal nature of this design helps us argue that the independent variable is responsible for variation in the dependent variable, rather than the other way around.

The other advantage of this design is that we measure (rather than randomize away) preexisting differences between groups on the dependent variable, which can help us argue against the selection threat to internal validity. Data analysis of the model involves a different statistical technique compared with the one used for static-group comparisons. Rather than ANOVA, this method uses analysis of covariance (ANCOVA), with the pretest score providing the covariate. Some researchers may suggest using raw change scores, but the adjusted change scores provided by ANCOVA are generally preferable (e.g., Judd et al., 2009). Some psychophysiology studies have used percentage changes as dependent variables. And still other researchers might use time as a second factor in a two-factor ANOVA, which yields results that are equivalent to a change score analysis. Our preference, however, is still ANCOVA or, more generally, a multiple regression analysis that includes both continuous and categorical (contrast-coded) predictors.

Consider the hypothetical results in Figure 11.2, comparing consumption of electricity in two groups – individuals who installed solar panels after the pretest and individuals who did not. In spite of nonrandom assignment, the results are fairly interpretable, thanks to the added pretest. It is quite likely, as Figure 11.2 shows, that

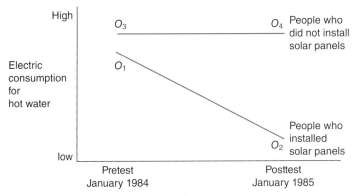

Figure 11.2   Effects of Solar Heating Panels on Electric Use.

people who install solar panels use energy more sparingly than other people to begin with. Their interest in solar energy is a further expression of their preexisting inclinations. Therefore, if we had only the posttest information, we would not know whether the difference reflected the natural conservation tendencies of the people who installed solar panels or whether it reflected the savings produced by the panels. When we look at the pretest differences, we see that those who installed the panels were conservers to begin with. They used less electricity even before they installed the panels. This difference became even larger after the treatment, however, which suggests that the solar installations had an effect.

Are there any alternative explanations? We might suspect that the people who became interested in solar energy would naturally have decreased their electricity consumption even if they had not installed the panels; because they were conscious of the need to conserve energy, they might have naturally used less hot water at the time of the posttest than at the time of the pretest. This design does not provide the information necessary to rule out this possibility – a *selection by maturation* threat to internal validity. Only if we had a longitudinal series of observations, including many observations taken before the solar panels were installed and many taken after, could we see whether the treated group was on a natural downward trend both before and after the solar panel installation.

This example illustrates how we must consider not only the design but also the content of a study and the pattern of results when ruling out alternative explanations. For some topics we might not consider it plausible that the treated group would have changed as it did to become increasingly different from the control group without the implementation of the treatment.

For some patterns of results, the most plausible explanation is that the treatment produced the effects. Imagine an energy conservation program imposed on people who live in states that use the most air-conditioning. Suppose the imposed conservation program consisted of higher electric rates for people in the high-consumption states. To study the effects of this program we could compare the electricity consumption by people in those states with consumption by people in neighboring states who had not consumed as much electricity for air-conditioning. We know that the

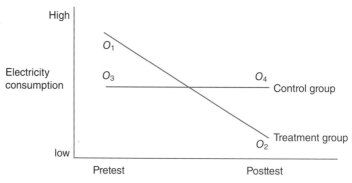

Figure 11.3   Electricity Consumption Levels by People Living in Treatment and Control States.

treatment group initially consumed more electricity than those in the comparison states, so their pretest levels would look like O_1 and O_3 in Figure 11.3. If the posttest showed that the treatment group reduced their consumption below the level of the control group, the most plausible explanation is that the program worked. A crossover pattern such as the one in Figure 11.3 is more difficult to explain with any of the alternative explanations, such as a selection by maturation threat. In this example, the constant trend of the control group can be considered the normal trend; the downward trend of the treatment group can be reasonably attributed to the treatment. To explain away the apparent treatment effect by calling it differential maturation (or differential development of energy consciousness), we probably would have to regard the people in the formerly high-electric-consumption states as an extraordinary group of late-blooming conservationists, who not only met but also surpassed the conservation levels of the people in the neighboring states. This is so unlikely for this case, and most others, that the crossover pattern shown in Figure 11.3 usually can be interpreted as a treatment effect.

One-Group Pretest–Posttest Design

Both of the designs discussed so far are those in which the independent variable varies between individuals. Thus, comparisons between treatment and control conditions involve comparisons of average scores on the dependent variable between different groups of individuals. The **one-group pretest–posttest design**, also known as a simple panel design in survey research, is based on within-individual treatment comparisons. The design is represented schematically as:

$$\text{Group 1} \quad O_1 \text{———} X \text{———} O_2$$

One group of individuals is observed (O_1), exposed to the treatment, X, then given a posttest (O_2) measurement. The treatment effect is then estimated simply by examining the average difference between O_2 and O_1. Here the analytic method is a one-sample t-test, comparing within-subject pre–post change scores. In other words, if the pretest–posttest difference is significantly different from zero, one could conclude that significant change occurred. Equivalently, one could conduct a t-test for correlated or dependent samples to compare pretest and posttest scores.

Although this design is not threatened by selection, it is subject to the internal validity threats of history, maturation, testing, and instrumentation. To see these threats, consider a design in which we want to evaluate the effects of taking yoga classes on an individual's serenity. We develop a measure of serenity and administer it to individuals both before and after they have taken yoga classes. Suppose we find higher average serenity scores after classes than before. Can we attribute this difference to the practice of yoga? No. The following alternative explanations are threats to this conclusion:

- *History*: Because the posttest observations are made after the pretest, the difference between them could be a result of historical events intervening during the period. For instance, the nation might have ended a war, a new presidential candidate might be talking about Eastern philosophies, or popular culture might be advertising new forms of meditation. Any of these historical events could be responsible for the increase in serenity instead of the yoga classes.
- *Maturation*: During the course of the study, the individuals became older. They might also have become more relaxed, retired from work, or matured in other ways that affected their serenity apart from any effect of the yoga classes.
- *Testing*: If the pretest measurement of serenity sensitized the people we were studying and made them believe that they should relax or slow down, the pretesting alone could have produced higher serenity scores on the posttest. The shorter the time between pretest and posttest, the more plausible are testing effects.
- *Instrumentation*: If we changed our serenity questions or scoring system between the pretest and posttest, these changes in the measuring instrument could account for a difference between pretest and posttest levels of serenity.

As discussed in Chapter 10, these threats to internal validity are all eliminated on average if participants are randomly assigned to different orders of treatment exposure. This can be done only with independent variables whose effects dissipate or wear off over short time periods. Presuming, for instance, that the effect of taking yoga classes on serenity occurs only for one week following the classes, we might measure the serenity of some individuals immediately after yoga classes and then again one week later (first treatment, then control), whereas for other individuals we would measure their serenity prior to classes and then immediately after (first control, then treatment). If we randomly decided which individuals to measure in which sequence, the preceding four threats to internal validity would be eliminated. Employing such a randomized experimental design is simply not feasible in this example because we would not expect such short-lived treatment effects.

Interrupted Time-Series Design

Group 1　O_1——O_2——O_3——O_4——X——O_5——O_6——O_7——O_8

Interrupted time-series designs are an extension of the one-group pretest–posttest design. They extend the design simply by having numerous pretests and posttests, spread out before and after exposure to the treatment. These designs are great if data can be readily collected, but if data collection is complex, having to collect data multiple times may make such a design impractical. For example, if data on students were collected, and each wave of data collection took 30 minutes, the loss of several hours of class time likely would not be allowed by the school. Nevertheless, this extension of the design sometimes enables the researcher to argue against the internal validity threats of maturation, testing, and history. Thus, this design is substantially stronger, from the point of view of internal validity, than the simple one-group pretest–posttest design. Traditionally, this design has been analyzed by time-series analysis, but it also could be analyzed through regression discontinuity analysis.

Consider the maturation threat. Suppose we find a marked difference between O_4 and O_5 and wonder whether the difference is truly a result of the treatment (X) or of maturation; we can inspect all the intervals before and after that point to look for maturation trends. Presumably, if maturation were occurring, it would show up as a long-term trend, producing similar differences between O_1 and O_2, between O_2 and O_3, and so on, along the entire series. If none of the other intervals shows such a trend and the only difference lies between O_4 and O_5, maturation is not a very plausible explanation, unless, of course, we are studying some phenomenon that happens to coincide with a particular maturational change such as puberty and that could also plausibly be affected by puberty. Only under such a special set of circumstances and coincidences would maturation pose a threat to the validity of a time-series study.

The same reasoning applies to testing as an alternative explanation. If we suspected that the difference between O_4 and O_5 resulted not from the treatment but from the sensitizing effects of the pretest (O_4), we could examine all the preceding and succeeding intervals to see whether the repeated testing produced similar differences along the entire series. If there were no differences at any other points, it would be highly implausible that the testing at O_4 alone would have created an effect at O_5.

Eliminating history as a threat to internal validity is a little more difficult because historical events that affect observations can have precipitous effects similar to exposure to the treatment (i.e., between O_4 and O_5). In such cases, the history threat is insurmountable. Many historical events, however, unfold slowly, with slowly accumulating effects rather than precipitous ones. These can be effectively argued against using an interrupted time-series design.

Sometimes the X occurs only once, and its effect is presumed to persist forever or for some specified time. A measles inoculation should last forever; a flu shot might have a limited period of effectiveness. Sometimes the X signals a permanent change in the situation – as when a state changes its laws to permit same-sex marriage or when the federal government introduces new air pollution standards. In cases like these, when the treatment occurs not only at a single time but also continues in force at following time periods, the time series may be more appropriately diagrammed as follows:

Group 1 $O_1 — O_2 — O_3 — O_4 — X — O_5 — X — O_6 — X — O_7 — X — O_8$

In either case, with a one-shot treatment or a continuing treatment, the virtue of time-series designs is that we can examine the trends in the data before the treatment, at the time of intervention, and after the treatment. This allows us to assess the plausibility of maturation, testing, and history as alternative explanations.

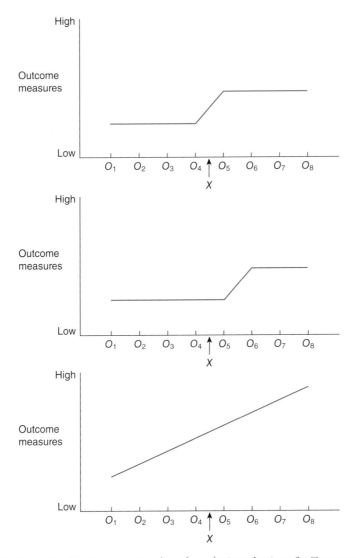

Figure 11.4   Some Possible Outcomes Resulting from the Introduction of a Treatment (*X*) into a Time Series of Measurements.

How easily we can interpret a time series and rule out alternative explanations depends not on the formal features of the design alone but also on the pattern of results. Some results are relatively easy to interpret – we can rule out most of the threats to validity and conclude that the treatment caused the effect. Other patterns are more vulnerable to alternative explanations. For instance, in Figure 11.4 three hypothetical patterns of results are plotted for an interrupted time-series design. The graph at the top of the figure probably shows an effect of the treatment, the results shown in the graph in the center of the figure are ambiguous, and the pattern illustrated in the bottom graph shows no effect of the treatment.

With results like those shown in the graph at the top of Figure 11.4, many alternative explanations can be eliminated. It appears that the treatment caused the shift in scores from the pretest level to the posttest level. There are no maturational trends in either the pretest (O_1 to O_4) or posttest (O_5 to O_8) observations, so maturation is not a persuasive alternative explanation. The most problematic and plausible threat is history – some event that coincided with the treatment. How plausible it is depends on the problem under study. If we were studying the effects of a foreign relations film on American students' attitudes toward people of other countries, and if the showing of the film coincided with international agreements about sharing the world's energy resources or with an international incident in which Americans were suddenly held hostage by another country, these historical events would be plausible alternative explanations. If there are no obvious external events that coincide with the treatment and could have produced the same effects, history presents no problem.

With results like those depicted in the center of Figure 11.4, it is not clear that the treatment caused the shift upward because the shift does not coincide with the treatment; it lags behind by one time interval. In some cases, there would be reason to expect such a lag and, therefore, to attribute the effect to the treatment. For instance, a rise in the world's petroleum export prices might not be felt immediately in domestic gas prices at the pumps because of an oil reserve that was bought at lower prices. Therefore, if we were studying the effects of world export oil price increases on American carpooling, the effect is likely to lag some months behind the cause. If, for instance, there was a 6-month lag in the effect, and the time-series observations were made at 3-month intervals, the effect would appear not in the first observation following treatment but in the second, and the pattern in the graph would be a convincing demonstration of the effect of the price increase on carpooling. If there is no such plausible mechanism and therefore no plausible lag for the cause to have its effect, the graph is more difficult to interpret, and other alternative explanations might be plausible. These alternative explanations would probably fall under the heading of history – other events that occurred after the treatment and produced the effect.

The pattern shown in the graph at the bottom of Figure 11.4 is the clearest case of no effect. The higher levels of O after the treatment merely reflect the prevailing trend that also produced increasingly higher levels of O before the treatment. This graph also shows most clearly why the time-series design is far superior to the one-group pretest–posttest design. If the pattern seen in the bottommost graph in Figure 11.4 were studied with only one pretest and one posttest (points O_4 and O_5), we would be tempted to conclude that the treatment had an effect – causing O_5 to be higher than O_4. Without the other data points, it would be impossible to distinguish between a real effect and the prevailing trend that we see in the graph.

By the addition of a series of pretest and posttest observations, the time-series design is much more interpretable than the one-group pretest–posttest design. Even though it lacks random assignment, it is a useful quasi-experimental design because the additional observations allow the investigator to test the plausibility of several alternative explanations. The chief threat to internal validity with this design is history, although on occasion this too can be eliminated as a threat. Another potential concern for all studies that require repeated measurement of participants is loss of participants over time, sample attrition or mortality. And, as suggested in Chapter 10, mortality is particularly challenging if it differs across conditions.

Replicated Interrupted Time-Series Design

The interrupted time-series design has several variations. In these variations there is more than one group of participants who are exposed to the treatment at different times or who are not exposed to the treatment at all. Thus, the **replicated interrupted time-series design** subsumes the following designs:

Design 1

Group 1 O_1——O_2——O_3——O_4—— X——O_5——O_6——O_7——O_8

Group 2 O_9——O_{10}——O_{11}——O_{12}——————O_{13}——O_{14}——O_{15}——O_{16}

Design 2

Group 1 O_1——O_2——O_3——O_4—— X——O_5——O_6——O_7——O_8

Group 2 O_9——O_{10}——O_{11}——O_{12}——O_{13}—— X——O_{14}——O_{15}——O_{16}

In the first design, we have two groups of participants, the first of which is exposed to the treatment following O_4, whereas the second is never exposed to it. In the second design, both groups are exposed to the treatment although at different times. The Palmgreen et al. (2001) antimarijuana PSA study we described earlier was of this design. It is important to remember that participants have not been randomly assigned to groups in these designs.

Although these are not randomized experimental designs, they are quite strong from the point of view of internal validity. As in the one-group interrupted time-series designs, threats of maturation, instrumentation, and testing can usually be eliminated as alternative explanations for treatment effects. In addition, the replication of the design with more than a single group permits most alternative explanations associated with history to be eliminated. If the treatment coincided with some historical event in one of the groups and if the various groups were presumably exposed to the same historical conditions, the effects of that historical incident should appear in both groups as a difference at the same time, so between-group differences could not be accounted for by history. In addition, in the first group it might be coincident with the treatment, but in the second it would not be.

Note that part of the strength of these replicated interrupted time-series designs comes from the fact that comparisons between treatment and control conditions can be made both within the same participants over time and between different groups of participants at the same time. Consider the first design shown above. There are numerous pairs of observations that can be used to estimate a treatment effect. Looking only within participants, we can treat the design as a single-group interrupted time-series design and estimate the treatment effect by comparing O_4 and O_5. If this difference is large and if the differences between adjacent pretests or adjacent posttests are relatively small (e.g., the topmost graph in Figure 11.4), we have evidence within participants of a treatment effect. Because this estimate of a treatment effect is within participants, a selection threat is eliminated.

To eliminate history, maturation, testing, and instrumentation threats, we would also like to estimate the treatment effect by examining the difference between treated and untreated participants at the same time. Thus, we can estimate the treatment effect between participants by comparing O_5 and O_{13}, O_6 and O_{14}, O_7 and O_{15}, and O_8 and O_{16}. Because each of these between-participant comparisons involves information gathered at the same time, presumably threats due to maturation and history can be eliminated. Of course, because participants have not been randomly assigned to groups, it could be that the two groups of participants are differentially sensitive to historical events that might intrude and cause changes in the posttest measures. In other words, in the absence of random assignment, we cannot eliminate all threats to internal validity. Nevertheless, this sort of replicated time-series design, because it permits both within- and between-participant treatment comparisons, is a very strong design.

Note that this design is the one used in the Panel Study of Income Dynamics described earlier. Longitudinal panel surveys permit comparisons both within individuals over time and between individuals at the same time. Such survey designs are particularly informative about the development of social behavior, particularly when the researcher is unable to control assignment to levels of the independent variable. Thus, in the Panel Study of Income Dynamics, we might well be interested in understanding the effects of unemployment, but we surely are not going to manipulate it experimentally. By observing numerous individuals over time, some of whom become unemployed during the course of the panel study, we have in essence a replicated time-series design that permits relatively strong inferences about the effects of employment status.

Single Case/Single Subject Designs

A variant of time-series designs is a **single subject or single case design** (e.g., Horner, Carr, Halle, Odom, & Wolery, 2005; Kratochwill & Levin, 1992, 2010). Performance before an intervention is compared with performance during and after the intervention. A couple differences from some time-series designs are, first, that the intervention can last more than one time period and, second, that performance during the baseline ideally stabilizes or displays consistency of pattern before entering the intervention stage. The approach involves multiple observations taken during the baseline and intervention stages. Horner et al. (2005) suggest that there be three cycles of baseline and intervention or that the intervention be replicated across individuals. Fidelity of the intervention is a critical aspect of the design.

Proponents of single case designs argue that the methods provide much greater rigor than do case studies. Internal validity is strengthened through replication, and, more recently, through randomization (Kratochwill & Levin, 2010). Replication can refer to either multiple intervention periods with a single participant or replication of the intervention with multiple single case participants. Although early designs may have had only a single baseline period and single intervention period (called an A-B design where A is a baseline period and B is an intervention period), current recommendations are for multiple baseline and intervention periods to gather more information about both the nature of the intervention (e.g., A-B-A-B design) and to see if the non-treatment baseline changes after interventions. For some instances, like learning tasks, the baseline might be expected to change after an intervention, while for others such as self-injurious behaviors, the suppression of behavior might in some instances be expected to immediately cease.

Over the past 20 years, the single case design approach has become increasingly popular, particularly in operant psychology and in education. Although the name suggests that each study has only a single participant, as noted above variants of the design have multiple participants, with each acting as her or his own control and generalizability information coming from comparing cross-participant consistency of results. Arguments could be made for placing some variants of single case designs in the experimental research chapter, but we have chosen to locate it here, for it shares much with time-series designs.

Key elements of a single case design as described by Horner et al. (2005) are:

- the level of analysis is the individual (or individual group, setting, etc.);
- a detailed description needs to be provided of the individual participants, the setting in which they are performing, and the criteria used to select them;
- the dependent variables must be clearly defined and measured with reliability and validity, including providing valid and consistent assessment and a replicable assessment process;
- the dependent variables must be measured repeatedly within and across conditions; the design is intended to document causal or functional relationships;
- recording of the dependent variable is monitored for consistency throughout the process and reliability assessed;
- dependent variables are selected for their practical significance;
- independent variables are interventions that are carefully described so that they can be replicated by others; and
- fidelity of the intervention is documented.

Participants are measured repeatedly until a stable baseline is established. Ideally, trends in the baseline will not already be producing a pattern of effects sought for the intervention. When there is only a single participant, the design involves implementing the intervention multiple times to determine whether changes in behavior correspond to changes in the treatment. For example, the A-B-A-B or reversal design involves gathering baseline data during the first phase (A), implementing the treatment while continuing to record the behavior (B), withdrawing the treatment again while continuing to record the behavior (i.e., a return to baseline A), and, finally, implementing the treatment again while continuing to record the behavior (B). If the treatment has an effect, one would expect to see changes in behavior that correspond to the implementation (better behavior) and withdrawal (worse behavior) of the treatment. An A-B-A-B design is viewed as the minimum high-quality single case design.

Unlike time-series analysis, interpretation may not involve formal quantitative analysis, but visual analysis, which is based on three elements: *level*, *trend*, and *variability*. Level is the mean, trend the slope, and variability the extent to which the data fluctuate about the mean and slope. Visual analysis also examines how quickly the changes occurred (immediacy), amount of overlap of adjacent time periods, magnitude of changes, and consistency of the differences across conditions. Conditions are established for the different elements that document the effectiveness of the intervention. Not surprisingly, adding multiple participants, locations/settings, dependent measures (e.g., behaviors), and stimulus materials increases the external validity of the results.

An alternative approach to the single case design for behaviors where withdrawal of a treatment would likely lead to re-emergence of negative behaviors might be alternating two different interventions. Rather than a baseline, conditions alternate between competing interventions. They could follow a baseline period, but that is not necessary. Such a design could be strengthened further if their implementation were to be randomized (Kratochwill & Levin, 2010). Further, although cases are often thought of as individuals, they can be groups, classrooms, or even community centers or clinics, businesses, social service agencies, or schools. The level of the case should match the level of the intervention. A rich description of the features of the case should be part of a single case design, regardless of how a case is defined.

The single case design is intended to provide a detailed and sensitive analysis across systematic introduction of specific interventions or changes in approaches into a particular setting. By following particular participants across time, one can compare the magnitudes of different intervention effects, impacts of combining interventions, and impacts of changing things like "dosage" of a treatment. By adding participants, generalizability of the intervention can be increased (think replication). Readers thinking about when single case research is most appropriate likely have thought about settings like clinical ones, either for medical or psychological services, and educational settings addressing needs of exceptional learners of all types. With only a single participant, the design is most appropriately kept in this chapter, for it shares concerns in common with interrupted time-series research.

Regression Effects: Challenges of Matching in Quasi-Experimentation

Researchers often are tempted to use a **matching** strategy in many nonrandomized research designs. Suppose we have a treatment and a control condition and we plan on using a pretest–posttest nonequivalent group design. We are not able to assign individual participants randomly to the treatment and control groups, but we intend to gather pretest data. We might consider the possibility of trying to eliminate preexisting group differences by matching the otherwise nonequivalent groups on their pretest scores. Although this might sound logical, there are substantial dangers in trying to match groups unless people can subsequently be randomly assigned from the matched pairs to a treatment and control group. The problem with matching is that even if researchers believe they have matched perfectly on a pretest, the preexisting group differences are likely to reappear on the posttest and make it impossible to determine whether the differences observed after the treatment are the result of the treatment or are the re-emergence of preexisting difference.

To show how this can happen, we introduce another threat to internal validity: regression toward the mean. **Regression toward the mean**, also called statistical regression, regression effects, or regression artifacts (e.g., Campbell, 1969), refers to the phenomenon that extreme scores are not likely to be as extreme on a second testing. Regression toward the mean appears whenever two sets of scores are not perfectly correlated, that is, when individuals' scores on one variable cannot be perfectly predicted from their scores on the other. Two sets of scores are never perfectly correlated if there is any measurement error in either variable, and, unfortunately, there is almost always error in measurement (recall Chapter 7). In this case, measurement error can be random error or even inaccuracy in measuring a theoretical variable of interest. Therefore, in practice, it is safe to assume that if individuals from groups with different means are matched, there always will be regression toward the mean.

Let us imagine giving a midterm and a final exam to a group of 58 students. The midterm we shall call our pretest and the final our posttest. In general, students who score in the upper half of the class on the pretest also score in the upper half on the posttest, and the students who score in the lower half on the pretest score there again on the posttest, although there is some shifting of scores from the first to the second test. The correlation is not perfect. This means that the students who received the highest pretest scores do not all receive the highest posttest scores, and those who received the lowest pretest scores do not all receive the lowest posttest scores. Figure 11.5 shows what scores these students received on the pretest and posttest. Of the four students who scored 100 on the pretest, only one received 100 again on the posttest. The other three students obtained scores of 90, 80, and 70. Therefore, the average posttest score of those students is closer to the mean than their pretest scores were. A similar movement toward the mean appears for the students who received the lowest pretest scores. They all received 40 on the pretest, but on the posttest their scores ranged from 40 to 70. At both extremes of the pretest, we find that the group's average posttest scores are closer to the mean. This is what we mean by regression toward the mean.

Regression toward the mean occurs whenever there is an imperfect correlation. To see this, compare Figure 11.5, which shows two measures that are imperfectly correlated, with Figure 11.6, which shows two measures that are perfectly correlated. There is no regression toward the mean in Figure 11.6 because everyone who received the highest score on the pretest also received the highest score on the posttest, and everyone with the lowest pretest score has the lowest posttest score. We never see perfect correlations such as this in reality because all our measurements contain a random error component – which means that observed scores are not perfectly reliable and will show fluctuations from one testing session to the next. Such fluctuations reduce the correlation, and the lower the correlation the more we find regression toward the mean as it appears in Figure 11.5.

The fact that extreme scores regress toward the mean does not imply that students become more homogeneous over the course of a semester. If we work backward and

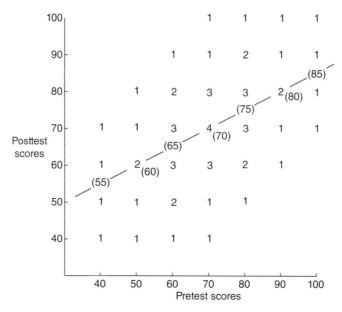

Figure 11.5   Scatterplot Showing Regression Toward the Posttest Mean from Pretest Scores.
Note. The numbers inside the graph (1, 2, 3, and 4) indicate how many students received each score on the two tests. The dashed line represents the average posttest score for each group of students who received a particular pretest score. The figures in parentheses are those averages. Turning the figure on its side shows the average pretest score for each group of students who received a particular posttest score. The regression toward the mean operates in both cases.

begin with final exam scores, we find the same regression effect of final exams on midterm scores. The students who received the highest scores on the final exam would not all receive identical midterm scores, and those who received the lowest scores on the final would not all receive the lowest scores on the midterm. If we turn Figure 11.5 on its side, we can see that the same regression toward the mean occurs when we look first at posttest scores and second at pretest scores.

Regression toward the mean occurs, therefore, not as a result of a homogenization process but as a result of scores being less than 100% reliable. Any change of the most extreme scores is of necessity a regression toward the mean. To see how regression toward the mean is a threat to internal validity when a matching strategy is used, consider a real example from public schools. A couple principals who were trying to make sense of their students' test score *changes* realized that the group of students who scored well above average at the beginning of the school year had change (gain) scores that were lower than those of students who scored well below average at the beginning of the school year. They worried that their educational programs were not as successful for their highest-scoring students as they were for their lowest-scoring students, and thought that they should redirect effort to provide more help for their above-average students.

Before we could tell if they were correct in their judgments, we needed to adjust the change scores for regression effects. The nice feature of the particular problem is

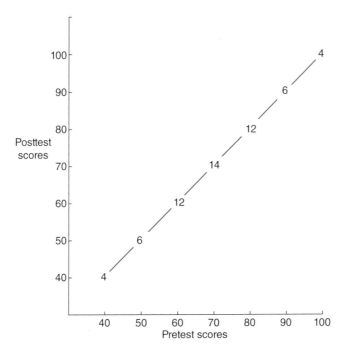

Figure 11.6 Scatterplot Showing No Regression Toward the Mean When There Is a Perfect Correlation Between Pretest and Posttest Scores.

Note. The numbers along the dashed line indicate how many students received each score on the two tests. The dashed line with all scores falling exactly on the line has no "scatter" of points around it. Therefore, there is no regression toward the mean. The posttest score is the same as the pretest score for each group of people.

that because scores were available for all students, the population means and standard deviations could be calculated, as could the reliability of the tests. The magnitude of regression effects is inversely related to reliability, with no regression for tests with perfect reliability and large effects for tests with low reliability. The formula for the size of a regression effect for a particular group is:

$$\text{Expected Change} = [1 - \text{reliability}] \times [\text{population mean} - \text{group mean}]$$

That means, for example, that even with a test with a reliability of .9, a group one standard deviation below the population mean would move 1/10th of the way back to the mean on a subsequent testing. A group two standard deviations below would move back 2/10th of a standard deviation. The average change score for those groups would be artificially increased by regression effects. In contrast, students starting above the mean would move back toward the mean, and have their change scores decreased by regression. In the example above, when we adjusted the change scores to take into account regression effects, students scoring above the mean actually showed greater gains than students scoring below it. In effect, when educational programs are evaluated, regression effects can obscure what actually is happening.

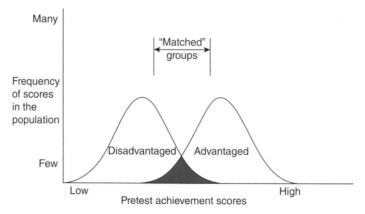

Figure 11.7   Hypothetical Distributions of Pretest Achievement Levels of Two Populations, One Considered Disadvantaged and One Advantaged.
Note. The darker region represents the "matched" groups from the two populations.

If we have a nonequivalent control group design where children are not randomly assigned to the treatment and control groups but are selected on the basis of some qualifications, we cannot assume that the children in the two groups come from the same population. In fact, the more reasonable assumption is that they come from two different populations or social groups, those who qualify and those who do not. In the case of compensatory education programs, those who qualify must usually demonstrate a disadvantage, such as having a low income. The children who qualify for the program come from a group considered disadvantaged; the comparison children do not. These two groups obviously differ in family income levels and in other ways related to income. They also likely differ in their average pretest achievement levels. As a result, even though students from two groups may be matched on their test scores, they will differ on other variables. In the process of matching, a researcher sets the conditions for regression artifacts to operate. Figure 11.7 shows the distributions of pretest scores for two hypothetical groups – one an advantaged comparison, the other a disadvantaged treatment group. The distributions overlap, but they have different means or averages. In an attempt to match individuals from the two groups, the researcher draws from opposite ends of each group – from the upper end of the disadvantaged group and the lower end of the advantaged group. The darker region of Figure 11.7 shows the matched portion of each group.

These two "matched" groups represent extreme scorers from their respective populations. Because the pretest scores are not 100% reliable, we know that the posttest scores of these children will not be equally extreme – they will regress in opposite directions, toward their population means. The advantaged group's posttest scores will be higher, for they represent the bottom end of their population; the disadvantaged group's posttest scores will be lower, for they represent the upper end of their population. Thus, regression artifacts alone can create a difference on the posttest, even if no compensatory program had actually been implemented. Unfortunately for researchers trying to show benefits of compensatory programs, regression effects can make a program look detrimental if the treatment and comparison groups are selected in such a way that they represent opposite ends of two preexisting groups. The same regression artifacts also can make a program look mistakenly beneficial if the treatment is given to the advantaged group and a presumably matched comparison group is drawn from a disadvantaged group.

Matching, therefore, is inadequate for removing preexisting group differences. Unless we randomly assign individuals from a common pool to treatment and control groups, it is always likely that the two groups represent different populations with different means. Attempts to match on either pretest scores or other variables are destined to be imperfect, and regression toward the mean is a potential explanation for subsequent differences. In a later section of this chapter, we describe a technique called propensity score matching, which uses an array of background and other variables to create a new score on which individuals from two different groups can be matched. The goal is to create a score that represents the individual's true score; by eliminating unreliability, regression effects should be eliminated. A successful matching approach produces matching comparable to that from random assignment to conditions.

Regression Discontinuity Analysis

Regression discontinuity analysis (RDA) is an analytic approach most often used when groups are assigned to conditions on the basis of a cut score. The idea is that the intervention changes the relationship between the pretest and the posttest for the treated group relative to a comparison group, and that a regression approach will expose that difference. The most common view of RDA is that a meaningful difference between conditions would result in a change in the intercept of the regression line (where the regression line meets the vertical axis). The logic can be used more widely, for example, to document shifts in the level of a regression line due to an intervention where there are multiple time points before and after a treatment, or to show that the relationship between two variables (the slope of the regression line) changes at some threshold due to a treatment or even due to increased or diminished capacity of individuals at particular levels to benefit or not.

The logic was articulated by Donald Campbell and colleagues (e.g., Campbell, 1969) in the context of an interrupted time-series design. In the analysis, Campbell argued for the importance of a comparison group, which led him to the two group pre–post design. Campbell used as an example a comparison of students receiving graduate fellowships with peers who did not receive them. Clearly, fellowships are not given randomly, although it may in some cases seem so to non-recipients given the complex and non-transparent approaches that sometimes are used. So the two groups are not equivalent.

All RDA approaches start by looking at a bivariate plot of pre- and posttest scores, carefully examining the pattern and spread of scores at different points along the distribution. The posttest is regressed on the pretest separately for the recipient and non-recipient groups, and the regression lines compared via an additional regression equation that includes recipient versus non-recipient group (contrast-coded), pretest (centered), and the pretest (centered) × group (contrast-coded) interactions as predictors. The latter regression equation tests whether the intercepts and the slopes in the two separate regression equations differ from each other (see Judd et al., 2009). An alternative comparison of the two regressions is provided by a Chow test, which adds to the two regressions a third regression with the full sample, and then compares differences in residuals when the two groups are analyzed together and separately (e.g., Lee, 2008). A common use of RDA occurs in a situation like the fellowship illustration above, where students above a certain level (threshold) receive awards and those below that level do not. Because the two groups do not overlap on the predictor variable, the two regressions could be placed together on a single diagram to see how their intercepts and slopes compare.

Although Campbell (1969) argued that a change in slope without a change in the intercept is not by itself evidence of effect, other more recent discussions of RDA include instances where the prediction is that an inflection or change in slope will occur at a threshold. So a meaningful RDA also could be manifested as a change in the slope of a regression line at a certain point (e.g., at a point of inflection). Regression discontinuity is commonly viewed as a shift in the intercept of the regression line; thus, the discontinuity in the regression line where the treatment either increases or decreases the intercept while leaving the slope unchanged.

RDA has several potential weaknesses. First, it assumes that relations between the pretest and posttest are linear; curvilinear relations could result in the appearance of an effect even if no effect occurred. Second, if the treatment group is small and/or has a small range of scores on the pretest, prediction may not have enough categories to establish a good regression equation. Third, if the cut points are not distinct, with overlap of groups around the threshold (called in RDA literature a "fuzzy" cut point), selection around the threshold may appear as an effect of the treatment. For example, if within a group at the threshold other measures of the selection criteria were available, and the most able people were selected, the higher-scoring people on the posttest (another measure of ability) would be in the selected group and the lower-scoring in the not selected group. So the two regression lines would appear to diverge in the area of the threshold. Finally, a larger sample size is needed compared to a study that uses random assignment to conditions (e.g., Shadish et al., 2002).

Propensity Score Matching

As noted earlier in this chapter, **propensity score matching** (PSM) is an approach that uses information in addition to pretest scores to create groups that are comparable when random assignment is not possible. Although this method has been employed widely in medical research, only recently has it become more widely used in the social sciences (e.g., Fan & Nowell, 2011). In principle, if a good set of propensity matching variables (covariates) is available, individuals with the same propensity score should be well matched, for their true scores should be comparable (unlike their observed scores, which contain error and are susceptible to effects like regression to their respective means). Using the language of PSM, a propensity score is the probability of exposure to a specific treatment conditional on observed variables (e.g., Austin,

Grootendorst, & Anderson, 2007). Regardless of whether individual participants are in a treatment or comparison condition, if their propensity scores are identical, they should have had the same probability of being in the treatment condition. Participants in the different conditions having identical likelihoods of being in the treatment condition is the cornerstone of random assignment; individuals matched by propensity score matching should approximate random assignment. We use "approximate" here because the effectiveness of the matching is dependent on the particular set of covariates selected (conditioned on the covariates). Propensity scores are a single numerical value calculated from the covariates. They are used to match participants enrolled in a program (or treatment) to similar individuals about whom the researchers have data but who did not participate in the program. By using statistical matching on key background and performance characteristics, bias due to all covariates is removed, allowing stronger inferences to be drawn from group comparisons (e.g., Rosenbaum & Rubin, 1983).

One thing that should be clear from the preceding discussion is that the set of covariates is critical. Not surprisingly, there are different views about how the set should be selected (e.g., Austin et al., 2007). One view is to include those variables that are related to treatment assignment. A second is to include all variables potentially related to the outcome variable. And a third approach is to include only variables that are associated with both treatment and outcome. Based on findings from a Monte Carlo study, Austin et al. (2007) suggest that the most effective approaches are those that include as covariates variables that are confounded with (or are related to) treatment assignment as well as variables that are related to the outcome variable.

An important challenge to propensity score matching that is true of any approach that tries to substitute for random assignment by matching on an array of background and other variables to make the two groups equivalent is that it may fail to eliminate preexisting group differences. In general, matching on variables known to be associated with the dependent variable errs in the direction of undermatching, and, therefore, may fail because we can never know when we have matched on enough variables to ensure that the two groups are equivalent. For instance, Head Start evaluators might match the treatment children with a comparison group on the basis of age, sex, race, kindergarten attendance, and parents' social status. Yet the children might still differ in the kinds of television programs they watch, in their grandparents' education levels, in the number of books in their homes, in the achievement levels of their friends, and so on. The numbers of variables on which they were not matched is infinite. As compensatory social programs are usually designed for populations that are defined as disadvantaged, the children from the treatment group had fewer natural "head starts" than the comparison group on many other variables. Because they were not matched on variables like grandparents' education, kinds of television programs watched, and many other variables, the treatment group probably would have scored lower on these unmatched variables, with an advantage probably going to the control group. Therefore, matching on variables known to be associated with the dependent variable is likely inadequate because it is incomplete. In studies of compensatory social programs, the resulting **undermatching** has usually favored the control group and has made the program look harmful or ineffective solely as a result of the failure to equate groups. Fortunately for PSM, there is some evidence (e.g., Rosenbaum &

Rubin, 1983) that PSM can control for bias from covariates. Whether that is true for all settings is not clear; researchers should plan carefully the covariates that are to be in the design.

Summary

Nonrandomized designs are the methods of choice either when establishing causality is not a primary concern in the research or when we cannot randomly assign participants to levels of manipulated independent variables of interest. In the former case, we might simply be interested in documenting the distribution of some variable of interest in some population. We also might be interested in establishing whether two variables are associated, regardless of whether that association is causal. For these sorts of goals, nonrandomized designs are perfectly suitable. Indeed, they might be more appropriate than randomized experimental designs because random sampling and other procedures to ensure external and construct validity sometimes are more easily accomplished in nonrandomized designs.

In other cases, we might wish to infer causality about the effects of an independent variable on a dependent variable, but we might not be able to manipulate the independent variable and randomly assign individuals to its level. In these cases, we use a quasi-experimental design and attempt to rule out threats to internal validity. Quasi-experimental designs are subject to a variety of threats to internal validity, such as selection, history, maturation, testing, and regression to the mean. Alternative designs differ in their susceptibility to each one of these threats, with perhaps the strongest design, from the point of view of internal validity, being a replicated interrupted time-series design.

Although we might get discouraged by the threats to internal validity that characterize these research designs, we must remember that the designs are nevertheless very useful tools. Research does not begin and end with randomized designs. For many purposes, nonrandomized designs are tools of choice rather than simply less desirable alternatives, particularly as newer approaches like propensity score matching and regression discontinuity analysis become more widely used and their advantages and limitations for different settings are identified.

Go online   Visit the book's companion website for this chapter's test bank and other resources at: www.wiley.com/go/maruyama

---

Key Concepts

Alternative explanation

Cross-sectional comparison

Interrupted time-series design

Longitudinal design

Matching

Nonrandomized research design

One-group pretest–posttest design
Panel design
Pretest–posttest nonequivalent control
   group design
Propensity score matching
Quasi-experimental designs
Regression discontinuity analysis
Regression to the mean, regression
   effects

Replicated interrupted time-series
   design
Selection
Single subject/single case design
Static-group comparison design
Survey research
Temporal ordering
Undermatching

On the Web

http://www.isr.umich.edu/src/psid/index.html The website for the Panel Study of Income Dynamics.

http://www.socialresearchmethods.net/kb/quasnegd.php Detailed discussion of the pretest–posttest nonequivalent control group design, emphasizing the threats to causal inference entailed in the design. Part of the Research Methods Knowledge Base web text written by William Trochim.

http://www.socialresearchmethods.net/kb/quasiexp.php Another part of Trochim's Research Methods Knowledge Base, this is a very nicely written description of variations of quasi-experimental designs, including some not described in this chapter.

http://www.fammed.ouhsc.edu/tutor/qexpdes.htm Another site with clear descriptions of various types of quasi-experimental designs, including research examples.

http://www.socialresearchmethods.net/kb/design.php Again on the Research Methods Knowledge Base, this article describes types of experimental and quasi-experimental designs.

Further Reading

Shadish, W. R., Cook, T. D., & Campbell, D. T. (2002). *Experimental and quasi-experimental designs for generalized causal inference*. Boston, MA: Houghton Mifflin.

Trochim, W. M. K. (Ed.). (1986). *Advances in quasi-experimental design and analysis*. San Francisco, CA: Jossey-Bass.

West, S. G., Cham, H., & Liu, Y. (2014). Causal inference and generalization in field settings: Experimental and quasi-experimental designs. In H. T. Reis & C. M. Judd (Eds.), *Handbook of research methods in social and personality psychology* (2nd ed., pp. 49–80). New York, NY: Cambridge University Press.

Single Subject Design Readings

Kazdin, A. E. (1982). *Single-case research designs: Methods for clinical and applied settings*. New York, NY: Oxford University Press.

Kazdin, A. E. (1998). *Research design in clinical psychology* (3rd ed.). Boston, MA: Allyn & Bacon.

Kennedy, C. H. (2004). *Single case designs for educational research*. Boston, MA: Allyn & Bacon.

Kratochwill, T., & Levin, J. R. (1992). *Single-case research design and analysis: New directions for psychology and education*. Hillsdale, NJ: Lawrence Erlbaum Associates.

Chapter 12

Non-Experimental Research

Research Methods in Social Relations, Eighth Edition. Geoffrey Maruyama and Carey S. Ryan.
© 2014 John Wiley & Sons, Inc. Published 2014 by John Wiley & Sons, Inc.
Companion Website: www.wiley.com/go/maruyama

In contrast to experimental and quasi-experimental research, in non-experimental research there usually is no manipulation or intervention that is planned and executed. Although studies where everyone is exposed to the same occurrence or intervention could be viewed as non-experimental because there is no untreated comparison group, such studies are not purely non-experimental, for they can be made into interrupted time-series studies as long as there are data available from before the occurrence of the event. And, in our data-rich world, there typically will be some pre-event data available that could be viewed across time to assess impacts of the event. Consider, for example, a situation where everyone was given a vaccine for a disease. We might think that the intervention could not lead to a quasi-experiment because there was no comparison group. And if everyone got the vaccine, "getting the vaccine" is no longer a variable but a constant, with no variability. But we know what the rates of occurrence of the disease were well before and after the vaccine was developed, so we might have a quasi-experimental design that allows us to examine whether or not the data are consistent with the vaccine having positive effects. Even though we might not be able to completely dismiss alternative explanations for the effects, we can learn a lot, for example, whether there was a change in rates of occurrence of the disease, particularly if we had multiple time points looking backward and forward.

If research like the study just described were the only type of "non-experimental" research, we wouldn't need a separate chapter to describe it. So, while recognizing a fuzzy line between quasi-experimental and non-experimental research, this chapter focuses on research that cannot be made quasi-experimental, including research where the researcher "comes late to the party" and the researchable issue is already ongoing or even completed. In some instances, the approaches described later in this chapter could be used as a way to collect data in an experiment, so they are not exclusively the domain of non-experimental research.

Although in any particular setting there may be many "interventions" going on, in most non-experimental research the researchers would not have a priori designed a study and purposefully collected the precise data needed to examine impacts of the intervention. But even in the absence of controlled experiments, there are great opportunities for non-experimental research to complement experimental and quasi-experimental research, for available data could be used to examine plausibility of different conceptual views or possible impacts of unplanned or unanticipated events. One example of such an event is Hurricane Katrina, which went through New Orleans in August 2005. In the aftermath, an array of research studies was done examining issues including: how race/ethnicity affected how people were treated, why planning failed, how the media covered the event, helping behaviors during the crisis, challenges in following disaster survivors, and why people failed to leave (see the special issue of *Analyses of Social Issues and Public Policy*, Volume 6, Issue 1 (2006)).

Getting away from thinking that one has to design all research studies allows researchers to make use of existing available data in creative ways. Non-experimental research complements other types by its opportunism; whereas an experiment takes careful planning, opportunities to examine plausibility of theoretical predictions and external validity of theories in real-world settings abound. In some instances, a researcher can be involved as a partner and help ensure that adequate measures are available to help assess possible impacts of a treatment or change in practices, but in other instances researchers find out about the change as or after it occurs. As was true for working in field settings, the opportunities are fraught with challenges, and require sleuthing as well as creative thinking and flexibility to maximize opportunities. Sometimes researchers are primarily detectives, sorting through available information and creating their own clues about the what, why, and when of events. Regardless of the specific approach, the rewards can be great, for the non-experimental work extends and informs experimental work. *Complement* is a key idea – science is most productive when multiple approaches address important conceptual and practical problems and evidence about convergence or lack of convergence of findings across approaches shapes theory, practice, public policy, and how future research is planned.

Types of Non-Experimental Research

Non-experimental research is of many types, and can be quantitative, qualitative, or mixed methods, combining both qualitative and quantitative. In this chapter, we focus largely on quantitative non-experimental approaches; the following chapter will cover qualitative research. Nevertheless, the types of non-experimental research described below can be used for both qualitative and quantitative research, although their forms will differ for the different approaches. For example, a questionnaire with all open-ended, narrative responses likely will be analyzed using qualitative methods to take advantage of the richness of the responses, whereas a questionnaire with fixed responses will be analyzed using quantitative methods to take advantage of summarization of the full set of responses.

Each type of non-experimental research described below will be covered in more detail elsewhere, but for now we provide an overview so readers can get a sense of the scope of possibilities for non-experimental research. One prominent type is **survey research**, described in detail in Chapter 14, where researchers use a particular research instrument and ask questions of respondents. Surveys range from as little as a single question to long and elaborate, assessing multiple domains and including branches so that respondents answer different questions depending on a prior response. Surveys provide an array of specific information that helps researchers understand relationships among variables as well as correlates of important outcomes, for example, predicting political outcomes or determining public opinion. Surveys can be administered through questionnaires or through interviewing. A second category is other **questionnaire research**, where instruments like achievement tests are administered to a sample to gather information on particular outcomes. Questionnaires are the approach of choice for inventories about topics like vocational interest or personality types. Third is **observational research**, described later in this chapter, where researchers record the behaviors of research participants, often using a structured template or framework that ensures collection of particular information on a consistent basis. And a fourth type is **archival research**, also described later in this chapter, where existing data are used in research. As was noted above, in today's data-rich world, "data mining" is an important way to extend research and gather useful information. As examples:

- grocery stores not only collect all their sales data, the use of "preferred buyer" identification allows them to create profiles of users and target them with promotions or special deals;
- healthcare providers now have their data stored electronically, allowing them to assess effectiveness of their educational, prevention, and clinical programs;
- Internet usage is tracked by "cookies," which allows advertisers to target users with specific information relevant to their usage patterns and preferences; and
- states are developing longitudinal data bases of educational outcomes of their students from preschool through college, in a federal effort called Statewide Longitudinal Educational Data Systems (SLDS or SLEDS, the latter acronym used in cold places like Minnesota – really!).

In research partnerships, researchers may collect some specific data using one of the approaches described above to enrich existing data. The new data are then linked to existing data already collected by partners in data sets like the ones just mentioned. For example, for educational research on college success, researchers might want information about student attitudes toward college to complement the outcome data already available.

Causal Thinking and Correlational Data

One of the challenges of non-experimental research is staying true to the limitations of the methods. Almost all research is developed with underlying ideas about causal relationships among the variables on which data are collected. And it's not just scientists, for, as noted in Chapter 1, causal thinking and hypothesis formulation and testing is part of our everyday lives. So when we leave the experimental domain where we are testing our ideas about causality and enter the domain of non-experimental research, it is easy to keep aspects of our causal reasoning and interpret correlations as consistent with our causal thinking about what the correlation means, and to use language like "affects," "changes," "determines," or even "causes." Yet the data do not support such an interpretation, instead supporting "is related to," and it is important for researchers to keep the distinction between correlation and cause clear, for too often the distinction is blurred.

Consider, for example, the world of public policy. Laws that are passed are usually driven by causal thinking about their impacts, and in casual usage the language is often language of cause and effect. Speed limits are changed to increase public safety, construction requirements modified to make buildings and roads safer, curfews imposed to decrease negative behaviors among young people, and early childhood programs expanded to increase school achievement. But do they work? Sometimes, but not necessarily, for often relationships are not causal.

For example, in Minnesota a law has been passed requiring all students to take Algebra no later than eighth grade. That law was based upon research showing that students who took Algebra before they started high school were on a track of high academic intensity leading to advanced math in high school beyond Algebra 2. Students taking a math course beyond Algebra 2 in high school had a high probability of graduating from a baccalaureate degree-granting institution of post-secondary education (e.g., Adelman, 2006). The law is a classic illustration of policy makers inferring causality from a correlation. Would they really believe that increasing the level of math courses required for all students would dramatically alter high school graduation rates and college attendance and completion rates? Perhaps some did, but a more pragmatic view would be that legislators wanted to increase academic preparation, and requiring all students to take Algebra in eighth grade was a clear way to do that.

Once the legislation is implemented, all students would be taking Algebra in or before eighth grade, which would make taking of Algebra a constant rather than a variable. So taking of Algebra will no longer correlate with other variables and can't predict later outcomes. If, however, college readiness or graduation rates increased dramatically for the cohort of students required to complete Algebra by eighth grade, one could do a time-series analysis (see Chapter 11) to make a case for its importance. But it would be by eliminating alternative explanations, and still unqualified causal language would not be justified. And, in this particular instance, in contrast to optimistic predictions, thus far requiring Algebra in eighth grade has not appreciably affected high school dropout or graduation rates or college attendance rates. And students not ready for Algebra in eighth grade may find themselves taking "Intermediate" Algebra in ninth grade to get them ready for Algebra 2.

The Algebra example is also a good one because it illustrates challenges in drawing inferences about present times using archival data. In order to have data available, it would have to be generated long enough ago that students who took Algebra in eighth grade had time to complete college. The quickest study possible probably would have a lag of at least 12 years (5 years of high school, 6 more to give most students time to complete college, and a year for data analysis and report writing). So even if the processes were causal when the data were collected, societal shifts (history) could have resulted in a different relationship between taking Algebra and academic outcomes. In the particular research, the data set used was the National Education Longitudinal Study of 1988, measuring students who were in eighth grade in 1988, so the lag was 18 years. And then there is the lag for the research to create an impact. The legislation started affecting students who were in eighth grade more than 20 years later. In fact, the proportion of students who took Algebra in eighth grade changed over time, and a much broader group of students was taking it by the time the policies were put in place, which could markedly change the relationship between taking Algebra and later academic success.

Exercise: Causal thinking and correlational data

One of the challenges of non-experimental research noted above is that because the thinking underlying the work is often causal, there is a tendency to view results consistent with the theorizing as confirming the thinking, when in fact the results simply fail to disconfirm the adequacy of the thinking. Such thinking is widespread in sports and in business. For the former case, when a sports team does well, sportscasters often point to things like locker room climate and team motivation, as if losing teams lack such climate and motivation (and not considering the opposite causal direction, namely, that when teams win motivation is good and climate is good). For the latter case, when the stock market goes up, information consistent with an improving market is pointed to as a reason for the market going up, while when it goes down, information consistent with a struggling market is pointed to, even though most days there is a combination of positive and negative information that could be selected to account for whatever the stock market does.

Think of examples where people think causally and act as if correlational data prove causal thinking. Share them with your small group members, and select one example to present to the class.

Analyzing Non-Experimental Quantitative Data

When doing quantitative analysis of non-experimental data, approaches examine the relations among the different variables. Analyses can range from being very restricted, testing plausibility of hypotheses that are guided by theory, to approaches that are very exploratory. A general linear model approach is most common. Multiple regression approaches are most often used, but the specific technique depends on the nature of the variables. If the dependent variables are continuous, the approach is regression, if dichotomous or categorical, logistic regression, with other variants of regression used in specific circumstances. The work can follow two different approaches.

The first, *prediction*, is one where what is most important is prediction – how much of the variability in some outcome variable (R^2) can be accounted for by the predictors. If the purpose is purely prediction (e.g., which students should we accept into our program, who should we hire?), then the particular variables that predict may be of little importance. Rather, what is important is accuracy of prediction, and the specific coefficients tied to each variable are of secondary importance. So the approach is regression with all predictors included in the regression to generate predicted scores for the applicants.

The second approach, *understanding*, is one that is conceptually driven, and that specifies why each of the predictors is related to a criterion variable. It focuses not only on what predicts the outcome, but also on how strongly and why. It allows researchers to use their conceptual models to define variables as predictor or criterion variables, or perhaps both in different models. And it often examines relations among predictors as more than just correlations in structural models, which specify hypothesized causal ordering among variables and then test plausibility of the hypothesized ordering.

Regardless of the approach, the first step is inspection of the distributions of the variables and the bivariate relationships among them. Although correlations are most often examined because they are in a metric (ranging from -1 to $+1$) that is easy to understand and compare one with another, the non-standardized coefficient (covariance) is the unit of choice, for it expresses relationships in actual score units rather than standardized units. If we wanted to see whether the relation between academic performance and self-concept were the same, for example, for U.S. students and British students, we should not compare their correlations, for those are affected by the variability of the measures in the different populations. The unstandardized relationship is the one to compare.

Once examination of distributions of variables and the relations among pairs of variables is complete, it is time to think about the multivariate nature of the relationships. Because many of the data sets, particularly archival, include multiple dimensions and variables, a multivariate approach that allows examination of relations of multiple predictor variables with some criterion variables is common. The specific analysis depends upon the purpose and conceptual underpinnings of the research, and may be for either prediction or understanding. In some cases, the analyses for understanding may include a system of equations that examines plausibility of a conceptual model. Those analyses are called structural equation modeling approaches, and include path analysis, panel analysis, multistage least squares estimation techniques (e.g., two-stage least squares), confirmatory factor analysis, latent variable structural equation modeling, and multilevel modeling. Detailed description of the techniques is well beyond the scope of this book, but there are many resources available for each of the approaches.

Longitudinal Panel Designs

We already have covered types of longitudinal data analysis in talking about repeated measures analysis and time-series designs. But when the same variables are available at more than one point in time, an additional type of model is created. The design becomes a **panel design** with multiple variables repeated across time (e.g., Pelz & Andrews, 1964; Rozelle & Campbell, 1969; Shingles, 1976). One advantage of panel designs is that plausibility of alternative models of causation (A causes B vs. B causes A) can be examined simultaneously, and a second is that because prior measures of each variable are included, relationships are examined while taking account of stability of variables across time. Stability refers to the amount of change in a variable across time. A third advantage is that challenges in "causally" ordering of variables can be improved by use of time differences; later variables cannot cause earlier variables. Imagine, for example, a simple two-variable, two-wave model with self-concept (X) and achievement (Y). (See Figure 12.1.)

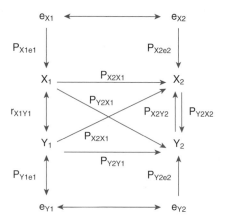

Figure 12.1   "Simple" Panel Model Illustration: Two-Variable, Two-Wave "Full" Panel Model.

Note that in Figure 12.1 there are paths across time from X at time 1 (X_1) to itself at time 2 (X_2) and from Y to itself (Y_1 to Y_2); those paths are referred to as *stabilities*, like measures of test–retest reliability. And there also are paths from X_1 to Y_2 and from Y_1 to X_2. In the model, each variable "causes" the other at a later point in time. If simultaneous "causal" paths are added within time 2 (p_{Y2X2} and p_{X2Y2}), a weakness of a two-variable panel model is that there are more parameters to estimate than there are degrees of freedom, so the model as it appears cannot be uniquely solved. A second challenge is the covariances of the residuals. If the same measure is repeated, there is measure-specific residual covariation that goes across time for any measure. It cannot be separated from the stability of the measures of the variables in Figure 12.1, and typically would be included as part of the stability of those variables. Although there are challenges from longitudinal designs, by adding more measures of the conceptual variables and more conceptual variables as well, all the different sources of variability can be modeled. As we have suggested for other statistical techniques, readers should find sources that go into more detail about structural equation modeling (SEM) techniques to learn about what can be done using SEM approaches, which are covered only briefly in this book (e.g., Maruyama, 1998).

Naturalness in Research

A major advantage of the observational and archival research approaches is that they can embody unobtrusive or nonreactive approaches to research procedures. With these methods, participants either are unaware of being observed (with **unobtrusive observation** or archival data) or are thought to habituate quickly to the presence of visible and open observers. Alternatively, they might be aware of being observed but unaware of the particular behavior they are emitting that is of interest. For example, studies of attraction among individuals might use as an indicator of liking how close the participant sits to the target. Although participants are presumably acutely aware of being observed, they do not realize that interpersonal distance is being measured and, therefore, are unlikely to modify their own behavior in that regard. By using a nonreactive measure, the researcher hopes that participants' responses will not be shaped by such considerations as a desire to impress the researcher or a belief that certain behaviors would support the research hypothesis. The drive for "naturalness" in research thus derives from the belief that participants are more likely to behave in the same way that they would in "real life" if they can be studied in the circumstances in which they are ordinarily found. In contrast, survey and laboratory-based research is more likely to elicit behaviors that are specific to the unnatural research context, such as socially desirable responses and behavior.

Relying on **nonreactive** forms of research to enhance the external validity or generalizability of results leads to a strategy of seeking naturalness in research. Three dimensions of naturalness have been emphasized: the behavior being studied, the setting of the behavior, and the event eliciting the behavior (Tunnell, 1977). Different researchers place different emphasis on these three dimensions, and the three do not always go together. The purest conception of natural research might involve all three dimensions, as was found in a study by Kraut and Johnston (1979): unobtrusive observation of a natural behavior (smiling) as it happened in its natural setting (a bowling alley) as the result of a naturally occurring event (getting a strike).

Natural behaviors are those that are "not established or maintained for the sole or primary purpose of conducting research" (Tunnell, 1977, p. 426). They reflect a concern with naturalness in the dependent variable in research. For example, committing suicide, gazing into one's lover's eyes, or smiling after bowling a strike are natural behaviors because they would have occurred without the researcher's presence. Conversely, questionnaire or interview responses occur only as a result of the researcher's questions and would not be considered natural behaviors. An example of a study of a natural behavior but neither a natural setting nor a natural event is one by Berry and Hansen (2000). Undergraduate women were videotaped while waiting in a psychology laboratory. The tapes were later coded for a wide variety of natural nonverbal behaviors, including gaze while speaking and listening, positive and negative facial expressions, gesture, and body orientation toward partner. Analyses showed that participants who devoted more visual attention to their partners, gestured more often, and oriented their bodies more toward their partners were deemed to have interactions of higher quality.

Natural settings are contexts that are not established for research purposes, such as shopping centers, private homes, racetracks, commercial aircraft, churches, or hospitals. For example, observation in the Kraut and Johnston (1979) study took place in a bowling alley, a natural setting. All forms of field research, by definition, occur in natural settings. At the same time, some settings, like mental health centers or community clinics, may be much more like laboratory settings insofar as research may be a regular part of the setting than are shopping centers or community centers.

Finally, a **natural event** is an incident that is not arranged for research purposes and that has some human consequences, that is, a natural independent variable in research. Examples of natural events include natural disasters, economic fluctuations, heat waves, and surgery. Note that "natural" here does not mean that the independent variable cannot have been produced by human beings, only that the independent variable was not produced solely for research purposes. In an archival study of the impact of a natural event, Anderson and Anderson (1996) examined the "long, hot summer" hypothesis to see whether there was an association between temperature (a natural event) and the incidence of violent crimes. Drawing data from government archives of weather and crime statistics, they found a strong positive association between increases in air temperature and incidence of violent crime.

Benefits and Costs of Naturalness

Natural behaviors, settings, and events are three distinct facets of naturalistic research, although they can go together in various combinations in practice. Naturalness in any of these forms can afford advantages for the social scientist. In particular, studying natural behaviors in natural settings can lead to greater external validity of research results because participants will not alter their behavior to take account of being studied. Naturalness can also contribute to construct validity because unobtrusively observed behaviors (such as racially integrated seating patterns in a lunchroom) are likely to reflect the desired construct (unprejudiced attitudes) to a greater extent than survey or interview responses obtained for obvious research purposes, which might be more subject to response biases.

Nevertheless, naturalness is not the sole criterion – or even the most important one – by which to evaluate research. Every study, not just those using observational or archival methods, must meet the fundamental criteria of reliability and validity of measurement, and naturalness in research can have drawbacks and costs in these and other respects. Conducting research in a natural setting often limits the researcher's ability to control extraneous factors that introduce error into observations and hence reduce reliability. Some research topics, such as the examination of patterns of gaze, might require an unnatural laboratory setting where precise measurement procedures such as carefully placed video cameras, observers behind one-way glass, and freedom from outside interruptions can be arranged. And archival data often fail to include the exact variables of interest; in such instances, researchers look for imperfect or "proxy" variables to stand in for the variables of interest. Such variables will be less able to reliably measure the variables of theoretical interest.

The relative importance of the advantages and disadvantages of naturalness in research depends on the type of research question. Questions that concern rates or patterns of natural behaviors in natural settings obviously require naturalistic research to answer them. For example, we might wonder about gender differences in the practice of "civil inattention" (aversion of one's gaze from the other person's face) when strangers pass each other on the sidewalk. Results from laboratory research on this behavior might not generalize to real street settings; however, we must remember that non-laboratory settings differ among themselves also. Results obtained on Broadway in New York City – however natural that setting – might not generalize to other locales (e.g., side streets of small towns, where strangers might be rare) any more than results obtained in a laboratory might. Ultimately, whether results obtained in one setting, natural or unnatural, will generalize to another setting is an empirical question, not one that naturalness in research can answer automatically.

When Might We Not Need Natural Settings?

Research questions concerned with causal associations among constructs or with hypothetical (if-then or what-if) questions often require specifically unnatural research settings and treatments. To estimate the causal effects of exposure to violent television programming on aggressive behavior among adolescents requires the participants to be given unnatural treatments (some caused to watch and others prevented from watching violent programming). Attempts to answer this research question with non-experimental methods (e.g., simply correlating people's reports of their television viewing with their aggressiveness) have low internal validity. We cannot be confident of the causal nature of the association unless random assignment to an experimental manipulation – unnatural by definition – is used. At the same time, if the data show no relation between the two variables, assuming that self-reports are valid measures of aggression and television viewing, we could argue that the data disconfirm the hypothesis, for there would have to be a relationship between them for the variables to be causally related. On balance, however, advantages of natural research in external validity are often counterbalanced by disadvantages in internal validity.

An example of how a hypothetical, or what-if, question might require an unnatural setting is the question of whether extensive experience cooperating with an African American person on some task would reduce negative racial attitudes among initially prejudiced Whites. Waiting for a prejudiced person to show such cooperative behavior spontaneously might take a long time, or even be missed if observations were not continuous but samples of behavior. In sum, although answering questions about the natural prevalence or patterning of behavior calls for natural settings, answering causal or hypothetical questions often requires the creation of an unnatural setting or treatment (Mook, 1983).

There is some evidence that the ability to generalize from research is not necessarily tied to its degree of naturalness. Dipboye and Flanagan (1979) reviewed hundreds of laboratory and field studies in industrial-organizational psychology and concluded: "Too often the assumption is made that because a study was conducted in a field setting, it is inherently more externally valid than a laboratory study" (p. 388). The generalizability of any research finding is ultimately an empirical question, to be settled only by replication of the research using different participants, behaviors, and settings. No specific feature of a study can guarantee generalizability.

The importance of naturalness depends on the target population of individuals, settings, or behaviors to which we wish to generalize. This involves the distinction between particularistic and universalistic research goals introduced in Chapter 5. The goal of drawing conclusions about a particular situation – for example, determining whether goal setting will improve the productivity of workers at the Acme Widget factory – is best attained by studying those particular workers performing their natural tasks in their natural setting. Many research questions do not so narrowly specify the target population or setting, however. For example, researchers who study helping behavior often have in mind a very broad intended target of generalizations (i.e., any person in any setting). For such research, naturalness is often irrelevant, and because it often interferes with experimental control and other important goals, it is often absent. The chief requirement in such research is **experimental realism**, the meaningfulness and impact of the situation for the participant, rather than **mundane realism**, the resemblance of the situation to some aspect of everyday life (Carlsmith, Ellsworth, & Aronson, 1976). Thus, helping has often been studied in an artificial laboratory setting with unnatural behaviors by the staging of accidents or emergencies that occur while the participant is working on some task (e.g., Latané & Nida, 1981). The researchers assume that individual participants' interpretation of their behavior, setting, and surroundings, rather than their naturalness per se, influences generalizability. That is, it is argued that the theories supported by this research should apply in other situations in which people think that help is required despite differences in the setting, type of accident that necessitates help, and so on.

Perhaps the most articulate and entertaining discussion of these issues is Mook's (1983) classic article, "In Defense of External Invalidity." In this article, Mook notes the heavy pressures on researchers to demonstrate validity: "Who wants to be invalid – internally, externally, or in any other way?" (p. 379). He argues that the emphasis on external validity is often misplaced and that what we really want to generalize is not participants or experimental settings or tasks but rather theories. Mook uses as an extended example the important and well-known studies by Harlow showing that baby monkeys reared in isolation prefer a terry-cloth "mother" to a wire "mother" that provided food. As Mook points out, Harlow's studies (e.g., Harlow, 1958) fail to satisfy virtually any criterion of external validity one might impose: The monkeys were not a representative sample, having been born and orphaned in the laboratory. The experimental setting itself was highly reactive. And there certainly are no examples of terry-cloth or wire mothers in the jungle. But Mook argues that we do not care whether wild monkeys in the jungle would prefer terry-cloth to wire mothers; instead, all that is important is to know that it happens in the laboratory. Harlow's findings were important because they disproved traditional drive-reduction theories of attachment that led to the prediction that baby monkeys would prefer the food-providing wire mother. In short, Mook argues that for theory-testing purposes, we do not need to show how people would behave in the real world, only that they behave in predictable ways in the laboratory.

In summary, naturalness has an important place in the design of research to answer certain types of questions. For other questions it is irrelevant. Just as it might be a mistake to create an unnatural setting for research if our goal were to assess a target behavior as it naturally occurs in everyday life, it would be a mistake to view naturalness as an overriding criterion for the validity of all research and try to do all our research in natural settings. Rather, natural settings provide ways to extend our research and to conduct complementary research to see whether and how the different approaches and settings converge. Although we have focused on external and construct validity, which are usually the chief issues raised by advocates of naturalistic research, other important goals might also be served by naturalistic research. It might lead to new hypotheses, which can be tested in more internally valid ways through laboratory or field experimentation. It might reveal previously unsuspected empirical associations. And it might identify limitations of theories. All these purposes are important for the advancement of knowledge in the social sciences.

Observational Research

Some of the observations made by social scientists appear to be mundane at first glance. For example, it has been noted that some restaurant diners salt their food before tasting it and others salt after they have had a first bite (McGee & Snyder, 1975); that some jail inmates socialize, whereas others perform isolated behaviors that are either active (e.g., reading or cleaning) or passive (e.g., just sitting or sleeping; Wener & Keys, 1988); and that some billiard players show their tongues while making difficult shots, whereas others do not (Smith, Chase, & Lieblich, 1974). These observations become scientific when the data are gathered systematically for the purpose of improving our understanding of human behavior more broadly. McGee and Snyder, for example, showed that individuals who ascribed more stable traits to themselves, as opposed to seeing their behavior as varying with context, were more likely to salt their food before tasting it. Wener and Keys found that increased crowding in one jail unit led to fewer active isolated behaviors and more passive behaviors, as well as to more sick-call rates – findings that are consistent with other research demonstrating negative physical and psychological effects of population density among both humans and nonhuman animals. Finally, Smith et al. observed that tongue showing occurs when one is engaged in a demanding activity and signals an unwillingness to interact. Good billiard players showed their tongues more often on hard than on easy shots and showed their tongues less than did unskilled players overall.

Observation thus becomes scientific when it

(a)   serves a formulated research purpose,
(b)   is planned deliberately,
(c)   is recorded systematically, and
(d)   is subjected to checks and controls on validity and reliability.

There are two major categories of observational techniques: physical trace measures, which involve assessing evidence of the behavior of interest after it has been expressed (e.g., counting beer bottles in a garbage can to estimate how much drinking went on during a party), and systematic observation, which involves structured or nonstructured assessment of the behavior of interest as it is occurring (e.g., posting an observer during the party to record the number of beers consumed). In the next two sections, we describe and give examples of these two categories of observational techniques.

Unobtrusive Measures Involving Physical Traces

Unobtrusive measures involving **physical traces** rely on "pieces of data not specifically produced for the purpose of comparison and inference but available to be exploited opportunistically by the alert observer" (Webb, Campbell, Schwartz, Sechrest, & Grove, 1981, p. 5). There are two major types of physical trace measures: erosion and accretion. **Erosion measures** look at the degree of selective wear on some material. The usual inference is that the greater the degree of erosion, the greater the popularity or liking for the object. One often-cited example is the finding that floor tiles around a museum exhibit featuring live, hatching chicks had to be replaced about every six weeks, whereas tiles around other exhibits in the same museum went months or years without replacement (Webb et al., 1981). This measure of erosion appears to show differences in the popularity of the exhibits. Note, however, that this inference might be in error. For example, viewers, possibly children, might move around and scuff their feet more at the chick-hatching exhibit, wearing out the tiles. Thus, the exhibit might not be seen by more people or for a longer time than other exhibits; it might just be seen by people whose feet are more active. Or, possibly, the erosion might have been caused by a small number of individuals who stayed at the chicken-hatching exhibit for long periods of time. These alternatives highlight one of the major disadvantages of physical trace measures – their interpretation is considerably more ambiguous than more direct forms of observation.

Accretion measures are the opposite of erosion measures and look at the selective deposit of materials. Going back to the museum example, a possible accretion measure of the popularity of the chicken-hatching exhibit would be to count the number of fingerprints and nose prints on the glass wall surrounding the exhibit. Measuring the heights of the fingerprints could even provide a means of estimating age differences in exhibit popularity. The inference is that the greater the accretion of fingerprints, the more popular the exhibit, although once again this inference could be in error if all of the fingerprints were contributed by one individual who loved chickens.

An interesting example of an accretion measure comes from Cialdini and Baumann (1981). They assessed people's attitudes toward presidential candidates by placing fliers that favored Jimmy Carter or Gerald Ford on the windshields of cars in a polling place parking lot and then observing whether the car's driver subsequently retained or littered the flier. Cialdini and Baumann also asked participants when they left the parking lot for whom they had voted. They found that participants were less likely to litter a flier that favored the candidate they supported. A second experiment demonstrated that participants' littering behavior was consistent with their responses to direct questioning when the topic was unlikely to be subject to social desirability concerns; however, when socially desirable responding was likely, littering behavior generated fewer responses in the socially desirable direction. In other words, the behavioral measure was less reactive.

More recently, Carney, Jost, Gosling, and Potter (2008) explored relationships among liberal versus conservative political ideology, personality, and the "behavioral residues" or contents of people's living spaces (e.g., apartments, rooms in private houses). Independent coders entered college students' spaces and recorded the presence of items, such as ironing boards, laundry baskets, books, sports paraphernalia, flags, music, and so forth. Participants also completed a measure of political ideology. The results revealed that conservatives and liberals differed in ways the authors predicted. For example, conservatives' living spaces tended to contain more conventional items, such as sports paraphernalia and flags, and organizational items, which reflect conscientiousness. In contrast, liberals' living spaces tended to contain a greater number of books and a greater number and variety of music CDs – items consistent with greater openness to experience.

Physical trace measures such as erosion and accretion can thus show the frequency or extent of some behavior. Despite their interest value and potential, however, such measures have not been widely used. One major impediment to their use is the lack of a standardized set of trace measures for which reliability and validity have been established, although some headway has been made, for example, the Personal Living Space Cue Inventory (Gosling, Craik, Martin, & Pryor, 2005) used by Carney and colleagues (2008). Further, the task of finding physical trace measures for constructs typical of the social sciences might seem daunting if not impossible. Nevertheless, as the examples we have highlighted indicate, a bit of creativity and a few moments of hard thought can bring to mind several potential physical trace measures for complex constructs.

Exercise: Erosion and accretion measures

Take a few minutes to imagine possible erosion and accretion measures for the following constructs: hunger, anxiety, sadness, and liking for another person. Do the exercise first, and then turn to Table 12.1 (page 338) to see some possibilities we considered. Finding physical trace measures is not always as difficult as it seems.

Inspection of Table 12.1 further illustrates the limitation we spoke of earlier regarding the inferential problems inherent in physical trace measures. Yes, there might be many tissues in a wastebasket if someone is feeling sad and thus crying a great deal. But it also is possible that the person just has a bad cold that day and is not feeling sad at all. Even though readers could imagine possible ways of distinguishing between the two different causes of tissues, the important point being revisited is that there often are competing explanations for the presence of particular physical trace measures that do not reflect the predictions, and the post hoc nature of the data collection prevents observers from drawing unequivocal conclusions. Physical trace measures may suffer greater threats to validity than more direct self-report measures. One should not necessarily conclude, however, that physical trace measures are less valid than self-report measures. As Cialdini and Baumann's (1981) work indicates, physical trace measures can be more valid than self-reports of those behaviors when assessing socially undesirable behaviors. Similarly, Rathje and Hughes (1975) compared participants' self-reported estimates of their beer consumption (obtained during interviews) with a count of beer cans in the same households' garbage. The "front door" interview data indicated that beer was consumed in only 15% of the homes, with eight cans per week being the maximum consumption reported. The "backdoor" data from garbage cans, on the other hand, found evidence of consumption in 77% of the households, with 54% of the homes having more than eight cans per week. Clearly, there was considerable underreporting of beer consumption in the self-report data.

In summary, physical trace measures such as erosion and accretion present both important advantages and disadvantages. They are generally nonreactive and can allow participants to remain anonymous. On the negative side, they require

Table 12.1 Examples of Possible Erosion and Accretion Measures for Assorted Constructs

Construct	Erosion Measure	Accretion Measure
Hunger	• Pieces of candy eaten • Amount of food consumed • Milliliters of saliva generated	• Number of candy wrappers discarded • Size of food portion placed on plate
Anxiety	• Extent to which fingernails chewed off • Degree of wear on hospital waiting room floor • Indentations from fingers on some soft surface • Amount of alcohol consumed	• Accumulation of fingernails torn or chewed off • Sweat stains on clothing • Cigarette butts in ashtray or on floor
Sadness	• Number of tissues taken from box • Number of antidepressant pills taken	• Number of tissues in wastebasket • Quantity of tears
Liking	• Wearing down of speed-dial button for target • Wearing down of tiles in hallway to target's room	• Fingerprints on speed-dial button of target • Number of email messages sent to target • Number and size of gifts sent to target • Number of photographs of target in room • Lip prints on photographs of target

considerable imagination and can pose significant validity problems. Thus, we recommend using physical trace measures as a complement to rather than a substitute for more traditional measures. In so doing, we echo a position we elaborated on in Chapter 7 – the best approach to measurement is *multiple operationism*, measuring a variable using more than one approach, each of which is imperfect in different ways.

Systematic Observation

Systematic observation involves the selection, recording, and encoding of a set of natural behaviors or other naturally occurring phenomena. In other words, systematic observation involves relatively objective measures of behavior (e.g., checklists, detailed coding systems for movements), often in conjunction with a systematic procedure for sampling time intervals or other units for observation. The observer can be open or hidden but usually makes an effort to avoid interfering with the ongoing behavior that is being observed. In contrast, participant observation, discussed in Chapter 13, involves unstructured recording techniques, such as open-ended verbal descriptions of behavior, and the observer's participation in the ongoing behavior is accepted. It is generally considered to be a method of hypothesis generation rather than of structured data collection.

Systematic observation has been used to study a wide range of behaviors such as interactions between general and special education students (Hughes et al., 1999); parents' verbal behavior during their children's sporting events (Kidman, McKenzie, & McKenzie, 1999); nurses' interactions with AIDS patients (Siminoff, Erlen, & Sereika, 1998); the sentencing of defendants in a magistrate's court (Hedderman, 1994); shoplifting behavior (Buckle & Farrington, 1994); and teacher–pupil interactions, pupil engagement, and pupil–pupil interaction (Blatchford, Bassett, & Brown, 2005). In the field of nonverbal communication, there is some evidence that certain subtle but observable behaviors signal whether a speaker is being deceptive (Zuckerman, DePaulo, & Rosenthal, 1981), although the evidence appears to be weak and somewhat mixed overall (Sporer & Schwandt, 2007).

Systematic observation studies differ considerably in how the behaviors or observations of interest are recorded and encoded (Weick, 1985). At one end of the continuum are methods that are relatively unstructured and open-ended. The observer tries to provide as complete and nonselective a description as possible. On the other end of the continuum are more structured and predefined methods, which itemize, count, and categorize behavior. Here the investigator decides beforehand which behaviors will be recorded and how frequently observations will be made. The investigator using structured observation is much more discriminating in choosing which behaviors will be recorded and precisely how they are to be coded.

Relatively Unstructured Methods: Ethological Approaches

The most unstructured and nonselective method of observation would be a complete descriptive account of everything that surrounded an event. This is not only an impossible goal but also not a desirable goal. The basic principle of any observational technique is that it summarize, systematize, and simplify the representation of an event rather than provide a complete replay of it. Even films and videotapes do not provide exact reproduction, for they are subject to biases introduced by camera angle, lighting, microphone placement, and lens. Nor does a "complete" description ever perfectly capture what occurred because of investigators' expectations, language structure, or other cultural biases that might unintentionally affect what is recorded. These issues will be discussed further but are noted here to alert the reader to the fact that all observational techniques involve selection and editing decisions, if for no other reason than the history, prior experiences, and perspective of the observer. The issue for researchers is to make their frames of reference and decisions as explicit as possible.

Ethological approaches opt for as little prior categorization as possible. Ethologists attempt to enter a scene to discover what is there. The object is to derive a detailed and comprehensive description about the nature of an animal's or person's behavioral repertoire. A basic assumption for ethologists is that the natural world is best approached through careful exploratory studies aimed at the generation of hypotheses rather than the testing of them (Blurton-Jones, 1972). Moreover, ethologists are concerned with the naturalistic behavior of the animal species being studied in its own right, whereas other scientists study animals primarily as a means for ultimately understanding human behavior (Lyman-Henley & Henley, 2000). Thus, ethologists are concerned with questions that have application only for animal behavior, as seen, for example, in the study by Phillips and Morris (2001) showing that cows avoid walking through dark passageways but do not mind walking through slurry- or excrement-coated passageways. This study has important implications for dairy farmers (they don't have to worry about cleaning their walls but should add lights to cows' walkways to improve their welfare), but benefits for understanding human behavior are neither obvious nor intended.

Ethologists concentrate on **molecular behaviors**, that is, behaviors tied to specific motor or muscular phenomena, and avoid descriptions that involve inference. For example, ethologists would not describe someone as looking "very pleased." That would entail too much interpretation. They would instead describe such details as facial expression, body movement, speech content, and the behavioral results of such a display rather than allude to some underlying state or intention. An example of this approach is seen in a study by Fridlund (1991), who measured the extent to which people smiled while watching a pleasant videotape under various conditions of sociality (alone, alone but friend nearby, alone but friend watching same videotape in another room, or friend present). Smiles were measured not through observers' judgments but rather quite precisely through muscular movements detected via electromyograph. Analyses indicated that participants displayed moderate to strong smiling while watching the tape with a friend or believing that the friend was watching the same tape, but only weak smiles were displayed in the other two conditions. Interestingly, though, participants' self-reported happiness did not differ across the four viewing conditions, leading the author to conclude that smiling is better predicted by the social context than by the emotion felt (Fridlund, 1991).

Another example of an unstructured type of systematic observation is **ecological observation**. Ecological psychologists assume that all behaviors depend heavily on settings. In their view, the best way to predict a person's behavior is to know where he or she is: "In a post office, he behaves post office, at church he behaves church" (Willems, 1969, p. 16). Thus, these researchers are centrally concerned with characterizing behavior settings in terms of such dimensions as their geographic character (rural, urban); practical functions (drugstore, garage); typical objects (chairs, blackboards); primary behavioral displays (singing, discussing); and temporal domain (morning, evening).

According to ecological psychologists, to understand behavior one must account for two qualities of the behavior setting, *constraints* and *affordances*, and two qualities of the behaving person or persons, *attunements* and *abilities* (Greeno, 1994, 1998). With regard to the behavior setting, constraints are those aspects of the setting that prescribe specific behaviors that result in predictable outcomes (e.g., rules and norms of appropriateness). Affordances are those aspects of a behavior setting that present opportunities for action by people in the setting. Attunements are tendencies on the part of a person to behave in particular ways given specific constraints and affordances associated with behavioral settings. Finally, abilities are aspects of the person that contribute to their behavior in settings. Using these four qualities, the ecological psychologist can describe in rich detail the interactive forces that bring about behavior by a person or group of people in a particular setting.

An example of ecological observation is a study of social support in children's friendships by Rizzo and Corsaro (1995). These researchers positioned themselves as participant observers, then "peripheral participants," in a university preschool, a Head Start center, and a first-grade classroom. Their goal was to evaluate the degree to which the dynamics of childhood friendship are shaped by the settings in which friends interact. Their analysis made use of dozens of videotaped interactions among children during free play and copious field notes. Rizzo and Corsaro illustrate the use of friendship to get what one wants in this excerpt from field notes:

> Jenny and Betty are seated at a worktable with several other children drawing pictures. Jenny tells Betty that she is copying her picture. Betty says: "I am not!" which leads Jenny to claim: "Yes you are, you always copy me." Betty then replies, "I do not and if you keep saying that, then I don't like you any more and you're not my friend." "OK," says Jenny, "I won't say it any more."

From this and other instances recorded during intense observations, Rizzo and Corsaro concluded that children adapt their behavior to fit the constraints of the behavior settings in which they interact with peers, an adaptation the authors refer to as "ecological congruence."

Other ecological studies focus more on behavioral settings themselves, with the goal of cataloging and organizing the many behavior settings that a person or group of people might inhabit. For instance, Barker and Schoggen (1973) comprehensively described all the behavior settings of a particular community, which were then organized in hierarchies of types and subtypes. The final step in this **behavior setting survey** is the description of the settings in terms of whichever of their many attributes and characteristics are of interest. Individuals are known then by the settings they inhabit as they conduct their daily lives. For the ecological psychologist, the lifestyles of individuals can be accurately grasped by listing the behavior settings that they inhabit. The listing of behavior settings is called the behavior range. For example, the behavior range for a particular person or group of persons reveals how active they are in community life, what interests they have, and where they spend most of their time.

Ecological observation is thus a type of systematic observation that emphasizes full and impartial recording of behaviors in their specific setting and context. As in participant observation (Chapter 13), the goal is the discovery of ecologically valid base-rate information rather than hypothesis testing. In contrast to participant observation, but like other forms of systematic observation, the emphasis is on the objective observation of specific actions rather than the inference of underlying processes.

Structured Methods: Checklists or Coding Schemes

The major difference between unstructured and structured observational methods is that in the latter, investigators know what aspects of social activity are relevant for their purposes before starting and deliberately set forth a specific and explicit plan to record them.

Most structured observational methods require an observer to code the appearance of the behavior, but some technological devices can record even in an observer's absence. For example, cable boxes are able to track how many and what television programs are turned on, and pedometers calculate the territory covered by people on foot during any given day. As another example, the electronic scanners in many grocery stores gather extensive data continuously, recording all the items bought by each customer at what times, thus allowing market researchers to uncover trends in buying behavior. For example, are diaper sales greater in the morning or evening? What other products are people who buy diapers likely to purchase? Finally, Internet usage is tracked, allowing advertisers to target ads and promotions specifically to individual users, and for algorithms to suggest to individuals that, based on their purchases, they would probably like specific products.

Checklists or **category systems** can range from simply noting whether or not a single behavior has occurred to multiple behavior systems. As an example of the first, Perrine and Heather (2000) recorded whether individuals contributed more money to a donation box that displayed the phrase "even a penny will help" compared to boxes that did not display that phrase. And Goldstein, Cialdini, and Griskevicius (2008) examined the effectiveness of signs requesting hotel guests to participate in an environmental conservation program on towel use, that is, whether hotel guests put their towels back on the towel rack or on the floor (to be replaced with clean towels). As an example of the use of multiple behavior systems, Strayer and Strayer (1976) classified initiation of antagonistic behavior by children in a playground into one of several categories: bite, chase, hit, kick, push–pull, and wrestle.

The construction of a reliable and valid checklist is crucial to its usefulness as an observational tool. Critical features of a good checklist include:

- Explicit definitions of behaviors. For example, in observing antagonistic behavior, observers would need to know when a friendly tap becomes a hit. This is accomplished more easily when the behaviors are classifiable on objective grounds rather than on inferential ones. The observer would code a behavior as a hit only if it actually met the explicit description for the act and not if it only appeared that the child "wanted" to hit.
- Categories that are mutually exclusive. Each behavior of interest must be able to be classified into one and only one category. A behavior would be either a "push–pull" or "wrestle" but not both.
- Categories that are exhaustive of the type (e.g., fighting), but limited in distinctions. The code should cover the sphere of interest but be sufficiently finite to allow meaningful assessments to be made.

Group processes and classroom interaction are enduring targets for checklist observational systems. Two systems that have received substantial use by social scientists are Bales's (1970) Interaction Process Analysis for studying group interaction and Flanders's (1970) system for analyzing teacher behavior. In Bales's (1970) system, each act by a group member is categorized into 1 of the 12 categories shown in Figure 12.2. Bales's checklist system uses a modified version of continuous time sampling; that is, each act by a person is coded into 1 of the 12 possible types, and an act is defined as

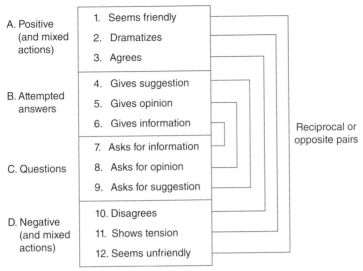

Figure 12.2   Bales's (1970) Interaction Process Analysis Coding Scheme for Interaction in Groups.
Source: Bales (1970).

Table 12.2 Flanders's (1970) Category System for Classroom Behavior		
Teacher Talk	Response	1. Accepts Feeling
		2. Praises or Encourages
		3. Accepts or Uses Ideas of Pupils
		4. Asks Questions
	Initiation	5. Lecturing
		6. Giving Directions
		7. Criticizing or Justifying Authority
Pupil Talk		8. Pupil-Talk Response
		9. Pupil-Talk Initiation
Silence		10. Silence
Source: Flanders (1970).		

"a communication or an indication, either verbal or nonverbal, which in its context may be understood by another member as equivalent to a single simple sentence" (p. 68). In Flanders's system, classroom behavior is classified according to the 10 categories shown in Table 12.2. The Flanders system, in contrast to the Bales system, uses very small interval time-point sampling to maintain a rendering of the original behavioral sequence in the classrooms. An observer codes ongoing behavior into one of Flanders's 10 categories every 3 seconds.

Structured methods such as checklists are particularly appropriate for testing specific hypotheses after the behaviors have been described and hypotheses generated, perhaps by less structured observational methods. Checklists also vary with respect to how general or specific they are. One of the advantages of Bales's (1970) coding scheme is that it can be used to code virtually any group interaction. More specific checklists might be constrained to a certain context, but that can be an advantage if the specific checklist contains behaviors of direct theoretical interest. In sum, the choice of checklist should be theoretically driven. If an existing checklist encompasses the desired behaviors, by all means use it. If not, a new checklist tailored to the research questions being investigated might need to be devised.

Software programs can greatly facilitate the use of checklists. These programs generally allow users to customize coding schemes, specifying what behaviors and how many targets are to be coded. The coder sits at the computer and strikes various keys corresponding to the behavior categories when appropriate. The computer keeps track of the time and records precisely at what times a given behavior occurs and for how long (if duration is being coded). Figure 12.3 shows such a coding entry screen

Figure 12.3 Event Recorder Screen from The Observer XT© Observational Coding Program.

from The Observer XT, one of the commercially available coding programs for observational data. As shown in the figure, this particular configuration is set up to code six separate activities (eat, kick, scream, play, avert, and other) and five types of position (sit, stand, walk, run, and other) expressed by a child. The coder strikes the appropriate key ("e" for eat, etc.) every time the behavior occurs. The program also allows the entry of modifiers that allow the recording of sequential data; for example, when the behavior "kick" is recorded, a modifier indicating who was kicked ("Derek") can be entered. These kinds of software programs possess several important advantages: First, they allow for much more organized, efficient, and hence more reliable coding than manual procedures. Rather than having to fumble with sheets of paper listing columns and memorizing special codes for each type of behavior, the coder merely needs to strike the appropriate computer key. Second, timing of events is done automatically and without error. Third, observations are entered directly into the computer, removing the need for manual data entry and thus avoiding an important source of error.

Steps in Conducting an Observation

In the final section on observational techniques, we provide a general sequence of steps/framework for studies using observational methods – particularly for quantitative approaches – to summarize decisions that must be made.

- Step 1: Arrive at Operational Definitions of the Desired Construct(s)

This step can be the most difficult, as it can require considerable imagination or creativity on the part of the researcher to decide to observe "fidgetiness" in doctors' waiting rooms as a measure of nervousness or floor-tile wear to measure an exhibit's popularity in a museum. The selection of the behaviors or physical traces to observe is guided both by the focus of interest and by practical and ethical concerns that limit what is observable. It is also important that the target of observation should be unambiguously definable, so that reasonable reliability and validity in measurement can be attained.

- Step 2: Select the Setting and Mode of Observation

Because settings exert a powerful influence on behavior, we must choose a setting in which the trace or behavior can be expected to occur with sufficient frequency to make observation worthwhile. For example, we would not try to code the time children spend running around during a religious service, though we probably would if we were observing the children at a park. The setting should, if possible, also permit relatively unobtrusive but reliable observations by an in-person observer or recording instrument (such as videotape equipment). For example, if fine, small behaviors are to be coded, the setting should permit the observers to be physically close to the participants or else permit the use of binoculars or telephoto lenses.

Mode of observation refers to whether the behavior will be coded online (i.e., live) or from videotapes. The choice between live coding and permanent recording for later coding is crucial. Videotaped and other recorded information facilitates the use of multiple coders for each behavior and therefore increases the reliability of measurement. Videotapes also carry the great advantage of producing a permanent record so that researchers can go back and code additional variables when desired. With online coding, the researcher must identify all the variables to be coded in advance of observation, and no changes can be made to this list. A permanent record such as videotape also allows the research team to review the behavioral information to resolve discrepancies between coders. Thus, if an initial reliability analysis indicates that coding is not sufficiently reliable, the coding scheme can be refined and observers trained until adequate reliability is reached. If the coding were done online, though, the researchers are stuck with any poor reliability that results. For all of these reasons, videotaping or otherwise permanently recording the behavior to be coded is preferred whenever possible. Online coding should be used only when permanent recording is not feasible. For example, researchers wishing to code children's play behavior at a park would perhaps find videotaping too difficult. The camera angle would have to be very wide to capture all of the park activities, and the resulting video images of children running about would be so complex that coding of the behavior of individual children would be difficult. Online coding using a large number of coders responsible for circumscribed sections of the park or individual children might be the only option in such a study.

Following recording, the next step entails encoding the observations. **Encoding** is the process of simplifying the observations through some procedure, such as categorization, and quantifying the categories for statistical analysis if that is a goal. Sometimes recording and encoding can involve a single operation, as when an observer counts whether a specific behavior has occurred when making a live observation. The observations are thus already encoded by virtue of being recorded. Sampling according to time-point procedures in vivo would yield this type of situation. In contrast, the recording of single or multiple behaviors through continuous time measurement would allow different types of encoding, such as frequency, rate, duration, percentage duration, and sequential analysis. The distinction between recording and encoding is a critical one in that the same recorded observations can be encoded according to different systems. In this regard at least, observations do not speak for themselves. The question that the researcher has in mind guides the encoding of the observations. Consider gaze behavior: Two pairs can look at each other for comparable total duration, thus seeming very similar if total duration of contact is a dependent measure. The first pair might have done so through one or two longer periods of eye contact, however, whereas the second pair might have attained their total through frequent but brief looks or even many glances.

• Step 3: Select a Sampling Strategy

The major decision here involves whether the entire interaction or event will be coded continuously or whether only portions of the interaction or event will be coded. The former method of coding is called **continuous real-time measurement** (Sackett, 1978). Continuous measurement occurs when every onset of a behavior (frequency) or elapsed time of a behavior (duration) is recorded during the observational session.

For example, researchers interested in coding friendliness during an interpersonal interaction might code the frequency of smiles. The entire interaction would be observed and the total number of smiles expressed by each participant recorded. In later analyses, the researchers probably would want to convert the frequency measure to a rate measure by dividing by interaction length so as to correct for any variation in interaction length. Otherwise, a person who smiled 10 times might be deemed twice as friendly as a person who smiled only 5 times, yet if the first interaction were twice as long as the second, the actual rate (and level) of friendliness would be the same.

The second major sampling strategy in deciding what parts of an event or interaction to code is called time sampling. There are two variations of time sampling. In **time-point sampling**, recording is done instantaneously at the end of set time periods, such as every 10 seconds or every sixth minute or every hour on the hour, with the number and spacing of points selected to be appropriate to the session length. This is like freezing time and then recording whether a particular behavior is present at that moment in time. Through film or videotape, the time point is literally accomplished by stop action on one frame. In contrast, **time-interval sampling**, like continuous measurement, records behavior in real time; but, as in time-point sampling, each observed behavior, such as smiling, is scored once and only once during successive intervals of the session (e.g., 60 seconds) regardless of the number of actual occurrences in each interval.

A third variation on sampling behavior is to use a combination of continuous and time-interval sampling. In this approach, only a portion of the total interaction or event is coded, but that portion is coded in a continuous fashion, that is, rather than scoring a given behavior only once if it occurs during the sampled time interval, the total frequency is tallied. This approach is particularly useful when the total amount of material to be coded is prohibitively large. Take, for example, a study looking at therapist and client behavior during a social skills training group that met weekly for 2 hours across a 12-week span. Assuming a rather small-scale study of 10 groups, consisting of 2 therapists and 8 clients each, we would be looking at 24 hours of coding per person, for a total of 2,400 coding hours if each person were coded independently. A reasonable alternative would be to code only a subset of those 24 hours, say, 3 hours randomly taken out of the 24 possible hours. Or, the times to be sampled could be deliberately chosen to be representative of the entire course of therapy, for example, 1 hour each from the beginning, middle, and last third of the group sessions.

Although some researchers initially express reluctance to use such time-sampling methods ("What? You mean you want me to throw out most of the data?!"), there often is no choice but to adopt such an approach. Moreover, research indicates that the information obtained from sampled subsets of an event or interaction represent well the information obtained from continuous sampling over the entire session. Indeed, Ambady and Rosenthal (1992) have shown that nonverbal ratings taken from extremely short video clips, even as short as 30 seconds, have impressive validity coefficients. They also found that studies using longer periods of coding (e.g., 5 minutes) did not differ in their accuracy of predictions compared to studies based on observations of less than 30 seconds in length. (See also Murphy, 2005, and Richeson & Shelton, 2005.)

The decision whether to use continuous or time-sampling methods thus depends partly on practicality concerns and partly on theoretical concerns. Continuous real-time observation allows the determination of the actual frequency or duration of particular behaviors, whereas time-sampling strategies require less coding effort and allow estimation of total frequencies and comparisons of subgroups. Time-sampling methods are thus particularly useful when there are many behaviors to code, long observational sessions to be recorded, or quick changes in the relevant behaviors. Time sampling tends not to be appropriate for behaviors that occur infrequently or briefly, when the sequence of the behavior amid other behaviors is significant, or when actual frequencies or durations are important to know. Consequently, continuous recording in real time is the method of choice when these concerns are paramount in the research.

- Step 4: Train the Observers

Observers need to be trained to code objects or events similarly and to avoid errors of commission and omission in scoring. Training can proceed in conjunction with the development of coding categories or checklists. Before actual coding begins, observers practice on sample behaviors until they reach acceptable levels of agreement (i.e., high reliability). As detailed in Chapter 7, the reliability of observational measures is usually assessed by documenting the extent to which two or more independent observers agree in their ratings of the same events or objects, expressed in statistics such as the inter-rater reliability coefficient or Cohen's (1960) kappa, which is based on the percentage of scored units on which the observers agree. If adequate reliability cannot be attained, the coding system or checklist needs to be revised, probably in the direction of more specificity in the definitions of the coding categories. Furthermore, **observer drift**, a decline in observer reliability or validity over time, is a common phenomenon. Because of fatigue or habituation, the use of coding categories can vary randomly or systematically over time so that behaviors are not coded in the same way. We cannot assume that high reliability at the beginning of a study implies high reliability at the end. When coding is done from videotapes or other permanent records, researchers can avoid a systematic bias due to observer drift by having participants coded in a random order that is different for each coder.

Observers also are subject to a number of biases (such as halo effects) that are characteristic of raters in general (see Chapter 7) and that can only be reduced, not totally eliminated, by careful training. The best control of such biases involves videotaped records of behavior and keeping observers as unaware as possible of potential biasing factors. It is sometimes possible to edit videotapes in a manner that would prevent halo and other potential biases through editing out information that identifies the conditions under which the observation was made. For example, if the research hypothesis is that male participants smile more while conversing with females than with males, and if the observers can see the other party to the conversation, their ratings of the participant's smiles might be influenced by their knowledge of the circumstances of the observation. This bias might even falsely lead to a seeming confirmation of the hypothesis. A strategy for dealing with this possible bias would be to record or edit videotaped observations so that the coders could see and hear only the participant, not the partner, removing any possibility of this form of bias. This also can be accomplished in some cases by the low-cost strategy of placing a piece of cardboard over half of the video or computer monitor, obscuring the other person. When interactions are audiotaped, a simple approach is to record each person's comments on separate tracks, thus facilitating preparation of editing tapes that contain only one participant's voice. As should be clear, it is often easier to arrange for naïve coding when videotape or other recording techniques are used than with live observers. In either case, it is crucial that observers are kept unaware of the hypotheses guiding the study. It is for this reason that researchers should almost never code their own observations.

• Step 5: Analyze the Data

After the coding system has been found or created, good reliability and validity have been achieved, and observations have been recorded on the research participants, analysis of the data is the final step. A common analytic approach is simply to use the coded behavior (i.e., frequency, rate, or duration of specific behaviors) as dependent variables in standard statistical analysis procedures. More sophisticated procedures are available, however, for the investigation of behavior streams and sequences (e.g., Bakeman & Gottman, 1997; Hall & Oliver, 1997). Although the statistical nuances of these strategies are beyond the scope of this book, basically they analyze the conditional probabilities of a given behavior predicated on a prior or subsequent behavior. In other words, given that Person A smiled, how likely is it that Person B smiled in return? An example of this kind of approach is given by Wehby, Symons, and Shores (1995), who coded a variety of prosocial and aggressive behaviors in classrooms for children with emotional and behavioral disorders. Analyses showed that students who displayed more aggressive behavior received fewer positive social interactions from their teachers. Teacher use of social or instructional commands elicited more aggressive behavior from students, whereas peer-directed aggression was usually precipitated by other peer aggression. Thus, a **sequential analysis** provides information not only on differences in mere frequencies of behavior but also on how certain behaviors relate to one another across time. Through sequential analysis, Wehby et al. (1995) were able to identify not merely which students were more aggressive but the precise events that elicited their aggression. In sum, as is the case with any form of social science data, the decision of what analytic strategy to pursue is a joint function of the conceptual questions that guided the research strategy and the nature of the information it generates.

Archival Research

The primary advantages of archival research are that the data are already collected, and that research hypotheses about what is occurring cannot affect data collection or participant responses. Said differently, archival research is nonreactive, for no data collection is required. As examples, we might want to:

- look at college admissions decisions for an applicant class;
- look at relations between state-level high school examination performance and college success;
- examine government records to determine suicide rates in social groups with differing levels of social integration;
- look at annual changes in traffic fatalities for different states;
- review Jefferson's writings to note the relative frequency of references to different ideological themes;
- examine relations of the type and amount of support services provided to families with child outcomes; or
- look at stock market performance under different situational pressures.

Archival data are often "there for the taking," easily accessible to the researcher without great physical or financial costs. Archives often provide aggregated measurements, often over time, of significant constructs drawn from millions of individuals, hundreds of organizations, or dozens of different societies – data that would be almost impossible to obtain in other ways. They also provide our only access to the thinking of people who are dead or otherwise unavailable for direct questioning. Finally, in today's world of "big data," archives promise access to breadth and depth of information not possible even a decade ago. For example, through the SLDS (Student Longitudinal Data Systems) supported by the U.S. Department of Education, there are many states with integrated K-16 data bases available for research.

Statistical archives and written records are kept by all literate societies for a variety of purposes, of which research is by no means the most important. However, such archives can be used by imaginative researchers for purposes that were never envisioned by the originators of the archives or documents, often in a way that takes advantage of the strengths of archival data. These strengths include the potential for (1) spanning long periods of time (including the ability to look *back* in time, which is not possible with other research methods); (2) covering large populations of people or other units of observation; (3) addressing important practical issues at a different level of analysis or scale; and (4) quantifying reactions to events, such as earthquakes, riots, or factory closings, that researchers cannot intentionally impose for practical or ethical reasons.

This section is divided into three parts, based on the nature of the archive that is the source of information. First we consider statistical records and other government or institutional records, such as those on hospital admissions, educational institutions, unemployment rates, daily temperatures, or population growth. Next, survey archives of data collected for research purposes by standard survey methods (usually by telephone or personal interviews) are considered; they generally include a range of sociodemographic information as well as attitudes on social and political topics, drawn from very large probability samples. Finally, the research use of written records, ranging from private diaries to mass-circulation newspapers, and the associated techniques of content analysis are presented.

Statistical Records

Of all the changes since this book was first published in 1951, perhaps the most amazing is the widespread availability of data in our current information age. Few if any researchers 60 years ago could have imagined the massive computing and storage power currently available. That capability has resulted in almost every kind of data imaginable being regularly stored on electronic record systems. Although in many data bases the historical data are incomplete, going forward the data bases should get better and better as record systems are in place and as storage capacity continues to expand. Potential data bases (some highly restricted) include shopping preferences of individual shoppers, educational performance from early childhood through college, financial transaction records and earnings and income of all U.S. taxpayers, health records, and criminal history. Many available statistical archives include socioeconomic information about age, sex, family size, occupation, residence, and other characteristics. Health statistics give birth and death rates and frequencies of operations and major illnesses; federal, state, municipal, and private economic institutions collect and publish information on wages, hours of work, productivity, absenteeism, strikes, financial transactions, and so on. Many small non-profit organizations have records not only of their own members but also of the people whom they serve. In addition, a smaller but increasing body of information is being collected by various institutions on psychological characteristics, such as aptitude, achievement/attainment, personality, and attitudes. For example, schools, hospitals, social service agencies, personnel departments in businesses, and similar institutions frequently administer tests of various kinds to their entire populations.

The variety of research questions that can be addressed using statistical archives is staggering. For example, Rubinstein and Caballero (2000) used archival data on the height and weight of Miss America pageant contestants to track social changes in standards of beauty. Fogg and Rose (2000) examined archival data on 2,288 astronaut applicants and determined that the best predictors of being accepted into astronaut training were undergraduate and graduate grade point averages and aviation experience. Intentions to remain in the military and their relation to family characteristics were examined in a study by Lee and Maurer (1999). Finally, archival analyses in South Africa of violent crime statistics and representative national surveys showed that although politically motivated violence had declined dramatically by the end of 1994, the levels of fear reported by citizens remained high (Barbarin, Richter, de Wet, & Wachtel, 1998).

Suicide is an example of a research topic that is difficult to study by any approach other than archival. Durkheim's (1897/1951) classic study of suicide tested the hypothesis that a basic cause of suicide is lack of integration into a social group. He examined three major kinds of social group integration: religious, familial, and political. He found suicide rates were lower among Catholics than among Protestants, lower among married people than among single people, lower among those with children than among those without children, and lower during periods of national fervor. All these findings, he argued, supported the hypothesis that belonging to a cohesive social group is a deterrent to suicide. A century later, Phillips, Carstensen, and Paight (1989) used statistical archives to document the "copycat effect" in suicides. There is a marked increase in suicides and traffic fatalities (which often reflect suicidal decisions) following a publicized suicide, but this effect is primarily restricted to individuals who are similar to the publicized suicide victim. In other words, more teenagers commit suicide after a teen suicide story is publicized, and more elderly people commit suicide after a story about an elderly suicide.

Available **statistical records** are used as social indicators to chart the status and change in the quality of life. The U.S. government gathers and reports statistics detailing various social indicators of human well-being, including employment levels, housing availability, and crime rates. Previously only accessible as heavy volumes with fine print in reference libraries, these reports can now be easily accessed on the Internet. For example, the FedStats site (www.fedstats.gov/) listed in the "On the Web" section at the end of the chapter provides links to a cornucopia of statistics from over 100 federal agencies, including information on social and economic conditions in the United States, national trends in educational statistics, birth and death rates, life expectancy, risk factors, and other health-related topics. The U.S. Census Bureau also publishes the *Statistical Abstract of the United States*, available on the web at http://www.census.gov/compendia/statab/. Table 12.3 lists the over 30 types of statistical tables that are available through the *Abstract*. Just about anything one might want to know about the lives of Americans can be found here. These reports are compiled to monitor present social conditions and to chart societal changes. Therein lies one of the singular advantages of using existing records. Many of these are collected regularly, thus enabling the user to measure associations among social variables across time. For example, is the socioeconomic standing of various racial or sex groups declining, rising, or sustaining the status quo, and to what other social factors is there a systematic tie?

Table 12.3   Categories of Statistics Available in the *Statistical Abstract of the United States*

1997 economic census	Industrial outlook
20th-century statistics	Labor force, employment, and earnings
Agriculture	Law enforcement, courts, and prison
Banking, finance, and insurance	Manufacturers
Business enterprise	National defense and veteran affairs
Communications and information technology	Natural resources
Comparative international statistics	Outlying areas
Construction and housing	Parks, recreation, and travel
Domestic trade and services	Population
Education	Prices
Elections	Science and technology
Energy	Social insurance and human services
Federal government finances and employment	State and local governments
Foreign commerce and aid	Transportation – air and water
Geography and environment	Transportation – land
Health and nutrition	Vital statistics
Income, expenditures, and wealth	

The U.S. Census, a truly massive data-gathering effort undertaken every 10 years, produces a variety of statistical records suitable for many research purposes. The variables include a fairly narrow range, being limited to basic characteristics of people (such as age, sex, race, ethnic background, education, occupation, and income) and housing units (such as location, value, inclusion of indoor plumbing, and occupants per room). The Census Bureau publishes a number of tabulations of data (e.g., income broken down by race and sex) for the United States as a whole and for states and smaller areas, and using these data for research is as simple as looking up the appropriate table. Kasarda (1976) has long argued that the information provided in various national censuses offers opportunities for secondary analyses that are limited only by the imagination of the researcher. Among these opportunities Kasarda mentions the chance to analyze educational attainment, ethnic and racial segregation, poverty, marriage and divorce, social mobility, and commuting patterns.

However, often the particular associations in which a researcher is interested are not among those tabulated by the government, so the researcher must turn to the original information. Public Use Microdata, samples of a tiny percentage of the actual census responses, are released by the government, coded in relatively gross geographic areas so that individual respondents' privacy is not threatened by the release of the actual data. From the original information, any desired tabulation or analysis of the existing variables can be prepared by an appropriate computer program.

Despite their unparalleled coverage of the U.S. population, census data have important limitations for research. Although the repetition of the census every 10 years provides a good basis for research over time, the researcher must be wary of changing conceptual and operational definitions that render some year-to-year comparisons problematic. For example, the entire scheme for coding occupations changed between 1970 and 1980; some change is necessary as new occupations appear and old ones vanish, but the changes can make comparisons over time inexact. Ethnic/racial categories have also been changed over time to reflect changing identities and demographic shifts. The boundaries of census areas within which information is accumulated (tracts and metropolitan areas) also change over time as population patterns shift. Again, examining social or economic changes within a city or other area can be difficult because of these noncomparabilities.

Finally, social change can affect the way people respond to survey items, even when data-gathering procedures remain unchanged. Between 1970 and 1980, it appears that a large number of people of Spanish origin shifted from indicating "White" to "Other" on a question about ethnicity; in 1970, 90% of this group indicated "White" compared to 58% "White" and 38% "Other" in 1980. Ethnic breakdowns across years would be confounded unless special precautions were taken because the "White" and "Other" groups would contain varying proportions of Spanish-origin respondents. The addition of the "multiracial" category to the 2000 census makes ethnic group comparisons across time even more difficult. The problem of changes over time in the ways variables are defined is, of course, not limited to the census. For example, social service agencies might change the ways that they define variables to reflect changes in the types of services offered, to be consistent with changes in available funding, or because new and better outcome assessments are available.

The relatively small number of variables measured by the census has already been mentioned, and it is this feature that poses the most important limitation on research content. No attitude or belief variables are included. Yet, for whole fields within the social sciences, including the study of fertility, educational and occupational differences in income, or characteristics of different areas within cities (e.g., residential segregation by race or income), the census is the single most valuable data source.

Characteristics of Archival Research

Archival studies have a number of common characteristics. First, they rely entirely on the analyses of information gathered for purposes other than those of particular studies of social behavior. Consequently, they require familiarity with known sources of information, such as the *New York Times Index*, and skill in uncovering less well known material, such as cemetery records. Second, archival studies often call for ingenuity in translating existing records into quantifiable indices of some general concepts. For example, objective public records of social integration do not exist, so Durkheim's (1897/1951) resourcefulness is evident in using existing material to indicate more general social psychological processes. Third, although the explosion of information archived on the Internet makes it more likely that the statistics one needs are only a mouse-click away, the sheer volume of information available is overwhelming, and it can take hours of frustrating searching before relevant information is identified. Fourth, researchers using archival information must make what in some instances may be a leap of faith, namely, that the data are accurate. If an archivist were careless in recording or describing data, later users might have no way of knowing that what they are using and finding is flawed.

Fifth, archival studies are particularly susceptible to alternative interpretations for the natural events and their effects. What is required, then, is care in using multiple measures or ruling out other explanations. For example, Durkheim (1897/1951) examined a number of alternative hypotheses – that suicide is the result of psychopathic states, imitation, racial or hereditary factors, or climate. He then demonstrated that the statistics are not in accord with any of these hypotheses. For example, in considering the hypothesis that suicide is influenced by climate, he started with the observation that in all countries for which statistics are available over a period of years, the incidence of suicide increases regularly from January until June and then declines until the end of the year. This observation had led other writers to conclude that temperature has a direct effect on the tendency to suicide. Durkheim examined this possibility in great detail and demonstrated that the statistics did not support it. He argued, for example, that if temperature were the basic cause, suicide would vary regularly with it, but this is not the case. There are more suicides in spring than in autumn, although the temperature is slightly lower in spring. Moreover, suicide reaches its height not in the hottest months (July and August) but in June. By a series of such analyses, Durkheim demonstrated that the seasonal regularities in suicide rates could not be accounted for by temperature and suggested the alternative hypothesis that social activity is seasonal and that the rate of suicide is related to the extent of social activity.

Research Survey Archives

An alternative source of information on social behavior is archives created specifically for research – **research survey archives**. Several organizations (including the Roper Center of the University of Connecticut, the Interuniversity Consortium for Political and Social Research, and the National Opinion Research Center at the University of Chicago) maintain and distribute data files drawn from large-scale surveys, often based on high-quality probability samples of the general U.S. population.

One research survey archive, the General Social Survey (Davis & Smith, 1992), illustrates the types of information that are available. This survey, conducted by the National Opinion Research Center, began in 1972 and has gathered face-to-face interview data on an annual or biennial basis since then (http://www3.norc.org/GSS+Website/). To date, over 40,000 randomly chosen respondents have answered more than 3,500 questions on a host of variables relevant to social behavior. Each sample is a national area probability sample of 1,500 to 3,000 noninstitutionalized adults. Response rates average 77% for the 20 administrations of the General Social Survey since 1972, an impressively high rate given the length of the survey and reflective of the great methodological care that has gone into designing and implementing the survey.

The General Social Survey contains a standard core of demographic and attitudinal variables that remain the same from year to year, and others appear in rotation every two or three years, offering valuable opportunities to make comparisons over time. The standard social and demographic characteristics include age, sex, education, income, religion, urban or rural residence, occupation, and marital status. Questions about beliefs, attitudes, and behaviors relevant to social and political topics include, for example, reported vote in the most recent presidential election, preferences for government spending on a range of programs, interracial attitudes, sexual behavior, political alienation, attitudes toward labor unions, gun ownership and attitudes toward gun control, and abortion.

Many excellent studies have been conducted using the General Social Survey or other research survey archives; the National Opinion Research Center's bibliography lists over 5,000 studies published using the General Social Survey alone. Some examples include studies of changes in sex-role attitudes among men and women from 1972 through 1978 (Cherlin & Walters, 1981); race and social class differences in support for the use of force by police (Arthur & Case, 1994); and the incidence of high-risk sexual behavior in the general population (Anderson & Dahlberg, 1992).

The use of such archives for research has obvious advantages and disadvantages. The advantages include the availability of extensive information obtained from high-quality samples over time, which would be beyond the ability of any single researcher to collect. Low cost is also a benefit; at many colleges and universities such archives are available through campus libraries or research offices, and the cost to obtain them is typically low if they are not already available. Finally, in contrast to most archives, research survey archives are created and maintained for research use so that they do not have many of the problems that must be faced by the user of government or institutional archives, with regard to which research use is often a mere afterthought.

The main limitations are, of course, those imposed by the method (sample surveys are clearly not an unobtrusive or nonreactive form of data gathering) and the topics. Although the questions cover a wide range of topics, a researcher who is interested in an issue that is not covered by the survey is simply out of luck. And even where questions are available, their format or wording may be less than optimal for later purposes. In addition, some older archives have annoying problems, such as incomplete or inaccurate codebooks (the documentation describing what variables are recorded where and what codes are used in the data) and obsolete recording methods. Newer archives are largely free of the last type of problem.

Verbal Records

Public and Private Documents.   **Verbal records** also provide a rich source of information about social behavior. For example, public documents such as the speeches made by Arab and Israeli political decision-makers have been coded (Astorino-Courtois, 1995). This analysis revealed that, in contrast to popular impressions of the Mideast conflict, the speeches tended toward cautious decision-making and restraint during times of uncertainty. Moreover, Arab and Israeli leaders attempted to minimize perceived conflict escalations by moderating their behavior. Similarly, an analysis of the public speeches by Presidents Bill Clinton and George H. Bush indicated that Clinton used a more flexible and cooperative approach to foreign policy, whereas Bush was relatively less cooperative (Walker, Schafer, & Young, 1999).

Personal documents, including autobiographies, letters, diaries, school essays, and the like, are also open to social scientific observation once obtained. For example, a classic study by Thomas and Znaniecki (1918) used letters sent between Poland and the United States, along with other information sources, to draw conclusions about Polish peasants who immigrated to the United States and, more broadly, the effects of culture on beliefs and attitudes. Snowdon and his colleagues (1996) used diaries written by nuns in their early twenties to predict their cognitive functioning 50 years later.

Ideally, the research use of personal documents can achieve for inner experiences, such as beliefs and attitudes, what observational techniques can achieve for overt behaviors: reveal them to the social scientist without the use of reactive questionnaires or other research instruments. However, personal documents are relatively rare and often pose problems for the researcher. Their authenticity can be uncertain – were the letters from Polish peasants actually written by the person in question or by somebody else (such as a village scribe)? If the latter, that person might have influenced the content. In addition, available samples of documents might be biased. If not all peasants are literate, conclusions about their thinking based on letters probably pertain to a biased sample of individuals, underrepresenting those who do not write.

Mass Communications/Social Media.   In addition to statistical records and autobiographical documents, every literate society produces a variety of material intended to inform, entertain, or persuade the populace. Such material can appear in the form of literary productions, newspapers and magazines, film, radio, television shows and commercials, and the Internet. Mass communications and social media provide a rich source of information for investigating a variety of questions. They can be used to shed light on some aspects of the culture of a given group, to compare different groups in terms of some aspect of culture, or to trace cultural change. For example, Lusk (1999) analyzed images of patients in 446 advertisements displayed in four nursing magazines and found that more men than women were portrayed, and most patients were White and under 65 years old. Men were shown more frequently as being critically ill or having heart disease. Lusk noted that these portrayals do not reflect actual patient demographics and that, more seriously, the underrepresentation of minorities and the elderly in such advertisements negates their healthcare presence and needs.

The popular press has over time become more attuned to opportunities of archival information as well. For example, as we were writing this book, a very popular show, *Breaking Bad*, aired its final season. Newspaper articles have tracked what has been called the "de-evolution" of the TV hero from good guy heros in the 1950s through 1970s (Perry Mason, Kojak) to the questionable during the 1980s (J. R. Ewing in *Dallas*) to the more recent Tony Soprano and *Breaking Bad*'s Walter White (e.g., Neal, 2013a, 2013b).

Television commercials often have been the topic of study. Greenberg and Brand (1993), for example, analyzed Saturday morning cartoons and commercials targeted toward young children. All these studies document trends in content in the mass media. All utilize with varying sophistication a technique called **content analysis**, which is "any technique for making inferences by systematically and objectively identifying specified characteristics of messages" (Holsti, 1969, p. 601). This is similar to the definition of systematic observation of natural behavior. Both techniques require objectivity of coding categories to ensure reliability, systematic application of these coding systems across a representative sample of material to control observer bias, and consistency in theoretical aims so that the findings can be related to some relevant variable.

Although content analysis is covered in Chapter 13, we summarize here the steps involved in doing a content analysis on mass media communications, which are very similar to the steps in systematic observation:

1. The phenomenon to be coded, such as the presence and portrayal of elderly people in the print media, must be chosen.
2. The media from which the observations are to be made must be selected. The issue here, as in systematic observation, is the selection of media that are typical or representative of what is available and with which people have contact. The issue is to find out what is out there and not to select so as to enhance or inhibit the possibility of obtaining particular findings.
3. In deriving the coding categories, as was the case with systematic observation, content analysis categories can range from a simple binary system, in which the presence or absence of people of a certain age are noted, to multicategory systems using mutually exclusive and exhaustive categories in which distinctions are made on a range of phenomena, such as the status of the portrayed character (e.g., high, middle, or low), background physical attractiveness (attractive, neutral, unattractive), or evaluation of context (positive, neutral, negative).

4. The distinctions in deciding on the sampling strategy are roughly comparable to the decisions involved in systematic observation. The task is to choose among strategies that code every reference to the phenomenon in question or to select a discontinuous though regular method of sampling, such as every other issue of several magazines over a year's period.

5. Training the coders ensures reliability of content analysis, an important consideration, particularly so when inferences are required to decide, for example, whether the portrayal of an elderly person is cast positively or negatively.

6. Sometimes the most straightforward statistical analysis is the tabulation and presentation of the characteristics in summary form such as frequencies and percentages.

Sampling material from mass communications requires much time and thought. The first task is to define the population – newspapers, magazines, radio, television, online, or social media. But even if we limited ourselves to newspapers (do we use the print version, or the electronic, and what about blogs of writers?), it would not be satisfactory to list all the newspapers published in a given country and draw every tenth or twentieth one. Even if we were also to introduce controls to ensure that newspapers representing different geographic areas, political orientations, economic groups, and ethnic groups were included in the proportion in which they are represented in the total population of newspapers, there would be a problem. The difficulty arises from the fact that newspapers vary tremendously in size and influence, and a realistic sample should not weight an obscure journal equally with a metropolitan daily. The situation is not the same as that of drawing a representative sample of a voting population, each member of which has equal influence at the polls – namely, one vote.

A study by Graber (1971) illustrates the complexity of decisions involved in sampling mass media sources. Graber wished to represent a cross-section of the newspapers used by the general public as sources of information in one study. She developed a complex sampling scheme that reflected where these newspapers would be found. First, it was decided that newspapers in each of the major regions in the country should be included in the sample. Cities in each region were then divided into three groups by population: over 1 million, 500,000 to 1 million, and fewer than 500,000. She decided to draw three-fourths of the sample from the most populous states in each region and the remainder from the less populous states to reflect voting power on the basis of population. Further decisions narrowed even more the potential newspapers that could be included in the sample. Half the newspapers were selected from states in which the Democratic Party was stronger; half from states in which the Republican Party was stronger. Newspapers were selected, moreover, to represent monopolistic as well as competitive newspaper market situations. Finally, two types of newspapers, appealing to either special or general audiences, were included in the sample. Graber then coded all the campaign stories in the newspapers.

Frequently, then, the sampling procedure in content analysis of mass communications consists of three stages: sampling of sources (which newspapers, which radio stations, which films, and so on are to be analyzed); sampling of dates (which time period is to be covered by the study); and sampling of units (which aspects of the communication are to be analyzed). In the sampling of units, decisions are often arbitrary and based on tacit assumptions about which feature of a medium best characterizes it. For example, is it the headline, the human interest story, the editorial, or some other feature that best indicates the policy of a newspaper?

To avoid such arbitrariness, content analysts frequently follow one of two possibilities: They analyze on the basis of several different units (e.g., they take samplings of headlines, of human interest stories, and of editorials and then count how many times a target person, behavior, or event is mentioned in each), or they disregard these "natural" units completely, dividing the issues of a newspaper mechanically into lines or inches of space from which they draw a sample. Note here the similarity to the distinctions among types of time sampling.

In summary, content analytic methods applied to verbal records, either personal communications (including social media) or the mass media, constitute an underused resource for research on social behavior. Content coding schemes for a variety of psychological states (such as anxiety, positive and negative feelings, and hostility) already exist and have been shown to have adequate reliability and validity (Bardi, Calogero, & Mullen, 2008; Viney, 1983). As we discuss in Chapter 13, content analysis can also be done via computer programs, with benefits of both lower cost and higher objectivity and reliability compared to human coders. As the previous examples illustrate, the range of issues that can be approached by content analytic techniques is wide indeed.

Issues in Archival Research

Archival research offers important advantages for some research questions. The use of archives is often economical, for the researcher is spared the time and cost involved in gathering and recording information. This advantage can be offset, though, by the effort involved in finding the relevant information as well as the search for materials that would allow the researcher to rule out alternative interpretations. Another important advantage is that much information is gathered by governments and other organizations as part of their everyday operations, and it is often collected repeatedly. This helps to avoid the difficulties associated with people's awareness of being participants in research (reactivity) and often makes possible the analysis of trends over time. Finally, archival research is particularly well suited to the investigation of large-scale or widespread social or natural phenomena that are not amenable to study in other ways.

Archival records give the opportunity to assess the impact of natural events and investigate many other issues. They are obviously strong on external validity because of the participants' unawareness of the research or its aims; however, they also characteristically offer certain problems of interpretation, centering on internal and construct validity. To give an oft-cited example, records are available on the two variables of ice-cream sales and crime rates, which turn out to be positively associated (i.e., as one increases the other increases as well; Kasarda, 1976). Can we conclude that eating ice cream increases the propensity to commit crimes? Obviously not, and this is an example of a **spurious association**: The two variables are associated only because they are both influenced by a third variable. Here, the variable is probably weather conditions – increasing temperature increases both ice-cream sales and crime, but the latter two variables probably do not affect each other. When using archival records, we must allow for the possibilities of internal invalidity or spurious associations (caused, for instance, by common influences of increasing population, inflation-induced price rises, or weather or other seasonal effects). This can require the collection of additional information, such as temperature records in this example, to rule out threats to internally valid causal inferences. We can never be sure we have ruled out all potential threats to internal validity, and thus it is difficult to arrive at a firm causal inference using archival methods.

Another major issue in archival research is the construct validity and reliability of the data for research purposes. The researcher does not control the gathering of information in archival research, so it can be subject to various sources of unreliability, bias, or invalidity. For example, organizations might keep records haphazardly, with little attention to consistency in recording similar events in the same way over time. Records also can be subject to systematic biases; for example, the crime reports published by universities under new reporting laws have been frequently criticized as reflecting an underreporting bias. Similarly, samples of written documents from some societies might overrepresent the literate (and therefore those with higher status) and underrepresent the illiterate. Even the *Congressional Record*, a rich source of information on speeches and official proceedings in government, is edited after the fact by the speakers, so that what appears in the record is not always what was spoken on the floor.

Finally, archives are subject to gaps and incompleteness that make it difficult to determine whether the available information adequately represents the population of interest. A demographer interested in the life span of ancient Romans investigated tombstones to find birth and death dates – but found biases. Tombstones that survive to the present are more likely to represent the middle and upper classes than the poor, and it even appeared that "a wife was more likely to get an inscribed tablet if she died before her husband than if she outlived him" (Durand, 1960). Researchers have examined suicide notes for clues to the mental states of suicide victims, but the majority of suicide victims do not leave notes. Are their mental states the same as those of note writers? And archives can contain information that is simply wrong. Stamp (1929) offered a friendly warning about the accuracy of archival records that is just as timely today as when he first said it:

> The government is very keen on amassing statistics. They collect them, add them, raise them to the nth power, take the cube root and prepare wonderful diagrams. But what you must never forget is that every one of these figures comes in the first instance from the *chowty dar* (village watchman), who just puts down what he damn pleases. (pp. 258–259)

Summary

This chapter began by describing the types of research that can be viewed as non-experimental. It focuses on quantitative non-experimental types of data, noting that causal thinking typically underlies these types of research. Therefore, it is important to avoid the trap of using language corresponding to the theory rather than the data, which do not support causal thinking. Longitudinal panel models were introduced, and predictive and explanatory types of analyses were described.

The latter part of the chapter focused on naturalness, a defining feature of many of the research methods considered in this chapter. In contrast to laboratory and survey research, many forms of observation and archival research stress natural behaviors, treatments, and settings so that some of the potential problems stemming from the respondent's awareness of being a research participant can be avoided. For certain types of research questions, particularly those dealing with the naturally occurring rates or patterns of behaviors, methods like those described in this chapter are the most appropriate. Observational methods give particular stress to natural behaviors and settings, although the specific methods vary in their emphasis. Archival methods (with the exception of research survey archives) also emphasize the use of records that are kept by or about individuals in the natural course of their activities, so they similarly offer access to natural behavior that is unaffected by the research process. Archives are particularly well suited for the analysis of the effects of natural treatments, such as natural or human-created disasters or social changes.

In this chapter, as elsewhere in the book, we emphasize the use of appropriate research techniques to improve the validity of findings. The specific technique that is most appropriate depends on the nature of the question as well as other factors, but for a wide range of research questions, observational and archival methods are certainly strong candidates for adoption. Naturalness in research can increase the external and construct validity of results, as many examples cited indicate, especially with respect to participants' awareness of research and associated problems like social desirability biases in responding. Yet, these methods are characteristically weaker in internal validity and other aspects of construct validity; we often cannot be certain that a measure is affected by only the single desired construct rather than multiple possibilities. It is when a research hypothesis has been tested, with converging results, by observational or archival methods and by laboratory, questionnaire, or other more reactive methods that we can be most confident of its validity.

Exercise: Serendipitous and opportunistic research

We have selected serendipitous and opportunistic to describe how researchers can use or build upon existing (archival) data to test hypotheses. As is noted in the text, one of the interesting features of today's grocery stores is their capacity to target individual shoppers. Stores reward frequent shoppers using "loyalty cards" by giving them discounts on selected merchandise. At the same time, those loyalty cards allow stores to track customers, including their frequency of shopping and patterns of purchases, which allows stores to target them for additional promotions. And, in the near future, consumers may be targeted from "cookies" from cell phones that provide recognition of customers and their buying patterns

(Continued)

whenever they enter a store. For us as researchers, being able to pair shopping and purchasing patterns with individual customers can produce all kinds of research opportunities. For example, we could use existing data to track ways that advertising affects purchasing of particular products, or how cultural changes in eating patterns affect total purchases of particular products as well as the demographics of the people whose patterns are changing most. Or we could hypothesize that really tall people buy different products than do really short people because they see different products on shelves (if you believe that reaching products might also account for differences, you could offer "extender" tools to shorter people so they can reach products on the highest shelf). Or, if we wanted to study attitude intensity and/or attitude change or persuasion, we could do that by changing prices or coupon discounts. If we know a particular shopper has a particular brand of a product that they purchase, we could examine the strength of their preference by providing discounts or coupons for alternative products.

Think about hypotheses you might have about shopping that you could test using or building on data already available at grocery stores. Working in groups, design one study that uses existing data, and a second that builds from existing data. Critique the study's threats to validity.

Go online   Visit the book's companion website for this chapter's test bank and other resources at: www.wiley.com/go/maruyama

Key Concepts

Accretion measures	Observational research
Archival research	Observer drift
Behavior setting survey	Panel designs
Checklists/category systems	Personal documents
Content analysis	Physical traces
Continuous real-time measurement	Questionnaire research
Ecological observation	Research survey archives
Encoding	Sequential analysis
Erosion measures	Spurious association
Ethological approaches	Statistical archives
Experimental realism	Statistical records
Mode of observation	Survey research
Molecular behavior	Systematic observation
Mundane realism	Time-interval sampling
Natural behaviors	Time-point sampling
Natural events	Unobtrusive observations
Natural settings	Verbal records
Nonreactive measures	

On the Web

http://www.nara.gov/ The website for the National Archives and Records Administration, an independent federal agency that oversees the management of all federal records. Includes links to the Federal Register, history/genealogy sites, and veterans' services archives.

http://www.dmoz.org/Reference/Archives/ Provides links to many different archives; themes include Arts, Medical, Personal, Social History, University, and Regional (organized by country).

http://www.fedstats.gov/ This site bills itself as "Celebrating over 10 years of making statistics from more than 100 agencies available to citizens everywhere." Very easy to navigate, allows searching by topic, state, or federal agency, but has not been updated recently.

http://www.norc.uchicago.edu/homepage.htm The official website of the National Opinion Research Center (NORC), including information about the General Social Survey as well as other large-scale sample surveys conducted by NORC.

http://www.noldus.com/ Website for the Noldus Company, originators of The Observer XT and other software programs for observational research.

http://nces.ed.gov/nationsreportcard/ The National Assessment of Educational Progress (NAEP) is a nationally representative assessment of students across many subject domains. This website contains information on NAEP assessments, various publications, and allows users to interact with some of the data.

http://www.iea.nl/data.html/ The website of the International Association for the Evaluation of Educational Achievement (IEA) contains international data covering a range of educational topics. The site provides access to these data, relevant publications, and tools to help with analysis of the data.

Further Reading

Agnew, C. R., Carlston, D. E., Graziano, W. G., & Kelly, J. R. (Eds.). (2010). *Then a miracle occurs: Focusing on behavior in social psychological theory and research*. New York, NY: Oxford University Press.

Bakeman, R., & Gottman, J. M. (1997). *Observing interaction: An introduction to sequential analysis* (2nd ed.). New York, NY: Cambridge University Press.

Bakeman, R., & Quera, V. (1995). *Analyzing interaction: Sequential analysis with SDIS and GSEQ*. New York, NY: Cambridge University Press.

Baumeister, R. F., Vohs, K. D., & Funder, D. C. (2007). Psychology as the science of self-reports and finger movements: Whatever happened to actual behavior? *Perspectives on Psychological Science, 2*, 396–403.

Heyman, R. E., Lorber, M. F., Eddy, J. M., & West, T. V. (2014). Behavioral observation and coding. In H. T. Reis & C. M. Judd (Eds.), *Handbook of research methods in social and personality psychology* (2nd ed., pp. 345–372). New York, NY: Cambridge University Press.

Hill, M. R. (1993). *Archival strategies and techniques.* Thousand Oaks, CA: Sage.

Mook, D. G. (1983). In defense of external invalidity. *American Psychologist, 38,* 379–387.

Russell, C. H., & Megaard, I. (1988). *The General Social Survey, 1972–1986: The state of the American people.* New York, NY: Springer.

Chapter 13

Qualitative Research

Qualitative research takes many forms and is called by many names. One form consists of open-ended questions embedded in structured interviews or questionnaires; we covered this form of qualitative research in Chapter 7. The other forms rely almost entirely on open-ended explorations of people's words, thoughts, actions, and intentions. This kind of research includes narrative analysis, focus groups, oral history, participant observation (sometimes referred to as **ethnography**), case histories, and many others. Although these research strategies vary in their goals and methods, they all share the critical defining characteristic of **qualitative research**: Rather than imposing hypotheses, themes, and categories on participants' responses, participants relate

Research Methods in Social Relations, Eighth Edition. Geoffrey Maruyama and Carey S. Ryan.
© 2014 John Wiley & Sons, Inc. Published 2014 by John Wiley & Sons, Inc.
Companion Website: www.wiley.com/go/maruyama

stories about their lives that enable researchers to generate hypotheses and themes and, more generally, to understand participants' social worlds from their perspectives. With respect to scientific approaches, these methods, although used for many different purposes, are the methods of choice for constructivist researchers. In this chapter, we describe several forms of qualitative research used frequently in the social sciences, beginning with the most structured form – narrative analysis – and concluding with the least structured – participant observation. In doing so, we hope to communicate a sense of the variety, creativity, spontaneity, and genuineness that qualitative research entails. Integration of qualitative and quantitative research methods is provided in Chapter 16, on mixed methods.

Narrative Analysis

Narratives are oral or written accounts of personal experience. They can be distinguished from simple responses to open-ended questions in that they have the structure of a story: There is a beginning and an end, protagonists and antagonists, and a plot. Narratives can even be fictional, as in the case of fairy tales or myths, although in social science research we are normally concerned with narratives that are accounts of actual events in people's lives.

Narratives can be accounts that are produced specifically for a given research study, or they can be derived from preexisting archives, for example, collections of letters, diaries, or autobiographies. In the former case, the researcher has considerable control over the conditions under which the narratives are obtained and can focus the narrative in a direction that best suits the goals of the research. In the latter case, the researcher has less control in terms of both sampling and content of the narratives; however, archival narratives are generally less likely to be biased by demand characteristics. Moreover, archival narratives, for example, suicide notes (Osgood & Walker, 1959), can be particularly well suited for some research questions and populations. Archival narratives might also be used when the research questions concern longitudinal processes. For example, Snowdon et al. (1996) analyzed the diaries written by nuns when they were in their twenties. Remarkably, a measure of "idea density" as reflected in the diaries predicted which nuns were likely to develop Alzheimer's disease over 50 years later. This kind of longitudinal evidence is both impressive and convincing, especially considering the fact that Alzheimer's disease was not even known as a separate diagnosis at the time the diaries were written.

Researchers use narrative analysis because they believe that narratives yield information that is not accessible by more traditional fixed response methods, which yield information summarizing respondent perspectives without identifying underlying cognitive processes. Questionnaires using fixed response scales are not optimal for eliciting people's innermost thoughts, hopes, and feelings, nor for capturing complex mental phenomena, such as moral reasoning or cognitive styles (Smith, 2000). Narratives can reveal themes that researchers did not even think to ask about. As such, narrative analysis may be particularly helpful in the early stages of a research program, when the researcher is trying to identify the variables that are critical to understanding a phenomenon or to uncover the motivations for particular ideas or behaviors.

Research Example of Narrative Analysis

The richness of narrative data is nicely illustrated in a study by Laura King and her colleagues on parents' adaptation to having a child born with Down's syndrome (King, Scollon, Ramsey, & Williams, 2000). The advantages of narrative analysis in a project of this nature are clear. It would be difficult, if not impossible, to capture the range and complexity of emotions felt by parents upon learning of their child's diagnosis with Down's syndrome using a traditional paper-and-pencil questionnaire. An item such as "On a scale of 1 to 7, how distressed were you when you found out that your child had Down's syndrome?" seems both naïve and insensitive.

King and colleagues (2000) recruited 87 parents of children with Down's syndrome from mailing lists of various Down's syndrome support groups. Participants first completed questionnaire measures of subjective well-being, ego development, and stress-related growth. Then parents were asked to write a narrative "about the moment when you first were told that your child had Down's syndrome." These narratives were subsequently coded by judges for various features of the stories, such as the presence of foreshadowing, happy beginnings, happy endings, degree of closure expressed, and degree of negative emotion experienced. Two years later participants were mailed another packet including the same questionnaire measures. The primary goal of the study was to determine whether features of parents' narratives were associated with changes in subjective well-being, ego development, and stress-related growth.

Analyses produced an interesting pattern of results. Foreshadowing and happy endings in the stories were associated with greater subjective well-being at both time periods. In contrast, a strong sense of closure and accommodation in the stories was associated with greater stress-related growth. In other words, the parents who felt best about their experiences were not necessarily the ones who exhibited the most personal growth. These findings led the authors to conclude that "the stories we tell about our life experiences may illuminate two pathways – one to satisfaction and one to maturity" (King et al., 2000, p. 530).

One advantage of narrative analysis is that researchers can provide excerpts from participants' narratives written to illustrate important conclusions or perspectives in addition to reporting more standard quantitative analyses of the coded variables. For example, King and colleagues (2000) provided the following quotes to illustrate happy and sad endings, respectively:

> I know my daughter is quite special. It's as if she's part of another race or from another planet. She's definitely wired differently. And I think those wires are hooked directly to God. She's the closest I've come to an angel on Earth. (p. 519)

> We were given an *Exceptional Parents* magazine ... I found a picture of a crib with a lid on it, like a cage. I remember wondering, what do we have? What are we faced with? I also remember thinking that now we'll never be normal. (p. 519)

The researchers also provided an example of a narrative showing the parents' attempt to accommodate to the diagnosis:

> I cried a lot. The pain was so deep. I felt cheated – I could hardly function. I was so absorbed with my own fears. But I did regroup. I did grow. And I did learn to accept the situation. That opened the door for me to bond and love my child. But it took time. (p. 521)

The narrative excerpts are much more vivid and informative than are the variable labels of "happy ending," "sad ending," and "accommodation." Narrative analysis thus aids importantly in demonstrating construct validity because the meaning of a variable is clearly communicated through the judicious reporting of narrative excerpts.

Analyzing and Reporting Narrative Data

Narrative analysis, unlike other qualitative methods we discuss in this chapter, can include coding participants' responses into variables that can be subjected to quantitative analyses. In such usage, excerpts from narratives are quoted to make points or illustrate important conclusions, but the primary analyses tend to be quantitative in nature – as in the King et al. (2000) study.

To perform quantitative analyses, the qualitative narratives must be translated into quantitative information using a content analysis. **Content analysis** is the process of extracting desired information from a text by systematically and objectively identifying specified characteristics of the text (Smith, 2000). Variables to be coded might be tentatively identified prior to gathering the data; however, researchers also consider **emergent themes** and ways of thinking, that is, ideas that come from participants' responses and that might not have been considered when the research was designed. Content analysis then takes one or both of two major approaches: coding the narratives according to discrete themes or categories and rating the narratives on continuous dimensions.

The King et al. (2000) study provides examples of both approaches to content coding. First, three coders read each narrative for the presence (coded 1) or absence (coded 0) of foreshadowing, happy beginning, or happy ending. In addition to these nominal variables, the narratives were rated on several interval-scaled variables. For example, raters scored each narrative, using 7-point scales, on such variables as how active the participant was in the story, how traumatic the experience was, and how much denial was present in the narrative.

The number and type of variables that are coded in a given study depend on the goals of the research. Variables can be identified on theoretical grounds before the narratives are obtained, or they can be derived after reading the narratives over and detecting recurring themes. In general, it is better not to fall into the trap of "overcoding" the narratives; the coding of open-ended responses is generally labor intensive and if too many variables are coded, the researcher is in danger of capitalizing on chance in the analyses, meaning that some of the results will be statistically significant but would not likely replicate using another sample from the same population. Capitalizing on chance can occur anytime researchers engage in many analyses of a lot of variables; the more analyses one does, the more likely it is that something will be significant. A better strategy is to outline a concise list of hypotheses prior to obtaining the narratives and to choose a limited number of coded variables that would test those hypotheses.

A critical aspect of content analysis is the reliability of coding. As described in Chapter 7, at least two raters should code all of the narratives, and the reliability among the raters should be estimated and reported. Raters should be carefully trained prior to working with the actual narratives. Variables should be explicitly defined, examples of categories (sometimes referred to as rubrics, particularly if there is a performance aspect to the ratings) should be provided, and raters should practice coding a sample set of narratives until satisfactory agreement has been demonstrated. Interval-scaled ratings are generally more subjective than nominal-scaled coding, and, depending on the judgment being made, as many as five or six raters might be needed to attain adequate reliability. Raters should make their judgments independently, and they should be unaware of the status of the participant on other relevant variables.

Another approach to content analysis is to use computer software specifically designed for that purpose. Examples are General Inquirer, Linguistic Inquiry and Word Count (LIWC), ATLAS.ti, Non-numerical Unstructured Data with powerful processes of Indexing Searching and Theorizing (NUD*IST), and Ethnograph. These programs compare the text of interest to **dictionaries**, which are either provided by the software or created by the researcher for a particular study. For example, the LIWC program (Pennebaker & Francis, 1996; Tausczik & Pennebaker, 2010) compares the target text against the program dictionary and, if the target word matches one of the entries in the dictionary, the corresponding word category is increased by one count. The LIWC program codes almost 4,500 linguistic variables relevant to linguistic processes (e.g., word count, personal pronouns, number of questions), psychological processes (e.g., positive and negative emotion words, sensory-related words, social processes), and personal concerns (e.g., leisure activities, work and household-related words). (Additional information is available at http://liwc.net/index.php.)

As with any methodology, computerized content analysis has its advantages and disadvantages. A major advantage of programs like LIWC is that they can perform a large amount of tedious work very quickly. It would take a crew of research assistants weeks to code an average-sized sample of narratives. The main disadvantage is that the variables provided by the program might not correspond exactly to researchers' needs. However, it is usually possible for researchers to build their own dictionaries. Also, content coding performed by computer generally involves tabulating words that fall into various categories; these methods of coding cannot handle verbal subtleties, such as sarcasm. A phrase like "Man, that show was bad," meaning that it was actually good, would be coded as a negative emotion instead by the computer. Lastly, programs such as LIWC might provide too much of a good thing; it might be tempting to code more variables than are theoretically relevant. Performing many analyses without compelling theoretical reasons for doing so is likely to result in nonreplicable findings that occur due to chance.

An additional means of generating information using narratives is to have participants respond to a set of questions after they have finished writing their narratives.

An example of this approach is seen in a study of how teasing is used in different types of relationships (Bollmer, Harris, & Dotson, 2001). Participants were asked to write three narratives about occasions on which they teased a friend, a romantic partner, and a family member. Immediately following the writing of each narrative, the participants completed a 10-item paper-and-pencil measure asking them to rate, on 9-point scales, their impressions of their own motives for teasing in that particular incident and how the target of the teasing responded. For example, participants were asked how hurt and annoyed the target was, how humorous the teasing was, how much they regretted the teasing now, and to what extent they teased the target for each of three motives: to "put them in their place," to point out a weakness, or to gain their attention.

There is a major advantage to obtaining this kind of information in addition to the content analysis provided by objective judges. Having participants respond to standardized questions following a narrative ensures that comparable information is obtained from everybody in the study. Researchers typically have very little control over exactly what will be written in the narratives. Although a researcher can provide explicit instructions to participants, requesting specific kinds of information, such instructions obviously cannot be enforced. For example, in the Bollmer et al. (2001) study, the researchers wanted a measure of the regret felt by the teaser. Many of the participants spontaneously mentioned feeling regret ("I feel really bad about it now"), but many did not. Does that mean they did not feel regret? Not necessarily; maybe it simply did not occur to those participants to write about their regretful feelings in describing the incident. Having all participants explicitly rate how much regret they felt ensured that all participants considered the issue and that information would be obtained to allow direct comparisons among them.

Of course, nothing prevents researchers from conducting both an objective content analysis and having participants complete standardized measures about their narratives; in fact, having both kinds of information can be informative as well as provide valuable evidence of convergent validity. That was the case in the Bollmer et al. (2001) example. In addition to the 10-item questionnaire that participants completed, a group of four judges read each narrative and rated them on how hurt and angry the target was, how much regret was shown by the teaser, how much the teaser enjoyed the teasing, how the target responded behaviorally to the teasing, and the overall positivity of the consequences of the teasing. Thus, there was some overlap between the constructs rated by the judges and those rated by participants, which enabled the researchers to assess the degree of convergence between self-reports and judges' ratings, and to identify areas of intriguing difference. For instance, what does it mean when the objective judges deem the target to have been hurt badly by the teasing but the teaser rates the target as not having been hurt at all?

Asking participants to relate stories from their lives that pertain to the research questions is a highly effective yet curiously underutilized research tool. Participants' stories convey emotion and detail that are impossible to reduce to numbers. It is this richness of emotion and detail that makes narrative analysis so appealing and informative. Narrative accounts are also relatively easy to obtain. The question, then, is not whether or why narrative analysis should be conducted but, rather, why so few researchers in the social sciences avail themselves of this rich source of information.

Exercise: Change in North Dakota

Not too long ago there were conversations about relocating people from a large part of western North Dakota and recreating buffalo prairie that would attract tourists and restore wilderness. Today, however, the population of western North Dakota is growing rapidly because of advances in oil extraction techniques. The changes caused by this oil boom have disrupted communities and taxed their human and social services. As examples, the volunteer fire departments of many communities lack the capacity to deal with the types of problems they might face, the roads are being used in excess of their capacity, and the schools are over-crowded. Wages for all jobs have gone way up, housing is short, and restaurants and stores are insufficient for meeting the needs of the people. Using one or more approaches described in this chapter, design an exploratory study to gain a better understanding of the nature of problems being experienced by the different populations within western North Dakota (long-term residents, new arrivals, oil companies, etc.).

Focus Groups

Focus groups are structured group interviews. They bring together a small group of interacting individuals who discuss, under the guidance of a moderator, the topic of interest to the researcher. The first documented use of focus groups occurred soon after World War II when groups were assembled in an effort to evaluate audience response to radio programs (Stewart & Shamdasani, 1990). Since that time, focus groups have enjoyed immense popularity in market research; they are, perhaps, the bread and butter of market research firms. In the past couple decades the use of focus groups has spread to other areas of social science research. For example, Parker et al. (2012) used focus group methodology to examine African American, European American, and Lumbee American Indian parents' beliefs about their children's emotions. In this section, we describe the typical format and process of a focus group, provide examples of how focus groups might be used to study social behavior, and conclude with a discussion of the advantages and disadvantages of using focus groups.

How Focus Groups Are Structured and Conducted

A typical focus group consists of 6 to 10 individuals. Fewer than 6 makes it less likely that the desired diversity of opinions will be elicited; more than 10 makes it difficult for everyone to express their opinions fully. In most cases, it is desirable for focus group members to be previously unacquainted with one another. Lack of familiarity promotes free expression of ideas and opinions that might not be forthcoming if members feel constrained by what they have said in the past to others in the group. However, sometimes it is not practical to have unacquainted members in the focus group. For example, suppose we wanted to conduct a focus group of high school principals to generate ideas for preventing school violence. Many, if not all, principals within a city would likely know each other. Conducting a focus group in which principals are flown in from a variety of cities would achieve the goal of unfamiliarity, but it probably would be prohibitively expensive, and may bring together people with such different experiences that little common ground would exist for discussion.

Focus group members usually are selected because they share something in common that is relevant to the topic being researched. In market research, for example, the focus group might be composed of individuals who use the product in question or who constitute the target population for the product (e.g., female teenagers and jeans). Theory-testing research using focus groups often has specialized populations in mind such as breast cancer patients, lesbians and gay men, military personnel, teachers, African Americans, depressed people, and so forth. Research looking at the interactions between members of different groups might require several different focus groups. For example, a study looking at the quality of doctor–patient interactions might arrange separate focus groups for doctors and patients as well as a few mixed doctor–patient groups.

In short, the membership of a focus group tends to be relatively homogeneous with respect to one or more characteristics relevant to the research questions. Thus, focus groups are not representative of the general population nor are they intended to be, and findings that emerge from a focus group cannot be assumed to be true for the rest of the population, or indeed, for anybody else. We return to this point later in the chapter when we discuss the limitations of focus groups as a research tool.

All focus groups are led by a **moderator** – the researcher or a hired professional – and it is the presence and activities of the moderator that distinguish a focus group from an unstructured group discussion. The moderator is the key to the success of a focus group. The quality of information obtained from a focus group is directly related to the moderator's ability to monitor and control the discussion and elicit insights and revelations from the group members. A useful analogy is that of psychotherapy: One can tell another person about one's personal problems, but real therapeutic progress is only likely to take place when the other person is a skilled clinician trained to bring about insight and behavior change.

The moderator must engage in considerable advance preparation to make a focus group successful. First, the research objectives must be identified and clarified. In applied research, clients often provide those objectives ("Find out why nobody is buying our widgets!"), but in any case, the objectives usually need to be redefined and narrowed. In other research contexts, considerable expertise with the topic of interest is required to define the objectives in ways that elicit theoretically useful information from participants. In addition to identifying the objectives of the focus group, a **focus group guide** is developed. The guide consists of the major topics and questions that will be raised in the focus group discussion. The number of questions that can be asked in a focus group is surprisingly small. The recommended maximum duration of a focus group is 1½ to 2 hours (even shorter with children) – much beyond that and group members' attention wanders. Thus, only two or three major issues with two or three subissues each can be considered by any focus group.

Table 13.1 Example of a Focus Group Interview Guide

Major Objective: Determine what encourages and discourages teenagers from drinking alcohol.
Question 1: What factors encourage or pressure teenagers to drink?
    Subissue 1: What do your friends think about teenage drinking? What do kids at your school typically do for fun? How is alcohol viewed by your friends and the other kids at school?
    Subissue 2: How is teen drinking portrayed in movies or on TV? What usually happens when teenagers drink in movies or on TV shows?
    Subissue 3: Under what circumstances is a teenager likely to have the opportunity to drink? When is a teenager likely to feel pressured to drink?
Question 2: What factors discourage teenagers from drinking?
    Subissue 1: What do your parents think about teenage drinking? What are your family rules? How does that affect your behavior?
    Subissue 2: What kinds of things have you learned about the effects of alcohol from school or the media? What are your school's rules regarding drinking?
    Subissue 3: What do you think parents or teachers could do to prevent teenagers from drinking? What do you think they *should* do?

The phrasing and sequencing of questions in the focus group guide are also critical. Obviously, moderators should avoid closed-ended, yes-no questions. Not so obvious, however, is the fact that moderators should also avoid asking "why" questions. The reason is that "why" questions usually elicit rationalizations, particularly socially desirable rationalizations. Participants might feel pressured to give what they perceive to be the response expected by the moderator or that will cast them in a positive light. More generally, "why" questions might be less fruitful because people are often not consciously aware of the motives underlying their choices and behavior (Nisbett & Wilson, 1977). A better way to get at participants' motivations is to ask about what they do and how they feel about it. From a detailed description of these actions, thoughts, and feelings, the reasons for behavior can be more easily and accurately inferred.

Table 13.1 shows an example of a focus group guide that could be used in a group of adolescents aimed at discovering factors that encourage and discourage teenage alcohol use. Note that all questions are open-ended and grouped in a logical manner. Note also that the questions regarding the factors that encourage drinking among teenagers are asked before the questions regarding the factors that discourage drinking; often it is more productive to discuss the emergence of a problem before discussing how to solve it.

Once the focus group guide has been developed, participants are recruited, often using convenience sampling or other nonprobability sampling techniques. Unless the topic of the discussion is of special interest or relevance to the members (e.g., a focus group of spouse abuse victims), incentives might be necessary to get people to participate. Focus group discussions are held in comfortable meeting rooms, which may be equipped with one-way mirrors through which the researcher or sponsoring client can observe the proceedings.

Most focus groups begin with the moderator making introductions and describing the **ground rules** for the discussion. These ground rules include explaining the purpose and format of the focus group; emphasizing that everyone's ideas count and that the moderator wants to hear from everyone; that only one person should speak at a time; and that people should refrain from criticizing others' opinions. Moderators should also address confidentiality, assuring participants that only group-level information will be reported and nobody will be individually identified. Participants also should be requested to keep what they hear during the focus group confidential; however, because researchers do not have control over what participants say after the session is over, it should be made clear to participants that their confidentiality cannot be guaranteed. Most focus groups are either audiotaped or videotaped, and participants sign a consent form in which they are told that the session will be recorded.

Then the focus group session begins. The moderator follows the focus group guide, but the discussion is not entirely scripted. Part of what makes the moderator's role so difficult is that a moderator must be able to guide the conversation while carefully processing what is being said. Moderators need to be able to identify when follow-up questions are needed and what those follow-up questions should be. It is through the careful probing and following up of statements that focus groups generate the most useful information; a moderator who sticks completely to the guide is likely to obtain only superficial material. Depending on what is said, the moderator might need to abandon the guide to pursue a promising avenue of discussion. Many focus groups include an observer who takes notes about the process and records impressions so that the moderator can devote full attention to guiding the conversation.

One of the moderator's main tasks is to make sure the conversation stays on track; with only 60 or 90 minutes to achieve its goals, a focus group cannot afford to digress often or for any length of time. In the event of digression, the moderator must refocus the conversation without annoying the person who digressed. The moderator also must prevent one or two individuals from dominating the conversation as well as make sure that even the shiest participant speaks up. The moderator therefore should be skilled at interpreting nonverbal behavior. There can be considerable conformity pressure operating in a focus group, and the moderator needs to be able to identify the subtle nonverbal signs of discomfort that indicate that a participant does not agree with what is being said. Prompts such as, "There might be other ways to view that issue. So-and-so, what do you think?" might be needed to elicit the dissenting opinion. The moderator should maintain friendly rapport with the participants throughout the discussion while taking care to avoid appearing to approve or disapprove of particular statements being made. Participants generally desire to please the moderator; any kind of verbal or nonverbal reinforcements (head nods, "uh-huhs," or "goods") might quickly bias the direction of the discussion and compromise the quality of the information.

Once the main discussion is completed, a "cooling down" exercise is often helpful. The moderator might ask each participant to describe the most important thing they heard during the discussion. The moderator then reminds participants to keep the discussion confidential and thanks them for their help. Immediately following the session, the moderator might consult with observers to ensure that they record their impressions of the discussion while it is fresh in their minds.

Generally, more than one focus group is conducted for a given objective. One rule of thumb is to keep having focus groups until few or no new insights are volunteered, which usually happens after four or five groups. The information yielded by focus groups rarely is in a format that can be subjected to inferential testing or statistical analysis. Rather, participants' comments are classified according to broad themes, and a report is written summarizing the contents. Thus, focus groups capture the true spirit of qualitative research – the emphasis is on hypothesis generation rather than hypothesis testing.

Case Study of the Strategic Use of Focus Groups

We turn now to a real-world example of using focus groups in social science research. The goal of this research was to develop televised public service announcements (PSAs) for use in an antidrug campaign (Palmgreen, Donohew, Lorch, Hoyle, & Stephenson, 2001). Past media campaigns featuring prevention PSAs have revealed disappointingly small effects (Rogers & Storey, 1987). One possible reason is that the PSAs have not effectively targeted the population most at risk. Therefore, a major goal of the research program by Palmgreen and his colleagues was to create antidrug PSAs that would appeal to high-sensation-seeking adolescents, a population that previous research has identified as being especially susceptible to drug experimentation and abuse (Zuckerman, 1994).

Palmgreen and his colleagues (2001) conducted three sets of focus groups; members were students in the eighth through eleventh grades. Participants in the focus groups were eighth- through eleventh-grade students who had scored highest on a paper-and-pencil measure of sensation seeking. The first set of focus groups was devoted to discussing the kinds of risks associated with drug use. For an educational campaign to be effective, its target audience must believe that the consequences of drug use portrayed in the campaign are credible and they must perceive those consequences as deterrents. A good example of how a portrayal can backfire if that is not the case is the movie *Reefer Madness*, which was originally designed as an antimarijuana film but is now regularly shown in college towns to the great hilarity of the audience. Thus, the first set of focus groups addressed two major questions: (1) What are the specific kinds of risks – physical, legal, social, economic – that are realistic for particular drugs? (2) To what degree do these risks influence people like themselves to use or not use drugs?

The goal of the second set of focus groups was to identify features of PSAs that would appeal to high-sensation-seeking teens. To accomplish this, focus group members were shown a variety of advertisements and PSAs that had been previously produced and were asked to comment on specific features of the spots that did or did not appeal to them. These focus groups enabled the researchers to derive high-sensation-seeking value criteria for producing PSAs; these criteria included characteristics, such as novelty, drama, surprise, and strong emotional appeals.

The last set of focus groups helped in selecting the final antidrug PSAs to be produced (Palmgreen et al., 2001). Using the results from the first two sets of focus groups, the research team and a professional television producer created storyboards sketching a variety of possible PSAs. These storyboards (rough impressions of what a PSA would look like, describing the scenes that would be shown and the verbal content but not entailing the full costs of a polished production) were then shown to a new set of focus groups, whose members commented on the aspects they liked most and least about each ad. Focus group members were also asked about the perceived attention value of the possible PSAs, as well as their emotional impact, perceived realism, and effectiveness in deterring drug use.

The PSAs identified as most effective by the focus groups were then professionally produced and aired in a large field experiment involving two metropolitan areas. Over a 32-month period, face-to-face interviews with randomly selected teenagers indicated that the targeted PSAs were highly effective in decreasing marijuana use among high-sensation-seeking teenagers; as predicted, marijuana use among low-sensation-seeking teenagers was at a very low rate and not affected by the media campaign (Palmgreen et al., 2001).

For several reasons the Palmgreen et al. (2001) antidrug campaign study is a good example of how focus groups can be used in social science research. First, it highlights the primary strength of focus groups, which is that they are very effective in the hypothesis and idea generation stage of research. Palmgreen et al. used them to discover the best ways of creating an antidrug message. Second, this example shows just how cost-effective focus groups can be. Focus groups are an economical way of doing research; even if one is paying participants (usually $15 to $25 per participant is sufficient) and a moderator to conduct the groups, a full set of focus groups can be conducted for under $2,000. Contrast that amount to what it costs to prepare antidrug PSAs professionally and then buy television time to air them (hundreds of thousands of dollars at least). With so much money at stake, it was crucial that the researchers only produce PSAs that were likely to be effective, and the focus groups enabled them to do that. Thus, focus groups are highly recommended at the formative stage of any large-scale or expensive treatment or intervention.

What Focus Groups Can and Cannot Do

The foregoing discussion should make clear a primary appeal of focus groups: They are relatively quick, easy, and cheap. Compare collecting data on hundreds of participants in a months-long study with running three focus groups with a total of 20 participants in one weekend, and getting the same answers. Phrased that way, the growing popularity of focus groups as a research tool is easy to understand. The catch, of course, is in the assumption that focus groups yield "the same answers" as do other research methods. The reality is that focus groups are very good at generating certain kinds of information but not at all good for certain other purposes.

Focus groups have theoretical advantages as well – they enable researchers to explore ideas and suggest hypotheses. The best uses of focus groups are in stages of research or product development. Focus groups can be especially helpful in early stages because researchers tend to latch onto favorite ideas early on and often cannot see other possibilities or drawbacks to their favored hypotheses or plans. A quick and decisive dashing of an idea in the context of a focus group discussion ("There's no way that would work!") can end up saving researchers considerable time and energy from pursuing an ultimately doomed hypothesis or product.

Focus groups also are invaluable for gaining access to the unique concerns and perspectives of the target audience, which can sometimes be difficult for researchers to grasp. Determining what kind of persuasive appeal would work best for 10-year-old boys, for example, can be challenging for 40-year-old female (or even male) researchers. Similarly, it might be difficult for researchers to guess the deepest hopes and fears of people who are 70 years old. Rather than trying to second-guess 10-year-old boys' preferences or 70-year-olds' fears, it is easier and more accurate to bring them in for a focus group session. Researchers almost always gain new insights and discover where their preconceptions were wrong. For example, researchers conducting one focus group discovered that some young children interpreted the phrase "alcohol-free" to mean free beverages that contained alcohol, a miscommunication that could have serious ramifications if not detected.

Focus groups also are helpful when designing experimental materials or questionnaires for more traditional laboratory or survey studies. Researchers can discover how to phrase questions using the everyday language of the target population, and this process can be quicker than the traditional procedure of creating a questionnaire, pilot testing it on a small sample, and revising the questionnaire when ambiguities are identified in pilot testing. Focus groups can be helpful in more than just the beginning stages of research. For example, focus groups have been used extensively in evaluation research, which is discussed in Chapter 15, to determine whether a given program or intervention has been effective.

Another advantage of focus group methodology that is not normally considered concerns the benefits that accrue to participants: Focus groups can be an empowering experience for many participants. Members of focus groups are treated not as low-status experimental "subjects" but rather as full partners in the research enterprise, working collaboratively with the researcher to address an important question. Many participants greatly appreciate being considered and treated as possessing expertise on the topic in question and are gratified to feel that they are involved in something that can make a real difference. In sum, participants generally leave focus groups feeling better about the scientific process than do participants in more traditional forms of research.

Every research methodology has limitations, however, and focus groups are not without theirs. The major limitation is one we touched on earlier in the chapter, the problem of generalizability. Unless members of a focus group are randomly selected, a focus group is not representative of the population, and conclusions drawn from the focus group cannot be safely generalized to the population. In this respect, market research firms perhaps rely too heavily on focus groups. They use focus groups to make decisions about which products are likely to be successful, which is a question that can best be, and maybe only, answered through careful sampling and surveying. For example, the first set of focus groups discussing a newly designed Ford Taurus reacted quite negatively, calling it a "jelly bean" on wheels (Silverman, 2011). If Ford had stopped right there, they would have abandoned one of the best-selling models in automotive history.

Moreover, focus groups are even less likely to be representative than other convenience samples found in social science research. This is because focus group sessions involve social groups and are thus vulnerable to all the biasing dynamics that can occur in groups. Although moderators attempt to encourage equal participation from all group members, one or two individuals can dominate a focus group discussion and set the tone for others' contributions. The results of a focus group could therefore reflect only one person's opinions rather than the desired-for diversity of opinion. Yet researchers or marketing firms who would never dream of going along with a single person's judgment often do not hesitate to accept the conclusions of a focus group.

Another disadvantage of focus groups is that the researcher has substantially less control over the information obtained than in other research contexts. In a questionnaire study, or even an individual interview, researchers can set the agenda and specify exactly the questions that will be asked and the data that will be elicited. In a focus group, however, the participants can and do talk to and ask questions of each other that may wander far astray of what the researcher intended. Of course, the very feature of focus groups that results in less control for the researcher also produces the synergy that makes focus groups such a powerful tool. Researchers who use focus groups thus make the conscious choice to surrender control in order to gain insight.

Oral History

Oral history is a method for learning about the past by interviewing individuals who have experienced that past. Oral histories might center around important historical events, for example, the civil rights movement or the Holocaust, or they might center around important life roles or rites of passage, for example, what it means to be African American or becoming a parent. Interviews usually are tape-recorded, and the tapes or transcripts of the interviews are usually deposited in archives, libraries, or special collections so that other researchers can access them in the future. By examining what people have to say about their past, it is possible to gain insights about universals of human experience as well as an appreciation of how human nature has changed.

As with other forms of qualitative research, no attempt is made to select a random or representative sample in oral history, although in a few notable cases (e.g., the oral history of Holocaust survivors), researchers might attempt to interview the entire population, that is, every relevant individual. Usually, however, a smaller and non-systematic subset of potential respondents is selected for interviewing, often using snowball sampling methods (see Chapter 9). The researcher generally contacts the respondent ahead of time, describes the project, explains why the respondent was chosen, and requests permission to conduct and record the interview. The researcher often mails the respondent an outline of the questions to be covered in the interview in advance so that the respondent will have had the chance to think about and mentally prepare for the interview.

On the day of the interview, the respondent signs an informed consent form and a **deed of gift form** that allows the researcher to use the interview tapes and transcripts for research purposes and to place the tapes in an archive for public use. The information obtained in oral history is unlike that usually obtained by social scientists. Usually, social scientists guarantee participants anonymity or assure them that their

Table 13.2 Example of a Deed of Gift Form for Oral Histories

Deed of Gift Form

I, [name of respondent] hereby give to [name of sponsoring organization] for scholarly and educational use the recordings of the interview(s) conducted with me on [date of interview], and I grant to [sponsor] all of the rights I possess in those recordings, including all intellectual property rights.

I understand that [sponsor] grants me a nonexclusive license to make and to authorize others to make any use I wish of the content of those recordings, and that [sponsor] will, at my request, make available a copy of those recordings for such use.

If I wish to remain anonymous in any interview transcript or reference to any information contained in this interview, I will specify this restriction here. The foregoing gift and grant of rights is subject to the following restrictions:

This agreement may be revised or amended by mutual consent of the parties undersigned.

Accepted by:

_____   _____
[interviewer's signature]   Date:

_____   _____
[interviewee's signature]   Date:

_____
[interviewee's address and telephone number]

responses will never be individually identified. The whole point of oral history, however, is to preserve each individual's story in its unique form. Participants generally are offered the opportunity to have their identities concealed in transcripts and to have sealed those portions of the interview tapes that identify them, but many participants choose to remain fully identifiable. It is important for researchers to explain clearly to interviewees what their choices and rights are regarding their identification and to document carefully the choices that were made. In many cases, participants choose not to sign the deed of gift until after they review the transcript of their interview and are satisfied that the transcript faithfully reproduces their experience. Table 13.2 contains a sample deed of gift form that could be used in oral history research.

We illustrate oral history methods using extended quotes from a study by Barbara Levy Simon (1987) on the lives of women who had never married. Fifty women talked with Simon about their never-married lives, and from their stories she examined their views of being single, of family, intimacy, and work. The women's names were omitted or changed when their accounts were published, but their words remained in their original voices. For example:

How dare I fail to marry? How peculiar. How brazen. How sad. Or so many believe. Were I weak in the knees, I might believe that too. But fortunately, my knees are steady and hold me up fine when people give me those patronizing looks and commiserating tones.

As an eighty-two-year old, it's easy to ignore the labels attached to those of us who stayed single. It used to be harder. For example, when I was about forty, my boss asked me out of the blue if I was still in love with my father. By then, I knew enough to make jokes about such foolishness. The only alternative to humor that I could think of was committing mayhem or worse. And how could I explain to the judge that I killed my boss because he saw me as a silly spinster? (p. 1)

The women did not all tell the same story, but neither did they give 50 unrelated accounts. Thirty-eight women told of being voluntarily single, as illustrated in this quote:

I loved my job running that office. I did it for twenty-seven years. It was not my whole life, certainly, but it was a highly significant portion. They wouldn't have fired me if I had gotten married. But I would have been unable to be a good wife and also do that job. It required nights, weekends, early mornings, and lots of disrupted plans. I didn't meet men in those days who would have understood my insistence that the job was as important to me as anything else. Now, I know that such men exist. But back then, they were nowhere to be found, at least not in my circles. (p. 44)

Among the 12 women who described themselves as involuntarily single, seven said that their responsibility for taking care of elderly parents conflicted with the demands of fiancés and the former took precedence:

Finally, he [fiancé] told me that I had to put my father in a home if he was going to marry me. The only homes we could afford were disgusting. I refused, and, after a while, Joe stopped coming by. (p. 52)

Simon (1987) did not use the discovery that 38 out of 50 women in her study described themselves as voluntarily single to conclude that 76% of never-married women are voluntarily single. Hers was not a random sample, and she did not set out to estimate the number of voluntarily single women in the population. Instead, her research described the ways never-married women constructed their lives and formed relationships with friends and family. The women were between the ages of 65 and 105 when they were interviewed, so they were able to report on their old age as well as youth. Simon undertook this study to reveal the diversity in the lives and views of women who might otherwise be considered "old maids." This diversity is vividly expressed in their own words:

I am the first to bristle when married people or youngsters bandy about old ideas about "old maids." I set them straight right away about what single women are like. Mostly I make sure that they comprehend that ten single women present at least ten different approaches to living.

But I also know that we single women do share some qualities in common out of necessity. For example, we tend to plan ahead; we're good savers; and we initiate lots of things. Emily Post, you see, never devised a trail guide for the single woman. One has to devise that trail guide for herself at each step. So we do. From the outside, that looks like we are independent in the extreme. From the inside, I would say instead that we are heavily dependent on ourselves as well as on those select ones we choose to lean on. (p. 151)

Simon (1987) concluded with the observation that these women entered retirement and old age not simply as self-reliant individuals. Rather, each woman had learned to create her own mixture of independence and reliance on others, and "this mix has proved to be invaluable in the last third of her single life" (p. 182).

In many respects, oral history is a logical extension of narrative analysis. The primary difference is that narrative analysis usually centers on short stories (one to two pages) about specific events in a person's life. Oral history is much more ambitious in scope; a typical 60- to 90-minute oral history interview can translate into 15 to 20 double-spaced pages of typed transcript. The intent, moreover, is usually to capture a much broader and more comprehensive story of a person's life, with more detail about the people, context, and events leading up to the topic of interest.

A second difference between oral history and narrative analysis concerns how the stories are subsequently analyzed. In narrative analysis, the stories told by participants are usually objectively coded and quantitatively analyzed, whereas in oral history, participants' stories often are the final product. Researchers might try to identify major themes in the life stories and draw conclusions about the factors that shaped participants' lives, but statistical analyses are generally absent and unnecessary. For example, in the report of her study of never-married women, Simon (1987) presented excerpts from her notes to show how the concept of a "spoiled identity," borrowed from Goffman's (1963) study of stigmas, was useful in understanding the lives of her sample of older women who had never married. She noted that 8 of the women had wished to marry and lead "normal" lives, 20 remained ambivalent about their "deviant" status, and 22 resisted in various ways the definition of themselves as "not normal." She did not draw any conclusions from the fact that 22 is greater than 20 or 8. The numbers are less important than the fact that the concept of "managing a spoiled identity" provided a useful framework for understanding the lives of the women. This theoretical construct and the various ways the women reacted to their marginal status provided a set of lenses through which to view the women. These are not the only possible frameworks or lenses, but they were useful for summarizing Simon's data.

Often there is an exciting sense of urgency associated with oral history. The job of the oral historian is to capture the firsthand experiences of an important group of people while they are still alive and able to report on their experiences. The memories of individuals who lived through major historical events and times are irreplaceable; once these individuals die, an important source of information regarding the event is lost forever. Through oral history methods, an interview takes place and the tapes are placed in a permanent archive so the memories live on and can be used for research in generations to come.

Participant Observation

In **participant observation** the researcher joins the social group that is the topic of study. As a participant observer, the researcher moves outside the controlled settings typical of experiments and interviews to the **field**, namely, the uncontrolled and sometimes unpredictable settings in which people live out their lives. Thus, in contrast to the experimenters and interviewers who try to maintain a professional distance from their participants or respondents, participant observers become engaged in the conversations, actions, and lives of the people they study. And unlike the standardized questions and procedures used by experimenters and interviewers, the questions and actions of a participant observer vary from one person and setting to the next. Instead of approaching each respondent with the same list of questions, as does an oral historian, a participant observer engages in conversations and observations that might continue for several days, weeks, or months. The conversations move in directions that cannot be anticipated, so the researcher's questions cannot be duplicated from one person to the next. To the extent that the researcher participates in the lives of the people under study, each day provides new opportunities as a result of the previous day's activities.

Some participant observers participate fully in the lives of the people they study by being or becoming members of the group. Others remain outsiders, purely observers. Between these two extremes are countless possibilities, with more or less emphasis on being a participant. A common arrangement in participant observation is for an outsider to become a limited participant in the lives of others. Someone who cannot become a bona fide member of a group can still become accepted as a trusted friend and confidante. William Foote Whyte, a member of the Harvard Society of Fellows, conducted field research with the Norton Street Gang (Whyte, 1943). He bowled with them, intervened when he thought he could help one of them, and benefited greatly as a researcher from their acceptance of him – he could go anywhere with them and observe and ask questions at will.

Sometimes complex exchanges occur between the researcher and those who are being researched. Tourigny (2004), for example, describes her experiences conducting research with 26 socioeconomically disadvantaged inner-city residents of Detroit who had HIV/AIDS and 88 caregivers whom the residents identified. Tourigny's goal was to understand how her participants "managed life with HIV/AIDS." Tourigny writes:

> My research involved lengthy field visits, including overnights and weekends at participants' homes, participation in family events, attendance at clinic visits and hospital bedsides, telephone updates, and reading of respondent diaries. I witnessed drug deals, I saw mothers cry for the children they would soon orphan, and I witnessed deaths. I visited shooting galleries, three-generational households where no one was yet thirty, and tenements where children wailed in hunger in front of empty refrigerators, until despairing AIDS-inflicted mothers took to street sex work to feed them; I listened to seropositively mixed couples debating how one partner's HIV might impede pregnancy. I tagged along, listening in and observing and asking questions and challenging interpretations until I felt respondents' realities were as much my own as possible..."
> (p. 115)

Such immersion in the lives of the people one studies is very different from the distance maintained by experimenters and survey researchers. The latter often do not know or ask for the names of their research participants, trying instead to assure them of anonymity and to treat all participants alike. Participant observers do the opposite; they become well acquainted with the people they study and consequently treat no two people alike.

This degree of immersion in the research setting is at odds with the distance and anonymity of experiments and surveys. Does it make participant observation more vulnerable to distortion? Not necessarily. In fact, the lack of anonymity of respondents can ensure that the researcher observes phenomena as they are and not as the respondent or the researcher wishes they were. Participants in laboratory experiments and anonymous respondents in surveys are freer to distort reality than are people whose identities are known and whose actions are observed in natural settings. The people studied by participant observers are constrained to act as they normally would, particularly if the research continues over many weeks or months. They cannot put on an act and continue to function with their friends, families, or fellow workers. Even if a participant observer could not recognize an act or a distortion, the associates of the people being observed would, and the participant observer would probably hear about it. Thus, we have a paradox: The more time participant observers spend with the people they study, the less influence the observers have as researchers because although research participants might wish to appear a particular way in an observer's eyes, they cannot act in unnatural ways if the observer stays with them very long. The more participant observers are immersed in research settings, therefore, the less likely research participants are to distort the research.

However, the same thing is not necessarily true from the perspective of the researcher: The more the participant observers are immersed in research settings, the more likely they are to affect (and therefore distort) what transpires within the group. And they also create their own expectations about the people around them, which can affect what they see and how they interpret different behaviors. Participant observers thus face a difficult challenge: They must become sufficiently integrated into the group to gain access to high-quality information, yet they must remain sufficiently detached so that they do not unduly influence the group's activities.

This dilemma is beautifully described in Festinger, Riecken, and Schachter's (1956) classic account of a participant observation study in which several researchers joined a small cult that had predicted the imminent flooding and destruction of the world and subsequent salvation by extraterrestrial beings. The major goal of the study was to describe how the cult members adapted when the prophecy of worldwide destruction did not come true. As Festinger and his colleagues explained, "We tried to be nondirective, sympathetic listeners, passive participants who were inquisitive and eager to learn whatever others might want to tell us," but as it turned out, "our initial hope – to avoid *any* influence upon the movement – turned out to be somewhat unrealistic" (p. 237).

The first problem was that the simple act of joining the cult altered its dynamics; having four new members (the observers) join the small group within a short period of time – which they did in order to gather information prior to the predicted date of the flood – boosted the confidence of the cult members, who interpreted the sudden rush of new members as evidence that their prophecy was correct.

The second, more serious, problem was learning how to juggle appearing friendly and interested enough in the group so as to be fully accepted while avoiding any act of commitment or proselytizing that might change the group's direction. This was very difficult because the observers were often directly pressured to take some kind of action in the group. For example, during one meeting, the cult leader insisted that one of the participant observers "lead the meeting" that night. The observer, thinking admirably under duress, suggested that the group "meditate silently and wait for inspiration" (p. 244). The observers were also pressured to quit their jobs and spend all their time with the group as the predicted flood date approached. The observers' evasive responses to questions about their plans and failures to quit their jobs might have raised doubts in the true cult members who had quit their own jobs. In short, as Festinger and his colleagues concluded, "the observers could not be neutral – any action had consequences" (p. 244).

Field Notes

How can research in the field be systematic if the procedures vary from one person or day to the next? The systematization occurs not by following uniform procedures but by recording faithfully what is seen and heard. The records are stored as **field notes**, that is, detailed records of everything participant observers hear and see, which the researcher subjects to systematic scrutiny and analysis. Thus, as with narrative analysis, focus groups, and oral history, the distinctive feature of participant observation is its reliance on the words and voices of the people being studied. Instead of recording people's thoughts and feelings on scales or in categories, researchers record their actual words, through notes or tape recordings. The goal of a participant observer is to record in as much detail as possible people's voices, actions, intentions, and appearances.

This requirement might strike the beginning participant observer as an impossible task, which in a sense it is because the term "everything" sets no limits. It can include endless details about the times and locations of interviews and observations, including descriptions of the building, the furnishings, the decor, the level of cleanliness, the amount of noise, the numbers of other people present, the facial expressions of the persons being observed, their appearance and dress styles, their behaviors, and so on. Only some of these details are relevant to the purposes of the research, but when participant observers begin, they do not know what form their final reports will take. The rule, therefore, is to try to remember "everything" and write notes that are as complete as memory allows.

Recording everything that is said is an equally arduous task. Participant observers generally do not record conversations on tape because a tape recorder would inhibit the researcher's participation in many situations. When a tape recorder would interfere with participant observation, the researcher must rely on memory to write the field notes as soon after the observations as possible.

Not all the details in these notes become usable information. Nonetheless, it is important to record them for two reasons. First, by trying to write down as much as possible, the researcher stands a better chance of having useful information available for analysis later on; deciding which information is useful should be done during the analysis rather than during the writing of the field notes. Second, writing even those details that seem irrelevant at the time helps the researcher recall other details that are clearly relevant; each piece of information acts as a cue for recalling other pieces of the setting and is, therefore, worth recording as a means of triggering memory.

Analyzing Field Notes

Analysis of information obtained by participant observers is markedly different from analysis in quantitative research. In quantitative research, analysis is often predictable in advance and straightforward once the data have been gathered: The researcher knows the design of the study, and there is generally a small set of optimal ways of analyzing the data. In participant observation research, the situation is different, and analysis involves considerable creativity and insight. The first step is to organize and transform field notes into a visual record, which the researcher can scan repeatedly and mark in some way to identify recurring events, themes, and explanations. Before the widespread availability of computers, participant observers would write or type their notes and then use color codes, make notes in the margins, or excerpt portions onto index cards, which could then be sorted into categories. Word processors now enable participant observers to enter key words into the text of their field notes to identify instances of various categories or themes. Using a search procedure, researchers can easily locate all instances of any category and print them, see in what contexts they appear, note how they are related to other events, and begin to piece together an argument about what the observation reveals. The computer facilitates the physical search for categories and themes, but it does not perform the conceptual work. Researchers must still read through the notes many times, constructing and assessing themes or categories, revising hunches, testing ideas against the notes, and finally piecing together the story that they believe the data tell.

Rather than design a study to test a hypothesis, participant observers gather information to generate hypotheses and theories. Such research has been referred to as **inductive research** or, more recently, as **constructivist research** or **grounded theory** because the theory is said to emerge from the data (Bryant & Charmaz, 2007; Ponterotto, 2005). In other words, researchers begin with observations and generate hypotheses and theories that fit the information they have obtained. This approach stands in contrast to **deductive research**, in which researchers begin with a theory, formulate a hypothesis, deduce what the results should be if the hypothesis is correct, and then gather information to test the hypothesis. As was noted earlier, little actual research is either purely deductive or purely inductive. Most social scientists use a combination of inductive and deductive logic. Nonetheless, we can characterize research methods as being predominantly deductive or inductive, and participant observation is predominantly inductive. Many participant observation researchers start from the view that as outsiders, their theories will not have the validity of ones generated within the community being studied, so they purposely do not generate a priori theories and hypotheses. Participant observers might begin their research with some preliminary ideas about what to expect, but as they proceed, they revise their ideas based on negative case analysis.

Negative case analysis involves looking for information that disconfirms a hypothesis. When a single negative case is found, the participant observer revises the hypothesis so that it accounts for that case. Cressey's (1953) classic study of embezzlers illustrates how negative case analysis works. He revised his hypothesis five times before he completed his analysis of what leads embezzlers to use other people's money. For example, one version of his hypothesis was that "positions of trust are violated when the incumbent defines a need for extra funds or extended use of property as an 'emergency' which cannot be met by legal means" (p. 27). However, after interviewing inmates convicted of embezzling, Cressey discovered that although some embezzlers said this was the case, others said that there had been no financial "emergency," yet they had still taken the money. Thus, Cressey developed new versions of his hypothesis, checking each one not only against subsequent interviews but also against previous ones. If cases were found that violated his hypothesis, he revised the hypothesis so that it could account for the negative case. This process resulted in the final version of Cressey's hypothesis:

> Trusted persons become trust violators when they conceive of themselves as having a financial problem which is nonshareable, are aware that this problem can be secretly resolved by violation of the position of financial trust, and are able to apply to their own conduct in that situation verbalizations which enable them to adjust their conceptions of themselves as trusted persons with their conceptions of themselves as users of the entrusted funds or property. (p. 30)

Cressey (1953) developed and tested this hypothesis with all cases of embezzlement found in one state prison. He then tested the hypothesis in three additional ways. He searched the literature on embezzlement to see if his hypothesis was consistent with other studies. He examined 200 cases of embezzlement collected by another researcher. And he went to a federal penitentiary and interviewed people convicted of federal bank and post office embezzlement. In each of these sources he looked for negative cases that would contradict his hypothesis and concluded that in all of the cases he identified, his hypothesized process was present.

Few other published reports reveal so clearly the process of forming, revising, and retesting hypotheses. Cressey's (1953) approach is typical, however, in its use of negative case analysis to revise and generate hypotheses. What makes qualitative research systematic, therefore, is not standardization but negative case analysis. Systematic participant observation research involves conducting a thorough search for cases that disconfirm the hypothesis. The search and the information gathering are not routinized; in fact, they usually require asking new and different questions in each search. The measurements are not standardized, the data are not uniform, and they do not yield numbers that can be added or averaged. But the *procedure* is systematic.

Generalization

Participant observers study how people behave in specific organizations, communities, or circumstances and conclude that others would likely behave similarly in those situations. It is important to realize that this is not the same thing as concluding that people in other organizations, communities, or circumstances behave in the same way. Unlike survey researchers, participant observers rarely ask, "What percentage of persons in the population would respond in this way?" Instead they say, "What I have found true of the people in this study is likely to be true of any people placed in this situation." Participant observers are like laboratory experimenters in this respect. Both assume that the environmental forces or situational constraints they have studied would affect most people the same way. Experimenters and participant observers share this assumption even though they conduct their research in dramatically different ways and places.

Participant observation might seem to have a priori external validity simply because it takes place in the "real" world. To have value beyond the particular setting, conclusions based on any research, including participant observation, must be shown to be valid beyond the specific conditions of the original study. Participant observers can begin to establish the external validity of their findings by analyzing their field notes and demonstrating that the people and situations in their study are similar to other people and situations. The ultimate test of the external validity of any research, however, is replicability. If no one can replicate the research and reach the same conclusions, no matter now helpful the findings might be in the local setting, the research cannot be considered to have external validity, no matter how vivid the data.

Ethical Concerns

Participant observation gives rise to more serious ethical dilemmas than does any other type of qualitative research. Because participant observers become integrated into the lives of the people they study, invasion of privacy and confidentiality become especially important to consider. Participant observers witness events in people's homes or other private settings, and they often hear sensitive information. There is almost never anonymity, so guaranteeing confidentiality becomes an ethical imperative. As we discussed in Chapter 3, these concerns can be addressed through a thorough informed consent process, during which participants are told about the study, the kinds of information that are to be gathered, the degree of access the observer wishes to have, and so on. Assuming that participants still wish to participate in the study, the researchers have fulfilled an important part of their ethical obligations. Researchers can preserve confidentiality by changing participants' names and changing or eliminating other identifying information when reporting the findings.

However, some instances of participant observation have involved considerable deception. In the Festinger et al. (1956) study described earlier, for example, the researchers joined the group undercover without informing group members they were researchers and were recording information about the group. The ethical concerns in this situation are not easily addressed. The current federal regulations allow researchers to avoid informed consent only if (1) the research involves no more than minimal risk, (2) the rights of the participants would not be adversely affected, and (3) the research could not be practically carried out without waiving informed consent. The degree of deception and invasion of privacy involved in undercover participant observation studies make it unlikely that Institutional Review Boards today would consider the three conditions to be met, and most would not approve such a study.

In sum, the classic form of participant observation, in which researchers do not inform individuals that they are being observed, would not pass ethical scrutiny in most cases today. Participant observation is therefore limited to cases in which the researcher joins the group with the full knowledge and consent of those being observed. The trade-off, of course, is that participants might not behave as they normally would once they realize their actions are being recorded for research purposes. (We have to note that the nonrandom sample of participants in today's reality shows suggests that many individuals seemingly are not affected by being observed and recorded.) More problematic from a research standpoint is that there might be some groups – especially those involved in illegal or socially undesirable behavior – that would not grant access to researchers under open consent processes. The burden then falls on researchers to create rapport with such group members and convince them of the benefits of participation. In the final analysis, though, conflicts between the goals of the researcher and the rights of participants must be resolved in favor of participants.

The involvement of participant observers in the lives of the people they study raises other ethical issues as well. For instance, Stack (1975), a White researcher, participated extensively in the lives of the Black women she studied. She provided some services:

> Once I had the car, people continually asked me to run errands – taking children, goods and gossip between households. For a while all I seemed to be doing was taking half a pot roast from one house to another, picking up the laundry from a home with a washing machine, going to the liquor store for beer, or waiting with mothers in the local medical clinics for doctors to see their sick children. (p. 18)

She also developed genuine friendships, not for the purpose of observing but as a consequence of being there. Did her services and her friendship make her observations more ethically correct or less so? In a laboratory or classroom context, giving or accepting favors is normally regarded as a conflict of interest that must be avoided. In contrast, in participant observation research, the researcher becomes a genuine part of the social network of the group being observed, and to refuse to do or accept such favors would be to violate the ethical rules of friendship. The bottom line is that participant observation involves a tangled web of roles and relationships, as opposed to the detached and relatively simple experimenter–participant relationship of the laboratory, and participant observers must balance the natural consequences of friendship and involvement in the lives of their participants with their roles and responsibilities as researchers.

Summary

In qualitative research, researchers do not impose structure or questions on participants but, rather, learn from listening to participants discuss issues in their own voices.

Different forms of qualitative research vary with respect to the degree of structure. In narrative research, participants provide short narratives, or stories, of important life experiences that objective judges later code on theoretically meaningful dimensions. Focus groups bring several participants together to discuss the research question of interest. They are particularly helpful in the early stages of research to help guide the preparation of experimental materials and questionnaires; they also are useful in program evaluation. Oral history is a method for recording extended life stories of individuals, usually individuals who have undergone some culturally important event or in some other way serve as important witnesses to history or national consciousness. The least-structured form of qualitative research is participant observation, in which researchers immerse themselves in the research setting and in the lives of the people they study. Participant observers generate and revise their hypotheses as they gather information, and they use negative case analysis to arrive at conclusions that hold true for every observation.

Go online   Visit the book's companion website for this chapter's test bank and other resources at: www.wiley.com/go/maruyama

---

Key Concepts

Constructivist research

Content analysis

Deductive research

Deed of gift form

Dictionaries

Emergent themes

Ethnography

Field

Field notes

Focus group guide

Focus groups

Ground rules

Grounded theory

Inductive research

Moderator

Narratives

Negative case analysis

Oral history

Participant observation

Qualitative research

On the Web

Onlineqda.hud.ac.uk/Introduction/index.php Provides information about various types of qualitative research methods and qualitative data analysis software.

http://www.baylor.edu/oralhistory/ Published by the Institute for Oral History at Baylor University. Excellent overview of oral history methods, including a web-based workshop full of useful tips for conducting oral histories.

http://www.indiana.edu/~cshm/techniques.html A pamphlet on oral history techniques, written by Dr. Barbara Truesdell, Assistant Director of the Indiana

University Center for the Study of History and Memory. Includes useful hints as well as sample informed consent and deed of gift forms.

http://mnav.com/focus-group-center/cligd-htm/ An entertaining and well-written summary of what focus groups are and how best to use them, written from an applied marketing perspective.

http://ctb.dept.ku.edu/en/table-of-contents/assessment/assessing-community -needs-and-resources/conduct-focus-groups/main Information about conducting focus groups from the Community Tool Box, a public service provided by the University of Kansas.

http://writing.colostate.edu/guides/guide.cfm?guideid=61 Provides an introduction to content analysis by Carol Busch, Paul S. De Maret, Teresa Flynn, Rachel Kellum, Sheri Le, Brad Meyers, Matt Saunders, Robert White, and Mike Palmquist at Colorado State University.

Further Reading

Bernard, R., & Ryan, G. (2010). *Analyzing qualitative data: Systematic approaches.* Thousand Oaks, CA: Sage.

Braun, V., & Clarke, V. (2013). *Successful qualitative research: A practical guide for beginners.* Thousand Oaks, CA: Sage.

Denzin, N. K., & Lincoln, Y. S. (Eds.). (2000). *Handbook of qualitative research* (2nd ed.). Thousand Oaks, CA: Sage.

Hume, L., & Mulcock, J. (2004). *Anthropologists in the field: Cases in participant observation.* New York, NY: Columbia University Press.

Krueger, R. A., & Casey, M. A. (2000). *Focus groups: A practical guide for applied research* (3rd ed.). Thousand Oaks, CA: Sage.

Leavy, P. (2011). *Oral history.* New York, NY: Oxford University Press.

Popping, R. (2000). *Computer-assisted text analysis.* Thousand Oaks, CA: Sage.

Smith, C. P. (2000). Content analysis and narrative analysis. In H. T. Reis & C. M. Judd (Eds.), *Handbook of research methods in social and personality psychology* (pp. 313–335). New York, NY: Cambridge University Press.

Chapter 14

Survey Research

In this chapter, we provide an introduction to survey research – a type of research in which the primary purpose is to describe the distributions of attitudes, behaviors, and other characteristics in groups of people and to examine relationships among those characteristics. For example, researchers might have an interest in determining the attitudes of state voters toward some legislation that limits abortions. They might select a probability sample of registered voters in the state and ask those voters to complete a questionnaire that assesses their attitudes toward the legislation, their gender, and the extent to which they consider themselves politically liberal versus conservative. The researchers would be able to describe the average attitude of voters, how much variability there was in voters' attitudes, and so forth. The researchers might also examine whether attitudes toward the legislation differ for women and men or as a function of liberal versus conservative political ideology. And, if you look at findings from surveys in the popular press, you might also see them subdivided by other variables like age of respondents or race/ethnicity.

Note that the researchers probably would not manipulate any variables in their research nor would their goal be to identify causal relationships; rather, the primary

Research Methods in Social Relations, Eighth Edition. Geoffrey Maruyama and Carey S. Ryan.
© 2014 John Wiley & Sons, Inc. Published 2014 by John Wiley & Sons, Inc.
Companion Website: www.wiley.com/go/maruyama

goal is to understand voters' attitudes and the factors (e.g., gender and political ideology) that are associated with them. For these reasons, survey research is usually considered non-experimental. We discussed this issue in Chapter 12.

However, survey research can sometimes be considered quasi-experimental. Consider Payne and colleagues' (2010) research on the relationship between prejudice and voting behavior in the 2008 American presidential election, which resulted in the first Black U.S. president. Payne et al. asked probability samples of American adults to complete measures of implicit (i.e., reaction times assessing automatic negative associations with Black Americans) and explicit (i.e., questionnaire items) prejudice prior to the election. Following the election, they contacted participants again and asked them how they voted. The researchers statistically controlled for potentially confounding variables, including political party identification, liberalism versus conservatism, and demographic characteristics. The results indicated that both implicit and explicit prejudice predicted subsequent voting behavior; participants who exhibited greater prejudice were less likely to vote for Barack Obama (the Black candidate) and more likely to vote for John McCain (the White candidate). In addition, when explicit prejudice was statistically controlled, greater implicit prejudice predicted a lower likelihood of voting for Obama and a greater likelihood of either abstaining or voting for a third-party candidate rather than for Obama.

The researchers' (Payne et al., 2010) use of probability sampling methods, which are typical of survey methodology, strengthens the external validity of the conclusions. Indeed, external validity was very strong because data were obtained from three separate probability samples of participants. Other aspects of the design strengthen the internal validity of the design – at least as compared to non-experimental research. The researchers gathered measures of their independent variables (i.e., implicit and explicit prejudice) well before the election. Recall that drawing causal conclusions requires demonstrating that the causal variable and the dependent variable are correlated, that the causal variable preceded the dependent variable in time (i.e., temporal sequence), and that there are no other explanations for the relationship between the independent variable and the dependent variable. The Payne et al. research met the first two criteria, but the lack of random assignment to levels of prejudice prevents us from drawing causal conclusions. Although statistically controlling for confounding variables improves internal validity, that is, as compared to ignoring alternative explanations altogether, this strategy is not a substitute for random assignment to conditions. Thus, this survey research can be considered quasi-experimental.

Other types of survey research methods might also be considered quasi-experimental because even though participants are not randomly assigned to conditions, the designs provide comparisons that are stronger in internal validity than is the case in non-experimental research. Examples of quasi-experimental designs that might involve survey methods include interrupted time-series designs and nonequivalent control group designs, which are described in Chapter 11.

Survey research can even be experimental. One might, for example, randomly assign survey research participants to complete questionnaires that differ in whether the term "global warming" or the term "climate change" is used (Schuldt, Konrath, & Schwarz, 2011). In other words, researchers can manipulate independent variables to determine their effects on dependent variables (e.g., support for environmental legislation) even in survey research. As another example, participants might be asked to think about different experiences in two versions of a questionnaire. Different participants might be asked to think about different types of regret they have experienced: regrets about actions they took (regrets of commission) or regrets about actions they did not take (i.e., regrets of omission). The researcher could then examine differences in the emotions participants experienced as a function of the type of regret. A unique advantage of such designs is that they maximize both internal and external validity (assuming that a probability sample of respondents is obtained); as we have noted, in most designs these two types of validity are inversely related.

In any case, the general point is that particular studies often make use of elements from different types of research designs. The overarching goal is to obtain data that are as strong as possible in terms of internal, external, construct, and conclusion validity given the constraints of available resources. Again, strategies that maximize one type of validity can undermine other types of validity so that difficult decisions must often be made about which strategies to utilize in a particular study. But research designs and methodology are not mutually exclusive; procedures used in one type of research can be incorporated into other types of research. With this caveat in mind, we focus in this chapter on what is traditionally considered to be survey research, that is, non-experimental research in which the goal is to describe the characteristics (e.g., attitudes, behaviors, or values) of a group of people, the relationships among those characteristics, and the relationships of those characteristics with other variables, such as individual background variables.

Major Components of Survey Research and Sources of Error

That survey research is non-experimental does not mean that it is easy to do. Obtaining data that enable one to describe accurately the characteristics of a larger group, particularly when those characteristics concern complex attitudes or socially undesirable attributes, requires careful planning as well as methodological sophistication. Error can arise from multiple sources, resulting in biased sample estimates of population values.

According to the **total survey error perspective** (e.g., Krosnick, Lavrakas, & Kim, 2014), overall **survey error**, that is, overall differences between sample estimates and true population values, comes from seven sources. We discuss four of these sources: coverage error, sampling error, measurement error, and nonresponse error. **Coverage error** refers to bias that might occur when the survey participants are selected from a pool of potential participants (i.e., the sampling frame) that does not include some portions of the population of interest. **Sampling error** refers to random differences between a sample and the sampling frame from which the sample was selected. We discussed these sources of error in Chapter 9.

Measurement error refers to bias that results from the ways in which the constructs of interest are assessed. We discussed measurement issues in Chapters 7 and 8. In this chapter, we discuss additional measurement issues that are inherent in the development of operational definitions, including the mode of data collection to be used. For example, will interviews be conducted or will questionnaires be administered? Will the survey be carried out in person, by telephone, over the Internet, or by mail? Participants might even be prompted to answer questions on an electronic device (e.g., a programmed smart phone) during a set period of time (i.e., experience sampling, which is described in Chapter 9). We also describe in this chapter additional methods for asking sensitive questions in survey research so that measurement error is minimized and the validity of responses is maximized.

Finally, **nonresponse error** refers to bias that can result when data are not obtained from all members of the sample. It can be problematic when the **response rate**, that is, the percentage of respondents in the initial sample from whom complete responses are obtained, is low. The response rate is the chief index of data quality in a survey because it defines the extent of possible bias from nonresponse. Nonrespondents might differ in important ways from respondents, so if only 25% or 50% of the sample actually responds, there is no way of knowing whether their characteristics can be generalized to describe the whole sample, let alone the population the sample is intended to represent. Therefore, particularly when the research is concerned with estimating prevalence of behavior or otherwise describing a population, a low response rate calls into question any conclusions based on the data. In contrast, a response rate of 80% or 90% means that even if the nonrespondents differ substantially from those who respond, the overall estimates are unlikely to be badly biased.

It is important to remember, though, that even a high response rate is meaningless unless the sample was selected using an appropriate sampling plan, for example, a random sample, as discussed in Chapter 9. We might hand out questionnaires to 20 of our friends and acquaintances and achieve a near-perfect response rate, but the results would not be meaningful because they do not constitute a representative sample of any larger population, but a convenience sample. Response rates are meaningful only when initial samples are properly drawn and the research questions involve estimating the prevalence of a behavior or the strength of an opinion in a specified population. When survey research addresses questions that do not demand such estimates, higher response rates might be important for different reasons, for example, because higher response rates might yield larger sample sizes at a lower cost (e.g., fewer questionnaires would be distributed and less time would be required to obtain an adequate number of completed questionnaires).

How can response rates be maximized and thus nonresponse error minimized? Presenting the research to potential respondents and asking them questions in ways that motivate them to participate help; we have discussed such issues throughout this book. For example, people are more likely to respond to questions that are well developed and seem important; they are also more likely to agree to participate if the researcher seems trustworthy (Dillman, Smyth, & Christian, 2009). In this chapter, we discuss additional ways to maximize response rates, depending on the mode of data collection. We begin, however, by describing the major types of survey research designs.

Major Survey Research Designs

The two most basic research designs in survey research are cross-sectional surveys and panel surveys. A **cross-sectional survey** involves the collection of data from a sample of participants at the same point in time. This design is most often used to estimate the prevalence of characteristics in a population, for example, the percentage of adult women who agree or strongly agree with a statement concerning the availability of abortion or the percentage of voters who plan to vote for a particular candidate. It is also often used to assess relationships among variables, for example, relationships between participant gender and agreement with abortion legislation. Such data are strictly correlational, however. One can conduct statistical analyses, such as path analyses and structural equation models, to determine whether the data are consistent with certain causal hypotheses. One can also identify moderators of relationships, which can help to clarify the causal processes that might be operating (Krosnick et al., 2014). However, such analyses cannot rule out alternative explanations for the relationships and there are many possible alternative explanations in cross-sectional data – respondents likely differ on many variables in addition to the independent variable of interest. Further, the temporal sequence of the independent and dependent variables is often unknown.

A **panel survey**, in contrast, is a longitudinal design in which data are collected from the same research participants at two or more points in time. Panel surveys are most often used to assess stability or change in attitudes, beliefs, and behaviors, for example, change in racial prejudice, beliefs about global warming, or the prevalence of single-parent households. They also allow tests of causal relationships that are stronger in internal validity than are tests of causal hypotheses in cross-sectional data. For example, researchers can determine whether individual-level changes over time in an independent variable correspond to the expected individual-level changes over time in a dependent variable or whether an independent variable assessed at one point in time predicts subsequent change over time in a dependent variable.

Panel surveys are more costly and difficult to conduct than are cross-sectional surveys. It is more challenging to recruit and retain respondents for longitudinal studies as such studies require respondents to make a long-term commitment, and even those who make the commitment can be difficult to locate later. Recruiting and retaining participants is, of course, more challenging for studies that occur over longer periods of time. Respondents who initially agree might move, become disabled, die, or simply decide they no longer wish to participate; these problems, which undermine the representativeness of the sample, are more likely the longer the study continues.

Panel surveys can also have other drawbacks, for example, carry-over effects, which can be problematic in any type of repeated measures design. Responding to questions about the research topic can affect respondents' attitudes, beliefs, and behaviors relevant to that topic, potentially altering the phenomenon under study. For example, answering questions about environmental issues might lead respondents to become more environmentally conscious. Or respondents might alter their responses to appear consistent over time, thereby concealing actual change.

Sometimes researchers attempt to take advantage of the strengths of cross-sectional surveys and the strengths of panel surveys in the same study. In other words, researchers use a **sequential design** that has both cross-sectional and panel survey components. A researcher might, for example, ask two independently selected groups of people to complete questionnaires at two or more points in time or ask one group of people to complete a survey at two time points and another group to complete only the second survey. These types of designs allow one to evaluate the plausibility of alternative explanations. The latter design, for example, allows the researcher to assess the plausibility of carry-over effects. A difference between the two groups – only one of which completed an assessment previously – would suggest the presence of a carry-over effect (Krosnick et al., 2014).

As always, the choice of design depends on the specific nature of the research questions and, more specifically, whether the potential gains in knowledge warrant the costs associated with otherwise desirable design features. It is generally wise, for example, to consider whether it might first be sufficient simply to demonstrate that certain relationships exist. Examining underlying causal processes generally requires a much greater investment of resources; such investments might not make sense if it is unknown whether the relationships even exist. And resources spent to strengthen one feature of a research design typically limit the choice of other design features, for example, the mode of data collection that can be used.

Modes of Data Collection

Survey research most often involves the direct questioning of respondents, for example, questionnaires, face-to-face interviews, and telephone interviews, rather than some of the other types of measures described in Chapter 8. We discussed developing items and measures used in direct questioning in Chapter 7. We therefore focus here on modes of direct questioning, discussing the advantages and disadvantages of asking questions in different ways, for example, by mail, in small group sessions, and over the Internet in the case of questionnaires. Although we talk about these **modes of data collection** as if only one mode is used in a particular study, different modes of data collection can sometimes be combined to improve response rates and data quality and thus the strength of the conclusions that can be drawn.

Questionnaires

The most common mode of data collection in any kind of research is the questionnaire. Low cost is the primary advantage, whether questionnaires are mailed, administered to small groups of respondents in a designated room, or administered via the Internet – an even more cost-effective mode of administering questionnaires. With programs like SurveyMonkey (http://www.surveymonkey.com), whose basic features are available without charge, some surveys can almost feel like they can be done for free. It might appear that printing and postage or other costs of distributing and collecting questionnaires, such as reply envelopes for mailed questionnaires or software for Internet surveys, are all that need to be taken into account. However, the steps needed to obtain high-quality data from any questionnaire involve additional costs. We discussed some of these issues, for example, the steps involved in developing valid questions and scales, in Chapter 7. Nevertheless, questionnaires are much less expensive than are interviews, and cost is not a trivial consideration. Cost often determines whether research can be done at all, and the lower cost of administering questionnaires might mean that available resources can be invested in other aspects of the research design, for example, developing better measures and gathering data from a greater number of people.

Questionnaires also eliminate interviewer bias when they are mailed or administered via the Internet, or greatly minimize interviewer bias when they are administered in person, for example, in group data collection sessions. Research has shown that the way interviewers ask questions and even interviewers' appearance or vocal qualities can influence respondents' answers. Although these biases can be minimized in interviews, they can be completely eliminated only with self-administered questionnaires.

When questionnaires are distributed by mail or the Internet, respondents can complete them as time allows, rather than feeling pressured to provide immediate responses. This factor might be important, for example, when participants have to search personal records for information to answer a question. Responses to attitude questions might also benefit if participants take time to consider each question carefully rather than giving the response that immediately comes to mind. The latter is more likely under the social pressure of long silences in face-to-face or telephone interviews or in small group sessions, for example, when one sees that others are completing the questionnaire more quickly. However, participants must also be motivated to give careful consideration to their responses, and interviewers and test proctors can generally motivate participants more than written instructions can.

Mail surveys often have poor response rates, usually less than 50% when the target population is the general public. This fact alone limits the usefulness of mail samples because the unknown bias from extensive nonresponse makes the sample estimates quite untrustworthy. However, when specialized populations are sampled, such as members of a particular profession or alumni of a particular college, response rates from mail surveys can reach respectable levels. In addition, Dillman (1972; Dillman et al., 2009) and others have developed techniques for carefully following up mail surveys with multiple waves of letters, postcards, and the like to attain as high a response rate as possible, sometimes reaching 70% or higher in samples of the general public with a short questionnaire. Many of these strategies are relatively simple. For example, creating appropriately personalized survey invitations and providing stamped return envelopes rather than business reply envelopes can improve response rates by several percentage points. However, these techniques also increase cost and can substantially reduce the cost advantage of a mail survey over a telephone interview, the next most costly alternative.

Response rates are generally worse for Internet surveys, partly because people have become suspicious of unsolicited email invitations – particularly those from unfamiliar sources (Dillman et al., 2009). Some strategies to increase response rates for mail surveys also increase response rates for Internet surveys. For example, potential respondents can be sent personalized email invitations that use respondents' names in the salutation rather than, for example, "Dear Student." Research has demonstrated improvements of 4.5 (Joinson & Reips, 2007) to 8 percentage points (Heerwegh, 2005) for more versus less personal invitations. Joinson and Reips also found that personalization was more effective when invitations were sent from more (vs. less) powerful people. Email invitations should also be sent individually rather than to groups of people at the same time not only to improve response rates and the quality of responses (Barron & Yechiam, 2002), but to decrease the likelihood that the email will be flagged as spam and to maintain respondent confidentiality (Dillman et al., 2009). Of course, researchers should also avoid the sorts of improper grammar, writing in all capital letters, and acronyms, such as FYI (for your information) or BTW (by the way), that are common in casual electronic communication.

For some types of Internet surveys, it might be impossible to calculate a response rate in the usual sense because it is not clear how many individuals could have responded but did not. When surveys are posted on a web page, response rates typically are calculated as the proportion of individuals who completed the survey among those who accessed the page. Williams, Cheung, and Choi (2000) reported that 1,486 of 1,720 individuals (86%) who accessed their pages went on to complete their study. In a second Internet-based study, these same researchers achieved a response rate of only 46%. McKenna and Bargh (1998) reached 64% of individuals who posted to the news groups they targeted; however, it is not possible to calculate the proportion of "lurkers" (individuals who read but did not post to the news group) who responded. In a formal study of this issue, Dillman et al. (2001) compared response rates to a questionnaire administered either by telephone, mail, or the Internet. Only after repeated telephone prods were they able to secure a response rate near 50% for the Internet. In comparison, response rates for telephone and mail surveys were 80% or greater.

Other factors also affect the quality of data gathered from questionnaires. Respondents must be motivated to provide accurate and complete responses. Motivation can be challenging to create and maintain when direct questions are posed in questionnaires as opposed to being asked by interviewers who can build rapport with respondents. In addition, questionnaires generally do not allow an interviewer or member of the research team to correct misunderstandings or answer questions that respondents might have. Respondents might answer incorrectly or not at all out of confusion or frustration, often without the researcher being able to tell that a question has been misinterpreted. Complex questions or instructions for some respondents to skip certain questions can lead to confusion, errors, or complete nonresponse. Writing long responses to open-ended questions is more work than giving the same responses orally to an interviewer, and can thus reduce response rates. Finally, some potential respondents might be unable to respond to questionnaires because of illiteracy, lack of proficiency in English, or other difficulties in reading or writing (e.g., poor vision).

When questionnaires are mailed to participants, question order cannot be controlled. It is often important that respondents answer one question before seeing another. For example, a questionnaire might begin by asking respondents what they see as the most important problem facing their community and then go on to ask questions about the availability of parks and recreation facilities. It is safe to assume that if the respondents were aware of the focus of the questionnaire, it would bias their responses to the initial open-ended question. There is no way to control question order in mailed questionnaires as respondents are likely to glance through the entire questionnaire before starting to answer.

It is also not possible to control the conditions under which respondents complete questionnaires when questionnaires are mailed or administered over the Internet. Respondents can complete the questionnaires in any setting or while engaging in other tasks, such as watching television, or they might complete the questionnaires in several stages rather than all at once, perhaps biasing their answers and increasing error. Respondents to a mail or Internet survey can also ask friends or family members to examine the questionnaire or comment on their answers, causing bias if respondents' own private opinions are sought. Indeed, there is no way to be certain that participants who respond to mailed or Internet surveys are the people they claim to be. Perhaps unique to the Internet is the possibility that some individuals would respond more than once to a survey without being detected. However, the rate of repeated participation in social behavioral research appears to be low (e.g., below 3%) and methods have been developed to avoid and detect multiple submissions, for example, providing access codes to respondents (Dillman et al., 2009; Reips, 2002). Additional advantages of the Internet over mail include the ability to restrict completion of questionnaires to single sessions and to certain IP addresses; researchers can also restrict the amount of time that respondents are allowed. Of course, such restrictions are also likely to reduce response rates. However, variables such as times and dates of completion can be recorded and perhaps analyzed to determine whether responses differ as a function of time, multiple completion sessions, and so forth.

Other, less serious disadvantages also characterize studies in which questionnaires are used, particularly those that are mailed to respondents. One is the requirement to use a short questionnaire. Dillman (1978) found that questionnaires up to about 12 pages or 125 individual responses produced response rates that did not depend on length. But for questionnaires exceeding that length, which represents a relatively short questionnaire for many research purposes, increasing length was associated with decreasing response rate.

A unique advantage of Internet questionnaires is the ability to reach diverse samples worldwide at a very low cost. However, other complications can arise. For example, researchers still need to make questionnaires available in the different languages represented in the population of people they wish to target or who are likely to access the questionnaire. (See Chapter 8 for a discussion of the issues involved in creating different language versions of a questionnaire.) Researchers also need to consider the diversity of web browsers, Internet service providers, and computers in use in the geographic areas of interest. Finally, researchers need to keep in mind that significant portions of the population do not have Internet access.

"Internet communities," which consist of like-minded individuals, also make it possible to target specific populations that might otherwise be very difficult to reach. News groups, chat rooms, and web rings provide access to potential respondents who have declared a particular interest, concern, or set of values. For example, McKenna and Bargh (1998) were interested in whether involvement in Internet news groups was associated with higher self-esteem, greater self-acceptance, and reduced feelings of social isolation among individuals with stigmatized identities. They surveyed participants in three news groups dealing with marginalized sexual identities. In addition to posting the 19-item survey to the news groups, they sent a copy via email to all individuals who posted a message during a three-week period. Of the 160 people in the latter group, 103 (64%) responded.

Another appealing feature of Internet-based research not shared with mail surveys is the degree of anonymity afforded the respondent. Although many websites require respondents to log in by providing an email address or other identifier, many respondents take on virtual identities that effectively render their true identity undetectable. This sense of anonymity is particularly important in research on sensitive topics in marginalized populations (e.g., McKenna & Bargh, 1998).

Face-to-Face Interviews

An alternative to questionnaires as a means of direct questioning is the face-to-face interview. Face-to-face interviews often are used when there is reason to believe that prospective research participants either would not be motivated to complete a questionnaire or would encounter difficulty reading the questionnaire or understanding how to indicate responses. They are also used frequently when the primary questions of interest are open-ended and longer, more in-depth responses are sought. Face-to-face interviews are more costly than are other modes of direct questioning and thus are used less frequently. Nonetheless, they can be particularly effective for certain types of research. Palmgreen, Donohew, Lorch, Hoyle, and Stephenson (2001), for example, were interested in the degree to which a televised antidrug campaign affected marijuana use by seventh to twelfth graders. Research on this topic and this population conducted in a school setting often meets with disapproval from school administrators and results in unacceptably low response rates from students. Palmgreen and colleagues therefore elected to dispatch interviewers to students' homes. Interviewers posed questions to students and their parents and recorded responses using a laptop computer and computer-assisted personal interviewing (CAPI) software. A key feature of this strategy is the ability to allow the students to input their responses to questions of a sensitive nature (e.g., "Have you used marijuana anytime during the last 30 days?") directly into the computer without divulging responses to the interviewer. As another example, in a study of the association between stress and emotions in older adults, Zautra, Reich, Davis, Potter, and Nicolson (2000) interviewed adults between the ages of 60 and 80 who had either recently experienced the death of a spouse, had recently experienced declining health, or were healthy and had not recently experienced the death of a spouse. Interviewers queried participants about their personality, health, and emotions. In both of these examples, the researchers deemed it important that members of the research team work directly with respondents in acquiring responses to direct questions.

As with questionnaires, there are trade-offs involved with the use of face-to-face interviews for direct questioning. Face-to-face interviews offer important advantages, some of which are shared by telephone interviews. The potential for interviewers to notice and correct respondents' misunderstandings, to probe inadequate or vague responses, and to answer questions and allay concerns is important in obtaining complete and meaningful responses. Interviewers can control the order in which respondents receive the questions, which is only otherwise possible with Internet questionnaires and telephone interviews. And, in general, the interviewer can control the context of the interview, including the possible biasing presence of other people.

Other advantages are specific to face-to-face interviews. Visual aids (photographs, maps, or show cards with response options printed on them) are useful in a number of contexts. For example, in surveys of prescription drug use it is helpful to show illustrations of different types of pills and capsules to aid respondents' memory for medications they might have used but whose names they have forgotten.

The most important advantage of face-to-face interviews, however, is that they yield the highest response rates of any survey technique, sometimes over 80%. Their advantage is particularly marked with special populations, such as low-income minority populations, who might not have telephones or Internet access or respond to mail surveys. Moreover, face-to-face interviewers can more readily establish rapport and motivate respondents to answer fully and accurately, improving the quality of data. Face-to-face interviews also allow the greatest length in interview schedules. An hour or so is typical, and interviews two to three hours long with samples of the general public have been done. The additional length permits extensive in-depth questioning about complex or multifaceted issues.

Although the opportunity for interviewers to build rapport with respondents has the potential to yield better information, it also introduces the potential for **interviewer effects**. The interviewer's expectations, training, and personal characteristics, such as ethnicity or sex (Frey & Oishi, 1995), voice inflection, and voice tone, can influence how respondents interpret and respond to interview questions. Consistent with the idea that face-to-face situations create the strongest rapport – and hence the strongest tendency for respondents to give invalid, socially desirable answers to suit the interviewer's expectations or desires – studies have found larger interviewer effects in face-to-face than in telephone interviews (e.g., Schuman, Bobo, & Steeh, 1985). Face-to-face interview respondents are also more likely than paper-and-pencil questionnaire respondents to adjust their answers to later questions based on how they answered an earlier question in order to appear fair. Such adjustments are more likely to occur in interview than in self-administered surveys because the fairness norm is less likely to be evoked in the latter case. And of course, respondents can usually look ahead to later questions and change responses to previous questions when questionnaires are paper-and-pencil and calibrate their responses accordingly (Dillman et al., 2009).

Various methods can be used to minimize interviewer effects although they must be used in ways that do not sacrifice the benefits of personal interviews. For example, standardized probes for additional information, standardized kinds of feedback to respondents, and standardized ways to ask questions can be developed. Interviewers can be trained in the use of these procedures and acceptable variations as well as in other aspects of the interview process more generally. Computer-assisted personal interviewing (CAPI), in which interviewers refer to scripts and enter responses directly into a laptop computer or other mobile computing device, can also minimize interviewer effects. Interviewers might also benefit from additional training during the data collection period, as some research indicates that interview length and interviewer-reported respondent interest decrease as interviewers conduct more interviews (Olson & Peytchev, 2007). Although the reasons for these relationships are unclear, it seems reasonable that interviewer behavior would be affected by respondents just as respondent behavior is influenced by interviewers and that these effects are more likely with greater exposure to respondents and more time between training and interviewing.

The primary disadvantage of personal interviews is their high cost, which depends heavily on the geographic coverage required by the study. For a city or other limited area, costs for face-to-face interviews might not greatly exceed those for telephone interviews; however, for larger geographic areas, travel and subsistence costs for interviewers in the field are large, and face-to-face interviews typically cost two to three times as much as telephone interviews of equivalent length (Groves & Kahn, 1979). Conducting interviews in people's homes has also become more difficult as gated communities, locked apartment buildings, and other safety-related practices have greatly increased in recent years (Dillman et al., 2009).

Telephone Interviews

The use of telephone interviews in social science research expanded rapidly as telephones in homes became more commonplace in the 1960s and 1970s. Now, it is hard to imagine that readers have not been asked at least once to submit to a telephone interview. However, the process of conducting telephone surveys has become more difficult in recent years. Safety and privacy concerns and the increase in unsolicited telemarketing calls have made people more reluctant to participate. In some instances, interviews have been used as a ruse to solicit information or pitch a product. Indeed, unlisted telephone numbers, answering machines, caller identification, and call blocking now enable people to avoid unsolicited telephone calls altogether. Further, the increased use of cell phones and concomitant concerns about the cost to respondents of completing lengthy telephone interviews as well as the likelihood of reaching respondents while they are engaged in other tasks (e.g., driving) has lessened the utility of traditional telephone surveys. Finally, a preference for electronic communication, such as texting and email, has decreased the likelihood that people will answer their telephones. In short, it has become more difficult to reach participants by telephone and those who are reached have become less willing to participate (Lepkowski et al., 2008). Thus, although telephone interviews have typically yielded high response rates, on the average just 5 percentage points lower than personal interviews (Groves & Kahn, 1979) and 10 to 15 percentage points higher than even the best conducted mail surveys (Dillman, 1978), response rates for traditional telephone surveys are now sometimes lower than those for mail surveys (Dillman et al., 2009).

As we have noted, however, similar problems apply to other modes of data collection; it is generally not possible to reach 100% of those who are sampled from a national population regardless of the mode of data collection. All types of surveys – regardless of the mode of data collection – tend to underrepresent the poor, socially isolated, transient, younger, and male members of society (Groves, 1987). And more recently the number of individuals with landlines has become even less representative of the general population. As an example, one of us recently contracted with a survey research firm to collect data from a "challenged" community. The age range of respondents varied substantially across the four years the survey was done, including one year in which 71% of the sample was made up of individuals 55 or over. In response to such challenges, researchers have developed other ways of improving response rates; some developments have improved other aspects of telephone interviews so that it might be better to characterize telephone surveys in research as undergoing dramatic change in the ways they are conducted rather than becoming altogether obsolete.

The use of the telephone interview as a mode of direct questioning is illustrated in these published research studies: In a study of relationship satisfaction and breakups, Arriaga (2001) used telephone interviews to determine whether couples were still intact four months after the conclusion of the paper-and-pencil portion of the study. The interview was brief and had been agreed to by participants during the first portion of the study. Participants were asked whether they still were dating the individuals they were dating at the beginning of the study and, if not, who was responsible for the breakup. In a more typical use of telephone interviews for direct questioning, Spoth, Redmond, and Shin (2000) conducted interviews of more than 1,200 parents of sixth-grade children in rural Iowa. Eligible parents were sent letters alerting them that they would be called for an interview and describing the goals of the study. About one week after parents received the letter, they received a call from an interviewer. When the initial call did not reach an eligible parent, additional attempts – up to 30 – were made to reach the parent. When an eligible parent was reached, the interview was conducted using computer-assisted telephone-interviewing (CATI) software. The researchers reported an impressive 84% response rate. As these examples illustrate, the telephone interview can be effective when very little information is needed from research participants and when the population of interest is scattered across a wide geographic area.

Telephone interviews do not impose strict limits on interview length, although they generally do not extend more than an hour, as do some face-to-face interviews. It was once believed that five minutes or so was an upper limit to the length of telephone interviews, but this belief has been thoroughly discredited (Quinn, Gutek, & Walsh, 1980). For example, Dillman (1978) reported that in one survey of the general public, with telephone interviews averaging over 30 minutes, only 4% of the respondents broke off after the interview started. Another large-scale study was successful in using interviews that averaged nearly an hour in length, covering topics that included beliefs about opportunity for racial minorities (Kluegel & Smith, 1982). In practice, however, telephone interviews are generally kept under 30 minutes, on average (Holbrook, Green, & Krosnick, 2003). Special populations (e.g., cancer survivors) might allow even longer interviews without major problems.

All the other advantages of face-to-face interviews, except the ability to use visual aids, are also available in telephone interviews. These include the interviewer's ability to correct misunderstandings, motivate the respondent, and probe for more detail when answers are vague. Although the ability to motivate the respondent might not be as great with telephone interviews as in person, this is compensated for by the somewhat smaller interviewer bias and tendency toward socially desirable responses in telephone interviews (Bradburn & Sudman, 1979). Carefully designed studies comparing face-to-face and telephone interviews using the same questions have found few if any differences in overall data quality (e.g., Quinn et al., 1980).

To overcome sampling concerns, researchers now routinely use random digit dialing techniques. These techniques are discussed in detail in Chapter 9 as an example of probability sampling strategies. Here it will suffice to note that **random digit dialing** is a means of including in a telephone sample the significant number of homes for which the telephone number is unlisted, including cell phones. The most rudimentary application of random digit dialing involves using a computer to randomly generate four-digit suffixes to the three-digit prefixes known to identify telephones in a geographic area of interest. This strategy can be improved upon by taking advantage of rules by which telephone companies assign telephone numbers and only generating numbers that satisfy these rules. But even here the portability of cell phones and policies allowing people who move to keep their landline numbers can create problems for place-bound sampling, and those problems are likely to increase.

Telephone interviews have several advantages over face-to-face interviews, besides the obvious one of substantially lower cost. The cost advantage is generally a factor of two to three, depending mainly on the geographic coverage needed. Larger areas give greater cost advantages to the telephone because costs of gathering information from respondents scattered geographically have become almost irrelevant; phone companies using the Internet to provide phone service (voice over Internet protocol (IP) services) typically offer unlimited free "long-distance" service. For business or other users, fixed-rate long-distance services, such as WATS lines, can also limit costs. Another advantage that is sometimes overlooked is the supervision of interviewers. Because interviewers can all work from a single room equipped with a bank of telephones and computers loaded with CATI software, their supervisors can be constantly available to answer questions, resolve problems, or even talk to difficult respondents. The problem of a dishonest interviewer faking data, which occasionally occurs with face-to-face interviews in distant geographic areas, is virtually ruled out by this type of arrangement for telephone interviewing. This arrangement also allows errors in the questionnaire or interviewing procedures to be corrected immediately upon discovery, which is usually impossible with face-to-face interviewing. All these factors contribute significantly to higher data quality as well as lower cost.

Another advantage of telephone interviews is speed. A questionnaire can be put together quickly and hundreds of interviews conducted almost overnight to assess public responses to a disaster, assassination, television program, or some other event. Mail or face-to-face interviews would reach respondents only many days after the event, greatly reducing the validity of data about people's immediate responses.

Finally, as noted, contemporary telephone interviews typically make use of CATI software. The interviewer sits with the telephone in front of a computer display and keyboard, reads questions displayed one at a time on the screen, and types in codes for the respondent's answer. The computer can check for valid data and signal the interviewer to recheck implausible responses, eliminating most coding and data-entry errors. Furthermore, the computer controls the sequence of questions, preventing interviewer errors in sequencing questions or in asking questions of the wrong subgroup of respondents (e.g., asking unmarried respondents about their spouses' occupation). Finally, biases deriving from question order can be reduced or eliminated by having a set of questions asked in a different, randomly selected order for each respondent; this would be difficult if not impossible for interviewers to do manually. As noted earlier, the same sort of computer assistance (CAPI) is now available and increasingly widely used in face-to-face interviews.

Telephone interviews also have disadvantages. Interviewer effects are possible. And, although they usually are smaller than with face-to-face interviews, in large-scale surveys involving national area probability samples and long questionnaires (i.e., longer than 30 minutes), random digit dialing telephone respondents have been shown to be more likely to satisfice (e.g., respond with "no opinion") and more likely to present themselves in socially desirable ways than face-to-face interview respondents (Holbrook et al., 2003). Telephone interviews also offer fewer opportunities to develop interviewer–respondent rapport than do face-to-face interviews.

Drawings, maps, show cards (i.e., cards on which response choices are printed) or other visual aids must be sent to respondents prior to telephone interviews or, as is more often the case, completely eliminated, and relevant questions reworded (or omitted) for telephone interviews. Some questions are difficult to ask on the telephone because of their complexity; if respondents miss even a single word, the entire question might become unintelligible. Interviewers do not have visual cues (a puzzled look, a shake of the head) when misunderstandings occur. As a result, more attention probably needs to be paid to question wording with telephone interviews than with other techniques. Finally, there are technical problems in the computation of response rates in random-digit-dialed telephone surveys because calls that are never answered on repeated calls are of uncertain status. If they are nonworking numbers, they should not be counted in the response rate calculations, but if they represent households or individuals who did not answer – for whatever reason – they should be counted as nonrespondents.

Asking Sensitive Questions

Survey research often involves asking participants to respond to sensitive questions, that is, questions that ask about socially undesirable, private, and/or illegal behavior. Consider, for example, efforts to understand child abuse, drug addiction, HIV/AIDs, or the experiences of undocumented immigrants. Obtaining valid responses to questions about such topics can be challenging. Sensitive questions can lower overall response rates, that is, potential respondents' willingness to participate in the survey; increase item nonresponse rates; and reduce response accuracy (Tourangeau & Yan, 2007). In addition to concerns about the extent to which responses are truly confidential or anonymous, that is, the extent to which researchers – whom respondents do not know – can be counted on to safeguard the information, respondents might feel embarrassed or threatened. In Chapter 7, we described issues that researchers should consider in developing questions and instructions, for example, introducing sensitive questions by transition statements that clarify the association of the questions to the study topic. In this section, we consider additional issues, including the importance of identifying sensitive questions and methods for assuring respondent confidentiality or anonymity.

It is not always clear what respondents might consider to be sensitive information, nor is it clear how respondents might react to such questions, because there are different types and degrees of sensitivity. Tourangeau, Rips, and Rasinski (2000) distinguished between questions that are perceived as **intrusive**; those that raise concerns about the possible consequences if the information were to become known outside of the research, that is, questions that are sensitive because of the **threat of disclosure**; and questions that require **socially undesirable** responses. For example, questions about both income and illegal behavior might be considered sensitive, but the former might be considered intrusive, whereas the latter would involve the threat of disclosure. The two types of questions are thus unlikely to elicit the same reactions and the strategies for dealing with them might therefore differ. An item assessing income might simply need to be placed elsewhere in the questionnaire, rewritten, for example, using different response options, or simply eliminated if it is not necessary to the research. In contrast, a survey concerning illegal behavior might require reworking entire sets of questions, more intensive training of those who gather the data, and so forth. Further, what is considered sensitive and the types of reactions that respondents might have can differ for different populations (Johnson & van de Vijver, 2002). One goal of pretesting a questionnaire should therefore be the identification of sensitive questions and the types of reactions that researchers might expect. If pretesting indicates that some respondents are likely to perceive certain questions as sensitive, researchers must decide whether the information is necessary and, if so, develop ways to ask those questions in ways that minimize respondents' discomfort and yield valid and therefore useful responses.

The use of potentially sensitive questions also needs to be considered in the context of the mode of data collection that is to be used. People are generally more willing to report sensitive information when the questionnaire is self-administered rather than administered by an interviewer. The reason, however, appears to be the anonymity of responses rather than the presence of the interviewer; in other words, participants appear to respond similarly when their responses are unknown to an interviewer (e.g., because they type their responses into a computer) whether the interviewer is physically present or not (Tourangeau & Yan, 2007). There appears to be little difference between computerized and paper-and-pencil self-administered questionnaires in terms of respondents' willingness to report sensitive information (Tourangeau & Yan, 2007). However, the difference may depend on whether respondents are promised anonymity as opposed to confidentiality. Some work suggests that when responses are not anonymous, respondents are less willing to report sensitive information in computerized than in paper-and-pencil self-administered questionnaires (Richman, Kiesler, Weisband, & Drasgow, 1999). Overall, respondents are more likely to report sensitive information to the extent that they believe their responses will remain anonymous.

Researchers have developed a variety of procedures for ensuring the anonymity of responses to sensitive questions. The **randomized response technique**, for example, allows participants to provide responses to questions without revealing the nature of the question to the interviewer. A variation of the technique allows participants to provide responses to a known question without revealing whether their answers are truthful. Participants use randomization devices, such as coins or a die, to determine whether they are to provide truthful responses or a specific forced choice from the range of possible response options. Because the properties of the randomizing device are known, the results can be statistically analyzed to reveal meaningful variations in responses to the sensitive question, such as differences among population subgroups. Such methods are useful when the research goals involve estimating population and subgroup prevalence, but make it difficult to examine relationships between responses to sensitive questions and many other respondent characteristics (Tourangeau & Yan, 2007). However, analytic procedures, for example, item randomized response theory or IRRT (de Jong, Pieters, & Stremersch, 2012), that extract participants' true scores on the construct that such questions are intended to measure, continue to be developed.

Interestingly, social desirability bias appears to be worse in telephone interviews than in face-to-face interviews (Tourangeau & Yan, 2007), even though the former might seem to provide greater anonymity than the latter. Perhaps it is because face-to-face interviewers are better able to develop a rapport with respondents and are thus also better able to assure respondents that their data are confidential. Indeed, some sensitive questions would seem to be best handled in face-to-face interviews in which participants respond to open-ended questions that allow them to qualify their responses and express themselves in greater depth. Face-to-face interviews also facilitate the assessment of respondent reactions so that immediate or long-term assistance (e.g., therapeutic services) can be provided when necessary. Such procedures might be important for particularly sensitive topics or potentially vulnerable populations, such as abuse victims.

Regardless of other procedures, it is especially important to assure participants that their responses will remain confidential when questions concern sensitive topics. Although complete anonymity also reduces the tendency to provide socially desirable responses, it may reduce accountability and thus the accuracy of participant reports (Lelkes, Krosnick, Marx, Judd, & Park, 2012). In any case, assuring participants of confidentiality (or anonymity) requires that respondents perceive the researchers and the sponsoring organization as trustworthy. Researchers can convey their trustworthiness through clear, straightforward, and professional communication (e.g., well-designed and carefully proofread questionnaires and prompt and courteous replies to questions) and by clearly telling potential respondents about the steps being taken to safeguard their data. For example, researchers can tell potential respondents about identification numbers on questionnaires and explain how the numbers are to be used. In addition to being necessary for ethical reasons, telling potential respondents that identification numbers enable the researchers to check names off of the mailing list, that the list of names will be destroyed, and that respondents' names will never be connected to their responses does not appear to affect response rates adversely (Dillman et al., 2009).

We have highlighted the importance of recognizing that researchers might not always know which questions or topics respondents consider sensitive and the need for researchers to assure respondents of the steps being taken to ensure the anonymity or confidentiality of data. However, it is also important to realize that, as with anything, too much focus on these issues can undermine the research effort, for example, by leading potential respondents to believe that they *should* be concerned about their responses when they might not otherwise be (Schwarz, Groves, & Schuman, 1998).

> **Exercise: Identifying commonalities in challenges facing North Dakotans**
>
> In the exercise in Chapter 13, you have (hypothetically) interviewed people from a number of communities in North Dakota, and decide that you now want to know which challenges are being most widely experienced. You decide to design a survey to give to people living in western North Dakota. First, decide on a sampling plan. Then, drawing from your interviews (and perhaps focus groups), identify questions for a survey (do this hypothetically, identifying what might be problems or challenges), constructing items that get at the problems/challenges that you have "identified." How might a web survey be different from a paper one? How does a web survey relate to a sampling plan?

Summary

We began this chapter by highlighting the variety of ways in which survey research methodology could be used, noting that survey research is most often used to describe the characteristics (e.g., attitudes, behaviors, or values) of a group of people, including the relationships among those characteristics and individual background variables. We also described the various sources of error that survey researchers must attempt to minimize in an effort to maximize the external validity of their research.

The three major types of survey research designs are cross-sectional, panel, and sequential designs. Cross-sectional designs involve the collection of data at one point in time, whereas panel designs involve the collection of data from the same participants at two or more points in time and are thus longitudinal designs. Each design has its strengths and weaknesses. Sequential designs include both cross-sectional and panel components and therefore take advantage of the strengths of both types of designs.

The remainder of the chapter focused on modes of data collection in survey research, that is, ways to directly question research participants. Modes of data collection in survey research include paper-and-pencil questionnaires, which can be administered in person (e.g., in small group sessions), by mail, or by the Internet. Other modes of data collection include face-to-face interviews and telephone interviews. The best way to gather information that involves direct questioning of participants depends on a variety of factors. Table 14.1 presents a schematic summary of the strengths and weaknesses of the different modes that we have discussed, so that readers can weigh specific considerations as they choose. Nevertheless, to give a general guideline, for surveys of the general population that cover more than a local geographic area, telephone interviews and, increasingly, the Internet are the methods of choice.

Exceptions to this generalization include a number of specific situations. Mailed surveys should be considered (1) for homogeneous groups – such as alumni of a

Table 14.1   Comparison of Different Modes of Direct Questioning

Dimension of Comparison	Paper-and-Pencil Questionnaire	Face-to-Face Interview	Telephone Interview	Internet
Cost	Low	High	Moderate	Low
Response rate	Low	High	Moderate to high	Low
Respondent motivation	Low	High	High	Moderate to high
Interviewer bias	None	Moderate	Low	None
Sample quality	Low, unless high response rate	High	Moderate to high, if directory; high, if random digit dialing	Low
Possible length	Short, if by mail; long, if in small groups	Very long	Long	Very long
Ability to clarify and probe	None, if by mail; some, if in small groups	High	High	None
Ability to use visual aids	Some (e.g., maps)	High	None	High
Speed of implementation	Low	Low	High	High
Interviewer supervision	–	Low	High	–
Anonymity	High	Low	Low	High
Ability to use computer assistance	None	High	High	High
Dependence on respondent's reading and writing ability	High	None	None	High
Control of context and question order	None	High	High	None

specific college or members of an organization – if they are widely scattered geographically; (2) if mailing lists are available, to minimize sampling costs; or (3) if cost constraints are maximal and low data quality is acceptable for the specific research purpose. With mail surveys, the techniques of Dillman and colleagues (2009) should be used to improve response rates, although they will incur additional costs. If, for a homogeneous group, one has access to a list of email addresses, then the Internet is a fast, low-cost method, sending the survey as an attachment or as a link. Also, if the target population is likely to have a strong virtual presence in the form of news groups, chat rooms, or web rings, then the combination of email and a well-designed website is a viable option.

Face-to-face interviews should probably be chosen (1) if maximal data quality is required and cost is no object; (2) if the study calls for special populations difficult to reach in other ways (e.g., low-income rural residents who might not have phones and might be too uneducated to respond well to mail questionnaires); or (3) if the population to be studied is geographically concentrated, making face-to-face interview costs comparable to telephone costs or only somewhat higher.

In deciding whether to use a paper-and-pencil questionnaire, face-to-face interviews, telephone interviews, or the Internet, researchers should consider the advantages and disadvantages of each mode as they relate to the purposes of the study. The nature of the target population and the sampling design chosen for the study also have implications for the mode of data collection.

Finally, we discussed some factors to consider when questions or entire surveys concern sensitive topics, noting that pretesting allows researchers to identify questions or topics that are likely to be considered sensitive by at least some respondents. Pretesting can also provide information about how researchers might best ask sensitive questions if the questions are deemed necessary to the research objectives. A variety of factors needs to be considered to minimize participants' discomfort and maximize the validity of responses, including the degree of sensitivity, question design and presentation, mode of data collection, and respondents' perceptions of the researchers' and sponsoring organization's trustworthiness.

Go online   Visit the book's companion website for this chapter's test bank and other resources at: www.wiley.com/go/maruyama

---

Key Concepts

Coverage error

Cross-sectional survey

Interviewer effects

Intrusive questions

Measurement error

Modes of data collection

Nonresponse error

Panel survey

Random digit dialing

Randomized response technique

Response rate

Sampling error

Sequential design

Socially undesirable questions

Survey error

Threat of disclosure

Total survey error perspective

On the Web

http://www.surveymonkey.com/ Create your own online survey and administer it via email and the web.

http://www.gallup.com/home.aspx The home page of Gallup, a polling organization that assesses public opinion on a variety of social, political, and economic issues.

http://www.src.isr.umich.edu/content.aspx?id=pub_methodology_109   Survey Research Center at the University of Michigan provides a list of publications on survey methodology. Click on the Data Resources link to learn more about public use data sets.

http://www.pewtrusts.org/our_work_category.aspx?id=288 The Pew Research Center conducts public opinion research on a variety of social issues. Click on the

Research Methodology link to see their research findings concerning survey research methodology.

Further Reading

Dillman, D. A., Smyth, J. D., & Christian, L. M. (2009). *Internet, mail, and mixed-mode surveys: The tailored design method* (3rd ed.). Hoboken, NJ: John Wiley & Sons.

Krosnick, J. A., Lavrakas, P. J., & Kim, N. (2014). Survey research. In H. T. Reis & C. M. Judd (Eds.), *Handbook of research methods in social and personality psychology* (2nd ed., pp. 404–442). New York, NY: Cambridge University Press.

Lepkowski, J. M., Tucker, C., Brick, J. M., de Leeuw, E. D., Japec, L., Lavrakas, P. J., . . .

Sangster, R. L. (2008). *Advances in telephone survey methodology.* Hoboken, NJ: John Wiley & Sons.

Patten, M. L. (2011). *Questionnaire research: A practical guide* (3rd ed.). Los Angeles, CA: Pyrzcak Publishing.

Tourangeau, R., & Yan, T. (2007). Sensitive questions in surveys. *Psychological Bulletin, 133,* 859–883.

Chapter 15

Evaluation Research

Research Methods in Social Relations, Eighth Edition. Geoffrey Maruyama and Carey S. Ryan.
© 2014 John Wiley & Sons, Inc. Published 2014 by John Wiley & Sons, Inc.
Companion Website: www.wiley.com/go/maruyama

Background

Evaluation research, also called program evaluation, is one type of applied research. It is distinct from other types of research not by the methods it uses, but by its purpose of answering practical, real-world questions about the impacts of some policy or program. Some researchers make a distinction between research and program evaluation, suggesting that program evaluation is not really research because its focus is not on seeking generalizable laws of behavior, but instead on how well a specific program works and what could be done to improve its effectiveness. Scriven (1973), for example, argued that evaluation has a single goal, namely, to determine the worth or merit of whatever is being evaluated. Consistent with such a view, sometimes program evaluation is treated differently by Institutional Research Review Boards, which may not require approval unless the researcher intends to publish the work as research. As has been described in discussions of different epistemologies that underlie research traditions, however, not all research has as a goal the identification of general laws or generalizable findings. Therefore, we see little if any reason for creating such a dichotomy, for program evaluations can enrich theories and identify generalizable elements of programs, even in cases where a research study is not intended. And many good program evaluations have a theoretical basis that is tested empirically. Deciding in advance that an evaluation project is not going to be research presumes knowledge of the outcomes, and could result in valuable information not being shared because no permission was sought when the work started.

Program evaluation covers a wide range of situations and settings. Different evaluations operate at very different scales, ranging from small scale and very local (e.g., examining effectiveness of a summer camp or an after-school program) to large scale and multisite (e.g., examining effectiveness of federal government jobs programs). While the former typically focus on helping programs to improve their effectiveness and funders to direct their resources toward programs that work, the latter can identify elements of effective programs that cross sites, providing information that guides new programs and develops generalizable knowledge. Even local information from small evaluations can help develop principles that guide practice and build theories. Although applied research can serve more broadly to define a social problem or explore alternative policies or programs that might be implemented to solve some problem, evaluation research has as its primary goal the description and evaluation of some existing social policy or program.

What is a program? In the broadest sense, a **program** is a set of procedures put in place by an organization in order to provide or improve services to its constituents (e.g., patients, customers, clients). In not-for-profit organizations (e.g., schools, social services), programs often map directly onto the goals of the organization – they represent mission-related work. In for-profit organizations, programs may be circumscribed efforts aimed at introducing and obtaining acceptance of a new product or line of products. In either case, programs and the organizations that underwrite them can benefit from evaluations that draw attention to their strengths, needs, and how they can be improved.

Defining Program Evaluation

Merriam-Webster's Eleventh New Collegiate Dictionary defines *evaluate* as (1) to determine or fix the value of, and (2) to determine the significance, worth, or condition of, usually by careful appraisal and study. The definition of evaluation is interesting, for in the definition is the idea of careful appraisal and study intended to determine significance, worth, or condition, which could refer to research as well as program evaluation. Definitions of **program evaluation** link even more strongly to goals and purposes of evaluation. Patton (1986) defined program evaluation as "the systematic collection of information about the activities, characteristics, and outcomes of programs for use by specific people to reduce uncertainties, improve effectiveness, and make decisions with regard to what those programs are doing and affecting" (p. 14). The Joint Committee on Standards for Educational Evaluation (1994) defined it as "systematic investigation of the worth or merit of an object."

Overall, social science definitions of evaluation show a high degree of consistency around issues of determining effectiveness and value. They are, however, vague about the role of theory, and avoid making theory a specific part of evaluation (for a contrasting view, see Chen & Rossi, 1999). Researcher definitions of program evaluation are consistent with the dictionary definition of evaluate, suggesting that the general public should readily understand what program evaluation is and why it is useful.

Program Evaluation and Accountability

Thinking of program evaluation as a tool for documenting the worth or value of a program links nicely with a current zeitgeist about accountability. Earlier, in Chapter 4, we discussed pressures on universities and researchers to show that they are using public money in effective ways. **Accountability** reflects general interest by the public, funders, and program supporters in knowing whether or not resources are being invested wisely and if programs are working, in effect using available information (data) as documentation. Viewed from a psychological perspective, the emphasis on accountability reflects movement of policy makers and the public from being "naïve psychologists" (Heider, 1958) who "test" their theories in imprecise and aperiodic ways – for example, accepting anecdotes and exemplars (Chapter 1) – to being more demanding and scientific in seeking available data to test accuracy of their expectations about how programs work and what is being accomplished. Successful accountability systems depend on frequent and effective program evaluation, so it should be no surprise that evaluations of various types are becoming a regular part of everyday life.

Accountability can be used to illustrate the scope of activities and fields in which evaluation is important, and where opportunities for program evaluation exist. Businesses, for example, have long valued the elements of "Total Quality Management" or "Continuous Quality Improvement." A central element of these approaches is making "data-driven decisions," recognizing and celebrating programs that work, improving others that are not working well, and eliminating programs that cannot be improved enough to make them effective. Similarly, in the world of non-profit social service agencies, documenting effectiveness has become almost a prerequisite for funding – or at least for continued funding. Organizations like the United Way are asking agencies that receive funds to demonstrate that the money they are receiving is making a difference, setting targets and showing that the programs have increased the numbers of people served and contributed to attainment of particular outcomes for those people. For example, food shelves may have to document the amount of food they distribute, the number of different individuals and families they serve (unique users, repeat users, low-income users, etc.), and even the ways that food is used to move clients into other services that they need. Agencies able to construct effective evaluations of their programs not only can respond to their funders and increase the likelihood of receiving continued support, they also can make their programs better.

In medical fields, finding effective treatments for medical problems and sharing them with practitioners has much in common with the accountability movements. The experimental approaches reflected in clinical trials are complemented by applied research looking at relations of many behaviors and attitudes with health and health risk factors, and of different types of programs with health behaviors. Regular reports in the media describe new correlates of health and risk that have been identified based upon evaluation types of studies that compare individuals choosing some intervention (e.g., type of diet regimen), practice (e.g., number of times engaging in vigorous physical activity per week), eating habit (e.g., consuming cured, salted meat like bacon), or drug regimen (e.g., taking a daily "baby" aspirin regimen) with others not using that approach. PreK-12 schools have been added in a major way to the accountability mix; policy makers have argued that schools should be able to demonstrate that they are successfully educating their students, with those that have not been able to document success being restructured (see illustration 1 at the end of Chapter 4) or even closed under No Child Left Behind (NCLB). Under NCLB there was in each state an accountability system that spelled out specific outcomes that needed to occur and consequences for not attaining them. Whether those outcomes were too ambitious and therefore unrealistic has been a challenge that has undermined the process; it illustrates the importance of stakeholder involvement in the decision process and developing outcomes that are aspirational and yet attainable. Accountability also has been making inroads into post-secondary education, with many universities being asked or told to identify learner outcomes their graduates have obtained.

Exercise: Evaluating college student learning

Imagine that you are asked to evaluate the learning produced by your university at undergraduate/graduate levels (choose the one that you currently are experiencing), setting learner outcomes – targets or goals that document effectiveness of your institution. Develop a process for establishing learner outcomes for your institution, and a method for collecting needed information.

Given demands for accountability and for using resources wisely, program evaluation is becoming widely used across a broad range of topic areas from business to social services to health care to education. The work occurs in field-based natural settings where the programs are rather than in laboratories. It typically is done collaboratively with practitioners, in their environments. In many instances the practitioners are partners in developing and even conducting the research, but in others external evaluators are brought in to review a program and how it is working. In the latter case, it is likely that the evaluators will be responsible for designing and conducting the evaluation, gaining perspectives of the practitioners before finalizing the design. Evaluation involves the process of designing investigations of how well different programs are working. Investigations attempt to be as unobtrusive as possible, for it would be a problem if the evaluation were so obtrusive that it changed what happened in the evaluation setting. Investigations may be experimental, quasi-experimental, or non-experimental, and involve both qualitative (e.g., interviews of key stakeholders) and quantitative (e.g., measurement of key outcome variables) methods. And, as will be explained in a later section of this chapter, they also may be formative, evaluations conducted as programs get under way to help guide their development and refinement, or summative, intended to assess effectiveness and impact of a program.

Steps in an Evaluation

Conducting an evaluation typically involves a series of steps. They include:

1. identifying the central issues of the program that is to be evaluated, the key elements of the program, and its expected outcomes;
2. planning and implementing an evaluation design with components that assess both program success/effectiveness and the ongoing processes that are occurring and that contribute to the processes;
3. collecting and analyzing the data; and then
4. using the findings to identify things that are going well and areas where changes might be needed, and, if the evaluation is summative, to judge success of the program.

The general process of conceptualizing issues, operationalizing variables, collecting and analyzing data, and interpreting the data parallels an orientation integral and foundational to most types of research. In contrast, the problem focus, the lack of control, imperfect comparison groups, and working collaboratively with practitioners to design the research distinguishes program evaluation and engaged and community-based research from most experimental research. As a result, even though many researchers have the research and technical skills needed to conduct effective program evaluations, they will face unexpected challenges unless they also have experience in the messy and less predictable world of engaged research and program evaluation.

Maruyama (2004) suggests several reasons that many researchers finish graduate school without much understanding about either program evaluation or engaged research and how it can be used to address problems and advance theory (see also

Maruyama, 1997). First, universities typically organize based upon disciplines and departments rather than problems, which de-emphasizes the need for skills that are focused on problems rather than disciplinary theories. Second, as has been mentioned, applied work is less predictable in terms of time and outcomes, which makes it unattractive for students on a structured timeline. It takes time to build relations with practitioners who work in applied settings, and many of the factors affecting the evaluation and how well it works are outside the control of the researcher. In the words of Schon (1995), applied work is work in the swamp rather than on the high ground, messy, slow, and potentially bad for getting publications and tenure. Third, the findings from program evaluations may have greater practical than conceptual importance, which makes them more difficult to publish. Fourth, if and when graduate students are exposed to evaluation, it is likely as one of a variety of methodological tools used for applied research, and one which they might not have occasion to use, particularly if their research is done primarily on campus. Finally, to some, evaluation has been viewed as useful primarily in specific situations where theory might be subordinate to social problems, which may seem not particularly desirable in graduate programs with a strong emphasis on theory and theoretical contributions.

Summative and Formative Evaluations

There are two general categories of evaluation research, summative and formative research (see, e.g., Scriven, 1967). **Summative evaluations**, otherwise referred to as outcome evaluations, examine the effects of a program and ask, "Does it work?" **Formative evaluations**, sometimes called process evaluations, ask, "What is it?" and "How does it work?" Although many evaluations have elements of both types of evaluation, it is easy to create a strong contrast between the two different types of evaluation, their methods, and their purposes.

Summative evaluations use experimental, quasi-experimental, and survey research designs. Formative evaluations use techniques more like the observational methods discussed in Chapters 12 and 13. Summative evaluations usually use statistical analysis of quantitative data. Formative evaluations are usually qualitative research and use case histories and observational or interview data rather than statistics to make a point. Summative evaluations are used to decide whether programs should continue, cease, or change; for this reason, administrators might resist and evaluators find it difficult to implement a summative evaluation. Formative evaluations seem more benign because they are used to help the administrators develop their programs, refine them, and improve them. Formative evaluations provide feedback to the program director and/or board of directors about how the participants react to the program, how the implementers are carrying out the program, and whether the actual program resembles the intended program. They define the program as it appears in action and describe how it works. This feedback often takes place during the early stages of a program, when there is still room for change and improvement – hence the name *formative* evaluation. By contrast, summative evaluations are done at the end of a program or after it has been in existence long enough to have produced some measurable effects that provide a fair test of the program's success. But because past completers of a program may have experiences very different from those of current participants, evaluators need to understand how the program has developed and changed over time; recommendations for the future cannot be based upon what "used to occur," but need to be based on what currently is. In this chapter, we focus primarily on summative evaluations; in Chapter 13 we described strategies like focus groups that can be used in formative evaluation research.

Consider an illustration of a program evaluation. The City of Minneapolis began a summer jobs program for youth, called STEP-UP, in 2003. It was named because it asked employers to "step up" to the plate and provide summer jobs for low-income youth living in Minneapolis. In 2010, we were asked to help evaluate the successes of their program. At that point, the program had been in existence for 8 summers, so there were lots of data available, for the various parts of the program (one for 14- to 15-year-olds, another for 16- to 19-year-olds) served about 1,000 students per summer. But the program was continually being refined and changed. For example, eligibility for the program changed in summer 2009, changing the pool of eligible students, and potentially changing markedly the outcomes that might be expected from the program. As a result, despite the age of the program, both formative as well as summative outcomes were needed. For formative parts, staff and participants were interviewed, while for the summative parts, summary information about backgrounds and experiences of participants was compiled and experience and post-experience outcomes of the participants were examined. We worked with program staff to identify key outcomes of the program. Those ranged from satisfaction of employers and students with the program, proportions of students successfully completing the program, and post-experience academic outcomes of participants. In order to provide a quasi-experiment, we used propensity score matching techniques to identify a comparison group of eligible students who did not participate in the program, and compared their school outcomes with those of participants. Consistent with an engaged action research model, we still are working with the program staff to continue evaluation efforts.

Detailed Description of Stages in Conducting a Program Evaluation

Because of the potential real-world impact of the findings from an evaluation study, it is important that the evaluation be sound in every respect. The Directorate for Education and Human Resources of the National Science Foundation, which provides funds for evaluation studies of programs designed to improve science, mathematics, engineering, and technology education, established a "user-friendly handbook" for program evaluation (Frechtling, 2010). The handbook suggests that an evaluation has six phases, which are:

- Develop a conceptual model of the program and identify key evaluation points
- Develop evaluation questions and define measurable outcomes
- Develop an evaluation design

- Collect data
- Analyze data
- Provide information to interested audiences

Developing a Conceptual Model

Starting with the first stage, program evaluators often develop **logic models** that describe the pieces of the project and expected connections among them. Frechtling (2010) suggests that a typical model has five categories, *project inputs, activities, outputs, short-term outcomes,* and *long-term outcomes,* which are connected by arrows that describe how the processes work. Inputs are funds and resources that support a program; activities are the services, materials, and actions that represent the actions of the program; short-term outcomes are immediate and proximal impacts; and long-term outcomes are the broader and more enduring impacts. A logic model identifies the different program elements and shows expected connections among them. It also can provide a framework both for evaluating a project and for managing it.

Based on our experiences, a focus on **inputs** is key, for many programs that are evaluated struggle at the inputs category, being forced continually to raise funds to support ongoing operations. Many people who start programs as non-profits don't anticipate the continuous effort needed to ensure ongoing funding. One reason is that funders rarely support infrastructure (e.g., Kania & Kramer, 2011), even though without a solid source of support for infrastructure needs, much time and energy are spent just keeping a program going. Consequently, many problems that small organizations face are a result of not being able to focus on the key activities because input issues consume time and energy. So if input measures are not collected, problems facing programs may be misidentified. The STEP-UP program described above is a fortunate program, for the Mayor was strongly supportive. But even in that case, part of the motivation for the evaluation is to document successes to increase effectiveness of fundraising appeals. (Incidentally, the literature review revealed that evidence supporting the effectiveness of summer jobs programs for youth like STEP-UP is not strong.)

Activities also are critically important, for those are the "manipulations," the independent variables in the work (services, materials, and actions) that produce outcomes. Without understanding what they are and how they really operate, it is difficult to identify the kinds of measures needed to assess their impacts. It is logical for program evaluations to focus on processes as well as outcomes. Unlike research in which the manipulations are well understood and the outcome measures are simply documenting effects of those manipulations, in program evaluation the nature and impacts of different aspects of the program are important to examine. Those impacts may not be operating in practice as they are in principle (note that we avoided saying "in theory," for not all programs are based on theory even though our preference would be for programs to have conceptually sound underpinnings). Such information is best gathered through approaches like observation, interviews, or even informal conversations with people using the program as well as with staff.

Outputs are the descriptions of the activities that describe their quantity and quality. They may measure intensity, duration, and other aspects of the activities that help decision-makers and outsiders understand what is happening in the program.

Short-term outcomes are the immediate outcomes that programs produce. If a goal is to educate 50 individuals from groups underrepresented in a field, or to serve 500 new program users, the outcomes can be numbers actually served. They also could be measures of climate or culture, for example, for a program that intends to revitalize an institution where morale is low or to increase worker motivation. If the goal is to increase motivation of workers, there also may be behavioral measures already available, like rates of absenteeism or of timeliness in arriving for work, or even in speed with which workers leave their workplace and socializing they do with coworkers outside of work. However, short-term outcomes can sometimes be challenging to assess and interpret – some programs might appear initially ineffective (or even detrimental) on certain measures as the programs get under way and problems are ironed out or as program participants and others adapt to changing expectations and processes.

Long-term outcomes are the most challenging, for few funders provide support of sufficient duration to allow assessment of long-term impacts. For example, a prison diversion program may want to look at five-year recidivism rates, an educational program for middle-schoolers at high school graduation rates, or a preschool program effectiveness in sustaining increased achievement. Typically, the long-term outcomes are the ones of greatest interest. As another example, food shelves were designed as emergency sources of food rather than as an ongoing part of the long-term ways that people avoid hunger. Short-term data on users provide only part of the picture, answering the question of how a program manages to meet immediate hunger needs. But without long-term outcome data, information about how hunger needs are being addressed is incomplete, for if food from food shelves becomes an integral part of the way that large numbers of people avoid hunger, food shelves are no longer "emergency" sources as they were designed, and, regardless of their short-term effectiveness, a different long-term solution is needed to address hunger needs. Food shelves are an interesting instance to consider, for they provide a critical service by addressing immediate hunger needs, which have been immense (an estimate from Hunger-Free Minnesota was that Minnesotans miss 100,000,000 meals per year), but do not affect the variables that force people to food shelves. As an evaluator of a food shelf program, (how) does one balance effectiveness of providing food against the point that food shelves cannot reduce long-term need?

Developing Evaluation Questions

The development of evaluation questions builds on the conceptual model of the first stage. According to Frechtling (2010), it consists of several steps:

- Identifying key stakeholders and audiences
- Formulating potential evaluation questions of interest to the stakeholders and audiences

- Defining outcomes in measurable terms
- Prioritizing and eliminating questions

One of the challenges is identifying who the **stakeholders** are. Some are obvious, for they have direct interest in what happens; they include users of programs, staff in the programs, and funders of programs. But there also may be people who *should be* using the program but for various reasons are not. Certainly, non-users would provide information that is different from the information provided by those using the program, but they might be very important in shaping a program for the future – particularly if they are much larger than the group that currently is using an under-subscribed program.

At the point where evaluation questions are designed, it probably is best to err on the side of inclusion, considering a broad array of questions of interest to various stakeholders as well as the researchers. Once they are articulated, the process of prioritizing and winnowing down can begin. Then, once the key research / evaluation questions are articulated, the process of operationalizing them occurs. That process engages stakeholders, for once questions are identified, they can be asked what success would look like, and how would they know if they were successful. As researchers, the outcomes that have been articulated need to be made measurable, and then the magnitude of difference that constitutes impact would need to be articulated. Perhaps the best way is to think in terms of **effect size** (magnitude of effect) rather than significance so that sample size is not the driver of success. Thinking in terms of prediction and nonstandardized coefficients is best. What size change in actual measured units would be viewed as meaningful? For example, if we could raise the grade point average of students 2/10ths of a grade (e.g., from a 1.8 to a 2.0), would that be sufficient? Or would we want to focus on a threshold, for example, how many more students have GPAs at or above the level that keeps them eligible for competing in interscholastic sports, or allows them to graduate from high school?

Developing an Evaluation Design

An **evaluation design** requires decisions about the methodological approach to be taken and the ways for collecting data. One consideration is whether the evaluation is quantitative, qualitative, or both. Today many evaluations take a **mixed methods** approach where both quantitative and qualitative data are collected. A second consideration is finalizing the data collection instruments. A third is selecting the sampling frame and how the sample will be drawn from that frame to avoid bias. Although random sampling is ideal, as noted earlier, in many instances random sampling just is not possible. Regardless, an important element of a program evaluation is developing a defensible approach to sampling. That approach may include a comparison group not experiencing the program or whose entry into the program was delayed.

Collecting Data

This stage is not much different from other research. Approval to conduct the research needs to be acquired, as do consent forms from participants so their data can be collected and analyzed. There may be more flexibility in a program evaluation to modify data collection techniques and questions. For example, if the initial results suggest that the measures are missing important information, questions could be added so the information is available for later participants. Collecting information unobtrusively is important for, as noted earlier, data collection ideally provides information that would be observable regularly in the program, not only when the program is under scrutiny from "researchers" or "evaluators." And, equally important, the data collection should minimally disrupt the program and its regular activities. Regardless of the method of data collection, the same issues of reliability and validity are true for program evaluation as would be true for any research study. For example, if observers are used, they need to be trained so there is high inter-rater reliability. Linking back to Chapter 4, program evaluation is a situation where using a combination of community and academic researchers and obtaining high inter-rater reliabilities helps researchers to be more comfortable about the quality of the data they are obtaining.

Analyzing Data

Data analyses are also much like any research, except that they need to engage the partners. Initial analyses should screen data for out-of-range responses or respondents who responded frivolously. Outliers need to be examined. Then analyses addressing research and evaluation questions need to be conducted, and the results shared with key stakeholders for their feedback and interpretation. After consulting with stakeholders, additional analyses may be important to clarify findings or to extend them. Then the final results should again be shared with stakeholders before preparing the report of the findings.

Providing Information to Interested Audiences

The report is a final stage. Once it becomes available, a plan for sharing the findings with the broad group of stakeholders needs to be developed. Unlike basic research, there often are immediate practical implications of the findings. The report should provide background and history to frame the report, a description of the program, the research design and research questions, the approach taken, the findings, and what the findings mean. An important part of the report is the section written last, an executive summary, for many readers will want to know the highlights of the evaluation without "wading through it." An executive summary should provide a concise summary of the purpose, the important questions asked, what the answers were to the questions, and what the answers mean. It likely becomes the "face" of the evaluation, and the information that makes its way into reports about the program and its success.

Viewed as a whole, the stages illustrate how program evaluation and other applied research differ from basic research. Although the principles of sampling, measurement, and research design discussed so far in this book apply equally to applied and basic research, applied research such as program evaluation involves additional considerations, some of which can be in conflict with the principles of good sampling, measurement, and design (see also the Appendix to this chapter on criteria for effective evaluations). In the end, the evaluation researcher must balance principles of good science and the practicalities of conducting research in an arena in which many, often conflicting, personal and political agendas are at play.

A Quasi-Experimental Program Evaluation: Compensatory Education

Head Start preschool education programs began in the 1960s on the assumption that "if children of poor families can be given skills and motivation, they will not become poor adults" (Economic Report of the President, 1964). Social critics have argued that this assumption is tantamount to "blaming poverty on the inadequacies of the poor versus blaming the poverty condition on the inadequacies of society" (Levin, 1978, p. 523). We agree and would argue that erasing the economic disparity between rich and poor requires much more than preschool educational programs. Nonetheless, recent research suggests that the benefits of preschool programs, including the economic return on money invested in such programs, are greater than any other investment we can make in the education of children (e.g., Heckman, Moon, Pinto, Savelyev, & Yavitz, 2010; Reynolds & Temple, 1998). Given those findings, advocates of early childhood programs are seeking government funding of universal early childhood programs, or at least funding for programs serving all low-income children – who are becoming an increasing proportion of the population. Evaluations of preschool programs are critically important, for programs that can produce results need to be identified. Consider the following straightforward questions of compensatory educational programs: Do they improve children's subsequent academic achievement or self-concept, and what do children and parents think of the programs? To answer such questions, actual evaluations of Head Start and other preschool programs have used children's subsequent academic achievement to determine program effectiveness – a short-term rather than long-term goal (e.g., lessening economic disparities) of the programs.

The evaluations of Head Start programs included three types: (1) summative evaluations of the overall effectiveness of all Head Start programs, (2) comparisons of different strategies and curricula within Head Start, and (3) on-site monitoring or formative evaluations of individual programs (Williams & Evans, 1972). We describe the first type of evaluation – summative evaluation of the overall effectiveness of the programs – and discuss some of the criticisms of it.

The first and most widely publicized evaluation of the overall effectiveness of Head Start was made by the Westinghouse Learning Corporation (Cicirelli & Granger, 1969). The evaluation included a sample of 104 Head Start centers from across the country and a sample of children from those centers who were then in first, second, and third grades. A comparison group was formed of children from the same grades and the same schools who had not been in preschool Head Start programs. These comparison children were selected to be similar to the Head Start children in age, sex, race, and kindergarten attendance. The evaluators tested both groups of children with a series of standardized tests to measure scholastic abilities and self-concepts. They also had teachers rate the children's achievement and motivation, and they interviewed the parents of both groups of children. The comparison group was not formed by random assignment, making this a quasi-experiment rather than a randomized experiment. The researchers tried to match the children in terms of their backgrounds; we discussed in Chapter 12 on non-experimental research how such attempts to match generally fail to eliminate group differences.

The results of this evaluation received wide attention because the findings were negative. The major conclusions were that (1) the summer programs were ineffective in producing gains that persisted in the elementary school years; (2) the full-year programs were marginally effective in producing cognitive gains and ineffective in producing gains in how the children felt about themselves; (3) Head Start children remained below national norms for standardized tests of language and scholastic achievement but approached national norms on school readiness in grade one. The most positive finding came from parents' testimonials: "Parents of Head Start enrollees voiced strong approval of the program and its influence on their children. They reported substantial participation in the activities of the centers" (p. 78). The Westinghouse report concluded that:

> the Head Start children cannot be said to be appreciably different from their peers in the elementary grades who did not attend Head Start in most aspects of cognitive and affective development measured in this study, with the exception of the slight, but nonetheless significant, superiority of full-year Head Start children on certain measures of cognitive development. (p. 78)

The criticisms of this study, even though it was not a true experiment with random assignment, include some of the criticisms made of randomized experiments: "the study is too narrow. It focuses only on cognitive and affective outcomes. Head Start is a much broader program which includes health, nutrition, and community objectives, and any proper evaluation must evaluate it on all these objectives" (Williams & Evans, 1972, p. 257). Cicirelli and Granger (1969) answered that "in the final analysis Head Start should be evaluated mainly on the basis of the extent to which it has affected the life-chances of the children involved. In order to achieve such effects, cognitive and motivational changes seem essential" (p. 257).

Another criticism was that the test instruments used to measure the cognitive and motivational changes were not developed for disadvantaged children and were therefore insensitive and inappropriate. The evaluators conceded that this was possible but that they had used the best instruments available.

A third criticism is that the study looked only for long-term effects by testing children in first, second, and third grades and ignored the immediate benefits that children might have derived from being in a preschool program. "Rather than demonstrating that Head Start does not have appreciable effects, the study merely shows that these effects tend to fade out when the Head Start children return to a poverty environment" (p. 259). The evaluators admitted that this, too, could be true, but they said the program must be judged not by its short-term effects alone if those effects disappear in a year or two; "the fact that the learning gains are transitory is a most compelling fact for determining future policy" (p. 259).

One other major criticism is the one we discussed earlier in this book. The results were probably contaminated by a **regression artifact**; because the children were not admitted to Head Start by a lottery, the "control" group of comparison children was not equivalent, making this a nonequivalent control group design. The researchers tried to match the Head Start and comparison children on age, race, sex, kindergarten attendance, and parents' social status, but matching does not eliminate the effects of preexisting differences between two populations. Matching is a good strategy only if it is followed by random assignment. If the investigators had originally tried to identify matched pairs of children and then from within each pair randomly assigned children to Head Start and the control group, they would have created equivalent groups. But matching alone is no substitute for random assignment, for it matches on observed scores rather than on true scores.

Let us compare the results of the randomized experiment in the Cambridge–Somerville Youth Study (e.g., McCord, 1978) and the quasi-experimental Head Start evaluations. The results of the Cambridge–Somerville experiment are difficult to dispute because the randomized experimental design made the treatment and control groups equivalent to begin with. Some aspects of the well-intentioned treatment hurt the life chances of the recipients. The question that remains unanswered about that evaluation is, why did the treatment hurt more than it helped? In the Head Start evaluation, the apparently negative results are not so convincing because there is an alternative explanation – regression effects alone could have made the program look ineffective. It could be the evaluation research rather than the compensatory program that failed in this case. Without random assignment, the Head Start researchers could not conclude that a treatment did or did not produce the intended effects.

Subsequent evaluations of elementary school compensatory education programs have yielded more positive and interpretable results. Follow Through is an elementary education program designed to continue the work of Head Start. It was conceived as a large-scale, federally funded program to provide for teacher training, parental involvement, and new instructional models of education for children from low-income families. When the funds needed to serve large numbers of schools and children were not made available, the program continued on a much smaller scale, including a research component to evaluate the effectiveness of 15 model programs (Wang & Ramp, 1987). The evaluation was based on a nonrandom assignment of students to Follow Through and control groups. Because participation in Follow Through was based on being "in need," the students in the comparison group most likely began with higher achievement scores and living conditions, favoring their subsequent scholastic achievement. The impossibility of equating the treatment and control groups persists in this research, as it did for the evaluation of Head Start. If the results had shown no differences between the two groups or had shown the Follow Through students performing less well than the comparison group, it would again be difficult to know whether their preexisting differences overshadowed any gains, but this was not the case.

The results of more than a dozen evaluations were positive and interpretable. Measures of the long-term effects showed that students from the Follow Through classes achieved higher academic scores; had better school attendance; and were less likely to drop out of school, repeat grades, or require special educational placement (Wang & Ramp, 1987). Given these results, which ran counter to expected effects of regression, the nonrandom assignment did not present problems in interpreting the effects of the Follow Through program. At the same time, it is possible that if regression effects could have been controlled, the findings would have been even more favorable than those reported.

The Politics of Applied and Evaluation Research

We started this chapter by stating that applied research, and particularly evaluation research, differs from basic research in the extent to which it can and intends directly to affect people's lives. The applied researcher designs studies with the ultimate hope of being useful in changing or affecting social policies and programs that have an impact on people's lives. Because policy change and formation are inevitably a political process, applied research must necessarily attend to and address the political realities within which it is conducted.

One of the most pressing political concerns in the conduct of evaluation research is the question of who benefits from the research. Although the issue may in many cases seem straightforward, it is shaped by decisions about what dependent variables the research should examine: What outcomes define whether or not a program or policy is "successful"?

Results with Immediate Impact

Because it is carried out to evaluate ongoing programs, evaluation research often is designed with a shorter time span than basic research. History has shown us that most complex social problems are not solved immediately, but at best "whittled away at" over time. In contrast, decisions about programs are made immediately because budget allocations and personnel decisions are frequently based on demonstrable "results." Despite the fact that implementing change is slow and warrants a long time window, policy makers often have "short time horizons" and wish to see immediate or at least short-term research results to justify continuing or terminating a program. The pressure to identify quick and definite answers makes much evaluation research different from basic research. Pressure for quick results is highly frustrating to practitioners building programs, for there inevitably is a period of review and refinement (a formative evaluation stage). But in a "results now" environment where budget trimming and "efficiency" are valued, it is difficult to separate effective programs from others.

Although evaluation research is intended to produce immediate results and have an immediate impact, two circumstances often prevent this from happening. The first arises when results are equivocal or contradictory so that it is not clear what the policy decision should be. For example, the many evaluations of preschool Head Start programs do not all agree about the program's success or failure (Campbell & Erlebacher, 1970; Cicirelli & Granger, 1969). If the planners and decision-makers are to use these results, which set should they use?

The second circumstance that interferes with using the results of program evaluation arises when the real effects of social programs are not immediately visible. For instance, Head Start preschool education was originally introduced to "break the cycle of poverty" by educating 3- and 4-year-old children so that they would become achieving, self-sufficient adults. Educational planners do not intend to wait 20 or 30 years for an evaluation, however, before they decide whether to continue with the preschool programs. Instead, they use immediate outcomes – the children's subsequent academic achievement in elementary school – and assume that adult occupational attainment will follow from childhood academic performance. In reality, there is a positive but weak connection between the two. Nevertheless, the illustration makes a point that when projecting long-term results, researchers need to think about the proximal and intermediate steps that would move to those outcomes. For example, a logical perspective is that Head Start programs prepare students for school, improve their academic performance, and eventually are manifested as better academic attainments and careers. If there were no effects of Head Start programs on kindergarten readiness or early school achievement, would we really want to wait 20 to 30 years to see if long-term impacts could be positive? If so, we had better have alternative explanations about ways in which Head Start programs could result in reduced poverty.

Returning to the positive but weak connection between occupational attainment and early educational success, Weiss (1972) argues that when immediate or short-term effects (which she called "proximate" goals) and the long-term effects (to her, "ultimate" goals) have been shown by prior research to have a direct and strong connection, short-term goals are sufficient. For instance, "in evaluation of a Smokers' Clinic, it is probably enough to discover that the program led participants to stop smoking. It is not essential to investigate the ultimate incidence of lung cancer" (p. 38). Many of our more ambitious social programs, however, are designed to have long-range effects. Short-term outcomes in such cases are unsatisfactory whenever their relation to long-term outcomes either has not been established or has been found to be weak. At the same time, regardless of how we behave, how well should we expect to predict events 20 or more years in the future? Realistically, given all that transpires over that time period and influences outcomes, not very well. Unfortunately, they are all that we have.

Vested Interests and Competing Criteria

The choice of dependent variables – the criteria for evaluating a program – makes evaluation researchers face this issue: In whose interests is the research? It is not sufficient to say "in the interests of science" because the outcome will influence more than science. Because the results of evaluation research are used to make funding decisions, there are vested interests in the criteria chosen for success. The evaluation could affect some people's jobs, education, or health; and the results could be in the interests of some people and perhaps to the detriment of others.

The scientific questions of selecting dependent variables become political questions in evaluation research. If there are competing views about appropriate outcomes, whose criteria will prevail? It is not always clear that one set of criteria is "better" than another. All evaluation research must address the question of whose values, whose criteria for success or failure, will prevail in designing the evaluation and in judging the outcome of a program. Different stakeholders have different perspectives and different goals. Evaluation researchers, therefore, even more than basic researchers, must ask themselves, "Whose side are we taking through our decisions?" (e.g., Becker, 1967).

Technical Decisions with Ideological Consequences

The technical issues involved in finding measurable criteria have ideological consequences. "Applied social researchers are more technically proficient in the study of individuals than in the study of organizations, and therefore, social research tends to be more social psychological than social structural" (Berk & Rossi, 1977, p. 81). The technical ease with which we can measure problems and outcomes determines which ones we recognize or attend to. Crime-prevention programs provide a case in point. One criterion for success is reduction in crime rates, which can be accomplished or attempted in several ways. If we consider the events leading to crime as forming a long causal chain, we could intervene at any point along that chain to prevent or reduce crime (Kidder & Cohn, 1979). We could intervene in the childhood experiences of "potential delinquents" and try to prepare them for noncriminal careers (McCord, 1978). Or we could focus on adult employment problems and provide job skills for the unemployed. Or we could seek alternatives to unemployment and layoffs as industrial options. Or we could focus on the doorsteps of victims of crime and promote better home-security measures, such as locks and burglar alarms. All these are reasonable starting points for explaining and preventing crime. Yet, they all suggest very different goals or solutions for crime-prevention programs, some of which would be much easier to implement successfully than others. Programs to install door locks and burglar alarms have higher success rates (if we simply count numbers of locks and alarms distributed) than do programs to restore community cohesion or job security; and as Berk and Rossi (1977) point out, "outcomes that can be counted easily tend to be listed as the outcomes desired" (p. 81). The technical decision – to count burglar alarms installed – has the ideological implications that the way to reduce crime is to prevent victimization. In schools today, similar issues are being debated. Is safety improved more by locking outside doors, placing armed guards in schools, and screening with metal detectors, or by engaging communities with schools and improving the educational readiness and engagement of youth to discourage disengagement and disenfranchisement from the educational system? Should money be spent on security or teacher salaries? It may be easier to calculate return on investment for money spent on security, but how much should ease of documenting impacts be the basis for making decisions? In addition, can one really isolate impacts of security systems when so many other variables and processes affect the outcomes (e.g., school violence) attributed to security systems?

The examples illustrate a larger point, namely, that establishing programs as successful does not guarantee that the problem or issue that produced the program will be solved. This point is often illustrated by the widely told tale of people seeing babies floating down a river and rushing in to pull them out. One man heads away, and another asks him where he is going when there still are babies to save. His answer:

"I'm going to go see who is throwing them in." Food shelves are a great illustration. They may be very efficient, serve a lot of people, and prevent a lot of hunger. But they are a "downstream" solution to an "upstream" problem and cannot solve the issue of hunger, only help address it. At some point, the demand for food shelves needs to be reduced. The best programs are ones that not only are effective, but also produce solutions to problems by reducing future demand for services.

Clients' and Other Stakeholders' Participation in Evaluations

In any program evaluation, there are likely to be numerous parties with different vested interests in the program and its outcomes. Those parties include policy makers who create and support programs, administrators who run them, frontline staff, and clients/users. Efforts to include stakeholders in the development of evaluations reveal the very political nature of the research (Farrar & House, 1986; Weiss, 1986). Each group of stakeholders has a different type of decision to make and considers different results to be relevant. Policy makers and funders who decide whether to continue funding the program want to know whether the program has produced the intended effects. (Think back to the first chapter, where we discussed how causal thinking leads policy makers and others to expect programs to lead inevitably to particular outcomes.) Program administrators who are interested in improving the program want to know what is going well and what is not, and whether they can continue things as they are or if they need to change staffing, approaches being used, or even target a different group of clients. The frontline staff want to know how they can be more effective in helping particular clients, but also want to have results that make them look good. And the clients themselves, if they have a choice, want a program that meets their needs and the opportunity to decide whether or not to continue participating in the program (Weiss, 1986). Each group considers different information relevant for its decision.

Bush and Gordon (1978) valued client participation in their research on children's placements in foster homes, institutions, or their families of origin. While reviewing records, they came across the description of a woman identified as a pyromaniac – a mother who set fire to her apartment and whose child was subsequently taken from her and placed in an institution as a ward of the state. When Bush and Gordon interviewed the child, they heard another version of that incident. The child said that during a cold winter, when the apartment heating was inadequate and the mother had repeatedly requested that it be repaired, the mother lit a fire in a waste-basket, which tipped over and set fire to the apartment. From an agency's point of view, this was pyromania; from the child's point of view, it was an effort to keep warm. Whichever version of the story you believe, there are at least two – and one is the client's.

Bush and Gordon (1978) advocate including clients' preferences not only in the evaluation of social programs but also in the decision of what treatment they should receive. Letting clients choose their own treatments naturally obviates random assignment, but we present the case because it also tells us something about using clients' satisfaction as a criterion for program evaluation. Bush and Gordon make three points:

1. that clients have more information about their past and present needs and a greater stake in choosing the right treatment than do "outsiders";
2. that clients who exercise such choice are more pleased with their treatments (in this case, foster placements for children) than clients who are denied the choice; and
3. that for the choice to be a real choice, it must be an "informed" choice.

Two factors sometimes limit people's ability to make an informed choice: Small benefits can look good to someone who has previously had no benefits at all, and restricted experience with alternative treatments in the past can limit people's ability to make an informed judgment about which treatment to choose. Some of the children in Bush and Gordon's study who could "only remember one kind of placement, institutions, were very reluctant to choose other forms of care when given a variety of options" (pp. 26–27). Only when the researchers made it clear to the children what the other placements were like were the children able to make an informed choice between living in an institution or a foster family.

Applying this logic to the McCord (1978) experimental evaluation of the Cambridge–Somerville social program casts doubt on the validity of the participants' positive subjective evaluations of the treatment. Would two-thirds of them still have said positive things about the treatment had they been told about the subsequent criminal records, poor health, lower occupational standing, and earlier deaths of the treatment group? For clients' satisfaction to be a useful evaluation, it must be an informed evaluation, with hindsight about the objective consequences of the treatment and not a simple judgment of whether it made the clients feel good. It is fair and reasonable to include clients as judges and evaluators of the services they receive, but if they are not fully informed, they might err in their judgments (see, e.g., Campbell, 1969). Like McCord's findings that clients' testimonials were contradicted by objective evidence, other researchers report inflated and sometimes misguided testimonials in evaluations of educational programs: "Studies of compensatory education programs have one 'universal finding': regardless of the type of program, duration, or actual results, parents are enthusiastic" (McDill, McDill, & Sprehe, 1969, pp. 43–44). Perhaps the participants in the Cambridge–Somerville experiment and the parents of children in compensatory education programs are telling us that they appreciate the special attention – the investment of resources and the good intentions.

We face a dilemma: We want to take into account clients' evaluations, criteria, ratings of effectiveness, and satisfaction; but those ratings do not always agree with objective indicators. If we resort to objective indicators, we face another problem: "The more any quantitative social indicator is used for professional decision making, the more subject it will be to corruption pressures and the more apt it will be to distort and corrupt the social process it is intended to monitor" (Campbell, 1979, p. 69). Moreover, objective indicators measure something quite different from satisfaction. The association between objective indicators, such as absenteeism or job turnover, and subjective ratings of satisfaction is weak. Gutek (1978) concludes, therefore, that we should not abandon subjective measures because "people live in a subjective world as well as an objective one… Satisfaction may not take the place of objective indicators, but neither can objective indicators take the place of subjective indicators such as satisfaction" (p. 50).

Summary

This chapter covers what some consider a type of applied research and others don't consider to be research at all, namely, program evaluation (research). We suggest that program evaluation is research, but with special attention given to the stakeholders of the process and the practitioners running the programs. We provide a sampling of the ways in which program evaluation has been defined, and discuss how important program evaluation is in the age of accountability where programs are being scrutinized for their effectiveness. We provide a detailed description of the steps of an evaluation and the stages that evaluations go through from beginning to end. We distinguish between formative and summative types of evaluation, and their differing methods, purposes, and data collection. We illustrate program evaluation by focusing on evaluations of compensatory education programs, and the challenges they face eliminating confounds like regression effects. Finally, we discuss some of the political aspects of program evaluation, including the importance of immediate impacts for sustaining programs, the effects of vested interests of different stakeholders on the questions they want to ask, the potential consequences of ideology underlying different approaches and even questions, and the importance of engaging stakeholders in the process of program evaluation. As part of that discussion, we discuss how researchers reconcile findings when perspectives and perceptions of different stakeholders vary.

Exercise: Evaluating the plan (Follows from an exercise in Chapter 14)

Now you have analyzed the surveys from respondents in North Dakota, and they suggest that you need to develop an intervention that helps communities refine their individual identities through town hall meetings. Construct an imaginary town hall meeting intervention, and then develop an evaluation plan to assess its effectiveness. Since you have the luxury of beginning the evaluation when the intervention begins, you can include both formative and summative measures. Follow the stages of conducting an evaluation described in this chapter.

Go online   Visit the book's companion website for this chapter's test bank and other resources at: www.wiley.com/go/maruyama

Key Terms

Accountability
Activities
Effect size
Evaluation design
Evaluation research
Formative evaluation
Inputs
Logic models
Long-term outcomes

Mixed methods
Outputs
Program
Program evaluation
Regression artifact
Short-term outcomes
Stakeholders
Summative evaluation

On the Web

http://www.eval.org/ The American Evaluation Association (AEA) is an international organization aimed at promoting the field of evaluation. AEA's website contains many useful links to evaluation-related information, such as relevant journals, conferences, and, for members, an opportunity to connect with other evaluators to discuss key issues in the field.

http://evaluation.umn.edu/evaluationland/ This site hosts an online quiz on evaluation topics, covering several topic areas for beginners and advanced students in the field.

http://www.evaluationcanada.ca/ The website of the Canadian Evaluation Society contains useful resources, such as an outline of program evaluation standards and various online textbooks. Unlike most countries, Canada has an accreditation process for evaluators; information on this process and the five evaluator competency domains is provided.

Further Reading

Alkin, M. C. (Ed.). (2012). *Evaluation roots: A wider perspective of theorists' views and influence* (2nd ed.). Thousand Oaks, CA: Sage.

Patton, M. Q. (2012). *Essentials of utilization-focused evaluation*. Los Angeles, CA: Sage.

Russ-Eft, D., & Presill, H. (Eds.). (2009). *Evaluation in organizations: A systematic approach to enhancing learning, performance, and change* (2nd ed.). New York, NY: Basic Books.

Scriven, M. (1967). The methodology of evaluation. In R. W. Tyler, R. M. Gagne, & M. Scriven (Eds.), *Perspective of curriculum evaluation* (pp. 39–83). AERA Monograph Series on Curriculum Evaluation, No. 1. Chicago, IL: Rand McNally.

APPENDIX: Criteria for Effective Evaluations

The National Science Foundation (NSF) also established a set of criteria that had to be met by any evaluation conducted using their funds. These criteria likely apply to any sound evaluation of a program or organization. The criteria fall into three categories: evaluation plan, evaluation instruments, and evaluation report.

Evaluation Plan.   Before an evaluation study can begin, a detailed plan that has been reviewed by all concerned parties must be developed. The plan should include the following information:

- What are the purposes of the program or organization to be evaluated? Without a clear understanding of the philosophy, goals, and procedures of the program, it is not possible to evaluate its performance in a fair and meaningful way.
- What is the purpose of the evaluation, and how will it be done? The justification for and procedure by which the evaluation will be done needs to be explained to all parties who might be affected by the results of the evaluation.
- Who are the stakeholders? That is, who stands to gain or lose from the evaluation? This might include program staff, clients served by the program, or the policy makers who will determine the future of the program.
- What is the scope of the evaluation? Will it focus on the overall performance of the program, or will it focus on specific goals or procedures within the overall purpose of the program? The evaluation can vary in the depth and breadth of its scope, characteristics that sometimes are influenced by the amount of resources available to conduct the evaluation.
- From whom within the organization will information be gathered, and how will it be gathered? Will the evaluation focus on management or other personnel within the organization, or will it focus on the clients for whom the program was designed? In what way will stakeholders be involved in developing a strategy?
- What measures will be put into place to ensure that the information obtained as part of the evaluation is of high quality? These concerns are not different from those for any type of empirical research; however, there is the additional concern that the measures are appropriate for the context in which the program is implemented. Also, it is important that ethical considerations, such as confidentiality of responses, are adequately addressed.
- Will the evaluation study include both qualitative and quantitative measures? Although quantitative measures are well suited to an evaluation of the productivity or performance of a program, qualitative measures can provide important information about how these outcomes are achieved.

Evaluation Instruments.   The second set of criteria concerns the means by which information will be obtained regarding the performance of the program that is being evaluated. These criteria focus primarily on the way in which respondents will be sampled and the approach to measurement that will be taken.

- The measures should be defensible. That is, they should evidence high construct validity in the context of the evaluation. It is important that the measures can be defended clearly and persuasively to all stakeholders and decision-makers.
- The measures should be comprehensive. They should not be biased in their coverage of the various goals, functions, and procedures of the program.
- The procedures for administering the measures should be standardized. Because respondents are likely to come from various constituencies associated with the program, the settings within which information will be gathered likely will vary. This variability must be overcome by strategies for administering the measures that ensure no influence of setting.
- The measurement strategy must be practical. Because the measurement process will be disruptive for some respondents, it is important that the procedure for administering and responding to the measures be as straightforward and efficient as possible.
- The measures should be balanced. They should be designed to detect both strengths and weaknesses of the program being evaluated.
- The measurement process must be done in such a way that respondents' rights are not violated. Although evaluation research varies in terms of goals and participants from most of the research described in this book, all of the ethical principles outlined in Chapter 3 apply. A particular concern in evaluation research is confidentiality of responses. Respondents cannot be expected to provide honest and meaningful answers to questions about the program if they worry that their honest opinions could get them in trouble.

Evaluation Report.   Perhaps the most critical feature of an evaluation study is the final report. As noted earlier, unlike research reports, which are intended for a relatively homogeneous audience of the researchers' peers, reports produced by evaluators must be appropriate for a heterogeneous audience. This audience can include program staff, clients, government officials, or other policy makers in whose hands the future of the program rests.

- The evaluation report begins with an executive summary, a succinct document that provides essential information about the evaluation report in a style that is easily understood by stakeholders. It should clearly summarize the primary content of the full report.
- The evaluation report should describe in detail the program that has been evaluated. The description should include the goals and objectives of the program, the procedures by which the program attempts to realize its goals and objectives, the rationale for the evaluation, and the stakeholders.
- The report should identify prevailing forces that need to be understood in order to interpret the results of the evaluation. These forces can range from timing to economic, political, and social conditions impinging on the organization during the period covered by the evaluation.
- The report should identify the stakeholders in the program and describe the different perspectives they will bring to a reading of the report.

- A proportionately large section of the report should describe in detail the procedures used in the evaluation. It is this section of the report that most resembles a research report typical of social science research. Measures should be described and justified, procedures detailed, and results of statistical analyses presented.
- Perhaps the most critical aspect of the evaluation report is "the bottom line" – the conclusions and recommendations offered by the evaluator based on the findings from the evaluation study. This section of the report should be balanced and circumspect. Both strengths and needs identified by the study should be highlighted. And potential limitations to the evaluation should be disclosed and discussed.

http://www.westat.com/westat/pdf/news/ufhb.pdf Link to the current NSF Handbook for Project Evaluations (December 2010).

Chapter 16

Mixed Methods Approaches
Learning from Complementary Methods

Overview

So which method(s) should I use?? This chapter attempts to bring together the preceding chapters by considering questions readers may have about picking a method or methods to use for their research. Certainly, the simplest answer to the question above is: Use the method that best matches the type of research that you want to do. In some instances the choice is obvious. For experimental studies, in which a key part is

Research Methods in Social Relations, Eighth Edition. Geoffrey Maruyama and Carey S. Ryan.
© 2014 John Wiley & Sons, Inc. Published 2014 by John Wiley & Sons, Inc.
Companion Website: www.wiley.com/go/maruyama

attaining significant differences between conditions and drawing causal conclusions, the analysis of quantitative data (e.g., using ANOVA or ANCOVA, both of which can be thought of as special cases of multiple regression) is typical. For more exploratory, non-experimental studies, researchers typically use correlational approaches or qualitative ones, depending both on their inclinations and on the nature of the problem being addressed. A researcher seeking to reflect the nuanced voices of the participants and convey their perspectives is likely to choose a qualitative approach. A researcher desiring to find out what the public thought about a social issue would likely choose a quantitative survey approach.

But for many research questions any single answer is just too simple, for many questions are complex and multifaceted and can be answered in a range of different ways. Studies examining complex problems within a dynamic social context may find that conclusions based on a single method are too narrow or limited in scope, missing some valid perspectives and overemphasizing others. Further, at times a researcher may want to blend different philosophical orientations in thinking about research. As a result, even in many "straightforward" instances, the best answer to the question of method could be to go beyond what is obvious, even when the choice of method seems clearly indicated. For example, even in experimental studies there are good reasons to collect qualitative responses that allow researchers to better understand the cognitive and social processes underlying the responses participants provide.

Blending qualitative and quantitative methods in a single research project is called using **mixed methods** approaches. Conducting research using mixed methods is in part epistemological and in part pragmatic, for the choice is guided by how researchers think about their research and their roles in it. As described by Fielding and Fielding (2008), it is "not a technique,... but an attitude of inquiry, an approach to quality standards and to what constitutes adequate explanations of social phenomena" (p. 566). Their definition reflects the more recent ways that writers have described mixed methods research. Originally definitions focused on collecting both quantitative and qualitative data, pretty much independently of the motivations for collecting them together. In contrast, more recent definitions have included the blending of the different philosophical orientations to, and **epistemologies** about, research that different methods manifest. If used correctly, researchers using mixed methods need to integrate different ways of making sense of the social world, of engaging in research, and in determining what is most important to study (see, e.g., Creswell & Plano Clark, 2011).

When to Use Mixed Methods

Creswell and Plano Clark (2011) suggest that there are several types of research problems that are well suited for mixed methods. They are ones where:

- a single data source is not sufficient;
- initial or preliminary results provide incomplete explanation;
- a secondary method can enhance a primary method;
- a particular theoretical stance warrants collection of both quantitative and qualitative information; and

- the research problem can be best addressed in stages or phases with a variety of methods.

Consider, as a relatively simple example, a study of the causal attributions that participants make for particular outcomes that they receive. Much of the research has relied on asking participants to rate how important the same widely accepted attributional dimensions (e.g., Weiner, 2010) are in accounting for their outcomes (e.g., How important, from not at all important, to extremely important, was your ability in determining your outcome?). A second, similar, approach is to ask participants to spread the attributions for their outcomes across a set of prescribed categories (What percent of your outcome was due to your ability? to your effort?...). These two response options capture a static and measurable set of common understandings of attribution responses. But attribution research either in place of the previous approaches or along with them may ask participants to explain what happened and why it happened, accepting open-ended responses not tied to pre-identified attributional categories. In such a case the open-ended responses ideally would be collected first so the responses are not shaped by prior questions identifying and possibly cueing particular responses. The open-ended responses may or may not conform to the researchers' expectations about how causes are assigned, but they certainly do not force respondents to fit their perceptions to predetermined categories and they might result in the identification of new and different patterns of responses (although not if the prior research has in fact effectively identified the dimensions that people use in forming attributions). We earlier referred to this general issue when discussing the advantages of open-ended versus closed-ended questions in Chapter 7 and emic versus etic approaches in cross-cultural measurement in Chapter 8. From a qualitative perspective, a researcher should not necessarily be able to anticipate the ways that participants think about and interpret their successes and failures. The open-ended responses may be analyzed quantitatively as well as qualitatively. For example, the proportion of respondents who attribute their successes or failures to their abilities could be compared across conditions through quantitative analyses of the open-ended responses. But specific responses made by individual participants also could be included in the results section as narrative responses exemplifying a particular type of response that some participants give, without comparison across conditions.

Consider as an example the classic Milgram (1974) studies of obedience,[1] in which subjects were asked by a lab-coated researcher to shock "co-participants" in a learning task when they gave an incorrect answer to a memory quiz. The results of this research are well known; regardless of the setting, substantial proportions of participants complied with the researcher and administered shock into the "Danger, severe shock" and "XXX" range. These results stimulated intense discussions about the motivations of participants. What if the studies had been mixed methods studies, and if each time an opportunity to shock the co-participant arose, the participants had been asked to write down any thoughts that passed through their mind? Such information, although probably much more reactive, might have offered a rich lens into the cognitions underlying an obedience or noncompliance mentality, and into the mixture of

---

[1] Thanks to our colleague Dr. Suzanne Russ for suggesting this example.

thoughts going through the minds of the participants. Interestingly, the Milgram (1963) study actually was mixed methods, for the researchers interviewed participants afterward about their motivations, but those findings are not reported in the article, nor are their questions listed. If they had asked particular questions, perhaps the researchers could have reported that those who shocked co-participants had been raised in authoritarian households, or that they were employed in jobs with no autonomy, and accustomed to paying consequences for disobedience to authorities. We would have gained an insight not only into whether or not participants would shock ostensible co-participants, but also into the factors that led them to do so. The addition of straightforward qualitative methods to an experimental study potentially offers a much more complete view of the phenomenon under exploration.

Exercise: Enriching past research studies

The Milgram study provides an illustration in which the findings of a quantitative study could have been enriched markedly by the addition of a qualitative component. Think of other research studies in your discipline that were either qualitative or quantitative, and how they might have been enriched by adding methods that made them mixed methods. Talk about triangulation (described later in this chapter), and how it might occur.

The point of the examples is that in many studies, researchers can collect quantitative and qualitative dependent measures in order to have both very specific information about how participants respond on specific tasks, and more general information about the complex ways that participants think about the issues. Ignoring opportunities to obtain both types of information may result in researchers not being able to tease apart different explanations for their findings. At the same time, we are not arguing that both types of information are needed in all instances. There are instances where the theorizing is clear, past results have already focused the research to a point where only particular dependent measures are needed, and to collect additional measures will not add to what is known, but may simply place additional burden on participants. So a balance to mixed method approaches is the principle of **parsimony**; in all research, respect for burden on participants should lead researchers to design studies that collect the information that is needed and additional information that could be important in helping understand what is found, but not to collect additional measures because they happen to be available, they might be interesting, or they aren't a lot of work to add or even analyze.

Regardless of how trendy use of mixed methods becomes, not all studies should be mixed methods. Said differently, even though at times researchers can get carried away with their creativity and desire to find out all kinds of information, it is important to minimize the burden on participants. And, if we collect additional measures, we will want to analyze those data, which may in some instances detract from or complicate the primary findings. Birth order, for example, is a variable that is easy to add to a study, but its inclusion needs to be guided by theory, not convenience. Its inclusion may lead to increased confusion rather than increased understanding, for it is difficult to determine the proportion of times that birth order yields meaningful outcomes (e.g., Schooler, 1972); the number of nonsignificant and unreported findings from studies that happened to include birth order as a "secondary" variable is difficult to estimate.

As an example of measures to collect and not collect, consider a study of the effects of a self-efficacy manipulation on student academic success. It definitely would want to collect appropriate measures of academic success. The study might even want to focus on particular subject areas of academic success. But it probably would not include measures of athletic accomplishment, for athletic and academic success are different dimensions. To the extent that prior research on self-efficacy had been vague about the underlying processes through which self-efficacy is related to other variables, it would consider adding qualitative measures that would increase our understanding of the processes, and the work would employ mixed methods. If, in contrast, those processes were well understood, mixed methods would not be needed.

Linking back to the reliance of research on underlying theorizing, we might have other reasons besides using mixed methods for wanting to collect additional measures. Some may result in mixed methods, others not. For example, if theorizing were to suggest that processes of mediation or moderation are occurring, measures should include variables that are viewed as either mediators or moderators of the relationship. If a self-efficacy intervention only affected students who had already experienced at least moderate academic success, we would need to include a prior measure of cumulative academic success so we could examine the prediction of moderation – which would be done through analyses that examine the presence of an interaction between the treatment and prior success. Alternatively, if in a study we hypothesized that only people upset by an intervention would be more likely to help others, we might want to interview them, asking them how they felt during and after the study, to identify those who should be affected by the intervention.

Thus far, we have largely illustrated a role for mixed methods in experimental research. We focused there first because use of mixed methods is less commonly thought of in such research, but even in experiments there are often good reasons for using mixed method approaches. Quasi-experimental and non-experimental research provides even more obvious reasons for using mixed methods, for such research is more exploratory and more likely to benefit from collecting different types of data that can provide multiple lenses for viewing what is occurring. When a phenomenon is not well understood, having available data of different types and from different sources is particularly valuable for extending our understandings. And drawing from multiple epistemologies can be valuable in forcing researchers to think more creatively about the phenomena being studied.

Triangulation

One term often used in mixed methods work is **triangulation**, representing the idea that confidence about a finding increases when different methods converge on similar findings. This idea has many roots. One is the idea of **convergent and discriminant validity**, the idea that constructs should relate to some things (convergent) and be very different from others (discriminant). (See Chapter 8.) We identify the specific place of a construct not only by what it relates to, but also by what it differs from. If we were to create a new construct and call it "the great self," to fulfill the concept of triangulation that construct would have to be similar, but not identical, to other measures of self, and also relate to other variables in some ways that differ from existing self measures. We would collect measures of that construct and others to examine its convergent/discriminant validity. We also might gather archival information to see whether the attribute of "great self" was reflected in people's actual lives, and interview family members about the "great self" levels of participants. If triangulation didn't support the construct, we would have to conclude that our wonderfully conceived measure really wasn't so great after all. From a mixed methods perspective, a construct operationalized in different ways should still show the same pattern of relationships regardless of how it is operationalized. To the extent that it does, our confidence in that construct increases.

A second root is the **multitrait–multimethod matrix** idea introduced by Campbell and Fiske (1959), which argues for collecting multiple measures of constructs using multiple methods. (See Chapter 8.) Although their examples used quantitative data and inspection of the nature of the correlation matrix generated by the data, the logic is readily extended to qualitative measures as well. To the extent that underlying logic about the nature of research, the sources of information, and the ways of collecting and analyzing information differ, convergence of findings can be particularly powerful, regardless of whether they can be represented in a single quantitative matrix. One uncertainty may be about the existence of methods factors for qualitative methods; some methods may show a distinct pattern of responses, as might be found in scales from a survey, but for others there may be no discernible methods factor underlying the responses.

A third root for triangulation can be drawn from the idea of the **nomological net** (e.g., Cronbach & Meehl, 1955), which argues that a nomological net is a mapping of interrelationships among theoretical constructs, the ways that they are operationalized and measured, and the nature of the observed relationships among measures. Whereas convergent and discriminant validity address relationships at the empirical level, the nomological net focuses on the conceptual level. With both approaches, different ways of operationalizing and measuring variables and of approaching research would ideally yield the same patterns of relationships across variables.

The point to take away is that using mixed methods allows stronger inferences to be drawn about relationships in those instances where the different measures yield similar conclusions about relationships among measures. Convergence of different approaches is a powerful type of replication of findings, for those findings are not limited to a specific approach or type of measure. And failure to converge, disconfirmation of expectations, is recognized by cognitive psychologists as a strong way to create reflection, reassessment, and refinement. Given the clear advantages of conducting studies that use mixed methods, it is not surprising to see great interest in developing mixed methods approaches.

The next sections provide some history on mixed methods approaches, and then describe different "types" of mixed methods approaches. Before turning to them, however, it is important to return to a point alluded to earlier, namely, that some types of research do not naturally fit together, for they are based on very different philosophies, rationales, and assumptions. In such instances, designs may pit pragmatism against epistemology; if a researcher is strongly wedded to a single approach and its orientation to research, the idea of incorporating competing perspectives may seem counterintuitive and prevent serious consideration of a multimethod approach. For example, experimentalists working in field settings might view them as alternative laboratories where they impose as many controls as they can, and collect traditional data about the interventions they design. In contrast, Lewinian action researchers build a partnership with practitioners to design research shaped by input from the practitioners and focused on application of existing theories to everyday problems in ways that help practitioners improve their practice while also informing theory. In yet a third very different approach, **grounded theory** researchers use qualitative data to generate a theory that explains processes as they occur in natural settings. Not surprisingly, the different approaches are not often combined in a single research project. If one were to attempt to merge the various approaches, it would most often be in some sequential and iterative way where different methods are used at different times. Further, the approach would likely have as a dominant orientation one where pragmatism overrides the different philosophical underpinnings of different approaches. Given the range of philosophical perspectives underlying research, it is not surprising that different methods are defined by the order and way in which they combine quantitative and qualitative data collection.

Brief Background of Mixed Methods Approaches

Articulation of the potential value of mixed methods can readily be traced back over 60 years to social scientists including Campbell, Fiske, Cronbach, and Meehl, and roots for mixed methods can be found in many examples throughout the social sciences of researchers combining qualitative and quantitative research. Nevertheless, the emergence of mixed methods research approaches did not capture widespread attention until around 1990. At that time, Greene, Caracelli, and Graham (1989) identified dimensions of methodological mixed methods design, Caracelli and Greene (1993) identified different strategies for integrating quantitative and qualitative research, and Hammersley and Atkinson (1995) framed combining methods as a way to counteract possible threats to validity. In 2003 publication of the *Handbook of Mixed Methods in Social and Behavioral Research* (Tashakkori & Teddlie, 2003) signified that mixed methods had become a serious method that surpassed its original focus of simply combining different approaches in a single study. Interest in mixed methods has expanded to the point where several journals (e.g., *Journal of Mixed Methods Research*) provide outlets for such research and strongly encourage authors to submit papers using mixed methods, and a number of textbooks focus solely on mixed methods approaches (e.g., Creswell & Plano Clark, 2011; Greene, 2007).

Types of Mixed Methods Approaches

Although there are several ways in which approaches to mixed methods research have been categorized, we present the approach suggested by Creswell and Plano Clark

(2011). They provide a number of framing perspectives, and then present six different approaches.

Framing Perspectives for Mixed Methods

First, Creswell and Plano Clark (2011) suggest a distinction between a **fixed design** in which the researcher has predetermined how quantitative and qualitative approaches will be used and sequenced, and an **emergent design** in which the methods used are identified in response to issues arising during the research process. For fixed designs, the research is always going to be mixed methods, whereas emergent designs may begin as a single method, but add additional methods to overcome obstacles encountered during the course of data collection. Creswell and Plano Clark view the two designs as anchor points on a continuum; some studies may be fixed, but change in response to participant responses, while others may always plan on using mixed methods and have a tentative plan, but decide on specifics only after some exploratory data collection.

Second, Creswell and Plano Clark (2011) suggest that researchers may choose between the a priori adoption of a particular well-established mixed methods approach, which they call a **typology-based approach**, and creating one's own approach driven by a design process in which one picks and chooses the elements that seem best to fit the particular setting and research question, called a **dynamic approach**. The typology approach could be characterized as "cook book," selecting a recipe and following it. In contrast, a dynamic approach weighs different components (purpose, conceptual framework, research questions, methods, and validity) in designing a study.

For a dynamic approach, Creswell and Plano Clark (2011) suggest that key considerations from the components described above focus on the research problem, the purpose of the research, and the research questions. Pragmatism is key, for the goal is to identify the methods that best address the questions and fulfill the purpose of the research. Selection of mixed methods should be an explicit choice. A list of reasons was proposed by Greene et al. (1989); they argued that broad reasons for using mixed methods were their capacity potentially to produce triangulation – convergence across methods; **complementarity** – broader understanding through elaboration and clarification that comes from different approaches; **development** – using methods to inform other methods; **initiation** – adding new perspectives and identifying contradictions; and **expansion** – extending breadth and range of the research. More detailed lists are now available, but the reasons of Greene et al. provide a sufficient introduction to the benefits that can be realized from use of mixed methods.

Decisions in Selecting the Type of Mixed Methods Design

Creswell and Plano Clark (2011) identify four decisions that have to be made in determining an appropriate mixed methods design. They are:

- *Level of interaction between the different methods.* Can the methods be kept separate, almost as if they are separate studies, or will they necessarily interact with one another? **Interaction** can be through one shaping the other in a sequential way, through collection of one type of information affecting collection and/or responses to the other type, through a framework imposed by one type of data collection, or even through converting one type to the other for analyses.

- *Relative priority of the different methods.* In some mixed methods studies, quantitative methods are primary, and will have **priority**. In others, the qualitative methods are primary with quantitative subordinate, and in still others, the two approaches have equal priority.
- *Timing of conducting the different approaches.* This refers to how the different parts of the research are ordered, but also can refer to sequencing of the analyses of the data or how the results are used. **Timing** can be concurrent, sequential, or multiphase – which may include both concurrent and sequential within the steps of the study.
- *Procedures for mixing the different components of the research.* **Mixing** refers to how the different components are combined and integrated. It includes when the different methods are "put together" as well as the way the data are combined. The various components may be mixed as late as when the different results are interpreted, and as early as when the research is designed.

Major Types of Mixed Methods Designs

Creswell and Plano Clark (2011) have identified six different designs that they refer to as "prototypes." They are the convergent parallel design, the explanatory sequential design, the exploratory sequential design, the embedded design, the transformative design, and the multiphase design. As noted earlier, these approaches, which we describe below, all assume that the researchers are skilled in both qualitative and quantitative research techniques.

Convergent Parallel Design

This design is the best known mixed methods design, with roots back to Campbell and others. It sometimes is called simply the convergent design or a triangulation design, and occurs when quantitative and qualitative components of a design are implemented concurrently. The two strands are of equal priority even though the data typically are *collected and analyzed independently* before being combined for interpretation. The goal is to obtain different yet complementary information addressing a single issue or question. A key idea is that the different data will complement each other and provide a richer source of information than either one could by itself. Although in some ways two separate studies, a goal is to merge the two sources of information to produce a single interpretation; it lends itself to a "single study" approach where timeliness of data collection is important and the research is needed quickly for decisions of policy or practice. Unless the researcher has strong quantitative and qualitative data analysis skills, taking a team approach for this type of research is recommended (Creswell & Plano Clark, 2011). This is the most popular mixed methods design. Challenges come in balancing both the different methods and the findings from the two approaches, particularly when the findings do not agree.

Explanatory Sequential Design

This design occurs in two separate stages, beginning with the quantitative data collection stage and followed by an explanatory qualitative data collection stage that helps explain the quantitative results. Given the role of the latter data collection to help interpret the former, this approach always is done sequentially. This sequence reflects the higher priority of the quantitative approach in investigating the questions addressed by the study. Sometimes the qualitative stage is motivated by unexpected findings, but in others it would be anticipated as a natural next step regardless of the findings. For example, the qualitative part may focus on interviewing outliers, who are identified by their responses to quantitative questions. In other instances, what initially was designed as a single methods approach can become a mixed methods study as researchers attempt to understand their findings, particularly in cases where the findings diverge from hypotheses. The explanatory sequential design approach appeals to quantitative researchers, is straightforward, and is readily amenable to report writing. A challenge of the approach is that the researcher needs to be able to return to the participants a second time to collect the second wave of data. In addition, sequential designs generally take longer to conduct, and likely require two different approvals from the IRB since the latter study is not designed until the former is completed.

Exploratory Sequential Design

The sequencing for this design is the reverse of the sequencing of the explanatory design. It begins with and prioritizes an exploratory qualitative study, and then designs a quantitative study to build on the findings of that exploratory study. An initial qualitative study could identify multiple themes from interviews, and the quantitative follow-up study could examine the rates of occurrence of the various themes across a representative sample. Alternatively, based on qualitative interviews, a quantitative instrument may be designed to survey a large group. Therefore, it is not surprising that this design has been referred to as the "instrument development design." A major purpose of this design is to generalize qualitative findings from a small sample that was interviewed or surveyed to a larger and representative sample. Because the study starts with qualitative data, its approach is likely to be constructivist, valuing multiple perspectives and gathering of information that can provide a deep, rich understanding of phenomena. It is used in instances where the researcher is not sure about the constructs that are important to study or how to go about assessing them. But in the latter stage it may shift back to a positivist perspective. Challenges are tied to the time it takes and in selecting information from the qualitative stage to quantify.

Embedded Design

An embedded design is the type of design we used as an illustration to begin this chapter. It was an experimental quantitative study in which qualitative data are gathered within a largely quantitative framework to increase understanding of the processes underlying the quantitative results. Embedded designs include those in which the second approach is added to enhance the overall design, and can be either largely quantitative or largely qualitative. The second type of information is subordinated within the design. Both types of information are collected within a single design, and the design can be predominantly either qualitative or quantitative. The example given earlier in which we suggested that Milgram's subjects could have been asked to identify their thoughts as they participated in the obedience study also illustrates this type of approach, as was the variant where they would respond to an interview or survey after the experience. As another example, a study of cognitive dissonance might not only collect measures that demonstrate dissonance-consistent results, but also ask open-ended questions to participants about how they perceived the situation and what they were thinking when they responded to ensure that the processes in fact represented dissonance. Alternatively, the researcher might embed a quantitative study within a broader qualitative study and framework. For example, an intervention to improve student achievement may begin by asking several focus groups of students what they think prevents them from doing better in school and what might help them do better. The responses could guide development and assessment of an intervention. The approach can be used by researchers who are largely trained in only one of the two approaches, but they do need experience in using mixed methods approaches. A challenge, suggested in our illustration of the Milgram study, is that the second type of data collection might introduce treatment bias that affects the outcomes of the experiment.

Hillard, Ryan, and Gervais (2013), for example, used what might be best described as an embedded design to examine college students' reactions to use of the Implicit Association Test (IAT) as a tool to raise awareness of racial bias. Participants received one of two sets of instructions about the IAT prior to completing it online; they then completed various quantitative measures about their affective reactions, perceptions of bias, and attitudes toward the IAT. Two types of qualitative data were also gathered. To the extent that the qualitative data were collected to augment the largely quantitative data and were subordinate to those other data, the study is an embedded design. Alternatively, if the two types of data collection were viewed as parallel, the study also could be viewed as a convergent parallel design. Participants provided short (3–5 sentences) written descriptions of their thoughts about the IAT and how they felt and thought about their IAT scores. A subset of participants provided longer reflection papers concerning their IAT experiences. Qualitative and quantitative data were first analyzed separately and then together to identify relationships between qualitative and quantitative responses. One of the most interesting findings was that participants who provided negative qualitative responses were subsequently *more* likely to help an African American individual (a quantitative measure). This relationship was only revealed as a result of the integrated data analyses.

Transformative Design

This design is shaped by the researchers in a transformative theoretical (e.g., feminist theory, critical race theory) world view or framework. Such researchers employ theoretical frameworks that advance the needs of underrepresented or marginalized populations. Such research is likely to produce recommendations for change, and is social justice oriented. Its goal often is empowerment of individuals. Creswell and Plano Clark (2011) suggest as an example how a researcher may use a critical feminist perspective and collect quantitative data to uncover consequences of stereotypes of women and then collect qualitative data to illuminate how the processes of stereotyping work. This design is somewhat controversial since it is defined by its ideologically driven decisions rather than methodological ones. It therefore stands in contrast to other approaches (e.g., experimental research) in which researchers actively subject ideas and perspectives to the possibility of falsification, using procedures that are accepted by others, and other approaches (e.g., grounded theory) in which theories or meaning are driven by participants' responses and behaviors. Challenges include developing strong relationships with participants, for trust is key when promoting a social change agenda. In addition, justifying the need for using the framework may be tricky and controversial, for it often presumes dissatisfaction with existing structures.

Multiphase Design

This category goes beyond basic designs, covering designs that have both concurrent and sequential elements. One early type was called a "sandwich" design, for it had three parts, with the different part in the middle (quant-qual-quant or qual-quant-qual). More recently, however, this design has been viewed as a possible way to deal with large studies with numerous research questions that are asked in a combination of concurrent and sequential approaches to advance a single programmatic objective. Thinking back to action research and its cycles of planning and action, one could imagine that a first cycle might concurrently collect quantitative and qualitative data to yield information that would help understand some phenomenon, but then the second might sequence the data collection to address the next set of questions, and a third might use only a single approach to try out an intervention suggested by the previous steps. A key idea for this design is that of a program of research that would require a series of studies and steps moving toward some goal. It is an approach for researchers interested in addressing the objective across a period of time. It is highly flexible, provides a framework within which a lot of different types of research can be conducted, and fits well with engaged research and program evaluation efforts.

Wrapping Up

Mixed methods approaches have become particularly popular among researchers doing applied work, to the point that it seems that there is almost an expectation that "good" research will use mixed methods. It is valuable for researchers to understand the different types of mixed methods research, the distinctions across different approaches to mixed methods research, and decision processes and criteria for determining an appropriate design. We believe a major attribute of mixed methods research is that it encourages researchers to step out of their epistemological comfort zone and seriously consider alternative perspectives and approaches. In addition, the sequential types of mixed methods research in which findings lead researchers to decide to add mixed methods exemplify a strength of basic scientific processes, namely, their capacity to explore even unanticipated findings in pursuit of knowledge. Finally, mixed methods allow the initial question answered by the quantitative data, often a "what" question, to be enriched by consideration of a "why" question through gathering of qualitative data.

Mixed methods are not appropriate in all instances. We would argue strongly that researchers should collect only measures that are needed to answer their questions, and that there are costs to using mixed methods, including complicating the research study, adding burden to participants, and lengthening the time needed to complete the research. These all need to be carefully weighed against the anticipated benefits that come from adding additional methods of any sort.

To the extent that research is viewed as a process in which each research project leads to the next, ideas about mixed methods are particularly appealing, for they provide tools that add to validity of findings. Even if many of the specific studies are not mixed methods, the idea of varying methods, in effect, using mixed methods *across* studies, is a compelling one. Varying methods across studies increases confidence in findings through triangulation, for conceptual replication across different methods and epistemologies is powerful evidence for the underlying theory. And even in very practical settings where theory may be largely emergent, the interweaving of research methods and broadening of information sources provides rich perspectives that should help researchers move iteratively toward better interpretation of findings and increased knowledge. It is hard not to like what seems so logical and straightforward; after all, an effective researcher is one able to draw upon a full "set of tools" to address issues and create knowledge. Maslow's (1966) statement, "if the only tool you have is a hammer, you treat everything as if it were a nail" (p. 15), may succinctly capture the essence of mixed methods.

Summary

Mixed methods have been advocated as desirable for over 50 years, yet widespread use of mixed methods has occurred only fairly recently. Early uses of mixed methods were largely practical decisions about combining qualitative and quantitative approaches. They made sense in a lot of instances, and even in largely single-method approaches there were "expeditions" using complementary approaches to enrich understanding of depth or breadth of particular findings. Mixed methods offer opportunities to supplement and explain findings, to add different data sources, and to move programmatic research forward. More recently, as different methods became more strongly tied to different epistemologies, the inherent conflicts between combining qualitative and quantitative methods became apparent. Greene et al. (1989) list opportunities that mixed methods provide to yield results that produce *triangulation, complementarity, development, initiation, and expansion.*

Decisions that have to be made once a researcher decides to move forward with mixed methods are about how the different approaches are integrated: Are the different methods used simultaneously or sequentially, is data collection integrated or kept separate, is one approach superordinate, and at what point in the study is the decision made to make it a mixed methods study? These decisions shape the type of mixed methods design that is used. Creswell and Plano Clark (2011) identified six different designs: the *convergent parallel* design, the *explanatory sequential* design, the *exploratory sequential* design, the *embedded* design, the *transformative* design, and the *multiphase* design.

Exercise: Reversing the order, quantitative and then qualitative

In the earlier North Dakota exercise, the analyses of what is happening in North Dakota went from qualitative to quantitative. Design a study that starts with a quantitative study, and then goes to qualitative. For example, the research could start with a survey of residents or with quantitative analyses of recent newspaper articles. Then interesting findings could be followed up by interviews or focus groups to provide much greater depth of perspective about the issues.

Go online   Visit the book's companion website for this chapter's test bank and other resources at: www.wiley.com/go/maruyama

---

Key Concepts

Complementarity

Convergent validity

Convergent parallel design

Development

Discriminant validity

Dynamic approach

Embedded design

Emergent design

Epistemologies

Explanatory sequential design

Exploratory sequential design

Expansion

Fixed design

Grounded theory

Initiation

Interaction

Mixed methods

Mixing

Multiphase design

Multitrait–multimethod matrix

Nomological net

Parsimony

Priority

Timing

Transformative design

Triangulation

Typology-based approach

On the Web

**http://obssr.od.nih.gov/scientific_areas/methodology/mixed_methods
_research/section2.aspx/** This website provides a nice overview of mixed methods research in health sciences. The site contains many useful references and resources.

http://mmira.wildapricot.org/ This website is for the Mixed Methods International Research Association. While this site is largely dedicated to its members, it does have a mixed methods resources section that they report will be available to the public in 2014.

Further Reading

Creswell, J. W., & Plano Clark, V. L. (2011). *Designing and conducting mixed methods research* (2nd ed.). Thousand Oaks, CA: Sage.

Johnson, R. B., & Onwuegbuzie, A. J. (2004). Mixed methods research: A research paradigm whose time has come. *Educational Researcher, 33*(7), 14–26.

Tashakkori, A., & Teddlie, C. (Eds.). (2003). *Handbook of mixed methods in social and behavioral research*. Thousand Oaks, CA: Sage.

Part III

Analysis and Writing

Chapter 17

Critically Reviewing Research Reports and Literatures

An important part of being a capable researcher is developing the skills to be able to critically evaluate and summarize the work of others. Effective criticism is a related skill, for being able to disagree agreeably about theory, methods, and research is a key part of scientific advancement. Disagreements need to be about ideas and not about personalities. We come to our ideas honorably, but they are best viewed as temporary perspectives on knowledge, open to refinement, modification, or even transformation. They are informed by the work and ideas of others, both through agreement and through disagreement. We should treat the ideas of others as we treat our own, representing their construction of reality, grounded in their epistemologies and data. As we discussed in the introductory chapters, science and theory are cumulative, with later studies adding to and building on the results of previous studies. Progress is made through this accumulation of knowledge, and reviews of the empirical literature are an essential part of this process.

This chapter focuses on two main topics: how to read and evaluate individual empirical research studies, and how to summarize the results of a group of studies bearing on the same topic. Ongoing assessments of individual studies, coupled with periodic assessments of a given research area, provide an evaluation of what has been found so far, point out weaknesses and limitations in the accumulated knowledge, and provide direction for future studies. In the same way that critiques of individual studies are done during the review process and again after studies appear in press, periodic reviews of the cumulative body of knowledge gathered about a particular research area synthesize what is known and are an integral part of the scientific process. The focus here is on quantitative research, with varying relevance for different types of qualitative research.

Reviewing Individual Research Studies

Most students experience something of a culture shock upon their initial forays into the social science literature. As undergraduates, they have become accustomed to reading textbooks, which tend to distill empirical research into a few pithy conclusions accompanied by color photographs or humorous cartoons. Methodological detail is limited, and statistical results are practically nonexistent. Contrast this approach with typical research reports in the social sciences, which are often packed with technical language (jargon), methodological detail, and dense statistical results that are virtually incomprehensible to those without training in graduate-level statistics. No cartoons or color photographs are to be found, only figures displaying three-way interactions or structural equation models that look like a Jackson Pollock painting. Given the nature of quantitative social science research, it is not surprising that qualitative articles, with rich descriptions, quotes, and generally understandable interpretations, are more accessible for readers.

Students generally get little practice reading original research reports. Our first goal, therefore, is to provide some pointers for getting the most out of reading empirical research reports, as one must be able to read and understand a single report before one can summarize a group of reports on a topic. While thinking about this chapter, readers should also imagine themselves being on the other side, writing up their findings, for that process parallels this one, and is the topic of the next and final chapter in this text.

Step One: Read the Abstract

This recommendation may seem like common sense, but many readers actually skip over the abstract. It is useful, however, to read it, because it should summarize the study succinctly in nontechnical language and provide a short "take-home" message for the study. Knowing ahead of time in general terms about the procedure and findings makes it easier to follow the more detailed description to come. However, readers must keep in mind that abstracts typically cast a study in the most positive light, and the actual findings might not be as impressive as conveyed in the abstract.

Step Two: Read the Introduction

The purpose of the introduction is to provide the theoretical background for the study and to review relevant past research. Thus it will – or should – tell why the questions being asked are interesting. A good introduction makes clear how the study builds on the previous literature and why this particular study is important. The introduction provides suggestions for other relevant articles to find and read. The introduction also usually points out weaknesses or inconsistencies in the past literature, and makes the case for any unusual methods or measures being introduced. Although the introduction should allow readers to anticipate the hypotheses being tested, a well-written introduction states these hypotheses explicitly. Lastly, many articles conclude the introduction with a summary of the methodology employed in the study. This paragraph can be very helpful, as it provides a sketch of the subsequent method section.

Step Three: Read the Method Section with a Fine-Tooth Comb

It is essential to read the method section with a critical eye. There can be considerable slippage between the hypotheses stated in the introduction and the methods used to test them. It is not unusual for an introduction to convey rather grandiose goals for the study, only for the reader to discover in the method section that a narrow subset of those goals is actually addressed. Here is a list of questions readers should ask themselves as they read the method section.

A. Participants. How many people participated in the study? If the number seems very small given the research design, then **statistical power**, that is, the likelihood of finding an effect that exists in the population (this is the opposite of Type II error, discussed in Chapter 2), is probably too low, which raises issues of conclusion validity of the study if nonsignificant results are reported. This is particularly the case if the authors try to interpret any nonsignificant findings as being substantively meaningful. Less frequently, extremely large samples (e.g., more than 1,000 participants) make even trivial differences statistically significant, so one cannot rely on a mere finding of statistical significance as indicating that anything theoretically interesting is going on.

In all instances, reporting of significant differences should be accompanied by a measure of the amount of variability accounted for by the various independent variables (i.e., an effect size).

For studies using clinical or field samples, inclusion/exclusion criteria should be stated explicitly. For example, what cutoff score on the Beck Depression Inventory was used in determining if somebody qualified as "depressed" and was included in the study? For all studies, relevant questions are, from how many participants were data excluded from analyses? And why were they excluded? In most experimental studies at least a few participants are dropped from the sample, usually for failure to follow instructions. In non-experimental research, individuals may withdraw for a range of reasons, including moving away, getting a job, and so on. What one does *not* want to see is a large proportion of participants being dropped ("large" can be defined as over 10%), especially if the reason has potential implications for interpreting the findings. For instance, if, in a randomized experiment, participants are dropped because of their suspicion regarding the experimental manipulations, the manipulation may not have been executed in a believable manner, which casts doubt on the entire study. Similarly, if, in a nonrandomized study, the initial sampling plan was not equally effective across groups or if there was greater attrition in one group versus the other(s), then apparent group differences might reflect a problem with the representativeness of the groups rather than real differences between the groups. In short, one also does not want to see **differential mortality**, that is, a higher percentage of people being dropped from one group compared to the others, as that threatens the internal validity of the study. In non-experimental research, the parallel is nonparticipation of a substantial part of the population in surveys or interviews. What were the characteristics of the sample, and how did it compare with the population from which it was drawn? Were those who participated very different from the population that was supposed to be sampled? Even for observational data collection, who are the individuals absent from the setting (e.g., students who do not come regularly to class), and how might their absence affect the observations?

Who are the participants? If they are college students, as is the case with most of the laboratory-based research in the social sciences, is the topic of the study one that is meaningful to address with a population of such limited generalizability? For example, if the study addresses the formation of political attitudes, a college student sample is highly appropriate. But if the study concerns factors that predict employee satisfaction, a sample of college students who are asked to role-play employer and employee roles would not be optimal.

B. Measures or Apparatus.   In this section, authors describe the paper-and-pencil measures, observational procedures, or – less commonly – the equipment by which scores on their independent or dependent variables were obtained. With respect to paper-and-pencil or observational measures, questions to ask are, "What is the name of this measure or scale? Is it a standardized measure, that is, one that was created earlier and has been extensively validated, or is it a measure that was created by the authors exclusively for this study, without prior independent validation?"

In the former case, the authors should provide a full citation for the measure so that it can be looked up if desired, as well as a summary of its basic **psychometric properties**. In the latter case, the authors need to provide more detail to demonstrate the adequacy of the measure. What is the reliability? Has it been shown to be valid? If this information is not included, it could mean merely that the authors were pressed for space or overlooked it – or it could mean that the measure has not been sufficiently validated.

Measures that were created for a given study should achieve minimum standards of reliability, which is normally around .75 for internal consistency indices such as coefficient alpha (Chapter 7). However, a lower reliability does not automatically mean the measure is poor; it is merely one piece of information used to evaluate conclusions. And remember that high reliability does not mean that the measure is valid. The authors should thus also report validity information (Chapter 8). Sometimes validity information is only available for the study that is being reported. Results showing that the measure was related to other measures as expected provide some evidence for the validity of the measure. A lack of significant results, however, might mean simply that the measure was poor.

C. Procedures.   Here, the major questions concern construct validity and the avoidance of methodological artifacts. What was the design of the study? How were the variables operationalized? If the study is an experiment, have the authors convinced readers that they did in fact manipulate the construct they wanted to manipulate? In other words, if the study involved making one participant feel envious of a target person, does it seem reasonable after reading the procedure that the participants did in fact feel envious? Is it clear that envy was manipulated, for example, rather than simply negative mood? And was only envy manipulated, or might other factors also have been changed?

Were participants and experimenters kept unaware of the experimental condition and/or hypotheses? In some cases, experimenters cannot be kept unaware (if, for example, they are administering the crucial manipulations orally). If that is the case, do the authors make a good case that experimenter bias is not operating? If it was non-experimental, how and why did the authors decide which variables were predictors and which dependent measures? What prior work guided the analyses? Are the authors making assertions about causality, or not?

If the study is a survey, what were the conditions under which the data were collected? In general, one trusts questionnaire data less that were provided by participants at home, under unknown conditions, than data collected under more controlled conditions. What kinds of data were participants asked to provide? Retrospective reports (e.g., How many times have you been sick over the past year? What kind of attachment did you have with your mother as a child?) are less accurate than reports about current behaviors.

If the study was observational, questions could include: What were the conditions under which the observations were collected, how were observers prepared to collect the information, how many observers were employed, and how were reliability and validity of the observations determined? If interviews, what was told to interviewees prior to and during the interview, how were the questions chosen and pretested, was the script strictly adhered to or were interviewers allowed to probe after responses, and how were responses analyzed? Were rubrics created to categorize responses, were quantitative analyses done, or were analyses exclusively qualitative?

Step Four: Evaluate the Results

What do the authors say they found? Are they asserting causality? Were participants randomly assigned to experimental conditions? If not, are the authors appropriately cautious in their conclusions about the findings? Are any **manipulation checks** reported to indicate that participants experienced the manipulation in the intended manner? How about other measures of effectiveness of the research design? For example, if a mood induction manipulation was used, do the authors demonstrate that the participants who were supposed to be in a good mood did in fact feel better than participants who were supposed to be in a bad mood?

How many analyses were conducted, and roughly what percentage of those analyses yielded significant results? A misleading tactic for researchers is to mention only those variables in the results section for which there were statistically significant results without bothering to mention the *other* dependent variables for which there were none. Yet this is important to consider: One's confidence in the validity of a conclusion is considerably strengthened if, say, effects involving all 3 of the relevant dependent variables are significant compared to if only 3 of 15 effects are significant. Research results rarely come out perfectly; the point is that one needs to consider each finding and also the set of findings as a whole.

The results section is generally the most difficult section for students to read, especially if the analyses reported go beyond correlational analysis or a basic one-factor comparison of means. Skip over the numbers and complex analyses if you must, but do at least skim the results section and try to evaluate whether the authors' hypotheses were supported by statistically significant results. Keep in mind that becoming better able to read and understand research results requires practice and familiarity (and perhaps looking up things you don't understand); skipping results sections will not help you learn how to read them. Well-written results sections usually explicitly restate hypotheses and provide a bottom-line assessment as to whether they were supported; be on the lookout for such summary/transition sentences.

Step Five: Take the Discussion Section with More than a Grain of Salt

Most students who are intimidated by statistical detail in the results section tend to rely on the discussion section as a verbal summary of the findings of the study. Such a reliance can be unwise. Authors tend to wax poetically in their discussion sections, and there can be many a slip between the statistical results and the conclusions drawn. Results sometimes are exaggerated, and inconvenient results (those that are nonsignificant or, worse, in the opposite direction) are often either summarily dismissed or completely ignored. A good analogy is carving a diamond: In the discussion section, rough edges are smoothed out, the original stone is cut down so that flaws and blemishes are excised, and everything is polished until it shines brilliantly.

Pay close attention to the limitations section that most articles contain; one occasionally encounters what we call the "mea culpa" strategy where authors acknowledge a crucial flaw (e.g., lack of a critical control group or addressing a longitudinal question with cross-sectional data), but then – having pointed out the shortcomings of their study – they go on to draw firm conclusions as if the flaw did not exist. The discussion should be more than just a summary of the results; it should also provide an explanation of the why and how of what was found. The authors should relate their findings to the previous literature; are the results consistent with past research, and if not, why not? Most discussion sections also include a section on directions for future research (more flaws or shortcomings of the current study might be revealed in this section), as well as a discussion of the implications of the study for the field.

Reviewing Bodies of Research on a Single Topic

The review of individual research reports is often part of the larger exercise of reviewing the entire body of research on a particular topic. Such **literature reviews** begin with a thorough search for all research conducted on the topic. The research literature devoted to many social science topics has burgeoned, making the task of finding and retrieving research reports on a given topic daunting. Fortunately, availability of online archives and journals (e.g., *Oxford Bibliographies*) coupled with the increasing power and accessibility of computers have made the task more manageable. Technology, however, is no substitute for thoughtful planning and execution of a literature search, and the quality of a literature review is more a tribute to the thoughtfulness and care of the scholar who produced it than the power and accessibility of computers or the availability of Google Scholar and other data retrieval tools.

Searching the Literature

The first step in any review of the literature is to search the relevant literature and locate and retrieve all of the research reports pertaining to the topic of interest. In many respects, this is the most important step, because a literature review is only as good as the coverage of the literature it provides. A literature review that summarizes only 10 studies when over 100 exist does not make any useful sort of contribution. This is not meant to imply that all literature reviews must include every single research report on the topic; there might be very sound reasons to restrict the number of reports included in a review. For example, it is not unusual to see reviews in established literatures that include only those reports published since the last major review of the topic. Or a review might be restricted to only those studies that used a particular operational definition or measure of key variables. Somewhat idiosyncratically, *Oxford Bibliographies* limit the number of times an individual author is cited and the number of articles cited within a subtopic area, focusing on the more important articles in a research area. As a result, their bibliographies would not provide optimal resources for conducting a quantitative synthesis. Regardless of the decision made, the decision to restrict the population of studies to be included in a review should be made for sound theoretical reasons, not out of laziness or an incomplete search.

   The good news is that searching and retrieving the literature has become infinitely easier as access to electronic databases has become more widespread. In the days before ready access to computers, searching the literature meant doing a manual search of available databases. For example, using *Psychological Abstracts* was a time-intensive effort that required looking a topic up first in one book, then looking at one- or two-line summaries in a second book, and finally looking up the complete abstract to a given article in yet a third book. Today, one can type in a key word in an **electronic database** such as PsycINFO or MEDLINE from one's office or home and obtain within seconds the full abstracts to hundreds or thousands of articles.

Such electronic searches are deceptively easy, however. There actually is an art to conducting a literature search, and the steps involved in an effective search of electronic databases are often arcane. Too often students report that they have searched the literature but found nothing on a topic that has been heavily researched. Also common is the opposite problem that occurs when a student enters a popular term (e.g., "aggression"), obtains thousands of abstracts (39,327 in PsycINFO at the time this chapter was written, to be exact), and does not know how to proceed from there. Thus, perhaps the best piece of general advice we can offer for searching the social science literature is to solicit the help of a reference librarian. These individuals can be most helpful in identifying the best combination of key words and Boolean operators (e.g., *and*, *or*, *not*, *near*) to get the articles needed.

The first step in a **literature search** is to identify the relevant electronic database, as specialized databases exist for each major discipline, for example, PsycINFO for psychology, *Sociological Abstracts* for sociology, *Social Work Abstracts* for social work, ERIC for education, and so on. Again, a reference librarian can be helpful. Depending on the topic, it might be fruitful to search more than one database as well as Google Scholar (which, incidentally, returns approximately 1,200,000 results for a search on "aggression," demonstrating the importance of more precise searches). For example, the key words "teacher expectancy effects" would elicit a large number of articles (overlapping, but some unique) in both PsycINFO and ERIC.

The next step is the most critical – deciding on the key words to be used in the search. When an electronic database is accessed, the search can be conducted by author, title, or subject. Key words are those words entered when one searches by subject, and it is the key words selected that contribute most to the success or failure of a search. Many universities have staff in their libraries who are expert in selecting key words. A short primer on abstracting services is in order here. Each electronic database or abstracting service compiles the abstracts published in the set of journals covered by that particular abstracting service. PsycINFO, for example, covers over 2,540 periodicals in over 25 languages, tracking articles published since 1597 (with comprehensive coverage since the 1880s). Standard information is coded from each article that is abstracted, such as the author(s), journal title, article title, volume, page numbers, language, complete abstract to the article, and the descriptors (key words) associated with the article. Sometimes the descriptors are determined by the authors of the article, and sometimes they are chosen by the employees of the abstracting service following a close reading of the article. In either case, the descriptors are taken from a set of terms specified by the thesaurus for that particular abstracting service.

The **thesaurus**, which lists the "official" phrasing for a key word topic and variations on the descriptor, is perhaps the most underused tool in the arsenal of a literature reviewer. Knowing the proper terms used for descriptors can make searching the literature much more accurate. Say, for example, one wanted to look up references on computing the reliability between two coders or judges. If one were to enter the phrase "interjudge reliability" in a PsycINFO search, only 228 abstracts would be retrieved (at the time this chapter was written); however, perusal of the thesaurus would reveal that the official descriptor terminology preferred by PsycINFO is "inter-rater reliability." Entering the official descriptor would yield 4,965 abstracts.

Thus, one should consult the thesaurus associated with a particular abstracting service prior to doing an electronic database search and compile a list of possible descriptors to enter. Depending on the topic of interest, the search might need to be narrowed (e.g., searching for "television violence and aggression" rather than merely "aggression") or widened (specifying broader terms – supplied by the thesaurus – if an insufficient number of abstracts is elicited). Most literature searches require several iterations of specifying different key words and combinations of key words before one can feel confident that the vast majority of the relevant published literature has been found. And, as we noted earlier, one might need to repeat this process on multiple databases.

Once a stack of abstracts has been amassed, each one must be read carefully to determine its appropriateness for the literature review. Searches are actually done in a rather crude manner; the computer scans the article abstract and descriptor fields for the relevant key words. It is possible to have an abstract retrieved that merely contains the words "teacher," "expectancy," and "effect" interspersed throughout it but which actually has nothing to do with the topic of interest, teacher expectancy effects. Searches might also retrieve articles that discuss the topic in general terms but do not report empirical data, articles that might be helpful as a source for identifying other references but not for the review.

Other decisions about the scope of the review need to be made. Will it exclude articles written in foreign languages? Will it include articles from all sources or only peer-reviewed journals? It is okay to restrict a review? The authors need to make explicit and justify to readers the criteria used to restrict the search and, equally important, authors need to apply those criteria consistently across all research reports. For example, if it were decided in general not to use doctoral dissertations in the review, it would not be appropriate to include a certain dissertation just because it obtained particularly strong results in the favored direction. Researchers need to be aware of the potential consequences of those criteria. As will be explained in more detail below, selecting only peer-reviewed published studies, for example, likely excludes some research with nonsignificant findings.

Other Ways of Locating Articles

A quick search of a relevant database is generally sufficient for writing term papers or empirical research reports that do not pretend to be exhaustive reviews of the literature. However, if one's primary goal is to summarize and review the existing literature on a given topic, one cannot rely solely on electronic searches. The major problem in doing so is that electronic databases like PsycINFO, by definition, include only the published literature in a field. Yet there are generally many relevant studies "out there" that are not detected by electronic searches for several reasons. Some are conference presentations that have not been published in journal form; others are still undergoing the journal review process; or still others are unpublished because the results were not statistically significant or because they merely replicated a previous finding.

Relying on the published literature therefore results in **publication bias**, which is the tendency to overstate the magnitude of a given effect because unpublished but relevant nonsignificant findings or failures to replicate are not included in the review. A good literature reviewer makes every attempt to gather *all* the existing literature on a topic, not just the published literature. There are several ways to go about this, none of them particularly easy. First, one should use what is called the **ancestry approach**, in which the reference lists of all the articles obtained so far are checked to see if they cite any potentially relevant manuscripts that the search missed (Cooper, 1984). Second, one can search *Dissertation Abstracts International* for relevant studies. *Dissertation Abstracts* can be a good source for several reasons.

- First, it often includes reports of relevant studies that were never written up for publication because the student chose to go into a career other than academia and lost interest in writing for publication.
- Second, dissertations are written up whether or not the results were statistically significant, so dissertations can be a good source of failures to replicate that never make it into the published literature.
- Third, dissertations tend to be of relatively high methodological quality (the study must pass muster with a doctoral advisory committee), so they are sources a literature reviewer would generally want to include.

Practically speaking, though, it is difficult to include dissertations in a review. The abstracts provided in *Dissertation Abstracts* rarely give sufficient detail to rely on them alone, and most libraries are reluctant to send dissertations through the mail. One possible solution is to write or email the authors of the relevant dissertations (tracking them down can be difficult, although one might try contacting the student's faculty advisor) and ask either for the relevant results or to borrow a copy of the dissertation.

A third approach to supplementing an electronic literature search is to rely on what is called the **invisible college**, the network of researchers working on the topic (Price, 1966). Every research area involves a cadre of scholars who have been writing regularly on the issue; the preliminary literature search should readily identify who those individuals are. Reviewers should write to each of them, explain that they are working on a literature review in the person's area of expertise, and request copies of all unpublished papers and manuscripts in press (i.e., accepted for publication but not yet in print). (**Publication lag** – the interval between manuscript acceptance and actual paper publication – often exceeds a year, but authors often are willing to provide preprints of in press reports. And publishers increasingly are providing prepublication or in press versions of papers online long before the papers are published in print.)

An approach somewhat broader than using the invisible college would be to solicit the help of individuals through an electronic mailing list of people belonging to a relevant professional organization. In psychology, for example, there are many LIST-SERVs. As examples, the society that sponsors this book, the Society for the Social Psychological Study of Social Issues (SPSSI), has one, as do other social psychological organizations: the Society of Experimental Social Psychology and the Society of Personality and Social Psychology. Such LISTSERVs often reach a high proportion of active researchers in the field and represent a quick and easy way to request copies of unpublished material.

A fourth approach, newer than the others and still somewhat in a developmental stage insofar as it still is evolving, is to use Google Scholar (www.scholar.google.com) or even regular Google to search for key words. As noted earlier, this can yield enormous numbers of articles, but it is easy to revise to see how the set of links changes as one looks at intersections and unions of different key words. And there are alternatives to Google Scholar that have been developing. For example, because libraries are now working more collaboratively in consortia, they increasingly have been developing and archiving resources, and housing the resources in multiple locations (creating multiple redundancies) so that resources cannot be lost. One of the exciting things looking forward is fully searchable articles so, for example, a reviewer can readily pick only studies employing particular methods, samples, or even instruments. In addition, availability of organizing and archiving tools like EndNote makes finding and organizing one's references much simpler.

Reviewing the Literature: "Traditionally" and Meta-Analytically

Once all the relevant articles bearing on a given topic have been located, the task is to summarize or integrate the findings in a comprehensive, comprehensible, and accurate manner. The first decision is whether to conduct a traditional, or narrative, literature review versus a meta-analysis, or quantitative literature review. In a **narrative literature review**, studies are described and summarized verbally. Usually, the review is organized among major theoretical themes or questions; for example, is psychotherapy effective? Which types of therapies are most effective? What kinds of therapist training result in the best outcomes? Often, a "box score" summary table is provided giving the frequencies of studies reviewed whose results significantly supported the hypothesis, were nonsignificant, or significantly opposed the hypothesis. Table 17.1 shows an excerpt from a narrative review by Leventhal and Brooks-Gunn (2000) on the effects of neighborhoods on child and adolescent outcomes; it illustrates how such a review might summarize and describe relevant studies.

A second feature of a narrative review is a narrative assessment of methodological features of different studies, often using the Cook and Campbell dimensions to assess internal and external validity (e.g., Shadish, Cook, & Campbell, 2002). A good narrative review organizes the research in a logical way and describes and summarizes the different subtypes of studies. It doesn't provide an endless summary and analysis of individual studies, but synthesizes the studies in a way that allows readers both to understand the types of studies that have been done and what they have found, attempts to reconcile different and conflicting findings, and draws conclusions about what is known, what still needs to be examined in greater detail, and what is lacking.

In contrast to a narrative review, in a **meta-analysis** the results of studies are combined and analyzed *quantitatively*. In other words, the individual studies themselves

Table 17.1 Example of Describing Studies in a Narrative Review

Study	Design	Sample	Neighborhood Data	Findings from Published Studies
National Longitudinal Survey of Youth	Children born to women in nationally representative study	673 children aged 3–4 and 5–6 (approx. 40% African American)	1980 census tract data; 70% only study child in tract	*Chase-Lansdale & Gordon (1996)*: SES positive association with 5- to 6-yr.-olds' internalizing problems; male joblessness positive relation with 5- to 6-yr.-olds' internalizing and externalizing (African American only) problems. *Chase-Lansdale et al. (1997)*: High SES positive association with girls' internalizing (ages 5–6 only) and externalizing behavior problems; low SES negative association with 5- to 6-yr.-old boys' internalizing behavior problems; ethnic diversity negative association with 3- to 4-yr.-old African Americans' internalizing behavior problems and positive association with 5- to 6-yr.-old boys' internalizing problems.
Drug Abuse Resistance Education Program	Students drawn from 36 Midwest schools	747 5th and 6th graders	1990 census block data	*Ennett et al. (1997)*: Residential instability negative association with school rates of lifetime alcohol use.
Infant Health and Development Program	Early intervention for premature infants at 8 sites	Approx. 1,000 children, diverse backgrounds	1980 census tract data; average 1.1 cases per tract	*Brooks-Gunn et al. (1993)*: Managerial/professionals negative association with 3-yr.-olds' behavior problems. *Chase-Lansdale et al. (1997)*: Male joblessness negative association with 3-yr.-olds', African Americans' and girls' internalizing and externalizing behavior problems. *Duncan et al. (1994)*: Low-income negative association with 5-yr.-olds' externalizing behavior problems.

Source: Adapted from Leventhal & Brooks-Gunn (2000), p. 319. Reproduced with permission from the American Psychological Association.

become the "participants," "observations," or units of analysis. As we explain later in the chapter, standardized effect-size indices are coded from the results of all studies, as well as other methodological and theoretical features of the studies, and these are subjected to statistical analyses that aim to show an overall combined effect size as well as conditions under which the effect is strongest and weakest.

From the first appearance of meta-analytic techniques, social scientists have debated the relative merits of narrative and meta-analytic reviews (e.g., Harris, 1991; Hoyle, 1993; Sharpe, 1997; Strube, Gardner, & Hartmann, 1985). In the early going, each side had strong proponents and opponents, and passion ran high, as shown by the title of Eysenck's critique of meta-analysis, "An Exercise in Mega-Silliness" (Eysenck, 1978). Critics of meta-analysis did not like the quantitative nature of meta-analysis and felt that it often "mixed apples and oranges" – too many disparate studies of varying quality using different operational definitions and dependent variables were being combined together without sufficient appreciation of their differences. Proponents of meta-analysis countered that "[o]ne compares apples and oranges in the study of fruit" (Glass, 1978, p. 395), and pointed to studies showing that meta-analyses were less biased and more likely to reach accurate conclusions regarding the presence and magnitude of an effect than were narrative reviews (Beaman, 1991; Cooper & Rosenthal, 1980).

In our opinion, asking which is better, a narrative literature review or a meta-analysis, poses a straw man. A meta-analysis is also a narrative review and can and should do everything a narrative review does, but adds more detail through analyzing and aggregating results quantitatively in addition to discussing and attempting to integrate the articles narratively. For some research topics, there might not be enough studies all bearing on the same focused hypothesis, in which case a meta-analysis is not really practical or very informative; thus, a narrative literature review might be the best one can do – at least until more studies have been done and more results become available.

However, in most of the cases in which a literature review is warranted, namely, where a substantial number of studies have accumulated that warrant synthesis, meta-analysis of that literature is possible and probably should be conducted in addition to a narrative review. Thus, in the discussion to follow, we concentrate on meta-analytic literature reviews, bearing in mind that a good meta-analysis also incorporates the best features of a narrative review – thoughtful analysis of the theory, methods, findings, and interpretations, and attempts to integrate the analyses of the studies.

In some ways, adding meta-analysis to a literature review parallels using statistical techniques to make sense of large data sets or sets of relationships. For example, inspection of a 25 by 25 correlation matrix and its 300 $((N * N–1)/2)$ individual correlations is not likely to provide much synthesis. In the same way, interpreting a large set of studies, trying to tease apart a number of factors that could account for differences across studies, is not likely to be effective unless the pattern is atypically simple and clear. In each case, employing quantitative techniques, in the former case factor analysis and in the latter meta-analysis, allows researchers to identify patterns in relationships and variables/studies that are important – or not.

Understanding the Concept of Effect Size: The Foundation of Meta-Analysis

The goal of a meta-analysis is to combine – statistically – the results of a group of studies all asking the same, focused question. As examples: Does psychotherapy work? Is this intervention for reducing employee turnover effective? Does parental involvement reduce substance use among teenagers? What is the magnitude of the relationship between academic self-concept and academic achievement? How does cooperative learning compare with competitive and individualistic learning in promoting students' peer social relationships? The importance of having a **focused question** cannot be overstated; meta-analysis works only if the group of studies all address the same hypothesis. In other words, one cannot do a meta-analysis on, say, aggression in general; one needs to choose a specific hypothesis about aggression on which to focus: Does media violence lead to aggression? Does frustration lead to aggression? Does aggression in schools lead to lower student achievement? Of course, the causal interpretation of the relationship is not determined by the meta-analysis, which only establishes that there is a (predicted) relationship between variables.

In order to combine the results of several studies quantitatively, the results must be made comparable one to another across studies by transforming studies to a common index. We cannot simply take the raw means of the assorted treatment groups, for example, across studies and compare them to the raw means of the corresponding control groups. Different studies use different dependent measures, and so a score of "20" could mean a positive outcome for one study but a poor outcome for another study using a different dependent variable. Thus, the first step in a meta-analysis is to convert the obtained results of each study into a **standardized effect-size index** that puts the results of all the studies on the same scale and therefore allows the reviewer to combine and compare results across studies meaningfully.

The term **effect size** can be defined as the strength or magnitude of an association in the population (e.g., Rosenthal & Rosnow, 2008). There are many ways of expressing the magnitude of an association; the Pearson correlation coefficient r is one of the most common. A correlation coefficient expresses the degree to which two variables are linearly associated, that is, as values of one variable increase, to what extent do the values of the other variable increase or decrease in a systematic way? The value of r can range from -1.0 to $+1.0$, with 0 meaning no association between the two variables and $+1.0$ and -1.0 meaning a perfect positive and negative association, respectively. Conventional standards for interpreting the magnitude of a correlation were given by Cohen (1977); in the social sciences, an r of .10 is considered to be a "small" effect; an r of .30 is considered "moderate"; and an r of .50 is considered to be "large."

Another popular effect-size index that is intuitively easy to understand is **Cohen's d**, which is computed by subtracting the mean of the control group from the mean of the experimental group and dividing by the pooled standard deviation of the two groups (or, in some instances, the standard deviation of the control group):

$$d = \frac{\overline{X}_1 - \overline{X}_2}{\sigma}$$

Readers who are familiar with Z-scores will notice the similarity between the formulas for Z and d; both express values in standard deviation units. The main difference is that Z compares an individual score against the group mean in standard deviation units; d compares the difference between *two* group means in pooled standard deviation units. According to Cohen's (1977) standards, ds of .20, .50, and .80 correspond to small, medium, and large effects, respectively. In other words, if an intervention raised the experimental group's mean by half a standard deviation (i.e., $d = .50$), we could infer that the intervention had a medium or moderate effect.

When doing a meta-analysis, it does not really matter which effect-size index is computed as long as the same index is used across all studies. Rosenthal (1991) recommends r over d for several reasons, primarily because of its flexibility and relative ease of calculation when d cannot be calculated (to compute d accurately one needs exact numbers of participants per condition, and authors do not always provide this information). However, d is more common and accepted in certain fields (e.g., medicine), and if the literature review is asking a question that is naturally suited to a two-group format (e.g., comparing treatment and control groups), then d is a logical choice of effect size. If the review is asking a more correlational question (is teacher warmth associated with student achievement?), then r is probably more appropriate.

Some authors report effect sizes in their research reports; however, most of the time a meta-analyst must compute effect sizes from other information provided in the report. Fortunately, it is fairly easy to extract effect sizes from research reports because effect sizes, significance levels, and sample sizes are all related to one another in a straightforward way. This basic relation has been termed the **fundamental equation of data analysis** and can be expressed as:

$$\text{Significance Level} = \text{Size of Effect} \times \text{Size of Study}$$

In other words, statistical significance of an effect can be determined by two factors: the magnitude of the effect in the population and the sample size. This equation makes clear two important points: First, we should not rely on significance levels alone to tell us whether an effect or association is practically important. Because significance is driven so much by sample size, a p value by itself is not very informative. A study with a very small effect can still be statistically significant if the sample is large enough, as is the case with the U.S. Census, for example. The Census Bureau does not bother computing significance tests in its analyses because every test would be significant. In contrast, a large effect, one that might be very important, could fail to produce a significant p value if the sample is very small.

The second major conclusion to draw from this equation is that as long as we know two pieces of the equation, we can calculate the third. Thus, effect sizes can easily be computed from the significance tests and sample sizes reported in the original research reports. So, for example, we could rewrite the general equation,

$$\text{Significance Level} = \text{Size of Effect} \times \text{Size of Study}$$

to reflect specific statistical tests:

$$t = \frac{r}{\sqrt{1-r^2}} \times \sqrt{df}$$

$$F = \frac{r}{1-r^2} \times df_{error} \quad \text{(with 1 } df \text{ in the numerator)}$$

$$\chi^2 = \phi^2 \times N$$

Using such equations, it is only a matter of minor algebraic manipulation to solve for effect size, for example:

$$r = \sqrt{\frac{t^2}{t^2 + df}}$$

$$r = \sqrt{\frac{F}{F + df_{error}}} \quad \text{(when } F \text{ has 1 } df \text{ in the numerator)}$$

$$d = \frac{t(n_1 + n_2)}{\sqrt{df} \sqrt{n_1 n_2}}$$

Textbooks on meta-analysis contain these and other equations for computing r, d, g, and other effect-size indices from a host of statistics, for example, t, F, X^2, Z, and so on (e.g., Rosenthal, 1991). We list at the end of this chapter some of the effect-size calculators that are available. Once the appropriate statistical tests to include in a meta-analysis have been identified, the actual computation of effect sizes is generally straightforward. The word "generally" conveys an important caveat, however: In any meta-analysis one will encounter a significant minority of studies in which the necessary information is not provided in a direct fashion. There will be many cases, especially in reports published before standards for reporting statistical results became widely implemented, in which the desired information (e.g., sample sizes, standard deviations) is not provided. There also will be cases in which the desired focused comparison is embedded in a larger design containing irrelevant conditions, and the meta-analyst will be forced to carry out secondary analyses to obtain the effect size of interest.

For these reasons, although the actual computations involved in a meta-analysis are not complicated, a fair amount of statistical sophistication is nonetheless required to do a meta-analysis. A meta-analyst needs to be able to understand exactly what the authors did and be able to extract what is needed from the results they reported. The meta-analyst also needs to be able to detect when the authors made mistakes in their statistical analyses, which happens with surprising frequency. Errors are more likely to emerge in older research reports and those published in journals with lower publication standards, but meta-analysts must be vigilant when coding all studies.

Coding Studies for a Meta-Analysis

The second stage in conducting a narrative or meta-analytic review is reading each research report and coding it for effect size and other relevant methodological and theoretical variables. One of the most difficult and subjective challenges in meta-analysis is deciding what results from a given report to include. On the surface, it seems simple enough: One knows ahead of time the focused hypothesis of interest in a meta-analysis, so all one needs to do is read the research report, find the appropriate statistical test, and compute an effect size. However, it is never that straightforward. Many subjective judgments are required, both on the independent variable side (Does a particular study even belong in the meta-analysis? Which ones of possibly many experimental groups correspond to the hypothesis of interest?) and the dependent variable side (Which dependent variables should be used in computing effect sizes?).

Decisions are particularly subjective with respect to deciding which dependent variables to include. Very few studies include and report findings for only one dependent variable, and generally there is a large number from which a meta-analyst must choose. The first challenge is to decide which dependent variables are relevant. This is harder than it appears. Take, for example, a meta-analysis of the effects of using quality circles in management on employee satisfaction. Obviously, we would want to include all dependent variables that are explicitly labeled "employee satisfaction." But should we include or exclude a study that measured employees' level of "happiness" with their work? Is "happiness" appreciably different from "satisfaction"? How about employees' intentions to remain in their job? What if a study included both a "satisfaction" *and* a "happiness" variable? As should be readily apparent, nearly every research report will confront the reviewer with such decisions. Ideally, criteria for including dependent variables should be established prior to coding the studies, and they should be explicitly described in the write-up so that readers can see and evaluate the scope of the review. If new challenges emerge, then researchers should consider adding a new variable to their analyses that discriminates studies using the "new" version of that variable from others, so they later can examine whether the results for that variable seem different from those of other measures of the dependent variable.

The second challenge, once the relevant dependent variables have been identified, is to decide how to treat them in the meta-analysis. Some authors (particularly in older meta-analyses) treat individual effect sizes as the unit of analysis and thus allow studies with multiple dependent variables to contribute more than one effect size to the meta-analysis. The extent to which this would produce results that differ from those that produce only a single effect size from each study depends on the number of findings from individual studies. The consequences of including all effect sizes are: (1) It disproportionately weights studies with more dependent variables more heavily in the meta-analysis, yet there is usually no compelling theoretical reason for doing so; and (2) it violates the independence of observations assumption underlying many of the statistical tests that are carried out in a meta-analysis (Rosenthal, 1991).

How, then, to treat multiple results from a single study? Some people select the dependent variable that most closely fits the topic of the meta-analysis. The danger here, of course, is that it is too tempting to define "best" as the result that yields the largest effect size. A more defensible strategy, and the one that is used most often, is to compute the average of all relevant effect sizes and use that average to represent each study. Less commonly used, but statistically more powerful, are approaches that compute average effect sizes or significance levels taking into account the degree of dependence or interrelation among the multiple results (Rosenthal & Rubin, 1986; Strube, 1985). Another strategy is to conduct separate meta-analyses for each type of dependent variable (behavioral, self-report, etc.). Many meta-analyses use a combination of these approaches, reporting not only the overall mean effect size but also mean effect sizes at different levels of important variables. The key is that for any given analysis performed in a meta-analysis, each study should contribute only a single effect size.

A related topic involves how to handle results for variables described in the method section but for which no results are reported or effects are described simply as "non-significant." It is tempting to ignore those variables in a meta-analysis, as insufficient information is provided to compute an exact effect size. But it would be misleading to do so because excluding nonsignificant effects could result in a greatly biased mean effect size. Thus, if an article reports that results for a given variable were nonsignificant, the meta-analyst must enter an r or d of zero in the meta-analysis. The true effect size is probably not exactly zero, but it is reasonable to assume in the absence of information that would suggest otherwise that the average of all nonsignificant effects *is* close to zero, as some of the nonsignificant results likely will be in the predicted direction and some likely will be in the opposite direction. In the absence of better information, zero is our best estimate of the effect size for a nonsignificant result, and it is better than not including the study at all.

A trickier situation is studies that mention collecting data on a relevant dependent variable in the method section, but the variable is *not* mentioned in the results section. This can mean one of three things: The authors measured the variable but did not analyze it; they analyzed the variable and it was involved in significant effects but they did not report it; or they analyzed the variable and it was involved in no significant effects. The first two cases are unlikely, but one cannot rule them out entirely. In such cases, a good course of action for the meta-analyst is to contact the author and ask for the results concerning the variable of interest. Such requests are often granted, but in some cases, especially with older studies, the authors either cannot be located or they no longer have access to the original data to perform the analysis. A conservative solution in those cases would be to code the effect size for that variable as zero and include it in the meta-analysis.

Yet another situation is one where authors report a comparison as significant but provide only the significance level. In such cases, the nominal significance level can be used, for example, if authors report a finding as $p < .05$, the effect size used would be one that corresponds to $p = .05$. That level again would be conservative, but would include the study as showing a significant difference.

We hope that this discussion has made clear just how subjective an "objective" quantitative literature review can be, and how important it is to clearly explain the decisions that were made. The decisions made in the coding process can greatly influence the magnitude of effect sizes computed from studies and the ultimate results of the meta-analysis. This influence was documented by Matt (1989), who compared the results obtained when several common decision rules for a meta-analysis were applied to the same set of 25 studies. Matt found that the obtained mean effect size varied widely depending on the decision rule adopted. Matt's pessimistic conclusion was that "average effect estimates derived from meta-analyses may depend heavily on judgmental factors that enter into how effect sizes are selected within each of the individual studies considered relevant to a meta-analysis" (p. 106). It also points to the importance of using more than one person to code the articles so that inter-rater reliability between the coders can be computed and reported. Agreement among raters at the very least ensures that the coding categories were used and interpreted consistently, and increases the likelihood that another independent coder would be able to replicate the findings.

What should researchers, practitioners, and consumers of meta-analysis conclude from the prior discussion? First and foremost, it does not mean that we should abandon meta-analysis. Just because the estimates that are obtained can vary depending on who is doing the coding and what subjective decision rules are used does not mean that the estimates are not useful; a quantitative effect-size estimate that has some known error associated with it is more useful than no quantitative estimate. And, importantly, the same subjective judgments affect narrative reviews to the same extent, although perhaps less visibly than they do meta-analyses; a narrative reviewer also must decide which variables are relevant and how to weight them when describing a study narratively. The main lesson to be drawn here is that meta-analysts and readers of meta-analyses need to be cognizant of the subjectivity that enters into the coding process. Decision rules should be stated explicitly so that readers know what judgments were made and how. Ideally, a researcher should be able to read the method section of a meta-analysis and extract the exact same effect sizes (or close to it) from original sources as those extracted by the authors.

Readers should be cautious in their interpretation and use of meta-analytic results. There is a danger of reification in meta-analysis; the obtained effect size is treated as "the" population effect size, with little consideration for the factors – such as the nature of the literature search and the decision rules for including effect sizes – that might affect the values that are obtained. Meta-analytic results are imperfect estimates of population values that reflect a host of subjective decisions as well as the domain of prior research; they are not and should not be treated as some sort of "objective" truth.

Coding Other Features of Studies

In addition to extracting effect sizes from an article, relevant theoretical and methodological features should be coded. A good literature review does more than simply report the mean effect size for a focused hypothesis. We want to know more; we want to know what factors are associated with larger or smaller effects. The choice of methodological and theoretical variables to be coded depends on the topic being studied. For example, in the developmental literature, whether a study was cross-sectional or longitudinal in design would probably be an important methodological feature to code, but it would not be useful to code in other areas where most research is experimental and where longitudinal studies are rare (e.g., cognitive psychology). Mean effect sizes can then be calculated for the separate subcategories of the **moderator variables**. For example, Table 17.2 shows the output of a meta-analysis by Turkheimer and Waldron (2000) of the research literature on the role of nonshared environment in determining sibling similarity. The median and weighted mean effect

Table 17.2   Example of Reporting Mean Effect Sizes by Levels of Moderating Variables

Study Design	Median	Environmental Correlation		
		Weighted Mean	Range	k
Genetic vs. nongenetic				
Genetic	.354	.340	.05–.83	5
Nongenetic	.523	.510	−.08–.96	12
Longitudinal vs. cross-sectional				
Longitudinal	.655	.440	.05–.78	3
Cross-sectional	.430	.460	−.08–.96	17

Source: Adapted from Turkheimer & Waldron (2000), p. 89. Reproduced with permission from the American Psychological Association.

sizes are reported separately for two different kinds of study design (genetic vs. non-genetic) and for longitudinal versus cross-sectional studies.

It is essential that meta-analysts have a good grasp on the literature prior to starting the review so that they know the important methodological issues relevant to the topic and the theoretical issues that remain unexplained. Variables that need to be coded should be identified prior to beginning the coding process or at the very least after a few of the studies have been read. Clearly, a reviewer would not like to finish coding 482 articles on a topic only to realize that he or she should have coded whether participants were randomly assigned or self-selected and thus have to read the articles again.

Because the choice of methodological and theoretical variables is so context-dependent, it is impossible to offer a definitive list of variables to code from studies. However, certain methodological features are applicable to a majority of possible research questions in the social sciences and are thus good candidates for coding. These include such things as: information on the participants (age, socioeconomic status, gender composition); nature of the dependent variables (reliability, self-report vs. behavioral, standardized vs. created specifically for the study); nature of the independent variable(s) (experimentally manipulated vs. naturally occurring, type – social, instructional, or environmental); presence of threats to internal and external validity; and type of design used. The meta-analyst also can provide a subjective rating (e.g., on a 7-point scale) of the overall methodological quality of the study; this overall score of study quality can then be entered into later analyses to assess the association between effect size and methodological quality. As always, definitions for variables to be coded should be stated explicitly, and a second coder should code at least a subset of the studies so that reliability of coding can be estimated and reported.

Basic Meta-Analytic Tests: Combining and Comparing Studies

The literature has been searched and the relevant articles read thoroughly and coded. What next? Here is where a narrative literature review and a meta-analytic review part

Table 17.3   Framework of Meta-Analytic Techniques and Formulas

	Results Defined in Terms of:	
	Effect Sizes	*Significance Levels*
Combining Studies	$\bar{z}_r = \dfrac{\sum z_r}{k}$	$Z = \dfrac{\sum Z}{k}$
Comparing studies (Tests of heterogeneity)	$\chi^2(k-1) = \sum (N_j - 3)(z_{r_j} - \bar{z}_{r_w})^2$ where $\bar{z}_{r_w} = \dfrac{\sum (N_j - 3) z_{r_j}}{\sum (N_j - 3)}$	$\chi^2(k-1) = \sum (Z_j - \bar{Z})^2$
Comparing studies (Focused contrasts)	$Z = \dfrac{\sum \lambda_j z_{r_j}}{\sqrt{\sum \dfrac{\lambda_j^2}{N_j - 3}}}$	$Z = \dfrac{\sum \lambda_j Z_j}{\sqrt{\sum \lambda_j^2}}$

Source: Adapted from Rosenthal (1991).

ways. In a narrative review, the authors attempt to organize and summarize the articles in a thematic manner, concentrating on questions of theoretical importance. Often, individual studies are described and criticized in detail. In a good meta-analysis, the authors also organize and summarize the articles in a thematic manner, but they go beyond verbal summary to offer quantitative analyses that yield mean effect sizes and tests of theoretical and methodological moderating variables. It also is less common (but not, in principle, impossible) for a meta-analysis to describe and discuss individual studies in great detail.

Rosenthal (1991) offered a useful framework for categorizing the various analytic approaches that are possible within a meta-analysis (see Table 17.3). He noted that the results of studies can be defined in terms of either effect sizes or significance levels. We have restricted our discussion of meta-analysis so far to effect sizes, for two compelling reasons. First, as we argued earlier, significance levels are driven so heavily by sample size that they are relatively uninformative. Second, the majority of meta-analyses report only effect sizes or, more rarely, effect sizes and significance levels. Very few report significance levels alone.

Most of the time we are concerned primarily with the magnitude of an effect, and thus effect sizes are the proper index of the results of a study to meta-analyze. However, there are some cases in which a meta-analysis of significance levels is both useful and necessary. These include cases in which considerable controversy reigns over the very existence of a phenomenon or, relatedly, in research areas marked by numerous failures to replicate. For example, research on expectancy effects was initially met with great resistance by scholars who doubted that teachers' and experimenters' expectations about their targets' behavior could result in self-fulfilling prophecies. Opponents of expectancy effects pointed to well-publicized failures to replicate as supporting their doubts. Rosenthal and his colleagues thus were obligated to demonstrate not only the magnitude of expectancy effects but also their statistical significance, that is, to show that the obtained effects could not have occurred on the basis of chance alone (Harris, 1991; Rosenthal, 1968; Rosenthal & Rubin, 1978). Another example of an area in which a meta-analysis of significance levels was deemed critical is seen in Bem and Honorton's (1994) meta-analysis of ESP studies using the Ganzfeld technique, given the widespread and heavy skepticism of the existence of ESP.

Again, the main point is that significance levels and effect sizes are related to each other in fundamental ways and that a meta-analysis can be performed on either type of index. We focus on effect sizes for the reasons given earlier, but readers should bear in mind that the same analyses can be carried out on significance levels that are conducted on effect sizes using formulas adapted for *p* values. For example, if there were 100 studies done in an area, we could determine the likelihood that any particular number of them (e.g., 70 of 100) would be significant in a particular direction, and we could calculate how many additional studies there would have to be that find no differences between conditions in order to make the likelihood less than chance. Rosenthal called this the "file drawer" problem, for many studies are unlikely to be found during the literature review because they remained in researchers' file drawers – electronic as well as physical ones – and were never published or otherwise shared. Such studies are more likely to have yielded nonsignificant findings, and it is therefore useful to consider how many such studies there would have to be to invalidate meta-analytic results.

The second dimension in Rosenthal's framework for categorizing meta-analytic techniques is whether the studies are being combined or compared. **Combining studies** refers to arriving at an overall, bottom-line answer to the focused hypothesis of interest: Does psychotherapy work? Is teacher warmth related to student achievement? Statistically, what is involved is simply the computation of a mean effect size, either unweighted or weighted by some index of choice, for example, sample size or methodological quality. (Some meta-analysts argue that effect sizes should always be corrected for unreliability prior to averaging. The arguments for and against such corrections are beyond the scope of this chapter, but interested readers can consult Hedges & Olkin, 1985, for a discussion of the issues and procedures involved.)

Because *r* is not normally distributed (having $+/-$ 1.00 as its boundaries), when the effect-size index being used is *r*, one should normalize the *r*s using Fisher's *r*-to-*Z* transformation prior to any analyses. (Tables or formulas for doing the *r*-to-*Z* transformation are found in most meta-analytic textbooks, e.g., Rosenthal, 1991; computer packages available for doing meta-analysis do the transformation automatically.) Following the transformation, finding the mean effect size is simple:

$$\bar{z}_r = \frac{\sum z_r}{k} \quad \text{or} \quad \bar{z}_r = \frac{\sum w_j z_{r_j}}{\sum w_j}$$

where *k* is the number of studies, z_r is the Fisher-transformed correlation coefficient, and *w* is the desired weight, for example, sample size. The resulting mean Fisher z_r

can then be transformed back to a Pearson correlation coefficient for presentation purposes.

The concept of **comparing studies** refers to analyses that seek to document and explain variability among the effect sizes of the group of studies. Rosenthal (1991) further differentiates between diffuse and focused tests. In **diffuse tests**, also known as **tests of heterogeneity**, the goal is to determine whether there is significant variability among a group of effect sizes. This can be tested quite simply using a X^2 test:

$$\chi^2_{(k-1)} = \sum (N_j - 3)(z_{r_j} - z_{r_w})^2$$

where

$$z_{r_w} = \frac{\sum (N_j - 3)z_{r_j}}{\sum (N_j - 3)}$$

What do such diffuse tests of variability tell us? Variability among effect sizes is akin to the individual difference variability one normally finds among people in a single study. Tests of variability in meta-analyses are more often significant than not, and essentially all they are saying when significant is that there is variability among the effect sizes that needs to be explained. The diffuse test does not identify for the meta-analyst the reason for the variability. Indeed, because heterogeneity tests are usually significant, it almost becomes noteworthy when they are not, for it suggests that a given effect is so robust that it is not influenced substantially by variations in study design and methodology.

More useful from a theoretical standpoint are **focused tests** that explicitly test hypotheses about the reasons for variability among effect sizes. These analyses can take several forms. Rosenthal (1991) advocates the use of a Z test:

$$Z = \frac{\sum \lambda_j z_{r_j}}{\mathrm{SQRT} \sum \dfrac{\lambda_j^2}{N_j - 3}}$$

where λ refers to the contrast weight applied to a given study. For example, if a meta-analysis consisted of 20 studies, half of which used college students as participants and half of which used children, one could compute a contrast comparing the effect sizes from studies involving college students versus those involving child participants, with the contrast weights being $+1$ and -1. (For ease of interpretation, the category to which the positive contrast weight is assigned should be the one predicted in advance to yield the largest effect sizes.)

There are other ways to approach focused tests of effect sizes. If the moderator variable of interest is continuous in nature, a logical analysis would be simply to correlate the moderator variable with effect size. For example, one could correlate obtained effect sizes with the meta-analyst's rating of methodological quality. A positive correlation would mean that better studies yielded larger effect sizes. As another example, if one wanted to test the hypothesis that a given effect should increase with

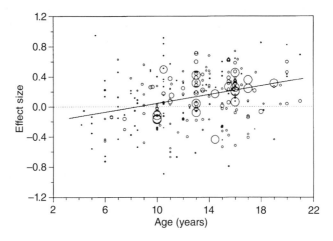

Figure 17.1   Example of a Scatterplot of Effect Size and Participant Age.
Source: Gray-Little & Hafdahl (2000), p. 35. Reproduced with permission from the American Psychological Association.

age, one could correlate obtained effect sizes with the mean age of the sample. Figure 17.1 shows a scatterplot of such an analysis that was conducted in a meta-analysis by Gray-Little and Hafdahl (2000) of racial differences in self-esteem.

Another common approach to conducting focused tests of effect sizes is to conduct analyses of variance (ANOVAs) or regression analyses, using study as the unit of analysis, effect size as the dependent variable, and the coded methodological and theoretical variables as the predictor variables. An example of this type of analysis would be a meta-analysis that had coded studies with regard to the type of dependent variable reported, say, self-report, behavioral, and peer-report. A one-way ANOVA might be conducted on the effect sizes, yielding an *F* statistic that compares effect sizes for different types of dependent variable. Mean effect sizes for each category could be reported, and, if there were an overall significant effect, post-hoc contrasts could be conducted among the three groups to see which types of dependent variables differed. This approach has some advantages, the most important being that it uses statistical procedures with which most readers are familiar; thus, readers can understand and interpret the results more readily than results from some of the more specialized meta-analytic techniques. The analyses also can be conducted quite easily using standard statistical packages, such as SPSS or SAS.

There are, however, a couple problems with using standard inferential statistics on meta-analytic effect sizes. First is the not so trivial problem that using effect sizes as the basic data in these types of analyses violates one of the major assumptions of the statistical models, such as ANOVA and regression, namely, the homogeneity of variance assumption. The error variances of effect-size estimates are directly and inversely proportional to the sample size of the study on which the effect size is based. Given the fact that sample sizes in a meta-analysis tend to vary widely, often by as much of a ratio as 50 to 1, this means that the error variances will not be identically distributed or homogeneous.

How much of a problem is this? Based on how often ANOVA and regression is used in meta-analysis, one might be tempted to conclude that it is not a big problem at all. After all, many studies have shown that ANOVA is robust to violations of the homogeneity of variance assumption. However, Hedges and Olkin (1985) point out, first, that the simulation studies that have demonstrated the robustness of ANOVA typically test violations of the assumption that are much less severe than the violations found in meta-analysis, and, second, that in ANOVA one is usually talking about homogeneity of variance within groups, whereas in meta-analysis the problem is homogeneity of error variance across individual cases (studies). In sum, Hedges and Olkin (1985) provide this grim conclusion: "There does not appear to be any rigorously defensible argument for the conventional use of *t* tests, analysis of variance, or regression analysis to analyze effect sizes or correlations" (p. 12).

However, the throwing of this gauntlet by Hedges and Olkin (1985) has not affected standard meta-analytic practice, as meta-analysts continue to perform *standard statistical tests* on their effect sizes with no apparent deference to the statistical violations involved. Hedges and Olkin provide multivariate models for testing hypotheses on effect sizes that do not violate the homogeneity of variance assumption. Their approach, however, is statistically complex and beyond the scope of this chapter. Our goal, instead, is simply to alert readers to the problem of conducting traditional analyses on effect sizes so that such analyses are interpreted with caution when encountered in the literature.

The second problem is one of non-representativeness of studies. Studies in no way could be considered a random sample of all possible studies, for studies in fact yield a very purposeful *nonrandom* set of data points reflecting systematic research following particular lines of reasoning. Many possible studies are never done, for even though they may represent a part of the possible domain of studies, they are trivial or uninformative. So researchers need to use caution when conducting statistical tests on a data set that is known not to represent a random sample.

That said, it is not our intent to cause readers to shy away from focused tests of effect sizes. Indeed, it is our belief that such focused tests are at the heart of a meta-analysis. Through the judicious coding of methodological and theoretical variables and subsequent contrast analyses, meta-analysis can help advance theory by testing new hypotheses and uncovering associations previously unknown in the literature, or to dismiss associations that have been considered likely and to diminish concerns about particular potentially confounding variables. For example, critics might argue that a given effect only occurs for studies done with children. If the meta-analysis finds no relation between age of participants and the size of the effect, such criticisms are not supported. In many ways, meta-analysis is even better suited for theory testing than are individual studies because individual studies cannot capture as many different levels of an independent variable or control variables as can a meta-analysis that encompasses hundreds of studies.

Writing and Reading Meta-Analyses

Once all analyses have been completed, the remaining chore is to report the results of the meta-analysis. Because the writing of research reports in general is addressed in Chapter 18, our remarks here are brief and restricted to concerns unique to meta-analysis. The first general recommendation is one to which we have alluded

Table 17.4   Example of Table Listing Study Features and Effect Sizes

Study	Sample Size	Target Gender	Perceiver Gender	Rater Type	Perceiver Age	Attract-iveness Measure	d
Dion & Berscheid (1979)	71	B	B	I	C	F	0.53
Felson & Borhnstedt (1979)	209	F	B	I	C	F	1.12
Felson & Borhnstedt (1979)	207	M	B	I	C	F	1.56
Kenealy, Frude, & Shaw (1987)	503	F	B	I	A	F	1.22
Kenealy, Frude, & Shaw (1987)	503	M	B	I	A	F	1.25
Lippitt (1941)	15	B	F	N	A	G	−0.66
Lippitt (1941)	21	B	F	N	A	G	−0.54
Lippitt (1941)	9	B	F	N	A	G	4.50
Rieser-Danner et al., (1987)	23	B	F	I	A	F	−0.14
Weisfeld, Block, & Ivers (1983)	50	M	F	N	C	G	0.94
Weisfeld, Weisfeld, & Callaghan (1984)	25	M	B	N	C	G	−0.18
Weisfeld, Weisfeld, & Callaghan (1984)	8	F	B	N	C	G	0.16
Weisfeld, Weisfeld, & Callaghan (1984)	24	F	B	N	C	G	0.75

Note: M = male; F = female; B = both; I = independent; N = nonindependent; A = adult; C = child; F = facial measure; G = global measure.

Source: Adapted from Langlois et al. (2000), p. 417. Reproduced with permission from the American Psychological Association.

throughout this chapter, namely that the meta-analyst must be detailed and precise in describing how the meta-analysis was conducted. The literature search should be described in detail, including what databases were searched using which key words. Criteria for excluding studies should be specified in detail, and the numbers of studies excluded for each reason should be given. Variables coded from the studies should be named and defined in detail. The method of extracting effect sizes should be described, as well as the decision rules for determining which dependent variables to use. Reliability of coding needs to be documented. Full citations for all studies used in the meta-analysis should be included in the reference section.

In terms of presentation of the results, a table listing all the studies and their corresponding effect sizes, as well as values on important methodological and theoretical moderators, is invaluable. Table 17.1 illustrated that format for a narrative review; Table 17.4 shows an analogous layout for a meta-analysis by Langlois et al. (2000) on judgments of attractive and unattractive children. For meta-analyses involving hundreds of studies, such a table might not be feasible, but one should be included whenever space permits. For smaller meta-analyses, a table or appendix can be prepared that provides even more detail about all the studies; for example, each study could be evaluated in a paragraph summarizing the methods, major findings, and contributions and limitations.

The organization of the results depends in part on the nature of the meta-analysis, but one general approach that works well in most cases is to start off with global summary analyses (mean effect size, tests of heterogeneity) and then move to more specific analyses that compute mean effect sizes by category or present tests of moderator or mediator analyses. Stem-and-leaf diagrams or other graphic displays

Table 17.5   Example of a Stem-and-Leaf Diagram of Effect Sizes

Self-Perceived Weight — Leaf	Stem	Actual Weight — Leaf
0	−2.2	
	−2.1	
	−2.0	
1	−1.9	
5	−1.8	6
	−1.7	
	−1.6	
4	−1.5	4
2	−1.4	
2	−1.3	
8	−1.2	
5 2 2	−1.1	
9 6 4	−1.0	3
0	−0.9	1 3 3 9
7 2 0	−0.8	5 7
7 7 5 0	−0.7	0 0 1 7 8
5 3	−0.6	0
8 4 0 0	−0.5	6 6 9
9	−0.4	1 2
9 7 7 0	−0.3	0 0 2 2
	−0.2	0 0 3 3 4 5 5 6 6 6 6 8
2	−0.1	1 2 6 7 8 8 9
6 0	−0.0	0 0 0 0 0 2 4
	.0	0 0 0 0 1 4 6 9
2 0	.1	0 0 0 8
9	.2	0
	.3	3 3
1	.4	

Note: Median effect sizes for each distribution are indicated.
Source: Adapted from Miller & Downey (2000), p. 75.

of effect sizes (overall or broken down by relevant categories) are helpful in conveying quickly and visually a gestalt of the findings in the area. Table 17.5 shows an example of such a stem-and-leaf diagram of effect sizes for a meta-analysis by Miller and Downey (1999) of the relation between self-esteem and weight. On the left-hand side of the diagram is the stem-and-leaf plot for studies looking at the association between self-esteem and self-perceived weight; on the right-hand side of the diagram is the corresponding plot for studies looking at the association between self-esteem and actual weight. Stacking stem-and-leaf diagrams side by side in this manner is an effective means of dramatically illustrating important points about differences across groups of effect sizes.

The discussion of the meta-analysis should summarize the basic findings and discuss in depth their theoretical implications. Limitations of the typical methods used in the area should be pointed out, and suggestions for improving research studies on this topic in the future should be offered. Revisions or extensions to the existing theoretical framework involving the topic should be made. In sum, a literature review, whether narrative or meta-analytic, ideally will make a significant contribution to the theoretical understanding of a research question.

Conducting a literature review, especially a meta-analytic one, is not an easy enterprise. It can take months or even years to gather the literature, analyze and encode/code the studies, perform the meta-analysis or organize and integrate the findings for a narrative review, and write the report. And this does not even account for the general high level of expertise that must be attained with respect to a research area before one can adequately review it. Further, insofar as additional studies will continue to be published, the article that is produced is only an intermediate outcome, one that will continue to be revised as additional research is added to the findings. As an example, see the work of David and Roger Johnson synthesizing research on cooperative learning. They continued to build from the first meta-analyses they did looking at academic outcomes of cooperative learning (Johnson, Maruyama, Johnson, Nelson, & Skon, 1981), coding studies and updating their meta-analysis (e.g., Johnson & Johnson, 1989; Qin, Johnson, & Johnson, 1995; Stanne, Johnson, & Johnson, 1999). Writing a literature review that is well received can be one of the most rewarding accomplishments of a social scientist's career. Literature reviews often are among the most frequently cited contributions in a research area, and a well-written review can influence the direction of an entire field (Garfield, 1992). Indeed, reviews hold the potential to change the face of a research area more than do individual studies. Thus, although the effort involved is enormous and the challenges great, the potential rewards are tremendous.

Summary

Reviewing the empirical research literature involves critically evaluating individual studies and summarizing multiple studies on a topic. Care should be taken in reading individual research reports. Readers need to determine that the authors' hypotheses were tested with methodologically sound designs and analyses, and that the conclusions drawn by the authors reflect the actual statistical results obtained. The first step involved in reviewing a body of literature is to conduct a thorough literature search to identify all the relevant articles. The literature search is accomplished largely through searches of electronic databases and abstracting services. Specifying the right combination of key words or descriptors is critical to a successful search. Electronic searches should be supplemented by other means of locating studies, particularly unpublished studies, such as circulating requests for manuscripts around the invisible college of researchers working on the topic or on relevant LISTSERVs.

Studies on a given research topic can be summarized via a traditional (narrative) review or meta-analytic (quantitative) review. Both types of review provide a summary of the main findings of a body of research and a critical evaluation of the methodologies employed in that area. Meta-analyses provide additional information from quantitative analyses of standardized effect-size indices extracted from the individual studies. A typical meta-analysis report includes an overall effect-size estimate for the group of studies as a whole, as well as moderator analyses that identify the important theoretical and methodological factors that significantly affect the magnitude of the obtained effect sizes.

Exercise: Narrative and meta-analytic reviews

Narrative reviews can be notable by their richness of description of particular studies. Meta-analytic reviews provide a means of empirically examining a range of research questions (how does a particular design flaw seem to affect study outcomes; are recent studies different from earlier ones, and why; are there patterns to the differences across studies, etc.). Look at recent review articles (it's easiest to look in journals focused on review articles, like *Psychological Bulletin* or *Review of Educational Research*) to find good illustrations of exemplars of the strengths of each type of review.

Go online   Visit the book's companion website for this chapter's test bank and other resources at: www.wiley.com/go/maruyama

---

Key Concepts

Ancestry approach
Cohen's *d*
Combining studies
Comparing studies
Differential mortality
Diffuse tests
Effect size
Electronic database
Focused question
Focused tests
Fundamental equation of data analysis
Invisible college
Literature reviews

Literature search
Manipulation checks
Meta-analysis
Moderator variable
Narrative literature review
Psychometric properties
Publication bias
Publication lag
Standardized effect-size index
Statistical power
Tests of heterogeneity
Thesaurus

On the Web

http://www.apa.org/psycinfo/ From this site you can get a personal subscription to PsycINFO®.

http://www.oxfordbibliographies.com/ This site offers annotated bibliographies that cover the scope of most major areas of research across many disciplines. Not intended to include every article in a field, but to cover the various areas of research within the domain. It provides a good starting point for researching many topics, and the number of areas is increasing.

http://www.ncbi.nlm.nih.gov/PubMed/ PubMed, a service of the National Library of Medicine, provides access to over 11 million citations from MEDLINE® and additional life science journals. PubMed includes links to many sites providing full-text articles and other related resources.

Download or use free software for doing meta-analyses on your computer at the following sites:

http://www.spc.univ-lyon1.fr/%7Emcu/easyma/

http://davidakenny.net/meta.htm

http://www.uccs.edu/~lbecker/

http://www.cebm.brown.edu/open_meta

Further Reading

Bem, D. J. (1995). Writing a review article for *Psychological Bulletin*. *Psychological Bulletin, 118*, 172–177.

Johnson, B. T., & Eagly, A. H. (2014). Meta-analysis of research in social and personality psychology. In H. T. Reis & C. M. Judd (Eds.), *Handbook of research methods in social and personality psychology* (2nd ed., pp. 677–709). New York, NY: Cambridge University Press.

Rosenthal, R. (1991). *Meta-analytic procedures for social research* (Rev. ed.). Thousand Oaks, CA: Sage.

Rosenthal, R. (1995). Writing meta-analytic reviews. *Psychological Bulletin, 118*, 183–192.

Shadish, W. R., Cook, T. D., & Campbell, D. T. (2002). *Experimental and quasi-experimental designs for generalized causal inference*. Boston, MA: Houghton Mifflin.

Chapter 18

Writing the Research Report

Research Methods in Social Relations, Eighth Edition. Geoffrey Maruyama and Carey S. Ryan.
© 2014 John Wiley & Sons, Inc. Published 2014 by John Wiley & Sons, Inc.
Companion Website: www.wiley.com/go/maruyama

Preface

We do not intend to provide here a comprehensive guide to preparing your research for publication. A comprehensive guide is provided by the *Publication Manual of the American Psychological Association* (sixth edition, http://www.apastyle.org/manual/index.aspx). We instead modestly revised the chapter previously written by Darryl J. Bem, who contributed this chapter for the fourth through seventh editions of *RMSR*, hopefully keeping the lively and thoughtful guidance he has provided to generations of experimentalists. Bem provides similar information in other places, for example, a chapter in *The Compleat Academic* (2002), and an article for writing review articles (Bem, 1995) that is part of a special section with other papers on writing meta-analytic reviews (Rosenthal, 1995) and methodological articles (Maxwell & Cole, 1995), and on critiquing published articles (Hyman, 1995). In addition, there are many books on how to write expository prose, covering grammar, word usage, punctuation, and style. A classic is *The Elements of Style* by Strunk and White (2000). It is brief, informative, and entertaining.

You have designed and conducted a study and analyzed the data. Now it is time to tell the world what you have learned, to write the research report. In most instances, even when your report is not for a professional audience, it makes sense to adopt the format used for research reports in the professional journals. Your language likely will differ for non-technical audiences and you may want to include a longer **executive summary** rather than a very brief abstract for readers (e.g., policy makers) who won't read the full report. But the format described is a general one that permits readers not only to read the report from beginning to end, as they would any coherent narrative, but also to scan it for a quick overview of the study or to locate specific information easily by turning directly to the relevant section. One caveat to remember regardless of the audience: Too much use of jargon is undesirable, for it limits readability for a general audience and for interested colleagues who are not experts in the area about which you are writing. Despite the standardized format, your individual style will find ample opportunity for expression. For empirical research the report is almost always divided into the following sections:

1. Introduction (What problem were you investigating and why?)
2. Method (What procedures did you use?)
3. Results (What did you find?)
4. Discussion (What do your findings mean? Where do we go from here?)
5. Summary or Abstract (A brief summary of points 1 through 4.)
6. References (An alphabetical list of books and articles cited in the report.)
7. Appendix (optional) (Copies of questionnaires, scales, observation forms, or stimulus materials used in the research or tables of data too extensive or too peripheral to include in the body of the report.)

In this chapter, we provide a structure and procedures for filling in the details of this outline as well as some stylistic suggestions for achieving maximum clarity in your report. The chapter follows the logic and sequencing developed for earlier editions by Bem, and therefore is oriented more toward experimental or quasi-experimental research.

Some Preliminary Considerations

Which Report Should You Write?

According to Bem, there are two possible reports you can write: (1) the report you had in mind when you designed your study or collected your data, or (2) the report that makes the most sense after you have seen the results. We think it is probably more realistic to think about a final report being some combination of the two. However, the report that makes the most sense after seeing the results can sometimes be very different from what one had in mind originally, and opinions differ about which of the two approaches should be chosen. Note that epistemologies matter here. For constructivists, this dilemma is of minimal importance, for they are expecting that the findings will inform and help develop the theory, a point that needs to be made clear to readers when using such an approach. In contrast, for positivists/post-positivists, this distinction goes to the heart of scientific processes of exploration and **confirmation/disconfirmation**. For experimental purists, the clear choice is (1), for that represents the theorizing that guided development of the research, and to make it seem otherwise is dishonest. Further, a post hoc fitting of theory and logic to findings may lead to unreplicable findings that have capitalized on chance. In contrast, Bem clearly opted for (2). He argued strongly that the goal in writing up research findings is to tell the research community what you found (rather than what you thought you would find) and why it is important and/or interesting. Further, because science is self-correcting, findings that are not replicable will be found out, and scientific discoveries will not suffer from such an orientation and presentation of findings.

We believe that there is merit in each position. We will not recommend choosing one approach or the other, but will describe each approach and encourage researchers encountering this challenge to consider both approaches while being cognizant of the strengths and challenges of each perspective, and to choose what makes sense to them. That may involve incorporating elements of both approaches.

Arguments for Position Number Two.   According to a traditional and popular view of the research process, an investigator begins with a formal theory, derives one or more hypotheses from that theory, designs and conducts a study to test the hypotheses, analyzes the data to see whether or not the hypotheses were supported (some might say confirmed, but we believe that term is too strong even for experiments), and then chronicles this sequence of events in the research report. If research actually proceeded according to this plan, most of the research report could be prepared before the data were collected. Research, however, frequently has a funny (or not so funny) habit of deviating from the plan the investigator had in mind at the outset – some might even say it has a mind of its own, unaffected by what you think or believe. Accordingly, those arguing for approach (2) recommend thinking about your report and what it should be beginning with your data.

Data analyses consist of more than simply checking to see whether your original hypotheses were confirmed or disconfirmed. They also involve describing the characteristics of the specific sample, exploring the data thoroughly to see if there are any interesting results that might not have been originally anticipated or that help understand and explain the major findings with respect to the hypotheses, and examining factors that may qualify primary findings. For example, examining the data separately for men and women might reveal an unexpected gender difference – would it be appropriate to present the findings as entirely consistent with prior expectations, knowing that the results were only true for women or for men?

You may even find some results that are far more informative than the confirmation or disconfirmation of your original hypotheses. Statistical tests and a review of literature relevant to those findings can help you decide just how much faith you should put in such discoveries. Perhaps you will only be able to mention these findings tentatively in your report and to suggest further research for following them up. But if these findings are more meaningful than findings from the initial hypotheses, you might be justified in deciding to focus your report around these new findings and to subordinate your original hypotheses. In making such a decision, you need to review the nature of the findings and consider alternative explanations for them. For example, if in an experiment random assignment is lost because the most interesting findings are related to a background variable (e.g., gender) that was not a basis for the random assignment, you would need to consider whether there are alternative explanations and whether the inferences you might want to draw are justified.

However, it is important to consider how hard you had to work to make sense of unanticipated results or how many times you had to conduct the same kind of experiment to obtain the results that you wish to report – the more difficult it is to obtain or explain results, the less likely they are to replicate. Such results may ultimately be shown to be **spurious**, and they hinder scientific progress when other researchers are led astray. At the same time, scientific progress is also hindered when researchers fail to share their results with others simply because the results were not expected.

We also want to be clear that approach (2) does not suggest that you suppress negative results or findings unfavorable to your theory. If your study was genuinely designed to test hypotheses derived from a formal theory or if the original hypotheses are of broad general interest for some other reason, the confirmation or disconfirmation of these hypotheses would be an important part of your report. The integrity of the scientific enterprise requires an investigator to report negative or disconfirming results no matter how personally disappointing this outcome might be.

But this requirement assumes that somebody out there cares about the disconfirmation of the hypotheses. Many studies in the social sciences are somewhat exploratory in nature, launched from some personal speculations or idiosyncratic questions of the "I wonder if . . ." variety. If your study is of this type, there may be little interest in whether you were wrong. Contrary to conventional wisdom, science does not care how clever or clairvoyant you were at guessing your results ahead of time. **Scientific integrity** does not require you to lead your readers through any or all your wrongheaded hunches only to show – voilà! – they were wrongheaded.

Your overriding purpose is to tell the world what you think you have learned about human behavior from your research. That might or might not be the same as telling the world about what you thought about human behavior before you began your study. If your results suggest an instructive or compelling framework for the presentation of your study, adopt that framework, making the findings that tell us the most about human behavior the centerpiece of your presentation. An appropriate metaphor here is to think of your data as a jewel. Your job is to cut and polish this jewel, to select the facets to highlight, and to craft the best setting for it. Good report writing is largely a matter of good judgment; despite the standardized format, it is not a mechanical process. So, think about your report by thinking about your data. You might even find that the easiest way to begin is to write the results section first.

Arguments for Position Number One. The popular view of scientific discovery is popular precisely because it represents the way in which science moves forward – through hypothesizing and testing. Research reports need to be about science and discovery, and post hoc rationalizations are not the way to move science forward in a systematic and consistent way. Indeed, a great deal of research indicates that people are adept at formulating inaccurate post hoc explanations for events that have occurred. Certainly, researchers are not immune, particularly given the investment they have in their formulations. For traditional experimental, theory-testing research, much of the research report can be written in advance. In fact, much of science proceeds this way, most notably, doctoral dissertations that are formulated and then approved by a committee of researchers before the research can be conducted.

Even though the write-up of any study is affected by the findings, the idea of reconfiguring one's research to emphasize the most publishable findings can contribute to a proliferation of nonreplicable findings that capitalize on chance. In nonexperimental research, it can focus on findings that are specific to the sample chosen. And, in an experimental study, the findings may be from "internal" analyses where random assignment is not maintained, and therefore subject to alternative interpretations. One might argue that the massive literature in the 1960s on birth order effects (e.g., Schooler, 1972) is an example of the consequences of such a focus. Only when the a priori conceptual arguments and rigorous methodologies "caught up" to interesting but often misinterpreted findings did the field make progress and create clarity.

Our interpretation of this perspective is not arguing that researchers should not publish interesting ancillary or **serendipitous findings**, but that those findings need to be explained as what they are, somewhat unexpected and warranting replication. Admittedly, taking such a perspective might provide editors a reason to reject very interesting and publishable findings, but such findings should motivate the researchers who found them to go further and strengthen their designs to follow up the research with additional studies that overcome the shortcomings. Corroborating findings through **replication and extension** is central to a cumulative science of behavior.

In summary, there are interesting and potentially compelling arguments for both positions (1) and (2) on writing up one's research. We leave it to individual researchers to decide which perspective is more persuasive to them. Our personal view is that one should not a priori reject either perspective, but consider the implications of each approach for communicating findings and informing readers about the research that was done.

Exercise: Report writing

The contrast between writing research reports backward from the results versus forward from the hypothesizing is an important and interesting one. Even though there undoubtedly is much pragmatism in how people decide to write up their findings, imagine for this exercise that in advance of your study you have to commit to one approach or the other. Which would you choose to do? Then construct a list of strengths and weaknesses of each approach. As a type of force field analysis, give weights to the different strengths and weaknesses. Get together with a small group and discuss your decisions and analyses.

The "Hourglass" Shape of the Report

A research report is typically written in the shape of an hourglass. It begins with broad general statements, progressively narrows down to the specifics of your particular study, and then broadens out again to more general considerations. Thus:

The introduction begins broadly:	"Individuals differ radically from one another in the degree to which they are willing and able to express their emotions."
It becomes more specific:	"Indeed, the popular view is that such emotional expressiveness is a central difference between men and women... But the research evidence is mixed..."
And more so:	"There is even some evidence that men may actually..."
Until you are ready to introduce your own study in conceptual terms:	"In this study, we recorded the emotional reactions of both men and women to filmed..."

The method and results sections are the most specific, the "neck" of the hourglass:	"(Method) One hundred male and 100 female undergraduates were shown one of two movies..."
	"(Results) Table 1 shows that men in the father-watching condition cried significantly more..."
The discussion section begins restating the important findings, linking them to the research questions and implications of your study:	"These results imply that sex differences in emotional expressiveness are moderated by two kinds of variables..."
From a "step back" it reviews the methods used and the nature of the sample, and notes limitations of the particular research study:	"Research conducted on undergraduates in an artificial setting may of course not generalize to real-world interactions, so future research needs to examine the extent to which the findings can be replicated..."
It becomes broader:	"Not since Charles Darwin's first observations has psychology contributed as much new..."
And more so:	"If emotions can incarcerate us by hiding our complexity, at least their expression can liberate us by displaying our authenticity."

This closing statement might be a bit grandiose for some scholarly journals – we're not even sure what it means – but if your study is carefully executed and conservatively interpreted, you deserve to indulge yourself a bit at the two broad ends of the hourglass. Being dull and noncontroversial only *appears* to be a prerequisite for publishing in the professional journals. To the extent that one's findings are presented cautiously, some liberty in interpretation of those findings is allowed in the discussion section, for creating controversy may more strongly motivate one's peers to respond and increase the rate at which discovery occurs. Whether advancement of a literature occurs through defining limiting conditions on research, by disconfirming findings or conclusions, or by producing findings that support a bold conclusion, does not matter.

Introduction

What Is the Problem Being Investigated?

The first task, or at least a very early task of any research report, is to introduce the background and nature of the problem being investigated. Even if your study were only asking a simple empirical question about human behavior or were directed toward a practical problem or policy issue, you must still place the question or issue into a larger context so that readers know why it is of any general significance. Here, for example, is an introduction to an article entitled "Does Sex-Biased Job Advertising 'Aid and Abet' Sex Discrimination?" (Bem & Bem, 1973):

Title VII of the 1964 Civil Rights Act forbids discrimination in employment on the basis of race, color, religion, national origin and sex. Although the sex provision was treated as a joke at the time and was originally introduced in an attempt to defeat the bill, more than 40 percent of the complaints warranting investigation in the first year of the Act were sex discrimination complaints. Nearly 6000 charges of sex discrimination were filed in 1971 alone.

Title VII extends as well to practices that aid and abet discrimination. For example, the Act forbids job advertisements from indicating a preference for one sex or the other unless sex is a bona fide occupational qualification for employment. In interpreting this provision, the Equal Employment Opportunity Commission (EEOC) has ruled that even the practice of labeling help-wanted columns as "Male" or "Female" should be considered a violation of the law.

Nevertheless, a large number of employers continue to write advertisements that specify a sex preference, and many more write advertising copy clearly intended to appeal to one sex only. Moreover, many newspapers continue to divide their help wanted advertisements into sex-segregated columns.

Do these advertising practices aid and abet discrimination in employment by actually discouraging applicants of one sex or the other from applying for jobs for which they are otherwise well qualified? The two studies reported in this article sought to answer this question empirically. Both were conducted and presented as part of legal testimony, the first in a suit filed by the EEOC against American Telephone and Telegraph Company, the second in a suit filed by the National Organization for Women against *The Pittsburgh Press*.

Note how this introduction conforms to the "hourglass" shape of report writing by beginning with the 1964 Civil Rights Act in general and then successively narrowing the focus to the sex provision of the Act, the aiding and abetting clause, and finally to the specific practices that are the subject of the studies to be reported. Regardless of the approach taken or type of study, readers want to know why the research is important and how it might change behaviors or attitudes. The same reporting strategy should be employed in a study designed to contribute to some theory of social behavior. In this case, you would need to summarize the theory or conceptual framework within which you are working. But no matter how theoretical, esoteric, or practical your study is, intelligent nonprofessionals should still be able to grasp the nature of the problem and understand why they should care. Here are four rules of thumb for helping readers out:

1. Write in English prose, not disciplinary jargon.
2. Don't plunge unprepared readers into the middle of your problem or theory. Take the time and space necessary to lead general readers up to the formal or theoretical statement of the problem, *step by step*.
3. Try to open with a statement about human behavior, not the behavior of social scientists or their research.
4. Use examples to illustrate theoretical points or to help introduce theoretical or technical terms. The more abstract the theory, the more important such examples become.

The following are examples of opening statements:

Wrong: "Recent research in the forced-compliance paradigm has focused on the effects of predecisional choice and incentive magnitude."

Wrong: "Festinger's theory of cognitive dissonance has received a great deal of attention during the past 15 years."

Right: "Individuals who hold two beliefs that are inconsistent with one another may feel uncomfortable. For example, people who know that they enjoy smoking but believe it to be unhealthy may experience discomfort arising from the disharmony or inconsistency between these two thoughts or cognitions. This feeling of discomfort has been called *cognitive dissonance* (Festinger, 1957)."

The Literature Review

After you have set the stage in your opening statement, summarize the current state of knowledge in the area of investigation. What previous research has been done on this problem? What are the pertinent theories of the phenomenon, if any? You should have familiarized yourself with previous work on the topic before you designed your own study, and hence most, if not all, of your literature search should have been done by the time you are ready to write your report. Of course, new literature may have been published since you did your initial review. And, if you are inclined toward approach (2), your results might have led you to recast your study in a slightly different framework or to introduce a new aspect of the problem. In this case, you might need to cite references you had not previously consulted, or even to go back to the literature to see whether other investigators have found such a difference or to see whether there are any related findings that might explain your unexpected result.

If based upon prior research you then decide to make the unexpected gender difference an important feature of your report, you should discuss the topic of gender differences in the introduction, including citations to the relevant previous findings. If you plan to mention the gender difference only as a subsidiary finding, however, postpone any discussion of gender differences until the discussion.

In reviewing previous work, you need not describe every study ever done on your problem. Your literature review needs to be focused, not comprehensive. Cite only articles pertinent to the specific issues with which you are dealing; emphasize their major conclusions, findings, or relevant methodological issues and avoid unnecessary detail. If someone else has written a review article that surveys the literature on the topic, you can simply refer readers to the review and present only its most pertinent points in your own report, unless of course you view it as flawed, in which case you might need to explain why and reinterpret its conclusions. Even when you must describe an entire study, try to condense it as much as possible without sacrificing clarity. One way of doing so is to describe one variation of the procedure in chronological sequence, letting it convey the overview of the study at the same time. Here, for example, is a description of a very complicated experiment on attitude change designed to test Festinger's theory of cognitive dissonance (Festinger & Carlsmith, 1959):

Sixty male undergraduates were randomly assigned to one of three conditions. In the $1 condition, the participant was first required to perform long repetitive laboratory tasks in an individual experimental session. He was then hired by the experimenter as an "assistant" and paid $1 to tell a waiting fellow student (a confederate) that the tasks were fun and interesting. In the $20 condition, each participant was hired for $20 to do the same thing. In the control condition, participants simply engaged in the tasks. After the experiment, each participant indicated on a questionnaire how much he had enjoyed the tasks. The results showed that $1 participants rated the tasks as significantly more enjoyable than did the $20 participants, who, in turn, did not differ from the control participants.

This kind of condensed writing looks easy. It is not, and you will have to write and rewrite such summaries repeatedly before they are both clear and succinct. The preceding paragraph was the eighth draft.[1]

Your Study

As you come to the end of the introduction, it often is useful to introduce your own study in a brief overview. The purpose is not to discuss procedural details but to provide a smooth transition into the method section, which follows immediately. The following example could have ended the introduction to the previously cited sex-biased advertising study:

The question, then, is whether or not such advertising practices discourage potential applicants from applying for jobs. The present study sought to answer this question by asking male and female high school seniors to read several telephone job advertisements and to rate their interest in each job. The interest ratings were analyzed to see whether men's and women's interest in jobs stereotyped for the "other" sex would be greater when advertisements were written in nonsexist language.

Method

What to Include

Readers need to know in considerable detail how the study was carried out. What was its basic design? If the study was an experimental one, just what were the experimental manipulations? (For example, was "threat" established by telling the participants that they were about to take a very difficult test that would determine their grades in a course, or by shouting "Fire!"?) If non-experimental, which variables were treated as predictor variables, and which as dependent? If observational, who was

---

[1] If your writing follows APA style, books and articles are cited in the text of the report by giving the author's last name and the date of publication; for example, "According to Festinger (1957), people find cognitive dissonance uncomfortable. Not everyone, however, agrees with this conclusion (e.g., Abelson, 1968; Bem, 1967; Kermit, 1979). Nevertheless, direct evidence for internal discomfort has actually been demonstrated in at least one study (Zanna, Freud, & Theophrastus, 1977)." Note that footnotes are not used for references or citations.

observed and what information was collected during the observations? At what point or points were the measurements taken? Who collected the information?

If the data were gathered through questionnaires or interviews, exactly what questions were asked? (Sometimes the questionnaire or interview schedule is reproduced in an appendix and sometimes sample questions are provided and the number of such questions asked is specified.) How much and what kind of experience had the interviewers had, and how were they trained for this particular study? If the measurements were based on observation, what instructions were given to the observers? Readers also need to know how the observations or replies to questions were translated into measures of the variables. (For example, which questions were taken into account in estimating "alienation"; what kinds of bystander behavior were classified as "helping"?)

With respect to the sample, readers should be told who the participants were, how many there were, and how they were selected. This information is crucial for determining the limits of generalizability of the findings and for understanding the context of the study. Are elaborate conclusions being drawn on the basis of responses of 10 college sophomores, selected because they happened to be friends of the investigator? Were only women interviewed? If so, is there any basis for extending the findings to people in general? Intensive study of a small number of cases, even if not representative of any specifiable population, can be quite valuable. However, the number and characteristics of the participants should be clearly stated so that readers can draw their own conclusions about the applicability of the findings to other groups and contexts.

If you conduct a fairly complex experiment with a sequence of procedures or events, it can be helpful to describe the study as seen from the participant's point of view. First give an overview of the study, including a description of the participants, the setting, and the variables assessed; then describe the sequence of events in chronological order so that the reader is carried through the experience as a participant was. Provide summaries or excerpts of what was actually said to participants, including any rationale or cover story that was given. Show sample items from questionnaires, labels or "anchors" for attitude scales, pictures of apparatus or stimulus materials, and so forth, even if you also include the complete questionnaires or rating scales in an appendix to your report. If you administered a standard personality test, describe its general properties and give a sample item even if it is a fairly familiar instrument; for example, "Participants then filled out the Marlowe-Crowne Social Desirability Scale, a true-false inventory that taps the degree to which people describe themselves in socially desirable terms (e.g., 'I have never lied')." The purpose of all this is to give the readers a "feel" for what it was like to be a participant. This factor often bears importantly on the interpretation of your results, and readers should be in a position to arrive at their own judgments about your conclusions.

Name all operations, variables, and measures with easily recognized and remembered labels. Do not use abbreviations (The AMT5% group) or empty labels (Treatment 3). Instead, tell us about the sex-biased ads and the sex-neutral ads, the success group versus the failure group, the teacher sample versus the student sample, and so forth. It also is better to label groups or treatments in operational rather than theoretical terms. It is difficult to remember that it was the high-dissonance group that was paid $1 and the low-dissonance group that was paid $20. So tell us instead about the $1 group and the $20 group. You can remind us of the theoretical interpretation of these variables again later when it is necessary. And finally, it often is helpful in a complicated experiment to end your description with a one- or two-sentence summary of the procedure and its purpose.

If your study involved a mail survey, here is where you need to tell us how many people returned the survey and to discuss the possibility that those who did not respond differed in some important way from those who did. If your study required observers to record behavior or judges to score written materials, you should present quantitative evidence for inter-observer agreement (kappa, intraclass correlation) or inter-rater reliability. If your study required that you misinform the participants about the nature of the procedures, you should have some evidence that they were not suspicious, that participants who participated earlier had not informed participants who participated later, and that your cover story produced the state of belief required for the test of your hypotheses. If you had to discard certain participants, either at the time of the study or later in the data analysis, you need to tell us why and how many and to discuss the possibility that this action limits or qualifies the conclusions you can draw.

Exercise: Reviewing method sections

At this point, we recommend either selecting the last empirical journal article you have just read or finding an article that you have been meaning to read. Turn to the method section and critique the article. Go back to the preceding sections of this chapter, and see how effectively the research addresses the issues we have covered.

Without trying to be comprehensive, we provide questions to illustrate ways in which method sections are reviewed. How well is the study described? If it is an experiment, is the description rich enough to understand what the participants experienced, and can you replicate the different experimental conditions? As you look for those, pay attention to stylistic features, organization of information, and the like. If you have an article that covers methods effectively, note what they have done. Where there are gaps or shortcomings, note those. How much detail is there about the subject population's demographics? About recruitment of and possible compensation for participants?

If the research is non-experimental, how well are the data sources described? Are they archival data from a different source? How well are issues of sampling, reliability, and construct validity addressed? To what extent are the conceptual underpinnings of the analyses explained? Are the authors talking about causal inferences? If observational, were there instruments used to guide and structure the observations? If they were generative, were there a priori areas that provide the focus of the observations? What were the keys for analyzing and summarizing the data? Were specific programs used to summarize the data?

Ethical Issues

The participants in our studies are human beings and, as detailed in Chapter 3, should be accorded respect and gratitude for their partnership in the research enterprise. Accordingly, as part of the "Participants" section of your method section, it is appropriate to tell readers how you compensated participants for their time and effort and how you dealt with any ethical problems. Procedures for ensuring the confidentiality and/or anonymity of participants' responses should be described, particularly if they deviate from standard procedures or are important to the interpretation of results. If your study raises ethical issues, you should be prepared to justify your procedures and to assure readers that your participants were treated with dignity and that they left your study with their self-esteem intact and their respect for you and social science enhanced rather than diminished.

Results

In short articles or reports of fairly simple studies, the results and discussion sections are often combined into a single section creatively entitled "Results and Discussion." The results are discussed as they are presented, and the section ends with two or three paragraphs that state the conclusions reached, mention qualifications imposed by problems encountered in executing or analyzing the study, and suggest what further research might be appropriate. Many empirical studies can be handled in this fashion. If, however, you need to present many different kinds of results before you can integrate them or draw any inferences or if you wish to discuss several different matters at length in the final discussion, you should separate the results and discussion sections. Even in this case, however, there is no such thing as a pure results section without any accompanying discussion. You cannot just throw numbers at readers and expect them to retain them in their memory until they reach the discussion section. In other words, the results section is still part of an integrated linear narrative about human behavior. It, too, is to be written in English prose, not numbers and statistical symbols.

Setting the Stage

Before you can present your main results, two preliminary matters must be handled. First, you need to present evidence that your study successfully set up the conditions for testing your hypotheses or answering your questions. If your study required you to produce one group of participants in a happy mood and another in a sad mood, here is the place to show us that mood ratings made by the two groups were significantly different. If you divided your sample of participants into groups, you need to assure us that these groups did not differ on some unintended variable that might bear on the interpretation of your results (e.g., social class, race, sex, age, intelligence).

Not all these matters need to be discussed at the beginning of the results section. Some of them might already have been mentioned in the method section (e.g., inter-rater reliabilities of scoring), and others might better be postponed until the discussion section, when you are considering alternative explanations of your results (e.g., the possibility that some participants became suspicious). Regardless of where you put this information, in some cases you might not have any hard evidence to cite, and you might have to fall back on plausible argument: "The possibility that those who did not return the survey were politically more conservative than those who did seems unlikely because surveys were returned in approximately equal numbers from the dormitories, the cooperatives, and the fraternities. If the survey had alienated conservatives, we would have expected a smaller return from the fraternities; moreover …"

The decision of what to include at the beginning of the results section to assure the reader that you have successfully set the stage for adequately testing your hypotheses or answering your questions is very much a matter of judgment. It is an important step, but don't overdo it. Get it out of the way as quickly as possible, and then get on with your story.

The second preliminary matter to deal with is the method of data analysis. First you need to describe any overall procedures you followed in converting your raw observations into analyzable data. (Sometimes, this information is provided in a measures section that is a subsection of the method section.) How were the responses to your mail survey coded for analysis? How were observers' ratings combined? Were all measures first converted to standard scores? (Some of these, too, may have been discussed in the method section and need not be repeated. Similarly, data-combining procedures that are highly specific can be postponed until those analyses are presented. For example, if you combined three measures of anxiety into a single composite score for analysis, you can tell us about that later when you are about to present the anxiety data.)

Next you need to tell readers about the statistical analysis itself. If it is quite standard, it can be described in very few words (e.g., "All data were analyzed by two-way analyses of variance with sex of participant and mood induction as the independent variables."). If your analysis is unconventional or requires certain statistical assumptions that your data might not meet, however, you need to discuss the rationale for it, perhaps citing an article or book for the reader who wishes to check into it further.

And finally, this is the place to give readers an overview of the entire results section if it is complicated or divided into several parts; for example, "The results are presented in three parts. The first section presents the behavioral results for the men, followed by the parallel results for the women. The final section presents the attitudinal and physiological data for both sexes combined."

Presenting the Findings

The general rule in reporting your findings is to begin with the central findings, and then move to more peripheral ones, and start with general findings and then get into more complex and detailed findings. It is also true within subsections: State the basic finding first, and then elaborate or qualify it as necessary. Similarly, discuss an overall measure of aggression or whatever first, and then move to its individual components. Beginning with one of your most central results, proceed as follows:

1. Remind us of the conceptual question you are asking (e.g., "It will be recalled that the men are expected to be more expressive than the women." Or, "We turn first to the question: Are the men or the women more expressive?"). Note that this is a conceptual statement of the question.

2. Remind us of the actual operation performed or the actual behavior measured (e.g., "Do the men produce more tears during the showing of the film than the women?"). Note that this is an operational statement of the question.

3. Tell us the answer immediately and in English. "The answer is yes." Or, "As Table 1 reveals, men do, in fact, cry more profusely than women."

4. Now, and only now, speak to us in numbers. "Thus, the men in all four conditions produced an average of 14 cc more tears than the women: $F(1,112) = 5.79$, $p < .025$."

5. Now you may elaborate or qualify the overall conclusion if necessary. "Only in the father-watching condition did the men fail to produce more tears than the women, but a specific test of this effect failed to reach significance: $t = 1.58$, $p < .12$."

6. As shown in the preceding examples, every finding that involves a comparison between groups or an association between variables should be accompanied by the appropriate statistic; degrees of freedom; level of statistical significance; *and a measure of the **effect size***, such as R^2, omega square, or eta square. This information allows readers to evaluate the strength of the findings; it also provides the necessary information to those who might later include your study in a meta-analysis. Despite the importance of inferential statistics for deciding which results are to be presented as genuine findings, they are not the heart of your narrative and should be subordinated to the descriptive results. Whenever possible, state the result first and then give its statistical significance, but in no case should you ever give the statistical test alone without indicating its meaning in terms of the substantive results. Do not tell us that the three-way interaction involving sex, esteem, and parent condition was significant at the .05 level unless you tell us immediately and in English that men are less expressive than women in the negative conditions if father watches but only for men with low self-esteem. Even something as simple as a correlation between two variables should be interpreted substantively. For example, women who had higher self-esteem expressed greater interest in male sex-typed occupations.

7. In selecting the descriptive indices or statistics, your purpose should be to show us the behavior of people as vividly as you can, to be as descriptive of the actual behavior observed as possible. If children in your study hit a Bobo doll, tell us how many times they hit it or the percentage of children who hit it. If an aggression score represents the mean on a 5-point rating scale, remind us that 3.42 lies between "slightly aggressive" and "quite aggressive." Just as the method section should give us a "feel" for the procedures employed, so, too, the results section should give us a "feel" for the behavior observed.

8. Important findings often are accompanied by a table, graph, or figure showing the relevant data (unless the entire set of findings can be stated in one or two numbers). An advantage of a visual display of the findings is that it helps readers grasp your major findings; they can do it either by reading the text or by looking

at the figures and tables. Tables and figures must be titled and labeled clearly and completely (e.g., "Mean number of tears produced as a function of participant sex, parental observation, and self-esteem"). Within the text itself, you must lead the reader by the hand through the table to point out the results of interest: "As shown in the first column of Table 2, men produce more tears (7.58) than women (6.34)... Of particular interest is the number of tears produced when both father and mother were watching (rows 3 and 4)..." Don't just wave in the general direction of the table and expect the reader to ferret out the information. It is not necessary to describe all numbers in a table or figure; instead, explicitly tell readers what you want them to take away from the table or figure.

9. End each section of the results with a summary of where things stand: "Thus, except for the father-watching condition, which is discussed later, the hypothesis that men cry more than women in response to visually depicted grief received strong support."

10. Lead into the next section of the results with a smooth transition sentence: "Men may thus be more expressive than women in the domain of negative emotion, but can we assume that they are also more willing and able to express positive emotions? Table 3 shows that we cannot..." (Note, again, that you should give the reader the bottom line immediately.) As the results section proceeds, you should continue to summarize and update the reader's store of information frequently. The reader should not have to keep looking back to retrieve the major points of your plot line.

By structuring the results section in this way, by moving from most important to other findings, by announcing each result clearly in prose before wading into numbers and statistics, and by summarizing frequently, you permit the readers to decide just how much detail they want to pursue at each juncture and to skip ahead to the next main point whenever that seems desirable. After you have demonstrated that your quantitative results are statistically significant, it is often useful to become more informal and to describe the behavior of particular individuals in your study. The point is not to prove something but to add richness to your findings, to share with readers the "feel" of the behavior: "Indeed, two of the men used an entire box of tissues during the showing of the heart operation but yet would not pet the baby kitten owned by the secretary." Such mixed methods reporting of results is valuable because it forces researchers to examine data from different perspectives and deepen their understanding of what is occurring.

We suggested above that important findings should be illustrated using figures and/or tables. Their format needs to parallel the discussion in the text, and be constructed to highlight the findings of interest. Tables are particularly useful if you have several categories or variables, which would make a figure too cluttered or visually confusing. You might have to try several different ways of displaying your own data until you find the one that conveys your findings most clearly and without excessive busyness.

Figures 18.1 and 18.2 show two different ways of displaying information about participants' interest in "opposite-sex" jobs, those in which the predominant sex of

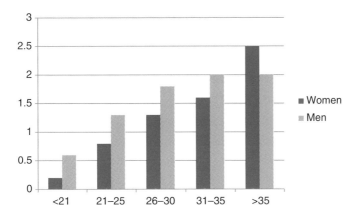

Figure 18.1 Bar Graph Showing Interest in Opposite-Sex Jobs as a Function of Participants' Age and Sex.

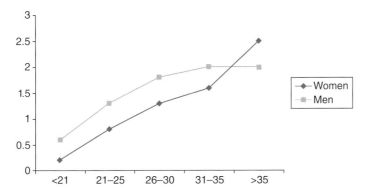

Figure 18.2 Diagram of Interest in Opposite-Sex Jobs as a Function of Participants' Age and Sex.

people holding those jobs differs from that of participants. For Figure 18.1, the x-axis represented discrete age categories. Alternatively, the x-axis could be used to represent the data as a quantitative scale using a line graph. Figure 18.2 shows how a line graph might display participants' interest in opposite-sex ads as a function of their age and sex.

Discussion

As noted earlier, the discussion section can be combined with the results section or, for studies with more complex results or implications, the discussion might appear separately. In either case, the discussion forms a cohesive narrative with the introduction, and you should expect to move materials back and forth between the introduction and discussion as you rewrite and reshape the report. Topics that are central to your argument will appear in the introduction and possibly again in the discussion. Points you have decided to subordinate might not be brought up at all until the discussion section. The closing discussion is also the "bottom" of the hourglass-shaped format and thus proceeds from specific matters about your study to more general concerns (about methodological strategies, for example) to the broadest generalizations you wish to make. The end of the discussion should be tied to the broad issues that motivated the research described at the beginning of the introduction.

Begin by telling us what you have learned from the study. Open with a clear statement on the support or nonsupport of the hypotheses or the answers to the questions you first raised in the introduction. Because some readers may only read the discussion, succinctly restate important points mentioned in the results. Additional statements should contribute something new to the reader's understanding of the problem. What inferences can be drawn from the findings? These inferences could be at a level quite close to the data or could involve considerable abstraction, perhaps to the level of a larger theory regarding, say, emotion, gender differences, or social behaviors. What are the theoretical and practical implications of the results?

It also is appropriate at this point to compare your results to those reported by other investigators and to discuss possible shortcomings of your study, conditions that might limit the extent of legitimate generalization or otherwise qualify your inferences. Remind the reader of the characteristics of your sample and the possibility that it might differ from other populations to which you might want to generalize, of specific characteristics of your methods that might have influenced the outcome, or of any other factors that might have operated to produce atypical results. But do not dwell compulsively on every flaw. In particular, be willing to accept negative or unexpected results without a tortured attempt to explain them away. Do not make up long, involved, pretzel-shaped theories to account for every hiccup in the data.

But suppose that, on the contrary, your results have led you to a grand new theory that injects startling clarity into your data and revolutionizes your view of the problem. Should that justify a long discussion section? Not necessarily! In this case, you should have either written the report to begin with your new theory (approach 2 earlier) or (approach 1) anticipate the theory as a part of your introduction. Try to provide an informative and compelling framework for your study from the beginning. If your new theory does that, do not wait until the discussion section to spring it on us. A research report needs to be a balance between a chronology of your theorizing and what the data show clearly.

The discussion section also includes a discussion of questions that remain unanswered or new questions that have been raised by the study along with suggestions for the kinds of research that would help to answer them. Indeed, suggesting further research is probably the most common way of ending a research report. Remember to avoid simple and obvious statements that more research is needed. More research is almost always needed; your job is to point people in potentially interesting directions with specific suggestions.

If you are following the hourglass-shaped format of the research report, the final statements should be broad general statements about human behavior, not precious details of interest only to social scientists. Consider: "Thus, further research will be needed before it is clear whether the androgyny scale should be scored as a single continuous dimension or partitioned into a four-way typology." No, no! Such a sentence might well be appropriate somewhere in the discussion, but please, not your final farewell. Why not: "Perhaps, then, the concept of androgyny will come to define a new standard of mental health, a standard that will liberate men and women rather than incarcerate them"? Yes, yes! End with a bang, not a whimper!

Summary or Abstract

A research report should include an **abstract**, that is, a brief (150–250 words) summary that appears at the very beginning of the article. An abstract permits potential readers to get a quick overview of the study and to decide whether they wish to read the report itself. It is difficult to write because it is so condensed; it requires slaving over every word to attain clarity. You cannot summarize everything in an abstract. Instead, you must decide what you wish to highlight, and this implies that you should write the abstract or summary last, after you have a firm view of the structure and content of your complete report.

The title of your report itself serves to summarize your study; it, too, should convey the content of your study as accurately and as clearly as possible so that a potential reader can decide whether or not to go further. The most informative titles for experimental research mention both the dependent and independent variables (e.g., "Emotional Responses of Men and Women to Visual Stimuli as a Function of Self-Esteem and Being Observed by Parents"). For non-experimental research, titles may both describe the conceptual issue and the specific study, with the first part stating the broad conceptual question, and the second more specifically describing the study (e.g., "Does Popularity Cause Achievement? A Test of the Lateral Transmission of Values Hypothesis"). Keep in mind that search engines rely on specific terms so that it is useful to consider the terms you use in both your title and abstract (in addition to key terms you might specifically provide), as they will determine when your article emerges in literature searches.

References

All books and articles cited in the text of a research report are listed at the end of the report under the heading "References." They are arranged alphabetically according to the first author's last name, a format that parallels the way in which they are cited in the text. The *Publication Manual of the American Psychological Association* includes a free tutorial that includes the basics of references (http://www.apastyle.org/learn/tutorials/basics-tutorial.aspx). Programs such as EndNote provide a great aid for creating your reference section.

Appendix

The appendix to a research report contains copies of materials used in the research that would be too extensive to include in the report itself. These might include questionnaires, attitude scales, stimulus materials, or photographs and drawings of experimental apparatus or the research setting. These are materials that would help someone else duplicate your experiment in detail. A second appendix might contain tables of data or additional data analyses that are too extensive or too peripheral to include in the report itself. This is information that would enable an interested reader to explore your data in fine detail or to answer questions about your results that you omitted or that might not even have occurred to you.

Because journal space is at a premium, most journal articles do not have appendixes. Some have websites for supplemental materials, or ask authors to provide a link to more extensive information on their web pages. Readers who have questions about the data or who wish to replicate the experiment themselves typically communicate directly with the original investigator. Doctoral dissertations, masters theses, and research reports for class assignments, however, usually do include such appendixes, for those are not restricted in the same ways.

In short, whether or not an investigator includes appendixes in a report depends a lot on who the readers will be and the likelihood that they will find the supplementary materials useful. But as we noted earlier, the report itself should still be self-contained; readers should not have to consult an appendix to understand the methods or results. For example, even if your entire survey questionnaire is contained in an appendix, you should still provide a few sample items from it in the method section.

Some Suggestions on Procedure and Style

Accuracy and Clarity

The overriding criteria for good scientific writing are **accuracy** and **clarity**. If your report is interesting and written with flair and style, fine. But flair is a subsidiary virtue. First strive for accuracy and clarity.

Work from an Outline

Even though the standardized format we have described here will go a long way toward organizing your report, you will be able to produce a more coherent report with a minimum of rewriting if you first organize the main points in outline form, examine the logic of the sequence, check to see whether important points are omitted or misplaced, and so forth. As we suggested earlier, it is sometimes helpful to write the results and method sections of the final article first, and then write (or rewrite) the introduction. It also is important to think of your introduction and final discussion as part of the same conceptual narrative.

Write Simply. Use Examples. Use Friends as Reviewers

As we noted earlier, it should be possible for nonprofessionals to read your report and comprehend what you did and why, even if they know nothing about statistics, research design, or the substantive area of your research problem. This goal is achieved by writing simply, with a minimum of jargon, and using frequent examples to illustrate and introduce technical concepts. The more abstract the subject matter, the more you need examples to tie it to the reader's own experience and previous level of knowledge. Read over your own writing, trying to take the viewpoint of an intelligent but nonprofessional reader. Ask at each point, "Do I know yet what this concept means?" "Is this clear?" The ability to take the role of a "naïve" reader or listener is the most important skill in writing or teaching. It is not easy. And because it is not easy, you should use your friends as reviewers, especially those who are unfamiliar with the subject matter. If they find something unclear, do not argue with them or attempt to clarify the problem verbally. If they have read carefully and conscientiously, they are always right: By definition, the writing is unclear. Their suggestions for correcting the unclarities might be wrong, even dumb. But as unclarity detectors, readers are never wrong.

Omit Needless Words

Virtually all experienced writers agree that any written expression that deserves to be called *vigorous writing*, whether it is a short story, an article for a professional journal, or a complete book, *is* characterized by the attribute of being succinct, *concise,* and to the point. *A sentence* – no matter where in the writing it occurs – *should contain no unnecessary* or superfluous *words*, words that stand in the way of the writer's direct expression of his or her meaning and purpose. In a very similar fashion, *a paragraph* – the basic unit of organization in English prose – should contain *no unnecessary* or superfluous *sentences*, sentences that introduce peripheral content into the writing or stray from its basic narrative line. It is in this sense that a writer is like an artist executing a drawing, and it is in this sense that a writer is like an engineer designing a machine. Good writing should be economical *for the same reason that a drawing should have no unnecessary lines, and* good writing should be streamlined in the same way that *a machine* is designed to have *no unnecessary parts*, parts that contribute little or nothing to its intended function.

This prescription to be succinct and concise is often misunderstood, and *requires* judicious application. It certainly does *not* imply *that the writer* must *make all* of his or her *sentences short* and choppy *or* leave out all adjectives, adverbs, and qualifiers. Nor does it mean that he or she must *avoid* or eliminate *all detail* from the writing *and treat* his or her *subjects only in* the barest skeleton or *outline* form. *But* the requirement does imply *that every word* committed to paper should *tell* something new to the reader and contribute in a significant and nonredundant way to the message that the writer is trying to convey.

You may well have figured out that the italics illustrate the point being made. You have just read a 303-word essay on brevity. It is not a terrible first draft, but a good writer or copyeditor would take its message to heart and, by crossing out all the nonitalicized words, cut it by 81%. Savor the result:

Vigorous writing is concise. A sentence should contain no unnecessary words, a paragraph no unnecessary sentences, for the same reason that a drawing should have no unnecessary lines and a machine no unnecessary parts. This requires not that the writer make all sentences short or avoid all detail and treat subjects only in outline, but that every word tell. [59 words]

This essay on brevity was written by Strunk and White (2000, p. 23) under the heading: "Omit Needless Words." Obey their injunction, for it is the most important piece of advice in this chapter. Research reports also should omit needless concepts, topics, anecdotes, asides, and footnotes. Clear any underbrush that clutters your narrative. If a point seems peripheral to your main theme, remove it. If you can't bring yourself to do this, put it in a footnote. Then when you revise your report, remove the footnote.

Avoid Metacomments on the Writing

Expository writing fails its mission if it diverts the reader's attention to itself and away from the topic; the process of writing should be transparent to the reader. In particular, the prose itself should direct the flow of the narrative without requiring you to play tour guide by commenting on it. Don't say: "Now that I have discussed the three theories of emotion, we can turn to the empirical work on each of them. I will begin with the psychoanalytic account of affect..." Instead, move directly from your discussion of the theories into the literature review with a simple transition sentence like, "Each of these three theories has been tested empirically. Thus, the psychoanalytic account of affect has received support in studies that..." Don't say: "Now that we have seen the results for negative affect, we are in a position to examine men's and women's emotional expression in the realm of positive affect. The relevant data are presented in Table 2..." Instead, use a transition sentence that simultaneously summarizes and moves the story along: "Men may thus be more expressive than women in the domain of negative emotion, but are they also more expressive in the domain of positive emotion? Table 2 shows that they are not..." Other guideposts can be supplied by using informative headings and by following the advice on repetition and parallel construction given in the next section.

If you feel the need to make metacomments to keep the reader on the narrative path, then your plot line is probably already too cluttered, the writing insufficiently linear. Metacomments will only oppress the prose further. Instead, copyedit. Omit needless words; don't add them!

Use Repetition and Parallel Construction

Inexperienced writers often substitute synonyms for recurring words and vary their sentence structure in the mistaken belief that this is more creative, stylish, or interesting. Instead of using repetition and parallel construction, as in "Men may be more expressive than women in the domain of negative emotion, but they are not more expressive in the domain of positive emotion," they attempt to be more creative: "Men may be more expressive than women in the domain of negative emotion, but it is not true that they are more willing and able than the opposite sex to display the more cheerful affects."

Such creativity is hardly more interesting, but it is certainly more confusing. In scientific communication, it can be deadly. When an author uses different words to refer to the same concept in a technical article – where accuracy is paramount – readers will justifiably wonder if different meanings are implied. This example above is not disastrous, and most readers will be unaware that their understanding flickered momentarily when the prose hit a bump. But consider the cognitive burden carried by readers who must hack through this "creative" jungle:

> The high-dissonance participants were paid a small sum of money while being given a free choice of whether or not to participate, whereas the participants we randomly assigned to the large-incentive treatment (the low-dissonance condition) were not offered the opportunity to refuse.

This (fictitious) author should have written:

> High-dissonance participants were paid a small sum of money and were not required to participate; low-dissonance participants were paid a large sum of money and were required to participate.

The wording and grammatical structure of the two clauses are held rigidly parallel; only the variables vary. Repetition and parallel construction are among the most effective servants of clarity. Don't be creative; be clear.

Be Compulsive. Be Willing to Restructure

The best writers rewrite nearly every sentence in the course of polishing their successive drafts. The probability of writing a sentence perfectly the first time is vanishingly small, and good writing requires a high degree of compulsiveness and attention to detail. But whether or not to worry about writing style in the course of producing the first draft is to some extent a matter of individual taste. Some experienced writers spend a long time over each sentence, carefully choosing each word. But when the purpose is to convey information rather than to achieve a literary production, it probably is true for most people that time is saved in the long run by writing the first draft as quickly as possible. Once it is written, you can go back and rewrite sentences and paragraphs, fortified by the knowledge that at least a first draft of the report has already been produced. In writing and rewriting, it is important to remember that a badly built building cannot be salvaged by brightening up the wallpaper. Rewriting often means restructuring, not just tinkering with sentences or paragraphs. Sometimes it is necessary to restructure totally a research report, even to go back and do more data analysis, just to iron out a bump in the logic of the argument. Do not get so attached to your first draft that you are unwilling to tear it apart and rebuild it. Rewriting often means restructuring.

Person and Voice

In the past, scientific writing employed the third-person passive voice almost exclusively ("The experiment was designed by the authors to test the hypothesis that...."). This is dull and clumsy and is no longer the norm. It is now permissible to use the first person and desirable to use the active voice. Do not refer to yourself as "the author" or "the investigator." Do not refer to yourself as "we" unless there really are two or more authors or investigators involved. You may refer to yourself as "I" as long as you do it sparingly; constant use of the first person tends to distract the reader from the subject matter, and it is best to remain in the background. Leave the reader in the background, too. Do not say, "The reader will find it hard to believe that..." or "You will be surprised to learn..." Perhaps you are wondering what you *can* do. You can let people and their behavior serve as the subjects of sentences: "Individuals appear to cling to their prejudices even when..." "Racial prejudice, then, diminishes when persons interact..." You may also refer to the reader indirectly from time to time: "Consider, first, the results for men..." You may also refer to yourself and the reader as "we" in some contexts: "We can see in Table 1 that most of the tears are produced..."

Tense

Use the past tense when reporting the previous research of others ("Bandura reported..."), how you conducted your study ("Observers were posted behind..."), and specific past behaviors of your participants ("Two of the group members talked..."). Use the present tense for results currently in front of the reader ("As Table 2 shows, the emotional film is more effective...") and for conclusions that are more general than the specific results ("Sex-biased advertising, then, leads qualified applicants to ignore...").

Avoid Language Bias

Like most publishers, the American Psychological Association now has extensive guidelines for language that refers to individuals or groups. Here is a summary of some of those guidelines. Although many of the examples may seem obvious given the social changes that have occurred and the attention today to the importance of language with respect to differences and sensitivity to others, similar kinds of problems still appear in writing. The guidelines therefore seem worthy as a reminder.

A. Research Participants.   It is no longer considered appropriate to objectify those whom we study by calling them *subjects*. Instead use descriptive terms that either identify them more specifically or that acknowledge their roles as partners in the research process, such as *college students, children, individuals, participants, interviewees,* or *respondents*.

B. Sex and Gender.   The issue of language bias comes up most frequently with regard to sex or gender, and the most awkward problems arise from the use of masculine nouns and pronouns when the content refers to both sexes. The generic use of "man," "he," "his," and "him" to refer to both sexes is not only misleading in many instances, but research shows that readers think of male persons when these forms are used (Martyna, 1978). Sometimes the results are not only sexist but humorous in their naïve androcentrism: "Man's vital needs include food, water, and access to females" (quoted in Martyna, 1978).

In most contexts, the simplest alternative is the use of the plural. Instead of writing, "The individual who displays prejudice in his personal relations is...," write, "Individuals who display prejudice in their personal relations are..." Sometimes the pronoun can simply be dropped or replaced by a sex-neutral article (e.g., *the*, *a*, or *an*). Instead of writing, "The researcher must avoid letting his preconceptions bias his interpretation of results," you can write, "The researcher must avoid letting preconceptions bias the interpretation of results."

If it is stylistically important to focus on the single individual, the use of "he or she," "him or her," and so forth is acceptable but clumsy if used very often. Alternating *he* and *she* is both confusing and distracting. Similarly, alternatives like *he/she* or *s/he* are unpronounceable and grate on the eye. Don't use them.

Stylistic matters aside, however, you must be accurate in your use of pronouns when you describe your research or that of others. Readers must be explicitly told the sex of experimenters, observers, and participants. When referring to males, use male pronouns; when referring to females, use female pronouns. (See, for example, the earlier description of the Festinger–Carlsmith study, which used male participants.) Under no circumstances should you omit or hide sex identity in a misguided attempt to be unbiased.

The problems of gender reference become easier when we move away from pronouns. Words like *man* and *mankind* are easily replaced by terms like *people* and *humanity*. Instead of manning projects, we can staff them. The federal government has already desexed occupational titles so that we have letter carriers rather than mailmen; in private industry we have flight attendants rather than stewardesses. And in life, children need nurturing or parenting, not just mothering. In all these cases, you will find it easy to discover the appropriate sex-neutral term if you think of the activity rather than the person doing it.

Next, watch out for plain old stereotyping. The author who asserts that "research scientists often neglect their wives" fails to acknowledge that women as well as men are research scientists, that some domestic partnerships are same sex rather than opposite sex, and that some couples, regardless of gender, are choosing not to marry. In all cases, the term wives would be better replaced by partners or domestic partners. If the author meant specifically male research scientists, he (she?) should have said so. Do not talk about ambitious men and aggressive women or cautious men and timid women if the use of different adjectives denotes not different behaviors on the part of men and women but your stereotyped interpretation of those behaviors. Insofar as this may be done unconsciously, reread your paper with a specific focus on gender stereotypes and terminology. Don't make stereotyped assumptions about marital sex roles by saying that "The client's husband lets her teach part-time" if all you know is that the client teaches part-time. If the bias is not yours but someone else's, let the writing make that clear: "The client's husband 'lets' her teach part-time." "The husband says he 'lets' the client teach part-time." "The client says her husband lets her teach part-time." "The client says sarcastically that her husband 'lets' her teach part-time." The client and her husband are allowed to say such things. You are not.

And finally, select examples with care. Beware of your assumptions about the sex of doctors, homemakers, nurses, and so forth. Why not "The athlete who believes in her ability to succeed…"? Let our writing promote the view that woman's vital needs are the same as man's: food, water, and access to equality, and readers can decide for themselves where sexual gratification appears in the list of needs.

C. Racial and Ethnic Identity.   Preferences for names referring to racial and ethnic groups change over time. For example, *African American* and *Black* are currently acceptable terms, whereas *Negro* and *Afro-American* are now obsolete. Similarly, *Asian* and *Asian American* are currently acceptable designations, whereas *Oriental* is not. As these examples illustrate, hyphens should not be used in multiword designations, and terms like *Black* and *White* are considered proper nouns and should be capitalized.

Depending on their historical countries of origin, individuals might prefer to be called *Hispanic, Latino,* or *Chicano* (*Latina* and *Chicana* for women). *American Indian* and *Native American* are both accepted terms for referring to indigenous people of North America; but, technically, only the latter category includes Hawaiians and Samoans. It often is relevant to be more specific in describing your participants. For example, it might be pertinent to know that they were *Cuban*, not just *Hispanic*; *Chinese, Vietnamese,* or *Korean,* not just *Asian.*

If you are uncertain about how to describe your research participants, ask them.

D. Sexual Orientation and Identification.   Like terms referring to racial and ethnic identity, terms referring to sexual orientation and identification also change over time. For example, the term *sexual orientation* itself is now preferred to the older *sexual preference* – which implies a temporary free choice rather than an enduring disposition. And for some, the term is not about who individuals find sexually attractive, but how they identify themselves independently of attraction. Although terms like *homosexual* and *homosexuality* are still technically correct, they should be avoided when referring to individuals or groups. Instead of referring to *homosexuals* or *bisexuals*, use *lesbians, gay men,* or *bisexual men and women.* In some contexts, the word *gay* can be used to include both men and women (e.g., "the gay rights movement"), but when referring to individuals or groups, retain the distinction between gay men and lesbians.

E. Disabilities.   When referring to individuals with disabilities, maintain personal integrity as individuals and human beings by avoiding language that equates individuals with their conditions. Don't use nouns such as *neurotics, schizophrenics, manic-depressives, the mentally retarded,* or even *the disabled.* Also avoid terms that imply victimization (e.g., "suffers from schizophrenia," "AIDS victim") or that can be interpreted as a slur (e.g., *cripple*). *Challenged* and *special* are often considered euphemistic and should be used only if preferred by those who participate in your study. In general the preferred forms of description are "person/people with _____" or "person living with _____" or "person who has_____."

For many groups of people with disabilities, language focuses on being differently able rather than not able. One group that illustrates ways in which sensitivity needs to be displayed is individuals who are deaf or hearing impaired. Many hearing impaired individuals do not regard themselves as disabled but rather as members of a distinctive culture, a linguistic minority who communicate using American Sign Language. If your study involves deaf participants, your description should honor their preferences as a subcultural group, for example, using the term they prefer from among terms including hearing impaired, deaf, hard of hearing, or Deaf.

Summary

There are differing views about how best to write a research report. One view is that the report tracks the hypothesizing and findings of the authors from beginning to end. The second is that the research report should reflect the findings of a study, rather than any preconceived ideas that the investigator might have prior to conducting the study. There are merits (and drawbacks) to each approach so we recommend that researchers consider both approaches as they write up their findings.

The structure of the research report can be described as an "hourglass" format. The introduction constitutes the top portion of the hourglass in that it begins with a general statement, followed by a narrower discussion of theories and literature that are most pertinent to the phenomenon being researched. The subject of the investigation is then more specifically outlined beginning with the central question to be explored and an explanation of its significance. The introduction can end with a brief paragraph describing the study itself in general terms, leaving the details to the method section.

Method and results sections form the neck of the hourglass. The method section describes in detail the participants, the way in which the study was conducted, and the methods employed to measure the behaviors under examination. The results section presents the findings, including any tables, figures, and statistical analyses of the data. The hourglass then widens again in the discussion. This section brings the research report to a conclusion, beginning with specific implications and ending with broad conclusions.

Journal articles typically begin with a short abstract that describes the research question, the method used to examine it, the major findings, and the primary implications of those findings. The title of the report also serves to describe the study and should reflect as much as possible the content of the report. The research report should be written in a clear, accurate style that can be understood by nonprofessionals.

The use of the first person and the active voice is now preferred over the third person and the passive voice. The past tense is used when reporting the past research of others and in describing your own procedures. The present tense is used to discuss results currently in front of the reader or conclusions that are more general than the specific results. Do not use generic masculine terms such as "he" or "man" when referring to both men and women. It is also important to avoid offensive language when discussing sex, gender, ethnicity, sexual orientation, and disability.

Go online   Visit the book's companion website for this chapter's test bank and other resources at: www.wiley.com/go/maruyama

Key Concepts

Abstract

Accuracy

Clarity

Confirmation/disconfirmation

Effect size

Executive summary

Replication and extension

Scientific integrity

Serendipitous finding

Spurious

On the Web

http://owl.english.purdue.edu/owl/section/2/10/ A valuable online research for all aspects of APA style and format.

http://www.apa.org/education/undergrad/student-research.aspx This site contains articles on how to write empirical essays, tools to help with research, tips on creating PowerPoint presentations, as well as information on research training opportunities. An equivalent page for doctoral students can be found at: **http://www.apa.org/education/grad/research.aspx**

http://www.ncfr.org/professional-resources/career-resources/craftways-writing-evaluating-theory-review-research-articles/ This website has many resources and suggested readings for all levels and many disciplines.

Further Reading

Becker, H. S. (1986). *Writing for social scientists: How to start and finish your thesis, book, or article.* Chicago, IL: University of Chicago Press.

Herr, K., & Anderson, G. (2005). *The action research dissertation: A guide for students and faculty.* Thousand Oaks, CA: Sage.

McNiff, J., & Whitehead, J. (2009). *Doing and writing action research.* London: Sage.

Sternberg, R. J. (1993). *The psychologist's companion: A guide to scientific writing for students and researchers.* New York, NY: Cambridge University Press.

Sternberg, R. J. (Ed.). (2000). *Guide to publishing in psychology journals.* New York, NY: Cambridge University Press.

References

Adair, J. G., & Epstein, J. S. (1968). Verbal cues in the mediation of experimenter bias. *Psychological Reports, 22,* 1045–1053.

Adelman, C. (2006). *The Toolbox revisited: Paths to degree completion from high school to college.* Washington, DC: U.S. Department of Education.

Ambady, N., & Rosenthal, R. (1992). Thin slices of expressive behavior as predictors of interpersonal consequences: A meta-analysis. *Psychological Bulletin, 111,* 256–274.

American Psychological Association. (2009). *Publication manual of the American Psychological Association* (6th ed.). Washington, DC: Author.

Anderson, C. A., & Anderson, K. B. (1996). Violent crime rate studies in philosophical context: A destructive testing approach to heat and southern culture of violence effects. *Journal of Personality and Social Psychology, 70,* 740–756.

Anderson, C. A., & Dill, K. E. (2000). Video games and aggressive thoughts, feelings, and behavior in the laboratory and in life. *Journal of Personality and Social Psychology, 78,* 772–790.

Anderson, J. E., & Dahlberg, L. L. (1992). High-risk sexual behavior in the general population: Results from a national survey. *Sexually Transmitted Diseases, 19,* 320–325.

Anderson, J. R. (2007). *How can the human mind occur in the physical universe?* Oxford, England: Oxford University Press.

Argyris, C., Putnam, R., & Smith, D. M. (1985). *Action science: Concepts, methods, and skills for research and intervention.* San Francisco, CA: Jossey-Bass.

Aronson, E. (1966). Avoidance of inter-subject communication. *Psychological Reports, 19,* 238.

Aronson, E., Stephan, C., Sikes, J., Blaney, N., & Snapp, M. (1978). *The jigsaw classroom.* Thousand Oaks, CA: Sage.

Arriaga, X. B. (2001). The ups and downs of dating: Fluctuations in satisfaction in newly formed romantic relationships. *Journal of Personality and Social Psychology, 80,* 754–765.

Arthur, J. A., & Case, C. E. (1994). Race, class, and support for police use of force. *Crime, Law, and Social Change, 21,* 167–182.

Asparouhov, T., & Muthén, B. (2009). Exploratory structural equation modeling. *Structural Equation Modeling, 16,* 397–438.

Astorino-Courtois, A. (1995). The cognitive structure of decision making and the course of Arab–Israeli relations, 1970–1978. *Journal of Conflict Resolution, 39,* 419–438.

Austin, P., Grootendorst, P., & Anderson, G. (2007). A comparison of the ability of different propensity score models to balance measured variables between treated and untreated subjects: A Monte Carlo study. *Statistics in Medicine, 26,* 734–753.

Bakeman, R., & Gottman, J. M. (1997). *Observing interaction: An introduction to sequential analysis* (2nd ed.). New York, NY: Cambridge University Press.

Bales, R. F. (1970). *Personality and interpersonal behavior*. New York, NY: Holt, Rinehart & Winston.

Bales, R. F., & Cohen, S. P. (1979). *SYMLOG: A system for the multiple level observation of groups*. New York, NY: Free Press.

Barbarin, O. A., Richter, L., de Wet, T., & Wachtel, A. (1998). Ironic trends in the transition to peace: Criminal violence supplants political violence in terrorizing South African Blacks. *Peace and Conflict: Journal of Peace Psychology, 4,* 283–305.

Bardi, A., Calogero, R. M., & Mullen, B. (2008). A new archival approach to the study of values and value – behavior relations: Validation of the value lexicon. *Journal of Applied Psychology, 93,* 483–497.

Barker, R. G., & Schoggen, P. (1973). *Qualities of community life*. San Francisco, CA: Jossey-Bass.

Barron, G., & Yechiam, E. (2002). Private e-mail requests and the diffusion of responsibility. *Computers in Human Behavior, 18,* 507–520.

Baum, F., MacDougall, C., & Smith, D. (2006). Participatory action research. *Journal of Epidemiology and Community Health, 60*(10), 854–885.

Baumrind, D. (1964). Some thoughts on the ethics of research: After reading Milgram's "Behavioral study of obedience." *American Psychologist, 19,* 421–423.

Beaman, A. L. (1991). An empirical comparison of meta-analytic and traditional reviews. *Personality and Social Psychology Bulletin, 17,* 252–257.

Becker, H. S. (1967). Whose side are we on? *Journal of Social Problems, 14,* 239–247.

Becker, L. J., & Seligman, C. (1978). Reducing air conditioning waste by signalling it is cool outside. *Personality and Social Psychology Bulletin, 4,* 412–415.

Becker, L. J., Seligman, C., & Darley, J. M. (1979, June). *Psychological strategies to reduce energy consumption*. Center for Energy and Environmental Studies, Report 90.

Behrend, T. S., Sharek, D. J., Meade, A. W., & Wiebe, E. N. (2011). The viability of crowdsourcing for survey research. *Behavior Research Methods, 43,* 800–813. doi: 10.3758/s13428-011-0081-0

Bekkers, R., & Weipking, P. (2011). Accuracy of self-reports on donations to charitable organizations. *Quality and Quantity, 45,* 1369–1383.

Bem, D. J. (1995). Writing a review article for *Psychological Bulletin*. *Psychological Bulletin, 118,* 172–177.

Bem, D. J. (2002). Writing the empirical journal article. In J. M. Darley, M. P. Zanna, & H. L. Roediger III (Eds.), *The compleat academic* (2nd ed.). Washington, DC: American Psychological Association.

Bem, D. J., & Honorton, C. (1994). Does Psi exist? Replicable evidence for an anomalous process of information transfer. *Psychological Bulletin, 115,* 4–18.

Bem, S. L., & Bem, D. J. (1973). Does sex-biased job advertising "aid and abet" sex discrimination? *Journal of Applied Social Psychology, 3,* 6–18.

Berk, R. A., & Rossi, P. H. (1977). Doing good or worse: Evaluation research politically examined. In M. Guttentag & S. Saar (Eds.), *Evaluation studies review annual* (Vol. 2, pp. 77–90). Thousand Oaks, CA: Sage.

Berkowitz, L., & Donnerstein, E. (1982). External validity is more than skin deep: Some answers to criticisms of laboratory experiments. *American Psychologist, 37,* 245–257.

Berry, D. S., & Hansen, J. S. (2000). Personality, nonverbal behavior, and interaction quality in female dyads. *Personality and Social Psychology Bulletin, 26,* 278–292.

Bertell, R., Jacobson, N., & Stogre, M. (1984). Environmental influence on survival of low birth weight infants in Wisconsin, 1963–1975. *International Perspectives in Public Health, 1*(2), 12–24.

Blaney, N. T., Stephan, C., Rosenfield, D., Aronson, E., & Sikes, J. (1977). Interdependence in the classroom: A field study. *Journal of Educational Psychology, 69,* 139–146.

Blascovich, J. (2014). Using physiological indexes in social psychological research. In H. T. Reis & C. M. Judd (Eds.), *Handbook of research methods in social and personality psychology* (2nd ed., pp. 101–122). New York, NY: Cambridge University Press.

Blascovich, J., Mendes, W. B., Hunter, S. B., Lickel, B., & Kowai-Bell, N. (2001). Perceiver threat in social interactions with stigmatized others. *Journal of Personality and Social Psychology, 80,* 253–267.

Blatchford, P., Bassett, P., & Brown, P. (2005). Teachers' and pupils' behavior in large and small classes: A systematic observation study of pupils aged 10 and 11 years. *Journal of Educational Psychology, 97,* 454–467.

Blurton-Jones, N. (Ed.). (1972). *Ethological studies of child behavior.* Cambridge, England: Cambridge University Press.

Bogardus, E. S. (1933). A social distance scale. *Sociology and Social Research, 17,* 265–271.

Bok, D. (1990). *Universities and the future of America.* Durham, NC: Duke University Press.

Bollmer, J. M., Harris, M. J., & Dotson, S. (2001). *We hurt most the ones we love: Differences in teasing across relationship type.* Unpublished manuscript, University of Kentucky.

Boruch, R. F. (1975). On common contentions about randomized field experiments. In R. F. Boruch & H. W. Riecken (Eds.), *Experimental tests of public policy* (pp. 108–145). Boulder, CO: Westview Press.

Boyer, E. L. (1990). *Scholarship reconsidered: Priorities of the professoriate.* New York, NY: John Wiley & Sons.

Bradburn, N., & Sudman, S. (1979). *Improving interview method and questionnaire design.* San Francisco, CA: Jossey-Bass.

Brannigan, G. G., & Merrens, M. R. (Eds.). (1993). *The undaunted psychologist: Adventures in research.* New York, NY: McGraw-Hill.

Brick, J. M., Brick, P. D., Dipko, S., Presser, S., Tucker, C., & Yangyang, Y. (2007). Cell phone survey feasibility in the U.S.: Sampling and calling cell numbers versus landline numbers. *Public Opinion Quarterly, 71,* 23–39.

Brickman, P., Folger, R., Goode, E., & Schul, Y. (1981). Micro and macro justice. In M. J. Lerner (Ed.), *The justice motive and social behavior.* New York, NY: Plenum.

Brickman, P., & Stearns, A. (1978). Help that is not called help. *Personality and Social Psychology Bulletin, 4,* 314–317.

Brislin, R. W. (1980). Translation and content analysis of oral and written materials. In H. Triandis & J. W. Berry (Eds.), *Handbook of cross-cultural psychology* (Vol. 2, pp. 389–444). Boston, MA: Allyn & Bacon.

Bryant, A., & Charmaz, K. (Eds.). (2007). *The Sage handbook of grounded theory.* Los Angeles, CA: Sage.

Buckle, A., & Farrington, D. P. (1994). Measuring shoplifting by systematic observation: A replication study. *Psychology, Crime, and Law, 1,* 133–141.

Buhmester, M., Kwang, T., & Gosling, S. D. (2011). Amazon's Mechanical Turk: A new source of inexpensive, yet high-quality, data? *Perspectives on Psychological Science, 6,* 3–5.

Burke, P. A., & Dollinger, S. J. (2005). A picture's worth a thousand words: Language use in the autophotographic essay. *Personality and Social Psychology Bulletin, 31,* 536–548.

Burnham, J. R. (1966). *Experimenter bias and lesion labeling.* Unpublished manuscript.

Bush, M., & Gordon, A. C. (1978). Client choice and bureaucratic accountability: Possibilities for responsiveness in a social welfare bureaucracy. *Journal of Social Issues, 34*(4), 22–43.

Bushman, B. J., & Huesmann, L. R. (2012). Effects of violent media on aggression. In D. G. Singer & J. L. Singer (Eds.), *Handbook of children and the media* (2nd ed., pp. 231–248). Thousand Oaks, CA: Sage.

Campbell, D. T. (1969). Reforms as experiments. *American Psychologist, 24,* 409–429.

Campbell, D. T. (1979). Assessing the impact of planned social change. *Evaluation and Program Planning, 2,* 67–90.

Campbell, D. T., & Erlebacher, A. (1970). How regression artifacts in quasi-experimental evaluations can mistakenly make compensatory education look harmful. In J. Hellmuth (Ed.), *Compensatory education: A national debate, Vol. 3: The disadvantaged child* (pp. 597–617). New York, NY: Brunner/Mazel.

Campbell, D. T., & Fiske, D. W. (1959). Convergent and discriminant validation by the multitrait–multimethod matrix. *Psychological Bulletin, 56,* 81–105.

Campbell, D. T., & Stanley, J. C. (1963). *Experimental and quasi-experimental designs for research.* Chicago, IL: Rand McNally.

Cannell, C. F., Fisher, G., & Bakker, T. (1965). Reporting of hospitalization in the health service interview. *Vital and Health Statistics, 2*(6).

Cantor, N. (2007, January). *Scholarship in action: Why community commitment matters.* Paper presented at the 50th anniversary of the Center for the Study of Higher and Post-Secondary Education, Ann Arbor, MI.

Caracelli, V., & Greene, J. (1993). Data analysis strategies for mixed-method evaluation designs. *Educational Evaluation and Policy Analysis, 15,* 195–207.

Carlo, G., Knight, G. P., McGinley, M., Zamboanga, B. L., & Jarvis, L. H. (2010). The multidimensionality of prosocial behaviors and evidence of measurement equivalence in Mexican American and European American early adolescents. *Journal of Research on Adolescence, 20,* 334–358.

Carlsmith, J. M., Ellsworth, P. C., & Aronson, E. (1976). *Methods of research in social psychology.* Reading, MA: Addison-Wesley.

Carney, D. R., Jost, J. T., Gosling, S. D., & Potter, J. (2008). The secret lives of liberals and conservatives: Personality profiles, interaction styles, and the things they leave behind. *Political Psychology, 29,* 807–840.

Carter, L. F. (1971). Inadvertent sociological theory. *Social Focus, 50,* 12–25.

Caspi, A., Begg, D., Dickson, N., Harrington, H., Langley, J., Moffitt, T. E., & Silva, P. A. (1997). Personality differences predict health-risk behaviors in young adulthood: Evidence from a longitudinal study. *Journal of Personality and Social Psychology, 73,* 1052–1063.

Chassin, L., Pitts, S. C., & DeLucia, C. (1999). The relation of adolescent substance use to young adult autonomy, positive activity involvement, and perceived competence. *Development and Psychopathology, 11,* 915–932.

Chein, I., Cook, S. W., & Harding, J. (1948). The field of action research. *American Psychologist, 3*(2), 43–50.

Chen, H.-T., & Rossi, P. H. (1999). *Theory-driven evaluation.* Newbury Park, CA: Sage.

Cherlin, A., & Walters, P. B. (1981). Trends in United States men's and women's sex-role attitudes: 1972 to 1978. *American Sociological Review, 46,* 453–460.

Cheung, C. S., & Pomerantz, E. M. (2012). Why does parents' involvement enhance children's achievement? The role of parent-oriented motivation. *Journal of Educational Psychology, 104,* 820–832.

Cheung, F. M. (2012). Mainstreaming culture in psychology. *American Psychologist, 67,* 721–730.

Cheung, F. M., van de Vijver, F. J. R., & Leong, F. T. L. (2011). Toward a new approach to the study of personality and culture. *American Psychologist, 66,* 593–603.

Chiao, J. Y., & Cheon, B. K. (2010). The weirdest brains in the world. *Behavioral and Brain Sciences, 33,* 88–90.

Christensen, L. (1988). Deception in psychological research: When is its use justified? *Personality and Social Psychology Bulletin, 48,* 252–253.

Cialdini, R. B. (2001). *Influence: Science and practice.* Boston, MA: Allyn & Bacon.

Cialdini, R. B., & Baumann, D. J. (1981). Littering: A new unobtrusive measure of attitude. *Social Psychology Quarterly, 44,* 254–259.

Cicirelli, V., & Granger, R. (1969, June). *The impact of Head Start: An evaluation of the effects of Head Start on children's cognitive and affective development.* A report presented to the Office of Economic Opportunity pursuant to Contract B89-4536. Westinghouse Learning Corporation, Ohio University. (Distributed by Clearinghouse for Federal Scientific and Technical Information, U.S. Department of Commerce, National Bureau of Standards, Institute for Applied Technology. PB 184-328.)

Clark, K. B., Chein, I., & Cook, S. W. (2004). The effects of segregation and the consequences of desegregation: A (September 1952) Social Science Statement in the *Brown v. Board of Education of Topeka* Supreme Court Case. *American Psychologist, 59,* 495–501.

Cohen, J. (1960). A coefficient of agreement for nominal scales. *Educational and Psychological Measurement, 20,* 37–46.

Cohen, J. (1977). *Statistical power analysis for the behavioral sciences.* New York, NY: Academic Press.

Conger, R. D., Cui, M., Bryant, C. M., & Elder, G. H., Jr. (2000). Competence in early adult romantic relationships: A developmental perspective on family influences. *Journal of Personality and Social Psychology, 79,* 224–237.

Conti, R. (2001). Time flies: Investigating the connection between intrinsic motivation and the experience of time. *Journal of Personality, 69,* 1–26.

Cooper, H. M. (1984). *The integrative research review: A social science approach.* Thousand Oaks, CA: Sage.

Cooper, H. M., & Rosenthal, R. (1980). Statistical versus traditional procedures for summarizing research findings. *Psychological Bulletin, 87,* 442–449.

Cooper, W. H. (1981). Ubiquitous halo. *Psychological Bulletin, 90,* 218–244.

Correll, J., Park, B., Judd, C. M., Wittenbrink, B., Sadler, M. S., & Keesee, T. (2007). Across the thin blue line: Police officers and racial bias in the decision to shoot. *Journal of Personality and Social Psychology, 92,* 1006–1023.

Crawford, J. R., & Henry, J. D. (2004). The Positive and Negative Affect Schedule (PANAS): Construct validity, measurement properties and normative data in a large non-clinical sample. *British Journal of Clinical Psychology, 43,* 245–265.

Cressey, D. R. (1953). *Other people's money: A study in the social psychology of embezzlement.* New York, NY: Free Press.

Creswell, J. W., & Plano Clark, V. L. (2011). *Designing and conducting mixed methods research* (2nd ed.). Thousand Oaks, CA: Sage.

Cromer, A. H. (1993). *Uncommon sense: The heretical nature of science.* New York, NY: Oxford University Press.

Cronbach, L. J. (1951). Coefficient alpha and the internal structure of tests. *Psychometrika, 16,* 297–334.

Cronbach, L. J., & Meehl, P. E. (1955). Construct validity in psychological tests. *Psychological Bulletin, 52,* 281–302.

Crowne, D. P., & Marlowe, D. (1960). A new scale of social desirability independent of psychopathology, *Journal of Consulting Psychology*, *24*, 349–354.

Darley, J. M., & Latané, B. (1968). Bystander intervention in emergencies: Diffusion of responsibility. *Journal of Personality and Social Psychology*, *8*, 377–383.

Davis, J. A., & Smith, T. W. (1992). *The NORC General Social Survey: A user's guide*. Thousand Oaks, CA: Sage.

Dawes, R. M. (1972). *Fundamentals of attitude measurement*. New York, NY: John Wiley & Sons.

Dawes, R. M. (1977). Suppose we measured height with rating scales instead of rulers. *Applied Psychological Measurement*, *1*, 267–273.

Dawes, R. M., & Smith, T. L. (1985). Attitude and opinion measurement. In O. Lindzey & E. Aronson (Eds.), *Handbook of social psychology* (3rd ed., pp. 509–566). New York, NY: Random House.

de Jong, M. G., Pieters, R., & Stremersch, S. (2012). Analysis of questions across cultures: An application of multigroups item randomized response theory to sexual attitudes and behavior. *Journal of Personality and Social Psychology*, *103*, 543–564.

Dempsey, J., Riley, J., Ryan, C. S., & Kelly-Vance, L. (in press). Evaluation of a summer reading program to reduce summer setback. *Reading and Writing Quarterly: Overcoming Learning Difficulties*.

Denrell, J. (2005). Why most people disapprove of me: Experience sampling in impression formation. *Psychological Review*, *112*, 951–978.

DeSantis, A. S., Adam, E. K., Doane, L. D., Mineka, S., Zinbarg, R. E., & Craske, M. G. (2007). Racial/ethnic differences in cortisol diurnal rhythms in a community sample of adolescents. *Journal of Adolescent Health*, *41*, 3–13.

Devine, P. G., Forscher, P. S., Austin, A. J., & Cox, W. T. L. (2012). Long-term reduction in implicit bias: A prejudice habit-breaking intervention. *Journal of Experimental Social Psychology*, *48*, 1267–1278.

Dillman, D. A. (1972). Increasing mail questionnaire response in large samples of the general public. *Public Opinion Quarterly*, *36*, 254–257.

Dillman, D. A. (1978). *Mail and telephone surveys: The total design method*. New York, NY: John Wiley & Sons.

Dillman, D. A., Phelps, G., Tortora, R., Swift, K., Kohrell, J., & Berck, J. (2001). *Response rate and measurement differences in mixed mode surveys using mail, telephone, interactive voice response and the Internet*. Retrieved March 15, 2014, from http://www.sesrc.wsu.edu/dillman/papers/2001/responserateandmeasurement.pdf

Dillman, D. A., Smyth, J. D., & Christian, L. M. (2009). *Internet, mail, and mixed-mode surveys: The tailored design method* (3rd ed.). Hoboken, NJ: John Wiley & Sons.

Dipboye, R. L., & Flanagan, M. F. (1979). Research settings in industrial and organizational psychology: Are findings in the field more generalizable than in the laboratory? *American Psychologist*, *34*(2), 141–150.

Dollinger, S. J., Preston, L. A., O'Brien, S. P., & DiLalla, D. L. (1996). Individuality and relatedness of the self: An autophotographic study. *Journal of Personality and Social Psychology*, *71*, 1268–1278.

Duncan, S., & Rosenthal, R. (1968). Vocal emphasis in experimenters' instruction reading as unintended determinant of subjects' responses. *Language and Speech*, *11*, part 1, 20–26.

Durand, J. (1960). Mortality estimates from Roman tombstone inscriptions. *American Journal of Sociology*, *65*, 365–373.

Durkheim, E. (1951). *Suicide* (J. A. Spaulding & G. Simpson, Trans.). New York, NY: Free Press. (Original work published 1897.)

Economic Report of the President. (1964, January). Annual Report of the Council of Economic Advisers, transmitted to the Congress. Washington, DC: U.S. Government Printing Office.

Endler, N. S., Macrodimitris, S. D., & Kocovski, N. L. (2000). Controllability in cognitive and interpersonal tasks: Is control good for you? *Personality and Individual Differences, 29,* 951–962.

Epley, N., & Huff, C. (1998). Suspicion, affective response, and educational benefit as a result of deception in psychology research. *Personality and Social Psychology Bulletin, 24,* 759–768.

Ericsson, K. A., & Simon, H. A. (1984). *Protocol analysis: Verbal reports as data.* Cambridge, MA: MIT Press.

Esquivel, S. L., Ryan, C. S., & Bonner, M. (2008). Involved parents' perceptions of their experiences in school-based team meetings. *Journal of Educational and Psychological Consultation, 18,* 234–258.

Eysenck, J. J. (1978). An exercise in mega-silliness. *American Psychologist, 33,* 5–17.

Fals Borda, O. (2001). Participatory (action) research in social theory: Origins and challenges. In P. Reason & H. Bradbury (Eds.), *Handbook of action research: Participative inquiry and practice* (pp. 27–37). London, England: Sage.

Fan, X., & Nowell, D. (2011). Using propensity score matching in educational research. *Gifted Child Quarterly, 55,* 74–79.

Farrar, E., & House, E. R. (1986). The evaluation of PUSH/Excel: A case study. In E. R. House (Ed.), *New directions in educational evaluations* (pp. 158–185). London, England: Palmer Press.

Farver, J. M., & Howes, C. (1993). Cultural differences in American and Mexican mother–child pretend play. *Merrill Palmer Quarterly, 39,* 344–358.

Fazio, R. H., Powell, M. C., & Herr, P. M. (1983). Toward a process model of the attitude–behavior relation: Accessing one's attitude upon mere observation of the attitude object. *Journal of Personality and Social Psychology, 44,* 723–735.

Fazio, R. H., & Williams, C. (1986). Attitude accessibility as a moderator of the attitude–perception and attitude–behavior relations: An investigation of the 1984 presidential election. *Journal of Personality and Social Psychology, 51,* 505–514.

Festinger, L. A. (1954). A theory of social comparison processes. *Human Relations, 7,* 117–140.

Festinger, L. A. (1957). *A theory of cognitive dissonance.* Stanford, CA: Stanford University Press.

Festinger, L., & Carlsmith, J. N. (1959). Cognitive consequences of forced compliance. *Journal of Abnormal and Social Psychology, 58,* 203–210.

Festinger, L., Riecken, H. W., & Schachter, S. (1956). *When prophecy fails.* Minneapolis, MN: University of Minnesota Press.

Festinger, L., Schachter, S., & Back, K. (1950). *Social pressures in informal groups: A study of human factors in housing.* New York, NY: Harper.

Fielding, J., & Fielding, N. (2008). Synergy and synthesis: Integrating qualitative and quantitative data. In P. Alasuutari, L. Bickman, & J. Brannen (Eds.), *The Sage handbook of social research methods* (pp. 555–571). London, England: Sage.

Fine, M. Torre, M. E., Boudin, K., Bowen, I., Clark, J., Hylton, D., . . . Upegui, D. (2001). Changing minds: The impact of college in a maximum security prison. Retrieved February 6, 2013, from http://web.gc.cuny.edu/che/changingminds.html

Flanders, N. A. (1970). *Analyzing teaching behavior.* Reading, MA: Addison-Wesley.

Fogg, L. F., & Rose, R. M. (1999). Use of personal characteristics in the selection of astronauts. *Human Performance in Extreme Environments, 4,* 27–33.

Frank, G., Johnston, M., Morrison, V., Pollard, B., & MacWalter, R. (2000). Perceived control and recovery from functional limitations: Preliminary evaluation of a workbook-based intervention for discharged stroke patients. *British Journal of Health Psychology, 5,* 413–420.

Frechtling, J. (2010). *The 2010 user-friendly handbook for project evaluation.* Washington, DC: National Science Foundation.

Frey, J. H., & Oishi, S. M. (1995). *How to conduct interviews by telephone and in person.* Thousand Oaks, CA: Sage.

Fridlund, A. J. (1991). Sociality of solitary smiling: Potentiation by an implicit audience. *Journal of Personality and Social Psychology, 60,* 229–240.

Gable, S. L., & Shean, G. D. (2000). Perceived social competence and depression. *Journal of Social and Personal Relationships, 17,* 139–150.

Gaertner, S. L., & Dovidio, J. F. (2000). *Reducing intergroup bias: The Common Ingroup Identity Model.* Philadelphia, PA: Psychology Press.

Gaertner, S. L., & Dovidio, J. F. (2012). The Common Ingroup Identity Model. In P. A. M. Van Lange, A. W. Kruglanski, & E. T. Higgins (Eds.), *Handbook of theories of social psychology* (Vol. 2, pp. 439–457). Thousand Oaks, CA: Sage.

Garfield, E. (1992, October 12). Psychology research 1986–1990: A citationist perspective on the highest impact papers, institutions and authors. *Current Contents,* pp. 5–15.

Gawronski, B., & De Houwer, J. (2014). Implicit measures in social and personality psychology. In H. T. Reis & C. M. Judd (Eds.), *Handbook of research methods in social and personality psychology* (2nd ed., pp. 283–310). New York, NY: Cambridge University Press.

Gawronski, B., & Payne, K. B. (Eds.). (2010). *Handbook of implicit cognition: Measurement, theory, and applications.* New York, NY: Guilford Press.

Gelsinger, P. (2000). *Jesse's intent.* Retrieved March 15, 2014, from http://www.circare.org/submit/jintent.pdf

Gentile, D. A., & Bushman, B. J. (2012). Reassessing media violence effects using a risk and resilience approach to understanding aggression. *Psychology of Popular Media Culture, 1,* 138–151.

George, W. H., Gilmore, A. K., & Stappenbeck, C. A. (2012). Balanced placebo design: Revolutionary impact on addictions research and theory. *Addiction Research and Theory, 20,* 186–203.

Gilovich, T. (1991). *How we know what isn't so: The fallibility of human reason in everyday life.* New York, NY: Free Press.

Glass, D. C., & Singer, J. E. (1972). *Urban stress: Experiments on noise and social stressors.* New York, NY: Academic Press.

Glass, G. V. (1978). In defense of generalization. *Behavioral and Brain Sciences, 3,* 394–395.

Glick, P., Fiske, S. T., Mladinic, A., Saiz, J. L., Abrams, D., Masser, B., … Lopez, W. L. (2000). Beyond prejudice as simple antipathy: Hostile and benevolent sexism across cultures. *Journal of Personality and Social Psychology, 79,* 763–774.

Goffman, E. (1963). *Stigma.* Upper Saddle River, NJ: Prentice Hall.

Goldstein, N. J., Cialdini, R. B., & Griskevicius, V. (2008). A room with a viewpoint: Using social norms to motivate environmental conservation in hotels. *Journal of Consumer Research, 35,* 472–482.

Gordon, R. A. (1968). Issues in multiple regression. *American Journal of Sociology, 73,* 592–616.

Gosling, S. D., Craik, K. H., Martin, N. R., & Pryor, M. R. (2005). The Personal Living Space Cue Inventory: An analysis and evaluation. *Environment and Behavior, 37,* 683–705.

Graber, D. (1971). The press as opinion resource during the 1968 presidential campaign. *Public Opinion Quarterly, 35,* 168–182.

Graham, J., Nosek, B. A., Haidt, J., Iyer, R., Koleva, S., & Ditto, P. H. (2011). Mapping the moral domain. *Journal of Personality and Social Psychology, 101,* 366–385.

Graham, J. M. (2008). Self-expansion and flow in couples' momentary experiences: An experience sampling study. *Journal of Personality and Social Psychology, 95,* 679–694.

Gray-Little, B., & Hafdahl, A. R. (2000). Factors influencing racial comparisons of self-esteem: A quantitative review. *Psychological Bulletin, 126,* 26–54.

Greenberg, B. S., & Brand, J. E. (1993). Cultural diversity on Saturday morning television. In G. L. Berry & J. K. Asamen (Eds.), *Children and television: Images in a changing sociocultural world* (pp. 132–142). Thousand Oaks, CA: Sage.

Greene, J., Caracelli, V., & Graham, W. (1989). Toward a conceptual framework for mixed-method evaluation design. *Educational Evaluation and Policy Analysis, 11,* 255–274.

Greene, J. C. (2007). *Mixed methods in social inquiry.* San Francisco, CA: Jossey-Bass.

Greeno, J. G. (1994). Gibson's affordances. *Psychological Review, 101,* 336–342.

Greeno, J. G. (1998). The situativity of knowing, learning, and research. *American Psychologist, 53,* 5–26.

Greenwald, A. G., McGhee, D. E., & Schwartz, J. L. K. (1998). Measuring individual differences in implicit cognition: The Implicit Association Test. *Journal of Personality and Social Psychology, 74,* 1464–1480.

Greenwald, A. G., Poehlman, T. A., Uhlmann, E. L., & Banaji, M. R. (2009). Understanding and using the Implicit Association Test: III. Meta-analysis of predictive validity. *Journal of Personality and Social Psychology, 97,* 17–41.

Groves, R. M. (1987). Research on survey data quality. *Public Opinion Quarterly, 51,* S156–S172.

Groves, R. M., & Kahn, R. L. (1979). *Surveys by telephone.* New York, NY: Academic Press.

Gutek, B. A. (1978). Strategies for studying client satisfaction. *Journal of Social Issues, 34*(4), 44–56.

Guttman, L. (1944). A basis for scaling quantitative data. *American Sociological Review, 9,* 139–150.

Hall, J. A., Carter, J. D., & Horgan, T. G. (2000). Gender differences in nonverbal communication of emotion. In A. H. Fischer (Ed.), *Gender and emotion: Social psychological perspectives* (pp. 97–117). New York, NY: Cambridge University Press.

Hall, S., & Oliver, C. (1997). A graphical method to aid in the sequential analysis of observational data. *Behavior Research Methods: Instruments and Computers, 29,* 563–573.

Hammersley, M., & Atkinson, P. (1995). *Ethnography: Principles in practice* (2nd ed.). London, England: Routledge.

Hannah, S. T., Balthazard, P. A., Waldman, D. A., Jennings, P. L., & Thatcher, R. W. (2013). The psychological and neurological bases of leader self-complexity and effects on adaptive decision-making. *Journal of Applied Psychology, 98,* 393–411.

Harkavy, I., & Puckett, J. L. (1994). Lessons from Hull House for the contemporary urban university. *Social Service Review, 68*(3), 299–321.

Harlow, H. F. (1958). The nature of love. *American Psychologist, 13,* 673–685.

Harmon-Jones, E., & Sigelman, J. (2001). State anger and prefrontal brain activity: Evidence that insult-related relative left-prefrontal activation is associated with experienced anger and aggression. *Journal of Personality and Social Psychology, 80,* 797–803.

Harris, M. J. (1991). Controversy and cumulation: Meta-analysis and research on interpersonal expectancy effects. *Personality and Social Psychology Bulletin, 17,* 316–322.

Harris, M. J., Milich, R., Corbitt, E. M., Hoover, D. W., & Brady, M. (1992). Self-fulfilling effects of stigmatizing information on children's social interactions. *Journal of Personality and Social Psychology, 63,* 41–50.

Hastie, R., & Stasser, G. (2000). Computer simulation methods for social psychology. In H. T. Reis & C. M. Judd (Eds.), *Handbook of research methods in social psychology* (pp. 85–114). New York, NY: Cambridge University Press.

Heckathorn, D. D. (1997). Respondent-driven sampling: A new approach to the study of hidden populations. *Social Problems, 44,* 174–199.

Heckman, J. J., Moon, S. H., Pinto, R., Savelyev, P. A., & Yavitz, A. (2010). The rate of return to the High Score Perry Preschool Program. *Journal of Public Economics, 94*(1–2), 114–128.

Hedderman, C. (1994). Decision-making in court: Observing the sentencing of men and women. *Psychology, Crime, and Law, 1,* 165–173.

Hedges, L. V., & Olkin, I. (1985). *Statistical methods for meta-analysis*. Orlando, FL: Academic Press.

Heerwegh, D. (2005). Effects of personal salutations in e-mail invitations to participate in a web survey, *Public Opinion Quarterly, 69*, 588–598.

Heider, F. (1958). *The psychology of interpersonal relations*. New York, NY: John Wiley & Sons.

Henrich, J., Heine, S. J., & Norenzayan, A. (2010). The weirdest people in the world? *Brain and Behavioral Science, 33*, 61–83.

Hillard, A. L., Ryan, C. S., & Gervais, S. J. (2013). Reactions to the Implicit Association Test as an educational tool: A mixed methods study. *Social Psychology of Education, 16*, 495–516.

Hirt, E. R. (1990). Do I see only what I expect? Evidence for an expectancy-guided retrieval model. *Journal of Personality and Social Psychology, 58*, 937–951.

Hofmann, W., Baumeister, R. F., Förster, G., & Vohs, K. D. (2012). Everyday temptations: An experience sampling study of desire, conflict, and self control. *Journal of Personality and Social Psychology, 102*, 1318–1335.

Holbrook, A. L., Green, M. C., & Krosnick, J. A. (2003). Telephone versus face-to-face interviewing of national probability samples with long questionnaires. *Public Opinion Quarterly, 67*, 79–125.

Holsti, O. R. (1969). *Content analysis for the social sciences and humanities*. Reading, MA: Addison-Wesley.

Horner, R. H., Carr, E. G., Halle, J., Odom, S., & Wolery, M. (2005). The use of single subject research to identify evidence-based practice in special education. *Exceptional Children, 71*(2), 165–179.

Hoyle, R. H. (1993). On the relation between data and theory [Comment]. *American Psychologist, 48*, 1094–1096.

Hughes, C., Rodi, M. S., Lorden, S. W., Pitkin, S. E., Derer, K. R., Hwang, B., & Cai, X. (1999). Social interactions of high school students with mental retardation and their general education peers. *American Journal on Mental Retardation, 104*, 533–544.

Humphreys, L. (1970). *Tearoom trade: Impersonal sex in public places*. Chicago, IL: Aldine-Atherton.

Hunt, M. (1999). *The new Know-Nothings: The political foes of the scientific study of human nature*. New Brunswick, NJ: Transaction Publishers.

Hyman, R. (1995). How to critique a published article. *Psychological Bulletin, 118*, 178–182.

Isen, A. M. (1984). Toward understanding the role of affect in cognition. In R. S. Wyer & T. K. Srull (Eds.), *Handbook of social cognition* (Vol. 3, pp. 179–236). Hillsdale, NJ: Lawrence Erlbaum Associates.

Isen, A. M., & Levin, P. F. (1972). Effect of feeling good on helping: Cookies and kindness. *Journal of Personality and Social Psychology, 21*, 384–388.

Jahoda, M., Deutsch, M., & Cook, S. W. (1951). *Research methods in social relations with special reference to prejudice, Vol. 1: Basic processes*. Fort Worth, TX: Dryden Press.

Janis, I. L. (1997). Groupthink. In R. P. Vecchio (Ed.), *Leadership: Understanding the dynamics of power and influence in organizations* (pp. 163–176). Notre Dame, IN: University of Notre Dame Press.

John, O. P., & Benet-Martínez, V. (2014). Measurement: Reliability, construct validation, and scale construction. In H. T. Reis & C. M. Judd (Eds.), *Handbook of research methods in social and personality psychology* (2nd ed., pp. 473–503). New York, NY: Cambridge University Press.

Johnson, D. W., & Johnson, R. (1989). *Cooperation and competition: Theory and research*. Edina, MN: Interaction Book Company.

Johnson, D. W., & Johnson, R. (2005). New developments in social interdependence theory. *Psychology Monographs, 131*, 285–358.

Johnson, D. W., Maruyama, G., Johnson, R., Nelson, D., & Skon, L. (1981). The effects of cooperative, competitive, and individualistic goal structures on achievement: A meta-analysis. *Psychological Bulletin, 89,* 47–62.

Johnson, T., Kulesa, P., Cho, Y. I., & Shavitt, S. (2005). The relation between culture and response styles: Evidence from 19 countries. *Journal of Cross-Cultural Psychology, 36,* 264–277.

Johnson, T., & van de Vijver, F. J. (2002). Social desirability in cross-cultural research. In J. Harness, F. J. van de Vijver, & Mohler, P. (Eds.), *Cross-cultural survey methods* (pp. 193–202). New York, NY: John Wiley & Sons.

Joinson, A. N., & Reips, U. (2007). Personalized salutation, power of sender, and response rates to web-based surveys. *Computers in Human Behavior, 23,* 1372–1383.

Joint Committee on Standards for Educational Evaluation. (1994). *The program evaluation standards.* Thousand Oaks, CA: Sage.

Judd, C. M., & Kenny, D. A. (1981). *Estimating the effects of social interventions.* New York, NY: Cambridge University Press.

Judd, C. M., McClelland, G. H., & Ryan, C. S. (2009). *Data analysis: A model comparison approach* (2nd ed.). New York, NY: Routledge.

Kania, J., & Kramer, M. (2011). Collective impact. *Stanford Social Innovation Review (Winter),* 35–41.

Kaplan, J. (1988). The use of animals in research. *Science, 242,* 839–840.

Karpicke, J. D., & Roediger, H. L., III. (2008). The critical importance of retrieval for learning. *Science, 319,* 966–968.

Kasarda, J. D. (1976). The use of census data in secondary analysis: The context of ecological discovery. In M. P. Golden (Ed.), *The research experience.* Itasca, IL: Peacock.

Kawakami, K., Dovidio, J. F., Moll, J., Hermsen, S., & Russin, A. (2000). Just say no (to stereotyping): Effects of training in the negation of stereotypic associations on stereotypic activation. *Journal of Personality and Social Psychology, 78,* 871–888.

Kazdin, A. E. (1982). *Single-case research designs: Methods for clinical and applied settings.* New York, NY: Oxford University Press.

Kazdin, A. E. (1998). *Research design in clinical psychology* (3rd ed.). Boston, MA: Allyn & Bacon.

Kelman, H. C. (1968). *A time to speak: On human values and social research.* San Francisco, CA: Jossey-Bass.

Kennedy, C. H. (2004). *Single case designs for educational research.* Boston, MA: Allyn & Bacon.

Kenny, D. (1976). An empirical application of confirmatory factor analysis to the multitrait–multimethod matrix. *Journal of Experimental Social Psychology, 12,* 247–252.

Kenny, D. A., & Berman, J. S. (1980). Statistical approaches for the correction of correlational bias. *Psychological Bulletin, 88,* 288–295.

Kenny, D. A., & Kashy, D. A. (1992). Analysis of the multitrait–multimethod matrix by confirmatory factor analysis. *Psychological Bulletin, 112,* 165–172.

Kidder, L. H., & Cohn, E. S. (1979). Public views of crime and crime prevention. In I. H. Frieze, D. Bar-Tal, & J. S. Carroll (Eds.), *New approaches to social problems: Applications of attribution theory.* San Francisco, CA: Jossey-Bass.

Kidman, L., McKenzie, A., & McKenzie, B. (1999). The nature and target of parents' comments during youth sport competitions. *Journal of Sport Behavior, 22,* 54–68.

King, L. A., Scollon, C. K., Ramsey, C., & Williams, T. (2000). Stories of life transition: Subjective well-being and ego development in parents of children with Down Syndrome. *Journal of Research in Personality, 34,* 509–536.

Kline, P. (1994). *An easy guide to factor analysis.* London, England: Routledge.

Kline, R. B. (2011). *Principles and practice for structural equation modeling* (3rd ed.). New York, NY: Guilford Press.

Kluegel, J. R., & Smith, E. R. (1982). Whites' beliefs about Blacks' opportunity. *American Sociological Review, 47*, 518–532.

Kogan, S. M., Wejnert, C., Chen, Y., Brody, G. H., & Slater, L. M. (2011). Respondent-driven sampling with hard-to-reach emerging adults: An introduction and case study with rural African Americans. *Journal of Adolescent Research, 26*, 30–60.

Koslowski, M., Pratt, G. L., & Wintrob, R. N. (1976). The application of Guttman scale analysis to physicians' attitudes regarding abortion. *Journal of Applied Psychology, 61*, 301–304.

Kratochwill, T., & Levin, J. R. (1992). *Single-case research design and analysis: New directions for psychology and education.* Hillsdale, NJ: Lawrence Erlbaum Associates.

Kratochwill, T. R., & Levin, J. R. (2010). Enhancing the scientific credibility of single-case intervention research: Randomization to the rescue. *Psychological Methods, 15*(2), 124–144.

Kraut, R. E., & Johnston, R. E. (1979). Social and emotional messages of smiling: An ethological approach. *Journal of Personality and Social Psychology, 37*, 1539–1553.

Krosnick, J. A., Lavrakas, P. J., & Kim, N. (2014). Survey research. In H. T. Reis & C. M. Judd (Eds.), *Handbook of research methods in social and personality psychology* (2nd ed., pp. 404–442). New York, NY: Cambridge University Press.

Langhout, R. D. (2014). Photovoice as a methodology. In X. Castañeda, A. Rodriguez-Lainz, & M. B. Schenker (Eds.), *Migration and health research methodologies: A handbook for the study of migrant populations.* Berkeley, CA: UC Press.

Langlois, J. H., Kalakanis, L., Rubenstein, A. J., Larson, A., Hallam, M., & Smoot, M. (2000). Maxims or myths of beauty? A meta-analytic and theoretical review. *Psychological Bulletin, 126*, 390–423.

Latané, B., & Nida, S. (1981). Ten years of research on group size and helping. *Psychological Bulletin, 89*, 308–324.

Lavine, H., Borgida, E., & Sullivan, J. L. (2000). On the relationship between attitude involvement and attitude accessibility: Toward a cognitive-motivational model of political information processing. *Political Psychology, 21*, 81–106.

Lee, H. B. (2008). Using the Chow test to analyze regression discontinuities. *Tutorials in Quantitative Methods for Psychology, 4*(2), 46–50.

Lee, T. W., & Maurer, S. D. (1999). The effects of family structure on organizational commitment, intention to leave, and voluntary turnover. *Journal of Managerial Issues, 11*, 493–513.

Lelkes, Y., Krosnick, J. A., Marx, D. M., Judd, C. M., & Park, B. (2012). Complete anonymity compromises the accuracy of self-reports. *Journal of Experimental Social Psychology, 48*, 1291–1299.

Lepkowski, J. M., Tucker, C., Brick, J. M., de Leeuw, E. D., Japec, L., Lavrakas, P. J., … Sangster, R. L. (2008). *Advances in telephone survey methodology.* Hoboken, NJ: John Wiley & Sons.

Leventhal, T., & Brooks-Gunn, J. (2000). The neighborhoods they live in: The effects of neighborhood residence on child and adolescent outcomes. *Psychological Bulletin, 126*, 309–377.

Levin, H. M. (1978). A decade of policy developments in improving education and training for low-income populations. In T. D. Cook (Ed.), *Evaluation studies review annual* (pp. 521–570). Thousand Oaks, CA: Sage.

Lewin, K. (1946). Action research and minority problems. *Journal of Social Issues, 2*, 34–46. Reprinted as Ch. 13 in Lewin (1948), pp. 201–216.

Lewin, K. (1948). *Resolving social conflicts.* New York, NY: Harper.

Lewin, K. (1951). *Field theory in social science.* New York, NY: Harper & Row.

Lewis, S. (1925). *Arrowsmith.* New York, NY: Harcourt Brace.

Likert, R. (1932). A technique for the measurement of attitudes. *Archives of Psychology, 140*.

Lincoln, Y. S., & Guba, E. G. (1985). *Naturalistic inquiry.* Newbury Park, CA: Sage.

Linville, P. W. (1987). Self-complexity as a cognitive buffer against stress-related illness and depression. *Journal of Personality and Social Psychology, 52*, 663–676.

Locke, E. A., & Latham, G. P. (2006). New directions in goal-setting theory. *Current Directions in Psychological Science, 15*, 265–268.

Lucker, G. W., Rosenfield, D., Sikes, J., & Aronson, E. (1977). Performance in the interdependent classroom: A field study. *American Educational Research Journal, 13*, 115–123.

Lusk, B. (1999). Patients' images in nursing magazine advertisements. *Advances in Nursing Science, 21*, 66–75.

Lyman-Henley, L. P., & Henley, T. B. (2000). Some thoughts on the relationship between behaviorism, comparative psychology, and ethology. *Anthrozoos, 13*, 15–21.

Mackenzie, N., & Knipe, S. (2006). Research dilemmas: Paradigms, methods, and methodology. *Issues in Educational Research, 16*(2), 193–205.

Marsaglia, G. (1984). *A current view of random number generators.* Paper presented at the 16th Symposium on the Interface between Computer Science and Statistics, Atlanta, GA.

Martyna, W. (1978). What does "he" mean? *Journal of Communication, 28*, 131–138.

Maruyama, G. (1997). Academics and action in research universities of the 21st century. *Journal of Public Management and Social Policy, 3*(1), 20–28.

Maruyama, G. (1998). *Basics of structural equation modeling.* Thousand Oaks, CA: Sage.

Maruyama, G. (2004). Program evaluation, action research, and social psychology: A powerful blend for addressing applied problems. In C. Sansone, C. C. Morf, & A. T. Panter (Eds.), *The Sage handbook of methods in social psychology* (pp. 429–442). Thousand Oaks, CA: Sage.

Maruyama, G., Jones, R. J., & Finnegan, J. R. (2009). Advancing an urban agenda: Principles and experiences of an urban land grant university. *Metropolitan Universities, 20*(1), 75–100.

Maruyama, G., Miller, N., & Holtz, R. (1986). The relation between popularity and achievement: A longitudinal test of the lateral transmission of values hypothesis. *Journal of Personality and Social Psychology, 51*, 730–741.

Maruyama, G., & Van Boekel, M. (2014). Action research. In Dana S. Dunn (Ed.), *Oxford bibliographies in psychology.* New York, NY: Oxford University Press.

Maslow, A. H. (1966). *The psychology of science: A reconnaissance.* New York, NY: Harper & Row.

Masters, J. R. (1974). The relationship between number of response categories and reliability of Likert-type questionnaires. *Journal of Educational Measurement, 11*, 49–53.

Matt, G. E. (1989). Decision rules for selecting effect sizes in meta-analysis: A review and reanalysis of psychotherapy outcome studies. *Psychological Bulletin, 105*, 106–115.

Maxwell, S. E., & Cole, D. A. (1995). Tips for writing (and reading) methodological articles. *Psychological Bulletin, 118*, 193–198.

McCall, R. B., Ryan, C. S., & Plemons, B. W. (2003). Some lessons learned on evaluating community-based two-generation service programs: The case of the Comprehensive Child Development Program (CCDP). *Journal of Applied Developmental Psychology, 24*, 125–141.

McCord, J. (1978). A thirty-year followup of treatment effects. *American Psychologist, 33*, 284–289.

McDill, E. L., McDill, M. S., & Sprehe, J. T. (1969). *Strategies for success in compensatory education: An appraisal of evaluation research.* Baltimore, MD: Johns Hopkins University Press.

McDowell, D. J., & Parke, R. D. (2009). Parental correlates of children's peer relations: An empirical test of a tripartite model. *Developmental Psychology, 45*, 224–235.

McGee, M. G., & Snyder, M. (1975). Attribution and behavior: Two field studies. *Journal of Personality and Social Psychology, 32*, 185–190.

McKenna, K. Y. A., & Bargh, J. A. (1998). Coming out in the age of the Internet: Identity "demarginalization" through virtual group participation. *Journal of Personality and Social Psychology, 75*, 681–694.

McTaggart, R. (1991). Principles for participatory action research. *Adult Education Quarterly, 41*, 168–187.

Meehl, P. E. (1978). Theoretical risks and tabular asterisks: Sir Karl, Sir Ronald, and the slow progress of soft psychology. *Journal of Consulting and Clinical Psychology, 46*, 806–834.

Milgram, S. (1963). Behavioral study of obedience. *Journal of Abnormal and Social Psychology, 67*(4), 371–378.

Milgram, S. (1974). *Obedience to authority: An experimental view.* New York, NY: Harper & Row.

Miller, C. T., & Downey, K. T. (1999). A meta-analysis of heavyweight and self-esteem. *Personality and Social Psychology Review, 3*, 68–84.

Minkler, M., & Wallerstein, N. (Eds.). (2008). *Community-based participatory research for health: From process to outcomes.* San Francisco, CA: Jossey-Bass.

Mohr, C. D., Armeli, S., Tennen, H., Carney, M. A., Affleck, G., & Hromi, A. (2001). Daily interpersonal experiences, context, and alcohol consumption: Crying in your beer and toasting good times. *Journal of Personality and Social Psychology, 80*, 489–500.

Mook, D. G. (1983). In defense of external invalidity. *American Psychologist, 38*, 379–387.

Mosler, H., Schwarz, K., Ammann, F., & Gutscher, H. (2001). Computer simulation as a method of further developing a theory: Simulating the Elaboration Likelihood Model. *Personality and Social Psychology Review, 5*, 201–215.

Murphy, N. A. (2005). Using thin slices for behavioral coding. *Journal of Nonverbal Behavior, 29*, 235–246.

National Institutes of Health Office of Behavioral and Social Sciences Research. (2011, July 1). Community-based participatory research. Retrieved March 6, 2014, from http://obssr .od.nih.gov/scientific_areas/methodology/community_based_participatory_research/ index.aspx

Neal, J. (2013a, August 10). Bryan Cranston and "Breaking Bad" get ready for the end. *Star Tribune,* pp. E1, E14. Retrieved August 14, 2013, from http://www.startribune.com/ entertainment/tv/218927041.html

Neal, J. (2013b, August 10). From Perry Mason to Tony Soprano: The de-evolution of the TV hero. *Star Tribune,* p. E14. Retrieved August 14, 2013, from http://www.startribune.com/ entertainment/tv/218927121.html

Newell, A., & Simon, H. A. (1961). Computer simulation of human thinking. *Science, 134*, 2011–2017.

Newton, P. E., & Shaw, S. D. (2013). Standards for talking and thinking about validity. *Psychological Methods, 18*, 301–310.

Nisbett, R. E., & Wilson, T. D. (1977). Telling more than we can know: Verbal reports on mental processes. *Psychological Review, 84*, 231–259.

Norman, G. (2010). Likert scales, levels of measurement and the "laws" of statistics. *Advances in Health Sciences Education, 15*, 625–632.

Norton, M. I., Sommers, S. R., Apfelbaum, E. P., Pura, N., & Ariely, D. (2006). Color blindness and interracial interaction: Playing the Political Correctness game. *Psychological Science, 17*, 949–953.

Nosek, B. A., Greenwald, A. G., & Banaji, M. R. (2005). Understanding and using the Implicit Association Test: II. Method variables and construct validity. *Personality and Social Psychology Bulletin, 31*, 166–180.

Nunnally, J. C., & Bernstein, I. H. (1994). *Psychometric theory* (3rd ed.). New York, NY: McGraw-Hill.

Olsen, R. B., Orr, L. L., Bell, S. H., & Stuart, E. A. (2013). External validity in policy evaluations that choose sites purposively. *Journal of Policy Analysis and Management, 32*, 107–121.

Olson, K., & Peytchev, A. (2007). Effect of interviewer experience on interview pace and interviewer attitudes. *Public Opinion Quarterly, 71*, 273–286.

Omoto, A. M., & Snyder, M. (1995). Sustained helping without obligation: Motivation, longevity of service, and perceived attitude change among AIDS volunteers. *Journal of Personality and Social Psychology, 68*, 671–686.

Orne, M. (1962). On the social psychology of the psychological experiment. *American Psychologist, 17*, 776–783.

Orne, M. T. (1969). Demand characteristics and the concept of quasi-controls. In R. Rosenthal & R. L. Rosnow (Eds.), *Artifact in behavioral research* (pp. 143–179). New York, NY: Academic Press.

Osgood, C. E., Suci, C. J., & Tannenbaum, P. H. (1957). *The measurement of meaning*. Urbana, IL: University of Illinois Press.

Osgood, C. E., & Walker, E. G. (1959). Motivation and language behavior: A content analysis of suicide notes. *Journal of Abnormal and Social Psychology, 59*, 58–67.

Oskamp, S. (2007). Applying psychology to help save the world: Reflections on a career in psychology. *Analyses of Social Issues and Public Policy, 7*, 121–136.

Page-Gould, E., Mendoza-Denton, R., & Tropp, L. R. (2008). With a little help from my cross-group friend: Reducing anxiety in intergroup contexts through cross-group friendship. *Journal of Personality and Social Psychology, 95*, 1080–1094.

Palmgreen, P., Donohew, L., Lorch, E. P., Hoyle, R. H., & Stephenson, M. T. (2001). Television campaigns and adolescent marijuana use: Tests of sensation seeking targeting. *American Journal of Public Health, 91*, 292–296.

Park, B., Wolsko, C., & Judd, C. M. (2001). Measurement of subtyping in stereotype change. *Journal of Experimental Social Psychology, 37*, 325–332.

Parker, A. E., Halberstadt, A. G., Dunsmore, J. C., Townley, G., Bryant, A., Thompson, J. A., & Beale, K. S. (2012). "Emotions are a window into one's heart": A qualitative analysis of parental beliefs about children's emotions across three ethnic groups: III. The current study. *Monographs of the Society for Research in Child Development, 77*, 34–42.

Parry, H. J., & Crossley, H. M. (1950). Validity of responses to survey questions. *Public Opinion Quarterly, 14*, 62–80.

Patton, M. Q. (1986). *Utilization-focused evaluation*. Newbury Park, CA: Sage.

Patton, M. Q. (2012). *Essentials of utilization-focused evaluation*. Los Angeles, CA: Sage.

Paulhus, D. L. (1991). Measurement and control of response bias. In J. P. Robinson, P. R. Shaver, & L. S. Wrightsman (Eds.), *Measures of personality and social psychological attitudes* (pp. 17–59). New York, NY: Academic Press.

Paulhus, D. L. (2002). Socially desirable responding: The evolution of a construct. In H. I. Braun, D. N. Jackson, & D. E. Wiley (Eds.), *The role of constructs in psychological and educational measurement* (pp. 49–69). Mahwah, NJ: Lawrence Erlbaum Associates.

Payne, B. K., Krosnick, J. A., Pasek, J., Lelkes, Y., Akhtar, O., & Tompson, T. (2010). Implicit and explicit prejudice in the 2008 American presidential election. *Journal of Experimental Social Psychology, 46*, 367–374.

Pelz, D. C., & Andrews, F. M. (1964). Detecting causal priorities in panel study data. *American Sociological Review, 29*, 836–848.

Pennebaker, J. W., & Francis, M. E. (1996). Cognitive, emotional, and language processes in disclosure: Physical health and adjustment. *Cognition and Emotion, 10*, 601–626.

Perren, S., Ettekal, I., & Ladd, G. (2013). The impact of peer victimization on later maladjustment: Mediating and moderating effects of hostile and self-blaming attributions. *Journal of Child Psychology and Psychiatry, 54*, 46–55.

Perrine, R. M., & Heather, S. (2000). Effects of a picture and even-a-penny-will-help appeals on anonymous donations to charity. *Psychological Reports, 86*, 551–559.

Pettigrew, T. F., & Tropp, L. R. (2006). A meta-analytic test of intergroup contact theory. *Journal of Personality and Social Psychology, 90*, 751–783.

Petty, R. E., Rennier, G. A., & Cacioppo, J. T. (1987). Assertion versus interrogation format in opinion surveys: Questions enhance thoughtful responding. *Public Opinion Quarterly, 51,* 481–494.

Phillips, C. J. C., & Morris, I. D. (2001). A novel operant conditioning test to determine whether dairy cows dislike passageways that are dark or covered with excreta. *Animal Welfare, 10,* 65–72.

Phillips, D. P., Carstensen, L. L., & Paight, D. J. (1989). Effects of mass media news stories on suicide, with new evidence on the role of story content. In D. R. Pfeffer (Ed.), *Suicide among youth: Perspectives on risk and prevention* (pp. 101–116). Washington, DC: American Psychiatric Association.

Ponterotto, J. G. (2005). Qualitative research in counseling psychology: A primer on research paradigms and philosophy of science. *Journal of Counseling Psychology, 52,* 126–136.

Pratto, F., Sidanius, J., & Levin, S. (2006). Social dominance theory and the dynamics of intergroup relations: Taking stock and looking forward. *European Review of Social Psychology, 17,* 271–320.

Pratto, F., Sidanius, J., Stallworth, L. M., & Malle, B. F. (1994). Social dominance orientation: A personality variable predicting social and political attitudes. *Journal of Personality and Social Psychology, 67,* 741–763.

Price, D. (1966). Collaboration in an invisible college. *American Psychologist, 21,* 1011–1018.

Qin, Z., Johnson, D. W., & Johnson, R. (1995). Cooperative versus competitive efforts and problem solving: A meta-analysis. *Review of Educational Research, 65*(2), 129–143.

Quinn, R. P., Gutek, B. A., & Walsh, J. T. (1980). Telephone interviewing: A reappraisal and a field experiment. *Basic and Applied Social Psychology, 1,* 127–153.

Rathje, W. L., & Hughes, W. W. (1975). The garbage project as a nonreactive approach: Garbage in … garbage out? In H. W. Sinaiko & L. A. Broedling (Eds.), *Perspectives on attitude assessment: Surveys and their alternatives.* Washington, DC: Smithsonian Institution.

Reicher, S. D., Haslam, S. A., & Miller, A. G. (Issue Eds.). (2014). Milgram at 50: The enduring relevance of psychology's most famous studies. *Journal of Social Issues, 70*(3).

Reips, U.-D. (2002). Standards for Internet-based experimenting. *Experimental Psychology, 49,* 243–256.

Reynolds, R. A., & Temple, J. A. (1998). Extended early childhood intervention and school achievement: Age thirteen findings from the Chicago Longitudinal Study. *Child Development, 69,* 231–246.

Richeson, J. A., & Shelton, S. J. (2005). Brief report: Thin slices of racial bias. *Journal of Nonverbal Behavior, 29,* 75–86.

Richman, W. L., Kiesler, S., Weisband, S., & Drasgow, F. (1999). A meta-analytic study of social desirability distortion in computer-administered questionnaires, traditional questionnaires, and interview. *Journal of Applied Psychology, 84,* 754–775.

Rind, B., Tromovitch, P., & Bauserman, R. (1998). A meta-analytic examination of assumed properties of child sexual abuse using college samples. *Psychological Bulletin, 124,* 22–53.

Rizzo, T. A., & Corsaro, W. A. (1995). Social support processes in early childhood friendship: A comparative study of ecological congruences in enacted support. *American Journal of Community Psychology, 23,* 389–417.

Rogers, E. M., & Storey, J. D. (1987). Communication campaigns. In C. R. Berger & S. H. Chaffee (Eds.), *Handbook of communication science* (pp. 817–846). Thousand Oaks, CA: Sage.

Rosch, E. (1988). Principles of categorization. In A. M. Collins & E. E. Smith (Eds.), *Readings in cognitive science: A perspective from psychology and artificial intelligence* (pp. 312–322). San Mateo, CA: Kaufman.

Rosenbaum, P., & Rubin, D. (1983). The central role of the propensity score in observational studies for causal effects. *Biometrika, 70,* 41–55.

Rosenthal, R. (1968). Experimenter expectancy and the reassuring nature of the null hypothesis decision procedure. *Psychological Bulletin Monograph Supplement, 70*(6, Pt. 2), 30–47.

Rosenthal, R. (1969). Interpersonal expectations. In R. Rosenthal & R. L. Rosnow (Eds.), *Artifact in behavioral research* (pp. 181–275). New York, NY: Academic Press.

Rosenthal, R. (1976). *Experimenter effects in behavioral research* (Enlarged ed.). New York, NY: John Wiley & Sons.

Rosenthal, R. (1991). *Meta-analytic procedures for social research* (Rev. ed.). Thousand Oaks, CA: Sage.

Rosenthal, R. (1994). Science and ethics in conducting, analyzing, and reporting psychological research. *Psychological Science, 5*, 127–134.

Rosenthal, R. (1995). Writing meta-analytic reviews. *Psychological Bulletin, 118*, 183–192.

Rosenthal, R., & Rosnow, R. L. (Eds.). (1969). *Artifact in behavioral research*. New York, NY: Academic Press.

Rosenthal, R., & Rosnow, R. (1984). Applying Hamlet's question to the ethical conduct of research: A conceptual addendum. *American Psychologist, 39*, 561–563.

Rosenthal, R., & Rosnow, R. L. (2008). *Essentials of behavioral research: Methods and data analysis* (3rd ed.). New York, NY: McGraw-Hill.

Rosenthal, R., & Rubin, D. B. (1978). Interpersonal expectancy effects: The first 345 studies. *Behavioral and Brain Sciences, 3*, 377–386.

Rosenthal, R., & Rubin, D. B. (1986). Meta-analytic procedures for combining studies with multiple effect sizes. *Psychological Bulletin, 99*, 400–406.

Rosnow, R. L., & Rosenthal, R. (1997). *People studying people: Artifacts and ethics in behavioral research*. New York, NY: W. H. Freeman.

Ross, L., Lepper, M. R., & Hubbard, M. (1975). Perseverance in self-perception and social perception: Biased attributional processes in the debriefing paradigm. *Journal of Personality and Social Psychology, 32*, 880–892.

Rozelle, R. M., & Campbell, D. T. (1969). More plausible rival hypotheses in the cross-lagged panel correlation technique. *Psychological Bulletin, 71*, 74–80.

Rubinstein, S., & Caballero, B. (2000). Is Miss America an undernourished role model? *Journal of the American Medical Association, 283*, 1569.

Ryan, C. S., Casas, J. F., Kelly-Vance, L., Ryalls, B. O., & Nero, C. (2010). Parent involvement and views of school success: The role of parents' Latino and White American cultural orientations. *Psychology in the Schools, 47*, 391–405.

Sackett, G. (1978). Measurement in observational research. In G. Sackett (Ed.), *Observing behavior, Vol. 2: Data collection and analysis methods* (pp. 25–42). Baltimore, MD: University Park Press.

Scambler, D. J., Harris, M. J., & Milich, R. (1998). Sticks and stones: Evaluations of responses to childhood teasing. *Social Development, 7*, 234–249.

Schon, D. A. (1995). Knowing-in-action: The new scholarship requires a new epistemology. *Change, 27*, 26–34.

Schooler, C. (1972). Birth order effects: Not here, not now. *Psychological Bulletin, 78*, 161–175.

Schuldt, J. P., Konrath, S. H., & Schwarz, N. (2011). "Global warming" or "climate change"? Whether the planet is warming depends on question wording. *Public Opinion Quarterly, 75*, 115–124.

Schuman, H., Bobo, L., & Steeh, C. (1985). *Racial attitudes in America: Trends and complexities*. Cambridge, MA: Harvard University Press.

Schuman, H., & Presser, S. (1996). *Questions and answers in attitude surveys: Experiments on question form, wording, and context*. Thousand Oaks, CA: Sage.

Schwarz, N., Groves, R. M., & Schuman, H. (1998). Survey methods. In D. T. Gilbert, S. T. Fiske, & G. Lindzey (Eds.), *The handbook of social psychology* (Vol. 1, 4th ed., pp. 143–179). New York, NY: McGraw-Hill.

Scriven, M. (1967). The methodology of evaluation. In R. W. Tyler, R. M. Gagne, & M. Scriven (Eds.), *Perspective of curriculum evaluation* (pp. 39–83). AERA Monograph Series on Curriculum Evaluation, No. 1. Chicago, IL: Rand McNally.

Scriven, M. (1973). The methodology of evaluation. In B. R. Worthen & J. R. Sanders (Eds.), *Educational evaluation: Theory and practice*. Belmont, CA: Wadsworth.

Sears, D. O. (1986). College sophomores in the laboratory: Influences of a narrow data base on social psychology's view of human nature. *Journal of Personality and Social Psychology, 51,* 1173–1182.

Sekaquaptewa, D., Vargas, P., & von Hippel, W. (2010). A practical guide to paper-and-pencil implicit measure of attitudes. In B. Gawronski & B. K. Payne (Eds.), *Handbook of implicit social cognition: Measurement, theory, and applications* (pp. 140–155). New York, NY: Guilford Press.

Seligman, C., & Hutton, R. B. (1981). Evaluating energy conservation programs. *Journal of Social Issues, 37*(2), 51–71.

Shadish, W. R., Cook, T. D., & Campbell, D. T. (2002). *Experimental and quasi-experimental designs for generalized causal inference*. Boston, MA: Houghton Mifflin.

Sharpe, D. (1997). Of apples and oranges, file drawers, and garbage: Why validity issues in meta-analysis will not go away. *Clinical Psychology Review, 17,* 881–901.

Sherif, M., Harvey, O. J., White, B. J., Hood, W. R., & Sherif, C. W. (1961). *Intergroup cooperation and competition: The Robber's Cave experiment*. Norman, OK: University of Oklahoma Press.

Shingles, R. D. (1976). Causal inference in cross-lagged panel analysis. *Political Methodology, 3,* 93–133.

Shweder, R. A., & D'Andrade, R. G. (1980). The systematic distortion hypothesis. In R. A. Shweder & D. W. Fiske (Eds.), *New directions for methodology of behavioral science: Fallible judgment in behavioral research* (pp. 37–58). San Francisco, CA: Jossey-Bass.

Sieber, J. (1992). *Planning ethically responsible research*. Thousand Oaks, CA: Sage.

Silverman, G. (2011). *Client guide to the focus group*. Retrieved March 21, 2014, from http://mnav.com/focus-group-center/cligd-htm/

Siminoff, L. A., Erlen, J. A., & Sereika, S. (1998). Do nurses avoid AIDS patients? Avoidance behaviours and the quality of care of hospitalized AIDS patients. *AIDS Care, 10,* 147–163.

Simon, B. L. (1987). *Never married women*. Philadelphia, PA: Temple University Press.

Sinclair, L., & Kunda, Z. (2000). Motivated stereotyping of women: She's fine if she praised me but incompetent if she criticized me. *Personality and Social Psychology Bulletin, 26,* 1329–1342.

Skloot, R. (2010). *The immortal life of Henrietta Lacks*. New York, NY: Crown.

Sleek, S. (2013). Attacking science: Trials of the inconvenient truth-tellers. *APS Observer, 26*(9, November), 24–29.

Smith, C. P. (2000). Content analysis and narrative analysis. In H. T. Reis & C. M. Judd (Eds.), *Handbook of research methods in social and personality psychology* (pp. 313–335). New York, NY: Cambridge University Press.

Smith, P. B. (2012). Cultural social psychology. In M. Hewstone, W. Stroebe, & K. Jonas (Eds.), *An introduction to social psychology* (5th ed.). Chichester, England: BPS Blackwell.

Smith, S. S., & Richardson, D. (1983). Amelioration of deception and harm in psychological research: The important role of debriefing. *Journal of Personality and Social Psychology, 44,* 1075–1082.

Smith, W. J., Chase, J., & Lieblich, A. K. T. (1974). Tongue showing: A facial display of humans and other primate species. *Semiotica, 11,* 201–246.

Snowdon, D. A., Kemper, S. J., Mortimer, J. A., Greiner, L. H., Wekstein, D. R., & Markesbery, W. R. (1996). Linguistic ability in early life and cognitive function and Alzheimer's disease in late life. *Journal of the American Medical Association, 275*, 528–532.

Snyder, M., & Omoto, A. M. (2008). Volunteerism: Social issues perspectives and social policy implications. *Social Issues and Policy Review, 2*, 1–36.

Sommer, K. L., Horowitz, I. A., & Bourgeois, M. J. (2001). When juries fail to comply with the law: Biased evidence processing in individual and group decision making. *Personality and Social Psychology Bulletin, 27*, 309–320.

Sporer, S. L., & Schwandt, B. (2007). Moderators of nonverbal indicators of deception: A meta-analytic synthesis. *Psychology, Public Policy, and Law, 13*, 1–34.

Spoth, R., Redmond, C., & Shin, C. (2000). Modeling factors influencing enrollment in family-focused prevention intervention research. *Prevention Science, 1*, 213–225.

Stack, C. B. (1975). *All our kin: Strategies for survival in a Black community.* New York, NY: Harper Colophon.

Stamp, J. (1929). *Some economic factors in modern life.* London, England: King & Son.

Stanne, M., Johnson, D. W., & Johnson, R. (1999). Social interdependence and motor performance: A meta-analysis. *Psychological Bulletin, 125*(1), 133–154.

Stanovich, K. E. (2013). *How to think straight about psychology* (10th ed.). Boston, MA: Pearson.

Stewart, D. W., & Shamdasani, P. N. (1990). *Focus groups: Theory and practice.* Thousand Oaks, CA: Sage.

Strayer, F. F., & Strayer, J. (1976). An ethological analysis of social agonism and dominance relations among preschool children. *Child Development, 47*, 980–989.

Strube, M. J. (1985). Combining and comparing significance levels from nonindependent hypothesis tests. *Psychological Bulletin, 97*, 334–341.

Strube, M. J., Gardner, W., & Hartmann, D. P. (1985). Limitations, liabilities, and obstacles in reviews of the literature: The current status of meta-analysis. *Clinical Psychology Review, 5*, 63–78.

Strunk, W., Jr., & White, E. B. (2000). *The elements of style* (4th ed.). Boston, MA: Allyn & Bacon.

Swim, J. K., Hyers, L. L., Cohen, L. L., & Ferguson, M. J. (2001). Everyday sexism: Evidence for its incidence, nature, and psychological impact from three daily diary studies. *Journal of Social Issues, 57*, 31–53.

Tajfel, H. (1982). Social psychology of intergroup relations. *Annual Review of Psychology, 33*, 1–39.

Tashakkori, A., & Teddlie, C. (Eds.). (2003). *Handbook of mixed methods in social and behavioral research.* Thousand Oaks, CA: Sage.

Tausczik, Y. R., & Pennebaker, J. W. (2010). The psychological meaning of words: LIWC and computerized text analysis methods. *Journal of Language and Social Psychology, 29*, 24–54.

Teige-Mocigemba, S., Klauer, K. C., & Sherman, J. W. (2010). A practical guide to implicit association tests and related tasks. In B. Gawronski & B. K. Payne (Eds.), *Handbook of implicit social cognition: Measurement, theory, and applications* (pp. 117–139). New York, NY: Guilford Press.

Thomas, W. I., & Znaniecki, F. (1918). *The Polish peasant in Europe and America: Monograph of an immigrant group.* Chicago, IL: University of Chicago Press.

Thompson, C. P., Skowronski, J. J., & Lee, D. J. (1988). Telescoping in dating naturally occurring events. *Memory and Cognition, 16*, 461–468.

Thorndike, E. L. (1920). A constant error in psychological ratings. *Journal of Applied Psychology, 4*, 25–29.

Thornton, G. C. (1980). Psychometric properties of self-appraisals of job performance. *Personnel Psychology, 33*, 263–271.

Thurstone, L. L. (1929). Theory of attitude measurement. *Psychological Bulletin, 36*, 222–241.

Tourangeau, R., & Rasinski, K. A. (1988). Cognitive processes underlying context effects in attitude measurement. *Psychological Bulletin, 103,* 299–314.

Tourangeau, R., Rips, L. J., & Rasinski, K. (2000). *The psychology of survey response.* Cambridge, England: Cambridge University Press.

Tourangeau, R., & Yan, T. (2007). Sensitive questions in surveys. *Psychological Bulletin, 133,* 859–883.

Tourigny, S. C. (2004). "Yo, bitch . . . " and other challenges: Bringing high-risk ethnography into the discourse. In L. Hume & J. Mulcock (Eds.), *Anthropologists in the field: Cases in participant observation* (pp. 111–126). New York, NY: Columbia University Press.

Trawalter, S., Adam, E. K., Chase-Lansdale, P. L., & Richeson, J. A. (2012). Concerns about appearing prejudiced get under the skin: Stress responses to interracial contact in the moment and across time. *Journal of Experimental Social Psychology, 48,* 682–693.

Trope, Y., & Ferguson, M. J. (2000). How and when preferences influence inferences: A motivated hypothesis-testing framework. In J. A. Bargh & A. K. Apsley (Eds.), *Unraveling the complexities of social life: A festschrift in honor of Robert B. Zajonc* (pp. 111–130). Washington, DC: American Psychological Association.

Tunnell, G. B. (1977). Three dimensions of naturalness: An expanded definition of field research. *Psychological Bulletin, 84,* 426–437.

Turkheimer, E., & Waldron, M. (2000). Nonshared environment: A theoretical, methodological, and quantitative review. *Psychological Bulletin, 126,* 78–108.

Turner, J. C. (1987). *Rediscovering the social group: A self-categorization theory.* Oxford, England: Blackwell.

Urbaniak, G. C., & Plous, S. (2013). Research Randomizer (Version 4.0) [Computer software]. Retrieved June 22, 2013, from http://www.randomizer.org/

Viney, L. L. (1983). The assessment of psychological states through content analysis of verbal communications. *Psychological Bulletin, 94,* 542–563.

Walker, S. G., Schafer, M., & Young, M. D. (1999). Presidential operational codes and foreign policy conflicts in the post-Cold War world. *Journal of Conflict Resolution, 43,* 610–625.

Wang, M. C., & Ramp, E. A. (1987, November). *The national Follow Through program: Design, implementation, and effects.* Philadelphia, PA: National Institute of Education.

Watson, D., Clark, L. A., & Tellegen, A. (1988). Development and validation of brief measures of positive and negative affect: The PANAS scales. *Journal of Personality and Social Psychology, 54,* 1063–1070.

Webb, E. J., Campbell, D. T., Schwartz, R. D., Sechrest, L., & Grove, J. B. (1981). *Non-reactive measures in the social sciences* (2nd ed.). Boston, MA: Houghton Mifflin.

Wehby, J. H., Symons, F. J., & Shores, R. E. (1995). A descriptive analysis of aggressive behavior in classrooms for children with emotional and behavioral disorders. *Behavioral Disorders, 20,* 87–105.

Weick, K. E. (1985). Systematic observational methods. In G. Lindzey & E. Aronson (Eds.), *The handbook of social psychology* (Vol. 1, pp. 567–634). New York, NY: Random House.

Weijters, B., Geuens, M., & Schillewaert, N. (2010). The stability of individual response styles. *Psychological Methods, 15,* 96–110.

Weiner, B. (2010). The development of an attribution-based theory of motivation: A history of ideas. *Educational Psychologist, 45,* 28–36.

Weiss, C. H. (1972). *Evaluating action programs.* Boston, MA: Allyn & Bacon.

Weiss, C. H. (1986). The stakeholder approach to evaluation: Origins and promise. In E. R. House (Ed.), *New directions in educational evaluation* (pp. 145–157). London, England: Palmer Press.

Wener, R. E., & Keys, C. (1988). The effects of changes in jail population densities on crowding, sick call, and spatial behavior. *Journal of Applied Social Psychology, 18,* 852–866.

Whyte, W. F. (1943). *Street corner society*. Chicago, IL: University of Chicago Press.

Willems, E. P. (1969). Planning a rationale for naturalistic research. In E. P. Willems & H. L. Rausch (Eds.), *Naturalistic viewpoint in psychological research* (pp. 44–71). New York, NY: Holt, Rinehart & Winston.

Williams, K. D., Cheung, C. K. T., & Choi, W. (2000). Cyberostracism: Effects of being ignored over the Internet. *Journal of Personality and Social Psychology, 79*, 748–762.

Williams, W., & Evans, J. W. (1972). The politics of evaluation: The case of Head Start. In P. H. Rossi & W. Williams (Eds.), *Evaluating social programs: Theory, practice and politics* (pp. 247–264). New York, NY: Seminar Press.

Wilson, T. D., Aronson, E., & Carlsmith, K. (2010). The art of laboratory experimentation. In S. T. Fiske, D. T. Gilbert, & G. Lindzey (Eds.), *Handbook of social psychology* (Vol. 1, 5th ed., pp. 51–81). Hoboken, NJ: John Wiley & Sons.

Wortman, C. B., & Rabinovitz, V. C. (1979). Random assignment: The fairest of them all. In L. Sechrest, S. G. West, M. Phillips, R. Redner, & W. Yeaton (Eds.), *Evaluation studies review annual* (Vol. 4, pp. 177–184). Thousand Oaks, CA: Sage.

Wyer, R. S., Chiu, C-Y., & Hong, Y-Y. (2009). *Understanding culture: Theory, research, and application*. New York, NY: Psychology Press.

Zautra, A. J., Reich, J. W., Davis, M. C., Potter, P. T., & Nicolson, N. A. (2000). The role of stressful events in the relationship between positive and negative affects: Evidence from field and experimental studies. *Journal of Personality, 68*, 927–951.

Zerhouni, E. (2003). The NIH roadmap. *Science, 302*(5642), 63–72.

Zimmer, C. (2013). A family consents to a medical gift, 62 years later. *New York Times*, August 7. Retrieved March 6, 2014, from http://www.nytimes.com/2013/08/08/science/after-decades-of-research-henrietta-lacks-family-is-asked-for-consent.html?hpw&_r=0

Zuckerman, M. (1994). *Behavioral expression and biological bases of sensation seeking*. New York, NY: Cambridge University Press.

Zuckerman, M., DePaulo, B. M., & Rosenthal, R. (1981). Verbal and nonverbal communication of deception. In L. Berkowitz (Ed.), *Advances in experimental social psychology* (Vol. 14, pp. 1–59). New York, NY: Academic Press.

Index

Note: Page numbers in *italics* refer to figures. Page numbers in **bold** refer to tables.

Research Methods in Social Relations, Eighth Edition. Geoffrey Maruyama and Carey S. Ryan.
© 2014 John Wiley & Sons, Inc. Published 2014 by John Wiley & Sons, Inc.
Companion Website: www.wiley.com/go/maruyama